The Craft
of Public Administration

Tenth Edition

The Craft
of Public Administration

George Berkley

University of Massachusetts

John Rouse

Ball State University

Mc Graw Hill **Higher Education**

Boston   Burr Ridge, IL   Dubuque, IA   New York   San Francisco   St. Louis
Bangkok   Bogotá   Caracas   Kuala Lumpur   Lisbon   London   Madrid   Mexico City
Milan   Montreal   New Delhi   Santiago   Seoul   Singapore   Sydney   Taipei   Toronto

The McGraw·Hill Companies

Higher Education

THE CRAFT OF PUBLIC ADMINISTRATION, TENTH EDITION

Published by McGraw-Hill, an imprint of The McGraw-Hill Companies, Inc., 1221 Avenue of the Americas, New York, NY 10020. Copyright © 2009, 2004, 2000, 1997, 1994, 1990, 1984, 1981, 1978, 1975. All rights reserved. No part of this publication may be reproduced or distributed in any form or by any means, or stored in a database or retrieval system, without the prior written consent of The McGraw-Hill Companies, Inc., including, but not limited to, in any network or other electronic storage or transmission, or broadcast for distance learning.

This book is printed on acid-free paper.

1 2 3 4 5 6 7 8 9 0 FGR/FGR 0 9 8

ISBN: 978-0-07-337895-4
MHID: 0-07-337895-X

Editor in Chief: *Michael Ryan*
Editorial Director: *Beth Mejia*
Sponsoring Editor: *Mark Georgiev*
Managing Editor: *Nicole Bridge*
Marketing Manager: *Bill Minick*
Developmental Editor: *Kate Scheinman*
Lead Media Project Manager: *Ronald Nelms, Jr.*
Senior Production Editor: *Karol Jurado*
Production Service: *Anne Draus, Scratchgravel Publishing Services*
Manuscript Editor: *Margaret Tropp*
Senior Production Supervisor: *Tandra Jorgensen*
Cover Designer: *Laurie Entringer*
Cover Image: *© BananaStock/PunchStock*
Composition: *10/12 Times Roman by ICC Macmillan Inc.*
Printing: *45# New Era Matte, Quebecor World, Inc.*

Library of Congress Cataloging-in-Publication Data

Berkley, George E.
    The craft of public administration / George Berkley, John Rouse.—10th ed.
       p. cm.
    Includes bibliographical references and index.
    ISBN-13: 978-0-07-337895-4 (alk. paper)
    ISBN-10: 0-07-337895-X (alk. paper)
       1. Public administration. I. Rouse, John E. (John Edward), 1942– II. Title.
JF1351.B47 2009
351—dc22

                                                                              2008030008

The Internet addresses listed in the text were accurate at the time of publication. The inclusion of a Web site does not indicate an endorsement by the authors or McGraw-Hill, and McGraw-Hill does not guarantee the accuracy of the information presented at these sites.

www.mhhe.com

Brief Contents

Contents

Preface

Four Pedagogical Segments

The four pedagogical segments of this textbook—federalism, public personnel administration, budgets, and government regulations—succinctly organize the study of partisan, policy, and system politics—and government bureaucracies. Conflicting, diverse values challenge *The Craft of Public Administration* in ways not yet envisioned. Despite this clash of civilizations, all cultures must determine how public bureaucracy is to be responsive and act as an effective catalyst for serving people.

The Craft of Public Administration, tenth edition, is not just a textbook; it is a pedagogical gathering of pertinent yet limited literature, assembled to inform and interest college students in the dynamics of the public, or government, sector in the United States. The literature is limited because we choose not to write a book that is "everything one wants to know about public administration but is afraid to ask." Local, state, regional, and federal governments are too overwhelming and far-reaching to attempt a dictionary approach to the field. To comprehend projected federal government spending (state and local government spending not included), the literature of public administration is divided into four pedagogical segments:

Federalism

Federalism covers craft of public administration; relationships to economic development, political and bureaucratic culture; the structure of politics; partisan, policy, and systems politics; equality; efficiency; synergy; formal organization; and human relations. Chapters 1 through 4 focus on the structure of American politics, or issues of U.S. federalism. Chapter 1 concerns "The Administrative Craft"; Chapter 2 deals with "The Ecology of the Administrative Craft"; Chapter 3 investigates "The Anatomy of Public Organizations"; Chapter 4 studies "The Physiology of Public Organizations."

Public Personnel Administration

Public personnel administration covers people, patronage, merit, equal opportunity, affirmative action, job classifications, labor relations, leadership, charisma, communication, technology. Chapters 5 through 8 address matters of public personnel administration. Chapter 5 explores "People and Personnel"; Chapter 6 reviews "Public Sector Labor-Management Relations"; Chapter 8 deals with "Communication and Leadership" in government bureaucracies.

Budgets

Budgets cover taxing, appropriations, spending, productivity, efficiency, effectiveness, motivation, privatization of government functions, planning, program evaluation. Chapters 8 and 9 examine priorities of taxing, budgeting, spending, productivity, and program evaluation. Chapter 8 addresses "Taxing, Budgeting, and Spending" and points out how partisan, policy, and systems politics affect the likelihood of higher taxes but fewer government programs and services. Chapter 9 probes "The Productivity Challenge" and outlines the pressures on government employees to do more with fewer resources.

Regulations

Regulations cover administrative law, administrative controls, administrative law judges, ethics, discretion, rules, procedures, administrative responsibility, administrative state, and clientele relations. Chapter 10 describes "Administrative Law and Government Regulations." It explores clientele relations, the impact of administrative growth on democratic ideals, administrative law judges, and how economic, social, and subsidiary regulations are affected by administrative rules and rule making.

Case Studies, Videos, and Taxpayer-State Chemistry

The narrative and case studies allow students to learn from analyzing the literature in conjunction with specific illustrations. Case studies force us to think about how the general (literature) affects the particular (case study) and how specific illustrations amend our perceptions of public administration literature. Examination of case study facts brings out the dynamic nature of the literature.

The Craft of Public Administration recognizes that effective teaching of partisan, policy, and systems politics occurs in a global world of images, videos, and films. Thus the tenth edition now includes in each chapter a Videos and Films box for instructional consideration, which follows the Summary. This new feature shows the many faces of public administration in action.

Also new to this edition is an end-of-book Appendix listing government and other Web sites that students will find helpful for completing homework assignments, conducting research, and seeking internships and post-college jobs.

Public administration constitutes the "chemistry" of the United States. The two key principles that have come to embody the American ideal, equality and efficiency, are likewise the crucial determinants of how well the public, or government, sector functions in the United States. Democratic capitalism does not flourish if public infrastructures, such as schools, highways, institutions of public safety, and similar taxpayer-funded government operations, are devalued and rendered ineffective.

Public sector functions, programs, and activities represent the "bottom line" expectations that society guarantees citizens. The domestic and military spending priorities of the 1980s have forced public administration as a field to be more accountable, adjust to economic realities, and evolve in unforeseen ways. The field is dynamic. The efficacy of *The Craft of Public Administration* depends upon people *effectively* relating to other people in the exchange of partisan, policy, and systems politics.

The actions and reactions of partisan, policy, and systems politics bring to life the "chemistry" of equality and efficiency and of public and private relations in the

United States. We encourage feedback from professors and students on the effectiveness of *The Craft of Public Administration,* tenth edition. Your contributions will make future editions of this text reflect the dynamic "chemistry" of U.S. life as it is played out in everyday relations between the "equality" of government programs and services and the "efficiency" of private opportunities.

Acknowledgments

As principal author of the tenth edition of *The Craft of Public Administration,* I wish to express my thanks and appreciation to:

- George Berkley, author of the first four editions of this textbook, for the opportunity to coauthor the fifth, sixth, seventh, eighth, ninth, and tenth editions.
- Mark Georgiev, Jeff Neel, and Kate Scheinman, McGraw-Hill Companies, for their encouragement and feedback on the development and evaluation of various stages of the writing and production.
- Joe Losco, chairman and professor, Department of Political Science, Ball State University, for his leadership in promoting a working environment conducive to integrating the tasks of teaching and research.
- Faculty colleagues in the Department of Political Science, Ball State University, for creating an atmosphere where consensus is valued and productivity is recognized.
- Max Walling, graduate assistant, for insisting on making certain that all insights, issues, and components of this effort are accurate, correctly stated, and fine-tuned; for assembling the Instructor's Manual/Test Bank and the Appendix; and for his consistency and technological expertise.
- The reviewers who provided feedback to help create this tenth edition: Morgan M. Laury, Kean University; Paul Melendez, University of Arizona; Amy Ramson, Hostos Community College; and Peter L. Sanzen, Hudson Valley Community College.
- Employees of the more than 87,000 units of government in the United States, whose craft constitutes the challenges of federalism, personnel, budgets, and government regulations.
- Thousands of Ball State University graduate and undergraduate students, past and present, who continually force me to think and rethink the dynamics of the public sector in the United States.
- The generous taxpayers of the State of Indiana, my employer, for access to a professional career that bridges the worlds of partisan, policy, and systems politics with the rich and varied literature of public administration.
- Barbara Maves, my wife, and for many years, executive director of a government-funded, not-for-profit east central Indiana health care agency, which daily confronts the challenges of the craft of public administration.

These contributions in many ways enhanced my research and the writing of the tenth edition of *The Craft of Public Administration.*

John Rouse
jrouse@bsu.edu

The Craft
of Public Administration

The Administrative Craft

Chapter Highlights

The Heart of the Matter

Art, Science, or Craft?

Capital, Government, and Myths

Trust in Government and Politics

Partisan, Policy, and System Politics

Adversarial Legalism

Bureaucratic Legalism and Hidden Law

American Constitutional Principles

Summary

FDNY Personifies Public Administration

Why does New York City need a public sector, civic-based, government-run, taxpayer-funded fire department?

The Fire Department of New York (FDNY) is not a private company. It is a taxpayer-based, rule-bound, culture-driven local government assembly of committed, skilled public administrators. So why not privatize New York City (NYC) fire fighting—reducing the city's commitment levels to the lowest common denominator?

Consider the possibilities for privatization. First, fire protection could be negotiated among owners of individual skyscrapers. But who would be responsible to fight a fire that starts in building A and spreads to building B? A second idea might be to privatize the FDNY's function. The agency's costs might be reduced if its fire-fighting functions were outsourced to private companies. However, it would be difficult to make private companies obey strict rules on hiring, promoting, and firing fire fighters.[1]

Moreover, the city cannot write contracts to cover all eventualities, and privatized fire-fighter companies would have incentives to cut costs at the expense of public safety. Minimum-wage fire fighters might well offer ineffective, barebones services. The bottom line is this: When the stakes are high, citizens want dedicated civil servants to do whatever it takes to protect them and the greater good.

On September 11, 2001, New York City was turned upside down at 8:46:26 A.M. when a hijacked American Airlines Boeing 767 superjet was flown into the North Tower of the World Trade Center (WTC). The jet, loaded with 92 people and 15,000 gallons of jet fuel, crashed into the North Tower at 500 mph. The plane exploded into the 93rd to 98th floors with a force equal to 480,000 pounds of TNT. No one above the 92nd floor survived.[2]

At 9:02:54 A.M., the suicide-bent hijackers flew a United Airlines 767 jet into the South Tower with a similar payload of explosive jet fuel, striking the 78th through 84th floors. The South Tower collapsed first, at 9:59:04 A.M.; the North Tower fell at 10:28:31 A.M. Chalk clouds rose 30-stories high as steel, concrete, and people collapsed to Ground Zero.

The WTC twin towers symbolized America's financial might. At 110 stories each, they were engineering miracles. The buildings housed both private and public clients, from financial firms to government offices. Subway and commuter trains rolled by below. The WTC was larger than many cities. The concrete and steel infrastructures housed a multitude of restaurants, a tremendous shopping mall, and a world-class hotel.

The New York City financial manager, Comptroller William Thompson, later forecast that the economic impact of the WTC attack could reach $95 billion and cost 83,000 jobs. "While this devastating event can never be reduced to numbers, it is clear that New York City and the nation will continue to suffer its economic ramifications for years to come," stated Thompson.[3] Thirteen million square feet of private office space was destroyed, and another 30 million square feet of office space was damaged. Half of the city's $6 billion budget deficit is directly attributable to the terrorist attack.

The morning of the attack, fire engines and rescue vehicles rushed to the scene. Fire fighters, police officers, and emergency personnel rushed up stairwells in a heroic effort to rescue the occupants of the towers. "I remember coming down the steps, in the smoke, with water pouring in the dark," said Peter Genova, who worked in the North Tower. "And all I saw was dozens and dozens of firemen and cops going up those steps to try to help people. Twenty minutes later, the building was gone."[4] The instinctive efforts of fire fighters to save others cost many their own lives.

Skyscrapers can be constructed to withstand almost any stress, but their aesthetic appeal would be diminished and the costs would become prohibitive. The WTC towers initially withstood the impact of the plane crashes. But they succumbed to the inferno of heat created by burning jet fuel. Temperatures of perhaps 1,000 to 2,000 degrees Fahrenheit likely weakened the buildings' steel supports. The external walls buckled, and the floors above fell straight down.[5]

The actual WTC death toll is 2,843, including 479 rescue workers and the 157 passengers and crew members on the two hijacked jets. Citizens from 67 countries perished in the attacks. Despite the huge loss of life, the evacuation was a success. Everyone who could get out did get out.[6]

Why were so many people able to escape from the two burning skyscrapers? The Port Authority of New York and New Jersey, owner of the WTC, had made crucial improvements after a bomb exploded in the basement of the North Tower in 1993, killing six people. Private and public entities worked together to improve safety. In accordance with NYC building code standards, stairwells were well marked. The WTC towers had excellent stair systems, and building management took evacuations seriously. Each floor had assigned fire wardens. In addition, on September 11, 2001, the towers were half-empty when the planes hit. Officials project that between 5,000 and 7,000 persons were in danger in each tower—not the 10,000 to 25,000 per tower that might have been endangered had the towers been fully occupied; tourists were also few in number at 8:46 A.M. The observation deck on the 107th floor of the South Tower did not open until 9:30 A.M.

The sacrifices made by the FDNY and New York Police Department (NYPD) typify the self-less, lifelong commitments of many of New York's public safety workers. The NYPD lost 23 officers and the Port Authority of New York and New Jersey lost 37, but the New York Fire Department sacrificed 343 firefighters.

Entire FDNY companies were lost. The total number of dead was nearly 30 times the number the department had ever lost before in a single event. All five of the elite Rescue Companies and five of the highest ranking chiefs were killed. The ultimate sacrifice was paid by these city government employees. And the effects of the WTC disaster on the FDNY go beyond lives sacrificed. The fire department as an organization suffered severe losses of leadership and institutional memory.[7]

The FDNY—overwhelmingly white, Catholic, and male—is under political pressure to become more diverse, more representative of the city. In 2000, 94 percent of the 10,860 members of the FDNY were white, 3 percent black, and 3 percent Hispanic. This ethnic disparity is partially explained by the tendency to "pass down" the job from father to son, with the dinner table serving as a recruiting station. However, 22 percent of recent applications came from minority groups, compared to 7 percent in 2000.

The 343 FDNY public sector employees lost in the WTC attacks died trying to save their fellow citizens. Then-Mayor Rudolph Giuliani had something to say to these civil servants at the New York City Fire Department promotion ceremony on September 17, 2001: "You're all my heroes."

Notes

1. Paul Krugman, "The Public Interest," *New York Times,* October 10, 2001; http://www.nytimes.com/2001/10/10/opinion/10KRUG.html.
2. Jane Spencer and Mary Carmichael, "Deadly Miscues: In the First Moments after the World Trade Center Attack, Miscalculations by Heroic Rescuers Probably Cost Lives," *Newsweek,* http://www.msnbc.com/news/627959.asp?0sp=w12b2.
3. Timothy Williams, "Economic Impact of WTC Attack Climbs," *News.Yahoo.com,* September 5, 2002, http://news.yahoo.com.
4. Michael Powell, "New York: A City Turned Upside Down," *Washington Post*, September 12, 2001, p. A16, http://www.washingtonpost.com/ac2/wp-dyn/a14164-2001Sept11.
5. James Glantz and Eric Lipton, "Towers Withstood Impact, But Fell to Fire, Report Says," *New York Times,* March 29, 2002, http://www.nytimes.com/2002/03/29/nyregion/29TOWE.html.
6. Dennis Cauchon, "For Many on Sept. 11, Survival Was No Accident," *USA Today,* December 20, 2001, http://www.usatoday.com/news/attack/2001/12/19/usatcov-wtcsurvival.htm.
7. David Schwartz and Christopher Stewart, "The Fire Department," *GothamGazette.com,* December 3, 2001, http://www.gothamgazette.com/iotw/firedepartment/.

Sources

E. J. Dionne, Jr., "No Time for Partisan Pleaders," *The Washington Post,* September 21, 2001, p. A37; http://www.washingtonpost.com/ac2/wp-dyn/A1148-2001Sep20; and Don Wyclif, "In Praise of Civil Servants," *Chicago Tribune,* November 8, 2001, http://www.chicagotribune.com/news/columnist/chi-0111080042nov08.column.

The words *public administration* express a concept that at first glance may seem abstract and nondescript. However, a closer look at the phrase helps relieve the ambiguity.

Public administration is grounded in partisan, policy, and systems politics. It links private and public citizen relations. It is both product and process. It acts on responsiveness and competence. It is administered under the legal auspices of federal, state, and local governments. American constitutional principles dictate its every move. Public administration is an art, uses science, but is mostly a craft.

In its varied activities, the centralization of power is accompanied by the decentralization of governmental function. A diversity of social values skews its uniformity. Its origins are political. It cannot operate without personnel. It is monitored by administrative laws. It regulates private citizens and their many activities. The political cultures of the 50 states penetrate its many behaviors in, of, and for American lives.

Public means the citizens of a given area—the people of a town, county, state, or country. If an issue is considered in the public domain, information and discourse about that issue are available to the people and can be known to all. The word *public* also refers to activities the state administers on behalf of the entire community.

Public administrators serve the people. Organized collectives of citizens constitute a variety of public communities in the United States. These publicly organized communities include national, state, and local governments. They include townships, state recreation areas, and public utilities. They include school, sanitary, and water districts. These communities administer public libraries, public parks, public defenders (police, fire, legal), public roadways, and public servants. In the event of war, citizens may be called upon to make the ultimate sacrifice to their national community—their lives. However, in peacetime, Americans are required only to pay taxes and obey the laws. When April 15 rolls around, citizens have a definitive economic opportunity to be patriotic by meeting their financial obligation to society. The one thing all public programs have in common is that they are financed by taxpayers, most of whom want a voice in how those dollars are spent.

U.S. taxpayers often pressure the government to reduce personnel and expenses for services. (There is correspondingly less demand to reduce services to citizens.) Since most services are delivered by local governments and their employees, the reduction of personnel and expenses must come first at the local level of operations, less so at the state level, and much less so at the centers of federal government operations.

As we study *public administration,* the abstract, nondescript, colorless images of public bureaucracies will fade away to be replaced by more concrete concerns about the development, evaluation, and implementation of programs that require our tax dollars. Such decisions are usually political in nature; a major function of politics is to allocate importance to numerous and often conflicting values in society. *Public administration,* then, is the process of implementing those diverse values in our complex and ever-changing society. This process plays a vital role in the daily lives of all citizens.

One issue that affects public administration is the size and role of government. How big is government? According to Michael Hodges, federal government spending in fiscal year 2006 ($2.8 trillion) consumed 26 percent of the economy, or $9,223 per man, woman, and child—or 36 percent of the economy if regulatory compliance is included. Social spending consumes 56 percent of total spending—and has increased 14 times faster than the economy. Individual incomes pay 82 percent of all federal revenue, compared to a 51 percent share in 1950. Compared to prior generations, today's economy is 8 times more dependent on federal government spending.[1]

Integrating economic, environmental, and social factors into the operations and management of governments challenges local, state, and federal executives— both elected and appointed. Sustaining, if not expanding, economic growth is but one priority of governments. Government spends about half what the nation "earns" each year. Is this amount excessive? The percentage of Gross Domestic Product (GDP) spent by the U.S. government is, in proportion to its economy, smaller than that of nearly any other industrialized nation.[2]

Government spending is more precisely evaluated in the context of population demographics, economic consumption, citizen production, and environmental consequences, all considered over time. To promote standards of a civil society, economic and political systems must proactively respond to population changes. The U.S. population increased from 151.3 million in 1950 to 281.4 million in 2000. Since the early 1800s, immigration has been a crucial component of America's growth and a periodic source of conflict. In recent years, immigration has surfaced as one of the most contentious issues on the nation's political agenda. According to Steven Camarota, about 1.25 million legal and illegal immigrants settle in the country each year. Net immigration into the United States has been increasing for five decades. The projected population increase comes mostly from legal immigration. Camarota estimates that the nation's population will increase from 301 million today to 468 million by 2060—a 167 million (or 56 percent) increase.[3]

Birth and immigration policies affect how the U.S. population grows, as well as affecting demands for limited resources, and pollution, deforestation, waste, and habitat choices. The more people, the more demand for government services—and the more government employees, bigger budgets, and higher taxes. Disparity in the tax burden may also increase, with some parts of the population shouldering more of the load.

While the U.S. population has expanded dramatically, federal tax levels have remained relatively stable over the past fifty years. The average tax level for the post–World War II period has been 18.5 percent of GDP. Federal tax composition, however, has generally shifted away from corporate income taxes and excise taxes toward social insurance taxes, with the individual income tax continuing to produce the most revenue. State and local taxes, unlike federal taxes, have doubled—from 5.3 percent of the GDP in 1947 to 10.7 percent in 1998.

The government sector is made up of publicly owned establishments. This sector includes 87,525 establishments of federal, state, and local government agencies that administer, oversee, and manage public programs and have executive, legislative, and judicial authority over other institutions within a given area. These agencies also set policy, create laws, adjudicate civil and criminal legal cases, provide for the public safety and for national defense. In 2007, 89,527 governments were counted, of which 89,476 were local governments.

Establishments such as public schools and public hospitals are also included in government. The information included here refers to civilian employment only. Counts from the Quarterly Census of Employment and Wages program show that, as a portion of the national economy, the federal government represents about 2.1 percent of all employment and 0.6 percent of all establishments. State government represents about 3.4 percent of all employment and 0.8 percent of all establishments. Local government is about 10.4 percent of all employment and 1.8 percent of all establishments.

Estimates from the Current Population Survey program show annual average employment in government was 19,664,000 in 1997. A decade later, during 2006, government employment averaged 21,990,000—an all-time high. According to the Current Population Survey, the 2006 unemployment rate of persons most recently employed in government was 2.3 percent—half the overall unemployment rate of 4.6 percent that year. Fiscal year 2006 recorded 20,292,000 federal, state, and local government employees. Of this total, 53.5 percent, or 10,908,000, were local employees; 30 percent, or 6,102,000, were state employees; and 16.5 percent, or 3,381,000, were federal employees.

The most common occupation in public administration is police and sheriff's patrol officers. In May 2005, there were 609,960 police and sheriff's patrol officers in public administration, with average annual wages of $47,440.[4]

The Heart of the Matter

In a classic textbook, Herbert Simon, Donald Smithburg, and Victor Thompson define *administration* simply but graphically in this opening sentence: "When two men cooperate to roll a stone that neither could have moved alone, the rudiments of administration have appeared."[5] That illustrates much about what administration is and is not. The first and foremost ingredient of administration is *people.* A stone on a hill is not in itself involved in any form of administration. If that stone rolls down the hill by some act of nature, administration is not involved. People have to be present before administration can take place.

Defining Organization

Chester Barnard

A formal organization is a system of consciously co-ordinated activities or forces of two or more persons.

> —*Chester Barnard*, The Functions of the Executive
> *(Cambridge, MA: Harvard University Press, 1938), p. 73*

Daniel Katz and Robert L. Kahn

The first problem in understanding an organization or a social system is its location and identification. How do we know that we are dealing with an organization? What are its boundaries?

> —*Daniel Katz and Robert L. Kahn,* The Social Psychology of
> Organizations *(New York: John Wiley & Sons, 1966), p. 14*

Philip Selznick

. . . formal organization is the structural expression of rational action.

> —*Philip Selznick, "Foundations of the Theory of Organizations,"*
> American Sociology Review *13, no. 1 (1948): 25*

Dwight Waldo

. . . organization may be defined as the structure of authoritative and habitual personal interrelations in an administrative system.

> —*Dwight Waldo,* The Study of Public Administration
> *(New York: Random House, 1955), p. 6.*

Source: Michael M. Harmon and Richard T. Mayer, *Organization Theory for Public Administration* (Boston: Little, Brown and Company, 1986). See "Defining Organization," pp. 17–21.

The second ingredient of administration is *action*. Two people looking at the stone are not, in that act alone, involved in administration. They must take some action regarding the stone before administration can enter the picture. There is no such thing as inactive administration (although many who have dealt with administrative agencies sometimes believe otherwise).

The third ingredient is *interaction*. If one person moves the stone, administration does not occur. At least two people must combine their efforts to move the stone for the activity to involve administration. The essence of administration is *people relating to people.*

People interacting with people to accomplish tasks—this is the essence of administration.

Art, Science, or Craft?

The title of this book clearly proposes that administration is a craft. Why this classification instead of another? Why not consider administration a science or an art?

Science is characterized by precision and predictability. A scientific rule is one that works all the time. In fact, rules in science are so rigid and final that they are not called rules at all, but laws. Two parts of hydrogen combined with one part of oxygen will *always* give us water, steam, or ice, depending on the temperature. While it is true that some sciences, particularly the social sciences, do not achieve such a 100 percent predictability level, it is also true that any scientific theory must stand up to rigorous, repeated tests to be considered valid. Administration uses scientific data, laws, and theories; for example, finance officers use mathematics and computers to keep a government agency's financial records. However, administration itself is not a science.

Although administrators use scientific laws, techniques, and data, they do so in ways that give individual imagination and temperament free rein. Usually a variety of successful solutions exist for dealing with a particular administrative problem, and a creative administrator may even devise a new solution on the spot. Administrative problems are rarely identical, and it is impossible to derive scientific equations that work the same way every time for such problems.

Administration shares traits with the arts as well as the sciences. Administrators often work in highly imaginative ways, employing a mix of methods, including intuition. Like painters and composers, administrators often find their own moods and personalities reflected in their work. There is, however, a vital difference that keeps administration from being characterized as an art: Artists create aesthetic works; administrators attempt to solve problems. The respective end products and the criteria for evaluating them differ.

Although public administration shares traits with both science and art, categorizing the field as one or the other obviously paints an incomplete picture. There is, however, a category more suitable—or at least more comfortable and workable. That category is *craft*.

There is never a precise formula that will invariably work best in all administrative situations. Not only do situations and people vary, but ideas for handling them are almost as infinite as the human mind. Still, we can establish an objective standard for most administrative situations: Did the solution result in more efficient completion of the desired task? Objective standards, a lack of precise formulas, changing situations, and problem solving are traits that best fall under the classification of craft. Whereas science uses unvarying methods to achieve predicted results, and art uses diverse methods to achieve diverse, unpredictable results, a craft uses diverse methods to attain a desired result.

Public administration deals with the ongoing pressing problems of American society. Government administrators—executives, civil servants, and others—may well employ artistry and imagination in dealing with the demands of a variety of interests. However, they are not creating works of art. Administrators rely on hard evidence to resolve dilemmas of consequence to citizens. Yet the possibilities for resolution are virtually limitless—so administration is surely not a science.

Public administration, therefore, is neither art nor science, but can be described as a craft. Working in their craft, executives and civil servants seek to achieve objective goals and standards—with all the creativity, capability, and civility they can muster. In the always evolving American administrative scene, the challenges of the craft of public administration are more demanding than ever before.

One of the toughest political challenges for any twenty-first-century president is shaping the modern welfare system. The term *welfare* originally referred to government as a "helper of the poor." The benefits the modern welfare state offers, however, reflect radical departures from the policy directives Franklin Roosevelt formulated in the 1930s. The current welfare state creates widespread dependency on government spending. Yet budget deficits and distrust of government accompany government programs, services, and spending.

According to *Newsweek* columnist Robert J. Samuelson, Americans are bereft of any consistent public philosophy by which to judge the effectiveness of

First Encounters of the Bureaucratic Kind

The ability to adapt to a bureaucratic system is necessary to be able to function in the American society. *Most young people first experience bureaucracy as college freshmen.* Their views regarding bureaucracy reveal the process of socialization that leads to the acceptance of or resistance to a system that can be inefficient or, at times, dysfunctional. Although the students experience frustration with the long lines and waiting as well as with the impersonality of the administrative staff, they develop coping mechanisms that enable them to accept the system and conform in the long run.

Source: Glen J. Godwin and William T. Markham, "First Encounters of the Bureaucratic Kind: Early Freshman Experiences with a Campus Bureaucracy," *Journal of Higher Education* 67, no. 6 (November–December, 1996):660–692.

their governments. In other words, no public philosophy spells out what governments should and should not do. Budget deficits and federal debt trace their origins to an inadequate taxing-and-spending philosophy. Though most taxpayers oppose tax increases, they cannot agree on which programs should face revenue cuts. Little consensus exists on which government programs are necessary for the common good.

"Sooner or later," Samuelson argues, "we need to come to terms with the welfare state. We need more rigorous standards for judging whose welfare is being advanced and why."[6] The welfare state emerged in the 1930s as an antidote to the insensitivities of free markets. More than 70 years later, middle-class government welfare is a subject of increasing anxiety and contention.

Capital, Government, and Myths

Public administration is grounded in capital, bureaucracy, and democracy. Effective government cannot exist without sufficient capital to finance buildings, programs, equipment, skills, knowledge, and expertise.

The poorer the country, the more inefficient government programs, services, and operations will be. Richer countries can better afford effective government bureaucracies. Legislatures tax the capital, profits, and wages that citizens earn. They pass laws and commission government organizations to implement those laws. Government bureaucracies, then, make use of the dollars collected by democratically elected legislatures. Government bureaucracies are created by taxing wealth.

Capital and bureaucracy depend on the political consensus created by democratic participation. In the 2000 presidential elections, when then Vice President Al Gore lost his petition to recount contested Florida votes by one vote in the U.S. Supreme Court, the losers accepted the verdict. George W. Bush's victory rested on the public's acceptance of democratic procedures in election politics.

Some call U.S. democracy a myth. Governments that create myths, sooner or later, are apt to shed them. Myths set ideals and standards governments cannot meet; self-government does not function effectively when citizens raise skepticism and continuous contest over these fundamental assumptions. Citizens must believe in the system, even when it is imperfect. They must agree to procedural rules for the democracy to function effectively. And no democracy can protect the rights of every individual when those rights conflict.

"The myths of our democracy are not delusions," says David K. Shipler. "They may be just part of the truth, or embellishment of an inner reality in our culture's creed. But coupled with our freedom to expose our flaws, the myths have power, because they celebrate the powerful ideas that government belongs to the people, that voting is a universal right, that all citizens are equal, that we are governed by the rule of law, that minority views are protected no matter how abhorrent to the majority."[7]

The myth of true democratic governance raises several difficulties. First, decreasing accountability of democratic institutions and processes fosters skepticism in the fairness and effectiveness of the system. Katherine Harris, Florida's Republican secretary of state during the 2000 election, appeared not to hold fast to the American myth of popular democracy when she denied Gore's request for a recount in certain Florida counties.

Second, the American middle class perceives itself as bearing more of the burden and receiving less of the benefits of government than it should. This perceived unfairness is important for public bureaucracy, because the bulk of the money collected to operate, finance, and expand government originates from the middle class. For a variety of reasons, many citizens insist that significant sectors of American society are increasingly excluded from democratic rule. This perceived "social apartheid" is creating serious economic disparities.

Third, the uniformity of intellectual thought on substantive policy questions closes out many economic and social options. The two political parties are often neither pragmatic nor flexible. They do not cope well with the ongoing, painful economic adjustment of the United States to its challenging role in the post–Cold War world.

Accountability, representation, and intellectual diversity challenge democratic rule. Public administrators are governed by laws, public bureaucracies are limited by the same, and freedom is manifested by a dynamic relationship between citizens and the state. If this relationship is not morally based, representative, and intellectually creative, government programs, services, and expertise suffer. The legitimacy of government functions becomes suspect.[8]

"For two generations, Government elites defined the great issues," writes Garry Wills. "Now, a tidal change in the culture is sweeping away traditional politics." In the title of an article in the *New York Times Magazine,* Wills asks: "Whatever Happened to Politics? Washington Is Not Where It's At."[9] What passes for politics, writes Wills, is Paula Jones's suit against former President Bill Clinton.

A stable structure for robust political debate is missing. Politics is no longer restricted to the political system; the electoral system no longer fosters sweeping, unprecedented change. In fact, the electoral system lags behind cultural change.

The controversial end of the 2000 presidential election and the trauma of September 11, 2001, raise even further questions about the viability of the American system of political economy. Prior to these events, the country often lacked the political machinery or public engagement to make progressive changes. The privileged, post–World War II elites could narrowly circumscribe what "politics" entailed.

However, politics cannot be separated from culture. Creative technologies, markets, and the courts relegate elections to johnny-come-lately arbitrators of political life. Consumerism and political rights emphasize individual prerogatives. Markets are driven by the purchases of consumer goods. Legal rights protect minorities—however they may be constituted—in the marketplace.

Wills argues that family and religion, as American institutions, promoted civic stability. Today, families are being redefined: Many children are born outside of marriage. Divorce is prevalent. These developments reflect definitive structural changes in family organization. Families are the first organized unit of of any society. Government programs are only as effective as the political consensus that arises when such social units agree on the common good; therefore, cultural changes effect political changes.

Public administrators respond and act in a cultural context. Whether fighting against terrorism or for more effective health care programs, politicians confront political—and cultural—wars. Television, radio, the Internet, cell phones, and other technologies give citizens access to information for making personal decisions. The average American may feel she needs neither priest nor politician to tell her how to conduct her life.

Freedoms make it ever more difficult to mold political consensus. Public administration programs and policies—ideally, at least—are populist concepts built through ideas to which citizens adhere. U.S. citizens enjoy both political and economic privileges. They live in a society that stresses individual rights. They make demands on industries in the public and private sectors. They therefore demand responsiveness and expertise of government employees.

Before the 2000 election and the attacks on the World Trade Center and Pentagon, what used to be called "the Establishment" was already disappearing. The agenda-setting elite is gone. Wise men, or for that matter wise women, do not exist in a society where sovereignty is less salient and where markets have more immediate impacts.

Marriage and family, as we have stated, are the fundamental institution of any society. In the United States, government and private industry likely come second and third; the media and religion are probably fourth and fifth. Why are the institutions of marriage, family, industry, religion, media, political parties, and governments under assault and constantly in flux?

Family structures and priorities changed once women became educated and realized a certain economic status. For two generations, as Wills notes, public policies encouraged citizens to make their own decisions—to not be bound by authorities in civic, religious, or private matters. The spread of egalitarianism has been slow but very persistent.

An Associated Press poll found that the United States is an impatient nation. Americans are demanding—wanting it all *now.* The Department of Motor Vehicles ranks high among places Americans hate to wait. Citizens feel more time poor than money poor. Waiting fifteen minutes in a line is the maximum. Public sector clients may resort to rudeness if they perceive government inefficiencies.[10]

Despite these changes in culture, citizens still think in terms of public and private sectors. But these distinctions are being called into question. Dwight Waldo offers long-term insights into the notions of *public* and *private:*

> The concepts of *public* and *private* are very central in the conceptual and emotional structuring of the Western world. A great deal of our thought and action concerning government, law, morals, and social institutions relates one way or another to this distinction, a distinction which the modern experience has taught us to make. But we need to appreciate public and private are not categories of nature; they are categories of history and culture, of law and custom. They are contextual and subject to change and redefinition.[11]

As cultural notions about public and private rights and responsibilities change, pressure is brought to bear on political and governmental systems to change as well. The myth of government as omnipotent provider and protector is collapsing; however, trust in the public sector soared as our society agreed to tackle the threat of terrorism. How will we carve out a new sense of the role of government? The answer partly depends on whether we as a society maintain this newfound trust in our system of government and those who administer it.

Trust in Government and Politics

When hijacked airliners exploded into the World Trade Center and Pentagon on September 11, 2001, the United States suffered the largest single-day loss of life ever on American soil. Public trust in government surged in the wake of the September 11 attacks. What had government done to earn it?

Perhaps you have heard the old adage: "Trust is something that must be earned. You have to show me you're trustworthy." The post–September 11 confidence level approached that of 1966 when the "Great Society" Democratic Congress, elected on Lyndon Johnson's coattails in 1964, passed the Voting Rights Act, put Medicare on the books, enacted the first large federal education assistance law, and created a host of social and environmental measures designed to improve American lives.

According to *Washington Post* columnist David Broder, government assumes two tasks. The first duty of government is to protect the people. The 2001 confidence-in-government surge reflected the belief that the U.S. government could employ its military, diplomatic, and economic skills to confront political terrorism and economic recession.

The second task of modern government is to promote economic growth, providing for stable incomes and job security. The events of September 11 produced disastrous results for transportation, tourism, and the service sectors of the economy.

How much do Americans trust government? Not very much. Trust increased to 61 percent in the early 1960s but plummeted to 27 percent by 1980. Trust and voter turnout decline when social spending and regulatory costs rise. The Vietnam War and the failure of Lyndon Johnson's war on poverty undercut patriotic idealism. The Watergate scandal crippled the Nixon administration—and confidence in government. Rising inflation and interest rates followed. That spiked faith in government in the 1970s.

President Ronald Reagan ushered in a strong rise in trust—topping out at 70 percent. His patriotic anticommunism became a catalyst for the fall of the Soviet Union. The Iran hostage crisis ended. Interest and inflation rates declined. Tax cuts juiced the economy into high gear. President George H. W. Bush first said no more tax hikes, then agreed to the largest tax increase in history. Health care failure doomed the Democrats in the 1994 elections.

The very low levels of trust today question the legitimacy of government size, emphasis, and debt. Indicating declining legitimacy, 63 percent of citizens do not trust government. This is a massive change in three decades. As of April 2006, the Zoby poll recorded that 58 percent have low respect for the media and 69 percent have low respect for corporate leaders, but 67 percent trust the courts. As of May 2006, 76 percent have low respect for Congress, 69 percent have low respect for the president, and 78 percent believe that the federal government has too much power.[12]

Confidence in American governments has been on the decline since the Vietnam War. In 1964, 75 percent of the American populace trusted the federal government to do the right thing. The end of the Cold War, the advent of the global economy, resentment over political scandals, incompetence of bureaucrats, and economic dislocations have led to government's fall from grace and the public's loss of faith in government.[13]

The skepticism about government has been directed most recently at former House Speaker Tom DeLay, former U.S. Senate Majority Leader Bill Frist, and former President George W. Bush. From 1994 until 2006, representing and reflecting the conservative milieu, Republicans guided government's very existence, but more often than not refused to take political responsibility for its action, inaction, indifference, and failures. The immigration challenge has been complicated by the citizenry's lack of confidence in the effectiveness of American governments.[14]

Writing in the *American Prospect,* Stanley Greenberg stated that "conservatives have failed in ways that have undermined Americans' sense of collective capacity. Their failure has communicated not just their own incompetence, but also the message that government is incompetent."[15] Government has been discredited by Republican malfeasance. In a milieu of disbelief, Democrats encounter trouble getting citizen backing for necessary programs. The American public is conflicted, once again, over trusting government. People's faith in the very instrument that progressives want to use to solve problems has been undermined.

Partisan, Policy, and System Politics

American government employees exercise their skills, knowledge, and expertise within the framework of a fast-paced and ever-changing society. Three of the dynamic forces at work in our society are partisan politics, policy politics, and system politics. Partisan politics is concerned with which political party wins office. Policy politics deals with deciding which policies to adopt. System politics examines how administrative systems (decision structures) are set up.[16]

Public administration emphasizes two of the three forms of politics: policy and system politics. However, it originates from partisan politics. Partisan, policy, and system politics are not separate, exclusive applications of the craft in practice—they are highly intertwined. In a nutshell, citizens elect political partisans to public office; partisans establish public policies; and administrative systems implement the policies partisans have established. Consider an example: the administration of Central Park.

Central Park in New York City is a public park. Located in the middle of Manhattan, the park runs from 59th Street to 110th Street, from 5th Avenue to 8th Avenue. In the midst of some of the most expensive private real estate in the world, the park somehow survives the marketplace values of New York City. Central Park affords the citizens of New York a wide variety of playgrounds, bicycle paths, wooded areas, jogging paths, swimming pools, picturesque lakes, and other natural scenery. The facilities of Central Park are offered to the public on a first-come, first-served basis.

Who's in charge of Central Park? Are the politicians in charge? Are the police in charge? Are the bureaucrats from the parks department in charge? These types of questions demonstrate the subtleties of how politics shapes life in the public sector. Similar analogies may be made to federal lands, state parks, and municipal buildings. So who is really responsible for the upkeep of the facilities of Central Park? In a general sense, the people of New York are responsible. In a more direct way, the New York parks department, the police, and the mayor are responsible because they are the custodians of this public interest.

Whereas the concept of political responsibility is often abstract, administrative aspects such as hierarchy, chain of command, unity of command, span of control, due process, regulations, rules, and even bureaucratic ineptness are more definitive and recognizable. Politics, in its varied definitions, may be vague to many citizens; on the other hand, citizens have concrete experiences with bureaucracies.

How is the study of public bureaucracy different from the study of elections, executives, legislatures, or the courts? The study of bureaucracy focuses on obeying authority; the study of elections, executives, legislatures, or the courts relates to the institutionalizing of democratic values. The study of public administration tells us what actually happens as bureaucracies carry out policies enacted by legislatures and approved by executives.

Decisions made by government officials, representing departments and agencies, reflect the policy and system politics that occur in public bureaucracies. Such decisions are monitored by political partisans within the framework of majority rule and minority rights.

Adversarial Legalism

Compared to other economically advanced democracies, the United States is uniquely prone to adversarial, legalistic modes of policy formulation and implementation, shaped by the prospect of judicial review. While adversarial legalism facilitates the expression of justice—allowing challenges to official dogma—its costs are often neglected or minimized.

A survey of existing research indicates the extent to which adversarial legalism causes (or threatens) enormous dispute-resolving costs and procedural delays, which in turn distort policy outcomes. Adversarial legalism, moreover, has increased in recent decades, as Americans have attempted to implement the ambitious, socially transformative policies of activist government through political structures, forms of legislation, and legal procedures that reflect deep suspicion of governmental authority.[17]

Public administrators rely on, and are vulnerable to, the law. Legalism in general, and laws in particular, tend to limit and influence the operation of a public institution much more than they do a private one. "This pervasive legal context is among the principal distinctions between public and private enterprise," note John M. Pfiffner and Robert Presthus. "In private management one is assured that he can do anything not specifically forbidden. In public administration, on the other hand, discretion is limited by a great number of laws, rules, and regulations."[18] To put it more succinctly, in private administration the law generally tells administrators only what they *cannot* do; in public administration, the law tells them what they *can* do.

The hiring and firing of employees, the purchase of equipment, and the adoption or even adjustment of a simple operational guideline have produced costly and frustrating litigation. To activist administrators, the law and its practitioners often seem to exist merely to tie their hands. Aggravating the problem for many public administrators is that their craft is becoming increasingly result-oriented. This contrasts sharply with the legalistic approach, which stresses the correctness of procedure. To the legal mind, justice is not a product but a process.[19]

The legal limitations placed on public agencies contribute to or create many of the other differences between them and private enterprise. Government organizations usually operate in a goldfish bowl, subject to scrutiny from politicians, the public, and the press. They must be ready to open their doors and their books to almost any outsider, even though the outsider's interest in the agency may be prompted by no more than idle curiosity.

The legal context within which the public sector functions also helps explain why its employees usually enjoy greater rights—and face greater obligations. Public agencies frequently possess less flexibility than private ones. The public organization must hold itself accountable. And new technologies have caused new legal dilemmas to sprout up.

The Internet and terrorism threaten to alter public and private boundary delineations. The Internet raises questions about applying laws to cyberspace communications; the legal principles surrounding this medium continue to evolve. In the 1960s, the U.S. Supreme Court cited the Fourth Amendment to the Constitution, which protects citizens against unlawful searches and seizures, as providing a "reasonable expectation of privacy" in telephone booths or street conversations. In the 1980s, the court reduced the scope of that protection.

In 1986, Congress passed the ECPA, or Electronic Communications Privacy Act. It outlawed nonconsensual interception and disclosure of electronic communications. Workplace privacy increasingly focuses on the Internet and electronic communications.[20]

However, the terrorist attacks of September 11, 2001, or the impacts, results, and implications thereof, now interfere with protections guaranteed by the ECPA. Former Attorney General John Ashcroft called for "sweeping authority" to investigate possible terrorists. Legislation known as the Patriot Act gives the attorney general flexibility to provide broad surveillance over the Internet.[21]

Yes, the latter is in contradiction to the former. This is where the issue of "civil liberties" comes to the fore. This is where partisan, policy, and system politics interact as debate continues.

According to Jeffrey Rosen, author of *The Naked Crowd: Reclaiming Security and Freedom in an Anxious Age* (2004), politicians, the media, interest groups, and an adversarial legal system contribute to an unhealthy state of panic. Rosen argues that risk aversion since the September 11, 2001, terrorist attacks erodes our freedoms. "The risk-averse democracies of the West continue to demand ever-increasing levels of surveillance and exposure in a search for an illusory and emotional feeling of security." [22]

In *The Unwanted Gaze: The Destruction of Privacy in America* (2000), Rosen writes that sophisticated surveillance technologies and strategies cannot absorb, analyze, and understand the sheer volume of information. New antiterrorist laws on wiretapping the Internet illustrate this point. This legislation vastly expands the FBI's ability to monitor foreign agents. The FBI must hire agents to listen to recordings from start to finish. Filtered or unfiltered, information taken out of context presents challenges for public administrators. Citizen privacy is held at bay.[23] In the interplay of partisan, policy, and systems politics, preservation of freedom, privacy, and security in a post-9/11 world tests the viability of essential American ideals.

Bureaucratic Legalism and Hidden Law

The establishment of law is one of the greatest achievements of human civilization. However, as Jonathan Rauch asks, what happens if law "starts getting off its leash"? Rauch portrays formal law as "bureaucratic legalism," with a focus on the legalistic bent of law in American society. Bureaucratic legalism posits that if citizens proceed through sufficient legal processes, the resulting outcomes will be procedurally correct and morally right. But does this always hold true when laws are applied to unique situations in American life?

What if the law is applied when an eight-year-old girl brings a nail clipper to school? Rauch points out that etiquette, norms, social codes, and customs exist to avert or resolve such conflicts. He says that these givens are "hidden laws." They are so deeply imbedded in our social structures that we forget they exist. Hidden law, says Rauch, entails everything from table manners to informalities by which neighbors settle land disputes.

Rauch believes that hidden law may be applied to issues such as adultery, pornography, assisted suicide, sexual harassment, and abortion, rather than relying on bureaucratic legalism. Bureaucratic legalism was in play when the Olympic athlete had to give back her gold medal because she took cold medication. It is also in force when a child is suspended or expelled for bringing a plastic squirt gun to school. The weapons policy did not include the word *plastic* when the city council outlawed guns.

When is hidden law relevant? Hidden law can be applied when we ask, "Is this offense worthy of notice? Maybe not. All right, we're going to pretend that it didn't happen." Bureaucratic legalism cannot make these distinctions. As Rauch explains regarding bureaucratic legalism:

> By its very nature, its standard of fairness is equal application, to absolutely everybody, all the time. It views Hidden Law as capricious and arbitrary and inequitable in that it makes distinctions between people based on very personal, local judgments. So, with Bureaucratic Legalism, it becomes virtually impossible to make exceptions.[24]

Bureaucratic legalism was manifest in the way the public responded to developments in the Monica Lewinsky–President Bill Clinton sexual affair. When a president or anyone else commits adultery, most folks do not particularly want to know. The Violence Against Women Act and the Independent Counsel law made certain that citizens had a right to know. It did not matter if they wanted to know or not.

As events turned out, much of the citizenry was more outraged with the law than with the personal conduct of former President Clinton. Clinton's personal behavior, many agreed, was odious. But they also found the application of the law and the behavior of the law's enforcers ridiculous and unrestrained. Conservatives applied a rigorous legal formalism to the Clinton-Lewinsky case, claiming that Clinton's answers in a legal case made him vulnerable to charges of perjury and subject to impeachment. Bureaucratic legalism won out over hidden law.

In the New Testament of the Bible, the hardline conservative religious party was known as the Pharisees. The Pharisees were a Jewish sect that observed the letter but not the spirit of religious laws. Denounced by Jesus as sanctimonious and self-righteous, the Pharisees viewed themselves as highly moral or virtuous based on their legalistic philosophy. The Pharisees not only rigidly observed the written law, but insisted on adherence to the oral, or traditional law, which grew out of popular usage.

Even in these days, law has religious origins. Laws may be applied with religious zeal, without exception, or not as precisely, upholding the spirit but not necessarily the letter of the law.

American Constitutional Principles

The craft of public administration is influenced by factors other than partisan, policy, and system politics and legalism. Our republican form of government, federalism, separation of powers, and constitutionalism—all of which will be discussed in the following pages—help put the craft into a larger perspective. Much is said pejoratively about public bureaucrats and their perceived power to operate without constraints in the American political system. However, a public administrator receives his or her authority for administrative decision making from certain constitutional principles. What are these principles?

C. Herman Pritchett cites four constitutional principles, embodied in the document signed September 17, 1787, that influence the lives of Americans every day.[25]

First, the Constitution established a *republican form* of government. Many Americans hold onto their grade-school conceptions of democracy in America, believing that we have a democratic form of government. We do have a democratic *philosophy* of government; however, the *structure* of our government is republican. What *is* a republican form of government? Simply stated, we send representatives—legislators and executives—to city hall, the general assembly, Congress, the governor's mansion, and the White House because it would be impractical for all citizens to vote and decide public policy on every issue. Although Article 4 of the Constitution guarantees "a republican form of government," the definition was left open-ended for future generations of Americans.

Second, the Constitution created a *federal system.* The original U.S. government set up in 1776 was a confederation, or a mere league, of states, in which each state retained its sovereign powers. Under the auspices of the 1787 Constitutional Convention in Philadelphia, the delegates formed a stronger central government that was to receive its authority from the people. Powers not transferred to the new national government were to be retained by the states. As the cornerstone of the U.S. governmental system, federalism encompassed a two-level structure of government that divided power between the central government and state governments, allocating independent authority to each level.

The condition of U.S. federalism has been altered by political conflicts and economic crises. The Civil War ended the political aspirations of those who wanted a confederate political system, and the economic collapse of the 1930s brought down a dual form of federalism in which states had been somewhat independent of the central government. Events culminating in the 1860s (Civil War) and 1930s (economic collapse) were stepping stones on the path to a more centralized American political economy in the twenty-first century. The Civil War was a crisis in federalism, as its effects encouraged greater centralization and caused the influence of the states to decline. The Great Depression of the 1930s was also a crisis in federalism, as the economic collapse caused the central government to intervene on behalf of the private economy. The Civil War and the economic depression thus had centralizing effects upon federalism. The federal government's influence expanded, as did the expertise, skills, and knowledge of public administrators. However, contrary to what the name implies, the United States are far from united on matters of politics and economics. Federalism, then, is the sometimes changing structure of federal and state politics in the United States.

Demographic federalism, a movement of the mid-1990s, redefined the relationship between the states and the federal government. Demographic federalism makes the federal government accountable for the health and financial security of the elderly and disabled. The states are responsible for human capital and programs for workers, families, and children. These changes will have a significant impact on decision making concerning economic and social policies.[26] As sovereign communities, states promote their own economic interests, seeking political advantage over each other; this sometimes results in a state public sector being able to offer a better quality of life to its citizens.

Third, the Constitution embodies the *separation-of-powers principle.* Each branch of government is assigned a particular task: Congress makes the law, the executive branch administers the law, and the judicial system enforces and interprets the law. The separation-of-powers concept operates in tandem with the goal of limiting governmental powers. Separation-of-powers doctrine restrains one branch from usurping the powers of the others; the limitation of government powers inhibits the national government from overpowering the rights of the states and restricts the intrusion of government into private lives.

A system of checks and balances enables each branch to have some influence on the operation of the others. Congress regulates the kinds of cases the Supreme Court will hear, and the Senate ratifies treaties and approves executive appointments. The president appoints federal judges and vetoes laws, but the Senate must approve his judicial appointments. The courts pass judgment on the validity of executive acts and interpret congressional statutes. With these checks and balances in place, abuse of power is less likely.

Former President George W. Bush declared that he had the power to set aside any statute passed by Congress when it conflicted with his interpretation of the Constitution—disturbing the balance between the branches of government. The Constitution clearly assigns to Congress the power to write laws and to the president the duty "to take care that the laws be faithfully executed." Bush claimed the authority to disobey more than 750 laws enacted while he was in office.

Bush challenged laws on torturing detainees, oversight provisions of the USA Patriot Act, and "whistle-blower" protections for federal employees. He ignored military rules and regulations, affirmative-action provisions, requirements that Congress be told about immigration problems, "whistle-blower" protections for nuclear regulatory officials, and safeguards against political interference in federally funded research.

Political opponents argued that the President was seizing for himself some of the lawmaking role of Congress and the Constitution-interpreting role of the courts. Bush refused to "execute" what he claimed to be unconstitutional laws. He challenged more laws than all previous presidents combined.[27]

Finally, basic to the concepts of republicanism, federalism, and separation-of-powers is the idea of *constitutionalism.* Constitutionalism includes such ideas as the rule of law, representative institutions, and guaranteed individual liberty. Two important elements of American constitutionalism are majority rule and minority rights. What happens when people disagree? The answer customarily given is "majority rule." It is here, however, that we must exercise caution. If 51 percent of the people voted to put the other 49 percent into concentration camps, we would hardly call this an exercise in democracy. When we think of constitutional democracy in American political culture, therefore, we must think not only of majority rule, but also of minority rights. This tenuous balance between the wishes of the majority and the rights of the few enormously complicates democracy, especially for public sector managers who must carry out the majority's mandate while simultaneously safeguarding minority interests. Public administration in a democratic society is a delicate and difficult task, requiring its practitioners to possess generous amounts of tolerance and tact. Those lacking such capacities may well do better in other fields.

Majority rule and minority rights even affect the workings of Congress. Because of the rules, the majority party can work its way more easily in the House of Representatives than in the Senate. In the Senate, regardless of which political party maintains a majority of U.S. senators, the leadership needs sixty senators to cut off debate. Until the magic number of sixty is reached, a minority can stall legislation. As the loyal opposition, the minority party has responsibilities to offer amendments to the suggested programs of the majority.

As previously emphasized, public administration uses art and science, but is essentially a craft. Considering public administration's grounding in constitutional principles incorporating majority rule and minority rights, the use of the term *craft* seems appropriate and realistic. With the limitations and diversity of constitutional guidelines, public administrators need to be "crafty" to fulfill their responsibilities.

In constitutional terms, then, public bureaucrats exercise power within the framework of a republican form of government, a federal system, the separation-of-powers principle, and constitutionalism. Federalism is the basis of the American constitutional system and American public administration.

William S. Livingston illustrates three ways in which the changing pattern of modern federalism has affected political bureaucracy.[28] First, he describes a cooperative federalism in which the *centralization of power* is accompanied by the *decentralization of governmental function.* The central government makes policy, then delegates the implementation of this policy to other levels of government. Since the New Deal era, the decentralization of governmental function has followed the centralization of governmental authority and power. State and national governments supplement each other and jointly perform a variety of functions. The federal food stamp program illustrates the centralization of power with the decentralization of administrative function.

Monies to finance the food stamp program are collected under the auspices of the federal purse and the Sixteenth Amendment. Congress authorizes the Department of Agriculture to organize the food stamp program—to pen its varied regulations and to monitor its progress—but depends on the county welfare offices in the fifty states for administration. So the national government, with its enlarged powers, supplements rather than supplants the tasks of the states and local jurisdictions.

State governors deal with issues ranging from education to energy to health care. Governors face tight budgets and rapidly rising costs for the joint federal-state Medicaid program. In regard to energy, President Bush's plan calls for the federal government to decide where electrical transmission lines are placed when state and local communities are stricken by the NIMBY ("not in my backyard") illness. According to Iowa Governor Tom Vilsack (D), "Governors want to maintain control of this."

A familiar question in the federal-state confrontations, at least for the nation's governors, is "How do we keep Washington from messing up our lives?" Governors often agree on education issues; that is, they agree until they must figure out how to pay for new government programs. Conflicts at the various levels of federalism transcend political parties or who occupies the White House. "Governors and mayors don't like to be told what to do," says Connecticut Governor John G. Rowland (R).[29]

Livingston's second illustration of how federalism affects bureaucracy considers the *highly decentralized* nature of the American political party system. Livingston concludes that the decentralization of power within the political parties enhances the decentralization of the political decision-making process and lends strength to federalism. The character of the parties supports federalism, and federalism, in turn, nourishes the decentralized character of the parties.

According to Livingston, American political parties are decentralized in three ways:

1. As discrete units, local parties exist to pursue control over state and local governments. Political parties are free associations of citizens who wish to influence the expenditure of taxpayers' dollars.
2. Because local parties are organized at the "grass roots," national parties exercise only periodic and ineffective control over local parties.
3. Local parties exercise considerable control over national parties. National political conventions are organized by collectives of state and local political parties. Forces of the religious right, for example, have captured many GOP local party organizations and insisted that certain social issues, such as abortion, pornography, homosexuality, and prayer in public schools become GOP priorities. The Republican National Committee (RNC) might think these concerns are divisive, but President Bush could not ignore the right wing's call for "family values."[30] These priorities originated at the grass roots of the GOP party structure. Political parties are private affairs; only public opinion constrains them.

The third, and final, feature that contributes to the increased vitality of modern day federalism is the *diversity of social values* in the United States. Livingston argues that the diverse people and values within a society determine the shape and character of political and governmental institutions. Federalism, as an arrangement of political power, responds to the changing values of society. What are the social values of American society?

Policies and values differ from state to state. Some states allow lotteries; others do not. Some states are restrictive in cigarette and alcohol sales; others are not. Some states maintain tough environmental standards; others do not. Some states have taken firm positions against racial and sexual discrimination; others back off. These illustrations indicate that public bureaucrats will have considerable difficulty enforcing laws mandated by the U.S. Congress if support for such policies does not emerge from the grass roots. From affirmative action to speed limits, public administrators have difficulty implementing laws that people do not support.

Public bureaucrats have been described as timid and ineffectual and at the same time as power-seeking and dangerous. In reality, their influence depends upon the consensus of political support for government laws and programs. Cooperative federalism, the grassroots nature of the political party system, and the diverse social values that Americans hold require public bureaucrats to share power and responsibility with federal, state, and local officials. Administrative federalism is the upshot of these political compromises.

People Without Organizations—Organizations Without People

No homogeneous conceptions of civil servants and public bureaucracies exist. These entities operate in the administrative worlds of behaviors, institutions, processes, and policies. These "worlds" significantly affect the lives of public administrators.

- The *behavioral world* entails an incredibly complex amalgam of personal needs, interpersonal relations, and small and large social groupings. The deportment, habits, and tendencies of individual men and women shape the context, structure, and functions of organizations.
- The *institutional world* reflects such institutions as the college environment in which students study, professors teach, and administrators implement academic programs. Institutions have histories. Policies and procedures are "institutionalized" into formats that develop over many years. Institutions are formally defined contexts in which administrators labor and in which clientele respond.

  Students achieve—or fail—within the contexts of formalized, institutionalized academic arrangements. The organizational context determines policies and procedures for selecting, monitoring, and promoting employees and delivering services. Police, fire fighters, schools, libraries, and universities formalize—even make routine—employee behaviors.
- *Processes* are often formalized by print in local, state, and federal government functions. Communicating with employees and clientele, coordinating people and programs, motivating employees, and controlling reporting and

budgeting procedures are all illustrations of the processes of public management.

Students encounter processes as they seek a college degree. Penalties occur if you fail to:

Register for classes on time
Pay your tuition fees on time
Attend and arrive at class on time
Study effectively and consistently
Meet prescribed—or even informal—
  academic deadlines

The college experience is a process for organizing your goals and objectives.

- *Policies* are developed, implemented, and evaluated by government administrators. Individuals may influence the policies and procedures of formal organizations. Students constitute an important clientele of any college or university. Campus bureaucrats and professors are employed by the institution, respond to the behaviors of clientele, develop and interact with collegiate processes, and formulate and amend institutional policies. Effective administration includes the development, implementation, and evaluation of public policies.

In summary, the individual and group behaviors of local, state, and federal government bureaucrats reflect *people without organizations*. Legal contexts, institutional arrangements, formal processes, and policy functions portray *organizations without people*.

Source: Robert T. Golembiewski, Frank Gibson, and Geoffrey Y. Cornog, *Public Administration: Readings in Institutions, Processes, Behavior, Policy* (Chicago: Rand McNally, 1976), pp. 1–10.

Summary

- The sacrificial and heroic performance of public servants in New York, Washington, D.C., and Pennsylvania on September 11, 2001, caused more Americans to express confidence in government employees.
- The more people, the greater the demand for government services.
- Federal spending consumes 26 percent of the economy, or $9,223 per man, woman, and child; or 36 percent of the economy when counting regulatory compliance.
- Approximately 87,525 units of governments employ 20,392,000 wage and salary workers. Of this national distribution, local government units employ 53.5 percent, or 10,908,000. State governments employ 6,102,000, or 30.0 percent of the total. Federal government employs 3,381,000, or 16.5 percent, of the nationwide government workforce.
- Administration involves people, action, and inter-action. People interacting with people to accomplish a task is what public administration is all about.
- Public administration involves artistry, but it is not an art. It makes use of science, but it is not a science. In these times of declining state, local, and federal budgets, government employees engage in a craft, seeking to achieve goals and meet standards with all the creativity, capability, and civility they can muster.
- Americans have no consensus on a public philosophy by which to judge the effectiveness of government-run, taxpayer-financed public sector programs.
- Compared to the growth of the United States economy, federal tax levels have remained relatively stable over the last fifty years.
- The percentage of Gross Domestic Product (GDP) spent by the U.S. government is, in proportion to the U.S. economy, smaller than that of nearly any other industrialized nation.
- Public administration is grounded in capital, bureaucracy, and democracy. In general, the poorer a country is in capital, the less efficient are its government programs, services, and operations.
- Politics cannot be separated from culture. Families are the first organizational unit of American life. Public administrators respond to and act in a cultural context.
- Delineations of *public* versus *private* are central to the conceptual and emotional structuring of the Western world.
- Trust must be earned. The American public is conflicted, once again, over trusting government.
- Partisan politics is concerned with which political party and personalities win office. Policy politics deals with deciding which policies to adopt. System politics examines how administrative systems (decision structures) are set up to implement policies.
- In private administration, laws generally tell administrators only what they cannot do. In public administration, laws tell them what they can do.
- The Internet and terrorism threaten to alter the boundaries between the public and private sectors.
- The establishment of law, rooted in religious thought, is one of the greatest achievements of human civilization.
- The U.S. Constitution established a republican form of government and a federal system. It enacted the separation-of-powers principle and established the rule of law, representative institutions, and individual liberty. Public administration is grounded in constitutionalism.
- In the interplay of partisan, policy, and systems politics, preservation of freedom, privacy, and security in a post-9/11 world tests the viability of essential American ideals.
- The centralization of power in U.S. federalism is not accompanied by the centralization of governmental function. Conflicts at various levels of federalism transcend political parties and who occupies the White House.
- Federalism is tempered by the diversity of social values in the United States.
- The worlds of behaviors, institutions, processes, and policies significantly affect the professional lives of public administrators.

In the next chapter, we will examine the environment in which public administrators practice their craft.

VIDEOS AND FILMS

Public Administration in Action

Legalism
12 Angry Men [1957]
A powerful indictment, denouncement, and exposé of the trial-by-jury system. Martin Balsam, Lee J. Cobb, E. G. Marshall, Jack Klugman, Henry Fonda, among others. [96 min].

U.S. Constitution
Our Constitution: A Conversation [2005]
How does the Constitution help Americans solve their problems? Do your moral values determine your decisions? Sandra Day O'Connor and Stephen G. Breyer. Annenberg Foundation Trust. [30 min]

U.S. Constitution
A History of the United States Constitution [2005]
Produced by Centre Communications. 4 videodiscs. Explores how the U.S. Constitution came to be; why it has protected Americans from abuse of power and tyranny; and how the principles set forth so long ago still set the framework for today's world. [236 min]

Partisan, Policy, System Politics
LBJ [1991]
PBS television series *The American Experience*. 2 videocassettes. Pt. 1: Beautiful Texas. My Fellow Americans. Pt. 2: We Shall Overcome. The Last Believer. Covers the span of Lyndon B. Johnson's political life from his early political career through the years of his presidency. David Grubin, producer. [239 min]

Partisan, Policy, System Politics
The Making of the President [1960, 1964, 1968]
Based on Pulitzer Prize books of Theodore H. White. [247 min]

Case Study

Public Administration as Chemistry*

The following case study illustrates how students encounter academic bureaucracies as they pursue their education on college or university campuses. Steady State University is located in College Corner, in the state of Commonwealth, USA.

Let us debate the issues and not the people.

> —*Gregory A. Darrah, former SGA President*
> *Steady State University, College Corner,*
> *Commonwealth, USA*

Steady State University students were about to get an indoctrination into the whys and wherefores of United States government bureaucracy. The mix of public and private concerns helps determine the "chemistry" of the United States culture—how people relate to others and

*Chemistry is defined here as the composition, structure, properties, and reactions of a substance, and/or the elements of a complex entity and their dynamic interrelation. See *The American Heritage College Dictionary*, 3rd ed. (Boston: Houghton Mifflin, 2000).

act or interact to reach a common goal. Students encounter cumbersome academic bureaucracies throughout their academic as well as extracurricular careers. Some of these bureaucracies are private colleges, but many are organized as government-funded and -regulated units.

A course in public administration is offered as part of the political science curriculum at Steady State University (SSU) in the town of College Corner, State of Commonwealth, USA. The college town is a uniquely American institution. The United States has a very institutionalized, economically developed, skilled population, within a society that strongly encourages individual initiative. To say that America is institutionalized is to emphasize that citizens soon find out their respective interests, then join groups or institutions to try to attain what they want for themselves and their families.

Postsecondary education in the United States is a study in decentralization. In 1800, there were 32 U.S. colleges, most of which had religious affiliations, none of which admitted blacks or women. Now there are 3,600 postsecondary institutions, including about 1,500 two-year colleges, 2,200 four-year colleges, and about 450 Ph.D.-granting institutions. In 1900, less than 3 percent of adult Americans age 25 or older had a bachelor's degree; by 1970, that figure climbed to 10 percent, and by 1997, about 25 percent. Data show that 70 percent of women, 64 percent of men, 68 percent of whites, and 60 percent of blacks enrolled at a four-year college eventually graduate.[1]

One way to attain what one wants in life is to seek the opportunities afforded by a college education. That is why 16,500 students are enrolled at Steady State University—a Ph.D.-granting university. U.S. Census Bureau figures indicate that a household headed by a baccalaureate degree holder earns, on average, $40,000 more in yearly income than a household headed by someone with a high school diploma.

Consumerism is at the core of college marketing today. A "full-service college" responds to the full range of student expectations. Cable television in all dormitory rooms is part of the package. Vending and laundry machines activated by student charge cards are perks that might give a competitive recruiting edge.[2]

On the other hand, legalism is at the core of legislative endorsement of higher education. In 1862, Congress passed the Land Grant College Act, or the First Morrill Act, to provide funding for institutions of higher learning in each state. Officially known as the Serviceman's Readjustment Act of 1944, the GI Bill was signed by President Roosevelt to boost opportunities for World War II veterans. In 1954, in *Brown v. Board of Educa-*

tion, the U.S. Supreme Court declared the "separate but equal" approach to education as unconstitutional, opening opportunities for members of minority groups when school districts were ordered to run a single school system for all students, regardless of color.[3] The National Defense Education Act (NDEA) of 1958 and the Elementary and Secondary Education Act (ESEA) of 1965 set legal landmarks for promoting American colleges and universities. Government programs do not function without the enactment of laws.

The social values of College Corner are shaped by its relative lack of heavy industry, its abundance of young people and highly educated adults, and its plethora of cultural opportunities more characteristic of larger metropolitan areas. College towns are typically more politically liberal than towns without prominent colleges. They tend to be more tolerant of unusual behavior and eclectic ideas. The distinctive residential landscapes of College Corner include the traditional faculty neighborhood, the fraternity district, and the off-campus student rental area.[4]

Steady State student life administrators prefer to ignore a report from the Harvard School of Public Health that marijuana use among U.S. college students increased by 22 percent during the 1990s. The county prosecutor in which Steady State is located refuses to prosecute students for violating certain norms of the "hidden law."

The county jail already suffers from overcrowding. Law officials know that increased marijuana usage at Steady State reflects the group of high school drug users enrolling in college. Jailing college kids for breaking "hidden laws" further crowds—and taxes—the criminal justice system. Lawyers make a dime or two, but almost everyone else simply gets caught up in more paperwork.[5]

To students of public administration, the words *inductive* and *deductive* may be only esoteric reasoning methods. But all citizens interested in the pursuit of a college degree should pay close attention to five national trends. An inductive gathering of facts and figures point out the following deductive arguments.[6]

1. Increases in tuition make colleges and universities less affordable for most American families. However, in weak economies, enrollments grow faster.
2. Student federal and state financial assistance does not keep pace with tuition increases. Federal and state governments offer low-income undergraduate students financial assistance, as provided in the federal Pell Grant program, the nation's largest need-based support program for college students.

3. More students and families at all income levels borrow more than ever before to pay for college expenses. Borrowing, however, is a much greater burden on low-income students and parents.
4. Times of economic hardships—economic recessions—adversely affect state government services and personal finances. Decreases in tax revenues correspond to lower funding of public services. Higher rates of unemployment may result in decreases in family income.
5. State government financial support for public higher education has increased. But tuition charges at state universities increased still more. From 1980 through 1998, state government appropriations rose 13 percent, but tuition revenues at state colleges and universities vaulted by 107 percent.

The challenges of SSU students occur in the portrait of political economy of attaining skills, knowledge, and expertise at taxpayer expense—and personal commitments. Human behaviors, policies, processes, and institutional arrangements take place and are organized in the mix of these trends.

Jacquette Glover is 19, an African-American political science major, pre-law student, and back bencher in deliberations of the Student Government Association (SGA) and the Black Students Association (BSA). She is also a first-generation college student and a single mother. Glover has heard through the SGA and BSA grapevines that public administration is a tough course. "What's with all this focus on concepts?" Jacquette asks her public administration classmate, Maynard Wilkins.

"Well, first off, you've gotta attend class every day. Not just most of the time, but constantly," Maynard advises. "The professor says that half of life is just showing up. And, despite being an old guy, his logic makes some common sense; I got a D in my first public administration class." Now, Maynard is making a second trip down bureaucracy boulevard. "Concepts, writing, thinking, analysis, and arguments—but only based on facts," sighs Wilkins. "Professor Jachim says that everything is organized, even our class. Well, at least sometimes he's organized."

In class that day, the professor states that college students mostly relate to college bureaucracies. Are they responsive? Are they efficient? "This is the ATM generation, with TV and the Internet," explains the professor. "Young kids don't comprehend the value of organization, laws, skills, and paperwork to help them be proactive against forces in sometimes very rigid organizations."[7]

Political Correctness as Intolerance

Political correctness, or an intolerance of criticism or debate, bothers both Glover and Wilkins. Jacquette's friends accuse Maynard of "antifeminist intellectual harassment." Professor Jachim, fully tenured, white, over fifty, jaded but not cynical, says, with some dismay, "Steady State could serve as a significant source of social criticism and an initiator of new modes and molders of attitudes. But our college president thinks it's more important to be true to our name."

Jacquette, revealing rare insight for her youth, blurts: "Almost no students value activity as citizens. They're passive in public, and hardly more idealistic in arranging their private lives. They settle for 'low success' and won't risk failure." Maynard chimes in: "SSU students don't give a damn about their apathy." Upon which Professor Jachim opines: "But apathy is not simply an attitude. It is a product of social institutions—namely, the structure and organization of Steady State itself."

SSU African-American students argue for more diversity in Steady State's social fabric. "The fallacy with this diversity stuff," says Jason Ashcraft, 23, a white, upper-middle-class economics major, "is that it's reverse racism. Diversity does not mean fixed percentages of students by race, but diversity in curriculum offerings and student interests."

Jacquette, Maynard, and Jason all agreed that Steady State should fire incompetent professors. But Professor Jachim appears to stump the threesome, at least for the moment, as he advises: "You can fire the incompetents—after your parents, the faculty, the taxpayers, the state legislators, the alumni, and the SSU bureaucrats figure out a stationary definition of competence."

A centralized bureaucracy—the Commonwealth Commission on Higher Education (CCHE)—sets university tuition increases. CCHE has statutory responsibility for the statewide planning and coordination of higher education in Commonwealth, the administration of student aid programs, establishment of tuition increases, and performance of designated regulatory functions.

Statutory responsbilities of the CCHE include the approval of new academic programs at public two- and four-year institutions, an annual funding recommendation to the governor of Commonwealth and the legislature on behalf of SSU and other public higher-education institutions, and the approval of off-campus offerings of public two- and four-year institutions. CCHE hires a professional staff, headed by a director, who orchestrate higher-education policies for all state colleges and universities. The commission is the midwife between the legislature and particular state institutions.

Administrative "worlds" encompass behaviors, institutions, processes, and policies. Jacquette and Maynard are about to encounter aspects of partisan, policy, and system politics. Partisan politics are neither recognized nor appreciated at SSU. State universities apparently grow in the middle of cornfields. Somehow they got placed there. Policy making refers to consuming alcohol at fraternity parties. System decision making focuses on drop-add dates for courses in which grades are declining. Steady State College life combines diverse processes, procedures, and rules.

Jacquette and Maynard, like most SSU students, are graduates of Commonwealth's high school system—and its limitations. Unfunded mandates come with federal grants. The Commonwealth state legislature has no way to measure the effectiveness of its subsidy to Steady State students. Steady State's football team is a deficit operation. Business, criminal justice, and communication majors are in demand. The humanities, liberal arts, and sciences are less popular. In the welfare state of SSU, students rely on the workings of the market as the "bottom line" decision maker.[8]

Steady State employs a very educated workforce. Students at Steady State, however, live in the State of Commonwealth, which is known throughout the region for tolerating a mediocre secondary education system. Steady State is not the flagship university of Commonwealth. SSU is perceived as an opportunity institution where hard work and achievement are devalued. Many SSU students do not come from families with high expectations for themselves. There is a disconnect between professors and students. Professors think students could achieve more than they do. The behaviors of professors and students, as the two major institutional components, are frequently at cross purposes. Professors and students contribute to the SSU behavioral world.

Who Pays the Bills—Clients or Taxpayers?

The institutional world of Steady State is influenced primarily by the fact that SSU receives most of its financial support from the Commonwealth General Assembly. Students at Commonwealth pay only 37 percent of the costs of their education. Tuition last year went up a stunning 13.8 percent. If this trend continues, students will pay more out of their pockets for college expenses, while the state legislature and Commonwealth taxpayers pay less.

"Public policy is clearly shifting," said Warren Madden, vice president for business and finance at Iowa State University, "from low tuition to expecting students to provide a larger share." Public institutions enroll 83 percent of the nation's college students. Budget cuts and price increases directly affect these students and their families.[9]

Federalism is also part of the dynamics of Steady State; the centralization of power is not accompanied by the centralization of governmental function. The state legislature makes the laws and finances the institutional operations at Steady State, but the governmental functions are decentralized to each academic department. Federal government agencies also provide grants to be allocated, then implemented, by professors and students at Steady State. Again, the functions are delegated to the most local level of human interaction.[10]

SSU is essentially a unit of local government, located in College Corner, 113 miles from the state capital. But there is little distrust, if any, among alumni and citizens of the State of Commonwealth toward the integrity of SSU. Rarely do partisan politics affect what is taught, how the classes are delivered, or the ideologies of those teaching college courses. Policy and system politics emerge as professors express in the Faculty Senate that too much money is being spent on a football team that competes at a very low level. Of the 1,934 total employees at Steady State, only 637 are tenured professors. Steady State is a product of the middle-class government-funded welfare state; local business leaders and elected legislators look the other way when asked how tenured professors should be evaluated.

Steady State administrators, professors, and students are heavily invested in processes, procedures, and rules. Professors are protected by tenure. Their freedom of speech is also protected by the First and Fourteenth Amendments. They can say pretty much what they want to in class. But professors are accountable as far as the processes by which they interact with students. Public administration consists of people, actions, and interactions, or people relating to people. Professors are bureaucrats who teach classes with certain knowledge, skills, and expertise. But procedures, rules, regulations and processes govern their interactions with students.

Administrators establish policies, and policy making affects both professors and students. The Steady State professors elect faculty representatives to the Faculty Senate, which forges curriculum policies. Steady State is governed by a complex arrangement of fragmented, yet egalitarian and somewhat democratic, committees of professors. The Faculty Senate decisions are advisory only. Faculty Senate decisions are not binding on Steady State's President or his administration. In essence, professors can have their say about university policy matters, but they possess no formal authority to change Steady State priorities.

Steady State affords personal choice and certain opportunities. Equality, diversity, and equity are immediate priorities, but personal achievements are recognized, respected, and rewarded.

Questions and Instructions

1. What "chemistry" is manifest in the instruction of your public administration class?
2. What impact does consumerism have on maintaining a clientele for Steady State University?
3. What force has legalism and law exerted in the history of American higher education?
4. Why is political correctness dishonest and unproductive? Is a commitment to diversity "reverse racism"?
5. What are the dynamics of federalism in the administration of Steady State University?
6. How do procedures and policies regulate the activities of Steady State students and professors?
7. Is public policy shifting at Steady State University?
8. How does culture affect the behavior of SSU students—and their professors?
9. How would you define teaching competence?
10. Why are U.S. colleges and universities admired throughout the world?

Insights-Issues/Public Administration as Chemistry

Clearly and briefly describe and illustrate the following concepts and issues. Interpret the word *role* in terms of impacts, applications, importance, effects, and/or illustrations of certain facts, concerns, or issues from the case study.

1. Role of consumerism and markets at Steady State University (private-sector decision making).
2. Role of partisan, policy, and system politics at Steady State University.
3. Role of legalism and laws for making activities at Steady State University "legitimate" and accepted by Commonwealth citizenry.
4. Role of federalism in the administration of higher education at Steady State University.
5. Role of procedures and policies at Steady State University.

Notes

1. Nick Gillespie, "The New College Try," *Reason,* December 1999, http://reason.com/9912/bk.ng .the.shtml.
2. Kristi L. Wiernicki, "Perspectives: Smorgasbord of Choices," NACUBO Business Officer, February 1998, http://www.nacubo.org/website/ members/bomag/9802/perspectives.html.
3. "Looking Back on Education: Historical Events That Still Affect Us Today," http://npin.org/ library/2000/n00484/lookingback.html; see also West Legal Directory, "Government Agencies and Programs: G. I. Bill," *West's Encyclopedia of American Law,* May 17, 2002, http://www .wld.com/conbus/weal/wgibill.htmg.
4. Blake Gumprecht, "The American College Town: A Research Prospectus," June 21, 2000, http://geography.ou.edu/collegetowns.html.
5. Robin Herman, "Survey Finds Increased Use of Marijuana and Other Illicit Drugs at U.S. Colleges in the 1990s," Harvard School of Public Health, Press Releases, October 27, 2000. http://www.hsph .harvard.edu/press/releases/press10272000.html.
6. "Chapter 1: Five National Trends," *Losing Ground: A National Status Report on the Affordability of American Higher Education,* May 2, 2002, http://www.highereducation.org/ reports/losing_ground/ar2.shtml.
7. Wiernicki, "Perspectives."

8. Ryan C. Amacher and Roger E. Meiners, "Empowering Students by Increasing Competition Among Universities," *VERITAS: A Quarterly Journal of Public Policy in Texas,* Winter 2001. See also James Engell and Anthony Dangerfield, "Forum: The Market-Model University: Humanities in the Age of Money," *The Harvard Magazine,* http://www.harvardmagazine.com/issues/mj98/forum.html; and John Rouse, "'Institution,' 'university' needs collide at Ball State," *The Muncie Star-Press,* May 5, 2000, p. 4a.

9. William Trombley, "Chapter 4: 2002 Update for the States: A Dire Situation, State Budget Shortfalls Trigger Escalating Tuition," *Losing Ground: A National Status Report on the Affordability of American Higher Education,* May 2, 2002; http://www.highereducation.org/reports/losing_ground/ar5.shtml.

10. Christen Baylis-Heerschop, "FEDERAL AID TO EDUCATION," http://www. nd.edu/~rbarger/www7/fedaid.html.

Sources

Ryan C. Amacher and Roger E. Meiners, "Empowering Students by Increasing Competition Among Universities," *VERITAS: A Quarterly Journal of Public Policy in Texas,* Winter 2001; Christen Baylis-Heerschop, "Federal Aid to Education," http://www.nd.edu/~rbarger/www7/fedaid.html; James Engell and Anthony Dangerfield, "Forum: The Market-Model University: Humanities in the Age of Money," *The Harvard Magazine,* http://www.harvardmagazine.com/issues.mj98/forum.html; Nick Gillespie, "The New College Try," *Reason,* December 1999, http://reason.com/9912/bk.ng.the.shtml; Blake Gumprecht, "The American College Town: A Research Prospectus," June 21, 2000, http://geography.ou.edu/collegetowns.html; Robin Herman, "Survey Finds Increased Use of Marijuana and Other Illicit Drugs at U.S. Colleges in the 1990s," Harvard School of Public Health, Press Releases, October 27, 2000, http://www.hsph.harvard.edu/press/releases/press10272000.html; "Looking Back on Education: Historical Events that Still Affect Us Today," http://ngpin.org/library/ 2000/n00484/lookingback.html; John Rouse, "'Institution,' 'University' Needs Collide at Ball State," *The Muncie Star-Press,* May 5, 2000, page 4a; "The Students," http://porthurontokentstate.tripod.com/TheStudents/The Students.htm; William Trombley, "Chapter 4: 2002 Update for the States: A Dire Situation, State Budget Shortfalls Trigger Escalating Tuition," http://www.highereducation.org/reports/losing_ground/ar5.shtml; "Truth or Consequences," HARDWICK, http://www.hardwickday.com/trends/enroll/default.htm; West Legal Directory, "Government Agencies and Programs: G. I. Bill," *West's Encyclopedia of American Law,* May 17, 2002, http://www.wld.com/conbus/weal/wgibill.htm; Kristi L. Wiernicki, "Perspectives: Smorgasbord of Choices," NACUBO Business Officer, February 1998, http://www.nacubo.org/website/members/bomag/9802/perspectives.html.

Notes

1. Michael Hodges, "Federal Government Spending Report," *Grandfather Economic Reports,* March 2007, http://mwhodges.hom.att.net/fed_budget.htm.

2. See William I. Buscemi, "Numbers? Borrrinnng!!!," *PS: Political Science & Politics,* no. 4 (December 1997): 738–739.

3. Steven Camarota, "100 Million More: Projecting the Impact of Immigration on the U.S. Population, 2007 to 2060," http://usinfo.state.gov/utils/printpage.html. See Roy Beck, *The Case Against Immigration: The Moral, Economic, Social, and Environmental Reasons for Reducing U.S. Immigration Back to Traditional Levels* (New York: W. W. Norton, 1996). See also Ben Wattenberg, *Fewer: How the New Demography of Depopulation Will Shape Our Future* (Chicago: Ivan R. Dee Publishers, 2004).

4. U.S. Department of Labor, Bureau of Labor Statistics, "Government," http://bls.gov/iag/government.htm.

5. Herbert A. Simon, Donald W. Smithburg, and Victor A. Thompson, *Public Administration* (New York: Alfred A. Knopf, 1950), p. 3.

6. Robert J. Samuelson, "Clinton's Nemesis," *Newsweek,* February 1, 1993, p. 51; "Our Love-Hate Relationship with Government," *Washington Post,* January 27, 1993, p. A19.

7. David K. Shipler, "The Myth of Democracy," *Washington Post,* December 3, 2000, p. B7.

8. Jorge G. Castaneda, "Three Challenges to U.S. Democracy," *Kettering Review* (Summer 1997), pp. 8–20.

9. Garry Wills, "Whatever Happened to Politics? Washington Is Not Where It's At," *New York Times Magazine,* January 25, 1998, p. 27+.

10. Calvin Woodward, "AP Poll Finds Americans in a Hurry," *Boston Globe,* May 28, 2006.

11. Dwight Waldo, *The Enterprise of Public Administration* (Novato, CA: Chandler & Sharp Publishers, 1980), p. 164.

12. Michael Hodges, "Report on Trust In Government & Media," March 2007, http://mwhodges.home.att.net/trust.htm.

13. Joseph S. Nye, Jr., Philip D. Zelikow, and David C. King, eds. *Why People Don't Trust Government* (Cambridge, MA: Harvard University Press, 1997).

14. E. J. Dionne, Jr., "Mistrust in Government Puts Up a Wall," *Washington Post,* July 3, 2007, p. A15.

15. Stanley B. Greenberg, "Democrats Are Back— But," *American Prospect,* June 18, 2007.

16. Aaron Wildavsky, *The Politics of the Budgetary Process* (Boston: Little, Brown, 1979), pp. 191–193.

17. Robert A. Kagan, "Adversarial Legalism and American Government," *Journal of Policy Analysis & Management* 10, no. 3 (Summer 1991): 369–407.

18. John M. Pfiffner and Robert Presthus, *Public Administration,* 5th ed. (New York: Ronald Press, 1967). In regard to the subsequent sentence in the text, Donald S. Vaughn, former chair, Department of Political Science, University of Mississippi, points out that the law also tells the public administrator what he or she cannot do. Professor Vaughn cites the first eight amendments to the U.S. Constitution as a case in point.

19. See Alan M. Dershowitz in *The Best Defense* (New York: Random House, 1982). However, the same theme runs through many other legal statements and writings. Oliver Wendell Holmes, for example, once said that his job as Justice of the U.S. Supreme Court did not require him to "do" justice, but merely to see that the rules of the game were followed.

20. Daniel J. Appelman, "The Law and the Internet: Emerging Legal Issues," http://www.isoc.org/Iamp/paper/222/abst.html.

21. Carrie Davis, "Terrorist Attacks Spawn Greater Surveillance Powers," *Internet Law Journal,* February 2, 2002.

22. Jeffrey Rosen, *The Naked Crowd: Reclaiming Security and Freedom in an Anxious Age* (New York: Random House, 2004), p. 7.

23. Jeffrey Rosen, *The Unwanted Gaze: The Destruction of Privacy in America* (New York: Random House, 2000).

24. Charlotte Hays, "TWQ Interview: Jonathan Rauch Talks about the Value of Hidden Law," *The Women's Quarterly,* Summer 2001.

25. C. Herman Pritchett, *The American Constitutional System* (New York: McGraw-Hill, 1981), pp. 7–8.

26. David Hosansky, "Reshaping the Federal-State Relationship," *Congressional Quarterly Weekly Report* 54, no. 40 (5 October 1996): 2824–2826; Bert Waisanen, "Demographic Federalism: Defining the New Federal-State Relationship," *Spectrum: The Journal of State Government* 69, no. 4 (Fall 1996): 53–58.

27. Charlie Savage, "Bar Group Will Review Bush's Legal Challenges," *Boston Globe,* June 4, 2006; "Bush Challenges Hundreds of Laws: President Cites Powers of His Office," *Boston Globe,* April 30, 2006.

28. William S. Livingston, "Federalism in Other Countries: Canada, Australia, and the United States," in *Federalism: Infinite Variety in Theory and Practice* (Itasca, IL: F. E. Peacock Publishers, 1968), pp. 131–141.

29. David S. Broder and Dan Balz, "Bush Agenda Concerns Governors Over U.S. Role," *Washington Post,* August 7, 2001, p. A2.

30. The term *right wing* is elusive. Almost without exception, "right wingers" are traditional thinkers on nearly every issue, value, and behavior confronting partisan, policy, and system politics. For example, they hold traditional views on abortion, religion, adultery, women in the workplace, sexual orientation, military spending, taxes, economic disparity, and foreign policy involvements. Therefore, a better description might be *traditionalists.*

The Ecology of the Administrative Craft

Chapter Highlights

Our Organized Society

Equality and Efficiency

Rights and Dollars

Democracy Often Unpleasant and Hard Work

The Growth of Public Bureaucracy

Comparing Public and Private Administration

Interest Groups and the Greater Good

The Gilded Age of the Internet Era

Summary

Congestion and Transportation Ecology

If you are going to travel from one city to another in the United States, you are not likely to take a train. Travel in the United States—for the most part—is by car or airplane. Local, state, and federal governments are committed to maintaining vast systems of taxpayer-supported highways and airports.

No public service challenges the ecology of our organized society as does the country's public transportation system. *Ecology* is the relationship between living organisms and their environment. Congestion fills a system to excess, whether we consider population or traffic. Reduced traffic congestion benefits the system—it improves air quality and conserves energy. If we apply the science of ecology to public transportation, we will gain an understanding of the relationships between transportation, people, and our environmental system.

Transportation is the lifeblood of American capitalism, the connector by which commerce takes place. Citizens venture into the marketplace by foot, bike, car, bus, subway, train, or plane. To sell and realize profits, businesses must be accessible to consumers. Public transit provides that access, as

well as promoting affordable mobility, congestion management, and support for neighborhoods.

Transportation in the United States comes in many forms. The trucking industry dominates America's interstate highways. Short-haul rail passenger service, though available in some cities, is not an option for most Americans. Car rentals provide flexibility but are costly. And the advent of wholesale terror makes airline travel ever more problematic and challenging.

All fifty states support taxpayer-funded and government-organized departments of transportation. State transit units supervise traffic patterns on the highways, for motorcoaches, for trains, and for airlines. Public transit systems help promote personal freedom and private commerce; ecology is the relationship between the private marketplace and the state's responsibilities for monitoring, supervising, and regulating personal freedoms and commercial activities related to transportation.

The power of the federal Department of Transportation (DOT) is limited by constitutional

Transportation Organizations in the United States

Federal Transportation Organizations

U.S. Department of Transportation
Bureau of Transportation Studies
Federal Aviation Administration
Federal Highway Administration
Federal Motor Carrier Safety Administration
Federal Railroad Administration
Federal Transit Administration
National Highway Traffic Safety Administration
Research and Special Programs Administration
U.S. Coast Guard

Transportation Interest Group Organizations

American Concrete Pavement Association
American Public Transportation Association
American Trucking Associations Foundation
Association of American Railroads
National Asphalt Pavement Association
U.S. Army Corps of Engineers
U.S. Department of Energy

The fifty states, the District of Columbia, and Puerto Rico administer government-regulated transportation depart-ments. Local public transit operators provide services in 319 urbanized areas with 50,000 or more residents each. Transit systems receive operating and capital funding from federal, state, and local governments—and even private sector sources. However, public transit remains essentially a public service provided and managed by local govern-ments. Federal and state officials give way to local authorities, who set and adjudicate the boundaries of transit-related issues for their communities.

Sources: Paul Hawken, *The Ecology of Commerce: A Declaration of Sustainability* (New York: HarperBusiness, 1994); Hawken, Amory Lovins, and L. Hunter Lovins, *Natural Capitalism* (Boston: Little, Brown, 1999); Norman Y. Mineta, "Hearing on Congestion in the United States Transportation System," U.S. House of Representatives, Committee on Transportation and Infrastructure, April 4, 2001, p. 8; and Don Phillips, "Mounting Congestion Is Challenge to DOT," *The Washington Post*, May 15, 2001, p. A15.

guarantees to the states. Federal transit budgets are limited. A major share of the federal transpor-tation budget "passes through" Washington, as major transportation-authorizing legislation must be renewed. The DOT Secretary has a major role in policy decisions. However, the Secretary is limi-ted as far as what he or she can do and spend.

Highway transit appropriations are con-tinually reauthorized. The Federal Highway Administration (FHA) administers DOT's high-way transportation programs as provided in legislation. The Administration is concerned with the operation and environment of highway systems, including highway and motor carrier safety. The Secretary must use federal, state, municipal, and private money to mold a coherent and efficient plan to permit people and freight to stay on the move.

Congestion is the toughest challenge facing the nation's transportation ecology, and it affects all modes of transportation. Our highway system is in heavy demand. Since the 1970s, highways have experienced a 143 percent increase in vehicle miles traveled. Over the same period, only a 5 per-cent expansion of roads has taken place. Mobility is declining in virtually every metropolitan area.

In addition to the FHA, the Federal Aviation Administration (FAA), Federal Transit Admini-stration, Research and Special Projects Admini-stration, and United States Coast Guard function under the authority of DOT. The FAA promotes—and regulates—the development and safety of air commerce. With a workforce of 49,000, including 15,000 air traffic controllers, the FAA has the most responsibility of any of DOT's units. As airline travel becomes increasingly common, air conges-tion contributes to the ecological challenges of travel in the twenty-first century.

Aviation traffic is expected to increase by almost 50 percent over the next several years, to more than one billion passengers by 2011. Since airline deregulation took place in 1978, air travel has become an essential form of transport. In the 1960s and 1970s, airline travel was a luxury. Now it is primarily a middle-class experience—connecting cities not just in this country, but throughout the world. Air travel has grown faster than any other mode of transportation.

In the early 2000s, average passenger boardings at U.S. airports was 728,712,000 per year. The next two decades are forecast to bring a threefold growth in the number of airline passengers. The rate of passenger traffic is expected to show an average 5 percent annual increase through 2026. This economic forecast results in a demand for around 24,300 new aircraft—accounting for revenues of $2,728 billion.[1]

This forecast is projected despite fears of a global recession, environmental concerns about aircraft emissions, runaway fuel prices, aniquated technology used by air traffic controllers, enormous communication gaps between air carriers and passengers, and lost, misplaced, and damaged baggage. In these commercial developments, the status of public sector special districts, namely airports, grows to meet consumer demands. Governments are not getting smaller. Time will tell if they get better.[2]

Seven major airports—New York-LaGuardia, Newark, New York-Kennedy, Chicago-O'Hare, San Francisco, Philadelphia, and Los Angeles—are often congested with "significant passenger delays." Because proposed airport construction projects must be submitted to environmental scrutiny, new runways cannot be built quickly enough to allow capacity to catch up with demands.

Other agencies support and regulate transportation. The Federal Transit Administration (FTA) plans, develops, and finances the development of improved mass transportation facilities. Federal support for transit depends upon revenue from motor fuel taxes. The U.S. Coast Guard, a uniformed force, engages in law enforcement activities along the coasts. The American Public Transportation Association (APTA) is a leading participant in research and legislation regarding the transportation industry and issues relating to it. Transit demands are growing at record levels in cities around the country, especially in the near-gridlocked areas of the East and West Coasts. However, ecology concerns and regulations place legal contraints on the ability of state governments to issue permits to build new highways.

Highway congestion forces states and cities to turn increasingly to rail commuter and transit services. Rail commuter services transport suburbanites into central cities. Urban subways and light rail trolley services are other alternatives.

Freight and passenger rail systems help relieve the overcrowding on highways and at airports. Rail capacity is utilized most extensively in the Northeastern states. California, Washington, and Virginia are increasing their freight and passenger rail capacity. Whatever the mode of transportation, the federal and state governments face tremendous challenges in providing safe, environmentally responsible, and accessible public transit to both consumers and commerce.

In May 2006, the U.S. Department of Transportation announced the National Strategy to Reduce Congestion on America's Transportation Network. The strategy acknowledges that "congestion is one of the single largest threats to our economic prosperity and way of life." Congestion costs America an estimated $200 billion a year. The strategy also notes that growing congestion reduces the economic benefits derived from the movement of freight.

For trucking companies, congestion diminishes productivity and increases the cost of operations. Drivers must be paid for time spent stalled or stopped in traffic. Additionally, congestion results in decreased fuel efficiency and increased vehicle maintenance costs resulting from stop-and-go traffic conditions. Congestion also contributes to societal costs such as decreases in air quality and increases in the cost of consumer goods.

Notes

1. "Air Passengers to Triple," *Travel News,* February 8, 2008, http://www.worldtravelguide.net/news/3042/news/Air-passengers-to-triple.html.
2. Dan Schlossberg, "Late-Winter Nor'easter Shuts Down East Coast Travel," March 17, 2007, www.ConsumerAffairs.com.

Our Organized Society

Ecology is the study of the relationships between organisms and their environments, and public administrators not acutely aware of how environmental factors influence administration are doomed to failure. This chapter describes the relationship between public administrators and the environment in which they work.

Public administrators do not operate in a vacuum: Countless environmental factors buffet administrators, making their tasks remarkably complex. Public administration occurs within the framework of an organized society. The principal barriers to the effective implementation of public programs are the conflicts between the political principles of democracy and the economic principle of capitalism.

Public administration is also carried out within the political cultures of states and communities. Culture, tangible and intangible, affects the environment in which public administration takes place.

A drive down Main Street, U.S.A., will take you past banks, dry cleaning establishments, cafes, and retail stores. Keep driving and you'll pass churches, shopping malls, fast food outlets, factories, gas stations, and schools. All are examples of organizations that affect our daily existence. Organizations must be managed or administered. We live in a complex society in which public organizations are needed if the smaller, private organizations are to thrive or operate at all. The alternative is anarchy.

Public organizations receive their lifeblood from legislative, executive, and judicial collectives in our organized society. Legislatures appropriate revenues to fund public programs. Presidents, governors, and mayors carry out the legislative will of the people. Courts adjudicate disputes between parties contesting, among other things, the delivery of government programs.

With its numerous organizations, modern America is the epitome of the organized society. The legislative, executive, and judicial branches of our national and state governments are the basic units of public organization. For example, Congress enacted the Social Security program for the elderly; the Social Security Administration implements the policy; and judges decide disputed claims.[1]

Questions constantly arise concerning the fairness and efficiency of public organizations—questions that contribute to these organizations' administrative entanglements.

Why focus on equality versus efficiency, rights versus dollars, democratic capitalism versus political economy, and other trade-offs in the organized society? The answer is that public administration enjoys a very conceptual grounding in partisan, policy, and system politics. To comprehend the interplay of these definitive aspects of the field, students need to understand how government programs, agencies, and departments operate.

Thinking about the many applications of public administration requires reading, focusing, illustrating, applying, and comprehending concepts, terms, trends, facts, and principles of the field. Before departments and agencies implement goals, directives, and processes, administrators must develop an understanding of what the community wants from these units. Communities direct their public administrators to fight wars on many fronts—terror, poverty, ignorance, sickness, and even incompetence. Government cannot operate effectively if the community is not in agreement with its goals and policies.

Understanding public administration and its varied applications requires a mix of conceptual and analytical thinking, as well as deductive and inductive reasoning. A concept is a general notion or idea; conceptual thinking involves the formation of ideas, the recognition of patterns and relationships. Analytical thinking requires one to examine the parts of some larger concept, to find out their nature, proportion, function, and relationship to one another as one breaks a whole puzzle into separate parts. A deductive thinker reasons from a general, known principle to a specific, unknown conclusion, or from a premise to a logical conclusion. An inductive thinker, by contrast, reasons from a particular fact or individual case to form a general conclusion.

Students learn to think by combining conceptual and analytical thought and deductive and inductive reasoning. This chapter and Chapter 1 are especially conceptual and inductive. In order to understand the principles (and principals) of public administration, students need to think conceptually and inductively, yet be analytical and, on occasion, deductive, as they think through the diverse challenges confronting public administrators.

Students cannot learn the dynamics of the organized society if they do not work to comprehend how, where, when, and why general concepts explain agency actions and how agency behaviors contribute to emerging conceptual definitions.

Equality and Efficiency

American society professes to provide equal opportunities for all citizens. This does not, however, guarantee that citizens will achieve equal results for their efforts. Your contribution in the competitive market depends on your skills, assets, and efforts and also on the supply of and demand for what you have to offer. As free speech does not guarantee an audience, free enterprise does not guarantee a demand for one's services. Effort does not guarantee excellence. Although a student studies long and hard for an exam, an "A" is not a foregone conclusion. It is easy to see that these factors, when applied to individuals in the marketplace, can result in unequal individual outcomes.

Our organized society, therefore, exists in an environment of equal rights and unequal outcomes. Conflicts between these two phenomena result in tensions between the *political principles of democracy* and the *economic principles of capitalism.*

The United States is a democratic society with a capitalistic economic system. In keeping with our democratic political philosophy, we hold elections. In keeping with our economic philosophy, we let supply and demand decide who achieves financial success. Arthur Okun describes contemporary U.S. society as a "split-level institutional structure" because of the combination of democracy and capitalism.[2]

We have a "split-level institutional structure" because private institutions value efficiency, while public sector institutions favor equality. Efficiency gives the top producers priority, and equality gives everyone priority.

The services provided by public administrators reflect the concept of *equality.* The concept of *efficiency* comes from letting the marketplace decide what goods and services are produced and purchased. Services and programs that governments produce are available to all citizens. Police, fire, and sewers are usually provided by government. Electricity, water, gas, garbage, and telephone services, although regulated by government, may be provided privately. Even though these utilities are produced privately, the government regulates their activities to assure "fairness" of delivery.

The rich and the poor have equal rights to travel on our network of interstate highways. The economic realities of the efficient marketplace may determine, however, that certain people lack any car to drive while others cruise along the turnpike in chauffeur-driven Mercedes. A public program is not maintained just for the very poor or the ultra-rich, but for the masses of middle-class citizens.

In that respect, America's highway system serves as an example of an efficient economy—the more we drive, the more road and gasoline taxes we pay. "With the great quarrel between capitalism and socialism in mothballs," says Suzanne Garment, "critics of the free market do not attack it by offering some grand, principled alternative. Instead, they march under the banner of prudence, calling for a pragmatic mixed economy that values markets but avoids the extremism preached by excessively principled free-market ideologues."[3]

The values of equality and efficiency are always in conflict. The pursuit of efficiency necessarily creates inequalities. Citizens make economic choices, such as buying a car or riding a bus. If we all choose to commute only by car, bus drivers will be out of work, the victims of our equal freedom of choice and the workings of our efficient economy. It is often the role of the public administrator to step in if one of these values begins to supersede the other. This is where the public administrator's regulatory powers come into play.

Through these powers, public administrators exercise great influence in determining the role of the marketplace. The public administrator does not, however, have unlimited regulatory power. As regulators of private interactions, public administrators are checked by limits on administrative power spelled out in laws such as the Administrative Procedure Act.[4]

In defending the state of affairs regarding equality versus efficiency, Okun says, "The market needs a place, and the market needs to be kept in its place."[5] The market is kept in its place by the limited regulatory powers of public administrators. So equality may be sacrificed for the sake of efficiency, and efficiency for the sake of equality. What provisions exist to protect the individual's equal rights in this market-driven economy? The issue of economic decision making in the late twentieth century focused on ensuring the right mix between government and private sector participation. A purely government-led or a pure market-dictated economy will not only be ineffective in economic terms but also in social and political terms. The market is usually more efficient than the public sector, but the latter is needed to ensure that the allocation of resources is balanced.[6]

American society promotes equality by allocating social and political rights equally and distancing these rights from the marketplace of supply and demand. For example, due process is a constitutionally mandated guarantee. Governments in the United States must act with fairness, justice, equity, and reasonableness, irrespective of economic considerations. Accused criminals have the right to seek fairness in prosecution through due process. Equal opportunity is protected in a court of law by constitutionally mandated due process. Due process is the legal cornerstone of the craft of public administration.

There are two types of due process, *substantive* and *procedural. Substantive due process* refers to the content or subject of a law. *Procedural due process,* the more commonly litigated of the two, refers to the procedures used in implementing a law or administrative practice. Deciding whether a law is constitutional is part of procedural due process.

The concept of equality is also demonstrated in the open admissions policies of many state universities. These policies require a university to accept students from all ethnic groups and income levels. The taxpayers subsidize public education to guarantee fairness, justice, equity, and reasonableness in the admission of students. The state university must pay careful attention to due process. On the other hand, a private college is not required to follow due process as stringently as a public university. A private college may, with some restrictions, select only those students who meet certain criteria that may not be used at a state institution. Their adoption of standards of excellence embraces the value of efficiency.

The value of equality is embodied in guarantees grounded in basic citizen rights. The value of efficiency is embodied in market productivity. Public administrators operate in a complex environment in which these two fundamental values often collide. The challenge of public administration must be to maximize efficiency without sacrificing equality, and vice versa.

Rights and Dollars

As we have already pointed out, a trade-off exists between our equal rights as individuals and the unequal distribution of wealth in our society. The United States pursues an egalitarian political and social system, yet it generates gaping disparities in economic well-being.

We acquire and exercise our rights without any monetary charge; rights cannot be bought or sold in the marketplace. Thus, in a sense, rights infringe on economic efficiency, and the marketplace infringes on rights. The poor are disadvantaged in terms of buying and political power. Campaign financing and lobbying regulations favor persons with access to wealth. Yet the poorest person has the right to challenge the wealthiest business, or even the government, in our system.

The conflicting values of equality and efficiency are manifest in government organizations. Everyone has an equal right to apply for public sector employment, but certain people will be more efficient in fulfilling the tasks of a given position. On the one hand, we emphasize individualism—rights, self-interest, liberty, freedom, choices, and rewards. On the other hand, we value community—consensus, agreement, sacrifice, altruism, and commitment to the greater good.

This mixture of equality and efficiency is crucial to American economic development. If one does not have the right to enter the marketplace, one is not going to be productive, on an individual basis or for the greater good. Therefore, if women, minorities, or other persons are denied equal opportunities, they have no chance to benefit themselves or society, and our productiveness as a nation suffers. Most citizens support equal access to opportunities. However, many question whether we can or should guarantee equal outcomes.

Equality and rights are the groundings for community consensus. Individual citizens agree on what elements constitute a satisfactory community for all. Markets value efficiency. Communities tax market profits and commit them to public administration programs—schools, streets, transit systems, parks, libraries, and other public services. Capitalistic markets depend upon community consensus, or democracy, and on the efficient use of community resources.

TABLE 2.1
Contrasting Equality and Efficiency

Equality	Efficiency
fairness	advantage
socialism	capitalism
public	private
community	individualism
government	business
inductive	deductive
democracy	bureaucracy
mediocrity	excellence
employees	executives
rights	responsibilities
chaos	order
collective bargaining	merit
accessible	restricted
common	elite
equal opportunity	affirmative action
republicanism	fascism
elections	courts
horizontal	vertical
egalitarianism	authoritarianism
tolerant	judgmental
incompetence	expertise
open	closed
level	hierarchical
modernization	traditionalism
decentralization	centralization
average	superior
diversity	homogeneity
Christianity	religion
April 15th	July 4th
Democrats	Republicans
female	male
bottom-up	top-down

Note: These terms are neither all-inclusive nor mutually exclusive as applied to American governments and politics. They are offered as discussion points in the ecology of American public administration. The mix of these concepts is witnessed in the development, implementation, and evaluation of government programs and functions.

Table 2.1 contrasts equality and efficiency. The terms listed in the table are neither all-inclusive nor mutually exclusive as applied to American politics, governments, parties, or leaders; they are simply meant to provoke thinking, discussion, questions, and commentary.

Two crucial questions for our democratic and capitalistic society are where and how the organized modern society establishes boundaries between the *domain of*

Equality as Investment?

Nations forge trade-offs between income equality and economic efficiency. Scholars and policy makers argue that greater equality reduces investment and dampens the incentive to work. Lane Kenworthy, however, argues that a more egalitarian distribution of income encourages consumer demand—as a greater number of workers become able to purchase consumer goods. If this premise is correct, egalitarian governmental policies would benefit efficiency, not dilute it.

Kenworthy offers evidence based on cross-sectional data from seventeen advanced industrialized economies over the period 1974–1990. He finds no adverse impact of greater equality on investment or work effort. According to his research, higher levels of equality associate with stronger productivity, growth, and trade performance. A national emphasis on equality does not adversely affect productivity, trade balances, inflation, or unemployment.

Source: Lane Kenworthy, "Equality and Efficiency: The Illusory Trade-off," *European Journal of Political Research* 27, no. 2(1995): 225–254.

rights (equality) and the *domain of the capitalistic marketplace* (efficiency). Conflicts between these domains are inevitable and pose dilemmas for our split-level, political economy.

Our democratic, capitalist society searches continuously for better ways to establish clear boundaries between the domains. The marketplace needs equality to put some *humanity* into *efficiency;* our democracy needs efficiency to put some *rationality* into *equality.* Capitalistic and bureaucratic systems will be more effective if they are more humane. Equality will be more acceptable to those who value efficiency, and hence, less chaotic, if consistent standards are applied to the diverse applications of the democratic principle.[7]

Democracy is characterized by equality, due process, fairness, participation, suffrage, and electoral politics. Capitalism implies efficiency, productivity, hierarchy, competition, and entrepreneurship. Public administration finds its origins in democracy but owes much to the fundamental principles of capitalism.

The modern organized society can also be described as a *political economy.* Our society is *political* in that citizens have the opportunity to organize and set priorities about what is important to them. The *economy* comprises the collective productivity of goods and services our society generates. The split-level structure of the political and economic systems affects public policy and administration. Communities cannot expect to have public services without providing an ample supply of *revenues,* raised by taxing citizens and businesses. Our organized society, therefore, depends upon the political system and the structure of the economic sector. The maintenance of the relationship between political power and economic structure is vital to the future of American democracy. Public administrators depend on capitalism to generate economic growth to pay their salaries and to finance the delivery of their services to the American people.[8]

The thrust of democratic capitalism comes from the opposing values of political power and economic structure. Middle-class citizens who do not possess the means of economic production agree to the private ownership of capital stock; meanwhile, wealthy citizens, who own the instruments of economic production, accept democratic institutions that allow interest groups to press for further allocation of resources and output. The large middle class thus permits members of the economic elite to own capital and organize production (the economy). The economic elite allows the general population to affect the allocation of resources and the distribution of the material effects of economic production.[9]

The craft of public administration occurs within the general economic shift from manufacturing toward services—in both outputs and employment. The upgrading of skills and gender balancing of the labor force triggered a major revolution in the field of education. A century ago, women received little or no education; now they constitute more than half of most student populations. The U.S. economy has also shifted from domestic to international competition, removing most forms of protectionism and heightening the importance of international communications through the World Trade Organization (WTO) and the United Nations (UN). Globalization and the removal or reduction of tariff barriers have resulted in the growth of gross domestic product (GDP) and worldwide efficiency. Workers, consumers, and the economy have benefited from competition with other countries.[10]

Still, the shift from a manufacturing-based to a service-based economy raises many concerns. The taxpayers, or our children through deficit federal spending, must raise revenues to pay salaries and benefits for the government employees providing services. The economic philosophy is that manufacturing jobs, not service sector jobs, are the core of any nation's political economy. We could argue that those government employees have a vested interest in deficit federal spending. After all, the Reagan-Bush years were devastating to public employees. However, the number of state and local employees increased by nearly one million, to 15.4 million. Since 1982, there has been a 20 percent growth in the workforces of state and local governments and an 8 percent increase in the federal workforce. The nation's industrial base is declining while demands for public services continue.

Americans opt for "market justice" over "political justice" as benefits are allocated by the economic marketplace, not by government programs and policies.[11] American participation in politics has declined as citizens do not perceive their economic well-being as being greatly dependent on political involvement.[12] The U.S. cultural emphasis is on individualism, not political participation. Citizens separate their personal lives and interests from other matters of national life. America is the country of *individualism par excellence*.[13] This culture of individualism negatively affects political participation among lower-income groups, causing an economic class bias to emerge. Citizens of higher economic status are much more politically involved than those of lower economic status.

Democracy Often Unpleasant and Hard Work

In 1994, Republicans swept to power with the zeal of self-described revolutionaries—limiting the size and reach of government, boosting the nation's security, and ending an era of a privileged, imperial Congress. The era of conservative ascendance witnessed business tax break extensions, trade measures, tax cuts time and again, expansions of government powers to combat terrorism, and growth of government discretionary spending. "It's a mixed bag," concluded former House Speaker Newt Gingrich, the political architect of the 1994 "Contract With America." "In a three-year period, we changed things fairly dramatically. We, candidly, then failed."[14]

The legacy of twelve years of conservative governance (1994–2006), with consolidated Republican Party control of Congress and the executive power of George W. Bush, is brief and relatively inconsequential, according to Julian Zelizer, a Boston University congressional historian. Zelizer concludes that the Republican era does not compete with the creation of Social Security, Medicare, voting rights, civil rights, the Marshall Plan, or Dwight D. Eisenhower's interstate highway system. The liberal ascendancy began with the New Deal, was renewed by the Great Society, but ran out of political steam at the Reagan revolution.[15]

Republican commitments to individual freedom, personal responsibility, and accountable government, all worthy principles, got trumped by the political principle's of arrogance, corruption, and preservation of power. Caleb Crain succinctly states the challenge of American partisan, policy, and systems politics:

> Democracy is unpleasant and hard work. It isn't enough to hold the right opinion. You have to speak to those who hold what you believe to be the wrong opinion in such a way as to convince them.
>
> Who wants to convince a horde of greedy, fearful, television watching philistines they ought to give up their fantasies of strength and righteousness? Who volunteers to take the lamb carcass from the hyena? Let's just go back inside and whine about how terrible hyenas are.[16]

David Brooks, conservative columnist for the *New York Times*, argues that voter "disaffection with the G.O.P. was not philosophical. It was about competence and accountability."[17] E. J. Dionne, in his 1991 book, *Why Americans Hate Politics*, opines that Americans are fed up with symbolic politics, dying ideologies, and false choices.[18] Brooks says that the 2006 election did not define a new political era; it marked the end of an old one. Republicans screwed up, says Brooks, and Democrats—as in the 1974 sweep—surged in. Conservatives enjoyed access to authority and power, but they were "out of sorts." They were losing the political fight for political consensus.[19]

Dan Balz, staff writer for the *Washington Post*, affirms that the voters in the 2006 midterm elections rejected President Bush's policies in Iraq and the Republican style of governance. He questions if the 2006 results rejected conservatism itself. In the view of strategists in both parties, the election was not a powerful affirmation of the Democratic Party.[20]

The political party that claims the electorate's shifting center—with its potential to change the balance of power—must gain the public's trust to keep Americans safe in a world of terrorism and rogue-state threats, keep the United States competitive in a global economy and restore the social contract that provides economic security to workers, and navigate the uncertain domains of social and cultural issues in a way that both preserves American values and accommodates greater tolerance in an increasingly diverse society.

In the contest of partisan, policy, and systems politics, terrorism and rogue-state threats gave Republicans historic political advantages. Globalization results in corporate restructuring. Worker economic security and the social contract are radically jeopardized. Health care, entitlement reforms, taxes, trade, immigration, and numerous social issues forecast battlegrounds for a much more even playing field. Elections will be more than a contest of personalities. They will include ongoing economic and cultural fights over policy making and government systems.[21]

Thomas Friedman writes of the power of green—reconnecting America abroad and restoring America to its natural place in the global order. Friedman, author of *The World Is Flat*, calls for redefining the term *green*. *Green* is often defined by its opponents as "liberal," "tree-hugging," "sissy," "girlie-man," "unpatriotic," and "vaguely French." Friedman's redefinition of *green* is geostrategic, geoeconomic, capitalistic, and patriotic.

Friedman insists that he is not trying to trump traditional Republican and Democratic agendas. He is attempting to bridge them as Americans confront three major issues: jobs, temperature, and terrorism. He asks: How do our kids compete in a flatter world? How do they thrive in a warmer world? How do they survive in a more dangerous world? Friedman offers his motto for seeking political consensus. "Green is the new red, white, and blue."[22]

According to Jonathan Rauch, partisans of George W. Bush claim that the greatness of their leader is "misunderestimated." In the end, they argue, President Bush will de vindicated. They argue that Bush will be to the war on jihadism what Harry Truman was to the Cold War. Truman was the plainspoken midwesterner who established the systems politics that guided subsequent decision makers through decades of post–World War II and post-Korea perils. The debate is whether Bush's course is less of a long road than a dead end.[23]

Rauch suggests that one of the best ways to judge a president's effectiveness is to ask: Did he solve more problems than he created? Presidents are prone to mischief and grandiosity. Rauch suggests that Bush leaves a legacy—in the form of four challenges or headaches:

- *The fiscal mess.* The Bush tax cuts and spending increases resulted in an astonishing reversal. A $236 billion federal surplus in fiscal 2000 became a $400 billion deficit four years later. With Baby Boomers retiring and expensive Medicare drug benefits in high demand, the country's fiscal challenges demand sacrifice, compromise, clarity, and direction.
- *The Iraq mess.* The gamble over war in Iraq has cost the United States in lives, money, prestige, and strategic focus. War, by its very definition, is full of controversy because young soldiers die before their time. The human toll of civilians killed in American's police action cannot be calculated. Money appropriated for Iraq cannot be spent on local steet maintenance. U.S. prestige is compromised by our arrogance, folly, and wrong-headedness. Longer-term foreign policy issues receive far less strategic attention.
- *International disgrace, scorn, shame, humiliation, ignominy.* The decline of America's image around the world means that we have less foreign policy leverage with friends and foes, their domestic power points, interest groups, citizens, educators, and diplomats. When the bad cop is ever too forceful, reckless, and uncaring, the good cop is met with suspicion, reluctance, and false hopes. The world is a difficult place to manage—even with George W. Bush off the political stage.
- *An extralegal terrorism war.* President Bush waged his terrorism war as a permanent state of emergency. The Bush administration has not been forthcoming on the details regarding the legal underpinnings of the surveillance program. The function is administered by the National Security Agency's eavesdropping program.[24]

The Department of Homeland Security supervises spying activities and detains and interrogates terror suspects. Legal adhockery is the norm in Bush policy making. The White House views Congress as a nuisance rather than a partner. Bush circumvents outmoded laws and treaties. The danger is that both American form (law abiding) and idea (democracy) are violated.[25]

Liberal columnist Frank Rich argues that the corruption of American partisan, policy, and systems politics

> grew out of the White House's insistence that partisanship—the maintenance of that 51 percent—dictate every governmental action no matter what the effect on the common good . . . the first M.B.A. president ignored every rule of sound management. Loyal ideologues or flunkies were put in crucial positions regardless of their ethics or competence. Government business was outsourced to campaign contributors regardless of ethics or competence."[26]

John DiIulio, the Bush administration's "compassionate conservative" political scientist on loan from the University of Pennsylvania, bemoaned an unprecedented "lack of a policy apparatus" in the Bush White House. DiIulio said: "What you've got is everything—and I mean everything—being run by the political arm. It's the reign of the Mayberry Machiavellis."[27] Every public initiative and all government programs originate with effective—or ineffective—politics. Examples of the arrogance of incompetence and personal prerogatives permeate policy making at the Bush White House:

- The unqualified political hacks and well-connected no-bid contractors who sabotaged the occupation and reconstruction of Iraq
- The outsourcing of veterans' care to a crony company at Walter Reed Army Hospital
- The politicization of science at the Food and Drug Administration and the Environmental Protection Agency
- The purge of independent United States attorneys by Alberto Gonzales's Department of Justice
- The inept response to hurricane Katrina by the Federal Emergency Management Agency[28]

According to Kevin Phillips, author of *The Emerging Republican Majority* (1969), three broad and related trends brought the Mayberry Machiavellis into power: first, the role of oil in defining and distorting American foreign and domestic policy making; second, the ominous intrusion of radical Christianity into politics and government; and third, the astonishing levels of debt—current and prospective—that both the American government and the American people continue to accumulate heedlessly.[29] The Republican Party became the vehicle for all three interests—a fusion of petroleum-defined national security; a crusading, simplistic Christianity; and a reckless credit-feeding financial complex.

The pursuit of oil has been one of the defining elements of American foreign policy since the 1970s. The Bush administration was unusually dominated by oilmen. The United States has embraced petro-imperialism, writes Phillips. The U.S. military has been transformed into a global oil-protection force. This political coalition includes Christian evangelicals, fundamentalists, and Pentecostals, who make up about

40 percent of the Republican Party electorate. Millions of their adherents believe that Armageddon, as described in the Bible, is coming soon. Oil price hikes, hurricanes, tsunamis, and melting polar ice caps verify and reinforce their religious beliefs.

The creation of a national debt culture leads, says Phillips, to the "financialization" of the American economy. This is manifested in an economy that has turned away from manufacturing and toward moving and managing money. The national debt tops $8 trillion. Huge trade imbalances contribute to an explosion of corporate debt, state and local bonded debt, trade-imbalance-induced international debt, and credit-card- and home-mortgage-driven consumer debt.

The president who assumes office in 2008 may be inclined to believe not in less or smaller government, but in better government. The Mayberry Machiavellis, from every indicator, had contempt for government. As electoral victors, they led government—but all the while looked down on it, disparaged it, and belittled its consensus role in American life. Disillusionment with President Bush's management of the Iraq war and the aftermath of Hurricane Katrina became the antithesis of smart, effective government.[30]

Instead of focusing on government being larger or smaller, the next president may signal to citizens what the role of government should be, highlight definitions of responsiveness and competence, guarantee honesty and transparency, and show support for federal government action in protecting the social safety net.[31]

The Growth of Public Bureaucracy

The organization of federal, state, and local jurisdictions is evidence of the fragmented nature of public administration in the United States. The concept of federalism, or the structure of politics in the United States, implies a system of authority apportioned constitutionally between the national and state governments.

Frederick S. Lane points out the three principal dimensions of federalism: *political, fiscal,* and *administrative.* The political dimension accounts for the ways in which local, state, and national jurisdictions participate in decision-making processes. The fiscal dimension indicates which jurisdictions pay what amount for services. The administrative dimension tells us which level will supervise the administration of various services. Lane concludes: "Federalism is a contradiction: it tries to marry diversity and central direction."[32]

According to U.S. Bureau of the Census figures for 2002, federal, state, and local governments number 87,900. They provide transportation, public safety, health care, education, public utilities, and an array of court systems. State and local governments employ about 7.5 million workers. Local governments—such as counties, cities, special districts, and towns—employ almost two-thirds of these workers. In many states, citizens are served by more than one local government unit.

There are 87,525 units of local government. Of these, 38,971 are general-purpose local governments.

- Counties (3,034) may contain cities or towns and often include unincorporated rural areas. There are 35,937 subcounty governments (townships and municipalities).
- Townships (16,504) often encompass suburban or rural areas and may or may not contain municipalities. Townships do not exist in some states. As of 2002,

the number of township governments had decreased by 696, or 4 percent, since 1952.

- Municipalities (19,429) are self-governing bodies or any formally created subnational government. Municipalities enact ordinances or local laws. Municipal courts have exclusive jurisdiction over violations of municipal ordinances. In 2002, there were 2,624 more municipal governments than in 1952—a 16 percent increase.
- School districts (13,506) include elementary, middle, secondary, and postsecondary government institutions. Postsecondary special districts provide academic or technical courses or both in colleges, universities, professional schools, community or junior colleges, and technical institutes. The educational services industry also includes libraries, vocational schools, and specialized training institutes. Over the past half-century, the number of school districts has decreased by 80 percent—from 67,355 in 1952 to 13,522 in 2002.
- Special districts (35,052) are independent, limited-purpose governmental units (see Table 2.2). They usually perform a single function or activity. Large

TABLE 2.2

Special District Governments by Function, 2002

Function	Number	Percent
Total	*35,356*	*100.0*
Single-Function Districts	*32,157*	*91.0*
Natural resources	7,026	19.9
Fire protection	5,743	16.2
Water supply	3,423	9.7
Housing and community development	3,413	9.7
Sewage	2,020	5.7
Cemeteries	1,670	4.7
Libraries	1,582	4.5
Parks and recreation	1,314	3.7
Highways	767	2.2
Health	743	2.1
Hospitals	735	2.1
Education*	530	1.5
Airports	512	1.4
Utilities other than water supply**	485	1.4
Other	2,194	6.2
Multiple-Function Districts	*3,199*	*9.0*

*Primarily school-building authorities.

**Includes electric power, gas supply, and public transit.

Note: These data have not been updated since 2002, but the Census Bureau indicates that they have changed little, if at all, as of March 2008.

percentages of special districts administer natural resource usage; examples include drainage, flood control, irrigation, soil, and water conservation services. Special districts have increased by 265 percent—from 13,340 in 1952 to 35,356 in 2002.[33]

Demands for government services have multiplied with an expanding population. The population of the United States in 1950 was 157,813,000; by 2000, it had increased to 283,230,000; in 2008, it was more than 303,600,000 (out of a world population of 6,656,000,000). The federal government has devolved, or decentralized, turning many services over to state and local governments; devolution is the practice whereby the federal government delegates to state and local governments the development, implementation, and management of government programs. The practice of welfare reform illustrates federal government devolution. The 1996 Welfare Reform Act provided block grants that gave state governments the prerogative to devise programs that meet their needs. The nature of government services, as provided by state and local governments, will continue to change as relationships between federal, state, and local jurisdictions shift in the political economy of the twenty-first century.

Comparing Public and Private Administration

Public and private administration differ in important ways. These differences can be compared in two areas: *substantive* and *procedural.*

Substantive issues of public and private administration include questions concerning politics versus profits, the measurement of objectives, and management versus administration. These are all areas of potential conflict.

Procedural issues address management as a universal process. Issues for procedural deliberation include open versus closed systems, methods of evaluation, criteria for decision making, personnel systems, planning, and efficiency.[34]

Substantive issues refer to conceptual or abstract concerns such as goals, objectives, means, ends, values, results, and priorities. Nobel Prize-winning author Herbert Simon argues that the means and ends of public administration differ significantly from those of private administration.[35] He maintains that the importance of an end or value should not be ignored and that the process, or means, of management is a value in itself and cannot be separated from other values.

The purpose of a college education, for example, is to seek learning, training, and knowledge about the significant values of life. The *end* is learning, training, and knowledge. Education is the *substance* and the institution is the *procedure.* The institution provides the procedural means for attaining the specific substantive ends. The *means* are provided by the curricula of the respective disciplines. In other words, the *means* for achieving the learning, training, and knowledge you seek are to meet the requirements of your discipline's prescribed curricula by attending classes and successfully completing exams.

Justice and the implementation of justice can also illustrate *ends* and *means.* Justice, in the philosophical realm, is an *end* in itself, a commonly held value. Justice can only be found in the United States by a *means*—due process of law. Justice is an example of a substantive issue; the matters of the judicial process constitute processes, authorities, and institutions that enforce procedural concerns. By unpacking the distinctions between substantive and procedural issues in public administration, we can clarify the differences between administration in the private and the public sectors.

Substantive Issues

1. **Politics versus Profits.** Decision making in public bureaucracies is achieved by meeting the objectives of compromise, consensus, and democratic participation. These objectives are different from the private sector's emphasis on the concepts of efficiency, rationality, and profit. Although the goals of public administration and private administration both respond to outside clientele pressures, their concepts of bottom-line accountability differ: one's god is a consensus of citizens concerned about the issues confronting an entire community, and the other's god is profit.

2. **Measurement of Objectives.** The private sector ultimately makes rational decisions based upon clear, concise, and quantifiable statements found in the sales ledger. The public sector deals with social intangibles such as health, welfare, and common defense.

3. **Management versus Administration.** In the private sector, the term *management* commonly refers to those persons in line *positions,* whereas in the public sector, the term *administration* refers to those in line *functions.* Line personnel command, have authority, and are generalists; staff personnel possess knowledge and skills, give advice, and are specialists. The term *management* is characterized by decision making in the private sector corporate model of hierarchy.

Procedural Issues

1. **Open versus Closed Systems.** Procedural concerns, such as accountability, reflect the dilemma of the open versus closed system, or the goldfish bowl of public administration versus the closed boardroom of private administration.

2. **Methods of Evaluation.** Community leaders seek consensus, agree to compromise, and advocate citizen participation to find support for policies. In contrast, efficiency, rationality, and concern for profit cause private sector entrepreneurs to view corporate evaluation differently. The public sector focuses on social good; the private sector emphasizes fiscal control. The two may, in some cases, be incompatible.

3. **Public versus Private Decision-Making Criteria.** Although the formal steps in decision making may be similar in both public and private administration, the criteria managers use to make decisions are not. The definition of the goal or problem, the desired consumer response, and the allocation of resources may apply similarly to both sectors: the logic, or mode of thinking, behind decision making differs.

      The public sector university's bookstore is, for example, under very different constraints from a privately run bookstore across the street. The public sector bookstore demands a higher standard in procedural process (the manner in which a function is carried out) and maintains certain expectations and guarantees in hiring, firing, promotions, and general conduct of bookstore business. The private sector bookstore can sell items based upon the supply and demand of the marketplace; the public sector bookstore must respond to every course, no matter how esoteric or obscure, and to every program offered by the state university.

4. **Personnel Systems.** Several differences exist in personnel systems. Unlike an applicant in the private sector, an applicant for a full-time civil service position governed by a merit system will go through a fixed process, monitored by law. Public sector employees also enjoy the privileges of administrative due process because laws prescribe guidelines for the recruitment, selection, promotion, and retention of employees. Merit plans that evaluate skills, knowledge, and expertise are a hiring tool, but they may differ greatly from agency to agency. Private enterprise employees have no guarantees of due process.

5. **Long-Term and Short-Term Planning.** Planning may be considered part of the process of decision making. The private sector manager does not need to seek consensus among employees before acting; the manager alone makes decisions, and the company's profit or loss ledger reflects success or failure. For the public sector employee, planning becomes hazardous if leadership is continuously changing after elections.

   Public officials need program continuity and political stability to carry out their responsibilities consistently. In the private sector, planning is easier because there are no automatic demands of due process or legally prescribed guarantees concerning hiring, firing, and promotion.

6. **Efficiency.** Hierarchical control, coordination, planning, meritorious performance, and lines of authority are emphasized in both the public and private sectors. However, the bottom line, or profit concern, of the private sector allows managers to realize success or failure immediately; in the public sector, with its less precise methods of evaluation, it may take longer to evaluate the efficiency and success of a public service.

Blurring or Bifurcation?

On the substantive issues we have discussed (politics versus profits, measurement of objectives, and management versus administration), a comparison of the public and private sectors reveals more blurring than bifurcation. A comparison of procedural issues (open versus closed systems, methods of evaluation, public versus private decision-making criteria, personnel systems, planning, and efficiency) reveals distinctions in regard to the accountability factor, but similarities in developing participative personnel systems to evaluate the expertise, knowledge, and skills of employees.

The public sector is grounded in *political equality* with consideration for everyone's opinion, seeking consensus, compromise, and democratic participation. The private sector is based on *economic efficiency,* seeking definitive results, rationality in decision making, and the maximization of profit. In practice, the realities of political equality and economic efficiency blend into what many call the "American System."

To a larger degree than most people realize, Alexander Hamilton's "American System" still plays a critical role in American economic development. The government uses investment and trade policies to promote American industry and create jobs. President Dwight D. Eisenhower's interstate highway system was a 1950s version of Hamilton's system of canals. U.S. Trade Representative Charlene Barshefsky followed Hamilton's lead when she signed agreements making certain that U.S. companies were able to access world telecommunications markets. Profits for the rich may mean jobs for the rest of us. If so, perhaps special interests and national interests are joined.[36]

Public administration, then, differs in significant ways from private administration. These differences hinge largely on the greater legal accountability of the former and the greater flexibility of the latter. Determining which sector is the most efficient remains a complex question, subject not only to differences in products and procedures but also to differences in purposes and processes.

Interest Groups and the Greater Good

The corps of Washington lobbyists has grown steadily since the New Deal, but especially since the early 1970s. This growth parallels the growth in federal spending and the expansion of federal authority into new areas. Voters may appear to demand political reform, but government is unlikely to change except in composition. The unwieldly size and contradictory complexity of modern governments has developed because of the cumulative inertia of entrenched lobbyists and special-interest groups. Reforms continue, but they come only gradually. Substantive change can come from the presidency or the electorate, but not unless individuals are willing to make personal sacrifices for widespread social welfare.[37]

Lobbyists compete vigorously to safeguard traditional spending in their areas of interest. Industries, labor unions, ethnic groups, religious groups, professional organizations, citizen groups, and even foreign business interests all periodically—and some continuously—seek to exert pressure on national and state legislatures to attain legislative goals. *Pressure by interest groups usually has a selfish aim: Their members wish to assert rights, win privileges, or benefit financially.* A group's power to influence legislation is often based less on its arguments than on the size of its membership, its financial resources, and the astuteness of its lobbyists. If there were any doubt about the increasing presence of special interests in American politics, within the Capital Beltway—the interstate highway that circles Washington, D.C.—there are 2,200 trade groups that employ more Washingtonians than any other organization except government or travel and tourism.

Expert articulation of particular citizen interests drives public bureaucracies in the United States. Legislatures write vague laws. Public administrators interpret those statutes with specificity in the *Federal Register.* The statutes are then codified in the *Code of Federal Regulations.* The public philosophy of the United States in the twenty-first century is no longer capitalism but *interest group liberalism,* a concept developed by Theodore J. Lowi. Lowi claims that capitalism has declined as an ideology and is dead as a public philosophy. Capitalism, the old public philosophy, has become outmoded since World War II because the elite, such as lobbyists, no longer agree on whether government should play a role in making policies for private citizens or for private sector businesses. Republicans and Democrats, as participants in interest group liberalism, fully agree that government should be a player in monitoring, if not directing, the relations among private citizens.[38] Interest groups reflect partisan bearings. Labor unions lean toward Democratic Party candidates, while many, but not all, business groups flock toward Republicans.

As the Great Depression ended and World War II began, U.S. capitalism came to be called "conservatism," but Lowi argues that this description is a misnomer. He states that capitalism never became conservative, but declined because it became irrelevant and erroneous. Capitalist ideology, according to Lowi, did not endure as the public philosophy because it could accept only one legitimate type of modern social control—competition. Lowi concludes that the old dialogue between liberalism and conservatism "passed into the graveyard of consensus," spelling the "decline of meaningful adversary political proceedings in favor of administrative, technical and logrolling politics. In a nutshell, politics became a question of equity rather than a question of morality. Adjustment comes first, rules of law come last, if at all."[39] As interest groups clash, the priority becomes equal opportunity for any group to put forth its unique version of how life should be conducted. The values of any particular organization are secondary.

In interest group liberalism, diverse groups check the values, or perspectives, of opposing interests by arguing for their own set of values in the great American marketplace of ideas. Milk producers, tobacco growers, billboard advertisers, moviemakers, bankers, physicians, broadcasters, cable TV operators, farmers, entrepreneurs, and energy interests are represented by a few of the more than two thousand lobbyists who insist that their concerns should be written into law. Whether liberal or conservative, the elite want to use the power and funding of government for their personal ends.

According to Lowi, the most significant difference between liberals and conservatives, Democrats and Republicans, can be found in the interest groups with which they identify. The values of organized interest groups guide Congress members in casting their votes, presidents in shaping their programs, and bureaucrats in exercising their administrative discretion. The only necessary guidelines for framing laws depend upon the validity or legitimacy of interest group demands.[40]

The philosophy of interest group liberalism is pragmatic, with government playing the role of broker, and is optimistic about government's role; that which is good for government is also good for society. The liberal process of private interaction with public officials is accessible to all organized interests and offers no value judgments concerning any particular claim or set of claims. Interest group liberalism defines the public interest as the amalgamation of claims of various interests. The principle of representation extends into public bureaucracy as administrators provide due process and a voice to all citizens.

To represent such diverse political, economic, and cultural interests, legislatures make open-ended, vague laws and issue broad delegations to public administrators to regulate interests in society. Says Lowi: "It [interest group liberalism] impairs legitimacy by converting government from a moralistic to a mechanistic institution. It impairs the potential of positive law to correct itself by allowing the law to become anything that eventually bargains itself out as acceptable to the bargainer. . . . Interest group liberalism seeks pluralistic government in which there is no formal specification of means or of ends. In a pluralistic government there is, therefore, no substance. Neither is there procedure. There is only process."[41] In other words, procedures and processes become vital, and substance and values are at the mercy of the strongest interests.

In recent years, private interests have contributed ever increasing amounts of money to participants fighting either to preserve the status quo of the political system or to change it, subsequently purchasing privilege, power, and profit. It would not be an exaggeration to assert that the American government—President, executive branch, and Congress—has been bought and sold. The Madisonian faction is firmly in the saddle and rides the nation.[42]

Quid pro quo (one thing in return for another) is a pragmatic approach to America's version of democratic capitalism. Access to capital dominates democracy. Do rich people and interest groups give large sums of money to politicians to promote good and just causes? Lee Hamilton, a Congressman from Indiana for more than a generation, reveals that "money, money, money, and the money chase" dominates political talk on Capitol Hill. As columnist Robert Higgs states, "the root of the problem lies not in the takers, who will always find a way to take, but in the givers. Foxes do not voluntarily evacuate the henhouse," Higgs speculates. "The hydra-headed government now dominating this country is inherently corrupt."[43]

In an era when politics seems, increasingly, to be the pursuit of self-interest under the banner of some high-sounding principle, one can be excused for doubting whether the opponents of campaign finance reform are really so passionately devoted to protection of the First Amendment. Nonetheless, the free speech argument is important enough to address on its merits.[44]

Interest group liberalism argues that national policy making is the province of organized lobbies. These groups work to the detriment of the overall public interest. They lead to an uncontrollable, amoebalike federal bureaucracy. Richard Nixon, Gerald Ford, Jimmy Carter, George H. W. Bush, and Ronald Reagan all governed under the auspices of interest group liberalism.

With Democrats controlling Congress, liberal interest groups pushed for new programs, added regulations, and expanded legal rights. Federal agencies implemented the new laws, regulations, and programs. The new governing philosophy, as noted, emerged as variations on interest group liberalism. Special-interest-driven government became the political norm.

The mid-1990s saw three balanced budgets. Under eight years of Bill Clinton, the size of the federal government shrank substantially in relation to the economy. However, the tune changed when George W. Bush and the Republicans won power. The governing philosophy became interest group conservatism. The people who professed to dislike the old version of interest group politics expanded, exploited, and substituted dominant conservative interests for the once dominant liberal interests.

Liberal officials were beholden to the Democratic Party's largest financial and political backers. They included public employees and teacher unions, lobbies representing women, civil rights, and gays, senior citizens, welfare advocates, the entertainment industry, and trial lawyers. The Democrats governed with disproportionate focus on policies that mattered far more to these groups than to the entire country.

However, the dominant conservative interests formed a rival constellation with Republican legislators. They served the special interests of corporations, energy and contracting sectors, evangelial Christians, wealthy investors, gun owners, and the conservative media.

The clients, patrons, and causes changed. Gay marriage, profanity, and indecency became targets of conservative Republican policy making. Job protection for teachers and government workers, affirmative action, abortion rights, the elderly, and malpractice reform mattered less to conservative lawmakers. The enterprise of governing Washington as a special-interest spoils system results in bloated, ineffective government.

Conservatives came into power believing in less government. Spending on the 101 largest programs that the Newt Gingrich Contract With America Republicans called for eliminating in 1995 rose 27 percent under a continuously Republican Congress. The hypocritical, corrupt, and ridiculous ruled. Conservative principles got lost in the arrogance of power.[45]

The Gilded Age of the Internet Era

Pressure groups manipulate the laws by which we live. A generation ago, lobbyists were portrayed as fat, cigar-smoking men who lined the pockets of lawmakers with $100 bills. This stereotypical description no longer applies, but the connotation of corruption persists. Rallying constituents through "grassroots" telemarketing has become as suspect as the old images of backroom bribery. The onslaught of a thousand identical postcards is discounted as a lobbying trick, and a hundred calls originating from a telephone bank arriving in the office on the same day are recognized for what they are. The new lobbying is much more subtle.

Researchers, rather than high-priced lobbyists, now inhabit the offices of Washington's most powerful interest groups. The clout of these groups depends on the sincerity of support they receive from actual voters back home. The ability to "buy" politicians or manipulate a groundswell of last-minute phone calls has less relevance than it used to. The "iceberg" principle of legislative success posits that the powerhouses of interest group persuasion are not very visible at the Washington "waterline" of influence. But these interest "icebergs" are very big and very menacing, and they "run" in deep political waters.

Interest groups are valued more for the votes they can deliver on behalf of certain candidates than for direct monetary contributions. Memberships are geographically dispersed and politically active. Members focus their activities on a narrow range of issues. They are true believers in the organization's cause. They turn out in droves on election day. In low voter turnout elections, committed voters may spell the difference between victory and defeat for partisans. And reelection is high on the priority agenda of partisans.

According to the Center for Responsive Politics, Washington's influence industry managed to build its lobbying business in 2006. However, growth was relatively flat in an election year. The profession of influencing public policy (lobbying) suffered ethical scandals of considerable magnitude and consequence. Federal lobbying overall increased just 1.7 percent in 2006—from $2.41 billion

TABLE 2.3
Total Lobbying Expenditures

Year	Billion
1998	$1.45
1999	1.44
2000	1.53
2001	1.61
2002	1.80
2003	2.03
2004	2.16
2005	2.40
2006	2.62
2007	2.54

Source: Center for Responsive Politics, http://www.opensecrets.org/.

in 2005 to $2.45 billion in 2006 (Table 2.3). Reported lobbying grew 10 percent in 2005.

The pharmaceutical, biotechnology, and health products industry spent more than $165 million in 2006, leading all industries for the eighth straight year. During the decade 1998–2007, insurance interests, electric utilities, computers/Internet, and business associations were the top lobbying spenders (Table 2.4). Among individual clients, the U.S. Chamber of Commerce reported spending $72.7 million on federal lobbying in 2006, up from $39.8 million in 2005. Top five spenders for 2006 were the American Medical Association, AT&T and its industry trade group, the U.S. Telecom Association, and AARP. The biggest spenders for the entire decade 1998–2007 are shown in Table 2.5.

Nearly 4,000 lobbyists worked on issues related to the federal budget and appropriations, more than on any other issue in 2006 (Table 2.6). The growth of this specialty was unusual. According to Sheila Krumholz, Executive Director of the Center for Responsive Politics, billions of dollars in federal government spending are earmarked to private interests. "To get money out of the government," says Krumholz, "or to save yourself some money in taxes, you need a lobbyist with the know-how and network to navigate the complicated budget process."[46]

The Center for Responsive Politics calculates spending on lobbying as defined under the Lobbying Disclosure Act of 1995. Spending by corporations, industry groups, unions, and other interests that is not specifically for lobbying of government officials, but is nevertheless meant to influence public policy, is not reported. This spending may exceed what is spent on direct lobbying. These activities include public relations, advertising, and grassroots lobbying.

Jeffrey Birnbaum, longtime observer of lobbying and government spending, speculates that influence peddling ranks with health care and home building as America's great growth industries. Between 2000 and 2005, the number of registered lobbyists more than doubled, to 34,750. Fees that lobbyists charge their new clients

TABLE 2.4

Lobbying: Industries Ranked by Expenditures, 1998–2007

Industry	Ranking
Pharmaceuticals/Health Products	1
Insurance	2
Electric Utilities	3
Computers/Internet	4
Business Associations	5
Education	6
Real Estate	7
Oil & Gas	8
Hospitals/Nursing Homes	9
Misc Manufacturing & Distributing	10
Health Professionals	11
Civil Servants/Public Officials	12
Securities & Investment	13
TV/Movies/Music	14
Air Transport	15
Automotive	16
Misc Issues	17
Telecom Services & Equipment	18
Telephone Utilities	19
Defense Aerospace	20

Source: Center for Responsive Politics, http://www.opensecrets.org/.

increased by as much as 100 percent. Birnbaum points out that the lobbying boom has been caused by three factors:

- Rapid growth in government
- Republican control of both the White House and Congress
- Wide acceptance among corporate executives that they need professional lobbyists to tap into federal government sending.[47]

In the 1990s, corporations fended off proposals that restricted them or cost them money. The endeavor was reactive. Pro-business political candidates were elected to run the executive and legislative branches. The process turned from defense to offense. Well-placed lobbyists were hired to go on the offensive to find ways of profiting from the many tax breaks and liberalized regulations.

Republicans were not just pro-business. They were also pro-government. Federal outlays jumped almost 30 percent from 2000 to 2004—to $2.9 trillion. Federal spending and budget deficits increased. Government functions in the areas of defense, homeland security, and medical coverage are paid for by taxpayers but often implemented by private sector entrepreneurs.

TABLE 2.5

Lobbying: Clients Ranked by Expenditures, 1998–2007

Client	Ranking
U.S. Chamber of Commerce	1
American Medical Association	2
General Electric	3
American Hospital Assn	4
Pharmaceutical Rsrch & Mfrs of America	5
AARP	6
Edison Electric Institute	7
Northrup Grumman	8
Business Roundtable	9
National Association of Realtors	10
Blue Cross/Blue Shield	11
Boeing Company	12
Freddie Mac	13
Exxon Mobil	14
Southern Company	15
Verizon Communications	16
Ford Motor Company	17
General Motors	18
Fannie Mae	19
Lockheed Martin	20

Source: Center for Responsive Politics, http://www.opensecrets.org/.

TABLE 2.6

Lobbying by Issue, 1998–2007

Issue	No. of Reports
Federal Budget and Appropriations	35,150
Taxes	31,508
Health Issues	28,703
Trade	21,183
Transportation	17,699
Defense	17,400
Energy & Nuclear Power	17,144
Medicare & Medicaid	16,259
Environment & Superfund	16,133
Education	14,328

Source: Center for Responsive Politics, http://www.opensecrets.org/.

The road to riches is called K Street, the lobbyists' boulevard in the nation's capital. The going rate for the political art of persuasion is $300,000 per year. Many legislators leave elected office on Capitol Hill to lobby their former colleagues from K Street. A former state governor and national political party chair now is compensated more that $1 million per year as president of an insurance association. As one lobbyist opines, Washington has become a profit center.

Under the Bush administration, the number of new federal regulations declined by 5 percent, to 4,100. The number of pending regulations costing businesses or local governments $100 million or more declined by 15.5 percent, to 135. According to Robert Livingston, Republican former chair of the House Appropriations Committee and now prominent Washington lobbyist, "Companies need lobbying help. . . . As government grows, unless you're right there to limit it, it can intrude in just about any industry. There are agencies that love to do things and acquire new missions. People in industry better have good lobbyists or they're going to get rolled over."[48]

Former Congressman Livingston's comments represent a skewed perspective on the U.S. Constitution. Elected presidents, governors, legislators, and judges—not selected bureaucrats of whatever personal skills, competence, and expertise—are supposed to make and implement laws. Elected legislators—not private sector lobbyists—are expected to enable, monitor, and restrict the work of those bureaucrats.

Opinion polls show that politicians are bought and sold by the rich and connected. Birnbaum concludes that campaign finance laws are really legal fiction. "Electoral donations are considered within the law even though they are actually bribes at root," concludes Birnbaum. "Think of them as 'legalized bribery.'"[49] Interest groups, industries, and labor unions give money to purchase votes.

The Gilded Age of a century ago featured corrupt railroad and oil barons. The audacious and shameless still act as if the public trust were a cynical joke—business as usual, the power of arrogance. David Safavian, former chief of the Bush White House federal procurement policy, who was convicted of false statements and obstruction of justice, worked for Jack Abramoff, who pleaded guilty to fraud, tax evasion, and conspiracy to bribe public officials.[50] Partisan, policy, and systems politics continue to suffer. Government functions as the end product of out-of-control democratic capitalism.

Summary

- Ecology is the relationship between private economic developments, or the marketplace, and the state's responsibility for monitoring, supervising, and regulating personal freedoms and commercial activities. Government employees do not operate in a vacuum, but in a complex environment.
- Modern America is the epitome of the organized society. The organized society exists in an environment of equal rights and unequal outcomes. Conflicts result between the political principles of democracy and the economic principles of capitalism.
- Students learn to think by a combination of conceptual and analytical thought and deductive and inductive reasoning.
- Congestion is the toughest challenge in the nation's transportation ecology.

- The craft of public administration is changing as the economy shifts from manufacturing toward services—in both outputs and employment.
- The political economy of the United States is one of democratic capitalism. The thrust of this ideology comes from the opposing values of political power and economic structure.
- Democracy is characterized by equality, due process, fairness, participation, suffrage, and electoral politics. Capitalism rests on efficiency, productivity, hierarchy, competition, and entrepreneurship.
- Rights are acquired and exercised without any monetary charge. Rights cannot be bought or sold in the marketplace, but they may infringe on economic efficiency.
- Public administration finds its origins in democracy but owes much to the fundamental principles of capitalism.
- The "body politic" of the United States is more pragmatic than ideological.
- Democracy is unpleasant and hard work. It isn't enough to hold the right opinion. You have to speak to those who hold what you believe to be the wrong opinion in such a way as to convince them.
- 89,527 governments were counted in 2007, of which 89,476 were local governments. Counties number 3,034, townships 16,506, municipalities 19,431, school districts 13,522, and special districts 35,356.
- Demands for government services have multiplied with an expanding population.
- The dimensions of U.S. federalism are political, fiscal, and administrative.
- As demands for government services have multiplied with an expanding population, the federal government has devolved, or turned over many services to state and local governments.
- Americans opt for market justice over political justice. Benefits are allocated by the economic marketplace—not by government programs and policies.
- The U.S. cultural emphasis is on individualism—not political participation.

Citizens separate their personal lives and interests from matters of national life. America is a country of individualism par excellence.

- Substantive issues of public and private administration raise questions concerning politics versus profits, measurement of objectives, and management versus administration. Procedural issues concern open versus closed systems, methods of evaluation, decision-making criteria, personnel systems, planning, and efficiency.
- Pressure groups manipulate the laws by which we live. The clout each of these groups yields depends on the sincerity and depth of support from actual voters back home.
- Quid pro quo (one thing in return for another) is the pragmatic approach that defines America's version of democratic capitalism. Access to capital dominates democracy.
- The public philosophy of the United States is interest group liberalism. Whether liberal or conservative, elites utilize the power and purse of government for personal ends.
- The philosophy of interest group liberalism is pragmatic—with government exercising its role as broker. In a pluralistic government, procedure and process may be as important as substance.
- The effectiveness of interest groups among elected officials, consumers, and government bureaucrats depends, in large part, upon the group's number of members, the size of its budget, and the expertise of its staff in Washington and/or any one of fifty state capitals.
- The president who assumes office in 2008 may be inclined to believe not in less or smaller government, but better government.
- One of the best ways to judge a president's effectiveness is to ask: Did this president solve more problems than he or she created?

Now that we have explored the ecology of the craft of public administration, we are ready to move to another important subject that public administrators must be aware of—the anatomy, or structure, of government organizations.

VIDEOS AND FILMS

Public Administration in Action

Interest Groups
Buying the War [2007]
A production of Public Affairs Television. Examines the reporting and political spin that shaped the public mind prior to, during, and following the 2003 invasion of Iraq. Princeton, NJ: Films for the Humanities & Sciences. Bill Moyers, host. [87 min]

Interest Groups
Free Speech for Sale [2004]
A Bill Moyers special, a production of Public Affairs Television, Inc., Princeton, NJ: Films for the Humanities & Sciences. Examines effect money has on free speech and political debate. [57 min]

Interest Groups
The Gun Fight: The Power and Politics of the NRA [2001]
Produced by ABC News, Princeton, NJ: Films for the Humanities & Sciences. Looks at the National Rifle Association, one of America's most powerful grassroots organizations. Examines where it derives its power and how it wields influence through lobbying and financing campaigns. [43 min]

Fairness
To Kill a Mockingbird [1962]
Due process of law. Based on Harper Lee's novel. In a dusty Southern town during the Depression, a white woman accuses black man of rape. [129 min]

Equality and Efficiency
The Great Depression and the New Deal [1996]
Examines the causes of the Great Depression, the stock market crash, the New Deal, the growth of unions, and birth of the modern welfare state. Schlessinger Video Productions. [35 min]

Equality and Efficiency
People Like Us: Social Class in America [2001]
Raises questions about ways Americans classify each other, how our inherited social class affects our self-perceptions and our expectations, and how race and other factors complicate an already complex arrangement of social distinctions in U.S. society. Center for New American Media. [124 min]

Case Study

Public Impacts of Private Interests

The following case study illustrates the public impact of private interests. It portrays how state and local government priorities are misdirected in favor of welfare for the rich. The ecology is evident in the minds of many. In this scenario, the rich get richer at the expense of the middle and lower classes.

It comes to why the ballparks matter to us—because exactly comparable people played a comparable game in this ballpark for generation after generation.

—*George Will*
The Washington Post

What is more Boston than Fenway Park?

—*Peter Gammons*
Boston native and ESPN-TV commentator

Almost a hundred years ago, when distinctions between the public and private sectors in the United States were far less complex, a baseball park was built in Boston. On April 20, 1912, Fenway Park officially opened for professional competition.[1]

After two rainouts, the Red Sox defeated the New York Highlanders (now parading around as the New York Yankees) 7–6 in 11 innings in the first professional baseball game played at Fenway Park. Baseball was pastoral in its origins, but the sport was an urban game.

Woodrow Wilson had not yet been elected by the smallest of margins over Bob Taft and Teddy Roosevelt. The Progressive Era had not yet begun. The Federal Trade Commission was not around to monitor unsavory business practices. Children were exploited in the labor force. World War I was yet to be played out on the hillsides of Europe, the federal income tax did not exist, and the Federal Reserve Board had not been created to regulate the American monetary system.

Except for Fenway and Wrigley Field in Chicago, the old parks of the golden age of American baseball are gone—victims of people's discomfort and inconvenience, their own obsolescence, and wrecking balls. They include Ebbets Field, Brooklyn; the Polo Grounds, Manhattan; Braves Field, Boston; old Comiskey Park, Chicago; Sportsman Park, St. Louis; Briggs Stadium, Detroit; Forbes Field, Pittsburgh; Crosley Field, Cincinatti; Shibe Park, Philadelphia; and Griffith Stadium, Washington.

The interiors of these fields of dreams were covered with advertising. No provisions were made for sanitation, the handicapped, or overcrowded seatings. Nothing was standardized. Conformity was not a concern.

Students do not have to be baseball fans to realize that this industry is permitted to operate as an economic cartel—better known as a monopoly. Organized baseball is an association of industrialists—and the industry is professional baseball.[2]

Major League Baseball (MLB) enjoys a complete monopoly of the sport. Franchise owners threaten to relocate their teams unless they receive large tax subsidies and related perks from their home cities. Institutional, ideological, and political factors prevent the repeal of baseball's antitrust exemption.

Next to the old North Church, Bunker Hill Monument, the U.S.S. *Constitution*, and Freedom Trail, the Red Sox—a baseball team that, until 2004, had not won a World Series since 1918—confuse public and private concerns about as much as any culture permits. The Red Sox are Boston's "800-pound gorilla." The Boston American League baseball club does—and gets—what it wants.[3]

The Red Sox are a beloved New England institution. But the team is part of a larger legalized, formalized, routinized, controlled, wealthy monopoly of American professional baseball teams. Major league baseball commissioner Bud Selig, also owner of the Milwaukee Brewers, strongly supported efforts to secure public monies for the private interests of Boston's American League baseball club.

Welfare for the Rich?

Red Sox management lobbied state and local government officials to soak the Boston and Massachusetts taxpayers to the tune of $352 million for a new ballpark. The team's plan relied heavily on ticket surcharges and game-day parking fees to repay the city's investment in the project. The team was to cover any cost overruns on the purchase of adjacent properties and pay for the cleanup for the $665 million project.[4]

But the power in Boston and Massachusetts is dispersed. The governor, mayor, state senate president, and state house speaker supported the appropriation of 352 million taxpayer dollars to destroy the old park and build a new stadium next door. The new stadium project needed the approval of the Boston City Council. The land would not come cheaply.[5]

The city was required to exercise eminent domain and compensate landowners adjacent to the 1912 structure. Not only did Boston's public sector elites lobby for large taxpayer spending for a new stadium, but the city's private sector elites called for "welfare spending" for the community's 800-pound gorilla—amounting to public welfare for the very rich. Prominent leaders from the Boston business community played behind-the-scenes roles in efforts to craft spending compromises.

Proponents for new sports facilities argue that infrastructure spending improves local economies in a number of respects:

- Building the new arena or stadium creates construction jobs.
- Fans and team employees generate new spending in the community—expanding local employment.

- The team brings in tourists and company personnel to the host city—also enhancing local spending and employment.
- A "multiplier effect" operates to increase local income—causing still more new spending and job creation.[6]

"Economic growth takes place when a community's resources—people, capital investments, and natural resources like land—become more productive," write Roger G. Noll and Andrew Zimbalist.[7] Most spending emerging from new stadium construction is a substitute for other local recreational spending—for example, at movie theaters and restaurants. Stadium construction is a consumption expense rather than an investment that produces more long-term jobs and local businesses.

Professional sports are popular with the American public. New stadium technology intensifies the tendency of sports teams to seek new homes. Approximately 115 professional teams aspire to move into new arenas or stadiums. The construction boom for housing these teams is heavily subsidized by federal and local taxpayers, and the tax bills will not stop until all payments are made. Taxpayer subsidies to pro sports are difficult to curb because the pro teams are so popular.[8]

Red Sox ownership wanted to demolish Fenway and replace it with a $665 million replica across Yawkey Way. The new place would include ten thousand more seats, more luxury boxes, more concessions, more merchandise-sales areas, in-stadium team offices, better clubhouse facilities, and a parking garage—all of the amenities found at modern-day ballparks.[9]

Enter Dan Wilson and Save Fenway Park (SFP)—an interest group with approximately 500 contributors. SFP, as a community, citizen-based group, sought a compromise that would meet the needs of the team, fans, and taxpayers. The interest group posed a question both pragmatic and sentimental: Why not just renovate Fenway Park?[10]

Age may be on the side of the old ballpark. Fenway is a national treasure; it is a historic landmark, the oldest baseball park in the major leagues. The park preceded Babe Ruth. Ted Williams swung his bat in the batter's box. Carlton Fisk homered off the foul pole. Bucky Dent homered over the wall. This baseball diamond is a living baseball museum and the number one tourist attraction in Massachusetts.

The Boston Globe commissioned a public opinion poll to gauge how citizens felt about investing their tax dollars in a private venture. Only 34 percent of those polled supported the ball club's financing plan—despite the team's promise to repay the public's $352 million investment. "The bottom line is Bostonians don't want public money used for this project," concluded Gerry Chervinsky, the CEO who conducted the survey.[11]

The SFP organization and Fenway Community Development Corporation (CDC) released a detailed plan to renovate the park as an alternative to the club's desire to build a new, nearly $1 billion stadium. The SFP renovation plan proposed building three decks, replacing nearly all the seating, and constructing parking garages and other related facilities on adjacent lots. The plan would preserve the Green Monster (the left-field wall) and the brick facade of the 1912 structure along Yawkey Way.

"This process has demonstrated that a public planning process can lead to something that satisfies everyone's needs," stated Fenway CDC president Lisa Soli. "It's in stark contrast to the backroom deals that surrounded the Red Sox plan." Boston is the cradle of American democracy. But Boston politics feature concentrations of political power and rigid economic structures. Fighting both city hall and the city's 800-pound gorilla is difficult! SFP and CDC have proven that participatory politics takes energy, commitment, time, and windows of opportunity. The SFP-CDC plan received favorable reviews from city council members and community groups.[12]

The Red Sox drew 2,970,755 fans in 2007, the best year in club history. The team is a very good market draw despite having the highest average ticket prices in all of

Red Sox Attendance by Decade

Decade	Total Attendance (in millions)	Average Annual Attendance
1912–1919	3.6	450,823
1920–1929	3.3	326,899
1930–1939	4.8	482,117
1940–1949	9.6	963,382
1950–1959	11.3	1,131,197
1960–1969	11.5	1,150,469
1970–1979	18.2	1,815,588
1980–1989	19.6	1,955,117
1990–1999	23.3	2,325,372
2000–2006	19.2	2,743,146

Source: www.redsoxconnection.com/fenwayattendance.html

major league baseball, a team that failed to make the playoffs, and the smallest ballpark in the major leagues—just 33,871 seats. The small park is regularly sold out, even though every home game is televised throughout New England. The new owners have been expanding Fenway Park, finding ways to increase capacity. Seating capacity as of 2008 is 36,984 for a day game and 37,400 at night. Sellouts began in 2004 and are ongoing.

What perspectives can this Fenway Park case offer students of public administration?

A review of history helps place current dilemmas into an expanded understanding. Baseball still is America's first sport, its national pastime. For many, after a day at the office, toiling for the boss and the all-American dollar, family and baseball come next.[13] The season is a daily process extending from February to almost November. Baseball is a democratic game, as even smaller athletes can play second base. The game has been exported to Cuba, the Carribean, and Asia. The golden era of baseball was a product of the Progressive Era, when President Wilson traveled through Europe trying to make "the world safe for democracy."

Fenway Park opened the same day the *Titanic* sank, when a ship's safety in a sea full of icebergs depended mostly on the captain's experience—not on technology. Television and the Internet were not yet around to blend notions of public and private.

Baseball and Ecology

How does the industry of organized baseball relate to its environment? Baseball and the ecology of American society share many common features. Equality is promoted if one can swing a bat and pitch a ball. Efficiency is ingrained in the baseball fabric, too: If you can really swing a bat and throw a ball with speed, a market may exist for your skills. At this juncture, supply and demand enter the picture. Professional baseball players average $2 million each season. Civil services may get a piece of this economic windfall as federal, state, and local governments tax baseball's *Titanic*-like salaries.

The decision to tear down Fenway Park—or to renovate it—points out public and private differences. In terms of politics versus profits, the governor, mayor, state legislature, and city council must balance economic interests with their own political goals. The baseball team, as a private sector endeavor, is mostly focused on the bottom line—profits. How do Boston citizens measure team versus city objectives? Is the trade-off World Series wins versus good garbage pickups?

Citizens may hear different points of view from "Red Sox management" and the "city administration."

When taxpayer dollars are spent, decision-making procedures must be open to everyone. "Last time I checked, this was a democracy," stated Rob Sargent of the Massachusetts Public Research Interest Group. "This is precisely the kind of thing that should be debated in public."[14] The Red Sox management, state and city administrations, well-connected media from the *Boston Globe* and the *Boston Herald,* corporate executives, and big labor engaged in convoluted attempts to secure $352 million to permit Boston's 800-pound gorilla to sit where it wanted. In the minds of many, subsidizing the Sox meant the "rich getting richer" at the expense of the middle class.

Boston is historic, wealthy, Irish, European, and sometimes sophisticated. The town's major industry is higher education. The state of Massachusetts is frequently referred to as "Taxachusetts." State and local governments prosper in these environs. As Tip O'Neill, late Speaker of the U.S. House of Representatives, famously pointed out, "All politics are local."

The Green Monster is part of a private domain—but also part of a very public park. The Big Dig is a $14-billion-dollar public-sector effort to bury Boston's expressways underground and make the city "richer in green"—not only in commerce and in federal dollars, but in trees, parks, and clean air. The people of Massachusetts are pragmatic, seeking compromises between the extremes of equality and market forces. Pragmatic Bostonians insist that the market needs a place, but also needs to be kept in its place.

The law of supply and demand is short-term, and sports is show business. The secret of Fenway's appeal may be based on the ecology of this confined field of dreams. If Fenway's 33,871 seats were not so scarce, perhaps not so many folks would make the effort to fill them. The long queues along Yawkey Way to buy tickets at $60 each are egalitarian: The line forms at the rear—regardless of one's race, sex, color, or creed.

Some things do not change. Teddy Roosevelt was the original Progressive thinker and actor. Industries—and markets—come and go. New concentrations of skills, expertise, and wealth emerge. A better method of community decision making in response to MLB's economic power might be to invoke antitrust laws to break up the cartel—forcing the American and National leagues to compete against each other.

Professional baseball salaries and schoolteachers' salaries are not even in similar ballparks. However, the prospects for reducing taxpayer subsidies to sports teams are not good. Karl Marx was wrong. Religion is not the opiate of the people; baseball is.

Principle and Principal Coincide?

The new Red Sox management determined that the old baseball park, after all, had both principle, or moral worth, and principal, or monetary value. Engineering designs to rebuild the 1912 structure deemed not feasible by the former owners are now more than probable. The nearly century-old park's capacity would be increased to almost 44,000. Renovations will be accomplished over a three-year span. Two new decks will be added.[15]

The principle of this case study is that the Boston baseball club is saving a sporting shrine of historical value. The new Red Sox management estimates the cost of building a new stadium at approximately $300 million.

A rough estimate of renovation costs is about 60 percent of that amount. The principal is the money the Red Sox and Massachusetts save by keeping Fenway adjacent to the Fens. Scarce taxpayer dollars may be directed to pay for public projects more directly benefiting citizens and the common good.

In 2008, Fenway Park, the oldest and smallest baseball park in the major leagues, still stands. The Red Sox have not lost a World Series game since 1986. In 2004 and 2007, they became not only American League Champions, but World Champions—defeating the New York Yankees, the St. Louis Cardinals, the Cleveland Indians, and the Colorado Rockies.

For Fenway Park fans, this case study has a happy ending. After years of tears, the Red Sox suddenly have an empire to call their own. Red Sox ownership is committed to improving and renovating Fenway Park. The old and the new have a marketplace in Boston.

Questions and Instructions

1. How might deductive and inductive thinking affect citizen decision making for and against industry monopolies?
2. "Rights are acquired and exercised without any monetary charge." What does this statement mean?
3. Explain the term *political principles of democracy* and *economic principles of capitalism* as they relate to the choices citizens confront in society.
4. In what circumstances should government employees apply principles of equality and efficiency?
5. "America is the country of individualism par excellence." What does this statement mean?
6. Public- and private-sector prerogatives differ on substantive and procedural issues. Explain why this is so.
7. In interest group liberalism, diverse groups check the values, or perspectives, of opposing interests by arguing for their own set of values in the marketplace of ideas. Explain and illustrate.
8. Is Major League Baseball a monopoly? If so, why? Explain and illustrate.
9. Baseball is pastoral in its origins, but the sport matured as an urban game. How did the ecology of the times affect baseball and the larger American culture? Explain with specific examples.
10. "Karl Marx was wrong. Religion is not the opiate of the people; baseball is." Explain this statement.

Insights-Issues/Public Impacts of Private Interests

Clearly and briefly describe and illustrate the following concepts and issues. Interpret the word *role* in terms of impacts, applications, importance, effects, and/or illustrations of certain facts, concerns, or issues from the case study.

1. Roles of equality and efficiency in making short- and long-term decisions for or against a new baseball park.
2. Roles of rights and dollars in affording all citizens procedural guarantees in regard to the effects of new construction plans.
3. Role of progressive thinking for opposing, reforming, or accepting baseball industry monopolies.
4. Role of substantive and procedural issues for determining public-private decision-making alternatives if historic Fenway Park should be taken down.
5. Role of special interest groups in promoting—and questioning—construction of a new baseball stadium in Boston.

Notes

1. Robert F. Bluthardt, "Fenway Park and the Golden Age of the Baseball Park, 1909–1915," *Journal of Popular Culture* 21, no. 1 (Summer 1987): 43–51.
2. Jerold J. Duquette, *Regulating the National Pastime: Baseball and Antitrust* (Westport, CT: Praeger Publishers, 1999); see also John Rouse, "Corporate Welfare, Taxpayer Subsidies, and Home Field Advantages," *Public Administration Review* 61, no. 5 (September/October 2001): 630–635.
3. Tom Farrey, "Historic Fenway Faces Uncertain Future," November 8, 2000, http://espn.go .com/mlb/s/2000/1031/849361.html.
4. Meg Vaillancourt, "Lawmakers, Red Sox Reach Tentative Agreement," *Boston Globe,* July 26, 2000.
5. Kathleen O'Toole, "Luxury Stadiums Point Up Problems with Pro Sports Monopolies, Economist Says," *Stanford [Online] Report,* http://www .stanford.edu/dept/news/report/news/ january7/stadiums.html.
6. Roger G. Noll and Andrew Zimbalist, "Sports, Jobs, & Taxes," *Brookings Review* 15, no. 3 (Summer 1997): 35–39, http://www.brook.edu/ pub/review/summer97/noll.htm.
7. *Ibid.*
8. Michael Gee, "Baseball's Fields of Bad Dreams: New Stadiums Not a Big Draw," *Boston Herald,* May 7, 2001; O'Toole, "Luxury Stadiums."
9. Darren Rovell, "Fenway: Classic or Clunker? Part II," *ESPN.com,* November 3, 2000, http://espn.go.com/mlb/s/2000/1103/854882.html.
10. Kimberly Anne Konrad, "Fenway Park's Green Monster," *CRM Online* 23, no. 10 (2000): 13–15, http://crm.cr.nps.gov/issue.cfm?volume= 23&Number=10.
11. Meg Vaillancourt, "Red Sox Plan Loses in City Poll; Public Funding for a New Ballpark Strikes Out," *Boston Globe,* July 10, 2000, p. A1, http:// www.boston.com/dailyglobe2/192/metro/Red_ Sox_plan_loses_in_city_poll%2b.shtm. See also Rouse, "Sox Plan Strikes Out: Ten Reasons/ Arguments for Saving Fenway Park," *Boston Phoenix,* April 6–13, 2000, http://www .bostonphoenix.com/archive/features/ LETTERS.htm.
12. Meg Vaillancourt, "Opponents Offer Alternative Fenway Plans," *Boston Globe,* August 23, 2000, http://www.boston.com/news/packages/ fenway/0813_alternative.htm.
13. See John Rouse, "Fenway and Family Values," *The Harvard Crimson,* April 20, 2000, http:// www.thecrimson.com/opinion.
14. Steve LeBlac, "Ballpark Opponents Critical of Closed-Door Meeting," Associated Press, May 9, 2000.
15. Gorden Edes, "Red Sox Explore Adding 10,000 Seats to Fenway," *Boston Globe,* October 11, 2002, p. A1.

Sources

Jim Caple, http://espn.go.com/mlb/columns/caple_jim/865956.html; Peter Gammons, http://espn.go.com/gammons/s/fenway_plan.html; Seth Gitell, "Talking Politics:Fenway Follies," *The Boston Phoenix,* June 14–22, 2000. http:// www.bostonphoenix.com; Vaillancourt, "Red Sox Adviser Shifts on Rebuilding Fenway," *The Boston Globe,* September 25, 2001; Scott Van Voorhis, "Polls Blast Sox Renovation Flip," *The Boston Herald,* September 27, 2001; "Welfare for the Wealthy: The Fight to Save Fenway Park, *Designer/Builder: A Journal of the Human Environment* (November 1999), copyright McGraw-Hill Companies, 2002.

Notes

1. Emmette S. Redford, Democracy *in the Administrative State* (New York: Oxford University Press, 1969), p. 3.
2. Arthur M. Okun, *Equality and Efficiency: The Big Tradeoff* (Washington, DC: The Brookings Institution, 1975), p. 4.
3. Suzanne Garment, "Making a Case for Regulation," *Washington Post,* February 2, 1997, p. A8.
4. Henry T. Abraham, *Freedom and the Court: Civil Rights and Liberties in the United States* (New York: Oxford University Press, 1977), pp. 110–129.

5. Okun, *Equality and Efficiency,* p. 119.

6. Ralph D. Christy, "Markets or Government? Balancing Imperfect and Complementary Alternatives," *American Journal of Agricultural Economics* 78, no. 5 (December 1996): 1145–1157.

7. *Ibid.*

8. Lester M. Salamon and John J. Siegfried, "Economic Power and Political Influence: The Impact of Industry Structure on Public Policy," *American Political Science Review* 71, no. 4 (December 1977): 1026–1043.

9. Adam Przeworski and Michael Wallerstein, "Democratic Capitalism at the Crossroads," *Democracy* 2, no. 3 (July 1982): 52–68.

10. John Pollacco, "Old Economy vs. New Economy," *Business Times,* January 31–February 6, 2001, http://www.businesstimes.com.mt/2001/01/31/focus.html.

11. Robert E. Lane, "Market Justice, Political Justice," *American Political Science Review* 80, no. 2 (June 1986): 383–402. See also Jennifer Nedelsky, *Private Property and the Limits of American Constitutionalism* (New York: Oxford University Press, 1990).

12. Harry Holloway with John George, *Public Opinion,* 2d ed. (New York: St. Martin's Press, 1986), p. 157.

13. William Watts and Lloyd A. Free, eds., *The State of the Nation* (New York: University Books, Potomac Associates, 1967), p. 97.

14. Jonathan Weisman, "GOP Laments Mixed Results As Control of Congress Ends," *Washington Post,* December 10, 2006, p. A1.

15. Julian E. Selizer, "The Conservative Embrace of Presidential Power," *Boston University Law Review* 88, no. 2 (April 2008): 499–503.

16. Caleb Crain, "'Democracy Matters': Plenty of Blame to Go Around," *New York Times,* September 12, 2004.

17. David Brooks, "The Middle Muscles In," *New York Times,* November 9, 2006.

18. E. J. Dionne, Jr., *Why Americans Hate Politics* (New York: Simon & Schuster, 1991).

19. David Brooks, "Running Out of Steam," *New York Times*, December 8, 2005.

20. Dan Balz, "Midterm Election Leaves Political Landscape Blurry," *Washington Post,* November 13, 2006, p. A8.

21. *Ibid.*

22. Thomas Friedman, "The Power of Green," *New York Times,* April 15, 2007.

23. Jonathan Rauch, "Comment: Unwinding Bush: How Long Will It Take to Fix His Mistakes?" *Atlantic,* October 2006, pp. 27–28; see also Colin Campbell, Bert A. Rockman, and Andrew Rudalevige, *The George W. Bush Legacy* (Washington, DC: CQ Press, 2008).

24. Rauch, "Comment."

25. *Ibid.*

26. Frank Rich, "Earth to G.O.P.: The Gipper Is Dead," *New York Times*, May 13, 2007.

27. Ron Suskind, "Why Are These Men Laughing?" *Esquire*, January 2003.

28. *Ibid;* see also Rich, "Earth to G.O.P."

29. Kevin Phillips, "How the GOP Became God's Own Party," *Washington Post,* April 2, 2006, p. B3.

30. Suskind, "Why Are These Men Laughing?"

31. Dan Balz, "Clinton Aims to Restore Public Trust in Government," *Washington Post,* April 13, 2007.

32. Frederick S. Lane, *Current Issues in Public Administration* (New York: St. Martin's Press, 1982), p. 156.

33. U.S. Census Bureau, Federal, State, and Local Governments, 2002 Census of Governments, Preliminary Report No. 1: The 2002 Census of Governments, GC02-1 (P), issued July 2002. See Ellis Katz, "Local Self-Government in the United States," *Issues of Democracy: An Electronic Journal of the U.S. Information Agency,* Vol. 4, No. 1 (April 1999), http://usinfo.state.gov/journals/itdhr/0499/ijde/ijde0499.htm.

34. Michael A. Murray, "Comparing Public and Private Management: An Exploratory Essay," *Public Administration Review* 35, no. 4 (July/August 1975): 364–371.

35. Herbert A. Simon, *Administrative Behavior* (New York: Macmillan, 1957).

36. Walter Russell Mead, "To Tether Big Business to the National Interest, Read Hamilton," *Los Angeles Times,* February 23, 1997, pp. M2, 6.

37. Jonathan Rauch, "The End of Government," *National Journal* 28, no. 36 (September 7, 1996): 1890–1896.

38. Theodore J. Lowi, *The End of Liberalism: The Second Republic of the United States* (New York: W. W. Norton & Co., 1969).

39. *Ibid.,* 43.

40. *Ibid.,* 51.

41. *Ibid.,* 63.

42. Richard N. Goodwin, "Perspective in Politics," *Los Angeles Times,* January 30, 1997, p. A9.

43. Robert Higgs, "The Futility of Campaign Finance Reform," The Independent Institute, 1997. http://www.independent.org/tii/content/op_ed/ahiggsscam.html.

44. Andrew Bard Schmookler, "When Money Talks, Is It Free Speech? PACs Give Big Bucks to Buy Access and Influence," *Christian Science Monitor,* November 10, 1997, p. 15.

45. Jacob Weisberg, "The Big Idea: Interest-Group Conservatism," *Slate,* May 4, 2005.

46. Center for Responsive Politics, "Despite a Flat Year for Lobbying, Business Booster's Advocacy Soared in 2006," March 15, 2007. http://www.opensecrets.org/pressreleases/2007/2006Lobbying.3.15.asp.

47. Jeffrey H. Birnbaum, "The Road to Riches Is Called K Street," *Washington Post,* June 22, 2005, p. A1.

48. *Ibid.*

49. Birnbaum, "The End of Legal Bribery," *Washington Monthly,* June 2006. http://www.washingtonmonthly.com/features/2006/0606.birnbaum.html.

50. Bill Moyers, "Delay, Abramoff, and the Public Trust," *Huffington Post,* February 26, 2006. See also Frank Rich, "Jack Abramoff and Guilded Age," *International Herald Tribune,* September 26, 2005; Peter H. Stone, *Superlobbyist Jack Abramoff, His Republican Allies, and the Buying of Washington* (New York: Farrar, Straus, & Giroux, 2006); Norman J. Ornstein, "The House That Jack Built," *New York Times,* January 14, 2007.

The Anatomy of Public Organizations

Chapter Highlights

The Basis of Organization	Centralization and Decentralization
Points about Pyramids	The Craft and Political Culture
Line and Staff	Summary

The Authority Never Changed—How We Managed Did

The following statement was made by Raymond W. Kelly, Police Commissioner, New York Police Department (NYPD), before the United States Senate Judiciary Committee, July 18, 2001. Kelly spoke regarding the management of the Federal Bureau of Investigation (FBI). He had served in twenty-five different commands for the NYPD.

From 1996 to 1998, Kelly, as Under Secretary for Enforcement at the U.S. Treasury Department, supervised the Department's enforcement bureaus— including the U.S. Customs Service; U.S. Secret Service; Bureau of Alcohol, Tobacco, and Firearms; Federal Law Enforcement Training Center; Financial Crimes Enforcement Network; and Office of Foreign Assets Control. As U.S. Customs Service Commissioner, Kelly directed more than 19,000 employees responsible for enforcing laws and protecting American citizens.

I came to federal law enforcement after a thirty-year career in the New York City Police Department. I also served in the United States Marine Corps. The one thing both organizations have in common is that they are very hierarchical. While both encourage initiative on the part of their front-line troops, the fact remains that both organizations insist on adherence to a strict chain of command.

They also maintain tight spans of control. For example, the span of control in the New York City Police Department begins with a sergeant and five police officers, lieutenants reporting to captains and so on through to the very top ranks of the organization. . . .

When I came to federal law enforcement, first as Under Secretary of the Treasury for Enforcement and later as Commissioner of U.S. Customs, I was struck by the relatively loose span of control and the horizontal structure of enforcement agencies.

Where my municipal and Marine Corps experience was very hierarchical, federal law enforcement tended to be more lateral. For example, when I first arrived at Customs, there were 20 Special Agents in Charge scattered across the United States, 100 Resident Agents in Charge offices, and 55 more attachés in twenty-four foreign countries—all reporting to one assistant commissioner in Washington.

The ratio of that span of control was more than surprising. It was unmanageable—certainly on a day-to-day basis. The result was that the investigative arm of the Customs Service was balkanized under the various Special Agents in Charge. Routine, centralized management in Washington was often weak and uninformed.

To correct the situation, we divided the country into three administrative regions: East, Central, and West. The Special Agents in Charge in each region had to report to a new director for each of the regions. Those three directors, in turn, reported to the assistant commissioner. Our attachés abroad were directed to report to a new deputy in the existing office of Foreign Relations. The result was a much more managable span of control.

The assistant commissioner in Washington could get a quick picture of what was happening nationally and internationally by talking to three people who reported to him, instead of forty. Similarly, with three deputies, the assistant commissioner could execute and follow up on policy, making certain his orders were not only transmitted, but also complied with. In addition, inspections on a much more frequent basis could be conducted.

With big, widely dispersed organizations, it is not enough for headquarters to send teams to the field to conduct periodic inspections every few years. There should be daily oversight. And a rational span of control allows that to happen.

The balkanization . . . was not limited to the Customs Office of Investigation. It affected the Office of Field Operations as well, where Customs personnel were assigned to 301 ports of entry located across the country. For a time, individual port directors tended to set their own policy. That led to "port shopping" by brokers and others who found that the rigor in which Customs regulations were being enforced varied from port to port.

The policy of "power to the ports" was encouraged for a time as managers tried to apply to the federal government the devolution of power that was becoming popular in American business. The problem is federal law enforcement is *not* a business enterprise. Its employees are responsible for enforcing the law, not making sales quotas. They are armed and have authority to conduct personal searches, make arrests, and use deadly force.

This kind of authority demands tight spans of control, close supervision, rigorous chain of command and oversight. . . . Internally, the lack of consistently executed policy led to complaints of unevenness and favoritism in disciplinary procedures and promotions. Discipline for the same transgression, for example, might be dispensed differently depending on the region of the country or whom an employee knew within the Service. We changed that by establishing an agency-wide Disciplinary Review Board with rotating membership.

One of the problems Customs experienced with the public was inconsistency in the way in which passengers arriving at various international airports were subjected to searches. Customs had broad authority to detain and search travelers, and did so. What was missing was a coherent policy that was closely supervised and uniformly adhered to. Once that policy was in place and closely supervised, the number of searches of law-abiding travelers plummeted, and the number of seizures of narcotics and other contraband increased.

The authority never changed. What changed was how we managed it. . . . Where none of the forty thousand police officers in the New York City Police Department is normally more than an hour or so away from headquarters, federal law enforcement has thousands of agents scattered across multiple time zones and even continents. . . .

The head of the agency must be persistent in demanding to know what is happening in the field and in making certain national policy is carried out there. Otherwise, power will devolve in a vacuum of leadership to the entrenched careerists in the field, where policy may be applied unevenly, if at all. . . .

[E]very law enforcement agency needs a robust internal affairs function within its ranks.

While inspector generals and other outside entities can play an oversight role, nothing is more effective in preventing and pursuing corruption within law enforcement than a credible Internal Affairs Unit. It takes a good insider to catch a bad one. . . . [I]nternal affairs needs to be staffed by the best and brightest investigators. . . .

An organization is only as good as the people who are recruited and trained to work for it. Federal law enforcement, and the FBI in particular, has a reputation for attracting highly skilled and highly motivated individuals. . . . The challenge is not who to manage, but how to manage them; how to manage a large, far-flung workforce with a broad and complex law enforcement mission. That's a heavy lift for anyone.

To lighten the load and manage effectively, I would recommend focusing on four essentials . . .

- Impose a strict managerial hierarchy.
- Maintain a tight span of control.
- Inspect regularly to make certain policy is being implemented in the field.
- Insure integrity through a robust internal affairs program within the agency.

Source

http://www.fas.org/irp/congress/2001_hr/071801_ kelly.html.

Every public administrator works within an organizational framework. Effective administrators have a solid understanding of general organizational principles and the structure of their particular organization. This chapter examines key organizational principles that have a major impact on public administration.

The *anatomy* of U.S. public bureaucracy—its organizational framework or administrative structure—owes much of its development to the 1933–1945 era of the Depression, World War II, and Franklin D. Roosevelt's leadership skills during the New Deal. In the 1990s, Republicans argued that the welfare state FDR created and nurtured had gotten out of control. Much of what FDR accomplished is thus now under attack. Many agencies in the federal bureaucracy that were created during the FDR era face privatization, consolidation, or elimination.

For Roosevelt, change was policy. "It is common sense to take a method and try it. If it fails, admit it frankly and try another. But above all try something," FDR said. Through the New Deal, Roosevelt built dams and brought electricity to millions, created farm subsidies and unemployment insurance, regulated a stock market gone out of control, set up a Social Security program for the elderly, and gave unions the right to organize. While many agencies no longer exist as they were created, other federal agencies and departments absorbed many functions in a greatly expanded welfare state.

The Basis of Organization

The structures of most public organizations are rather complex. These complexities can be simplified, however, by taking a look at the fundamental principles of organization outlined by Luther Gulick, who classified organizations into four categories. These categories are based on an organization's *raison d'être*—the reason it was established. The categories are *purpose, process, place,* and *clientele.*[1]

United States Federal Government Basics

Significant Points

- With more than 1.8 million civilian employees, the Federal Government, excluding the Postal Service, is the nation's largest employer.
- About 9 out of 10 Federal employees work outside the Washington, DC metropolitan area.
- Job growth generated by increased homeland security needs will be offset by projected declines in other Federal sectors; however, many job openings should arise from the need to replace workers who retire or leave the Federal Government for other reasons.
- Competition is expected for many Federal positions, especially during times of economic uncertainty, when workers seek the stability of Federal employment.

Nature of the Industry

The Federal Government is an organization formed to produce public services. We use some of these services every day, such as streets and sidewalks, police to maintain order, and parks, to name a few.

Goods and Services

The Federal Government's essential duties include defending the United States from foreign aggression and terrorism, representing U.S. interests abroad, enforcing laws and regulations, and administering domestic programs and agencies. U.S. citizens are particularly aware of the Federal Government when they pay their income taxes each year, but they usually do not consider the government's role when they watch a weather forecast, purchase fresh and uncontaminated groceries, travel by highway or air, or make a deposit at their bank. Workers employed by the Federal Government play a vital role in these and many other aspects of our daily lives. (While career opportunities in the U.S. Postal Service and the Armed Forces are not covered here, both are described in the 2008–09 edition of the *Occupational Outlook Handbook*. See the *Handbook* statements on Postal Service workers and job opportunities in the Armed Forces.)

Industry Organization

More than 200 years ago, the founders of the United States gathered in Philadelphia, PA, to create a constitution for a new national government and lay the foundation for self-governance. The Constitution of the United States, ratified by the last of the 13 original States in 1791, created the three branches of the Federal Government and granted certain powers and responsibilities to each. The legislative, judicial, and executive branches were created with equal powers but very different responsibilities that act to keep their powers in balance.

The legislative branch is responsible for forming and amending the legal structure of the Nation. Its largest component is Congress, the primary U.S. legislative body, which is made up of the Senate and the House of Representatives. This body includes senators, representatives, their staffs, and various support workers. The legislative branch employs only about one percent of Federal workers, nearly all of whom work in the Washington, DC area.

The judicial branch is responsible for interpreting the laws that the legislative branch enacts. The Supreme Court, the Nation's definitive judicial body, makes the highest rulings. Its decisions usually follow the appeal of a decision made by one of the regional Courts of Appeal, which hear cases appealed from U.S. District Courts, the Court of Appeals for the Federal Circuit, or State Supreme Courts. U.S. District Courts are located in each State and are the first to hear most cases under Federal jurisdiction. The judicial branch employs more than one percent of Federal workers; unlike the legislative branch, its offices and employees are dispersed throughout the country.

Of the three branches, the executive branch—through the power vested by the Constitution in the office of the President—has the widest range of responsibilities. Consequently, it employed 98 percent of all Federal civilian employees (excluding Postal Service workers) in 2005. The executive branch is composed of the Executive Office of the President, 15 executive Cabinet departments—including the newly created Department of Homeland Security—and nearly 90 independent agencies, each of which has clearly defined duties. The Executive Office of the President is composed of several offices and councils that aid the President in policy decisions. These include the Office of Management and Budget, which oversees the administration of the Federal budget; the National Security Council, which advises the President on matters of national defense; and the Council of Economic Advisers, which makes economic policy recommendations.

Source: U.S. Department of Labor, Bureau of Labor Statistics, "The 2008–09 Career Guide to Industries," http://www.bls.gov/oco/cg/print/cgs041.htm.

Purpose

Organizations established on the basis of *purpose* are oriented toward the accomplishment of specific tasks. Examples of organizations developed on this basis are school systems, fire departments, and the branches of the military. These organizations engage in purpose-specific activities and seldom extend beyond their purpose.

Process

A *process* organization is oriented not so much toward accomplishing specific goals but toward performing certain functions. From our understanding of the law as process, we might guess that a good example of such an agency is a city legal department. Process organizations concern themselves almost completely with the procedural aspects of administration.

Place

Organizations under this heading serve particular locales. These agencies provide a variety of services to the people in a particular neighborhood, city, county, or other region.

Clientele

Closely linked to *place* organizations, *clientele* organizations are a less common feature of our administrative landscape. These agencies serve particular groups of people, such as seniors, children, or people of a particular ethnic background.

Obviously these categories overlap, and many organizations fall into more than one. Fire departments are not only established for the purpose of putting out fires, but are also organized to serve particular geographic areas; yet purpose, not place, is the main reason for establishing a fire department. Most organizations are established not on the basis of just one of Gulick's categories, but through a combination of purpose, process, place, and clientele, regardless of which factor dominates.

Of the three branches of government, the executive, legislative, and judicial, the executive has the widest range of responsibilities. Through the power vested by the U.S. Constitution in the office of the President, the executive branch includes the Office of Management and Budget (OMB), National Security Council (NSC), and Council of Economic Advisers (CEA). OMB oversees administration of the federal budget. NSC advises the President on matters of national defense. CEA offers economic policy recommendations.

Each of the fourteen executive cabinet departments administers programs that oversee an element of American life. The highest official of each cabinet department is a member of the president's cabinet. Each department is described here; Table 3.1 lists the number of employees in each.

- **Defense (DOD):** Manages the military forces that protect the country and its interests, including the Departments of the Army, Navy, and Air Force, as

TABLE 3.1

Federal Government Executive Branch Civilian Employment, Except U.S. Postal Service, January 2007

(in thousands)

	United States	Washington, DC area
Total	1,774	284
Executive departments	1,593	234
Defense, total	623	65
Army	223	19
Navy	168	24
Air Force	152	6
Other	80	16
Veterans Affairs	239	7
Homeland Security	149	20
Treasury	109	14
Justice	105	23
Agriculture	92	11
Interior	66	7
Health and Human Services	60	28
Transportation	53	9
Commerce	39	21
Labor	16	6
Energy	15	5
State	14	12
Housing and Urban Development	10	3
Education	4	3
Independent agencies	179	48
Social Security Administration	62	2
National Aeronautics and Space Administration	18	4
Environmental Protection Agency	18	5
Tennessee Valley Authority	12	0
General Services Administration	12	4
Small Business Administration	6	1
Office of Personnel Management	5	2
Other	45	30

Source: U.S. Office of Personnel Management, http://www.bls.gov/oco/cg/print/cgs041.htm.

well as a number of smaller agencies. The civilian workforce employed by the Department of Defense performs various support activities, such as payroll and public relations.

- **Veterans Affairs (VA):** Administers programs to aid U.S. veterans and their families, runs the veterans' hospital system, and operates our national cemeteries.

- **Homeland Security:** Works to prevent terrorist attacks within the United States, reduce vulnerability to terrorism, and minimize the damage from potential attacks and natural disasters. It also administers the country's immigration polices and oversees the National Guard.
- **Treasury:** Regulates banks and other financial institutions, administers the public debt, prints currency, collects federal income taxes, and carries out law enforcement in a wide range of areas, including counterfeiting, tax, and customs violations.
- **Justice (DOJ):** Enforces federal laws, prosecutes cases in federal courts, and runs federal prisons.
- **Agriculture (USDA):** Promotes U.S. agriculture domestically and internationally and sets standards governing quality, quantity, and labeling of food sold in the United States.
- **Interior:** Manages federal lands, including the national parks; runs hydroelectric power systems; and promotes conservation of natural resources.
- **Transportation (DOT):** Sets national transportation policy; operates the Coast Guard (USCG) except in time of war; plans and funds the construction of highways and mass transit systems; and regulates railroad, aviation, and maritime operations.
- **Health and Human Services (HHS):** Sponsors medical research, approves the use of new drugs and medical devices, runs the Public Health Service, and administers Medicare.
- **Commerce:** Forecasts the weather, charts the oceans, regulates patents and trademarks, conducts the census, compiles statistics, and promotes U.S. economic growth by encouraging international trade.
- **Energy (DOE):** Coordinates the national use and provision of energy, oversees the production and disposal of nuclear weapons, and plans for future energy needs.
- **Labor (DOL):** Enforces laws guaranteeing fair pay, workplace safety, and equal job opportunity; administers unemployment insurance; regulates pension funds; and collects and analyzes economic data at the Bureau of Labor Statistics.
- **State:** Oversees the nation's embassies and consulates, issues passports, monitors U.S. interests abroad, and represents the United States before international organizations.
- **Housing and Urban Development (HUD):** Funds public housing projects, enforces equal housing laws, and insures and finances mortgages.
- **Education:** Provides scholarships, student loans, and aid to schools.

Numerous independent agencies perform tasks that do not originate within the jurisdictions of executive departments or that are more efficiently executed by an autonomous agency. Some smaller but well-known independent agencies include the Peace Corps, Securities and Exchange Commission (SEC), and Federal Communications Commission (FCC). The majority of these agencies employ fewer than one thousand workers, and many count fewer than one hundred.

Local Government as Plural, Not Singular, Noun

The concept, local government, incorporates more than cities. The term may include a county, a city, a school district and community college district—plus numerous specialized and politically independent entities whose purposes entail regional mass transit, wastewater treatment, firefighting, mosquito abatement, and flood control. Los Angeles County, for example, includes 88 cities.

Policymakers, periodically, get alarmed by the proliferation and complexity of local government. County-level commissions monitor annexations and formations of new cities and special districts. The effects of highly decentralized land-use powers on growth patterns concern policymakers. Community leaders debate regional reorganizations. Government fragmentation questions the responsiveness of coordinated government action. Cries of "wasteful duplication" and "local control" fail to probe the structure of local governance.

Partisan, policy, and system politics produces political fragmentation—or the geographic and functional division of power among local governments. Political fragmentation affects government services and land use regulation. Proliferation of local governments frustrates policy coordination of transportation, housing, and environmental protection initiatives. Government structures may separate fiscal needs from resources. Citizens become confused and dissensus emerges.

Four distinct roles suggest differences in local government structure.

1. *Service provision.* Local government is the primary provider of routine public services. Trash collection, fire protection, and public education are illustrations. Competitive economic theories function in tandem with political fragmentation. Fragmentation sorts citizens into "communities of interest." Similar tastes for services and tax levels result.

2. *Land use and economic development.* The so-called "police power" affords cities and counties the power to create zoning ordinances, rules for subdividing land, and building regulations. Partisan politics decide land-use patterns for constructing growth-supportive infrastructures, such as sewer lines. Localities often regulate land use in their narrow self-interests, yet they may slight area-wide concerns.

3. *Equity.* Political fragmentation may separate fiscal resources from social needs. Equity distributes and redistributes life's chances. Separate taxing-and-spending jurisdictions may lead to service disparities. Unequal service distributions may reflect government fragmentation per se. Or different "tastes" for services may emerge from inequality. Redistributive policies attempt to rectify disparities among local governments.

4. *Representation.* Government fragmentation emphasizes effective political representation and accountability. Decision making closer to home builds faith in government services. However, general purpose governments focus on more global budgeting. Overall taxing and spending levels are set. Tradeoffs are made between competing services. Community service demands competition between services shared by larger populations in an interconnected region.

Source: "The Controversy over Local Government Structure," http://www.ppic.org/publications/ PPIC112/ppic112.chap1.html.

The largest independent agencies are:

- **Social Security Administration (SSA):** Operates various retirement and disability programs and Medicaid.
- **National Aeronautics and Space Administration (NASA):** Oversees aviation research and conducts exploration and research beyond the Earth's atmosphere.
- **Environmental Protection Agency (EPA):** Administers programs to control and reduce pollution of the nation's water, air, and land.

- **General Services Administrations (GSA):** Manages and protects federal government property and records.
- **Tennessee Valley Authority (TVA):** Operates the hydroelectric power system in the Tennessee River valley.
- **Federal Deposit Insurance Corporation (FDIC):** Maintains the stability of and public confidence in the nation's financial system by insuring deposits and promoting sound banking practices.

Points about Pyramids

The organizational structure of most institutions is best thought of as a pyramid. The organization must delegate its work to a number of employees. To make sure that these employees do the work and to see that their efforts are coordinated, the organization appoints supervisors. These supervisors may be numerous enough that they, in turn, require supervisors. As a result, one or more levels of hierarchy tend to emerge in any sizable organization, with the number of persons at each level dwindling until the tip of a pyramid is reached. The pyramid model brings with it the concepts of *unity of command, chain of command,* and *span of control.*

Unity of command describes the exclusive relationship between those who follow orders and those who give them orders. No one can serve two masters. This maxim has held true for work organizations, particularly those operating under the bureaucratic norms of delegation, specialization, and accountability, and accounts for much of their success.

Requiring an individual or a group to respond to the orders of two or more superiors may produce conflict, confusion, and even chaos. If unity of command does not exist, conflict and confusion will not only characterize those being commanded but those doing the commanding. In other words, multiple superiors will not only confuse their subordinates but also each other.

The unity of command principle may conflict with the methods of some boards and commissions. Such multiple-headed bodies are considered suitable only for semijudicial organizations (such as regulatory commissions) or for certain policy-making or advisory functions. If an organization is administering a program, if it is *doing* things, then the reins of its authority should converge eventually into one pair of hands. Responsibility can then be pinpointed, and conflicting orders, internecine warfare, and a host of other organizational ills can be avoided.

Unity of command usually requires a *chain of command,* the second concept in the pyramid model. In any large organization, the person at the top cannot oversee all that is going on below; he or she needs others to help do this. Frequently, these helpers cannot supervise all those beneath them. As a result, several echelons of command may emerge, theoretically allowing commands to proceed downward in a neat, orderly flow. Unity of command means that the captain of A Company does not give orders to the soldiers of B Company. Within a chain of command, the battalion major does not give direct orders to soldiers from either company, but works instead through their company commanders.

Even less structured organizations observe, to some degree, the same principle. The college dean, if he or she has reason to be disturbed by the behavior of a particular professor, will usually first contact the professor's department chairperson before taking any direct action against the faculty member. In this way the chain of command at the university streamlines the administrative process.

A third concept linked to a pyramidal structure is *span of control*. Span of control refers to the number of units, whether individuals or groups, that any supervising unit must oversee. Unlike unity of command and chain of command, span of control does not constitute a principle of organization; instead, it serves as a frame of reference. Put another way, span of control is not something that organizations *ought* to have, but something they *do* have. Usually, a government organization develops guidelines for span of control based on an organization's mission. A challenge exists in making sure that the number of subunits to be supervised is neither too many nor too few—to make sure that the supervisor's span of control is neither too great nor too small. Unfortunately, public administration provides no hard-and-fast criteria for determining such things. As with so many other questions concerning this capricious craft, the only intelligent answer is the highly unsatisfactory, "It all depends."

Public administrators in America have functioned with relatively narrow spans of control. It is rare to find a manager overseeing more than twelve subordinates or subunits, and it is not rare to find a manager overseeing as few as three. The tighter the span of control, the more intervening levels between top and bottom, increasing paperwork and procrastination. A tight span of control also leads to decisions made and policies formulated too far from the scene of action. It can lead to difficulties in acquiring and retaining the services of top-notch people in vitally important, but no longer top-rated, positions.

As with so much in public administration, span of control becomes a question of finding a proper balance for each situation. In finding this balance, we must assess the specific circumstances, keeping in mind that a gain achieved by moving in one direction may be offset by some losses. These losses do not, however, necessarily cancel the gain. If an executive has 100 agencies under his or her tutelage, some consolidation is almost always needed, even at the expense of creating more administrative levels. However, every consolidation carries a price tag that we must be willing to pay if we wish to reap the benefits.

Figure 3.1 illustrates how the principles of unity command, chain of command, and span of control need to be grounded in political compromise, consensus, and democratic participation.

Line and Staff

The individuals working in the pyramid examples discussed earlier—U.S. Army companies and large state universities—are called *line personnel*. Another group of people to be considered are *staff personnel*.

While line personnel are primarily concerned with implementing policy, staff personnel are the working members of an organization who do not implement policy. Line agencies and employees are directly responsible for furthering an organization's goals. Staff employees are primarily concerned with assisting senior administrators in the determination of policy and the effective operation of the agency.

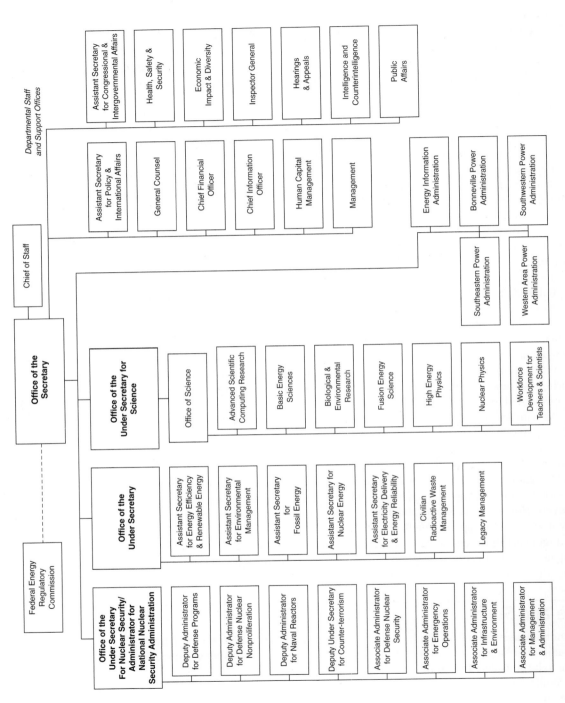

FIGURE 3.1 Department of Energy, as of March 2008

Source: http://www.doe.gov/organization/orgchart.htm.

Line people are generalists who occupy positions of authority in the organiza-tion and command implementation of the organization's operations. The Depart-ments of Agriculture, Commerce, Defense, Education, Energy, Health and Human Services, Housing and Urban Development, Interior, Justice, Labor, State, Transpor-tation, Treasury, and Veterans Affairs constitute the major line agencies of the federal government. These organizations administer clientele programs and deal directly with the public.

The primary line officers are members of the president's cabinet. These line and staff departments and agencies were established in the following order:[2]

1789: State, War, Treasury, Attorney General
1798: Navy
1829: Postmaster General
1849: Interior
1870: Justice
1889: Agriculture
1903: Commerce and Labor
1913: Commerce, Labor (split)
1939: Office of Management and Budget
1947: Defense (replaced Navy and War)
1953: Health, Education, and Welfare (HEW)
1965: Housing and Urban Development
1966: Transportation
1971: Postmaster General removed from cabinet
1974: Office of the U.S. Trade Representative
1977: Energy
1979: Health and Human Services, Education (HEW split into HHS and Education)
1989: Veterans' Affairs
1993: Environmental Protection Agency, United Nations Ambassador
2003: Department of Homeland Security

Note: The Office of Management and Budget and the Office of U.S. Trade Repre-sentative are part of the Executive Office of the President and are not executive departments.

The expansion of the president's cabinet has occurred over time. The U.S. Constitution does not specifically provide for a cabinet, but Article II, Section 2 stip-ulates that a president may seek advice from heads of the executive departments. Cabinet status puts an agency on a stronger footing when dealing with the Office of Management and Budget on fiscal and policy matters. In 1993, President Clinton proposed that the Environmental Protection Agency receive cabinet status. He also elevated the position of Ambassador to the United Nations to cabinet level.

Staff people are specialists who provide skills, knowledge, and expertise to line personnel. For example, staff personnel draw up job classifications, program computers, or provide legal services. These are the employees who are most accu-rately referred to as the "staff." Staff agencies aid the chief executive and line per-sonnel in developing, evaluating, and implementing public policies. Within the Executive Office of the President of the United States, for example, the main staff

The Department Head versus Your P.A. Professor— Line versus Staff

A student of political science need go no further than his or her university bureaucracy to note the tensions inherent between staff and line personnel. Faculty members in the Department of Political Science are selected, retained, and promoted based upon their skills, knowledge, and expertise in a subfield or subfields of political science. Political science faculty are hired to teach a certain specialty, such as political theory, political parties, legislative studies, the presidency, constitutional law and jurisprudence, law and courts, federalism and intergovernmental relations, state politics, public policy, urban politics, comparative politics, foreign policy, or public administration.

As experts in particular aspects of political science, faculty are "staff" advisors in your college or university to the chairperson of the Department of Political Science, a "line" official. Line officials are in command; they have authority as specified in the university's administrative guidelines. In the political science department the chairperson is a generalist in the discipline of political science. The dean, provost, and president of your college or university are also line officials.

A certain amount of tension between the political science department chair and a certain faculty member who teaches a specialty in political science is almost a given. An individual political science professor might consider courses in public policy and administration to be most important in the department's academic curriculum. The department chair must evaluate and balance this and other recommendations of the political science professors under his or her supervision as he or she makes decisions as to what courses to offer students.

The faculty member, as specialist, promotes student interest in a certain subfield or subfields of political science. The department chair, as generalist and the administrative authority in command of the political science administrative unit, has the responsibility to see that all subfields of political science receive appropriate emphasis in course offerings. Department heads, implementing line functions, and faculty, carrying out staff teaching assignments, have different program priorities. It is not difficult to imagine that they, as line and staff employees of your college or university, would often come into conflict as each person seeks to do his or her job as responsibly and as ably as possible.

agencies are the White House Office, Office of Management and Budget, Council of Economic Advisors, National Security Council, Office of Policy Development, Office of the U.S. Trade Representative, Council on Environmental Quality, and Office of Science and Technology Policy.

The essence of staff work is thought, fact-finding, and planning.[3] Staff units are usually formed on the basis of process. An organization's computer center, for example, is typically comprised of people engaged in a process while serving a variety of purposes, places, and clientele within the larger organization. In a school system, the computer center prepares attendance figures for principals, correlates statistics on children with learning disabilities for the director of special education, and pinpoints certain cost trends for the budgeting department. This last function illustrates that staff agencies may serve not only line departments, but also other staff units.

The bureaucratic pyramid, in its pure form, makes no provision for staff units and their personnel. Traditionally, staff units have played only a small and shadowy role in the structure of work organizations. The place they occupied was usually at the hands or feet of the organization's leader, providing advice and assistance. However, staff services and personnel have increased tremendously. They now occupy a greater place in an organization's structure, play a greater role in its activities, and consume a greater portion of its budget. In so doing, they provide the organization with new benefits and new problems.

Problems stem from the model pyramid's lack of provision for staff units. It is difficult, at times almost impossible, to establish the correct niche for staff within an organization's hierarchy. Staff people tend to be specialists whose expertise does not lend itself to a graded ranking except, possibly, within their own ranks. The authority of a line unit is fairly definite. Its personnel know which units are above them and which ones are below. The authority of a staff unit is, by contrast, much more nebulous and elusive. Such authority is determined by whatever need the line units have for the staff group at a particular time, the proficiency the staff can demonstrate in meeting this need, the administrative and political skills the staff demonstrates in its relationships with other units within the organization, and a variety of other factors.

Specialization tends to destroy hierarchy. The more the members of an organization are differentiated from each other in terms of separate, specific skills, the more difficult it becomes to position them on a hierarchical scale. Knowledge, in and of itself, knows no hierarchy. There is no "higher" or "lower" knowledge. Thus, the increasing presence of staff personnel is disrupting many bureaucratic organizations as specialists begin to dominate generalists in making agency policies. Staff people are undermining the cherished bureaucratic principles of unity of command, chain of command, and span of control.

Unity of command requires one channel of authority, but specialization creates several channels. The specialists, in one way or another, start giving orders relating to their areas of expertise. That these orders are not labeled as such and stem not from rank but from expertise does not fundamentally alter the situation. If the organization intends to use the energies and abilities of specialists, it must respond to what they say. To the extent that the specialists' capabilities are used, the authority of line personnel, particularly those in a supervisory capacity, is undermined.

The contrasting assignments of line (generalist) and staff (specialist) personnel generate a good deal of conflict and tension in organizations. At times, line people will complain that staff people are not sharing enough responsibility. More often, however, line personnel resent the intrusions of staff people. To line employees, the activities of staff personnel frequently seem more subversive than supportive.

To reduce the rivalry and rancor that may creep into line-staff relationships, organizations try to integrate the two as much as possible. They may make staff people spend time familiarizing themselves with line functions and line personnel, sometimes requiring staff personnel to perform some line functions for a time. They may recruit their staff people from the ranks of the line personnel, giving them special training for their new positions.

There is no "correct" organizational arrangement of *unity of command, chain of command, span of control,* and *line and staff.* These organizational principles vary from organization to organization and are based upon the most satisfactory way to serve the needs of clientele.

Centralization and Decentralization

One issue that has bewildered public managers since the beginning of public organization is *centralization.* Arguments have been raised on the devolution affecting the balance between nation and state as states have undertaken policy reforms that work to their individual advantage at the expense of national interest. *Devolution* is perceived to be an attempt to simplify incentives for common interests. However, reforms should balance multiple interests within the framework of the larger government.[4] In early times, concern focused largely on how to achieve this, for even the simplest communication between headquarters and the field often took weeks, months, or, in a few instances, years. Egyptian pharaohs, Roman emperors, and Chinese mandarins spent a good deal of time wondering how to control and use the energies of subordinates in distant subunits.

The emphasis has shifted. Now the number one concern often centers on how much centralization should be achieved. Centralization is no longer viewed as an unmixed blessing. Its opposite, decentralization, has become the watchword, if not the battle cry, of many theorists and practitioners involved in the administrative craft. Several movements throughout U.S. history have tried to downsize and decentralize government. Assaults on big government began with Thomas Jefferson and continued with the Jacksonian Democrats, the states' rights movement, and the antistatism movements of the twentieth century.[5]

The "citizen legislator" is a quaint vestige of early American democracy that continues to dominate state government. Forty-one states have legislatures that meet part-time—some for as little as thirty days a year—and their members spend the rest of the time practicing law, tilling fields, or staffing shops as ordinary citizens. However, the federal government's desire to send power to the states is increasing these legislators' workload and making it tough for them to keep up.[6] Only months after Congress turned control of welfare over to the states, legislatures around the country began considering whether to hand off responsibility for the poor once again, this time to county and local governments.[7]

We have seen how decentralization has characterized our country's *political* system since its inception. While such political decentralization may facilitate and foster *administrative* decentralization, it does not necessarily ensure it—at least not in all instances.

Political decentralization calls for policies to be developed as much as possible at the lower levels (the "grass roots"). *Administrative decentralization* requires that the organizations charged with carrying out these policies allow their subunits a great deal of autonomy in interpreting and applying them. When a city institutes its own health program, political decentralization is at work. If at the same time the health department refuses to set up neighborhood centers or insists that even the centers' most minor decisions must be made at headquarters, the program is not administratively decentralized.

Centralization and *decentralization* are relative terms. Nearly every organization of any size and scope must, to some extent, decentralize, for once it sets up subunits, it must grant them some discretion in carrying out their functions. The question, therefore, becomes a matter of deciding how far this independent discretion should go. Many argue that it should be pushed to the maximum limits.

Decentralization, or its lack, is no abstract concept in public organizations. An organization's *tasks, values,* and *organizational structures* are related to unique political, administrative, and economic characteristics. And the structural arrangements of an organization are never value-neutral. The locations of decisions affect an administrator's objectives and values. The perspectives of federal employees located in Washington are different from the perspectives of those implementing services in Peoria. As Miles's Law states, "Where you stand depends upon where you sit."

Who Controls Welfare?

Neither the president nor governors have as much control over welfare as they would have us believe. Welfare recipients are affected more by cyclical economic forces than by government regulations. Perhaps more important, welfare is ultimately a local matter. Lawmakers in Washington or the state capitals may pass grandiose reforms, but low-level officials have a lot of discretion in carrying them out.

Source: Bradley R. Schiller, "All Welfare Is Local," *New York Times,* January 28, 1997, p. A21.

States respond to increased marginal expenditure costs and reduced federal aid. States may also have to overcome spending limits and short-term policy perspectives. State finance research should focus on state spending determinants, interactions with local governments, federal aid changes, discretionary tax changes, and whether budgets are structurally balanced.[8] It is believed that state governments will gain control of many social programs presently run by the federal government. Legislators and other state officials will finally have the flexibility to choose which programs will work best for their situation. Experts believe that no single pattern of welfare and Medicaid reform will emerge. They also believe that reforms will evolve over time as states learn from their experience and that of other states.[9]

The structure of an organization affects the delivery of services to its clientele. Public organizations must mobilize resources to perpetuate themselves and their values. Decisions cannot be imposed from the top down if people in the subunits do not subscribe to the values and methods of implementing particular services. Administrators sometimes entertain *reorganization* plans to gain more control over the structure of the organization's policies and programs. Since any reorganization is implemented by the permanent bureaucracy, or the employees in the field accomplishing the everyday tasks of the organization, any decisions to decentralize or recentralize are of great consequence to the organization. These decisions should be made with sensitivity to the skills, knowledge, and expertise of field employees who must carry out the organization's values and purposes.[10]

The Reagan administration saw centralization as the best way to put its values into action and to achieve its goals. For most of the 1980s, the administration "devised a strategy for centralizing unprecedented decision-making power in the White House."[11] The Reagan administration centralized the budgetary process, the federal appointments process, decision making in the executive branch, and control of federal regulation.[12] A future president may take the opposite approach and opt for decentralization as a way of expressing a different set of values and achieving different goals. As we have mentioned, two types of decentralization exist: *political* and *administrative.*[13]

Political Decentralization

Political decentralization describes the allocation of powers among territories, which in this context refers to states, provinces, counties, municipalities, and other local governments. According to this approach to governing, general-purpose government officers residing in a specific territory coordinate public sector activities, because they are in closer contact with citizens and may alter programs according to particular territorial priorities. Political decentralization advances few real restrictions for guidelines and control, keeping them at a minimum to allow for local discretion. The territories, or subunits, possess considerable power, coordinating and reshaping resources coming into their geographic areas to meet local needs. Manifestly parochial and unable to formulate and act on national goals, politically decentralized systems experience difficulty "vertically" integrating a diverse set of governmental activities. The transfer of political power from nation to state to community constitutes a vertical pass-through of influence at each level. How is this vertical pass-through frustrated in a decentralized system?

Issues such as equal opportunity, the environment, and occupational safety illustrate the barriers to vertical pass-through that the parochialism of local jurisdictions poses. Congress may, for example, impose affirmative action criteria for implementing equal opportunity goals for every state in the union. If local groups of citizens are opposed to civil rights, however, equal opportunity policies may be frustrated.

Likewise, when administrative specialists in the Environmental Protection Agency (EPA) interpret U.S. environmental statutes to mean that private industry must control its waste emissions, EPA field officials may be frustrated in their efforts to enforce these laws if a community values the economic status of that industry more than clean air or water. If occupational safety is a concern of federal officers but not of local government, industry, and labor leaders, then Congress and the Occupational Safety and Health Administration may be wasting their time attempting to convince local residents otherwise. Groups of citizens in every political jurisdiction must be committed to the goals of the organization, at least in some fashion, for procedures and processes to be effective in implementing these goals.

Administrative Decentralization

Administrative decentralization occurs when a public organization delegates powers to subordinate levels within the same department or agency. The delegating authority may revise or retract such delegations at will. The central office of a bureaucracy in Washington may transfer federal government functions to regional or state offices, for example.

Whereas political decentralization pertains to powers allocated among geographic areas, administrative decentralization emphasizes functions, or specialties, and lines of authority for implementing agency functions. Functional and professional specialties of the central office bureaus and agencies are held in high regard in the field offices.

Politically decentralized jurisdictions grapple with "vertical" integration of governmental activities; *administratively decentralized* systems experience difficulties with "horizontal" integration of governmental activities. While a city might relate to a vertical hierarchy of state and federal governments for policy determination in political decentralization, federal administrators might horizontally coordinate the activities of several agencies within the same geographic area in an example of administrative decentralization. In such operations, problems are often addressed in a fragmented manner with specialists (staff) dominating the narrowly focused programs, and generalists (line) concerned for the whole project and guidelines emanating from the central office.

For example, the issue of civil rights concerns several federal departments and agencies; specific policies need horizontal coordination for implementation at the grassroots level. Departments challenged to coordinate civil rights regulations based upon the administrative discretion of bureaucrats include the Departments of Commerce, Education, Health and Human Services, Housing and Urban Development, Justice, Labor, and Transportation. Independent agencies also involved include the Commission on Civil Rights, the Equal Employment Opportunity Commission, and the Small Business Administration. The line officials of these departments and agencies could be in agreement on general purposes, desiring to implement civil rights statutes; however, the more narrowly focused specialists within each bureaucracy may disagree on the specifics.

Governmental Structure and American Values

Decentralization has its proponents in every political camp. Suspicion of the dangers inherent in a strong, centralized government dates back beyond the American Revolution. Participation, access, and responsiveness are characteristics of decentralized systems that in principle promote flexibility and democracy within federal organizations at the grass roots. By allowing flexibility within federal guidelines, political decentralization helps state and city officials to meet the needs of their constituents. Rigid functional categories of administratively decentralized systems restrict the options of leaders representing general-purpose governments.

Students of political decentralization argue that governors and mayors are better able than nonelected bureaucrats to allocate available resources effectively according to local priorities. But cogent arguments exist *against* political decentralization as well. Local jurisdictions may be fragmented and ineffective; states sometimes refuse to grant sufficient resources for local bureaucracies to implement functions in a professional and effective manner. Accusations of unprofessional behavior and political graft undermine citizens' confidence in the legitimacy of local governments. Regional and national concerns may be overlooked, ignored by smaller jurisdictions, or may be unmanageable for them.

Conflicts between political and administrative decentralization models pit the values and priorities of geographic area (Peoria) against administrative function (Washington). Local partisans champion the political will of the former; national leaders insist upon the dominance of the latter. A balance between the extremes usually results. The vertical and horizontal mixing of political and administrative decentralization illustrates that values, tasks, and organizational structure interrelate in an effective organization.

Structural arrangements selected for implementing a task directly affect the success administrators enjoy in achieving their objectives and values. Decentralization moves government closer to citizens, offering elected officials and voters opportunities to witness more closely the programmatic and fiscal consequences of their decisions. Decentralization also gives decision makers the flexibility to meet local conditions.

However, centralization of functions at the state level may promote more uniform policies, resulting in certain economies of scale, and may eliminate the impact of local fiscal disparities on the quality and cost of services. The ebb and flow of centralizing and decentralizing decisions in individual states is constant.

Decisions to centralize or decentralize public organizations cannot, therefore, be divorced from values, tasks, and organizational structure. An appropriate organizational design facilitates an administrator's values and objectives; an inappropriate organizational structure frustrates his or her purposes.

A variety of political, administrative, and economic characteristics typify public program functions. As new values and technologies emerge, organizational objectives change; new technologies affect community values. Issues affecting governmental centralization and decentralization include political, administrative, economic, and technological factors that may point the agency in conflicting directions as it attempts to integrate its values, tasks, and organizational structure into an effective organization.

In a dynamic society espousing democracy and capitalism, we may ask: an effective organization for whom, what, when, where, and how?

The Craft and Political Culture

Many are claiming that the United States is in the midst of a culture war over moral values and lifestyles.[14] Therefore, an understanding of culture is of great value to public administrators. To recognize the expectations and guidelines for professional behavior in one's culture is to promote understanding of the organization.

The culture of an organization provides guidelines for member behavior and performance. For example, class size is one feature of academic culture. The number of students in a class influences the type and number of assignments professors may require. If the number of students in your class reaches into the hundreds, you may assume that your professor will emphasize short-answer examinations instead of essays. However, the culture of small classes allows your professor to be more personal in his or her approach to teaching and gives the professor more flexibility for evaluating your writing skills and critical thinking abilities. An understanding of classroom culture can help you steer toward classes where you are likely to perform best.

For our purposes, *culture* is defined as "that complex whole which includes knowledge, belief, art, morals, law, custom, and any other capabilities and habits acquired by man as a member of society."[15] An awareness of culture is crucial for understanding the development, implementation, and evaluation of public administration.

Culture, or ways of life common to a society, government organization, or interest group, includes the *ideal* and the *real*. Ideal cultural patterns focus on what citizens do or say if they adhere completely to recognized cultural standards. Real behavioral patterns refer to actual citizen observations and behaviors. Various aspects of culture, such as religious rituals, work habits, beliefs, ideologies, and marriage relationships, relate to and affect one another.

Culture may be divided according to:

- *Technology,* or the ways in which people create and use tools and other material artifacts
- *Economics,* or the patterns of behaving relative to the production, distribution, and consumption of goods and services

- *Social organization,* or characteristic relations among individuals within a society, including the division of labor, the social and political organization, and the relationship between a society and other societies
- *Religion,* or ways of life relative to the human concern for the unknown
- *Symbolism,* or systems of symbols (such as language, art, music, and literature) used to acquire, order, and transfer knowledge[16]

The nature of our organized society and developments in the history of public administration underscore the importance of political and bureaucratic culture in the public administration environment. Partisan, policy, and system politics operate within a larger framework of political culture. *Political culture,* according to Daniel Elazár, is "the particular pattern of orientation to political action in which each political system is embedded."[17]

Culture puts limits on individuals in organizational settings. An organization is a subculture. For example, your public administration class is a subculture of the Department of Political Science, which is a subculture of a larger academic unit—usually a college of humanities, a subculture of the university or college. An understanding of the concept of culture is vital because we must recognize that an organization's members or employees are not free agents in any society.

Any organization is part of a larger social system. At least indirectly, its employees are thus subject to a larger set of values. Certain cultural patterns of conduct and belief can be found in any organization. The culture of an organization reflects a consensus of the particular values of that organization, but no organization can be isolated from its cultural environment.[18]

An understanding of culture can provide an advance indication of how people will act in a situation. A keenly developed sensitivity to culture can also be a substitute for experience. If you expect to climb the ladder of managerial success, pay close attention to your organization's culture. Traditions, customs, and patterned modes of behavior run through organizations. If you understand such structuring influences, you may even be able to facilitate changes in the organization.

According to J. Steven Ott, there are three levels of organizational culture and their interaction (Figure 3.2).[19] Level 1A involves artifacts, including both technology and art. Level 1B entails patterns of behavior, including familiar management tasks, visible and audible behavior, and norms. Level 2 focuses on values, whether testable in the physical environment or only by social consensus. Level 3 comprises basic assumptions regarding relationship to the environment; the nature of reality, time, and space; the essence of human nature; the nature of human activity; and the nature of human relationships.

On your college or university campus, examples of artifacts (Level 1A) are abundant. The administration building, main library, health center, basketball arena, football stadium, and parking garage all qualify. The technology of the shuttle bus that circulates to and from the dorms and classroom buildings and the artwork of plant life maintained by the grounds keepers also illustrate organizational culture Level 1A.

Certain norms of deportment are expected of students and faculty. Visible and audible expected behavior patterns include arriving at class on time. Familiar management tasks comprise daily routines for college classroom productivity and performance. These types of behaviors illustrate Level 1B.

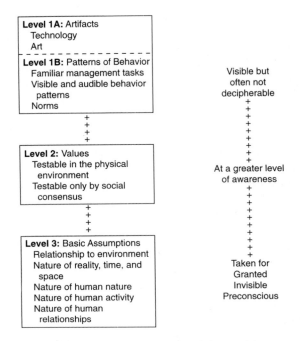

FIGURE 3.2 Levels of organizational culture and their interaction

Source: J. Steven Ott, *The Organizational Culture Perspective,* 1989. Reprinted with permission of the author.

Level 2 includes values that are testable in the physical environment and by social consensus, providing greater levels of awareness about organizational culture. The classroom limits or promotes effective exchanges between students and professor. The heating or cooling systems may malfunction, the lighting may be poor, the acoustics may be weird, the chairs may have splinters in them, or the roof may leak. The physical environment of the classroom contributes to the culture of the academic exercise. The social consensus may well be that the class should adjourn pronto, but that's not Professor Jones's decision; in fact, the professor insists that hot or cold air, lighting, acoustics, splinters, or rain should *not* interfere with the exciting revelations of public administration! The physical environment is now suspect; therefore, the social consensus for continuing the class tests the culture, dictated to the students by the professor.

After students sit in a cold (or hot) classroom, follow the professor's lecture in near darkness; listen to the professor's voice as it bounces off the ceiling, to the radiator, to the concrete floor, back up to the ceiling, and finally into their brains; pull splinters from their hands and other extremities from a forty-year-old chair; and see a $50 public administration textbook ruined by rain pouring through a hole in the roof, students question basic assumptions about the nature of reality, time, and space concerning the culture, or ways of life, common to a college classroom. The questioning of these basic assumptions, at Level 3, examines the relationships of students to their cultural environment. The components of culture are *material* and *nonmaterial.* As Figure 3.2 shows, the basic assumptions of Level 3 are often invisible and outside of consciousness.

Physical layout and organizational techniques are illustrations of material culture. Both contribute to the environment of public administration by focusing on the interaction between habitat and culture and by emphasizing how and why certain actions occur. As students attend different classes, they move from one classroom culture to another. In chemistry, a chart showing the elements is part of the material culture. In biology, a skeleton hangs for the professor's demonstration to students. In architecture, drawing boards are a common feature of material culture.

Technology plays a key role in influencing material culture. Equipment and techniques affect the character of an organization. Personal computers are likely to be more helpful to you than typewriters when you are conducting research or writing a paper. The use of a videocassette recorder or DVD player in college classrooms expands teaching methods. If technology becomes increasingly complicated, an organization may have more difficulty in entering a new field of endeavor.

Not all culture is observable in the same way as material culture. Nonmaterial culture includes beliefs, systems of communications, and modes of conduct. Rituals, taboos, and jargon are modes of conduct that influence important aspects of nonmaterial culture. All organizations follow these prescribed formulas when employees act in ritualistic unison, observe a system of taboos, or speak in a peculiar jargon. One of the rituals of college classes is to arrive on time; cheating on examinations is taboo. Public administrators communicate in an "alphabet soup" jargon of acronyms for departments, agencies, and programs.

Material and nonmaterial culture may conflict if organization members confuse patterns of conduct with changes occurring in the world outside the organization. In other words, your nonmaterial value system, or beliefs, may not line up with the realities of the material world, which can result in *cultural lag*. Our organized society is constantly changing. Our values and preferences, however, tend to remain the same. The challenge is to respond appropriately to the changes in society without altering core values.

Material and nonmaterial bureaucratic cultures reflect a larger political culture. Political culture, as Elazár notes, includes perceptions held by the general public and politicians concerning the nature of politics and the perceived role of government in society. A statewide political culture gives citizens a framework for what to expect from government and for how they perceive officeholders, bureaucrats, and campaign workers. Political culture outlines the boundaries and practices of citizens, politicians, and public officials. Elazár carves out three types of political culture in the United States and describes the relation of bureaucracy to each type. The three types of political culture are *individualistic, moralistic,* and *traditionalistic.*

- *Individualistic.* In this type of political culture, politics is viewed as dirty. Only professionals participate in politics, and parties dole out favors and responsibilities among them. Party cohesiveness is strong; competition arises between parties, not over issues. New programs are not to be initiated unless public opinion demands them. Political competition focuses on winning office to reap tangible rewards. Government is viewed as a marketplace, and economic development is favored. The appropriate spheres of activity are largely economic. Bureaucracy is viewed ambivalently. A loosely

The Culture of Corruption

It has not just been Ulysses S. Grant, Warren G. Harding, and Richard M. Nixon—our most famously scandal-burdened presidents—who wrestled with accusations of corruption. John Adams and John Quincy Adams, two of the most incorruptible men in U.S. political history, were also harried throughout their presidencies by accusations of corruption and abuses of power. Rutherford B. Hayes, a paragon of propriety, was known during his unhappy administration as "His Fraudulency" for having allegedly stolen the 1876 election from Samuel J. Tilden.

Harry S. Truman, a folk hero today for what Americans like to remember as his plain-speaking honesty, was buffeted by charges of "cronyism" and "corruption"—for creating what Nixon and many others in 1952 liked to call the "mess in Washington." Even Dwight D. Eisenhower, famously genial, enormously popular, legendarily honest, suffered from embarrassing revelations about his chief of staff, Sherman L. Adams, and other improprieties. What happened in the late 1990s to Bill Clinton is in many respects part of the ordinary pattern of U.S. political life.

In an era when charges are made—in the media and in courtrooms—against government officials on a rather frequent basis, the terms *corruption* and *scandal* become virtually synonymous in the minds of many Americans. But they have different implications. While both signify moral unsoundness, corruption denotes legal violations, or the breaking of laws, whereas scandal simply offends someone's moral values.

So, as the Monica Lewinsky scandal offended notions of sexual morality (personal lies) to millions, incidences of abortions, poverty, racism, economic disparity, lowering of education standards, and social welfare policies (institutional lies) are scandals to others. Officials in the Clinton administration offended the moral feelings of many citizens, creating scandal, but not necessarily resulting in corruption, or the breaking of laws.

Source: Alan Brinkley, "The Culture of Corruption," *Los Angeles Times,* November 2, 1997, p. M1.

---

implemented type of merit system is favored. Indiana, Nevada, New Jersey, and Pennsylvania are states that reflect the individualistic political culture.

- *Moralistic.* In a moralistic political culture, the practice of politics is viewed as healthy and as every citizen's responsibility. Everyone can participate. Political parties are vehicles to attain goals believed to be in the public interest. Party cohesiveness is subordinate to principles and issues. Competition is over issues, not parties. Political orientation focuses on winning office to implement policies.

  Government in a moralistic system is viewed as a commonwealth, answering directly for the general welfare and common good of the people. Appropriate spheres of activity include any area that will enhance the community through nongovernmental action. New programs are initiated without public pressure if they are believed to be in the public interest. Bureaucracy is viewed positively, bringing desirable political neutrality. A strong merit system is favored. Colorado, Michigan, Minnesota, North Dakota, Oregon, Utah, Vermont, and Wisconsin reflect the moralistic political culture.

- *Traditionalistic.* Politics is viewed as a privilege in which only those with legitimate claim to office should participate. Participation in politics is limited to the appropriate elite. Political parties serve as vehicles to recruit people for public offices not desired by established power holders. Party cohesiveness depends upon family and social ties and is highly personal. Competition is between the elite-dominated factions within a dominant party. The orientation to politics depends upon the political values of the elite.

Government is viewed as a means of maintaining the existing order. Appropriate spheres of activity are those that maintain traditional patterns. New programs are initiated if the program serves in the interest of the governing elite. Bureaucracy is viewed negatively, as it depersonalizes government. Merit should be controlled by the political elite, so no merit system is favored. Mississippi, South Carolina, Tennessee, and Virginia are states reflecting the traditionalistic political culture.

Some states fall into more than one type of political culture. Those states that are mainly moralistic political cultures yet also have individualistic traits are California, Iowa, Kansas, Montana, New Hampshire, South Dakota, and Washington.

States that are mainly individualistic but have moralistic traits as well are Connecticut, Illinois, Massachusetts, Nebraska, New York, Ohio, and Rhode Island.

States that are individualistic yet traditional are Delaware, Hawaii, Maryland, and Missouri. Those that are traditionalistic yet individualistic are Alabama, Arkansas, Florida, Georgia, Kentucky, Louisiana, New Mexico, Oklahoma, Texas, and West Virginia. States that are traditionalistic yet moralistic are Arizona and North Carolina.[20]

Political culture, then, can be said to encompass a state's orientation to political action. Culture includes knowledge, belief, art, morals, law, customs, capabilities, and habits institutionalized within an organization's environment. Material culture is observable, focuses on relationships of people distributed in space, and includes tools and techniques for fulfilling organizational purposes. Nonmaterial culture is not so obvious because it incorporates belief systems and patterns of conduct. No organization can be isolated from its cultural environment. This means the bureaucratic culture of the government organizations in a particular state cannot be divorced from that state's political culture.

When one examines the various aspects of public or government organization, one must look beyond mere facts and seek out factors that define reality or the culture of government, including:

1. The history of government, or how it developed
2. The role of government as perceived by members of society
3. The structures and processes considered proper to government
4. The values, mores, and habits of the primary people, especially the elected and appointed officials and the bureaucrats working beneath those officials[21]

Culture affects the everyday operations of a government organization. Culture resides in the ideas, values, norms, rituals, and beliefs of *socially constructed realities,* or organizations. Patterns of belief or shared meaning cause organizations to adopt their own ways of perceiving problems and resolving them.[22] The dynamics of culture incorporate traditions, perceptions, attitudes, assumptions, perspectives, values, and behaviors.

Summary

- The *anatomy* of public bureaucracy is its organizational framework or administrative structure.
- *Purpose, process, place,* and *clientele* explain why an organization was established.
- Of the three branches of government, the executive, legislative, and judicial, the executive has the widest range of responsibilities. As of 2005, the executive branch employs about 98 percent of all federal civilian employees, excluding the postal service.
- Principles for building a new agency are to keep it flat, focus on performance, and prepare for quasi-government status.
- *Unity of command* shows the relationship between those who order and those who follow orders. Unity of command usually requires a *chain of command,* because in any large bureaucracy, the person at the top cannot oversee all that is going on below. *Span of control* refers to the number of units—individuals or groups— that any supervising unit must oversee.
- *Staff personnel* are specialists who provide skills, knowledge, and expertise to line personnel. Staff functions to provide planning, fact finding, and support for line executives.
- Staff units in the Executive Office of the President include the White House Office, Council of Economic Advisers, Office of the U.S. Trade Representative, Office of Management and Budget, National Security Council, Council on Environmental Quality, Office of Policy Development, and Office of Science and Technology Policy.
- *Line personnel* are primarily concerned with developing, implementing, and evaluating policy. Line administrators are generalists. They legitimize authority and are in command. Line employees are directly responsible for furthering an organization's goals. Staff and line employees sometimes come into conflict. This should come as no surprise because their goals and functions are inherently different.
- Line departments in the federal government include Agriculture, Commerce, Defense, Education, Energy, Health and Human Services, Homeland Security, Housing and Urban Development, Interior, Justice, Labor, State, Transportation, Treasury, and Veterans' Affairs.
- *Decentralization* occurs when an organization delegates powers to subordinate levels within the same department or agency. Political decentralization allocates power among states, counties, cities, and other local governments. Decisions to centralize or decentralize cannot be divorced from the values, tasks, and structure of an organization. Americans seem to agree that governmental power should be shifted to the states. However, a 10 percent increase in efficiency as a result of state control would reduce government costs by less than 0.5 percent.[23]
- *Political culture* consists of the pattern of political action within a political system. Any organization is part of a larger social system. Indirectly, an organization's employees are therefore subject to a larger social system. Its employees are also subject, indirectly, to a larger set of values. No organization can be isolated from its cultural environment.
- Physical layout, organizational techniques, and technology illustrate material culture. Beliefs, systems of communication, and modes of conduct illustrate nonmaterial culture. Our nonmaterial values or beliefs may not line up with the realities of the material world, which can result in cultural lag.
- Corruption and scandal signify moral unsoundness. Corruption denotes legal violations, or the breaking of laws. Scandal simply offends moral values. Scandal surrounding sexual immorality may be emblematic of personal lies. Poverty, racism, economic disparity, lowering of education standards, and social welfare policies may be symbolic of institutional lies.
- Culture may be divided according to technology, economics, social organization, religion, and symbolism.

    The next step in understanding the craft of public administration is to examine some key theories about organizations. That is the focus of the next chapter.

VIDEOS AND FILMS

Public Administration in Action

Political Culture

Good Night, and Good Luck [2005]

Portrays 1953 ideological conflicts between veteran radio and television journalist Edward R. Murrow and U.S. Senator Joseph McCarthy of Wisconsin. Anticommunist witch-hunting spree is in full sway. [90 min]

Culture

Hoosiers [1986]

A basketball coach gets one last chance at redemption at a rural Indiana high school. Primer for Bobby Knight and Hoosier culture case study. [115 min]

Political Decentralization

Can the States Do It Better? [2004]

Explores the history and anatomy of current political debate over the idea of shifting power and authority from the federal government to the states and individuals. Examines the split between Thomas Jefferson and Alexander Hamilton over how much power the federal government should have. Welfare reform and school vouchers receive scrutiny. Princeton, NJ: Films for the Humanities & Sciences. Ben Wattenberg, host. Panel includes Robert Bork, Frances Fox Piven, Alan Brinkley, John Dilulio. [56 min]

Culture

10 Days That Unexpectedly Changed America [2006]

Presents pivotal moments in American history and often unforeseen repercussions. The Manhattan Project, television's emergence, teenage independence, sexuality, race relations, and new forms of music are emphasized. History Channel broadcast. [134 min]

Staff and Line

Rumsfeld's War [2004]

Frontline coproduction with the *Washington Post* and the Kirk Documentary Group, Ltd. Details the challenges of U.S. military occupations in Afghanistan and Iraq. [90 min]

 ## Case Study

Bobby Knight and Hoosier Culture

This case study illustrates potential conflicts in chain of command, unity of command, and span of control; line and staff and administrative decentralization; real and ideal cultures; material and nonmaterial cultures; traditionalism and individualism; and cultural identity. How could Indiana University President Myles Brand *have "played" basketball coach Bobby Knight as a one-to-ten scenario, not a zero-sum outcome?*

What makes a university better is what you get out of it. The essence to getting an education is creating advantages for yourself.

—*Bobby Knight*
Texas Tech basketball coach

As men's basketball coach at Indiana University (IU) from 1971 to September 2000, Bobby Knight led the Hoosiers to three NCAA titles (1976, 1981, and 1987) and eleven Big Ten championships. He also coached U.S. teams to gold medals in the 1984 Olympics and 1987 Pan American Games. Knight's teams won 763 games over the duration, and not once was the Indiana basketball program on NCAA probation.

At IU and then Texas Tech, Knight is a state government employee; his salary is paid by the taxpayers of Texas. As head of the Department of Men's Intercollegiate Basketball at Texas Tech University, Knight is regulated by provisions of state and federal laws. With certain skills, knowledge, and expertise, Knight is a government bureaucrat—and a basketball coach par excellence.

Born October 25, 1940, in Massillon, Ohio, Robert Montgomery Knight grew up in nearby Orrville, where he played basketball, football, and baseball for the Orrville Red Raiders. He played college basketball for three seasons (1960–1962) at Ohio State University. (Freshmen did not play varsity sports.) He started only two games. As a bench player, Knight was the "sixth man" on OSU's national championship team.

Knight coached high school basketball in Cuyahoga Falls, Ohio. He subsequently joined the Army to coach the U.S. Military Academy team at West Point. He arrived at Indiana University on April Fools day, 1971. He taught a class on basketball fundamentals while he was coach at Indiana. He is known to some as a jerk, bully, and abuser. Al Neuharth, founder of *USA Today,* says that Knight often reminds him of the great World War II Army general, George S. Patton, Jr. Neuharth points out that Knight

- Teaches discipline, as well as winning
- Develops team players, not just run-and-gun hotshots
- Makes sure most players graduate from college[1]

Knight never apologizes. "If my kids left and weren't successful, if they were on the bread line or selling drugs or in jail for one thing or another, then I would have a lot of questions about what my methods were leading to," Knight insists. "But when I have kids come back and talk about their experience here, what it's meant to them and I see what they're doing, then I'm just not sure what there is that I'm supposed to apologize for."[2]

Others disagree. Knight's quick temper and aggressive behavior toward players and others finally cost the legendary coach his job. On September 10, 2000, IU President Myles Brand fired Knight for a continuing pattern of "defiant and hostile" behavior. Paragraph 9 of Knight's contract read: "If the university at any time desires, Coach Knight shall cease to serve as head basketball coach when so advised in writing."[3]

Brand stated: "He is a legendary coach who has won three national championships, had graduation rates among the highest in the country, run a crystal-clean program with no NCAA violations, and been a great philanthropist. But he has failed to live within the guidelines by which he promised to abide."[4]

Why Did Myles Brand Fire Bobby Knight?

As IU President, Brand is a generalist, occupying a position of authority and commanding the organization's operations. As men's basketball coach, Knight was a specialist who provided coaching skills, knowledge, and expertise to line personnel director President Brand in IU's chain of command. Why did President Brand fire Coach Knight?

President Brand fired Coach Knight because:

- Knight refused to work within the "normal" IU chain of command in the athletics department.
- The coach made angry remarks about university officials and trustees.
- Knight refused to participate in previously scheduled events for IU alumni.
- He did not abide by sanctions as catalogued in IU's "zero tolerance policy" (ZTP).[5]
- Finally, of course, Knight confronted freshman IU student, Kent Harvey, 19, regarding proper manners and civility.

Harvey claimed Knight grabbed and intimidated him. (Knight is known for his intimidating presence.) Harvey is the stepson of Mark Shaw, a former Bloomington radio talk-show host and a critic of Knight. Harvey spoke to the coach, referring to him as "Knight." Knight reportedly said to young Harvey: "Son, my name is not 'Knight' to you. It's 'Coach Knight' or it's 'Mr. Knight.' I don't call people by their last name, and neither should you."[6]

Knight's run-in with Harvey resulted in "inappropriate physical contact," which violated IU's zero tolerance policy and was cause for immediate termination. IU's ZTP did not include due process guidelines.

Brand insisted that a half-dozen accusations against Knight were on record, and that no single offense reached the level for firing Knight. Taken together, however, all the offenses resulted in a pattern of conduct outside the boundaries of the zero tolerance policy guidelines.

As head of IU's chain of command, Brand asked Knight to resign. The coach refused, violating Brand's unity-of-command order. Brand then fired Knight. As the word filtered out to IU students, two thousand people—mostly students—marched on the athletic complex, Showalter Fountain, and at the president's home. During campus unrest, Harvey and Brand were hanged in effigy. The next day Knight bade farewell to the students at a talk in Dunn Meadow; crowd estimates ranged from six to ten thousand. Brand called Knight's talk "gracious."

Culture is defined as "that complex whole which includes knowledge, belief, art, morals, law, custom, and any other capabilities and habits acquired by man as a member of society."[7] Cultural awareness is crucial for understanding the development, implementation, and evaluation of any government program, including that of the men's basketball program at IU, funded by the Indiana taxpayers. Culture—or ways of life common to a society, government organization, or interest group—includes the ideal and the real.

Ideal cultural patterns focus on what citizens do or say if they adhere completely to the recognized standards of the culture. Real behavioral patterns refer to people's actual observations and behaviors.[8] In 2000, 52 percent of white college basketball players and 35 percent of black players graduated from college; yet the graduation rate for IU men's basketball players was 79 percent during the 1990s. What happens if one of Knight's players cuts class? "I'm too scared to find out," a smiling 7-foot, 285-pound Texas Tech center, Mickey Michalec, told ESPN. In the Knight-IU academic world, the real culture approximated the ideal.[9]

Culture places limits on individuals in organizational settings. An organization is a subculture within a larger culture. An understanding of the larger culture is vital because we must recognize that an organization's members or employees are not free agents in any society—including that of Indiana University.

One-to-Ten and Zero-Sum Games

College basketball is no one-to-ten game. Players do not get credit in the media for playing hard. Instead, NCAA college hoops is a zero-sum game: One team wins, the other loses. Stamina, conditioning, physical abuse, hard work, long hours, mental toughness, and competition make the difference—this is the culture of college basketball. In Knight's career at IU, the Hoosiers had no NCAA violations for recruiting or academics. They made it into the NCAA tournament for fifteen straight years. IU won more basketball games in the 1970s, 1980s, and 1990s than any team in the Big Ten conference.

Any organization, whatever its limits or prospects, is part of a larger social system. At least indirectly, its employees are subject to a larger set of values. Certain cultural patterns of conduct and belief are found in any organization. Culture reflects a consensus of the values of that organization.

In an era when charges are made—in the media—against controversial public figures on a daily basis, the terms *corruption* and *scandal* become virtually synonymous in the minds of many Americans. How many times has a TV clip portrayed Knight throwing chairs? Perhaps hundreds. How many times did Knight throw a chair? Once. How many times did Knight intimidate players or others? Many. Has Knight been convicted of assaulting anyone? No. Has he been charged in a court of law? No. Knight's behavior may be a scandal, but so far, none of it has ever proved illegal. Knight is certainly no criminal.

Bobby Knight and Bill Clinton

Bobby Knight and Bill Clinton have one thing in common. The left wing—grounded mostly in government-funded colleges and universities—abhors physical violence. The right wing—originating in private wealth and status and in small-town America—abhors sexual misdeeds. The left accuses Knight of physical abuse. The right accused Clinton of sexual misbehavior. Both extremes employ the media to make their cases known.

But no organization can be isolated from its cultural environment.[10] Understanding culture gives one an advance indication of how people may act in a given situation. Traditions, customs, and patterned modes of behavior are common to all organizations. Knight is a bright, hardworking, high-achieving, and charismatic college basketball coach. Clinton is a bright, hardworking, high-achieving, and charismatic former president. But going beyond what tradition, customs, and modes of conduct permit is sometimes a matter of smart people doing dumb things.

Physical layout and organization techniques are examples of material culture. Technology plays a key role in influencing material culture; equipment and techniques affect the character of an organization. College basketball is played between two teams of five players each, with players trying to throw the ball through an elevated basket precisely ten feet from the floor on the opponent's side of the rectangular court. Lighting technology for every arena varies. The size of the court is standard—54×90 feet. The three-point goal line is 19.9 feet from the end of the court. The free throw circle is a radius of six feet. These dimensions reflect college basketball's material culture.

Nonmaterial culture includes beliefs, systems of communications, and modes of conduct. All organizations follow prescribed formulas. Employees may act in ritualistic unison, observe a system of taboos, or speak in peculiar jargon. If our nonmaterial value system is not in sync with the realities of the material world, the result is *cultural lag*.[11]

Society is constantly changing, but many human values and preferences remain much the same. The challenge is to respond appropriately to changes in society without altering core values. Knight is a talented coach because he has developed techniques to defeat teams with varying skills. Yet his players learned and graduated.

Indiana culture is primarily traditionalistic south of U.S. highway 40 and especially individualistic north of that demarcation. Except for the region near Chicago, nowhere in Indiana is the culture moralistic. Participation is limited to the appropriate elite in traditional politics. Party cohesiveness depends upon family and social ties and is highly personal. Government is viewed as a means of maintaining the existing social order.[12]

Traditionalism versus Individualism?

Traditionalism conflicts with individualism in the Knight–IU case. Traditionalism implies that IU should have terminated the controversial coach a long time ago. An upright, conservative, and successful foul-mouthed megalomaniacal boor is still a foul-mouthed megalomaniacal boor. No assault or battery should be accepted in sport. Knight personifies a person of means who feels he is above the law and norms of society.

Individualism gives Knight a lot more rope. The ends, at least in part, justify the means. Bad language and screaming obscenities are contextual; record and performance are the bottom line. The players get educated. They win, they don't cheat, and they do well in life. You know where he stands. Knight is honest, productive, and loyal to IU. Politics is viewed as dirty in individualistic politics. Only professionals participate. Parties dole out favors and responsibility; government is a marketplace.

In the 1960 *Webster's New World Dictionary of the American Language, College Edition* (predating current definitions of *political correctness*) the word *Hoosier* is defined as a "mountaineer, dirty person, or tramp; a native or inhabitant of Indiana."[13]

Terms such as mountaineer, dirty person, tramp, or vagrant bring to mind the phrase "white trash." The United States, historically, is a "white trash country." Immigrants fled here from other countries to find opportunities in capitalism, democracy, and personal flexibility.

Bobby Knight became head basketball coach at Indiana University in 1971. Knight arrived in Bloomington approximately a decade after Webster published its interpretations of the word *Hoosier*. Knight assumed leadership of a college basketball program in a state called the "Appalachia of the Midwest." Indiana has more in common, demographically, with Kentucky than it does with Ohio, Michigan, Wisconsin, Iowa, and parts of Illinois.

While Knight coached IU, Indianapolis discarded its image as Indiana-no-place. The Lilly Corporation emerged as the world's most prominent drug company. Late-night-talk-show host Dave Letterman invented "stupid pet tricks." Two Republicans (Otis Bowen and Bob Orr) and two Democrats (Evan Bayh and Frank O'Bannon) were elected governor of Indiana during Knight's twenty-nine years as IU's coach. None affected the culture as much as Knight.

Knight gave Indiana University and the state of Indiana a new cultural identity. He redefined the word *Hoosier*—as a determined, focused, well-trained, skilled, hardworking, respectful, all-for-the-team, loyal, overachieving college student—who also happened to be a basketball player. Knight taught hard work and 100 percent effort, and he inspired confidence and loyalty that allowed IU teams to excel beyond their natural abilities.

Bobby Knight retired from coaching college basketball in the middle of the 2007–2008 season. Pat Knight, his son, replaced him as head basketball coach of the Texas Tech Red Raiders. In his forty-two-year career, Bobby Knight won 902 games—the most by any coach in the history of Division I college basketball. At age 67, Knight quit—and did it "his way." "Hate him or love him," one fan stated. "You must respect him."

Culture resides in the ideas, values, norms, rituals, and beliefs of socially constructed realities, or organizations. Belief patterns or shared meanings cause organizations to adopt certain ways of perceiving and resolving problems. Culture includes traditions, perceptions, attitudes, assumptions, perspectives, values, and behaviors.

Moralistic politics is viewed as healthy and as every citizen's responsibility. Political parties are vehicles to attain goals believed to be in the public interest. Competition takes place over issues, not parties. Indiana, as a state government, does not practice moralistic politics. In traditionalism and individualism, the bottom line is authority (line) and power (Brand) versus specialist (staff) and talent (Knight).

Could a moralistic ideology have ushered in compromise and consensus between Brand and Knight?

- Indiana culture pays attention to traditionalism and individualism. The moralistic idea of the greater good, if active in Indiana, is imported in from elsewhere.
- President Brand defended his power and position. Brand and the IU trustees fired the intimidating Coach Knight.
- Just because Knight was not paranoid does not mean that they were not after him. No bureaucrat, however talented, can ignore the culture outside his or her immediate organization.

Questions and Instructions

1. Define *culture*. Apply the definition in this case.
2. Name some ideal cultural patterns in this case.
3. Name some real cultural patterns in this case.
4. Culture places limits on individuals. What limits did it place in this case?
5. An organization is a subculture within a larger culture. How do staff and line come into play in this case? Explain.
6. Physical layout and organization techniques illustrate material culture. How is this true in this case?
7. Nonmaterial culture includes beliefs, systems of communication, and modes of conduct. How did these elements play out in Knight's case? Explain.

8. How might moralistic precepts at IU have brought the traditionalism of Brand (authority/line) and the individualism of Knight ("I did it my way"/staff) into compromise and an escape from the zero-tolerance, zero-sum game? Explain.
9. How did the cultural identity of Indiana change during Knight's twenty-nine-year tenure as IU's basketball coach? Explain.
10. Why did Knight have more influence on the culture of Indiana than Otis Bowen, Bob Orr, Evan Bayh, and Frank O'Bannon—all governors of the Hoosier state?

Insights-Issues/Bobby Knight and Hoosier Culture

Clearly and briefly describe and illustrate the following concepts and issues. Interpret the word *role* in terms of impacts, applications, importance, effects, and/or illustrations of certain facts, concerns, or issues from the case study.

1. Role of culture in the firing of Knight.
2. Role of chain of command, unity of command, and span of control in the firing of Knight.

3. Role of traditionalism and individualism in arguments for and against firing Knight.
4. Role of staff-line conflicts in arguments for and against firing Knight.
5. Role of Knight in developing a new cultural identity for the state of Indiana.

Notes

1. Al Neuharth, "Would You Want Your Son on Knight's Team?" *USA Today*, November 1, 2000, http://www.usatoday.com/news/comment/columnists/neuharth/neu044.htm.

2. "Knight Defends Record After Choking Accusation," http://espn.go.com/ncb/news/2000/0317/430679.html.

3. Indiana University, "IU Announces Removal of Basketball Coach Bob Knight," September 10, 2000, http://www.iuinfo.indiana.edu/ocm/releases/knight0910.htm.

4. *Ibid.*

5. Zero tolerance did not begin with Miles Brand and Bobby Knight. In the 1980s, the state and federal governments fought illegal drugs. By 1994, the Safe and Drug-Free Schools and Communities Act required schools that received federal funds to expel students who brought weapons to school. Brand and the IU Board of Trustees adopted their zero tolerance policy to encourage Knight to temper his "pattern of inappropriate behavior" with fans, student athletes, and basketball officials. Knight was fired, in part, because he lectured a student on the proper way to address an adult.

6. Rex W. Huppke, "Indiana Investigating Knight Again," Associated Press, September 8, 2000, http://sports.yahoo.com/ncaab/news/ap/20000908/ap-knight-student.html.

7. John M. Pfiffner and Frank P. Sherwood, *Administrative Organization* (Englewood Cliffs, NJ: Prentice-Hall, 1960), pp. 249–272. See also Rhys H. Williams, "Is America in a Culture War? Yes—No—Sort of," *The Christian Century,* 114, no. 32 (November 12, 1997): 1038–1043. Quotes from Tylor's Primitive Culture in Leslie A. White, "The Concept of Culture," *American Anthropologist,* Vol. 61, No. 227 (April 1959). White reports that there is great divergence of view among anthropologists as to a definition of culture.

8. Thomas R. Dye, *Power & Society: An Introduction to the Social Sciences* (Monterey, CA: Brooks/Cole, 1987), p. 39.

9. Don Williams, "Grad Rates Focus of TV Special," *The Lubbock Avalance-Journal,* March 1, 2002, http://www.redraiders.com/stories/030102/mbb_030102104.shtml.

10. Pfiffner and Sherwood, *Administrative Organization,* p. 252.

11. *Ibid.,* p. 264.

12. Daniel J. Elazár, *American Federalism: A View from the States* (New York: Harper & Row, 1984), p. 109.

13. *Webster's New World Dictionary of the American Language, College Edition* (Cleveland and New York: World Publishing Company, 1960), p. 699.

Sources

"Bob Knight—former Indiana University Basketball Coach," *Indianapolis Star,* September 15, 2000, http://www.starnews.com/library/factfiles/ people/k/knight_bob/knight.html; "Knight Offers Life Lessons, Dodges Controversy in Appearance at Ball State," Associated Press, April 20, 2001; Myles Brand, "Academics First: Reforming Intercollegiate Athletics," January 23, 2001, http://www.indiana.edu/~pres/speeches/press_club.html; Myles Brand "Open Letter to the Media," February 2, 1998; Graham Couch, "Keeping Knight Keeps IU from Becoming a Basketball Factory," *Columbia Chronicle Online* 33, no. 27 (May 22, 2000), http://www.ccchronicle.com/back/00may22/sports2.html; Jonathan Grossberg, "The Ironic End to a Great Era in Indiana," *Brown Daily Herald,* September 19, 2000, http://www.browndailyherald.com; Bobby Knight with Bob Hammel, *Knight: My Story* (New York: St. Martin's Press), 2002; John Laskowski, "Playing for the General," *Indiana Alumni Magazine* (November–December 2000), http://www.indiana.edu/~alumni.magtalk/nov.dec00/thegeneral.html; Mike Leonard, "Professor May Help Redefine 'Hoosier,'"

Bloomington Herald-Times, January 28, 2001; Rhonda Chriss Lokeman, "Indiana U. Should Hit Knight Where It Hurts," *Kansas City Star,* May 21, 2000, http://www.positivecoach.org/news/20000521_lokeman.html; Gareth Morgan, *Images of Organization* (Beverly Hills, CA: Sage, 1986); John Rouse, "Knight Not the Insidious Element at IU by Far," *Evansville Courier & Press,* September 21, 2000, http://www.courierpress.com; Chris Suellentrop, "Assessment: Bob Knight," March 15, 2002, http://slate.msn.com; "Suit Contends Indiana Broke Law in Firing Knight," *Sports Illustrated,* October 3, 2000, http://sportsillustrated.cnn.com/basketball/college/news/2000/10/03/knight_lawsuit_ap/;Steve Wilstein, "Knight May Be Asked to Quit," Associated Press, May 12, 2000, http://www.onlineathens.com/stories/051200/dog_0512000045.shtml; Mike Wright, "A Knight to Remember," *Indiana Alumni Magazine* (November–December, 2000), http://www.indiana.edu/~alumni/megtalk/nov-dec00/knightremember.html.

Notes

1. Luther Gulick and L. Urwick, *Papers on the Science of Administration* (New York: Institute of Public Administration, 1937), p. 15.
2. Barbara J. Saffir, "Evolution of Cabinet," *Washington Post,* February 9, 1993, p. A15.
3. John M. Pfiffner and Frank P. Sherwood, *Administrative Organization* (Englewood Cliffs, NJ: Prentice-Hall, 1960), pp. 170–188.
4. John D. Donahue, "The Devil in Devolution," *The American Prospect* 8, no. 32 (May–June 1997): 42–48.
5. Mary O. Furner, "Downsizing Government: A Historical Perspective," *USA Today* 126, no. 2630 (November 1997): 56–58.
6. Dana Milbank, *Wall Street Journal,* January 8, 1997, p. A1.
7. Judith Havemann, "After Getting Responsibility for Welfare, States May Pass It Down," *Washington Post,* January 28, 1997, p. A1.
8. Steven D. Gold, "Issues Raised by the New Federalism," *National Tax Journal* 49, no. 2 (June 1996): 273–287.
9. Hal Hovey, "The Challenges of Flexibility," *State Legislatures* 22, no. 1 (January 1996): 14–19.
10. David O. Porter and Eugene A. Olsen, "Some Critical Issues in Government Centralization and Decentralization," *Public Administration Review* 36, no. 1 (January/February 1976): 72–84.
11. Harold Seidman and Robert Gilmour, *Politics, Position, and Power: From the Positive to the Regulatory State,* 4th ed. (New York: Oxford University Press, 1986), p. 127.
12. *Ibid.*
13. Herbert Kaufman, "Administrative Decentralization and Political Power," *Public Administration Review* 29 (January/February 1969): 3–15.
14. See Rhys H. Williams, "Is America in a Culture War? Yes—No—Sort of," *The Christian Century* 114, no. 32 (November 12, 1997): 1038–1043; Leslie A. White, "The Concept of Culture," *American Anthropologist* 61, no. 227 (April 1959). White reports that there is great divergence of view among anthropologists as to a definition of culture.
15. Thomas R. Dye, *Power & Society: An Introduction to the Social Sciences,* 4th ed. (Monterey, CA: Brooks/Cole, 1987), p. 39.
16. *Ibid.,* p. 40.
17. Daniel J. Elazár, *American Federalism: A View from the States* (New York: Harper & Row, 1984), p. 109.
18. Pfiffner and Sherwood, *Administrative Organization,* pp. 249–272.
19. J. Steven Ott, *The Organization Culture Perspective* (Chicago: Dorsey Press, 1989), p. 62.
20. Elazár, *American Federalism,* p. 136.
21. Harold F. Gortner, Julianne Mahler, and Jeanne Bell Nicholson, *Organization Theory: A Public Perspective* (Fort Worth, TX: Harcourt Brace, 1997), p. 71.
22. Gareth Morgan, *Images of Organization* (Beverly Hills, CA: Sage, 1986).
23. John D. Donahue, "The Disunited States: 'Devolution'—Shifting Power from Washington to the Fifty States—Is No Cure for What Ails American Government," *Atlantic* 279, no. 5 (May 1997): 18–21.

The Physiology of Public Organizations

Chapter Highlights

Democracy in Bureaucracy	Human Relations Theories
Baseline Originals in Organizational Life	Summary
Neoclassical Theories	

Public Service as Organization Theory

Individualism is a priority in American life. Consumerism and the market follow close behind, with notions of "the greater good" and community bringing up the rear among citizen expectations and concerns. From the vantage point of organization theory, public service derives its support from community commitments—not selfish notions of individualism.

What is a public service career? Public servants today often have exciting careers. College professors, fire fighters, police officers, air traffic controllers, schoolteachers, diplomats, sanitation inspectors, elected representatives, moon walkers (of the NASA variety), soldiers, sailors, jet fighter pilots, Peace Corps volunteers, economic development specialists, mayors, governors, and presidents are engaged in public service careers. They represent and are employees of the community.

Dedication, work, tolerance, and love forge the depth, width, and psychological boundaries of community. "The United States is by definition a place on the map, but is not intrinsically a community," writes former Colorado governor, Richard D. Lamm. "A community is not geography—it is not who lives in an area—it is the web of human relationships of the people who live in a particular

place. Every house is not a home, and every spot on the map is not a community."

Public servants earn academic degrees in many disciplines, including aerospace technology, geology, environmental science, business, law, criminal justice, sociology, social work, computer science, finance, journalism, telecommunications, military science, political science, public administration, accounting, natural resources, history, economics, law enforcement, and civil engineering. Workplaces include local, state, and federal governments, along with nonprofit organizations. Bureaucrats, as government employees are often called, do not always have boring jobs. They shape urban designs, school curricula, immigration procedures, environmental regulations, air safety, railroad crossings, and Middle East peace accords. The marketplace fails to effectively function without the trust and safety instilled by public servants.

In terms of organization theory, working for the Children's Defense Fund, Habitat for Humanity, or the statewide Transportation Planning Region requires a different set of values than does working for oil companies, accounting firms, banking, real estate, or other profit-seeking enterprises. Lobbying for the rights of children, ensuring that families have homes, and organizing citizen input before building new interstate highways are all examples in which public servants work for the long-term interests of community, region, state, and nation.

Satisfying short-term, private consumer wants does not make the list of organizational priorities for public servants. Answering the needs of people and community does.

Source

Richard D. Lamm, "The Elusive Concept of Community," *Kettering Review,* Spring 2001, 28–36.

Physiology is the study of life processes, activities, and functions. Just as a medical student must study physiology to understand how the human body works, students of public administration must be familiar with *organizational theories* so they will be prepared to confront the realities of bureaucracy. This chapter provides a look at the most influential and helpful organizational theories and theorists.

Democracy in Bureaucracy

Bureaucracy and *democracy* are the central pillars of the public and private organizations of our society. Bureaucratic hierarchy and democratic equality influence the vital processes and functions of all organizations. Despite the apparent paradox, bureaucracy and democracy are both antithetical and complementary.

In partisan politics, we periodically elect presidents, governors, and mayors. In such electoral processes, we take advantage of the fundamental principle of democracy. While in office, however, presidents, governors, and mayors depend upon principles of bureaucracy, which apply formalism, strict rule adherence, impersonality, unity of command, chain of command, span of control, and similar values to the exercise of authority. Authority in a bureaucracy is checked by democratic voting procedures, but only on a periodic basis. As we consider the functions and processes of organizations, therefore, an understanding of the philosophical differences between bureaucracy and democracy is crucial.

The development of our organized society underscores the need for democracy in the administrative state. We, the voting public, come into contact with numerous public and private organizations each day. Government constantly exercises its influence on the public. Legislatures allocate public functions to administrative structures. What input should employees and clientele have in internal decision making within public organizations? Can there be democracy in bureaucracy? How democratic should life in organizations be?

If you are not already employed, in a matter of years, even months, you will probably enter the American workforce. You may be employed by a business, labor, social, or public organization. You may be full of ideas and energy to tackle your employer's challenges and problems, and you will want to be heard. How much democracy will exist in your bureaucratic workplace? The *authoritarian tenets of bureaucracy* and the *egalitarian tenets of democracy* are major forces shaping life and the pursuit of happiness in the twenty-first century. These concepts interact with

Bureaucracy and Democracy Are Not Esoteric

Bureaucracy and democracy—concepts, terms, ways of working life—may seem esoteric, even to government employees. They are key aspects of government-operated, taxpayer-financed, public sector organizations. Capital is a necessity if public bureaucracy is to function well and if democracy is to realize a diversity of expression.

The respective definitions of capital, bureaucracy, and democracy, are economic wealth, employee skills and responsiveness, and the relatively free articulation of opinions. Capital does not necessarily mean money, but it often does. Money is wealth, or economic access to what one wants in life. And, simply stated, wealth is power.

Wealth also implies having good health and access to good health systems, educational and economic opportunities, high expectations for youth, transportation options, viable communities, strong family structures, respect for the aged, and meaningful religious beliefs.

Wealth is very different, of course, from income. Most government workers have incomes. We support ourselves and our families through our incomes. We also contribute to health insurance and retirement plans, as do our taxpayer-based employers. But most government employees—public safety officials, teachers, military personnel, transit workers, and not-for-profit employees, among others—maintain incomes, yet have very limited access to wealth.

Of the three concepts—capital, bureaucracy, and democracy—democracy is the most challenged or threatened, even pleading for its very existence. Most government workers are not likely to speak out or exercise their due process rights if they suspect that their salaries may be affected—even indirectly.

Bureaucracy, according to Max Weber's theories, is structured by hierarchy, chain of command, specialization of task, a specified sphere of competence, established norms of conduct, and records, paperwork, or similar documentation. Government employees are expected to be responsive to citizen-clients. A certain level of competence is demanded.

Any citizen can file to compete for elective office. That's the democratic way. But how many political candidates have access to skilled campaign officials

and large bank accounts (wealth) to make their candidacies competitive?

Definitions of *public* and *private* regulate the relationships between capital, bureaucracy and democracy. As Dwight Waldo wrote in *The Enterprise of Public Administration* (1980), "Concepts of public and private are very central in the conceptual and emotional structuring of the Western world. . . . A great deal of our thought and action concerning government, law, morals and social institutions relates one way or another to this distinction. . . . But we need to appreciate public and private are not categories of nature; they are categories of history and culture, of law and custom. They are contextual and subject to change and redefinition." (p. 164)

Professor Waldo suggests redefinition, reevaluation, and restatement of the nature, culture, and context of capital, bureaucracy, and democracy as they are played out on the public and private stages of American governments and politics. Do partisan political leaders advocate space shields or provide a Patients' Bill of Rights? The Departments of Health and Human Services, and Defense, are governed and administered according to laws. Nurses, medical doctors, and other caregivers are private sector entrepreneurs or employees of not-for-profits. The U.S. government provides soldiers and strategy for military missions. Private sector groups produce tanks, airplanes, missiles, ships, guns, uniforms, and boots. In both health and defense administration (HHS and DOD), the government produces little or nothing. In wars on disease, in military conquest and economic advantage, citizens make sacrifices for the common good.

On matters of life (health) and death (military power), priorities of capital, bureaucracy, and democracy are vigorously debated. In efforts to redefine, reevaluate, and restate the parameters of public and private life, citizens determine what they owe the state (society), and what the state owes them. In determining such boundaries, democracy is as prevalent—and as effective—as citizen access to incomes and wealth.

Source: "Bureaucracy and Democracy Are Not Esoteric" by John Rouse, as appeared on ASPA Online Columns, http://www.aspanet.org, July 17, 2001. Reprinted by permission of the author.

other organizational philosophies, such as capitalism, nationalism, industrialism, and socialism, all historical antecedents to democracy and bureaucracy.

Defining democracy is not easy. We live in a democracy. In the classical sense, though, our system of *political economy,* or politics and economics, is not a democracy, but a republic. We have a democratic *type* of government; however, we have a republican *form* of government: In our republic, elected officials represent us in our state and national legislatures. Other tenets of democracy call for "rule by the people." However, who are "the people"? How, and by what means, do they "rule"?

Democracy is not an economic, social, or ethical concept, but a political one. It emphasizes the values of liberty, equality, human worth, human dignity, and freedom by guaranteeing the right to secret voting. With these values come free expression of ideas, free association of persons, representation, legislatures, due process of law, and the privilege of assuming our soap box and speaking our minds about virtually anything.[1]

While democracy has a leveling, or *horizontal,* feature about its application, bureaucracy is *vertical.* Democracy implies equality and equal opportunity; bureaucracy denotes hierarchy. Every four years American citizens vote for or against a presidential candidate because of the candidate's support of political principles as expressed in the party's platform. The party platform serves as a voters' guide to how its leaders should address the nation's challenges during the next term. Voting, which espouses equality, is a political right in a democratic society.

However, once a candidate becomes president, the direct democratic powers of voters are diluted. Voters may encourage members of Congress to oppose the president's new programs, for example, but the rights of suffrage in our electoral democracy come up only periodically. Except for those periodic elections, the premises of bureaucracy, or hierarchy, assume preeminence in our system. Public institutions—ranging from health to defense—develop, evaluate, and implement public policies.

The oft-used term *bureaucracy* has two meanings. In its most popular sense, the concept refers to any substantial public organization or group of organizations, as in "federal bureaucracy" or in "welfare bureaucracy." The other meaning is more specialized; it refers to a particular method or manner of administration. A bureaucracy in this sense is an organization or group of organizations that operates in a particular way.

What constitutes the bureaucratic way of doing things? The German sociologist Max Weber (1864–1920) was the first to define it. He saw bureaucracy as an impersonal system operating on the basis of "calculable rules" and staffed by full-time and professional (as opposed to political) employees. Bureaucracy presupposes hierarchy, but this hierarchy is based on organizational rank, not on social status or other considerations.

The chief characteristic of a bureaucracy in Weber's sense of the word is its uniform, nonarbitrary, and nonpersonal method of administering public affairs. "Bureaucracy," wrote Weber, "is like a modern judge who is a vending machine into which the pleadings are inserted along with the fee. The machine then disgorges the judgment based on reasons mechanically derived from the code."[2]

In Weber's view, bureaucracy is a bloodless mechanism devoid of the capriciousness and color we associate with human activity. Yet the positive features of such an administrative approach, characterized by impersonality and

Protestant Ethic and Capitalism

Max Weber wrote *The Prostestant Ethic and the Spirit of Capitalism* in 1904–1905, with the intention of showing why a total revolution in the organization of society, or the rationalization of life, occurred only in the West and not in other parts of the world. However, Weber's intention has been obscured by much philosophizing and myth making about the so-called "Protestant Ethic."

Source: Daniel Bell, "The Protestant Ethic," *World Policy Journal* 13, no. 3 (Fall 1996): 35–38.

professionalism, must not be overlooked. Impersonality implies impartiality, and professionalism opens the possibility of an employee selection system based less on social status and more on personal skill.

This bureaucratic ideal has made headway in Europe, especially in Germany. As such, it has brought more uniformity, predictability, and equality to public administration.

Because bureaucratic systems rest upon a highly systematized administrative arrangement, they often show resistance to change. The devotion to calculable rules often causes rule-conscious bureaucrats to "go by the book," regardless of the situation. Such routinized organizational behavior may, however, prove advantageous. France, with its long history of unrest and upheaval, has often been held together by its plodding but enduring bureaucracy.

Although the bureaucratic style has conquered the public sector in Western Europe, it has scored somewhat less decisively in this country. The dynamics of U.S. political bureaucracies, especially in state and local jurisdictions, are highly personal. It is often *who* one knows rather than *what* one knows that affects the administrative system. Just as personalities often count for more than parties or principles in policy making, so personalities often outweigh "calculable rules" in policy execution. This is not always true, but it happens often enough to differentiate U.S. administration from that of other economically developed democracies such as England, France, or Germany.

Lessened concern for abiding by the rules provides many rewards. Although U.S. administration has often been accused of stodginess, and rightly so, it is perhaps less than its Western European counterparts. It is much easier to bend, if not break, the rules in the United States than elsewhere in the world of modern democratic capitalism. The U.S. administrative setup, reflecting vast differences in bureaucratic cultures, can more easily accommodate individual idiosyncrasies and initiatives.

Before breaking out into cheers, the antibureaucratic enthusiast should note some of the benefits that we thereby forego. A system more open to the influence of individual personality is open to caprice and whim. As calculable rules become more easily manipulated, the system is also more vulnerable to corruption. If change can sometimes come more quickly, then such change may spring not only from public demand but from personal desire as well.

The distinctiveness of U.S. administration should not be overstated: The bureaucratic way of doing things is scarcely a stranger to our shores. And the systems of other countries are certainly not incapable of capriciousness or change. Yet for both good and ill, bureaucracy in Weber's sense characterizes the U.S. public sector less than it does that of many other modern developed nations.

Normative Vectors

The norms or values of public administration are grouped into three general areas, or normative vectors.

- *Concerns about efficiency and effectiveness.* These areas of concern focus primarily on the workings of government and the way its goods and services are distributed and delivered. A public dollar should be expended with as much care and deliberation as feasible. This attitude toward government values the ability to mobilize, organize, and direct resources.
- *Concerns about rights and the adequacy of governmental process.* These themes scrutinize a government's relationship with its citizens. Individual liberties provide a sense of equity; each citizen should be treated as an individual, according to his or her circumstances. As concerns arose about the manner in which governments treat people, the notion of due process emerged. Rights, due process, and equity

focus on measuring the quality of interaction between an agency and its clientele. This focus is rooted in democratic theory. It reaches as far back as Aristotle.

- *Concerns about representation and the exercise of discretion.* These themes point toward controls the citizenry has over the workings of government and its agents. Accountability implies external standards of correct action and is thus institutionalized. Legal, political, and bureaucratic sanctions induce competent and conscientious administrative performance. Administrators must act in accordance with moral obligation. Accountability, responsibility, and responsiveness put representation into operation.

Source: Michael M. Harmon and Richard T. Mayer, *Organization Theory for Public Administration* (Boston: Little, Brown, 1986). See Chapter 3, "The Normative Context of Public Administration," pp. 34–53.

Interpretations of Bureaucracy

According to Dwight Waldo, the term "bureaucracy" has two interpretations. The *popular-pejorative* interpretation is widely recognized in society: Bureaucracy is bad because bureaucrats are timid, ineffectual, power-seeking, and dangerous.

A second interpretation of bureaucracy is *descriptive* and *analytical.* This interpretation says that bureaucracy fosters advanced legal and economic systems and, therefore, advances civilization. Descriptive and analytical terms related to this interpretation include *form of government, formalism, rules, impersonality, hierarchy, expertise, records, large-scale, complex, efficiency,* and *effectiveness.*

In reality, the concept of bureaucracy is neither good nor bad. Bureaucracy simply is; it exists. The concept of bureaucracy encompasses procedures for organizing people within a certain culture in order to achieve a particular set of goals and objectives. *Bureaucracy exists for accomplishing tasks.* The tasks range from fighting dictators to fighting poverty.

How, then, are the societal values of democracy and bureaucracy antithetical, yet complementary?

According to Waldo, there are two problems in reconciling democracy and bureaucracy. One concern focuses on the definition of the *administrative unit.* Any organization able to respond to clientele is a unit. The function of a unit of bureaucracy may be defined by the manner in which the organization responds to its clientele. Academic departments, as administrative units at a college or university, are organized depending upon college and student demands for certain skills, knowledge, and expertise.

For example, English and math may be the largest departments on campus because most colleges mandate that students take courses in these subjects. Meanwhile, the departments of philosophy, anthropology, and foreign language may be smaller because the demand for courses taught by those departments is lower.

Waldo's concern is the status and weight accorded to *nondemocratic values*. Liberty and equality are democratic values; nondemocratic values include national security, personal safety, productivity, and efficiency. If the chairperson of an academic department is elected by members of that unit, the values of democracy have predominated. However, if the department head is selected by the dean of the college, then the values of bureaucracy—efficiency and productivity—have taken precedence.

Baseline Originals in Organizational Life

Max Weber, Frederick Winslow Taylor, Elton Mayo, and Chester Barnard form an intellectual baseline of early classical thinkers concerned with the anatomy and physiology of private and public organizations. Thinking of the organization as a "rational machine" provides a useful metaphor in understanding this approach to organizational behaviors.[3]

Max Weber

Weber's work on the nature of bureaucracy is considered by many the most important of its kind. Weber was trained in law, history, and economics. He viewed action as both individual and social. Weber postulates the *ideal-type* of bureaucracy, not referring to "goodness" or "badness," but suggesting a standard or model for organizational environment. Characteristics of the ideal-type may be found in any organization.

In the following list, John M. Pfiffner and Frank P. Sherwood summarize components of Weber's ideal-type. These components contribute to our understanding of the functions and vital processes of organizations.

- *Emphasis on form.* Bureaucracy's first, most cited, and most general feature, according to Weber, is its emphasis on form of organization. In a sense, the rest of the components are examples of this.
- *The concept of hierarchy.* The organization follows the principle of hierarchy, with each lower office under the control and supervision of a higher one.
- *Specialization of task.* Incumbents are chosen on the basis of merit and ability to perform specialized functions within a total operation.
- *A specified sphere of competence.* This flows from specialization of task. It suggests that the relationships between various specializations should be clearly known and observed in practice. In a sense, the job descriptions used in many American organizations are a practical application of this requirement.
- *Established norms of conduct.* There should be as little unpredictability as possible in the organization. Policies should be clearly enunciated, and the

---

Shame versus Official Censorship

Moral censorship is a strong weapon of the culture-war propaganda that can intrude upon a person's privacy in ways unmatched by any kind of bureaucracy. Some observers believe that conservatives try to use shame as an alternative to official censorship and as a means to instill a sense of fear and self-loathing among free-thinking individuals. The true meaning of shameful behavior is somewhat obliterated. Moral censorship applies more to nonconformity and nonacceptance of prevalent trends than to immorality. Real shame and repentance come from within, and not from outside pressures.

Source: Carl F. Horowitz, "The Shaming Sham," *The American Prospect,* no. 31 (March–April 1997): 70–76.

---

individuals within the organization should see that these policies are implemented.

- *Records.* Administrative acts, decisions, and rules should be recorded to ensure predictability of performance within the bureaucracy.[4]

Weber emphasized the universality of bureaucracy by emphasizing its rationality. His observations on bureaucracy coincided with the industrial revolution in Germany at the turn of the century. In seeking rationality in human behavior, Weber concluded that the ideal-type is the best means for achieving rationality at the institutional level.

Weber also assumed freedom for bureaucrats. Far from promoting a master-slave relationship, he emphasized that people were free agents, even within nineteenth-century economic bureaucracies.

Finally, Weber forecast a general separation of policy making and administration. The ideal-type organization is grounded in predictable decision-making processes and is staffed by professionals; therefore, its bureaucracies should not be subverted by nonprofessionals, according to Weber. In this view, professionals organize and implement expertise. Nonprofessionals, armed only with opinions about expertise and goals, do not fit into Weber's game plan. Neither the monarch ruling by divine right nor the elected American president would be part of Weber's ideal-type framework.[5]

Frederick Winslow Taylor

Mass production suffered a long and fitful birth when it appeared in America in the eighteenth century and slowly developed thereafter. Oliver Evans, Linus Yale, Lillian and Frank Gilbreth, and Henry Ford later made huge contributions to its development. But it was Frederick Winslow Taylor who developed the underlying theory of scientific management that gave mass production its enduring form. Scientific management captivated the American consciousness and catapulted Taylor's ideas onto center stage, where they have remained. Yet until the publication of Wellford Wilms's "The One Best Way," little was known about the man who revolutionized the workplace.[6]

Frederick Taylor (1856–1915) is often called the father of scientific management. He recognized the importance of technology, work, and organization to the functions and vital processes of bureaucracies. In the opening of his classic, *The Principles of Scientific Management,* Taylor wrote:

> The principal object of management should be to secure the maximum prosperity for the employer, coupled with the maximum prosperity for the employee.
>
> The words *maximum prosperity* are used, in their broad sense, to mean not only large dividends for the company or owner, but the development of every branch of business to its highest state of excellence, so that prosperity may be permanent.[7]

According to Taylor, scientific management is both liberating and economically rational. Employees and employers are assumed to be rational. Through rationality in the work process, labor and management determine the proper way to complete a task.

Taylor, like Weber, assumed the importance of the individual and foresaw the shift of power from both the *bourgeoisie* (economic elites) and the *proletariat* (masses) to the *expert* (possessor of skills and knowledge).

Taylor emphasized cooperation in the workplace and spoke of making life better for each employee. He represented a pre–World War II line of thought that there are principles and laws that order our knowledge of the world. By seeking to use the scientific method, organizations become impersonal but rational.

Elton Mayo

In 1932, Harvard Business School professor Elton Mayo (1880–1949) and a team of researchers completed a five-year study outside Chicago, Illinois, at the Hawthorne plant of the Western Electric Company. Later published as *The Human Problems of an Industrial Civilization,* Mayo's research found that many problems in worker-management relations are caused not by insufficient task specialization or inadequate wages, but by social and psychological forces. The Hawthorne Experiments, as they were subsequently known, were the first systematic research to expose the *human factor* in work situations. The study marked a major turning point in the history of administrative theory and practice.[8] The Hawthorne Experiments encouraged management to conceptualize organizations as *social institutions.*

According to Pfiffner and Sherwood, Mayo's Hawthorne findings contributed to the ideological revolution in organization and management in two ways: by challenging the physical or engineering approach to motivation, and by becoming the first real assault on the purely structural, hierarchical approach to organization. In other words, Mayo felt there was no scientific or best way to motivate employees to be productive. The "father knows best" authoritarian way of running an organization was seen as only one of several approaches available. The whims of scientific management were no longer accepted as gospel; the human relations movement was underway.[9]

Elton Mayo concluded from studying the Hawthorne Experiments that informal organization is more important than formal organization in determining worker cooperation; that output is set by social norms, not individual abilities; and that the group heavily influences the behavior of individual workers. Mayo's experiment showed how a group of young female employees at Western Electric reacted positively to every change made in their working conditions while they were working in the test room. However, another experiment conducted along the same lines produced quite different results.

Mayo and his colleagues persuaded the management of the company to put a group of men engaged in making parts of telephone switches on a piece-rate incentive system. This new system would allow the men to increase their earnings without undue physical strain, and these were depression times when most workers seemed desperate to earn more money; therefore, the researchers and the company expected a great jump in productivity. Their expectations came to naught. Output remained the same.

The research group then began to investigate why the workers responded or, rather, failed to respond. Unlike the young female relay assemblers, most of whom expected to get married and leave their jobs before too long, the male workers had developed a work culture of their own. They had become a cohesive and compact group with their own codes, rules, and norms. Among these rules were prohibitions against doing too much or too little work. So solidly entrenched were these understandings among the male employees that they remained impervious to any enticements from management. The men rationalized that the incentive plan was an attempt to eventually cut out some jobs or reduce wage rates. The company assured them that this was not the case and pointed to its record, which indicated no instance of its ever having acted in such a manner. The men remained unconvinced, and productivity remained at the same level.[10]

Mayo and his associates had come up against the informal organization, grounded in large part on informal communications. This phenomenon has interested and intrigued organizational theorists ever since, and their research shows far-reaching ramifications.

Chester Barnard

Chester Barnard (1886–1961) is the final member of the baseline foursome. Intrigued by the experiments at the Hawthorne plant, Barnard formulated a theory of organizational life that focuses on the organization as a system, formal and informal organizations, and the role of the executive. In *Functions of the Executive,* Barnard distinguishes between *organizational purpose* and *individual motive.* He postulates that each person in the organization reflects a dual personality, one organizational and the other individual. As an individual leaves home and enters the workplace, he or she becomes "the organization man or woman."

An organization is a collection of actions focused toward a purpose; an equilibrium is necessary for an organization to sustain itself. A successful equilibrium must exist between the organization and its employees. The organization receives energies and productive capacities from employees, and employees receive compensation, benefits, and meaning from their work.[11]

Although the distinction between formal and informal organization is now commonplace, Barnard introduced these concepts in the late 1930s as new analytic tools for examining organizational life. According to Barnard, *formal organization* is comprised of the consciously coordinated activities of people, while *informal organization* entails the unconscious group feelings, passions, and activities of the same individuals. Informal organization is essential to the maintenance of formal

structures and relationships. The formal organization cannot exist without its informal counterpart. Not all activity can be structured by a chain of command because
of the reality of informal organization.

Finally, Barnard addresses *executive functions* of organizations. These functions are:

- Maintaining organization communication
- Securing essential services from individuals
- Formulating the purpose and objectives of the organization

Barnard writes that the functions of the executive are "those of the nervous
system, including the brain, in relation to the rest of the body. It exists to maintain the
bodily system by directing those actions which are necessary more effectively to
adjust to the environment. But it can hardly be said to manage the body, a large part
of whose functions are independent of it and upon which it in turn depends."[12]

The writings of Weber, Taylor, Mayo, and Barnard form an axis around which
the theory and practice of public organizations revolve. Focusing on three early organizational themes—system, hierarchy, and structure—writers who follow these classical thinkers assume that understanding human rationality is central to theorizing
about organizational physiology.

Neoclassical Theories

The neoclassical perspective on organizational theory is represented by the works of
Luther Gulick and Herbert Simon. "Decision-set" organizational theory is characterized by several important themes, including decision making as the heart and soul of
administration; administrative capacity as measured by efficiency; an emphasis on
organizational roles, not individual roles, as they relate to decision making; and
instrumental rationality as the center of operation.

Luther Gulick

In 1937, Luther Gulick and Lyndall Urwick edited the *Papers on the Science of
Administration,* a collection of eleven papers reflecting the predominant thinking
concerning organizations in Europe and the United States prior to World War II.
Divided into two groups, the papers examined structural aspects and social and
environmental aspects of organization.[13]

Gulick's "Notes on the Theory of Organization," in which he introduced the
acronym POSDCORB, has influenced teaching and thinking about public administration for more than seventy years. Gulick's POSDCORB (Planning, Organizing,
Staffing, Directing, Coordinating, Reporting, and Budgeting) helped shape the Wil-
sonian separation of politics from administration, the need for a division of work to
reach organizational objectives, and the efficiency criterion for judging governmental activities. In POSDCORB, Gulick outlines the work of the chief executive:

- *Planning* is working out in broad outline the tasks that need to be done
  and the methods for doing them to accomplish the purpose set for the
  enterprise.

- *Organizing* is establishing the formal structure of authority through which work subdivisions are arranged, defined, and coordinated for the defined objective.
- *Staffing* is bringing in and training the staff and maintaining favorable work conditions.
- *Directing* is the continuous task of making decisions and embodying them in specific and general instructions as well as serving as the leader of the enterprise.
- *Coordinating* is the important duty of interrelating the various parts of the work.
- *Reporting* is keeping the top executive informed as to what is going on, and keeping subordinates informed through records, research, and inspection.
- *Budgeting* includes fiscal planning, accounting, and control.[14]

Herbert Simon

After World War II, in 1947, Simon illustrated the decision-set perspective in "The Proverbs of Administration," later incorporated into his classic, *Administrative Behavior.* Simon viewed the decision as the central act of organization, and instrumental rationality as the basis for decision making. By *instrumental rationality,* Simon meant that the individual is rational and responsible only within the environment of a particular organization. The organizational environment encompasses the purposes of rational behavior; autonomous individuals behave only within the confines of those organizational purposes.

In emphasizing the decision as the basis for administrative theory, Simon distinguished between *value* premises and *factual* premises of public administrators. He wrote, "The process of validating a factual proposition is quite distinct from the process of validating a value judgment. The former is validated by its agreement with the facts, the latter by human fiat."[15] In other words, the facts of any circumstance are validated within a given set of values in which those facts, or actions, occur.

Simon focuses on the *means-end* sense of rationality as most significant. Administrators weigh the means, ends, and consequences of acting; therefore, Simon suggests, decisions may prove objectively rational, subjectively rational, deliberately rational, organizationally rational, or personally rational. Regardless of adverb, to be rational means to consider *only* those choices present within a prescribed system of values. Government employees are not autonomous individuals. The organizational environment of the department or agency articulates the values that determine rational behavior. In other words, an employee is rational and responsible only within the environment of a particular department or agency. A government employee acts rationally only within the framework of the department's preestablished goals and purposes.

Values, on the other hand, are arbitrary, regardless of their origins. Human decree, sanction, or authority validates a certain set of organizational values. Executives, legislatures, and judges decide by fiat that a set of values, encompassed in laws and implemented by bureaucrats, are of importance to organizations and to society.

Miles's Law

Rufus E. Miles, Jr., proudly claims to have parented Miles's Law. The law states that "Where you stand depends on where you sit." Miles says he discovered the law while serving as a division director of the former Bureau of the Budget. He noted that a budget examiner might be a constant critic of an agency whose budget he oversaw, yet if the examiner were to be later hired away by the agency, he would promptly do a 180° turn and become one of the agency's most adamant advocates. The position a bureaucrat takes thus depends on what position he is in, or "Where you stand depends on where you sit."

Miles points out in illustration how John Gardner, as chairman of President Johnson's Task Force on Education, authored a report strongly favoring the removal of Education from the Department of Health, Education, and Welfare (HEW). Shortly thereafter, Gardner was appointed secretary of HEW. When asked whether he now planned to push for Education's removal, he firmly and flatly rejected any such nonsensical idea.

Citizens of public organizations then respond to the rules and regulations and the boundaries these values impose upon them.

All decisions in organizations only satisfy and suffice—that is, they *satisfice.* Our focus on choices and decision making and our acceptance of organizational premises brings us to the limit of administrative rationality. This final Simon theme, that of *satisficing,* recognizes that rationality, or human reasoning, is bounded by administrative settings. After analyzing the problem and considering the complexities of the situation, administrators "satisfice," surveying their options and selecting the first one they find at least minimally satisfactory.

With respect to employee "satisficing," Simon concludes that rationality is bounded. In describing *bounded rationality,* he concludes that an administrator's reasoning options are limited by unconscious habits and skills, values and conceptions of purpose, and degree of information and knowledge.[16]

Human Relations Theories

As we have seen in the previous passages, Max Weber speaks in *bureaucratic* terms; Frederick Taylor writes in *productivity* terms; Chester Barnard thinks in *organizational* terms; and Herbert Simon stresses *decisional* terms. Writing histories of the increasing bureaucratization of society, each of these authors emphasizes *efficiency* in some form as a potent force in any organization, but also concludes that organizations embody not just task but social purposes. In other words, they believe that if conflict exists within the organization, individuals must subordinate their interests to those of the organization.

For example, if students are not learning in a classroom, the onus usually is placed upon the students to change their behavior or study habits to respond to the professor's demands. Likewise, if the college's basketball team is losing, the assumption is that the players are not responding to their coach's leadership. Student athletes must subordinate their actions to the coach's instructions for the benefit of the team.

Systems Theory Characteristics

Systems theory was built on the previous commentary of Max Weber, Chester Barnard, and Herbert Simon. Michael M. Harmon and Richard T. Mayer constructed systems theory—probing organizations as purposive entities. Closed systems experience little or no vulnerability from external forces. Open systems emerge as social and technological changes bring uncertainty and interdependence.

According to Harmon and Mayer, five characteristics form the basis of systems theory:

1. Each part of an organization can only be understood in terms of its relation to the other parts.
2. The parts of the organization, including their interrelatedness, are important insofar as they contribute to the overall functioning of the organization.
3. Organizations, conceived as wholes, may be thought of metaphorically as biological organisms, replete with needs and goals that are superordinate to and conceptually separate from the conscious needs, purposes, and goals of individual parts or members.
4. The needs and goals of organizations may be conceived either statically (in terms of survival or maintenance of order) or dynamically (in terms of purposive change).
5. Organizational activity is understandable only in the context of the external environment, which provides the resources and conditions the organization depends on for its survival and the realization of its purposes.

Systems theory originates from structural-functional sociology and promotes understanding of the social system or organization as a whole.

Source: Michael M. Harmon and Richard T. Mayer, *Organization Theory for Public Administration* (Boston: Little, Brown, 1986), p. 158.

Human relations theories question such assumptions, placing responsibility on the professor to change his or her teaching methods and on the coach to change his or her leadership style and set up a new strategy for winning games. This shift in responsibility makes for several new ways of envisioning organizational structure and function.

Mary Parker Follett

An early prophet of human relations thinking was Mary Parker Follett (1868–1933). While the classical and neoclassical writers were attempting to construct a field of public administration along systematic and somewhat mechanical lines, Follett was marching to the beat of a different drummer.

She had become impressed with the psychological factors she had seen at work in her active life as an organizer of evening schools, recreation agencies, and employment bureaus and as a member of statutory wage boards. Already the author of two books on political science, *The New State* and *Creative Experience,* she embarked on a series of speculations in the 1920s concerning the functions and vital processes of organizations. Her work signaled the advent of a new era in administrative theory.[17]

In various papers and articles, Follett depicted administration as essentially involved with reconciling the agendas of both individuals and social groups. An organization's principal problems, in her view, were not only determining what it wanted its employees to do, but guiding and controlling the employees' conduct in such a way as to get them to do it. This, she indicated, was a much more complex task than previous writers had suggested.

Follett not only anticipated what was to become the human relations school of administration, she also foreshadowed the humanistic school that was to grow out of it. She urged organizations to stop trying to suppress the differences that may arise within their boundaries and to seek instead to integrate those differences, allowing them to contribute to the organization's growth and development. She advocated replacing the "law of authority" with the "law of the situation," admonishing organizations to exercise "power *with*" rather than "power *over*" their members.

A philosophical analysis of Mary Parker Follett's writings on democratic and organizational theories reveals similarities with the feminist theory of the time. These similarities include the notion that human relations supersede individual rights, the theory that knowledge is context specific, her sensitivity to the role of power as an obstacle in the development of knowledge claims, and her method of conflict resolution through the integration of opposing interests. Her writings provide important insights into modern organization and management principles.[18]

While Follett's writings did not go unnoticed, they failed to score the impact that similar ideas would later achieve. This was perhaps due partly to the fact that she was a woman writing in a society not yet willing to take women thinkers seriously. A more serious obstacle, however, may have been that she was an iconoclast, challenging the sacred credos of her time. She died during the same year Elton Mayo wrote on the Hawthorne Experiments. Mayo's work was the first systematic research to expose the "human factor" in work situations. Mayo's study, as we have seen, marked a major turning point in the history of administrative theory and practice.

Maslow, McGregor, and Likert

Like Follett, organizational psychologists Abraham Maslow, Douglas McGregor, and Rensis Likert wrote from a progressive, humanistic viewpoint. They have profoundly influenced the teaching and practice of public administration concerning the role of democracy in bureaucracy, advocating an expanded scope and encouragement of individual initiative by allowing employees to make many of their own decisions on the job. These authors call for *less hierarchy and more humanity in organizational life* and emphasize *the integration of individuals in organization.*

Writing in *Motivation and Personality* (1954), Maslow identifies a hierarchy of personal needs that the organization must contend with to successfully integrate the individual. He writes that food and shelter are the first needs humans seek to meet. Once these needs are met, people seek freedom from physical harm and deprivation. Next, the desire for affectionate and supportive relationships with family, friends, and associates becomes a priority. Then people seek to gain the recognition of worth from their peers. Finally, when all these needs have been met, humans can seek to actualize their inner potential, to release their creative abilities, to achieve everything they hope for in life.[19]

Like Maslow's, McGregor's thinking is essentially optimistic concerning individuals' capacity for self-actualization. McGregor examines the possibilities for merging individual and organizational demands in ways that would prove satisfactory to both. In *The Human Side of Enterprise* (1960), McGregor outlines management's conventional view of harnessing human energy to meet organizational requirements. McGregor calls this Theory X, and then boldly steps forward with a new theory of administration he calls Theory Y.

Theory X is based on these assumptions:

- The average person is by nature lazy. He or she will work as little as possible. Such an individual lacks ambition, dislikes responsibility, and prefers to be led.
- By nature resistant to change, such a person is gullible, not very bright, and the ready dupe of the charlatan and the demagogue. This person is furthermore inherently self-centered and indifferent to organizational needs.

Theory Y, or McGregor's new way of merging individual and organizational demands, takes a more humanistic approach:

- People are not naturally passive, lazy, and dumb. They are, on the contrary, eager for opportunities to show initiative and to bear responsibility.
- Work is a natural activity, and people by nature want to perform it.
- People work best in an environment that treats them with respect and encourages them to develop and use their abilities.
- There is no inherent and intrinsic conflict between the goals of the organization and the goals of the individual member. Meeting the goals of the individual will only result in a more productive organization.[20]

Rensis Likert, writing in *The Human Organization* (1967), develops four systems that positively or negatively influence the integration of individuals into organizations:

- System 1 is *punitive authoritarian* and closely resembles McGregor's Theory X. System 1 administrative leaders have no confidence or trust in their subordinates.
- System 2 is *benevolent authoritarian* and is more generous and humanitarian toward the employee. While System 1 takes everything from the individual and gives little in return, System 2 rewards employee behavior only if prescribed directives are followed. If the employee does his or her tasks as prescribed, he or she is dutifully rewarded. System 2 leaders are condescending in bestowing their confidence and trust, engaging in something resembling a master-servant relationship with subordinates.
- System 3 is *consultative* and allows still more participation by employees. Administrative leaders in such an organization may be democratic, allowing

Airport Security as American Community

Community is defined as ownership or participation in common. People live together and share work and social interests within a community. The events of September 11 put a large dent into the excesses of American individualism and brought to light the generosity of our national community that had previously been taken for granted and even abused.

Post–September 11 American flag waving may be a superficial gesture, but it nevertheless indicates that new community paradigms are emerging. These new forms must be nourished and continuously examined. Airport security may be an important catalyst for developing this new consciousness of country and community.

This journey is not linear. The Afghanistan war, terrorism, and travel safety prove once again that necessity is the mother of invention. If everything were rational in this politically right-of-center nation, the question of federalizing baggage screening at 142 major airports would be a no-brainer. Airport and plane safety should be the responsibility of federal public administrators—of federal bureaucrats, if you will!

There is nothing wrong with equipping public servants with the appropriate skills, knowledge and expertise to protect the citizenry from insidious attack. This task, however, should not be handled by local or state government employees. Like the Central Intelligence Agency (CIA), the Drug Enforcement Agency (DEA), the Federal Aviation Agency (FAA), the Federal Bureau of Investigation (FBI), the Internal Revenue Service (IRS) and the Secret Service, airport inspectors should be federalized. Possible reforms include a new Justice Department workforce of 28,000 federal employees to screen passengers and to inspect luggage and carry-on bags at airports. A $3.00 surcharge on each ticket would cover the costs of security reforms.

The late Aaron Wildavsky distinguished between policy politics, or which policy should be adopted; partisan politics, or which political personality will win office; and system politics, or how decision structures will be set up. National security is a system and policy concern. Federalizing airport security should not be partisan. Yet partisans vehemently oppose efforts to move from privatization to federal employees.

Yeshiva University Professor of Law John McGinnis offers insights to the advantages of federalization. Federalization creates a marketplace for governments. Government decisions are improved as they are pushed closer to the people they affect, and federalization increases civic responsibility.

A variety of interest groups, including government and flight attendant associations, have offered policy inputs on this issue. The *Washington Post* reported that 93 percent of respondents from a Business Travel Coalition survey—including 216 executives—say that airport security personnel should be federal employees.

Senators Fritz Hollings (D-S.C.) and John McCain (R-Ariz.) are leading the reform efforts on Capitol Hill. "Overwhelming majorities of the American people believe that [screening passengers] is now a law enforcement function, and law enforcement functions, like the Border Patrol and other functions to ensure security, are federal responsibilities," said McCain on a *Fox News Sunday* program.

Critics of these efforts may not realize that federalized airport security personnel could be fired or suspended by the Department of Justice. Regardless of Civil Service laws, they would not be permitted to strike.

Certain conservatives fear employee federalization would benefit organized labor and work against the House Republican majority. The way to improve airport security, they say, is to threaten to fire inefficient low-wage workers.

Before September 11, 2001, the American public distinguished their personal lives from events of national life. The citizenry chose *market justice* over *political justice*. Personal benefits are gained primarily through the economic marketplace. In the establishment of community, political justice and government policies are important.

The threat of terrorism upset the American cultural myopia of *individualism par excellence* as never before. Airport and plane safety serves the greater good as well as the individual citizen. The effective exercise of capitalism depends on the safety—and opportunities—of the entire community. The terror watch is a civic responsibility—by government jurisdictions, public sector employees, and airport consumers. System and policy politics must dominate as terrorism explodes. Short-term partisan politics come in a distant third to policy priorities and system concerns.

Believers in effective government should promote the skills, knowledge and expertise of public sector employees. Selecting public employees for airport security—with career proficiencies not unlike those of the CIA, FBI or Secret Service—is the most effective way to protect citizens, enhance commerce, and rebuild community.

Source: "Airport Security as American Community" by John Rouse, as appeared on ASPA Online Columns, http://www.aspanet.org, November 15, 2001. Reprinted by permission of the author.

Conflicts and Organization Character

Organization character is not divorced from an organization's ideological orientation. Labor-management differences may make ideologies more prominent. Conflicts over organization change often reflect ideological struggles.

Roger Harrison identifies competing organization ideologies, which in turn specify goals and values. What should employees expect of the organization? What should the organization expect of its employees? Who is valued, who is vilified, who is rewarded, and who is punished?

Harrison's four ideologies are:

1. *Power orientation.* Power-oriented government employees seek to dominate the organization, maintain absolute control over subordinates, compete for territory, expand control at the expense of others, bargain to their own advantage, justify abrogating agreements, and value growth for its own sake.
2. *Role orientation.* Role-oriented public sector employees are preoccupied with legality, legitimacy, and responsibility. They aspire to be as rational and orderly as feasible. Agreements, rules, and procedures replace or regulate competition and conflicts. These employees carefully adhere to defined rights and privileges.
3. *Task orientation.* Task-oriented government employees value goals, programs, and policies—and their accomplishment—as supreme. The aspiration need not be economic. Authority is legitimized if it is grounded in appropriate knowledge and competence. If power is based solely on position, it is not legitimate.
4. *Person orientation.* Person-oriented public sector employees serve the needs of their members. The unit exists to meet needs that members cannot meet by themselves. Individuals influence others through example, helpfulness, and caring. Person-oriented employees prefer consensus methods of decision-making.

The interests, values, and structural qualities of people are often juxtaposed against the interests, values, and structural qualities of organizations. Ideological tension and struggle are manifest in people and organizations.

free discussion regarding policy making, but still assume final responsibility for all decisions. System 3 illustrates substantial but not complete confidence and trust in subordinates.

- System 4 is a *participative group model* and closely resembles McGregor's Theory Y. Senior bureaucrats promote complete confidence and trust in employees in all matters. Employees provide guidance and participate in coordinated problem solving. Employees are not treated punitively.

According to Likert, administrative leaders adopting the participative style achieve from 10 to 40 percent greater productivity, experience much higher levels of employee satisfaction and much better employee health, enjoy better labor relations, suffer less absence and less turnover, obtain better product quality, and, finally, record better customer satisfaction as a result of better products and services than managers operating with System 1, 2, or 3 styles.[21]

Summary

- Individualism is a priority in American life, with consumerism and the market following close behind. Satisfying short-term, private consumer wants is not a priority for public organizations. Meeting the needs of people and the community is.
- In efforts to redefine, reevaluate, and restate the parameters of public and private life, citizens determine what they owe the state (society)—and what the state owes them.
- Bureaucracy and democracy are not esoteric. They are at the center of what occurs in the public and private organizations of American society.
- *Physiology* is the study of life processes, activities, and functions.
- In a classical sense, our system of political economy, or politics and economics, is not a democracy, but a republic. We have a democratic *type* of government, but a republican *form* of government.
- Democracy implies equality, while bureaucracy implies hierarchy. Bureaucracy exists to accomplish tasks ranging from fighting dictators to fighting poverty.
- While democracy has a leveling, or horizontal, quality in its application, bureaucracy is vertical.
- The popular view of bureaucracy tends to be pejorative. The descriptive-analytical approach promotes our understanding of behavior, policies, processes, and institutions. Bureaucracy is neither good nor bad; it exists for accomplishing tasks.
- The norms or values of public administration entail concerns about efficiency and effectiveness, the adequacy of governmental processes, and representation and the exercise of discretion.
- Max Weber's *ideal-type* of bureaucratic organization emphasizes form, hierarchy, specialization of tasks, specified spheres of competence, established norms of conduct, and record keeping.
- The advent of large-scale bureaucracy has seen the shift of power from both the bourgeoisie, or economic elite, and the proletariat, or the masses, to the experts, those who possess valued skills and knowledge.
- The Hawthorne Experiments of the 1930s encourage managers to conceptualize organizations as social institutions.
- The functions of the executive are to maintain organizational communication, secure essential services from individuals, and formulate the purposes and objectives of the organization.
- The acronym POSDCORB outlines the work of the chief executive in terms of planning, organizing, staffing, directing, coordinating, reporting, and budgeting.
- Formal organization is only part of the study of bureaucracy. Every organization has its informal counterpart—the unconscious group feelings, passions, and activities that exist in any group of people. Informal organization is essential to the maintenance of formal structures and relationships.
- Systems theory originates from structural-functional sociology and promotes an understanding of the social system as a whole. Closed systems experience little or no vulnerability from external forces. Open systems emerge as social and technological changes bring uncertainty and interdependence.
- Weber stresses bureaucratic terms, Taylor productivity terms, Barnard organizational terms, and Simon decisional terms. Weber, Taylor, Barnard, and Simon all emphasize efficiency.
- Human relations thinkers—Follett, Maslow, McGregor, and Likert—emphasize principles of equality. They call for less hierarchy and more humanity in organizational life.
- *Community* is defined as ownership or participation in common. People live together and share work and social interests in a community. National security is a system and policy concern. Federalizing airport security is not partisan.
- Organization ideologies relate to power, role, task, or people.

VIDEOS AND FILMS

Public Administration in Action

Systems Theory

Divided Highways: Interstates and the Transformation of American Life [1997]
Princeton, NJ: Films for the Humanities & Sciences. Describes the impact of the interstate highway system. Explores effects of the highways on community, culture, regionalism, and freedom. [85 min]

Organizational Theory

Formal Organizations and Bureaucracy [2002]
Examines processes by which sociologists study group behavior. Addresses how these processes differ from everyday observations and conclusions. Telelearning promotion by the Wadsworth Group. [30 min]

Systems Theory

The Big Dig [2002]
Transportation renaissance in Boston. Originally broadcast on PBS as one of four episodes of the television program *Great Projects: The Building of America.* Documents the building of the most expensive highway project in U.S. history. [60 min]

Bureaucracy and Democracy

Saving Private Ryan [1998]
Realistic recreation of World War II's D-Day invasion at Omaha Beach. Based on Stephen E. Ambrose's 1994 best-seller *D-Day: June 6, 1944.* Probes the logic of losing more lives to save a single soldier. Combines values of citizen initiative and administrative hierarchy. [170 min]

Organizational Theory

The Bureaucracy [2001]
Reviews characteristics, roots, types, and roles of bureaucracy. Cerebellum Corp. [20 min]

Case Study

Transportation Infrastructures as Organization Theory

The United States interstate highway system organizes roadway commerce. The layout of the U.S. highway network explains how Americans travel from one state to another. Even-numbered interstates go east and west; odd-numbered interstates go north and south. These highways are formalized by maps depicting public organizations—easily recognized as the fifty American states. Highways provide access to forty-four major airports throughout the country. Systems theory promotes an understanding of the social system as a whole. In this case study, how do organization theories promote or demote the development of commerce?

Commerce is really as interesting as nature.

—*Henry David Thoreau (1817–1862)*
U.S. philosopher, author, and naturalist

Transportation modes reflect theories of organization. The organization values of a national transportation system, by necessity, are every citizen's values.

Terrorism and security threats have caused Americans to probe how we conduct our domestic commerce, commute to our jobs, react to social organization and institutions, mobilize amid crisis, and shape our culture and politics in conflict and cooperation.

"The country would be better off if citizens flew flags of sacrifice, discipline, and tolerance in memory of those who perished on September 11," argues Tony Foster, two-term mayor of Big Burb. "Big Burbians must reduce our energy dependence on countries where no religious reformation, no industrial revolution, and no guarantee of individual rights typify values of everyday life."

Responding to pressures for responsiveness and efficiency, Americans invest billions of dollars in interstate highways, private railroads, state-of-the-art airports, and a technology-sensitive airline industry. Cars, trucks, trains, and airplanes move goods and people. The economics of airlines, trucking, and rail lines reflect incredible investments of human skill, infrastructure, and commerce.

Formal organization theory stresses the formal, structural arrangements within public organizations. The globalization of work environments, demands of the corporate world, and diversity of family life make the soul searching of post–September 11, 2001, ever more meaningful.

Physiology is the study of life processes, activities, and functions. Similarly, the physiology of an organization is the study of its vital structures and functions. Bureaucracy and democracy are central pillars of both private and public organizations. Our system of political economy, or politics and economics, is not a democracy, but a republic. All of these structural arrangements affect the workings of American organizations.

The more modes of transportation available to the citizenry, the more the potential for freedom. Transportation policy promotes the participative group model of decision making. If freedom of movement is a value, safe modes of transport are essential. The means of commerce are primarily highways and planes, but not trains. The ends are determined by the means.

Normative vectors—efficiency and effectiveness, rights and the adequacy of governmental process, and representation and the exercise of discretion—are challenges that face Big Burb and the state of Commonwealth. Efficiency and effectiveness are planning issues. Citizen participation and stronger partnerships require a focus on rights and the adequacy of the governmental process. Big Burb or central city priorities depend on representation and the exercise of discretion.

"Local governments can help reduce air pollution, fuel consumption, and traffic congestion," Mayor Foster points out. "Most traffic congestion is the result of work-related commuting: too many people driving too many cars within the same area at the same time."

The Intermodal Surface Transportation Efficiency Act of 1991 (ISTEA) requires the coordination of state transportation decisions with state goals for land use, energy conservation, environmental protection, and community vitality. ISTEA, reflecting a federal point of view, mandates a new state planning process and stronger partnerships with local officials to achieve this coordination.

In Commonwealth's largest metropolitan city, Big Burb, auto-dependent urban growth threatens environmental quality, requires an expensive infrastructure, and promotes the worst features of democracy—namely, fragmentation—and of bureaucracy—namely, unresponsiveness and excessive routinization. ISTEA legislates "flexible use" transit alternatives—including commuter rail, light rail, and subway developments.

Systems theory suggests that governments function like biological organisms. Inputs from the environment are crucial to effective decision making. Open systems theory examines relationships, questions structures, and promotes interdependence. Open systems interact with their environments—promoting constant feedback.

Planning Inclusive Decision Making

The State of Commonwealth Department of Transportation (COMDOT) employs two separate but parallel processes to bring citizens and local officials into transportation decision making. The Strategic Management Strategy attempts to involve the public in bringing a fresh perspective to the agency's operations. Reflecting systems theory, COMDOT created an internal department, the Office of Strategic Initiatives, and a Strategic Management Committee comprised of COMDOT senior management to oversee the strategic process, guide its implementation, and evaluate its results.

"Our approach was that everyone is an expert," said Barbara Tompkins, Director of COMDOT's Office of Strategic Initiatives. "We wanted to assure that all participants were able to contribute equally, and that we looked at transportation from a broad range of perspectives."[1] In the philosophy of Frederick Taylor, COMDOT elicited expertise, but the agency defined the term rather broadly. In the state of Commonwealth, citizens are the experts.

Participants identified the forces affecting transportation, including trends in education, the economy, health care needs, demographics, the environment, technology, globalization, resource availability, cultural values, and government. Citizens were asked to discuss future transportation needs in the context of this larger picture. They were discouraged from focusing on specific transportation projects.

After World War II, railroads connected the political economy of the United States. Today, interstate highways and airports orchestrate the flow of social and economic commerce. These infrastructures were organized on Max Weber–Luther Gulick theories: form, hierarchy, task specialization, competence, norms of conduct, records, planning, organizing, staffing, directing, coordinating, reporting, and budgeting.

Soon after ISTEA was enacted, about three hundred people gathered at the state capital to discuss how to implement the act. The Process for Transportation Investment Decisions (PTID) is a method for making state transportation project decisions based on long-range planning and regional cooperation. The PTID process places priority on:

- Preserving existing transportation facilities and improving operations
- Promoting shared authority and responsibility for decisions between state and local agencies
- Broadening the decision-making process and increasing public involvement in the process[2]

Urban and rural areas compete for scarce dollars. Two-thirds of the state's population resides in the heavily populated areas near the capital city of Big Burb. Big Burb must confront urban congestion, air quality violations, increased single-occupancy vehicle use, and aging physical infrastructures.

"Transportation is key to the productivity, and therefore the success, of virtually every business in America," emphasizes Norman Mineta, U.S. Secretary of Transportation. "Congestion and delay not only waste our time as individuals, they also burden our businesses and our entire economy with inefficiency and higher costs." Transportation, as an industry, accounts for 11 percent of the U.S. economy. (Health care accounts for 15 percent.) In 1999, transportation-related goods and services produced between $980 billion and $9.3 trillion for the U.S. gross domestic product.[3]

In Commonwealth, the railroad industry contributes to the development of state and local transportation plans. New regulations permit railroads to be members of Metropolitan Planning Organizations (MPOs). Railroads have significant roles in setting local transportation policies. ISTEA mandates the development of state and metropolitan transportation plans that consider freight movement and shape transportation decisions through a planning process.

Short-line railroads are making extensive infrastructure improvements. They operate approximately 50,000 miles of track. Unlike highways, they control right-of-way and the timing of traffic, making them more efficient for freight movement. "Replacing rails and ties and rebuilding equipment is an ongoing process for railroads," says Frank Turner, president of the American Short-Line and Regional Railroad Association (ASLRRA). "It's just a matter of money."[4]

Intermodal Management Planning Coordination

Commonwealth Governor Mike Rush and the General Assembly adopted a twenty-year transportation plan as required for each urbanized area of more than 50,000 people throughout the United States. Railroad interests influenced strategies and projects in the Big Burb metro area. The Intermodal Management System (IMS) and Safety Management System (SMS), reflecting systems theory, promote passenger and freight system connections.

President Dwight Eisenhower is credited with origination of the interstate highway system in the mid-1950s. The interstate highway plan includes 42,000 miles of limited-access modern highways. The Federal Aid Highway Act (FAHA) of 1956 commenced what is known today as the interstate system. FAHA provided for federal funding of 90 percent of the cost of the interstates. States contributed the remaining 10 percent.[5]

Standards were highly regulated—lanes 12 feet wide, shoulders 10 feet wide, 14-foot minimum bridge clearance, grades 3 percent or less, and travel speeds designed for 70 miles per hour. The first stretch of interstate—eight miles—opened in Topeka, Kansas, on November 14, 1956. The last link was completed in Los Angeles in 1993. In 1957, the red, white, and blue shield symbol for Interstate numbering began. Highways running north-south are odd-numbered, while highways running east-west are even-numbered. Three-digit interstate highway numbers designate beltways or loops.

The number of airline passengers in the United States is projected to rise from 733 million in 2000 to 1.2 billion in 2012. "The system is close to a saturation point," said Daniel D'Agostino, president of the Newark, New Jersey, Tower local of the National Air Traffic Controllers Association (NATCA). "There are plenty of routes up in the air. The unfortunate thing is these planes have to come down to the ground."[6] Flight cancellations are not uncommon. New FAA regulations, projected and real equipment failures, and turbulent weather conditions can all result in cancelled flights.

Airplane delays and cancellations are now virtually routine. In recent years, bad weather and faulty electrical wiring have grounded planes. All airlines must keep statistics on flight delays and cancellations. COMDOT's Web site and the FAA's Web site, by law, allow citizens access to relevant data. Citizens may be annoyed by delays, even cancellations, but airlines, COMDOT, and the FAA are commissioned to protect the citizenry from poor decision making. In one week, 2,000 cancellations occurred. Organized chaos results from the mix of expensive airplanes, skilled pilots, unpredictable weather conditions, nervous passengers, and changing levels of supply and demand.

In response to the systems theory–based 1998 revisions of ISTEA, Mayor Foster and the Big Burb City Council enacted a three-year program to reduce the number of cars on city streets (promoting ride sharing and preferential parking for high-occupancy vehicles). The Big Burb City Council and state of Commonwealth General Assembly found consensus to finance construction of a twelve-mile light rail system (LRT) on an abandoned rail line. By reducing automobile volume, LRT is expected to provide cleaner air, reduce traffic congestion, and increase efficiency.

Estimated costs of the project are $625 million. Half the costs are to be paid by the taxpayers Big Burb and the state of Commonwealth; the remaining portion will be financed with federal grants. LRT is to extend from the Big Burb International Airport to the Big Burb branch of Steady State University to Citizen Park, home of the Big Burb Braves, a major league baseball team.

Systems theory promotes resource planning—stressing delineations of efficiency and effectiveness. Citizen inputs to the intermodal approach to transportation reflect the salience of rights and the adequacy of the governmental process. Equity, discretion, and representation are reflected in the planning process and its commitment to fairness for Big Burb and its surrounding bedroom communities.

The United States is an organization of immense political economy, affected by capital, human and material wealth, public and private sector bureaucracies, and the fragile play of democracy and opportunities, all organized in appropriate philosophical fashion. The challenges of Big Burb and the state of Commonwealth typify citizen choices in other states. Freedom of movement is grounded in commerce and ease of transportation.

Physiology includes life processes, activities, and functions. Democratic capitalism, as an organizing theory in the United States, promotes citizen decision making. Air, rail, highway, and water infrastructures operate within the rules of democracy, but they also respond to laws of supply and demand. Freedom is based on access, capital, technology, and human skills. Applications of systems theory can either promote or restrict the human side of enterprise.

Questions and Instructions

1. Describe theories of public and private organization emerging from reforms of transportation infrastructures. Illustrate your ideas.
2. How are the writings of Max Weber and Luther Gulick realized in the Intermodal Surface Transportation Efficiency Act of 1991 (ISTEA)?
3. Frederick Taylor saw the shift of power from the bourgeoisie (economic elite) and the proletariat (masses) to the experts (possessors of skills and knowledge). How do the facts of the Big Burb case illustrate this shift?
4. The Process for Transportation Investment Decisions (PTID) calls for promoting shared authority and responsibility and broadening the decision-making process. The writings of which organization theory authors likely influenced the organizations in this case study to develop the PTID?
5. Systems theory originates from structural-functional sociology and promotes an understanding of the social system as a whole. Explain the salience of systems theory for light rail alternatives in Big Burb and the state of Commonwealth.
6. How do normative vectors play out in this case study? Explain.
7. How is freedom of movement grounded in commerce and ease of transportation? Explain.
8. If effective rail modes do not emerge as transportation alternatives, what are the prospects for airplane and airport saturation of personnel, equipment, and costs? Explain and illustrate.
9. How do highway, rail, and air infrastructures contribute to redefinitions of the United States political economy? Explain.
10. Elton Mayo encouraged the perception of organization as a social institution. How would the development of intercity passenger rail systems contribute to new ways of organizing the political economies of Big Burb and the state of Commonwealth? Explain and illustrate.

Insights-Issues/Transportation Infrastructures as Organization Theory

Clearly and briefly describe and illustrate the following concepts and issues. Interpret the word *role* in terms of impacts, applications, importance, effects, and/or illustrations of certain facts, concerns, or issues from the case study.

1. Roles of bureaucracy and democracy as central pillars of private and public organizations in developing intermodal management planning coordination for Big Burb and state of Commonwealth transportation infrastructures.
2. Roles of facts versus values, ends versus means, satisficing, and bounded rationality in developing Big Burb and state of Commonwealth transportation infrastructures.

3. Role of systems theory in understanding the development of intermodal management planning for Big Burb and state of Commonwealth transportation infrastructures.
4. Roles of bourgeoisie (economic elite), proletariat (masses), and experts (possessors of skills and knowledge) in developing and coordinating intermodal management planning for Big Burb and state of Commonwealth transportation infrastructures.
5. Roles of the writings of Max Weber, Luther Gulick, and Elton Mayo in developing intermodal management planning coordination for Big Burb and state of Commonwealth transportation infrastructures.

Notes

1. See National Transportation Library, *Surface Transportation Resource Guides: Case Studies:* Jenny Wilson, "Minnesota DOT's Strategic Management Process: Reorienting Daily Decisions," pp. 5–7, http://ntl.bts.gov/DOCS/TID.html.
2. *Ibid.,* p. 2.
3. Lee Bruno, "Transportation: The Future of Commuting," *Redherring,* February 8, 2002, http://www.redherring.com/insider/2002/0208/1713.html.

4. See FleetOwner, Online Exclusive, *PRIMEDIA* Business Magazines & Media, October 8, 2001.
5. "Interstate Highways," May 24, 1999; http://geography.about.com/library/weekly/aa052499.htm.
6. "No Relief in Sight for Travelers, More Flights, Passengers to Tax Overburdened Airports," Associated Press, March 13, 2001, http://abcnews.go.com/sections/us/DailyNews/airlines010313.html.

Sources

U.S. Department of Energy, National Renewable Energy Laboratory, "Beating the Traffic with Commuting Alternatives," DOE/GO-10095-171, May 1995, http://www.eren.doe.gov/cities_countries.beattra.html; Jolene M. Molitoris, Rodney E. Slater, and Gordon J. Linton, Bureau of Transportation Statistics, National Transportation Library, "ISTEA Regulations and Railroads," http://ntl.bts.gov/DOCS/395ISTEA.html. "Surface Transportation Policy Project Resource Guide: Case Studies," http://ntl.bts.gov/DOCS/TID.html; *The Columbia Dictionary of Quotations* (New York: Columbia University Press, 1995); Lawrence Dwyer,

"Intermodalism and ISTEA: The Challenges and the Changes," *Public Roads On-Line* (Autumn 1994), http://www.tfhrc.gov/pubrds/fall94/p94au1.htm; Erik Ledbetter, "Railroad Preservation and ISTEA: Are You on Board?" April 10, 2001, http://www.rypn.org/Editorials/010410ISTEA/; Martin Ringle and Daniel Updegrove, "Is Strategic Planning for Technology an Oxymoron?" *Cause/Effect* 21, no. 1 (1998): 18–23; Jochen Schneider, "Public-Private Partnerships for Urban Rail Transit," September 1, 1999, http://faculty.washington.edu/~jbs/itrans/todsch1.htm.

Notes

1. Dwight Waldo, *The Enterprise of Public Administration* (Novato, CA: Chandler & Sharp, 1980), pp. 33–47.
2. H. H. Gerth and C. Wright Mills, eds., *From Max Weber: Essays in Sociology* (New York: Oxford University Press, 1946), p. 197.

3. Michael M. Harmon and Richard T. Mayer outline the most important contributions to conceptual theories of public organizations. They describe six perspectives that bridge the theoretical with actual practice in public organizations. These perspectives, as

analyzed by various authors, focus on three organizational themes—system, hierarchy, and structure. See Harmon and Mayer, *Organization Theory for Public Administration* (Boston: Little, Brown, 1986).

4. John M. Pfiffner and Frank P. Sherwood, *Administrative Organization* (Englewood Cliffs, NJ: Prentice-Hall, 1960), pp. 56–57.

5. *Ibid.,* p. 217.

6. Wellford W. Wilms, "Father Time: The One Best Way," *Los Angeles Times,* June 1, 1997, p. 6.

7. Frederick Winslow Taylor, *The Principles of Scientific Management* (New York: W. W. Norton, 1947), p. 9.

8. Elton Mayo, *The Human Problems of an Industrial Civilization* (New York: Macmillan, 1933). Also see F. J. Roethsberger and William J. Dickson, *Management and the Worker* (Cambridge, MA: Harvard University Press, 1946).

9. Roethsberger and Dickson, *Management and Worker*, p. 552.

10. Pfiffner and Sherwood, *Administrative Organization,* p. 102.

11. Chester Barnard, *Functions of the Executive* (Cambridge, MA: Harvard University Press, 1938).

12. *Ibid.,* p. 217.

13. Luther Gulick and Lyndall Urwick, eds., *Papers on the Science of Administration* (New York: Institute of Public Administration, 1937).

14. Gulick, "Notes on the Theory of Organization," in Gulick and Urwick, *Science of Administration,* p. 13.

15. Herbert A. Simon, "The Proverbs of Administration," *Public Administration Review* 6 (Winter 1946): 53–67.

16. Herbert A. Simon, *Administrative Behavior: A Study of Decision-Making Processes in Administrative Organization,* 3rd ed. (New York: The Free Press, 1976).

17. Mary Parker Follett, *The New State: Group Organization—The Solution to Popular Government* (New York: Longmans, Green, 1918); *Creative Experience* (New York: Longmans, Green, 1924); and *Dynamic Administration: The Collected Papers of Mary Parker Follet,* Henry C. Metcalf and L. Urwick, eds. (London: Sir Isaac Pitman, 1960).

18. Noel O'R. Morton and Stefanie A. Lindquist, "Revealing the Feminist in Mary Parker Follett," *Administration & Society* 29, no. 3 (July 1997): 348–372.

19. Abraham Maslow, *Motivation and Personality* (New York: Harper and Brothers, 1954).

20. Douglas McGregor, *The Human Side of Enterprise* (New York: McGraw-Hill, 1960).

21. Rensis Likert, *The Human Organization: Its Management and Value* (New York: McGraw-Hill, 1967).

People and Personnel

Chapter Highlights

Conflicting Doctrines in American Public Administration

Procedures and Policies

Dynamics of Federal Government Employment

Merit-Based Recruitment

The Postrecruitment Phase

The Challenges of Public Personnel Administration

The Changing Demographics of the Federal Workforce

Equal Opportunity and Affirmative Action

Performance Rating and Measurement

Position Classifications

Summary

We Are Not Welcome the Way Whites Are

New York City, by far the largest municipal government in the United States, has a population of approximately 7.5 million and 411,651 full-time-equivalent government employees. Of those local government employees, the New York Police Department (NYPD) employs 465 captains—a group of senior officers whose ranks include the most prominent and powerful commanders.

Of the 465 police captains, only 9 are black males. Why, in a city where the 2000 census reports 25 percent of the population is African-American, are so few police captains of African descent?

The answer lies not only in the numbers and percentages of whites and blacks, but in history, culture, aptitude, and motivation.

In 1990, 7.7 percent of NYPD's sergeants were black. By the end of the decade, the percentage of front-line black supervisors decreased to 5.7 percent. Black men are likewise absent in the elite commands. Major case detectives, Emergency

Service, Mounted, Aviation, and Harbor units—almost all white—constitute the elite commands (see table below).

Data indicate that the percentages of uniformed black males increased from 7.7 percent (1974) to 9.2 percent (2000). Uniformed females at the NYPD have enhanced their numbers sixfold since 1974. Black women made significant

NYPD Demographics of Black Males in Elite Commands

	Total	Black Males
Emergency Service	501	37
Mounted Unit	124	3
Major Case detectives	43	3
Harbor Unit	159	2
Aviation Unit	59	1
Totals	886	46

advances within the NYPD ranks, too. Black women at the NYPD have increased from near statistical insignificance in 1974 to almost 5 percent in 2000. Black female supervisors have increased likewise, and Hispanic representation jumped by nearly 500 percent.

Why, then, has the proportion of black male officers been in decline since 1990?

A brief history lesson provides some context. Upon being rebuffed by the Anglo-Saxon culture, New Yorkers of certain ethnicities formed other organizations, which contested the dominance of white Protestants. Many Irish men, speaking English but not part of the dominant Protestant culture, became cops. Some Italians formed the Mafia. Therefore, the Irish long ago began a public service employment pattern that continues to this day. They have a long-standing tradition of becoming NYC police officers. It's all in the family— fathers, brothers, uncles, and now, perhaps, mothers and daughters have joined the NYPD.

The oldest organization in the history of humanity is the family. Government is likely second. While Irish-Americans were encouraged to join the ranks of the NYPD, African-Americans did not enjoy either the family prodding or the access their Irish neighbors had. But is it the fault of the organization, namely the NYPD, that black men have not become NYPD officers—at least not in proportions reflecting the city's demographics? After three decades of trying, the NYPD—in pursuit of a fully representative workforce—has failed to attract and advance black men.

This disparity between black and white exists despite the election of a black mayor, David N. Dinkins; the appointments of a black police commissioner, Lee P. Brown, and chief of patrol, Wilbur Chapman; and an affirmative action program advocated by both Democratic and Republican mayors. The City leadership explicitly promoted the belief that more black NYPD officers would improve the force's effectiveness. Even with black political and administrative leadership supporting that goal, the number of black males barely increased.

Geography is also a factor with NYPD officers. New York lacks a residency requirement for its officers, so white men from the suburbs

dominate each police academy class. Without a fully representative force, tensions between the NYPD and residents persist. Are black officers better prepared than white officers to negotiate the behavior of lower-economic-class African-Americans and immigrants? Are the tensions and confrontations racial—or economic?

The NYPD hierarchy believes in diversity, and in fact champions it, perhaps exaggerating its successes, while the NYPD white rank-and-file officers resist demographic changes in the force. Diversity is a community value. But the NYPD function, in itself, is not grounded in diverse representation. Its structural-functional operations are anchored in the skills, knowledge, and expertise of officers.

As we have discussed, American society reflects a tension between the values of equality and efficiency. The struggle for more black male NYPD officers is more of a challenge to efficiency than equality. The right to apply for a NYPD position reflects a commitment to equality; the city relies on civil service rules, which reflect efficiency, to gauge the qualifications of officers. After the Civil War, reforms designated that such rules replace a system of political spoils with objective hiring measures. However, controversy surrounds the civil service tests.

The civil service exam controversy surrounds their value as predictive tests. The primary arbiters of promotion to sergeant, lieutenant, and captain are multiple-choice exams. These tests focus on police-related knowledge, including NYPD rules, regulations, tactics, and criminal law. Top scorers are ranked on an eligibility list.

C. J. Chivers, a *New York Times* reporter, asks: Do these tests actually measure police aptitude? Do the exams predict supervisory skills? The value of the tests is questioned by many officers and police officials. Leadership—courage, judgment, and integrity—is crucial at the station houses and on the police beats. Civil service rules, over which the NYPD has limited control, reflect merit-based standards for public service at the NYPD. Civil service rules, or standards, have stymied the promotions of a large proportion of potential black officers.

In any bureaucracy, "who one knows" may be as important as "what one knows." At the

NYPD, connections within the police hierarchy are critical. Friends in high places whom officers rely on to get what they want are called "hooks." Police officers insist that hooks are directly related to choice assignments, and maintaining a good set of hooks is essential to a successful career. Even in equality, some are "more equal" than others.

"We are not welcome the way whites are," says a NYPD black police recruiter. "We do not have the same opportunities."

What the recruiter may be saying is this: The overt racism of yesteryear is gone. However, young black male professionals likely do not have the same advantages as their white counterparts in terms of

- Background (family encouragement)
- Education (reminders of merit requirements)

- Motivation (personal drive to become a police officer)
- Culture (police station as mini-city hall)
- Hooks (friends in all the right places)

Equality, as such, provides no guarantees—it only provides access. Affirmative action—without paths to achievement—is limited. The NYPD, reflecting efficiency, is a government-regulated opportunity structure for all races. The NYPD promotes merit. Merit affords mechanisms for achievement. As achievements increase, manifestations of race and sex discrimination decrease.

Source

C. J. Chivers, "For Black Officers, Diversity Has Its Limits," *New York Times,* April 2, 2001.

"Let me control personnel," George Kennan has said, "and I will ultimately control policy. For the part of the machine that recruits and hires and fires and promotes people can soon control the entire shape of the institution."[1]

Few administrative theorists or practitioners would dispute this statement, and in the course of history, few able administrators have thought or acted otherwise. Their attitudes and approaches to the subject, however, have often differed.

Thomas Jefferson, for example, believed that civil servants should be provided with "drudgery and subsistence only" so that they would not want to stay too long in office.[2] This would enable the country to escape the establishment and growth of an administrative class, a development that Jefferson greatly feared. Other public administrators have taken a different tack, working toward strengthening the competency and professionalism of civil servants.

Conflicting Doctrines in American Public Administration

Herbert Kaufman provided a foundation for describing conflicts in the doctrines of public administration—a foundation that remains solid in the twenty-first century. He notes that different values are reflected in different periods in American history. The quests for representativeness, for neutral competence, and for executive leadership reflect succeeding norms of public personnel administration.[3]

The quest for *representativeness* has its roots in the colonial period. In our republican system, government bureaucrats are accountable to policies initiated by representatives of the voters. The quest for *neutral competence* originated in the 1880s with abuses of legislative supremacy, the long ballot, and the spoils system.

The goal of this quest was "taking administration out of politics." The quest for *executive leadership* was an effort to deal with such governmental issues as budgeting, reorganization, fragmentation, and the size of the bureaucracy. The personnel function is an essential part of these issues.

In addition to these "quests," it is helpful to examine Donald E. Klingner's and John Nalbandian's description of factors affecting public personnel practices that may contribute to the conflicting values in public administration. These factors are:

- *Value influences.* These considerations especially concern the rights of the individual, administrative efficiency, responsiveness, and social equity.
- *Mediating activities.* These interventions include affirmative action, human resource planning, productivity, and labor relations.
- *Core functions.* These essentials focus on the procurement, allocation, development, and sanction of human resources.[4]

Procedures and Policies

Public organizations in this country use essentially one of two different methods of establishing and operating personnel systems. One method stresses *political appointment and election;* the other emphasizes an *objective determination of merit.*

The selection of civil servants by merit and by political patronage are not mutually exclusive, argues James E. Leidlein. Fears that any relaxation of a merit-based system will lead to the returned dominance of political patronage are not warranted.[5]

Units of the Revolutionary army frequently elected their own officers, and once the hostilities ended, states and communities elected most of the administrators they would need. Many cities and towns, particularly older ones, continue to follow this practice. Some New England communities elect as many as fifty officials. Newer areas of the country, such as the Far West, disdain such practices, but even they maintain county organizations with many elective posts. No other major country in the world elects so many of its administrators as does the United States. Most state governments elect some officials whose tasks would be regarded in Europe or Canada as purely administrative.

Although election, dating back to the foundations of U.S. government, is supposed to give the people a deciding voice in determining who will administer their government, it can lead to abuses such as misleading promises and a reliance on campaign funding from special interests. Most of the electorate finds it impossible to know all the candidates for whom they must vote.

Political appointment also has a long history in the United States, dating back to colonial times. Even John Adams, who considered himself something of a paragon of political propriety, felt constrained to provide his ne'er-do-well son-in-law with a government job. Such practices gained increased favor with the arrival of Andrew Jackson at the White House. Jackson strongly adhered to Jefferson's views on rotating public servants in office. At the same time, Jackson did not believe that this would entail any loss of public confidence. As he put it, "The duties of all public servants are, or at least admit of being made, so plain and simple that men of intelligence may readily qualify themselves for their performance."[6] Old Hickory's espousal of this philosophy was fortified in that he had a virtual army of job seekers at his back clamoring loudly for the plums of patronage.

From Jackson's time on, U.S. presidents frequently found themselves besieged by persons seeking positions on the public payroll. One aggressive appointment seeker jumped into Abraham Lincoln's carriage to ask for a job while the president was riding through Washington. Lincoln started to listen to him but then drove him away, saying, more in despair than in anger, "No, I will not do business in the street."

When a disappointed job seeker assassinated President James Garfield in 1881, the nation's appetite for such administrative practices began to dampen. Political appointment continues to play a prominent role in U.S. administrative life, however. Our presidents, for example, fill nearly one hundred times more appointments than do British prime ministers.

The assassination of President Garfield did have its effect: It gave rise to an alternative method of recruitment, namely the *merit system.* Two years after the president's violent death, Congress passed the Pendleton Act, setting up a systematized procedure for hiring and employing vast numbers of federal civil servants in nearly every category. The merit system principle has continued to grow. It not only encompasses more than 90 percent of positions in the federal government, but includes increasing numbers of employees in state and local governments. About two-thirds of our states have comprehensive merit systems that cover the vast majority of their job holders. Even those states without comprehensive merit systems make some provision for merit-style appointments. The federal government has helped prod states and municipalities to move in this direction, for federal grants-in-aid frequently require the recipient agency to operate a merit system of some sort.

The Pendleton Act, passed in 1883, provided the substance of modern merit principles:

- First, administrative reform focused on *nonpolitical appointments* in attempting to neutralize the civil service. Such nonpartisanship in selecting, promoting, and regulating public bureaucrats was a reaction against the evils of the spoils system.
- Second, the Pendelton Act embraced *egalitarianism,* the most important legacy of Jacksonian democracy. Congress, in adopting civil service reform, refused to pattern the U.S. career system after the British. The American merit system would be open to all applicants of appropriate aptitude and skills. Theoretically, at least, all classes of citizens may contest for government employment.
- Third, *competence*, as determined by competitive examinations, was instituted in the Pendleton Act's provisions. The requirement was that exams be practical, related to the duties to be performed, and not grounded in theoretical or scholarly essays based on academic achievement.[7]

More recently, the Civic Service Reform Act of 1978 established the key *merit system principles* that the government employs today: recruiting, selecting, and advancing employees on the basis of their abilities, knowledge, and skills; providing equitable and adequate compensation; training employees to assure high-quality performance; guaranteeing fairness for applicants and employees; and protecting against coercion for political purposes.

The Act states, in addition to many other merit principles:

Recruitment should be from qualified individuals from appropriate sources in an endeavor to achieve a workforce from all segments of society, and selection and

The Plum Book and the Prune Book

College students may aspire to become Washington policy makers. Two books that provide guidelines, facts, and positions for postgraduate students seeking jobs in the upper ranks of the federal government are the "Plum Book" and the "Prune Book."

The Plum Book, released every four years alternately by the Senate Committee on Governmental Affairs or the House Committee on Government Reform, carries the formal title of *United States Government Policy and Supporting Positions.*

The Prune Book, published by the Council for Excellence in Government, profiles fifty-six of the most important U.S. Senate–confirmed government positions. It details five senior management jobs common to most agencies—chief operating officer, chief

information officer, chief financial officer, general counsel, and inspector general.

The Plum Book catalogs more than seven thousand jobs at the prerogative of the president. They usually are appointed positions—including agency heads, immediate subordinates, policy executives, and advisors. The Prune Book examines issues relating to staffing the upper echelons of the executive branch and probes the challenges that face presidential appointees.

The Plum Book and the Prune Book are designed to facilitate presidential transitions every four years. They combine interests of partisan, policy, and system politics.

Source: Katy Saldarini, "2000 Plum Book Lists Sought-After Jobs in Next Administration," *Government Executive,* November 10, 2000.

advancement should be determined solely on the basis of relative ability, knowledge, and skills, after fair and open competition which assures that all receive equal opportunity.

Another key part of the 1978 law states:

Employees should be retained on the basis of the adequacy of their performance, inadequate performance should be corrected, and employees should be separated who cannot or will not improve their performance to meet required standards.

Despite the law, the merit system has its detractors, who say that such a system eventually leads to a triumph of mediocrity, with initiative and enterprise sacrificed to the pressures of security and the forces of stagnation. Even when a merit system encourages merit, the argument continues, it may lead only to a *meritocracy* that shuts out otherwise capable people who cannot pass the tests or meet formal and sometimes fatuous requirements of the system.

Supporters argue that even if it leads to a "meritocracy," it is still likely to be more egalitarian and democratic than a system built on political contacts and allegiances.

In a 1990 decision, the United States Supreme Court ruled that the U.S. Constitution prohibits partisan political considerations in hiring, promoting, or transferring most public employees. The ruling clearly prevents a mayor or local chief executive from reserving non-policy-making jobs such as road equipment operations, prison security, highway repair, or parks department positions for the party faithful. Although the practical impact of the ruling is difficult to assess, the Supreme Court dealt a sharp blow to political patronage at all levels.

Dynamics of Federal Government Employment

In 2007, the federal government, excluding the U.S. Postal Service, employed about 1.8 million civilian workers, or about 1.3 percent of the nation's workforce. The federal government is the nation's single largest employer. Because data on employment in certain agencies cannot be released to the public for national security reasons, this total does not include employment at the Central Intelligence Agency, National Security Agency, Defense Intelligence Agency, and National Imagery and Mapping Agency.

The federal government makes an effort to have a workforce as diverse as the nation's civilian labor force. The federal government serves as a model for all employers in abiding by equal employment opportunity legislation, which protects current and potential employees from discrimination based on race, color, religion, sex, national origin, disability, or age. The federal government also makes an effort to recruit and accommodate persons with disabilities.

Even though the headquarters of most federal departments and agencies are in the Washington, D.C. area, only 16 percent of federal employees worked in the vicinity of the nation's capital in 2007. In addition to federal employees working throughout the United States, another 92,000, which includes foreign nationals, are assigned overseas, mostly in embassies or defense installations.

Occupations in the Federal Service

The federal government employs workers in every major occupational group. Workers are not employed in the same proportions in which they are employed throughout the economy as a whole, however (Table 5.1). The analytical and technical nature of many government duties translates into a much higher proportion of professional, management, business, and financial occupations in the federal government, compared with the economy as a whole. Conversely, the government sells very little, so it employs relatively few sales workers.

Professional and related occupations accounted for about 33 percent of federal employment in 2006 (Table 5.2). The largest group of professional workers worked in life, physical, and social science occupations, such as biological scientists, conservation scientists and foresters, environmental scientists and geoscientists, and forest

TABLE 5.1

Percent Distribution of Employment in the Federal Government, Excluding the Postal Service, and for All Industries by Major Occupational Group, 2006

Occupational Group	Federal Government	All Industries
Total	100.0	100.0
Management, business, and financial	33.2	10.2
Professional and related	32.8	19.8
Office and administrative support	14.3	16.2
Service	8.0	19.2
Installation, maintenance, and repair	4.7	3.9
Transportation and material moving	2.9	6.8
Construction and extraction	1.7	5.5
Production	1.5	7.1
Sales and related	0.5	10.6
Farming, fishing, and forestry	0.4	0.7

Source: http://www.bls.gov.

TABLE 5.2

Employment of Wage and Salary Workers in Federal Government by Occupation, 2006, and Projected Change, 2006–2016

(*thousands*)

Occupation	Employment, 2006		Percent Change, 2006–2016
	Number	Percent	
All occupations	1,958	100.0	–4.6
Management, business, and financial occupations	650	33.2	–2.9
General and operations managers	29	1.5	–0.4
Financial managers	12	0.6	–5.5
Purchasing agents, except wholesale, retail, and farm products	30	1.5	–14.9
Claims adjusters, examiners, and investigators	42	2.2	–5.5
Compliance officers, except agriculture, construction, health and safety, and transportation	91	4.6	–5.5
Human resources, training, and labor relations specialists	23	1.2	3.8
Logisticians	23	1.2	4.0
Management analysts	45	2.3	–5.5
Accountants and auditors	24	1.2	–14.9
Budget analysts	14	0.7	–5.5
Tax examiners, collectors, and revenue agents	36	1.8	1.2
Professional and related occupations	642	32.8	–3.2
Computer specialists	77	3.9	2.0
Engineers	90	4.6	–4.4
Engineering technicians, except drafters	29	1.5	–5.1
Biological scientists	23	1.2	–5.5
Conservation scientists	8	0.4	12.2
Chemists	6	0.3	–5.5
Environmental scientists and specialists, including health	6	0.3	–5.5
Biological technicians	12	0.6	–5.5
Forest and conservation technicians	26	1.3	–4.9
Lawyers	31	1.6	–5.5
Paralegals and legal assistants	14	0.7	5.5
Education, training, and library occupations	32	1.6	–5.5
Physicians and surgeons	25	1.3	–5.5
Registered nurses	54	2.7	4.0
Health technologists and technicians	40	2.1	–5.6
Licensed practical and licensed vocational nurses	14	0.7	–5.5
Occupational health and safety specialists	7	0.3	–5.5
Service occupations	157	8.0	2.9
Fire fighters	8	0.4	–5.5
Correctional officers and jailers	16	0.8	13.4

continued

TABLE 5.2

Employment of Wage and Salary Workers in Federal Government by Occupation, 2006, and Projected Change, 2006–2016, *continued*
(*thousands*)

Occupation	Employment, 2006		Percent Change, 2006–2016
	Number	Percent	
Service occupations			
Detectives and criminal investigators	39	2.0	13.4
Police and sheriffs patrol officers	12	0.6	3.9
Building cleaning workers	12	0.6	–3.4
Office and administrative support occupations	279	14.3	–15.5
Bookkeeping, accounting, and auditing clerks	21	1.1	–5.5
Procurement clerks	15	0.7	–14.9
Eligibility interviewers, government programs	26	1.3	6.3
Human resources assistants, except payroll and timekeeping	14	0.7	–5.5
Secretaries and administrative assistants	34	1.7	–15.4
Word processors and typists	14	0.7	–24.4
Farming, fishing, and forestry occupations	9	0.4	–11.5
Agricultural inspectors	6	0.3	–14.7
Installation, maintenance, and repair occupations	93	4.7	–6.1
Electrical and electronic equipment mechanics, installers, and repairers	15	0.8	–2.0
Aircraft mechanics and service technicians	19	1.0	–14.9
Transportation and material moving occupations	56	2.9	–1.0
Air traffic controllers	22	1.1	9.1

Note: Columns may not add to totals due to omission of occupations with small employment.

and conservation technicians. They do work such as determining the effects of drugs on living organisms, preventing fires in the national forests, and predicting earthquakes and hurricanes. Many health professionals, such as licensed practical and licensed vocational nurses, registered nurses, physicians, and surgeons, are employed by the Veterans Administration (VA) in VA hospitals.

Large numbers of federal workers also held jobs as engineers, including aerospace, civil, computer hardware, electrical and electronics, environmental, industrial, mechanical, and nuclear. Engineers are found in many departments of the executive branch, but the vast majority work in the Department of Defense. Some work in the National Aeronautics and Space Administration as well as other agencies. In general, they solve problems and provide advice on technical programs, such as building highway bridges or implementing agencywide computer systems.

The federal government hires many lawyers, judges, and related workers, as well as law clerks to write, administer, and enforce many of the country's laws and regulations.

Computer specialists—primary computer software engineers, computer systems analysts, and network and computer systems administrators—are employed throughout the federal government. They write computer programs, analyze problems related to data processing, and keep computer systems running smoothly.

Management, business, and financial workers make up another 33 percent of federal employment and are primarily responsible for overseeing operations. Managerial workers include a broad range of officials who, at the highest levels, may head federal agencies and programs. Middle managers, on the other hand, usually oversee one activity or aspect of a program. One management occupation—legislators—is responsible for passing and amending laws and overseeing the executive branch of government. Within the federal government, legislators are entirely found in Congress.

Other occupations in this category are accountants and auditors, who prepare and analyze financial reports, review and record revenues and expenditures, and investigate operations for fraud and inefficiency. Management analysts study government operations and systems and suggest improvements. Purchasing agents handle federal purchases of supplies, and tax examiners, collectors, and revenue agents determine and collect taxes.

About 14 percent of federal workers are in office and administrative support occupations. These employees aid management staff with administrative duties. Administrative support workers in the federal government include information and record clerks, general office clerks, and secretaries and administrative assistants.

Compared with the economy as a whole, workers in service occupations are relatively scarce in the federal government. About seven out of ten federal workers in service occupations are protective service workers, such as correctional officers and jailers, detectives and criminal investigators, and police officers. These workers protect the public from crime and oversee federal prisons.

Federally employed workers in installation, maintenance, and repair occupations include aircraft mechanics and service technicians, who fix and maintain all types of aircraft, and electrical and electronic equipment mechanics, installers, and repairers, who inspect, adjust, and repair electronic equipment such as industrial controls, transmitters, antennas, radar, radio, and navigation systems.

The federal government employs a relatively small number of workers in transportation; production; construction; sales and related; and farming, fishing, and forestry occupations. However, it employs almost all the air traffic controllers in the country and a significant number of agricultural inspectors and bridge and lock tenders.

Government Employment Outlook

Wage and salary employment in the federal government is projected to decline by 4.6 percent through the 2006–2016 period. Job growth generated by increased homeland security needs may be largely offset by projected slow growth or declines in other federal sectors resulting from governmental cost-cutting, the growing use of private contractors, and continuing devolution—the practice of turning over the development, implementation, and management of some federal programs to state and local governments.

Staffing levels in government, though relatively stable in the short run, can be subject in the long run to changes in public policies legislated by Congress that affect spending levels and hiring decisions for the various government departments and agencies. In general, over the coming decade, domestic programs are likely to see cuts in their budgets as Congress seeks to reduce the federal budget deficit. Cuts are likely to affect some agencies more than others.

Any employment declines, however, are generally carried out through attrition—simply not replacing workers who retire or leave federal government employment for other reasons. Layoffs, called "reductions in force," have occurred in the past, but they are uncommon and usually affect relatively few workers. In any case, numerous employment opportunities will still be available in many agencies because of the need to replace workers who leave the workforce, retire, or accept employment elsewhere.

Job openings are forecast in all types of federal service employment over the coming decade. In particular, demand continues to grow for specialized workers in areas related to border and transportation security, emergency preparedness, public health, and information analysis.

A study by the Partnership for Public Service, which surveyed federal department and agency hiring needs through 2009, found that most of the new hires in the federal government will come in five areas:

- Security, enforcement, and compliance, which includes inspectors, investigators, police officers, airport screeners, and prison guards
- Medical and public health fields
- Engineering and the sciences, including microbiologists, botanists, physicists, chemists, and veterinarians
- Program management and administration
- Accounting, budget, and business, which includes revenue agents and tax examiners needed mainly by the Internal Revenue Service.

The Department of Health and Human Services needs health insurance specialists and claims and customer service representatives to implement the Medicare Prescription Drug benefit. Patent examiners, foreign service officers, and lawyers also are in high demand.

The distribution of federal employment will continue to shift toward a higher proportion of professional, business and financial operations, and protective service workers. Employment declines will be greatest among office and administrative support occupations and production occupations, because of increasing office automation and contracting out of these jobs.

Competition is expected for some federal positions, especially during times of economic uncertainty, when workers seek the stability of federal employment. In general, federal employment is considered to be relatively stable because it is not affected by cyclical fluctuations in the economy, as are employment levels in many private sector industries.

Earnings

In efforts to provide agencies more flexibility in how they pay their workers, several pay systems are in effect. The two largest departments with new pay systems are the Departments of Defense and Homeland Security. The new systems incorporate fewer, wider pay "bands" instead of grade levels. Pay increases under these new systems are based almost entirely on performance, as opposed to length of service.

TABLE 5.3

Federal Government General Schedule (GS) Base Pay Rates, 2007

GS Level	Entrance Level	Step Increase	Maximum Level
1	$16,630	varies	$20,798
2	18,698	varies	23,527
3	20,401	$680	26,521
4	22,902	763	29,769
5	25,623	854	33,309
6	28,562	952	37,130
7	31,740	1,058	41,262
8	35,151	1,172	45,699
9	38,824	1,294	50,470
10	42,755	1,425	55,580
11	46,974	1,566	61,068
12	56,301	1,877	73,194
13	66,951	2,232	87,039
14	79,115	2,637	102,848
15	93,063	3,102	120,981

Source: U.S. Office of Personnel Management.

The majority of professional and administrative federal workers are still paid under the General Schedule (GS). The General Schedule, shown in Table 5.3, has fifteen grades of pay for civilian white-collar and service workers, and smaller within-grade step increases that occur based on length of service and quality of performance. New employees usually start at the first step of a grade. However, if the position in question is difficult to fill, entrants may receive somewhat higher pay or special rates. Almost all physician and engineer positions, for example, fall into this category.

In an effort to make federal pay more responsive to local labor market conditions, federal employees working within the United States receive locality pay. The specific amount of locality pay is determined by survey comparisons of private sector wage rates and federal wage rates in the relevant geographic area. At its highest level, locality pay can lead to an increase of as much as 30 percent above the base salary in 2007. Every January, a pay adjustment tied to changes in private sector pay levels is divided between an across-the-board pay increase in the General Schedule and locality pay increases.

In March 2007, the average earnings for full-time workers paid under the General Schedule were $65,463 (Table 5.4). General attorneys, who earned $111,304 on average, were one of the highest paid occupations, while nursing assistants on average earned only about half the average for all occupations.

Federal employees in craft, repair, operator, and laborer jobs are paid under the Federal Wage System (FWS). This schedule sets federal wages so that they are compatible with prevailing wage rates for similar types of jobs in the private sector. As a result, wage rates paid under the FWS can vary significantly from one locality to another.

In addition to base pay and bonuses, federal employees may receive incentive awards. These incentive awards can be cash rewards; quality step increases, meaning a

TABLE 5.4

Average Annual Salaries for Full-Time Workers under the General Schedule in the Federal Government in Selected Occupations, 2007

Occupation	Salary
All occupations	$65,463
General attorney	111,304
Financial management	101,022
General engineering	100,051
Economist	94,098
Computer science	90,929
Chemistry	89,954
Criminal investigating	88,174
Microbiology	87,206
Architecture	87,128
Statistics	85,690
Information technology management	81,524
Librarian	80,873
Accounting	78,665
Chaplain	78,030
Ecology	76,511
Human resources management	76,503
Mine safety and health	73,003
Air traffic control	72,049
Budget analysis	71,267
Correctional officer	67,140
Nurse	65,345
Engineering technical	63,951
Border patrol agent	63,550
Medical technologist	59,840
Customs and border protection	59,248
Legal assistance	46,912
Fire protection and prevention	43,407
Secretary	42,334
Police	42,150
Tax examining	38,290
Human resources assistance	37,835
Nursing assistant	33,134

Source: U.S. Office of Personnel Management.

faster than normal progression of steps on the GS pay scale; and time-off awards, allowing time off without using leave or loss of pay. The one-time cash awards may be as high as $25,000 but are typically significantly smaller. They are bestowed for a significant suggestion, a special act or service, or sustained high job performance. Some workers may also receive "premium" pay. This allocation is granted when employees work overtime, on holidays, on weekends, at night, or under hazardous conditions.

Merit-Based Recruitment

Although the merit principle has become the most widely accepted basis for personnel operation in U.S. public administration, it nevertheless continues to arouse controversy and pose problems. In terms of recruitment, there is first the task of making sure that the system truly rewards merit. Most civil service systems make extensive use of comparative examinations to bring this about. Though such exams may weigh the merits of the various candidates more impartially than a system built on favoritism would, they present difficulties of their own.

To be valid measures, the exams must be *predictive*. In other words, high scores on the examinations should correlate with high performance on the job, and vice versa. This is not necessarily the case. The issue of validity (whether test results are accurate or appropriate) and other recruitment criteria have come to the fore because of the increased effort to recruit members of minority groups into government service. Civil rights supporters claim that many of these criteria serve to exclude blacks, Puerto Ricans, Chicanos, and others. Specifically, they charge that these tests fail to measure the true capability of a job applicant. A study in Chicago found that a black police recruit would perform as well on the job as a white recruit who scored 10 percent higher on the entrance exam.[8] In other words, the entrance test failed to measure black applicants' true ability for police work.

The federal government encourages test validation as a means of ensuring and expanding equal opportunity. The move to include more members of minority groups in public administration is part of a larger movement aimed at making government agencies more representative of the public they serve. This brings us to another issue in administration. Government agencies have at times become "captive" to one or more sectors of society. The *captive agency,* a term used by public administration scholar Brian Chapman, tends to recruit heavily from one particular ethnic, religious, social, or geographical group.

Limitations to Merit

A pure merit system for all public service appointments would be grounded in competition based on merit rules. However, no administration functions on a pure merit system. Exceptions always exist, including:

- *Elected officials.* Some officials are elected, not appointed. No civil service gauge is employed in an election.
- *Political appointments.* Elected officials may choose friends, neighbors, or college roommates as political advisers. No civil service gauge is employed for these appointments.
- *Affirmative action.* To hasten the advancement of members of a disadvantaged group such as women or certain ethnic minorities, that group receives hiring preference. No civil service gauge is employed for such hirings.
- *Internal appointments and transfers.* Sometimes promotion is restricted to existing staff. The search is conducted inside the organization, not externally, to minimize transaction costs. In such cases, opportunities are provided for insider career development.[9]

Government Jobs for Students

The Web site www.studentjobs.gov provides a wealth of data on federal job openings and information on the federal government's hiring processes, programs, and employment benefits. The Web site has an e-mail notification system that posts new vacancies every twenty-four hours. The openings are designed to match a student's personal job-search profile. The site offers links to student employment pages for more than fifty agencies and to articles describing student job opportunities.

The Office of Personnel Management (OPM) and Department of Education created *www.studentjobs.gov,* which is designed for high school and college students seeking temporary employment with the federal government. Applicants must be at least sixteen years old. Only 5 percent of government employees are under age thirty; about half are between forty-five and sixty.

Source: Stephen Barr, "Website Encourages Young People to Think About Working for Uncle Sam," *Washington Post,* July 13, 2001, p. B2. "Government Jobs for Students: New Website Helps Find Summer and Temporary Jobs," http://usgovinfo.about.com/library/weekly/aa071301a.htm.

Recruitment Procedures

Merit-based recruitment arrangements include these elements:

- A job analysis leading to a written statement describing duties, or a job description, and the knowledge and skills required of the job holder (the person specification)
- An advertisement disseminated to affected groups—including a summary of the job analysis
- A standard application form
- A scoring scheme based on the personnel specification
- A short-listing procedure to reduce applications, if pertinent, to a manageable number
- A final selection procedure based on the person specification. A panel interview is included in the process
- An appointment procedure based on the scoring scheme
- Notification of results to selected and rejected candidates[10]

Qualifications

The government hires people with nearly every level of education and experience—from high school students with no experience to Ph.D.'s with established careers. Jobs in some occupations, such as engineer, ecologist, and lawyer, require that workers have a bachelor's or graduate degree and credit for specific college classes. Other occupations require experience, education, or a combination of both. A few, such as office clerk, require no education or experience to start.

The qualifications needed for each job are described in detail in the vacancy announcements that advertise job openings. Each job also has a code that corresponds to its minimum requirements. Understanding these codes will speed your search.

The coding systems used to classify jobs vary by agency, but the most common system is the General Schedule (GS). The GS assigns every job a grade level from 1 to 15, according to the minimum level of education and experience its workers need. Jobs that require no experience or education are graded a GS-1, for example. Jobs

TABLE 5.5
GS Levels by Education

GS-1	No high school diploma
GS-2	High school diploma
(GS-3 for clerk-steno positions)	
GS-3	1 year of full-time study after high school
GS-4	Associate degree or 2 years of full-time study after high school
GS-5 or GS-7 depending on agency policy and applicant's academic credentials	Bachelor's degree or 4 years of full-time study after high school
GS-7	Bachelor's degree plus 1 year of full-time graduate study
GS-9 (GS-11 for some research positions)	Master's degree or 2 years of full-time graduate study
GS-9	Law degree (J.D. or LLB.)
GS-11 (GS-12 for some research positions)	Ph.D. or equivalent doctorate or advanced law degree (LL.M.)

Source: http://www.federal-resume.org/gs-levels-explained.aspx.

that require a bachelor's degree and no experience are graded a GS-5 or GS-7, depending on an applicant's academic credentials and an agency's policies.

Table 5.5 shows the GS levels for entry-level workers with different amounts of education and little or no work experience.

College degrees only qualify you for a particular grade level if they are related to the job. For occupations requiring general college-level skills, a bachelor's degree in any subject can qualify you. But other occupations require a specific major.

After gaining work experience, people often qualify for higher GS levels. In general, one year of experience related to the job could raise your grade by one GS level in most clerical and technician positions. In administrative, professional, and scientific positions, GS level increases in increments of two until you reach a GS-12. After that, GS level increases one level at a time. With each additional year of experience at a higher level of responsibility, your GS level could continue to increase until it reaches the maximum for your occupation.

The Postrecruitment Phase

After a recruit qualifies for and receives an employment appointment, he or she still has obstacles to overcome before claiming full-fledged membership in the agency or organization. During the *probationary period,* agency personnel measure the skills, knowledge, expertise, and responsiveness of every employee. During this time, the recruit can be dismissed without the safeguards that protect those who have successfully completed such a phase. Probationary periods vary in length from six months to as long as seven years. Shorter terms are common in state and local governments, while the federal government and some other subnational jurisdictions require longer probations. The time frames may also vary depending on the nature of the position. While a fledgling sanitation person may acquire permanent status in six months, a police officer may have to wait a full year, and a teacher may not be awarded tenure until three years have passed. The longest probation periods are usually found at colleges and universities, where new faculty members may be scrutinized for seven years before achieving tenure. Some positions, such as high-level political appointments confer no privileges or permanency.

Training is also an aspect of the postrecruitment phase. Some agencies do nearly all their own recruit training; these include police departments, fire departments, and the like. Other public bodies, such as school systems and public health agencies, expect the newcomer to have the needed basic skills. Usually, the higher the professional level of the position, the more likely it is that the recruit will have obtained the essential training prior to appointment.

Training of all types is receiving increasing attention in public administration. A fast-moving and fast-changing society exhibits a strong need for, and must place increasing emphasis on, wide-ranging and high-level skills. Not so long ago, a police officer's training consisted of some on-the-job supervision. Today an officer is likely to receive many weeks or months of schooling at a police academy. The same holds true for many other public positions. Street cleaners are now apt to operate fairly complicated equipment where previously they may have pushed brooms, and so they, too, must receive a certain level of instruction to cope with once-simple tasks.

A survey on welfare reform conducted by the Public Agenda Foundation among eight focus groups nationwide and a national, random telephone survey of 1,000 American adults found that 77 percent of the respondents—black, white, and welfare recipients—believed that enrollment in job training and education programs is absolutely essential. Only a minority of the respondents (19 percent) believed that reducing the benefits of most welfare recipients would be effective welfare reform.[11]

The fastest growing area of attention in recent years may be *in-service training*. The upsurge of interest in this training method arises from the growing realization that in a modern society scarcely anyone is ever fully trained for the rest of his or her career. Not only must skills be continually upgraded, but new skills must be acquired if the employee and the organization are to meet changing demands and work patterns. Administrators are progressively accepting the notion that education is a lifelong process and that the organizations they manage must provide training on a nearly nonstop basis throughout an employee's career.

Promotion

Once an employee achieves tenure as a member of the organization, promotion possibilities may emerge. Advancement may come in the form of a pay increase; an increase in grade at the present level; or a move up to a new level, usually with at least some new duties and responsibilities.

Merit systems customarily provide two basic criteria for promotion: *seniority* and *merit*. In the majority of instances, both factors enter into consideration. The question in evaluating this system is, "Which of these, seniority or merit, is more conducive to effective administration?"

The answer at first seems obvious: Merit is usually deemed the most effective method for determining who shall rise. But *who determines what is meritorious?* Seniority presents obvious drawbacks. It rewards the incompetent along with the competent. James E. Brennan argues that it is far better to raise the salaries of low-paid employees who have proved worthy to competitive averages while decelerating salary increases among the more highly paid. Once inequities are resolved, Brennan emphasizes, merit increases should be based on job values rather than human values.[12]

According to the Merit Systems Protection Board (MSPB), 1 of every 8.8 employees is promoted over a three-year period. In any given year, 11.4 percent of the federal workforce receive promotions. About 1 in 8 employees assigned to professional or administrative jobs is promoted from a GS-11 to a GS-12 position each year. At GS-13, the rate is 1 in 20, and at GS-14, about 1 in 25. Compensation for a GS-12 is about $79,178 (locality pay included) in the Washington area. (See Tables 5.3 and 5.4 for other salary examples.)

Once a person reaches the middle grades of most federal occupations, it is normal to spend ten to fifteen years at a given grade level. These promotion rates mean that many of the persons working in professional and administrative jobs will never advance—over the entirety of their career—beyond the GS-12 level. Employees working in Washington have a better chance for promotion than employees assigned to field offices, where the offices are smaller.[13]

A *promotion* is a change to a position at a higher grade level within the same job classification system and pay schedule, or to a position with a higher rate of pay in a different job classification system and pay schedule. A promotion is always a change to a higher grade and should not be confused with periodic within-grade increases, quality step increases, or merit salary increases, which provide salary increases within the scheduled step rates of a particular grade.

Promotions may occur through several processes. Employees compete for promotion when they apply for higher-graded positions. All applicants are evaluated and ranked for the position on the basis of their experience, education, skills, and performance record. Selections from among the best qualified applicants are based upon management's needs and the overall objectives of the organization. This type of promotion is characterized as a promotion through competitive procedures. A promotion may result from position reclassification to a higher grade due to a gradual accretion of responsibilities. The position to which an employee is promoted is clearly either an outgrowth of his/her present position or a successor to their present position.

The Rationale for Job Tenure

Remuneration for government employment is based on position rather than performance. Good performance originates from an employee's sense of duty, not from incentive pay. A tenure system can be wholesale or piecemeal: Tenure may be provided for all existing civil servants who have held a particular position for a certain number of years, or awarded to any public employee who holds a position for a certain amount of time.

Government employees enjoy greater protection from dismissal than do private sector employees. Tenured employment in the civil services is grounded in three elements:

- *Civil servants serve the state.* They must be responsive to the government, but they have longer-term concerns than elected government officials.
- *Long-term career paths encourage discipline within work.* The risk of losing secure future employment is a serious threat.
- *Long-term career paths publicly associate a civil servant with his or her job.* This job identity make civil servants want to safeguard their reputations. More generally, long-term career paths encourage discipline and good community.[14]

The Challenges of Public Personnel Administration

Federal, state, and local governments employ 20,392,000 wage and salary workers. Of this national distribution, local government units employ 53.5 percent, or 10,908,000, workers. State governments employ 6,102,000, or 30.0 percent. The federal government hires 3,381,000, or 16.5 percent, of America's government employees. Almost all government employees are paid with tax dollars. Given the costs, the public has a real interest in keeping governments efficient, effective, and economical. To serve that interest, local, state, and federal governments must:

- Attract high-quality job applicants
- Hire a reasonable share of the high-quality applicants
- Train and develop employees
- Motivate employees to perform at their best
- Retain good performers and remove poor ones

Any employing organization's ability to achieve these goals is closely linked to its personnel policies, systems, and procedures. For the federal civil service, those policies, systems, and procedures are inextricably bound to the concept of merit as defined through various laws and regulations. Today the U.S. civil service is experiencing a "quiet crisis" in its inability to meet government goals. Evidence suggests that "the government is not perceived as an 'employer of choice' by many graduates of the country's most highly rated academic institutions."[15] Ironically, "since the federal government employs relatively more managers, professionals, and technicians than other U.S. employers, the skills required of federal workers are greater, on average, than those employees in the nation as a whole."[16] This negative attitude toward federal employment is therefore damaging. Results of one survey said that less than half of senior-level federal managers and executives would work for the government again if they had a choice.[17]

The Changing Demographics of the Federal Workforce

Federal civilian employment reached a peak of nearly 3.4 million persons during World War II, receded to 2.0 million in 1947, and subsequently rose to 2.5 million in 1951. After nearly fifteen years of only minor fluctuation, federal government civilian

TABLE 5.6

Characteristics of Salaried Full-Time Permanent Federal Civilian Employees, by Occupational Category, December 2005

	All Categories	Professional	Administrative	Technical	Clerical	Other*
Average Age	46.9	47.3	47.5	46.8	47.5	38.4
Average Years of Service	16.5	16.0	18.4	14.8	15.3	10.9
Educational Attainment						
Bachelor's degree	48.9%	89.1%	50.3%	14.6%	11.3%	16.3%
Graduate degree	17.4	42.2	13.9	1.6	1.0	1.0
Sex						
Female	47.1	39.8	44.5	57.8	79.9	11.7
Male	52.9	60.2	55.5	42.2	20.1	88.3
Selected Ethnic Groups						
Black	17.5	9.7	16.9	24.7	30.0	16.5
Hispanic	7.5	4.9	7.3	8.9	8.0	18.1
Disabled	6.0	4.8	5.5	7.6	11.2	2.8
Veteran	21.5	13.3	25.1	22.6	19.5	36.0

Source: Congressional Budget Office, *Characteristics and Pay of Federal Civilian Employees* (Washington, DC: CBO, March 2007), p. 12.

*Mostly employees in protective services occupations, such as uniformed police officers and customs and border patrol officers.

employment reached almost 3.0 million in 1967 and fluctuated in the range of 2.8 to 3.0 million between 1968 and 1984. Beginning in 1985, federal government civilian employment again exceeded 3.0 million, increasing to 3.2 million in 1990. By 2005, however, the total had decreased to 2.7 million.

The demographic composition of the labor force has changed and will continue to change. The Office of Personnel Management and U.S. Bureau of Labor Statistics data indicate that many workforce changes and conditions are more prevalent in the federal workforce than in the nonfederal sector of government employment. The nonfederal workforce includes private sector employees and state and local government employees.

The federal workforce, once primarily composed of workers in clerical positions, is now made up predominantly of salaried full-time civil servants—more highly educated and proportionately more inclusive of professionals and administrators than in the past. The Office of Personnel Management (OPM) projects that high numbers of full-time permanent workers will retire between 2008 and 2010, and OPM forecasters are concerned about the loss of institutional knowledge with those retiring employees.

As of 2005, permanent full-time civilian federal employees had an average age of forty-seven, with an average sixteen years of federal service (see Table 5.6). More than 60 percent of federal employees were between the ages of forty and sixty-five.

Attracting the Next Generation

Who are federal agencies hiring to fill entry-level positions? Why do these people come to work for the federal government? What were they looking for in a job when the agency recruited them?

The Merit Systems Protection Board (MSPB) conducted a study of federal entry-level new hires in professional and administrative occupations to identify how the government can improve its entry-level hiring. MSPB surveyed almost 2,000 GS-5, 7, and 9 new hires in professional and administrative occupations to find out why they came to work for the government and what barriers they experienced during the hiring process. The MSPB also explored the perceptions younger generations have of federal employment to identify the obstacles the government faces in attracting and hiring high-quality applicants.

"Our research points to a number of positive conclusions about the Federal Government's ability to attract the best and the brightest," observes Chairman Neil A. G. McPhie. The federal government offers what many new hires—regardless of age or generation—want in an employer, including job security, good benefits, and the ability to make a difference with their work. In addition, many of the new hires faced fewer obstacles in the hiring process than expected, were fairly determined to obtain a federal job, and planned to stay with the government for a long time.

Chairman McPhie also notes, however, that "there are some troublesome trends that could thwart merit-based hiring over time." For instance, it appears that agencies are relying more on excepted service appointment authorities to hire new employees. The report cautions that these authorities can inadvertently circumvent merit because they often narrow recruitment sources, potentially short-circuiting fair and open competition.

The MSPB recommends that agencies and federal policy makers should consider its report when reflecting on how to improve the federal hiring process. The results indicate that the federal government competes for entry-level new hires better than some contemporary research suggests.

Source: Merit Systems Protection Board, "New MSPB Report Finds That Federal Entry-Level New Hires May Not Be What Most People Expect," February 8, 2008.

The average federal worker retires from the federal service at age fifty-nine. Almost 60 percent of federal workers had fifteen or more years of federal service, while only about 10 percent had tenures between ten and fifteen years.

The total number of federal employees, including part-time, temporary, and blue-collar workers, decreased from 3.2 million in 1990 to 2.7 million in 2005. This last figure is a little smaller than the size of the federal workforce in the mid-1970s. The distribution of occupations in the total federal workforce encompasses more professional and administrative positions and fewer clerical positions. The average age, tenure, and educational attainment of federal employees have all increased since 1975.

The demographics of full-time permanent civil servants vary by occupational category in the government's personnel system (Table 5.6). Clerical occupations are staffed by substantial proportions of women and blacks. The representation of minority groups has been increasing over time, and the diversity of a full-time permanent federal workforce has increased. The proportion of African-Americans in the civil service increased modestly from 1975 to 1990 but has changed little since then. The proportion of Asians and Pacific Islanders in the workforce has expanded in recent years. Military retirees make up about 6 percent of the full-time permanent workforce.[18]

Occupational Categories for Salaried Full-Time Permanent Federal Civilian Employees

In the 1970s, the Civil Service Commission (now the Office of Personnel Management, or OPM) created a system of occupational categories for all white-collar employees of the federal government. The five categories—Professional, Administrative, Technical, Clerical, and Other—are distinguished by their education requirements, the level of responsibility that employees must assume, and the nature of the work.

Positions that require an advanced degree or, in the case of a scientific field, significant experience are classified as *Professional*. More than 89 percent of workers in such occupations have a bachelor's or more advanced degree, by far the highest percentage of degree holders in any category. Examples of occupations that OPM designates as professional include accounting, nursing, physical therapy, architecture, engineering, law, library sciences, and economics. In December 2005, almost 450,000 federal employees were classified as professionals.

Although the positions in the *Administrative* category do not necessarily require higher education, many of the duties of administrators involve skills that are most often gained through undergraduate or postgraduate studies. In fact, more than 50 percent of employees in the administrative category hold a bachelor's or higher degree. Such workers are often required to perform research and exercise judgment in their work and must possess good analytical and writing skills. Physician's assistants, paralegal specialists, air traffic controllers, technical writers and editors, financial analysts, and information technology managers are jobs that OPM classifies as administrative. The largest occupational category in December 2005, it comprised roughly 640,000 employees.

Employees whose occupations place them in the *Technical* category often provide support for colleagues in the Professional and Administrative categories. The duties of technical employees require broad knowledge that is often gained through practical experience. Fewer than 15 percent of employees in this category have a bachelor's degree. Among technical workers are medical technicians, dental assistants, safety technicians, photographers, cartographic technicians, and food inspectors. In December 2005, about 370,000 employees were classified as technical workers.

Support work essential for the functioning of offices and operations is performed by employees in the *Clerical* category. The skills required of such workers are gained primarily through experience, although slightly more than 11 percent of those employees have a bachelor's degree. Occupations in this category include those of typist, data transcriber, dispatcher, correspondence clerk, sales store clerk, and intelligence aid. In December 2005, the federal government employed 130,000 clerical workers.

Positions that cannot be assigned to any of the other four groups fall into the *Other* category. More than 90 percent of the occupations so classified are related to law enforcement or protective services; the category also includes trainees for various occupations. Sixteen percent of employees in the Other category hold a bachelor's degree. Occupations under this heading include customs patrol officer, firefighter, police officer, security guard, border patrol agent, correctional officer, and U.S. marshal. This occupational category was the smallest in December 2005 with about 60,000 employees.

In most cases, occupations fall into a single category, but sometimes an occupation's classification depends on the General Schedule (GS) pay grade of an employee. For example, the position of park ranger is categorized as technical if the employee's pay grade is from GS-1 to GS-4. But if the grade is between GS-5 and GS-15, then the position is classified as administrative.

Source: Congressional Budget Office, *Characteristics and Pay of Federal Civilian Employees* (Washington, DC: CBO, March 2007).

Comparing Federal and Private-Sector Workers

In 2005, according to the Current Population Survey (CPS), 44 percent of federal workers were in management, professional, and related occupations, compared with 32 percent of private-sector workers. In the same year, the average age for federal workers was 45 in the CPS data, and the average age for private-sector employees was 40. Among management, professional, and related occupations, the average ages of federal and private-sector workers were 46 and 42, respectively. Among all federal workers, 43 percent held bachelor's degrees compared with 28 percent for all private-sector workers, and 46 percent of federal workers versus 42 percent of private-sector workers in management, professional, and related occupations were college graduates.

Additionally, the CPS data show that workers in the two sectors differ by demographic background. Most notably, the federal sector has a higher proportion of black workers than does the private sector—18 percent versus 11 percent for all occupations and 14 percent versus 8 percent for management, professional, and related occupations. In contrast, the federal sector employs proportionately fewer women (39 percent) than does the private sector (42 percent) in all occupations, with the difference being more pronounced in management, professional, and related occupations (42 percent among federal employees and 47 percent among private-sector workers). There are fewer Hispanics in all occupations in the federal sector as compared with the private sector (8 percent versus 15 percent), but the proportions in the two sectors are similar for management, professional, and related occupations (6 percent and 7 percent, respectively).

Source: Congressional Budget Office, *Characteristics and Pay of Federal Civilian Employees* (Washington, DC: CBO, March 2007.)

Equal Opportunity and Affirmative Action

Equal employment opportunity refers to the idea that "no person should be denied the opportunity for employment because of discrimination based on race, color, religion, sex, national origin, or physical disability."[19] While *equal opportunity* is essentially a passive concept, *affirmative action* is an active one. Affirmative action *implements* equal opportunity for minorities and women.

In some ways, equal employment opportunity redefines the merit system to emphasize that the merit philosophy not only recruits, selects, and advances employees on the basis of their relative abilities, but also calls for a workforce representative of all people. Equal opportunity is principal among the ideas that fuel the American way of life. Honest people often agree on the lofty goals of equal opportunity but disagree on the manner in which such a sometimes vague philosophy is carried out.

As a passive strategy, equal opportunity implies nondiscrimination. Equal opportunity and nondiscrimination are passive instruments of public policy because they rely on families, schools, and pertinent forces in U.S. society to abolish stereotypes and prejudices that prohibit the creation of a balanced workforce. Affirmative action is an active strategy, intended to ensure equal opportunity.

With the possible exception of trade unionism, which we shall examine in a subsequent chapter, no issue in the post–World War II era has engaged public personnel administration as has the quest for equal opportunity. Public administration is an integral part of modern society and, as such, is not impervious to society's pressures and concerns. As the campaigns for the rights of women and minorities emerged and accumulated legitimacy and recognition, they shook and buffeted public personnel administration along with the rest of American life. There is no question that personnel administration needed the shake-up. The federal government has a somewhat questionable record in equal opportunity.

The controversy over affirmative action arises from the noble aspiration of providing equal employment opportunity for all Americans. As noted earlier, in private administration the law tells administrators only what they *cannot do,* and in public administration the law tells administrators what they *can do.* The implementation of equal employment opportunity and affirmative action is, therefore, grounded upon a host of federal, state, and local laws.

Certain pieces of legislation have been crucial in the attempt to achieve *social equity* through proportional representation in the nation's workforce: the Civil Rights Act of 1964, Executive Order 11246 of 1965, and the 1972 Equal Employment Opportunity Act.

The development of the affirmative action concept began in the mid-1960s with the passage of the most far-reaching civil rights law since Reconstruction following the Civil War. The Civil Rights Act of 1964 prohibits job discrimination on the basis of race, sex, religion, national origin, age, or physical disability, and the Equal Employment Opportunity commission was simultaneously created for the purpose of administering the law. The law gives operational meaning to the 1954 Supreme Court desegregation case of *Brown v. Board of Education,* which holds that the previous doctrine of "separate but equal" facilities for the races will no longer satisfy constitutional requirements and specifically that blacks everywhere are permitted to attend the same public schools as whites.

President Lyndon Johnson signed Executive Order 11246 in 1965. It repeated nondiscrimination and affirmative action language used earlier, requiring government contracts to prohibit discrimination by the contractor and to use affirmative action to ensure that workers are employed without regard to race, creed, or color. The 1972 legislation also requires state and local governments to develop affirmative action plans.

Other pieces of legislation with an impact on affirmative action include the Equal Pay Act of 1963; amendments to the Fair Labor Standards Act of 1938; the Age Discrimination in Employment Act of 1967, amended in 1978; Title VI of the Vocational Rehabilitation Act of 1973; and the Vietnam Veteran's Readjustment Assistance Act of 1974.[20]

In the government workplace of the twenty-first century, the modernist feminist agenda squarely confronts conservative traditionalism. Tradition calls for women to focus and commit their energies to "kitchen, children, and school," expecting women to find satisfaction in feeding their families, comforting their husbands, raising children, praying and obeying, and teaching youngsters about God and country. This traditional view runs against the new and increasingly important presence of women in the marketplace.

The 1990s brought the Clarence Thomas/Anita Hill sexual harassment hearings before the U.S. Senate Judiciary Committee and the Paula Jones and Monica Lewinsky charges against President Clinton out of the closet and placed them on the political agenda—thrusting them into the *marketplace of ideas.* The broader issues raised include a woman's evolution and/or liberation from the more restrictive roles of children, church, and school. A woman's right to choose abortion and economic opportunities and protections in the workforce (including freedom from sexual harassment and other forms of discrimination) constitute the *new moral values.* The sexual harassment controversies featuring Thomas, Hill, Jones, and Clinton are

Americans with Disabilities Act

The purpose of the Americans with Disabilities Act (ADA) is to provide a clear and comprehensive national mandate for the elimination of discrimination against individuals with disabilities. The ADA gives people with disabilities access to employment, housing, public accommodations, education, transportation, communication, recreation, institutionalization, health services, voting, and public services. This affects more than 43 million Americans with one or more physical or mental disabilities. The ADA defines "qualified individual with a disability" as a person with a disability who, with or without reasonable accommodation, can perform the essential functions of the job that such individual holds or desires.

The ADA prohibits discrimination on the basis of disability in employment, public services, and public accommodations. The Equal Employment Opportunity Commission (EEOC) issues regulations to carry out the requirements of the Act. New buses and trains must be accessible to the disabled. If not handicapped accessible, existing transportation facilities must be altered and rendered accessible. This regulation includes access to rapid and light rail systems. Telecommunications companies now operate relay systems that allow hearing- and speech-impaired Americans to use telephone service.

Employers with fifteen or more employees are prohibited from discriminating against qualified individuals with a disability in job application procedures; hiring, advancement, or discharge of employees; employee compensation; job training; and conditions or privileges of employment. Absence of persons with disabilities in the decision-making process impairs tenets of democratic values and deprives society of talents that contribute to economic and social developments. The United States Census Bureau reports that nearly 20 percent or about one in every five Americans experience some level of disability.

Both de jure and de factor discrimination against the disabled occurs. Social and cultural norms, institutionalized by laws, may be a catalyst to discriminatory practices against persons with disabilities. Legislation is recognized as a mechanism for social change. Although costly and entangled in government regulations, the ADA enjoys support from partisan, policy, and system politics.

Sources: United States Office of Personnel Management, *Federal Civilian Workforce Statistic: Demographic Profile of the Federal Workforce as of September 30, 1996* (Washington, DC: U.S. Government Printing Office, 1997), 6. "Census: 1 in 5 Americans Has Disability: 53 million reported some level of disability in 1997, Census reports," March 17, 2001, http://usgovinfo.about.com/library/weekly/aa031701a.htmn3032901i; "Understanding The Americans with Disabilities Act," "The Consumer Law Page," http://consumerlawpage.com/article/disact.shtml.

symbolic of greater, more significant economic changes in U.S. society. Women exert more power than ever before in America's political economy.

Social conservatives call for government to put the "father knows best" genie back into the bottle of traditional values. But attempts by either the right or left to "legislate morality" confront a pragmatic political culture and economic realities. Economically and politically, women—as their power in society grows—will cast aside the arbitrary nature of male authority. The issues of sexual harassment and affirmative action plans in the workplace divide males and females of all races. Women do not want to be exposed, patronized, fondled, or harassed. They seek respect for their professionalism, and, indeed, demand it. The sexual harassment arguments of Hill and Jones reverberated throughout American politics and government workplaces.

Reverse Discrimination

The problem of reverse discrimination emerged in the Supreme Court cases of *Regents of the University of California v. Allan Bakke* (1978) and *Weber v. Kaiser Aluminum and Steel Corporation and United Steelworkers Union* (1979). The *Bakke* case was a *public sector* concern; the *Weber* case was a *private sector* matter. The distinction is crucial, because legalism in general and laws in particular circumscribe and influence the operation of a public institution more than a private one.

Bakke was a white male suing the medical school of the University of California at Davis for admission, claiming that the medical school rejected his application in favor of less qualified minority students. In a voluntary attempt to correct years of minority discrimination, the medical school established a quota for minority students for each entering class. The Supreme Court's ruling agreed that Bakke had been unfairly denied admission, but the scope of the decision was carefully narrowed.

First, the medical school is a public institution, supported by taxpayers. Second, the case was one of admission to a public university, not a public sector employment matter. Third, although the court outlawed the quota system, it played a different kind of judicial politics. If public sector bureaucracies avoided an inflexible quota system, affirmative action programs would remain constitutional. In this way, the court allowed public organizations to consider racial and sexual differences in accepting students. In other words, quotas were made illegal for the public sector; but race and sex remain acceptable for consideration in entrance requirements. The *Bakke* decision confused employers, bureaucrats, lawyers, and court watchers.

If the *Bakke* case left the constitutionality of affirmative action in doubt, the *Weber* decision made at least some headway in settling the issue. Because the *Weber* case was a private concern, no public sector monies were involved. As free agents in a democratic society, the Kaiser Aluminum Company and United Steelworkers Union cooperated in establishing an affirmative action program for minority employees.

Brian Weber, a white lab technician with more seniority than two black applicants, filed suit, claiming reverse discrimination against him by the company and the union. By placing minorities in 50 percent of the openings in a training program, thereby establishing a quota system, management and labor created a voluntary program that gave special preference to blacks. The Louisiana plant was located in a region where 39 percent of the local workforce was black. Fifteen percent of the employees of the plant were black, but only 2 percent of the skilled craft workers were black. Therefore, the *Weber* case raised not only the issue of equal employment opportunity, but also concerns about a representative workforce.

The Supreme Court decided in favor of the affirmative action program sponsored jointly by management and labor, concluding that Title VII of the Civil Rights Act of 1964 was passed for the particular purpose of improving the economic plight of black Americans. In other words, private sector employers could voluntarily establish a hiring and promotion program grounded upon improving the employment skills of blacks. To repeat an earlier distinction, the law tells managers in the private sector only what they *cannot* do, as in the *Weber* case; however, the law tells administrators in the public sector what they *can* do.

Technically, courts address only the particular set of facts of any case brought before them. To a large degree, the courts in the United States are passive units of fragmented and decentralized federal and state judicial bureaucracies. Courts consider only cases that merit jurisdiction before particular tribunals. Plaintiffs must take their particular set of grievances into court. To do so, plaintiffs need the skills of talented lawyers, money to finance such actions, and the patience and ego strength to see things through, win or lose.

Affirmative action issues concern *quotas, layoffs, work environments,* and *compensation.* The most controversial issue affirmative action raises is whether an employer can establish quotas for making employment decisions. Quotas, of course, specify that a precise percentage of appointments have to be minorities, women, and/or handicapped persons.

The Declining Importance of Affirmative Action

David H. Rosenbloom maintains that the importance of affirmative action began declining in the 1980s for at least three reasons:

1. There is *no strong consensus* favoring affirmative action, which reduces the organizational coherence and political integrity of affirmative action programs.
2. There is a *continuing constitutional stalemate* concerning affirmative action, as shown by the nonlinear direction of various Supreme Court cases.
3. There are *priority internal demands* such as executive leadership, retrenchment, and productivity that affect the commitment to affirmative action.[21]

What is the significance of affirmative action in our society? Affirmative action challenges public sector managers and some employees, but it also promotes representativeness in government bureaucracies. Affirmative action raises issues of potential and real discrimination that confront women, minorities, and disabled employees. The visibility of affirmative action issues heightens our awareness of discrimination in the workplace.

Perceptions about affirmative action produce a great deal of political and administrative rhetoric. However, the impact, in terms of concrete results, for the purported beneficiaries is questionable. Until the affected groups attain more education and experience, changes will come slowly and progress will likely be incremental. To its credit, however, affirmative action forces government departments and agencies to broaden and intensify their recruiting efforts, to examine the validity of their examinations, and to question the value of recruitment and promotion criteria. It stimulates innovation and makes governmental organizations more open. The administrative branch becomes, as a result, more representative of the population it serves.

Affirmative action, referred to as *equal opportunity* under the Civil Rights Act of 1964, means to many Americans in the twenty-first century the use of practices such as setting quotas and giving preferential treatment. Many argue that affirmative action should be based on criteria of *class* instead of considerations of *race* or *sex*.[22] To others, affirmative action is a policy aimed at eliminating discrimination in employment based on race, color, religion, sex, or national origin. It does not encourage the hiring or promotion of unqualified people just because they are minorities or women, nor does it impose quotas. It is not reverse discrimination, because it promotes equal opportunity.[23]

Bill Clinton argued that affirmative action must be reformed rather than eliminated. Despite its flaws, affirmative action has been effective in providing equal opportunity to women and minorities. It must be eliminated only when discrimination is finally abolished.[24] Critics of affirmative action are often silent about the veterans' preference program, which benefits mostly males. Since 1944, federal agencies

The Origins of Affirmative Action

Affirmative action, the set of public policies and initiatives designed to help eliminate past and present discrimination based on race, color, religion, sex, or national origin, is under attack.

- Originally, civil rights programs were enacted to help African-Americans become full citizens of the United States. The *Thirteenth Amendment* to the Constitution made slavery illegal; the *Fourteenth Amendment* guarantees equal protection under the law; the *Fifteenth Amendment* forbids racial discrimination in access to voting. The 1866 Civil Rights Act guarantees every citizen "the same right to make and enforce contracts . . . as is enjoyed by white citizens. . . . "
- In 1896, the Supreme Court's decision in *Plessy v. Ferguson* upheld a "separate, but equal" doctrine that proved to be anything but equal for African-Americans. The decision marked the end of the post–Civil War Reconstruction era as Jim Crow laws spread across the South.
- In 1941, President Franklin D. Roosevelt signed Executive Order 8802, which outlawed segregationist hiring policies by defense-related industries which held federal contracts. Roosevelt's signing of this order was a direct result of the efforts of black trade union leader A. Philip Randolph.
- During 1953, President Harry S. Truman's Committee on Government Contract Compliance urged the Bureau of Employment Security "to act positively and affirmatively to implement the policy of nondiscrimination. . . . "
- The 1954 Supreme Court decision in *Brown v. Board of Education* overturned *Plessy v. Ferguson.*

- The actual phrase *affirmative action* was first used in President Lyndon Johnson's 1965 Executive Order 11246, which requires federal contractors to "take affirmative action to ensure that applicants are employed, and that employees are treated during employment, without regard to their race, creed, color, or national origin."
- In 1967, Johnson expanded the Executive Order to include affirmative action requirements to benefit women.
- Other equal protection laws passed to make discrimination illegal were the 1964 Civil Rights Act, Titles II and VII of which forbid racial discrimination in "public accommodations" and racial and sex discrimination in employment, respectively; and the 1965 Voting Rights Act adopted after Congress found "that racial discrimination in voting was an insidious and pervasive evil which had been perpetuated in certain parts of the country through unremitting and ingenious defiance of the Constitution."

Much of the opposition to affirmative action is framed on the grounds of so-called "reverse discrimination and unwarranted preferences." In fact, fewer than 2 percent of the 91,000 employment discrimination cases pending before the Equal Employment Opportunities Commission are reverse discrimination cases. Under the law as written in Executive Orders and interpreted by the courts, anyone benefiting from affirmative action must have relevant and valid job or educational qualifications.

Source: "The Origins of Affirmative Action" by Marquita Sykes, as it appeared on the Web site www.now.org, April 2, 2002. Reprinted by permission of the National Organization for Women, Inc.

have provided preferential hiring consideration to veterans as a means of rewarding them for service to their country. Many argue that women are especially disadvantaged by veterans' preferences.[25] Opponents of affirmative action may have an easier time removing affirmative action from government offices and institutions than from American culture. In the following instance, even conservatives accepted the merits of an affirmative action candidate:

> The curtailment of affirmative action may mean less than is generally expected. . . . Affirmative action is now a firmly established institutional practice, indeed virtually a reflex of many university, corporate, and political decision makers. (As Mr. George Herbert Walker Bush's appointment of Clarence Thomas illustrates,

---

The U.S. Senior Executive Service and Diversity

A diverse Senior Executive Service (SES) corps may be an organizational strength that contributes to achieving results. Diversity brings a wider variety of perspectives and approaches to influence policy development and implementation, strategic planning, problem solving, and decision making.

The Senior Executive Service was established by the Civil Service Reform Act of 1978. The Act states that the policy of the federal government is to ensure equal employment opportunity in the workforce. Agency heads may set salaries of SES members at any one of six rates. In 2000, SES basic salaries ranged from $104,927 (ES-1) to $158,100 (ES-6), not including locality payments.

During the 2000–2007 time frame, white males at SES declined from 67.1 percent to 62.1 percent, white females rose from 19.1 percent to 23.1 percent, and minority males and females rose from 13.8 to 14.6 percent. From 2000 through 2007, 55 percent of SES employees governmentwide retired or left office. Replacing more than half of the SES corps presents a challenge and an opportunity for the federal government. The federal government is confronted with senior personnel losses that have a direct impact on leadership continuity, institutional knowledge, and expertise.

A number of federal organizations oversee federal efforts to achieve diversity in the workplace. The Equal Employment Opportunity Commission (EEOC) and the Office of Personnel Management (OPM) ensure that federal policies, laws, and regulations (1) protect federal workers from unlawful employment discrimination and other unlawful work practices and (2) promote equal opportunity, fairness, and inclusiveness.

OPM provides Congress with an annual report on employment of minorities and women in the federal government. Overall, the proportion of minority employees in the federal workforce increased slightly in 2005. Black employees represented 17.5 percent, Hispanics 7.5 percent, Asian/Pacific Islanders 6.2 percent, and Native Americans 2 percent.

Source: U. S. General Accounting Office, *Enhanced Agency Efforts Needed to Improve Diversity as the Senior Corps Turn over,* October 15, 2003, GAO-04-123T.

---

even conservatives need the legitimacy of multiracial representation.) Just as discrimination did not end with formal rulings against it, neither will affirmative action end with formal rulings.[26]

The bottom line is that affirmative action has contributed to the process of public administration, if not to its substantive content. Affirmative action forces governments to hire, promote, and fire employees under the auspices of legal procedures and administrative due process.

Performance Rating and Measurement

If an organization is going to use merit rather than seniority as a standard for promotion or demotion, how does one determine job performance? The most common method is for a superior to give a subordinate a *performance rating*. The system seems simple, but in practice it generates complications and controversies.

The essence of the performance rating problem lies in the absence of objective data and procedures for making these systems work effectively. Even when a supervisor attempts to be fair and impartial, neutral criteria are often scarce. Administrative decision makers too often give into personal whims and capricious actions. However difficult these ratings systems are to administer, they are universally part of the government workplace and culture.

Workforce morale and *government performance* are closely related. The ability of a government to function effectively and efficiently is related directly to the quality, competency, and motivation of its workforce. Despite positive attitudes toward their jobs and the work they do, only about half the respondents in a survey of federal workers would recommend the federal government as an employer, and more than one-fourth say they definitely would not. Several factors traditionally viewed as reasons to remain in federal employment lost strength as retention factors in one three-year period, according to surveys conducted for the Merit Systems Protection Board. These included the intrinsic value of the work; salary; current health insurance benefits; and the opportunity to have an impact on public affairs.

Many employees argue that the federal government's performance management program does not create an atmosphere that strongly encourages quality performance. Large percentages of employees believe their work units can increase the quantity and quality of the work they perform with the same people.[27]

All public organizations find it necessary to measure employee performance. As the demands of governments have changed, the meaning of the term *performance management* has changed as well. Rating employees once involved using a trait-based form. Factors such as neatness, punctuality, politeness, and sociability were important indicators of performance satisfaction. Public sector managers were less focused on work outputs. The evaluation process, even in the public sector, was often secretive. The employee did not participate. In some cases, he or she never knew the rating received.

This format is no longer considered good practice for the organization, the employees, or the citizen-consumers of public service. Instead, public sector performance management should be:

- *Task-oriented.* The evaluation must be grounded in results—not in personal traits. Results are measured against predefined goals and targets.
- *Participative.* The employee is involved in the evaluation alone with his or her supervisor. Both engage in setting goals at the start of the rating period. Employee and supervisor appraise results together at the end.
- *Developmental.* Evaluation processes do more than rate employees; they help employees to improve performance, identifying resources for training and support required to achieve this end.

Performance appraisals may define expectations, make clear when job performance is successful, specify when improvement is needed, and be used to set future goals. Taking responsibility for performance appraisals in local governments, developing performance standards, evaluating the appraisal system, distributing bonuses and cash awards, and implementing incentive plans all make significant differences in creating productive governments.

Employee performance must be linked to promotion; the best people must rise to management levels. Managers are paid more to make difficult personnel and policy decisions. Do servicewide performance schemes deliver worthwhile improvements in employee performance? The evidence is inconclusive. Budgetary constraints often limit the amounts of performance pay enhancements. A large lag-time occurs between the appraisal period and the payment of rewards.

Performance-pay schemes permit managers to make variable payments. However, most employees receive similar ratings; managers are often unwilling to make distinctions regarding subordinate skills. Employees often perceive their pay as inadequate. Small performance-pay bonuses are thus unlikely to motivate employees, especially since more employees are left out than included in pay enhancements and the majority may resent any process that gives the minority more compensation. Finally, management's performance-pay decision-making methods may be skewed. Overall, employee morale may suffer under such programs.

Position Classifications

Public sector personnel organizations have systems of position classifications. The premise for adopting position classification schemes is that different positions require varying degrees of ability and amounts of responsibility. The adoption of a classification plan has long been considered essential for the effective operation of a merit system, for it places the emphasis on *what* rather than *who* a person knows. An effective position classification program provides a basis for a fair and workable personnel operation that may reward good performance and penalize poor performance without fear or favor. In principle, such a position classification framework is open and objective.

One crucial question is, "How many classifications should there be?" Should the various jobs be distributed throughout a large number of separate grades and levels, or should they be compressed into a comparatively few broad categories? If the federal government's personnel system features fifteen grades with ten steps each, is this too many, too few, or about right?

The problem has no precise answer. There are no specific criteria defining narrow and broad classifications. To some, the federal government's fifteen grade levels may seem too numerous. To others, they may seem too few. We do know, however, that moving in either direction will yield both advantages and disadvantages.

A personnel system employing numerous narrow classifications organizes its job structures more precisely at each level. If there are two classifications for typists rather than one, better typists can be placed in the upper class and less capable typists can be put in the lower one. In principle, if typist A does better work than typist B, then A can be given a higher rating than B. It is further assumed that A will be given not only more money and more status, but also more difficult and more responsible assignments. In this sense, using many relatively narrow categories can be fairer to all concerned. Narrower categories also permit more extensive use of promotion as an incentive. More levels mean more possibilities for promotion, and at the same time, such promotional opportunities can be used as a sanction against those who fail to perform adequately.

Many public organizations have relatively few classification levels, particularly in the lower range of jobs. Postal workers, police officers, fire fighters, and others can usually move up only to a position of command. There are relatively few such positions in most organizations, so opportunities for promotion are limited.

Narrow and numerous job classifications also present distinct difficulties, however. The more classifications there are, the more personnel work the organization must do. Each classification must be carefully described and demarcated, and each job must be carefully plugged into the right classification. This results in a system that is not only costly but that can be cumbersome and complicated.

Personnel Bureaucracies

The Civil Service Reform Act of 1978 (CSRA) constitutes a major restructuring of federal civil service in the United States, and the Civil Service Commission (CSC), in particular. The functions once administered by the CSC (1883) are now allocated to three separate personnel bureaucracies. The Office of Personnel Management (OPM), as the central personnel agency directly answerable to the president, aids the president in establishing rules for administering civilian employment; advises the president on employment matters; executes, administers, and enforces civil service laws, rules, and regulations; coordinates research to enhance public personnel administration; and maintains and upgrades existing personnel practices such as examinations, executive development, and performance evaluations.

OPM has no authority over employee appeals. The appellate and quasi-judicial responsibilities previously implemented by the CSC are now vested in the Merit Systems Protection Board (MSPB). The MSPB decides most appeals and complaints, issues regulations regarding the nature and scope of its review, establishes time limits in which appeals must be settled, and orders corrective and disciplinary action against employees, departments, agencies if appropriate. As an independent federal agency, the MSPB is constituted as a bipartisan organization, consisting of three board members appointed by the president and confirmed by the Senate.

The CSRA's final structural change created the Federal Labor Relations Authority (FLRA). The FLRA determines appropriate units of representation, supervises labor organization elections, decides unfair labor practice cases, rules on negotiability issues, rules on exceptions to arbitration awards, mediates disputes, settles impasses, and prosecutes unfair labor practices.

Source: Joseph R. Grima, "Administrative and Civil Service Reform," The World Bank Group, http://www1.worldbank.org/publicsector/civilservice/individual.htm.

Use of numerous and narrow classifications may alleviate problems because those performing somewhat more demanding tasks can more easily receive recognition. This pattern can, for the same reasons, create tensions and prompt questions such as "Why should he be classified higher than I am when my job requires as much or more responsibility as his?"

The application of state and federal position classification plans is documented in the appropriate codes of laws. For example, in Texas, the position classification plan, the salary rates, and provisions in the General Appropriations Act apply to hourly, part-time, temporary, and full-time salaried employments in the state departments, agencies, or judicial entities specified.

The position classification system in the federal government is based on two fundamental principles:

- There should be substantially equal pay for substantially equal work.
- Variations in pay should be proportionate to substantial differences in the difficulty or responsibility of the job and in the qualifications required.

The classification of a civilian position consists of the position title, pay plan, series, and grade.

Classification decisions, whether made by managers or by human resources specialists, are based on the

- Nature and variety of the work
- Difficulty of the work
- Authority and responsibility exercised
- Extent of supervisory controls over the work
- Qualifications required to do the work

Assistant Professor Faculty Position

The University of Texas School of Social Work

The School of Social Work at the University of Texas at Arlington invites nominations and applications for a tenure-track faculty position for annual year (AY) 2004–2005. Applications from persons from underrepresented groups are especially encouraged.

Qualifications: A Doctorate in Social Work or related field and an MSW (Master in Social Work) with at least two years post-MSW full-time practice experience is required. ABDs (all but doctorates) may be considered. In addition, applicants for the faculty position must also have an identified area of scholarship and a strong commitment to funded research and publication.

Teaching Areas for Faculty Position: The ability to teach across the BSW, MSSW, and PhD levels is highly desirable, and the ability to teach in at least two areas of the curriculum is required. Emphasis will be placed on teaching Human Behavior and the Social Environment and/or Research.

The University of Texas at Arlington is a 100-year-old Institution with approximately 20,000 students. It has Carnegie classification of Doctoral/ Research University—Extensive. The second largest of fifteen institutions in the University of Texas System, it is located on a 388-acre campus in the heart of the Dallas/Fort Worth Metroplex. The School of Social Work enrolls approximately 204 students in the BSW program, 490 in its MSSW program, and 51 in its PhD program. In addition, the School houses the Community Services Clinic; The Center for Child Welfare; The Center for Research and Technology; The Community Services Development Center; and the Legislative Internship Program. The School also has a Dual Degree PhD Program in Comparative Social Policy with the Universidad Autonoma de Nuevo Leon in Monterrey, Mexico and a distance education MSSW program with West Texas A&M University in Canyon, Texas.

Review of applications will begin immediately and continue until the position is filled. E-mail or mail a letter of interest, curriculum vita, and names and full contact information for three references to:

Tom Smith
Ph.D. Professor and Search Committee Chair
The School of Social Work, The University of Texas at Arlington
Box 19129, Arlington, Texas 76019-0129
Telephone: 817-272-3964; Fax: 817-272-5227; E-mail: tsmith@uta.edu (See website: http://www2.uta.edu/ssw/ad.htm.)

Sources: "Assistant Professor Faculty Position" ad posted by the University of Texas at Arlington, School of Social Work at www.uta.edu/ssw/ad. Reprinted by permission of the University of Texas at Arlington, School of Social Work.

Summary

- The quests for *representativeness, neutral competence,* and *executive leadership* are norms of public personnel administration. Value, mediation, and core functions are factors affecting public personnel practices.
- Public organizations in the United States use two methods of establishing and operating personnel systems: (1) *political appointment* and *election* and (2) an objective determination of *merit.*
- The Pendleton Act of 1883 questioned the practice of *nonpolitical appointments,* embraced *egalitarianism,* and recognized *competence,* as determined by competitive examinations related to duties performed.
- The expansion of the merit system and development of public service are closely associated with the passage of legislation and presidential leadership.
- Key *merit system principles* are recruiting, selecting, and advancing employees on the basis of their abilities, knowledge, and skills; providing equitable and adequate compensation; training employees to assure high-quality performance; guaranteeing fairness for applicants and employees; and protecting against coercion for political purposes.

- Equality provides no guarantees; it only provides access. Affirmative action—without ways to achieve—is limited.
- The Plum Book and the Prune Book are designed to facilitate presidential transitions every four years. They combine the interests of partisan, policy, and system politics.
- *Test validity* for predicting on-the-job performance and other selection criteria pose problems for public agencies grounded in merit principles.
- A pure merit system for all public service appointments would be grounded in competition based on merit rules. However, no administration functions on a pure merit system.
- Two basic criteria for promotion are *seniority* and *merit.*
- Training is receiving increasing attention. A fast-moving and fast-changing society exhibits a high need for wide-ranging and high-level skills.
- Federal, state, and local governments employ 20,392,000 wage and salary workers. Of this national distribution, local government units employ 53.5 percent, or 10,908,000, workers. State governments employ 6,102,000, or 30.0 percent. The federal, or national, government hires 3,381,000, or 16.5 percent, of America's government employees.
- A promotion is the change of an employee to a position of a higher grade level within the same job classification system and pay schedule, or a position with a higher rate of basic pay in a different job classification system and pay schedule.
- Remuneration for government employment is based on position rather than performance. Good performance originates from an employee's sense of duty, not from pay.
- The average salary for all occupations in the federal government in 2007 was $65,463.
- The federal government hires people with nearly every level of education and experience—from high school students with no experience to PhD's with established careers. The qualifications needed for each job are described in detail in the vacancy announcements that advertise job openings.
- Private contractors provide public services for a price. Civil servants labor for a wage. Drawing

lines between public and private may be especially difficult in such cases.
- Representative bureaucracy is a basic policy goal that public personnel managers pursue. A separate but related policy choice is whether to pursue that goal *passively* or *actively.* A passive strategy is *equal opportunity.* An active strategy is *affirmative action.*
- The importance of affirmative action is declining because: (1) no strong consensus exists favoring affirmative action; (2) U.S. Supreme Court decisions regarding affirmative action are nonlinear; and (3) executive leadership, retrenchment, and productivity take priority over affirmative action programs in government agencies.
- Public sector performance management must be task-oriented, participative, and developmental.
- The demographics of the federal, state, and local workforces are changing.
- The average age of federal civilian nonpostal employees is 46.9 years; the average length of service is 16.5 years. About 66.3 percent of civilian employees have bachelor or higher degrees; 52.9 percent are men; 47.1 percent are women; 25.0 percent are minorities; and 6.0 percent are disabled. Within the overall workforce, 17.5 percent are black, 7.5 percent Hispanic, 6.2 percent Asian–Pacific Islander, and 2.2 percent American Indian–Alaskan natives.
- The premise underlying *position classification* schemes is that different positions require varying degrees of ability and impose varying amounts of responsibility.
- The position description is a record of duties assigned to an individual position in a class. It compares positions to ensure uniformity of classification and describes assigned duties and responsibilities.
- Public personnel administration, more than anything else, is a process encompassing *procedures, rules,* and *regulations.*
- The recruitment, selection, and promotion phases are grounded in *legislation* and *law,* reflecting the values of accountability and responsiveness to the public.

VIDEOS AND FILMS

Public Administration in Action

Equal Opportunity
In the Heat of the Night [1966]
A small Mississippi town's small-minded police chief (Rod Steiger) arrests a black suspect (Sidney Poitier) at the train station. The suspect soon reveals himself to be a homicide detective from Philadelphia. [109 min]

Affirmative Action
Affirmative action under fire: *Black Teacher, White Teacher: When Is It Reverse Discrimination?* [1999]. Princeton, NJ: Films for the Humanities & Sciences. Originally broadcast as a segment of the ABC television program *Nightline*. Host, Cokie Roberts. [22 min]

Affirmative Action
Beyond Black and White: Affirmative Action in America [2000]
Princeton, NJ: Films for the Humanities & Sciences. All sides in this debate say that they believe in the constitutional right to equality regarding race, creed, and sex. Very different interpretations emerge to what that means. Panel experts include Charles Ogletree, Ward Connerly, Ann Coulter, Ann F. Lewis. [58 min]

Affirmative Action
Legislating Morality: Affirmative Action and the Burden of History [1996]
Princeton, NJ: Films for the Humanities & Sciences. Explores whether affirmative action promotes racial balance, or fights discrimination of the past with reverse discrimination in the present. [29 min]

Race Relations
Understanding Race [1999]
Princeton, NJ: Films for the Humanities & Sciences. Examines the history and power of the artificial distinction called "race," viewing it within historical, scientific, and cultural contexts. Learning Channel video broadcast. [52 min]

Affirmative Action
Affirmative Action: The History of an Idea [1996]
Princeton, NJ: Films for the Humanities & Sciences. Explores historical roots of affirmative action and the current debate over its usefulness. Ben Wattenberg, host. Panel includes Stanley Fish, Dinesh D'Souza. [56 min]

Case Study

Is Equality for Women at VMI Real?

The military is a classic example of government bureaucracy—it includes hierarchy, a pyramidal form, task specialization, spheres of competence, norms of conduct, and paperwork. West Point, Annapolis, and Colorado Springs assimilated women into their corps decades ago. VMI, or Virginia Military Academy, did not. U.S. *Supreme Court Justice Ruth Bader Ginsburg, was "skeptical" about this and VMI was under "scrutiny."*

The history of American freedom is, in no small measure, the history of procedure.

—*Felix Frankfurter*
late U.S. Supreme Court Justice

Seven members of the U.S. Supreme Court, in *United States v. Virginia* (1996), "struck a blow" for equal opportunity for women at single-sex, government-funded military colleges. The all-male Virginia Military Institute (VMI), the nation's oldest military college, was declared open to female applicants. "Save the Males" was the plea of VMI leaders and alumni who wanted to keep VMI segregated by sex.

Regardless of sex, race, or disability, every citizen has the right to apply to a public college. The ideology of equal opportunity is as American as apple pie; affirmative action plans and programs implement equal opportunity. The tenets of diversity, representativeness, competence, and a merit system are matters of consequence in this regard.

The military is a classic example of a government bureaucracy. Hierarchy, a pyramidal form, task specialization, spheres of competence, norms of conduct, and paperwork all characterize military organizations. West Point and Annapolis integrated women into their corps decades ago. When would it happen at VMI?

Justice Ruth Bader Ginsburg Writes the Decision

Writing the 7–1 decision (one Justice recused himself), Justice Ginsburg concluded: "There is no reason to believe that the admission of women . . . would destroy" VMI.[1] The Court affirmed that VMI had violated the Equal Protection Clause. Justice Clarence Thomas did not participate in the decision because his son, Jamal, attended VMI at the time. Justice Antonin Scalia was the lone dissenter. The High Court opined that the state-supported VMI's all-male policy violated women's constitutional right to equal protection.

The Virginia Military Institute (VMI) was established in 1816 as one of three Virginia state military posts. During that era, VMI was known as the Lexington Arsenal. VMI, the emerging military bureaucracy of the nineteenth century, stored arms for Western Virginia. Two decades later, the arsenal emerged as a military college.

George C. Marshall, VMI class of 1901, five-star General of the Army, author of the Marshall Plan, winner of the 1953 Nobel Prize for Peace, was a VMI citizen-soldier.

In 1839, VMI was established as the nation's first state-supported military college. Union troops shelled and burned the Institute in 1864. VMI men fought in World War I, World War II, Korea, Vietnam, Grenada, Panama, and Operation Desert Storm. VMI remained all-male from its founding.

As the late Justice Felix Frankfurter stated, "The history of American freedom is, in no small measure, the history of procedure." In 1990, a complaint was filed with the United States Attorney General, and the United States then sued the Commonwealth of Virginia and VMI. The allegation was that VMI's all-male admissions policy violated the Equal Protection Clause of the Fourteenth Amendment.

The federal courts demanded that the state of Virginia remedy the equal protection violation. A six-day trial ended when the court ruled that VMI could: (1) admit women to the corps of cadets, (2) abandon state support and continue its admissions policy as a private institution, or (3) establish parallel institutions or programs. The Commonwealth created the Virginia Women's Institute for Leadership (VWIL) at nearby Mary Baldwin College as a parallel program for women. VWIL was designed to achieve the same end results as VMI—but by different means. VMI uses the adversative model of education, while VWIL used the cooperative model. The VWIL program did not adhere to the grueling rat line and spartan barracks life typified by the VMI culture.

VWIL then proposed a Cooperative Confidence Building Program. The Mary Baldwin program included an ad hoc physical training program and a nonmilitary VWIL House. But the intangibles were also important. VMI had a $131 million endowment and more than 150 years of tradition, history, and alumni support. Mary Baldwin College had a less illustrious history and a $19 million endowment. Six years after the VMI litigation commenced, the U.S. Supreme Court decided the merits of the VMI-VWIL solution. The VWIL program at Mary Baldwin College did not remedy the violation; in fact, Ginsburg wrote, the VWIL program was "significantly unequal" and a "pale shadow" of VMI.

Levels of Scrutiny

The Equal Protection Clause exists to prohibit invidious discrimination—arbitrary, capricious, and unjust behavior against a protected group. Equal protection brings on debates about reverse discrimination, hate crimes, and gay rights. The courts employ a variety of judicial tests called *levels of scrutiny* to evaluate equal protection cases. The levels of scrutiny are rational basis, intermediate scrutiny, and strict scrutiny.

Rational basis analysis is the most lenient level of scrutiny. For example, the streets are made for automobile traffic—not as sleeping grounds for homeless people—so a court would not be likely to find that a homeless person was discriminated against when forced to sleep elsewhere. Intermediate scrutiny comes into play when the government discriminates on the basis of certain suspect classifications such as gender or illegitimate birth; the court would scrutinize such an action carefully. Strict scrutiny comes into play when the government discriminates on the basis of highly suspect classifications such as race or national origin. The government would have to have a very compelling reason to overcome strict scrutiny.

Justice Ginsburg announced a new standard of equal protection review of gender classification—skeptical scrutiny. Skeptical scrutiny is distinguished from strict scrutiny, the equal protection standard applied to race classifications. Skeptical scrutiny favors the female sex only. It affords women (as a class) a degree of legal protection not available to any other group in American society.[2]

Under skeptical scrutiny, no qualified individual can be denied an opportunity on the basis of his or her sex. Ginsburg utilized the standard of intermediate scrutiny—concluding that Virginia provided no evidence of a substantial interest in diversity or equal opportunity for women historically.

In response to the Supreme Court decision against VMI, Janet Gallagher, director of the American Civil Liberties Union's (ACLU's) Women's Rights Project, said, "The decision is a historic blow to government-sanctioned discrimination against women." Eleanor Smeal, President of the Feminist Majority Foundations, stated, "At last, 'separate but equal' for women and girls in military academies goes to the dustbin of history—where it belongs."[3] The National Organization for Women (NOW) National Secretary, Karen Johnson, a retired U.S. Air Force lieutenant colonel, stated, "Finally, we have an affirmation that the qualities important for military leaders—integrity, tenacity and bravery—have nothing to do with a person's sex."[4]

Theodore Olsen argued the case before the Supreme Court on behalf of VMI. According to Olsen, the VMI style of education benefits certain young males who cannot do as well in a coeducational environment. The boot-camp, uniquely adversarial-style education builds confidence in these males. If even a few women are admitted, the benefits—the uniqueness—of VMI would largely be destroyed. Accommodating women would force VMI cadets to respect personal privacy. Abuse and harrassment by upperclassmen toward underclassmen, considered valuable to the VMI experience, might be viewed as sexual harassment if applied to female cadets.

Not all women agreed with Ginsburg's opinion. Phyllis Schlafly, President of Eagle Forum, a conservative group, opined: "Feminists want to gender-neutralize society so they can intimidate and control men. The feminists' long-time, self-proclaimed goal is an androgynous society. Repudiating constitutional intent, history, tradition, and human nature, they seek to forbid us, in public or private life, to recognize the differences between men and women."[5] Anita K. Blair, General Counsel of the Independent Women's Forum and a member of the VMI Board of Directors, stated, "If women as a class had disapproved of VMI's all-male status, they could easily have caused the state legislature to change it or even stop funding VMI."[6]

VMI Considers Privatizing

VMI leaders and alumni considered going private to preserve the school's 157-year all-male tradition. The Court decision directed VMI to admit women or forfeit state funding; a private institution can, of course, be all-male or all-female. VMI spent $14 million defending its all-male policy. "Why must a school with a 157-year-old tradition of leadership and excellence in the education of young men be sacrificed on another altar of gender rights and political correctness?" asked Michael Brook, a VMI board member.[7]

Josiah Bunting, VMI Superintendent, stated that he could make ten phone calls to wealthy alumni and raise millions to convert VMI to private status. However, privatizing VMI was not a very good option. The state of Virginia owns the VMI campus and its buildings. The property value was $137 million in 1995. VMI would have to increase its endowment to $180 million just to go private.

The annual revenue provided by the state of Virginia—$10 million—would also have to be accounted for from private sources. The Virginia General Assembly would need to approve any VMI privatization, and VMI would have acquired the real estate and buildings at full-market value. "If the state just handed VMI over to a private foundation, the state would be participating in the discrimination (against women) by directly supporting it," according to Allen Ides, a Washington and Lee University law professor.[8]

On September 21, 1996, VMI announced that, in a 9–8 vote, the Board of Visitors had decided that VMI should admit women. VMI formed the Coeducation Group—divided into seven subcommittees studying the challenges associated with coeducation. VMI alumni, faculty, staff, cadets, and Board of Visitors members were subcommittee members. They visited other coeducational colleges to learn about the mistakes that had been made in their transitions to coeducation.

Some of the gender challenges at VMI were unique:

- Barracks are the center of corps activities and crucial to the VMI experience. All cadets are required to live in barracks during their years at VMI. Barracks life, however, is characterized by a total lack of privacy.
- Physical training and stress are commonplace at VMI. Cadets must complete a one-and-one-half-mile run in twelve minutes, sixty sit-ups in two minutes, and five pull-ups. All cadets undergo identical physical training and performance evaluations.
- The adversarial system of education, described as both doubting and confrontational, permeates VMI's education. Freshmen "Rats" regularly endure workouts, sweat parties, flaming, and Rat-challenge activities. Upperclass cadets have a free hand in initiating Rats to life at VMI.

Rats are treated like the lowest creatures on earth. The purpose of this treatment is to build the individual Rat into a citizen-soldier. More than 20 percent of freshmen drop out.

However, some women did well at VMI. "Female VMI cadets measure up and excel," reported a 2000 story in the Associated Press. Women constituted less than 5 percent of the student body—53 females among the 1,200 cadets at VMI. In the fall of 2000, all of VMI's classes were coeducational for the first time. Erin Claunch broke a gender barrier by becoming the first woman to rise to battalion commander—the second-highest military post.

"I just wanted to blend in and be a good cadet," said Claunch, who led half of the 1,200-member cadet corps during her senior year.[9]

The 5-foot-4, 125-pound Claunch outperformed men on VMI's stringent physical fitness requirements. "Not a day goes by that you don't read something about how there should be changes in certain standards for men and women," Superintendent Bunting noted. "But this young woman and the others in her class said, 'Judge us as cadets and recognize us if we achieve in your system.' And she has."[10]

According to Claunch, she did not experience sexual harassment or discrimination. Rumors of harassment, she admitted, made her nervous. In 1999, VMI's top cadet was dismissed for allegedly demanding sex from female cadets.

Matters of Consequence

Diversity, equality, representativeness, competence, affirmative action, and merit system tenets are matters of consequence in the case *United States v. Virginia*. A culture that has not been diverse at any time in its 157-year history is unlikely to become so on its own volition. Women account for more than half of the United States population and half of U.S. college students. Once women were permitted to attend, they mastered the merit system skills at VMI.

Equal opportunity is essentially a passive concept. As a passive strategy, equal opportunity simply implies nondiscrimination. Equal opportunity and nondiscrimination are passive factors in policy making. They rely on families, schools, and the forces of good will in society to abolish stereotypes and prejudices. The courts are a catalyst, too.

Affirmative action is an active strategy. It is intended to ensure—even implement—guarantees of equal opportunity. At VMI, once equal opportunity was accepted, women benefited from affirmative action procedures. The history of American freedom is, in no small measure, the history of procedure.

Questions and Instructions

1. Feminists, according to conservatives, want to redistribute power from the "dominant" class (the male patriarchal system) to the "subordinate" class (nominally women, but actually only the feminists). What data support this division—that men are the "dominant" class, women the "subordinate" class?

2. According to conservatives, feminists call for adherence to the "unreasonable woman" rule, allowing the victim rather than the law to define the offense. Explain.

3. Skeptical scrutiny provides an unprecedented degree of legal protection to individuals—without

regard to the needs of society or civilizations itself. Explain this assertion in reference to the VMI case.

4. Theodore Olsen, representing VMI before the Supreme Court, argued that the VMI style of education (adversative boot-camp methods) benefits certain males who do not compete as well in coed college settings. What do you think this statement means?

5. VMI's adversative system of education is described as both "doubting" and "confrontational." How can this be so? Explain.

6. Intermediate scrutiny recognizes interference or discrimination on the basis of suspect classifications—sex or illegitimate birth, for example. Government action in such a case must be no more extensive than necessary. Explain how this statement applies in the VMI case study.

7. Equality provides no guarantees; it only provides access. Affirmative action—without pathways to achievement—is limited. Even when denials to access based on sex no longer exist, achievement may remain a challenge. Explain this from the perspective of women attending VMI.

8. The U.S. Supreme Court has a nonlinear record regarding affirmative action–related cases. No strong consensus exists, and the constitutional stalemate is continuing. How did the internal demands of VMI prompt new breakthroughs—if there were any? Explain.

9. Should admittance to VMI be based on the criteria of class—but not sex or race? How do class—and/or sex—discriminations matter? Explain.

10. Justice Felix Frankfurter said, "The history of American freedom is, in no small measure, the history of procedure." Explain and illustrate.

Insights-Issues/Is Equality for Women at VMI Real?

Clearly and briefly describe and illustrate the following concepts and issues. Interpret the word *role* as meaning impacts, applications, importance, effects and/or illustrations of certain facts, concerns, or issues from the case study.

1. Role of skeptical scrutiny for providing legal remedies to VMI female applicants.

2. Role of the quests for representativeness and neutral competence for admitting women to VMI.

3. Role of equal opportunity and/or affirmative action for admitting women to VMI.

4. Roles of the "dominant class" (males) and the "subordinate class" (females) in regard to equality at VMI.

5. Roles of Justice Ruth Bader Ginsburg, single-sex colleges, and gender classifications in the VMI case.

Notes

1. "VMI Must Admit Women, Supreme Court Rules; Decision Also Likely to Affect Citadel," June 26, 1996, http://www.cnn.com/US/9606/26/scotus .vmi.update/.

2. Anita K. Blair, "*United States v. Virginia:* The New and Improved Equal Protection Clause," Spring 1997, The Federalist Society, 2001, http://www.fed-soc-org/Publications/ practicegroupnewsletters/ civilrights/cr010203 .htm.

3. "U.S. Supreme Court Overturns VMI's All-Male Policy: ACLU Says Ruling Ends Chapter in Sex Discrimination," June 26, 1996; http://www.aclu .org/news/n062696a.html.

4. "NOW Leaders call Supreme Court Decision on VMI a 'Mixed Bag' Victory," June 26, 1996, http://www.now.org/press/06-96/06-26-96 .html.

5. "Feminist Assault on Reasonableness," *The Phyllis Schafly Report* 30, no. 4 (December 1996).

6. Blair, "*United States v. Virginia.*"

7. "The VMI Decision: VMI Considering Going Private," *Charleston News & Courier,* June 28, 1996, http://www.charleston.net/news/citadel/ vmi28.html.

8. Ibid.

9. Kia Shant'e Breaux, "Female VMI Cadets Measure Up and Excel," *Detroit News,* April 16, 2000. http://detnews.com/2000/nation/0004/16/ all-37533.htm.

10. Ibid.

Sources

"Equal Protection of Law and Other Concepts Related to Equality, Justice and Fairness," February 12, 2001, http://faculty.ncwc.edu/toconnor/325/325lect03.htm; "Exclusionary Policies," January 17, 1996 transcript, http://www.pbs.org/newshour/bb/law/vmi_1-17b. html; Colleen M. McFeely, "Letters to the Editor," *Washington & Lee University Law News*, 24, no. 3 (September 3, 1996): 3–4, http://www.wlu.edu/~lawnews/vol24no3-page3 .html; "One More Male Bastion Bites the Dust, Women Must be Admitted to All-Male Virginia Military Institute," The Feminist Majority Foundation and New Media Publishing, Vol. 8, No. 2 (1996), http://www.feminist .org/research/report/82_eleven.html; Tracy "Archie" Taylor, "VMI Decision '96," *Washington & Lee University Law News* 24, no. 4 (October 22, 1996): 4–7, http://www.wlu.edu/lawnews/vol24no4-page4.html; "VMI Must Give Up State Funds to Stay All-Male," June 27, 1996, http://centralohio thesource .net/Files3/9606279.html; "Top VMI Cadet Dismissed for Allegedly Demanding Sex," *Joplin Globe* (online edition), June 27, 1999, http://www.joplinglobe .com/archives/1999/990627/natnwrld/story1.html.

Notes

1. Quoted in John Franklin Campbell, *The Foreign Affairs Fudge Factory* (New York: Basic Books, 1971), pp. 139–140.

2. *Ibid.,* p. 47.

3. Herbert Kaufman, "Emerging Conflicts in the Doctrines of Public Administration," *American Political Science Review* 50 (December 1956): 1057–1073.

4. Donald E. Klingner and John Nalbandian, *Public Personnel Management: Contexts and Strategies* (Englewood Cliffs, NJ: Prentice-Hall, 1985).

5. James E. Leidlein, "In Search of Merit: A Practitioner's Comments on 'The Staffing Function in Illinois State Government after Rutan' and 'Curbing Patronage Without Paperasserie,'" *Public Administration Review* 53, no. 4 (July–August 1993): 391–392.

6. Quoted in Paul Van Riper, *History of the United States Civil Service* (New York: Harper & Row, 1958), p. 36.

7. Steven W. Hays and T. Zane Reeves, *Personnel Management in the Public Sector* (Boston: Allyn and Bacon, 1984), p. 16.

8. Cited in Patrick V. Murphy, *The Criminal Justice System in Crisis* (Syracuse, NY: Maxwell School of Citizenship and Affairs, 1972).

9. The World Bank Group, "Administrative & Civil Service Reform," http://www1 .worldbank.org/publicsector/civilservice/ recruitment.htm.

10. Ibid.

11. "The Values We Live By: What Americans Want from Welfare Reform," *Spectrum: The Journal of State Government* 70, no. 3 (Summer 1997): 5–6.

12. James E. Brennan, "Merit Pay: Balance the Old Rich and the New Poor," *Personnel Journal* 64, no. 5 (May 1985): 82–85.

13. Stephen Barr, "Expectations of Promotion Are Not So Great, Study Finds," *Washington Post,* February 21, 2002, p. B2.

14. The World Bank Group, "Administrative & Civil Service Reform."

15. U.S. Merit Systems Protection Board, *Attracting Quality Graduates to the Federal Government: A View of College Recruiting* (June 1988), p. vii.

16. The Hudson Institute, *Civil Service 2000, A Report Prepared for the U.S. Office of Personnel Management* (June 1988), p. 10.

17. *The Washington Times,* May 25, 1989, p. B5.

18. Congressional Budget Office, *Characteristics and Pay of Federal Civilian Employees* (Washington, DC: CBO, March 2007), pp. 3–7.

19. Ralph C. Chandler and Jack C. Plano, *The Public Administration Dictionary* (New York: John Wiley & Sons, 1982), p. 246.

20. Klingner and Nalbandian, *Public Personnel Management,* pp. 62–69.

21. David H. Rosenbloom, "The Declining Salience of Affirmative Action in Federal Personnel Management," *Review of Public Personnel Administration* 4 (Summer 1984): 202–205, 248–249.

22. Raymond W. Mack, "Whose Affirmative Action?" *Society* 33, no. 3 (March–April 1996): 41–44.

23. Nancy Stein, "Questions and Answers about Affirmative Action," *Social Justice* 22, no. 3 (Fall 1995): 45–53.

24. "The Future of Affirmative Action: President Clinton's Remarks," *Congressional Digest* 75, nos. 6–7 (June–July 1996): 166–169.

25. Ann Crittenden, "Quotas for Good Old Boys," *Wall Street Journal,* June 14, 1995, p. A18.

26. Paul Starr, "Civil Reconstruction: What to Do Without Affirmative Action," *The American Prospect,* no. 8 (Winter 1992): 7–14.

27. *Working for America: A Federal Employee Survey* (Washington, DC: U.S. Merit Systems Protection Board, 1990).

Public Sector Labor-Management Relations

Chapter Highlights

A Social-Work Model of Unionism

Decline, Transformation, or Reformation?

Union Members in 2007

State and Local Government Labor Issues

Alternatives for Avoiding a Work Stoppage

Collective Bargaining for Federal Employees

Conflicts in State Civil Service and Collective
Bargaining Systems

Zero-Sum versus One-Ten Power Games?

Radical Individualism and Labor Unions

Public Sector Labor Law Impacts

Reasons for Union Prominence

Summary

The Collective Bargaining Hodgepodge

American unions may have the best songs, but for decades, management has held the best cards. Labor rights of Americans lag behind those of other nations. The legal bottom line varies widely in local, state, and federal government labor relations and collective bargaining.

Support for unions is growing, according to a poll commissioned by the Associated Press. The poll showed that 51 percent of women under age 65, 48 percent of men under age 65, and 59 percent of adults aged 18 to 34 were more pro-union than adults over 65 (38 percent). The importance of protecting workplace rights is increasingly recognized.

A hodgepodge of statutes, ordinances, attorney general's opinions, executive orders, and court decisions govern worker rights in the public sector. Not even federal government employees are regulated by a single policy governing labor-management relations.

Until 1967, public sector workers were denied the right to form and join unions. The power of a government to implement the terms and conditions of employment for government workers was absolute. However, federal courts in 1967 gave the First Amendment freedom-of-association clause priority over government sovereignty claims. The courts protected the constitutional right of public employees to organize and join unions, discarding the sovereignty doctrine in the process.

The great majority of federal employees were granted unionization and collective bargaining rights under the Civil Service Reform Act and Postal Reorganization Act. State and local labor relations laws reflect the diversity of the fifty states. The mid-1970s witnessed debates on national labor legislation for state and local government employees. However, agreements to standardize labor relations in the states never materialized. More than 110 separate state statutes govern public sector labor relations. Numerous local ordinances, court decisions, attorney general's opinions, and executive orders augment the statutes.

Unionization in government usually occurs along professional lines. Public education is the largest public employer by far at the state and local levels; college and university professors initiated collective bargaining in 1967. Major faculty unions include the National Education Association (NEA), American Federation of Teachers (AFT), and American Association of University Professors (AAUP). Fire fighters are the most highly organized of municipal employees. The large majority belong to the International Association of Firefighters (IAFF). Health care, transit workers, and prison workers offer prospects for future government union growth.

State labor legislation ranges from a single comprehensive statute providing coverage to all public employees (Iowa) to coverage for fire fighters only (Wyoming) to the complete outlawing of collective bargaining (North Carolina). Wisconsin was the first state (1959) to establish collective bargaining rights for local government employees. Legislation or related policies mandate bargaining, meeting, or conferring with at least one group of public workers in forty-two states. State legislatures enacted most of the bargaining laws from the mid-1960s through the mid-1970s.

The District of Columbia and twenty-nine states provide bargaining coverage by statute for all major employee groups. This coverage may be realized through a single comprehensive public employee relations policy or through separate policies for different functions. "Bargaining laws are the single most important factor in determining the tone and character of public employer-employee relationships in state and local government," writes Richard C. Kearney. States sponsoring comprehensive bargaining laws are industrialized, urbanized, and relatively affluent jurisdictions.

Arizona, Arkansas, Colorado, Louisiana, Mississippi, North Carolina, South Carolina, and Virginia permit no formal collective bargaining. In these states, fire fighters and teachers benefit from some form of bilateral relations for one or more employee groups. At the other end of the spectrum, California, Connecticut, Delaware, Florida, Hawaii, Illinois, Massachusetts, Michigan, New Mexico, New York, Ohio, and Rhode Island have comprehensive collective bargaining laws. Since the 1970s, only Illinois, Ohio, and New Mexico have passed major collective bargaining laws.

The comprehensive-bargaining states catalog the following provisions in labor-management relations legislation:

1. Employee rights
2. Employer rights
3. Administrative agency (or machinery for administering public sector labor relations)
4. Unit determination
5. Recognition procedures
6. Scope of bargaining
7. Impasse resolution procedures (as strikes are prohibited or severely restricted)
8. Union security (or options for securing a union as the exclusive representative of a bargaining unit): closed shop, union shop, agency shop, fair share, dues checkoff, or maintenance of membership
9. Unfair labor practices (ULPs) of both employers and unions

The tables in this section outline labor-management essentials of bargaining laws in the states. The first table lists whether each state has bargaining legislation in place for state public employees, local government workers, police officers, fire fighters, and K–12 public school teachers. The second relates bargaining status to state political ideology and union density.

Sources

Richard C. Kearney, *Labor Relations in the Public Sector*, 4th ed. (New York: Taylor and Francis, 2009). See chapter 3, "The Legal Environment of Public Sector Labor Relations"; "Support for Unions Growing While a Majority of Workers Want More Protection of Workplace Rights, According to Labor Day Polls (September 1, 2001)," *Labor Research Association (LRA) Online*, September 1, 2001, http://www.lraonline.org/labor.php. See also http://www.workinglife.org.

State Bargaining Status, 2007
(X = Collective Bargaining Provisions; Y = Meet and Confer Provisions)

State	State	Local	Police	Fire Fighters	K–12 Teachers
Alabama	—	Y	—	Y	—
Alaska	X	X	X	X	X
Arizona	—	—	—	—	—
Arkansas	—	—	—	—	—
California	Y	Y[1]	Y[1]	Y[1]	X
Colorado	X[3]	—	—	—	—
Connecticut	X	X	X	X	X
Delaware	X	X[1]	X	X	X
Florida	X	X[1]	X	X	X
Georgia	—	—	—	X	—
Hawaii	X	X	X	X	X
Idaho	—	—	—	X	X
Illinois	X	X	X	X	X
Indiana	—	—	—	—	X
Iowa	X	X	X	X	X
Kansas	Y	Y[1]	Y[1]	Y[1]	X
Kentucky	—	—	X	X	—
Louisiana	—	—	—	—	—
Maine	X	X	X	X	X
Maryland	X	X[2]	—	—	X
Massachusetts	X	X	X	X	X
Michigan	X	X	X	X	X
Minnesota	X	X	X	X	X
Mississippi	—	—	—	—	—
Missouri	X[4]	X	X	X	X
Montana	X	X	X	X	X
Nebraska	X	X	X	X	Y
Nevada	—	X	X	X	X
New Hampshire	X	X	X	X	X
New Jersey	X	X	X	X	X
New Mexico	X[3]	X	X	X	X
New York	X	X	X	X	X
North Carolina	—	—	—	—	—
North Dakota	Y[2]	Y[2]	Y[2]	Y[2]	X
Ohio	X	X	X	X	X
Oklahoma	—	X	X	X	X
Oregon	X	X[1]	X	X	X
Pennsylvania	X	X	X	X	X
Rhode Island	X	X	X	X	X
South Carolina	—	—	—	—	—
South Dakota	X	X	X	X	X
Tennessee	—	—	—	—	X

continued

State Bargaining Status, 2007, *continued*

State	State	Local	Police	Fire Fighters	K–12 Teachers
Texas	—	—	X[1]	X[1]	—
Utah	—	—	—	—	X
Vermont	X	X	X	X	X
Virginia	—	—	—	—	—
Washington	X	X	X	X	X
West Virginia	Y[2]	Y[2]	Y[2]	Y[2]	Y[2]
Wisconsin	X	X	X	X	X
Wyoming	—	—	—	X	—

[1]Local option permitted.

[2]Meet and confer established by attorney general opinion.

[3]Collective bargaining established through executive order.

[4]Court-ordered collective bargaining.

Source: Richard C. Kearney, *Labor Relations in the Public Sector,* 4th ed. (New York: Taylor and Francis, 2009).

Bargaining Status, Political Ideology, and Union Density, 2006

State	State Collective Bargaining Law	Local Bargaining Rights	State Political Ideology Score*	State Union Density**
Alabama	—	Local Gov't	23.1	28.9
Alaska	X	All	15.6	49.2
Arizona	—	None	13	24.6
Arkansas	—	None	24	10.3
California	X	All	2.6	52.6
Colorado	X[3]	None	8.6	22.8
Connecticut	X	All	0.9	59
Delaware	X	All	3.7	39.2
Florida	X	All	11.1	22.6
Georgia	—	MARTA/Fire Fighters	18.5	9.6
Hawaii	X	All	0	55.1
Idaho	—	Teachers/Fire Fighters	21.7	15
Illinois	X	All	6.9	49.5
Indiana	—	Teachers	19.2	27.8
Iowa	X	All	15.4	30.9
Kansas	Y	All[2]	22.1	19.4
Kentucky	—	Police/Fire Fighters	17.5	16.3
Louisiana	—	None	23.7	15.5
Maine	X	All	8.4	46.3
Maryland	X	Education/Park Police/ Local Gov't	4.4	31.5
Massachusetts	X	All	−3.5	59.1

continued

Bargaining Status, Political Ideology, and Union Density, 2006, *continued*

State	State Collective Bargaining Law	Local Bargaining Rights	State Political Ideology Score[*]	State Union Density[**]
Michigan	X	All	10.9	55.8
Minnesota	X	All	8.2	52.1
Mississippi	—	None	30.2	12.2
Missouri	X[4]	All[4]	16.5	20.3
Montana	X	All	18.9	34.8
Nebraska	X	All	20.7	25.5
Nevada	—	All	16.3	32.9
New Hampshire	X	All	7.4	44.9
New Jersey	X	All	2.4	64.4
New Mexico	X[3]	All	8.8	17
New York	X	All	1.5	68.8
North Carolina	—	None	19.6	10.8
North Dakota	Y[2]	Teachers/All Local Gov't[2]	26.9	17.3
Ohio	X	All	14.3	43.5
Oklahoma	—	All	26.7	18.7
Oregon	X	All	9.1	48.5
Pennsylvania	X	All	11.5	51
Rhode Island	X	All	2.6	65.5
South Carolina	—	None	22.2	8.2
South Dakota	X	All	25	21.1
Tennessee	—	Teachers	21.6	21.7
Texas	—	Police/Fire Fighters	22.1	15.5
Utah	—	Teachers	24.9	18
Vermont	X	All	−8	40.7
Virginia	—	None	14.5	8.4
Washington	X	All	9	56.3
West Virginia	Y[2]	All[2]	14.1	30
Wisconsin	X	All	14.4	53.6
Wyoming	—	Fire Fighters	11.7	15.6

[*]Political ideology

Method of calculation: pooled raw data from CBS News/*New York Times* polls

Range of scores: a score of higher positive numerical value indicates increased conservative ideology, a score of zero indicates moderate ideology, a score of negative numerical value indicates liberal ideology. These scores have been reformatted from the original source.

Source: Correction for Appendix data to Chapter 12 of *Public Opinion in State Politics,* Jeffrey Cohen (2006). http://mypage.iu.edu/~wright1/CorrectAppendixTable12.1.txt.

[**]Union density is the percent of state and local employees that belong to unions.

Source: Barry T. Hirsch and David A. Macpherson, "Union Membership and Coverage Database from the Current Population Survey," 2007, http://unionstats.gsu.edu.

[1]Local option permitted.

[2]Meet and confer.

[3]Collective bargaining granted through executive order.

[4]Collective bargaining through court decision.

A Social-Work Model of Unionism

U.S. organized labor has never opposed American capitalism. In that, at least, labor leaders maintain an anti-ideological orientation. Labor leaders view themselves as a powerful interest group in a pluralistic U.S. society; in their view, unions serve the interests of dues-paying members. They rarely form alliances with social movements where rights and freedoms extend beyond their legal dimension.

The year 1973, considered a crossroads, signified the end of thirty-five years of U.S. economic dominance, during which Americans enjoyed the highest living standards in the world. After this time, union bargainers could no longer depend on the growth and stability of the nation's economy to justify their wage and benefits demands. A new global megastate replaced, in part, the nation-state. The new reliance on transnational capital and the development of networks outside the frameworks of nation-states forged close-knit, autonomous economic entities.

"At stake in labor's decline," writes Stanley Aronowitz, "is, in addition to its economic character, nothing less than the political and social climate of American society. That we have growing inequality in America—income differences are greater than in any advanced industrial society—may be ascribed mainly to the erosion of trade union power rather than to some mysterious market mechanism."[1] The old social compact was no longer in force—a compact that promoted close wage and price regulation along with high levels of mass personal and social consumption. A kind of social-work model of unionism replaced the more militant labor versions. The demise of labor unions as democratic institutions is a crucial factor, too. The absence of a genuine sovereignty for rank-and-file members contradicts the basic rationale for unions.

The viability of public sector unions depends on this historical context. Organized labor, in the past, carried out mass strikes and elections to gain recognition. Unions advanced race and gender demands, and union leadership included blacks and women. Unions engaged in solidarity struggles with other workers. They were committed to civil rights. However, union membership and power in the private sector declined as the corporate offensive accelerated. The organization of public employees in the 1960s and early 1970s was the exception to the ineffectiveness of private sector union activities.

Public sector union leaders and employees are challenged as never before. They must convince taxpayers of the justice of their position and their economic worth. The larger electorate is inundated with high taxes and anti-welfare propaganda. But public sector labor executives rarely educate the citizenry with broader understandings of the economy and portraits of the country's future. Picket lines can educate taxpayers and consumers. Individualism within the movement and worldwide economic dynamics waylay effective union responses. Organized labor movements often appear "disarmed, outflanked, and bewildered" by the challenges of these times.

Unionization is greater in the public sector, worldwide, than in the private sector. The United States fits that pattern—and increasingly so. Differences in collective bargaining coverage between the public and private sectors are more evident in the United States than in other advanced countries. The demographic and occupational composition of workers in both sectors explains why this is so. Though public sector union members outnumber their private sector counterparts, public sector workers, in fact, are more likely *not* to be union members. They are more likely to be women, nonwhite, older, more educated, white collar, or professional.

Federal laws govern the workplaces of federal government employees, while state and local laws govern the domains of state and local government employees. State laws vary across states and across occupations. According to Richard B. Freeman, U.S. public employee union members do not outnumber private sector union members because of a more favorable legal framework. Legal differences governing unionization and collective bargaining between the two sectors do not explain the mobilization of public sector unions. Instead, different management responses to similar laws provide an explanation. Public sector employees desire influence on workplace decisions. More so than in the private sector, government workers seek decision-making prerogatives on how to

- Do and organize work
- Promote training access
- Decide on pay raises for work group personnel
- Set goals for the work group
- Establish safety standards and practices

In other words, public sector employees promote an employee organization that is more independent of management than do private sector workers.[2]

Unionization rates in the public sector outnumber those in the private sector by about four to one. Members of private sector unions number about 7.4 percent of the workforce. Of the 20,392,000 government workers in the United States, a number that includes local, state, and federal workers, 36.2 percent are represented by labor unions. At the federal level, 28.4 percent of the 3,381,000 employees (16.5 percent of the total U.S. government labor force) are represented by labor unions. Labor unions represent 41.9 percent of local government employees—10,908,000 workers, accounting for 53.5 percent of the total workforce. State government workers—numbering 6,102,000, or 30 percent of the total workforce—register a 30.2 percent labor union membership. Teachers, fire fighters, and police officers are heavily unionized.[3]

Enhanced power for public employees is grounded in politics. Public sector employees possess power outside the collective bargaining process because government workers may attain power through the political process. As voters and through unions, government employees are a force in electing public sector leaders. In the private sector, employees are rarely stockholders who vote and select management. As budgets of school board members, fire departments, or police departments are increased, all parties—management, labor, and clientele—benefit.

Public sector employees are constrained by civil service regulations. Government activities cannot be easily moved from state to state. However, the privatization of certain government functions may be changing this prospect. Military bases sometimes close; as demographics change, public schools may close, too. Differing economic environments and differences in labor-management interactions between the sectors cause public sector management to be less resistant to unionization.

Union organizing is increasing in the service sector, which includes hotels, motels, and nursing homes, and in government. In contrast, union activities are sluggish in most of the private sector. This is partially due to fears that if employees try to unionize, companies may close and move their operations to another town, state, or even country.

Leo Gerard, a steelworkers' union president, concludes that the difference in union membership is due more to this factor than to the intense antiunion campaigns orchestrated by private employers. Why is it easier to organize workers in government offices, hospitals, and hotels than in factories? "You can't threaten to move the public sector out of Ohio," Gerard pointed out. "You can't threaten to move a hospital or nursing home to Mexico or China."[4]

Economic downturns, falling tax revenues, and privatization efforts confront public sector workers and their labor unions. Declining corporate profits, a lousy stock market, nervous consumers, and tax reductions undercut state government budgets. Soaring health care costs and public demands for improved schools also drain public coffers. In a country based on individualism and personal rights, anti-government rhetoric is frequently at a high pitch.

Challenges facing public sector labor include:

- Using positive government balance sheets to secure gains for the future during collective bargaining
- Gearing up to fight against privatization, which means utilizing enhanced research, mobilization, legal, and public relations or communications capacities
- Expanding political power—promoting increased voter registration, increased political action fundraising, and enhanced grassroots mobilization
- Working with private sector labor organizations to build a labor movement consensus on the importance of public services
- Expanding efforts to organize the unorganized in collective bargaining states and focusing energies to win bargaining rights in key nonbargaining states[5]

Decline, Transformation, or Reformation?

The decline, transformation, or perhaps reformation of public sector unionism occurs within the context of our changing political culture. With the decline of the middle classes, lack of real wage increases, and growing numbers of high-income families and families below the poverty line, the U.S. political economy is increasingly becoming more segregated into the wealthy and the poor. The decline of trade unions, the greater numbers of women in the workforce, the loss of manufacturing jobs to overseas workers, and growing immigration are often blamed for our country's woes. Higher wages, lower taxes, job training, barriers to foreign trade, and business recruitment of the poor are suggested to end the trend toward economic disparity.[6]

Unions in the United States originally arose to combat the terrible work and wage conditions of the early Industrial Revolution. After the Great Depression of the 1930s, organized labor, which then existed only in the private sector, was thriving and calling for macroeconomic policies advocating high employment and high wages. Since then, membership in public sector unions such as teachers' and fire fighters' unions has grown, while unionism in general is declining.

Is Work Less Economic and More Social?

Jobs should not just improve our incomes, we think. Like candy and cars, they should also enhance psychic well-being. They should be gratifying and stimulating . . . the boundaries between work and leisure are blurring . . . work has become less manual and more mental, less regimented and more collaborative and—as an activity—less economic and more social.

—*Robert Samuelson, "Work Ethic vs. Fun Ethic,"*
The Washington Post, *September 3, 2001, p. A21*

Public opinion surveys that span fifty years show a major transformation in labor union membership demographics and politics. In 2008 the Bureau of Labor Statistics reported that the number of American workers belonging to labor unions climbed in 2007 to the largest number since 1983. Union membership as a share of the total work force inched up to 12.1 percent from 12 percent the year before . Totals of 7.5 percent of private-sector workers and 35.9 percent of public-sector workers were in unions. In 1983 unions represented 20.1 percent of the U.S. work force.

Public sector unionism is a product of the Great Society of the 1960s and has changed the overall labor movement emphasis from high employment and high wages to an emphasis on the redistribution of society's economic resources. Today, public sector unions represent a larger percentage of the U.S. labor movement than ever before.

Private union membership has ebbed as public unions experienced meteoric membership increases. The enhanced importance of public sector unionism as a component of the overall U.S. labor movement is leading to increased demands for more government intervention in the economic arena.

Leo Troy, in describing the rise and fall of American trade unions, argues that organized labor has changed its philosophy of "more" for its clients to a philosophy of "more government intervention" in America's political economy.[7] Troy claims a philosophical division between America's private sector and public sector unions concerning the definition and implementation of "more government intervention" in our economy and society. Private sector unions wish to enhance their clients' incomes. Public sector unions, says Troy, argue for raising taxes so that client salaries may be increased.

Troy claims that public sector unions and private sector unions are on a collision course. "On one hand, private sector unions want government to vigorously apply macroeconomic policies to stimulate economic growth and avoid depression; on the other hand, public sector unions want a redistribution of the national income from the private to the public sector in the form of social services and transfer payments."[8]

Despite being larger than private sector unionism, public sector unionism is most likely in transformation. The rise of public sector organized labor activities in the 1960s and 1970s was followed by a leveling, or maturation, through the 1980s and 1990s, and into the twenty-first century.

With the growth of unionism in the 1970s, the challenges began to overshadow the benefits. Public employee organizations began to arouse increasing anxiety and alarm. The power of public sector unionism proved most powerful at the state and local levels. The growing number of collective bargaining rights did not occur simply because of political pressures. Union leaders had become more proficient in using bargaining strategies.

Union Members in 2007

In 2007, the number of workers belonging to a union rose by 311,000 to 15.7 million. Union members accounted for 12.1 percent of employed wage and salary workers, essentially unchanged from 12.0 percent in 2006. In 1983, the first year for which comparable union data are available, the union membership rate was 20.1 percent. Some highlights from the 2007 data are:

- Workers in the public sector had a union membership rate nearly five times that of private sector employees (see Figure 6.1).
- Education, training, and library occupations had the highest unionization rate at 37.2 percent, followed closely by protective service occupations at 35.2 percent.
- Among demographic groups, the union membership rate was highest for black men and lowest for Hispanic women.
- Wage and salary workers ages 45 to 54 (15.7 percent) and ages 55 to 64 (16.1 percent) were more likely to be union members than were workers ages 16 to 24 (4.8 percent).

The union membership rate for public sector workers (35.9 percent) was substantially higher than for private industry workers (7.5 percent). Within the public sector, local government workers had the highest union membership rate, 41.8 percent. This group includes many workers in several heavily unionized occupations, such as teachers, police officers, and fire fighters. Private sector industries with high unionization rates include transportation and utilities (22.1 percent), telecommunications (19.7 percent), and construction (13.9 percent). In 2007, unionization rates

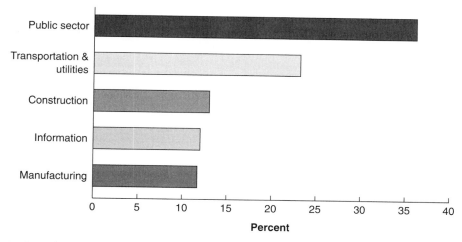

FIGURE 6.1 Union membership of employed wage and salary workers, selected industries, 2006.

These 2006 data on union membership are from the Current Population Survey. Unionization data are for wage and salary workers.

Source: U.S. Department of Labor, Bureau of Labor Statistics, http://www.bls.gov/opub/ted/2007/feb/wkl/art05.htm.

were relatively low in agriculture and related industries (1.5 percent) and in financial activities (2.0 percent).[9]

The power of public sector labor unions is tenuous; government labor unions retain their membership levels, but their power is suspect. The best organized government employees are teachers; teachers have the right to strike in eleven states. Teacher strikes are illegal in twenty-four other states, but local governments are permitted to bargain with school boards. In the other fifteen states, school boards do not have to bargain with teacher unions. Local governments position teacher bargaining rights midway between powerful industrial unions such as the United Auto Workers (UAW) and groups such as farm laborers, domestics, supervisors, managers, and independent contractors not protected by labor regulations at all.

The labor rights of Americans lag behind those of other nations. Employers enjoy a virtually unlimited right to enforce their perspectives in the workplace. Union organizers are prevented from articulating their point of view on workplace production. U.S. labor-management standards do not meet the criteria established by the International Labor Organization (ILO). The ILO, an arm of the United Nations, affirms workers' right to organize, to bargain collectively, to promote the speedy resolution of grievances, and, with limitations, to strike and conduct sympathy strikes. The ILO opposes the hiring of permanent replacement workers during strikes. U.S. labor laws permit employers to replace workers permanently if they strike for higher wages.[10]

According to Richard D. Kahlenberg, the decline of labor promotes U.S. economic inequality. Organized labor declined as a percentage of the nonagricultural workforce from 35 percent in 1954 to 13.5 percent in 2000. "The United States," Kahlenberg writes, "has about three times more inequality than European countries and Japan when measuring the wage gap between the top 10 percent of workers and the bottom 10 percent."[11] The decline of organized labor strength leads to rising economic inequality. In addition, as the U.S. population grows, more stress is placed on the political and economic systems to meet citizen expectations.

Union bargaining gives employees higher wages and benefits, slicing them a larger portion of the economic pie. Unions, representing a great array of employees, articulate different points of view on workplace issues. They engage business in battle over political and economic policies. They contest management's stand on the minimum wage, the Earned Tax Credit, health care, and Social Security. Weak labor laws contribute to the decline in labor and progressive politics, argue the anti-neocapitalists. Social change cannot take place without a strong labor movement.

How do private sector labor relations and macroeconomics impact public sector labor relations? To paraphrase Dwight Waldo again, the distinctions between public and private center on the structure, or organization, of U.S. society. Our constructions of public and private find their origins in the First and Fourteenth Amendments to the U.S. Constitution and in the opportunities provided by American capitalism. Americans are taught to think in terms of public and private differences. But, as Waldo points out, public and private sectors are not categories of nature. They are constructs of history and culture, of law and custom. They fit into the context of U.S. and international macroeconomics and are subject to continual change and redefinition.[12]

Public and private unions may be in some decline and not as strong as they once were, but neither shows signs of extinction. The United States is not unique in the decline of private sector unionism. Contrary to some assertions, unionism in the

---

Public Sector Unions

Teachers Unions
> American Federation of Teachers/National
>   Education Association
> American Association of University Professors
>   (AAUP)

Protective Services Unions
> International Association of Firefighters
>   (IAFF)
> Fraternal Order of Police (FOP)
> Police Benevolent Association
> Service Employees International Union
>   (SEIU)

Local Transit Employee Unions
> Amalgamated Transit Union (ATU)
> Transport Workers Union (TWU)
> United Transportation Union (UTU)

State and Local Government Employee Unions
> American Federation of State, County, and
>   Municipal Employees (AFSCME)
> Assembly of Government Employees (AGE)

Source: Michael Ballot, with contributions from Laurie Lichter-Heath, Thomas Kail, and Ruth Wang, *Labor-Management Relations in a Changing Environment,* 2d ed. (New York: John Wiley & Sons, pp. 474–478, 1996).

---

private sectors of Canada and Western Europe has also declined, and for the same reason—because of structural changes in the labor market.[13]

David Lewin cites key factors for the rise in public unionism during the decline of overall unionism.[14] Among those factors at work from 1960 to 1975 were the passing of state laws permitting collective bargaining by state employees and the rapid growth in public employment.

During the late 1970s and throughout the 1980s, however, political and economic factors changed. From a political and economic environment that promoted employee unionism and collective bargaining rights, the situation shifted to the current attitude, which emphasizes imposing penalties for illegal strikes by public employees.

Leo Troy, Distinguished Professor of Economics at Rutgers University, Newark, calls private sector unionism the "*Old Unionism*" and public, or government, sector unionism the "*New Unionism.*" The Old Unionism shares about 7 percent of the nonfarm labor market, the percentage it had at the start of the twentieth century. While the Old Unionism is in decline, the New Unionism continues to expand. In the first year of the Clinton presidency, New Unionism rose nearly 5.5 percent, or 370,000, to more than 7 million members. The New Unionism is more widely distributed across the country than the Old Unionism ever was.

According to Troy, public, or government, sector unionism constitutes attempts to "organize the organized." The most organized of full-time public employees are fire fighters, teachers, police officers, and sanitation workers. Why is Old Unionism in a permanent state of decline? Markets produce structural changes in labor arrangements. The shift from a goods-dominated to a service-dominated labor market assists the transformation. Increasing substitution of "high tech" for traditional manufacturing accompanies the decline of Old Unionism.

Competition abhors monopoly. State and local governments account for the bulk of public employees. As these governments extend their encouragement of unionization and bargaining, the disparities in the strength of the New and Old Unionism will grow. Troy states that a great potential exists for the unionization of state and local government employees.

The permanent decline of Old Unionism (the private sector model) is attributed to market competition, fundamental structural changes, and market "repeal" of the National Labor Relations Act. The NLRA states and defines the rights of employees to organize and to bargain collectively with their employers through representatives of their choosing. Union leadership and its supporters were late in recognizing the new environment confronting the Old Unionism.[15] The reform of labor relations and the steady increase in the number of labor unions show that Old Unionism is in a continuous decline and that New Unionism is rapidly taking over. Aside from profound changes in the structure of the labor market, New (public sector) Unionism will also increase the strength of organized labor.[16]

State and Local Government Labor Issues

Collective bargaining has been used by state and local government employees since the 1960s. Arguments questioning collective bargaining for government employees include the following:

- *Sovereign power and public accountability.* Many believe that public sector collective bargaining infringes on the sovereign power of the state. Unions directly affect the sovereign power of the state to determine service levels of different programs (police, fire, library, and sanitation, for example) and rules and regulations (production, benefits, and vacation days, for example).

  The government unions, as private interest groups, would unduly influence public, or communitywide, decisions. The union seeks to increase the pay and benefits its members receive. Unionized municipal departments are likely to have higher expenditures (budgets) than nonunionized departments. Also, private interest groups, in this case government unions, are not accountable to the public or community. Elected officials are accountable to the electorate or the populace that elects them. The electorate may vote the government officials out of office, but not government workers.

- *Fiscal responsibility and public budgeting.* Public sector unions soon encountered fiscal realities. In the 1960s and 1970s, union demands caused state, county, and municipal budgets to inflate, raising taxes, especially property taxes. States began to impose tax and/or spending limits. Elected officials operated with fixed budgets and small reserves. Union monetary demands were curtailed. These fiscal constraints slowed the growth of public sector unionism. Funds were reallocated, employment was cut, and citizens faced lower levels of public services.

- *Public goods and monopoly.* Government as a monopoly supplier is of concern to the citizenry. Government is the only supplier of certain public goods (police and fire protection, for example). In elementary and secondary education, public schools significantly outnumber private schools and maintain "near-monopoly" powers.

  Obviously, a strike or work stoppage would completely interrupt the provision of these services to customer citizens. However, citizens are not without redress. They may flee the city, county, or state if they are not pleased with the level of government services provided and/or the taxes charged to support that level of services. This flight reduces the community's tax base, causing reductions in the level of services government provides.

- *The right to strike.* If government is monopolist and, therefore, the only supplier of essential services, strikes by government employees may endanger the health and safety of the population. The tasks of police, fire, and sanitation workers are perhaps more paramount than the functions of teachers and transit workers. In the public sector, the costs are primarily on the users of the service. However, with government employees, the users, or citizens, are also the employers.

  Strikes are legal for some government workers in twelve states: Alaska, California, Hawaii, Idaho, Illinois, Minnesota, Montana, Ohio, Oregon, Pennsylvania, Vermont, and Wisconsin. In twenty-four states, strikes are either not covered by public sector labor relations laws or are prohibited. But no sanctions or penalties are specified for striking in violation of antistrike laws. Fifteen states penalize striking workers severely, including their employee association or union.[17]

Near-monopolies, however, occur in the private sector as well. If employees of private airline companies went on strike, their actions would not only inconvenience millions of travelers but could cost the U.S. economy billions of dollars. When UPS (United Parcel Service) employees walked out, the USPS (United States Postal Service) could not adequately handle the overflow of packages. If employees of private sector utilities agreed on a work stoppage, telephone, gas, electricity, and cable television services might come to a sudden halt.

State and Local Government Working Conditions

Working conditions vary by occupation. In some instances, they vary by size and location of the state or local government (see Table 6.1). For example, executives in very small jurisdictions may work less than twenty hours a week. In larger jurisdictions, they often work more than forty hours per week. Chief executives in large jurisdictions work full-time year-round, as do most county and city managers. Most state legislators work full-time only when in session, usually for a few months a year, and work part-time the rest of the year. Local elected officials in some small jurisdictions work part-time.

TABLE 6.1

Wage and Salary Employment in State and Local Government, Excluding Education and Hospitals, 2006

(thousands)

Jurisdiction	Employment	Percent
State and local government, total	8,018	100.0
Local government	5,594	69.8
State government	2,424	30.2

Source: U.S. Department of Labor, Bureau of Labor Statistics, http://www.bls.gov/oco/cg/print/cgs042.htm.

Most professional, financial operations, and office and administrative support workers in state and local government work a standard forty-hour week in an office environment. However, workers in some of the most visible local government jobs have very different working conditions and schedules.

Fire fighters' hours are longer and vary more widely than those of most workers. Many professional fire fighters are on duty for several days in a row, working more than fifty hours a week, because some must be on duty at all times to respond to emergencies. They often eat and sleep at the fire station. Following this long shift, they are then off for several days in a row or for the entire next week. In addition to irregular hours, fire fighting can involve the risk of death or injury. Some local fire districts also use the services of volunteer fire fighters, who tend to work shorter, regularly scheduled shifts.

Law enforcement work also is potentially dangerous. The injury and fatality rates among law officers are higher than in many occupations, reflecting risks taken in apprehending suspected criminals and responding to various emergency situations such as traffic accidents. Most police and detectives work forty hours a week, with paid overtime when they testify in court or work on an investigation. Because police protection must be provided around the clock, some officers are subject to call any time their services are needed and are expected to intervene whenever they observe a crime, even if they are off duty.

Most driver/operator jobs in public transit systems are stressful and fatiguing because they involve dealing with passengers, tight schedules, and heavy traffic. Bus drivers with regular routes and subway operators generally have consistent weekly work schedules. Those who do not have regular schedules may be on call and must be prepared to report for work on short notice. To accommodate commuters, many operators work split shifts, such as 6 A.M. to 10 A.M. and 3 P.M. to 7 P.M. with time off in between.

A number of other state and local government jobs also require weekend or night work. Because electricity, gas, and water are used continuously throughout each day, split, weekend, and night shifts are common for utility workers.

State and Local Government Occupations

Service occupations make up the largest share of employment in state and local governments, accounting for 31 percent of all jobs (see Table 6.2). Of these, police and sheriff's patrol officers, bailiffs, correctional officers and jailers, and fire fighters, concentrated in local governments, were the largest occupations. Professional and related occupations account for 21 percent of employment; office and administrative support occupations account for 20 percent; and management, business, and financial occupations constitute 12 percent. Local governments employ almost four times as many service workers as do state governments (see Figure 6.2).

State and local governments employ people in occupations found in nearly every industry in the economy, including chief executives, managers, engineers, computer specialists, secretaries, and health technicians. Certain occupations, however, are mainly or exclusively found in these governments, such as legislators; tax examiners, collectors, and revenue agents; urban and regional planners; judges, magistrates, and other judicial workers; police and sheriff's patrol officers; and correctional officers and jailers.

TABLE 6.2

Employment of Wage and Salary Workers in State and Local Government, Except Education and Health, by Occupation
(thousands)

Occupation	Employment, 2006		Projected change, 2006–2016
	Number	Percent	Percent
All occupations	8,018	100.0	7.7
Management, business, and financial occupations	942	11.7	6.3
General and operations managers	73	0.9	–3.4
Legislators	64	0.8	1.0
Compliance officers, except agriculture, construction, health and safety, and transportation	58	0.7	3.7
Human resources, training, and labor relations specialists	71	0.9	9.1
Accountants and auditors	81	1.0	16.1
Appraisers and assessors of real estate	28	0.4	6.6
Tax examiners, collectors, and revenue agents	45	0.6	2.9
Professional and related occupations	1,655	20.6	8.0
Computer specialists	142	1.8	12.7
Civil engineers	59	0.7	5.2
Civil engineering technicians	39	0.5	3.9
Urban and regional planners	26	0.3	10.7
Counselors	71	0.9	4.7
Social workers	175	2.2	5.4
Probation officers and correctional treatment specialists	92	1.1	9.9
Social and human service assistants	90	1.1	–0.5
Lawyers	88	1.1	27.6
Judges, magistrate judges, and magistrates	27	0.3	5.1
Legal support workers	58	0.7	8.2
Librarians	45	0.6	0.9
Library technicians	60	0.8	12.0
Registered nurses	90	1.1	5.9
Health technologists and technicians	123	1.5	8.4
Service occupations	2,508	31.3	10.9
Nursing, psychiatric, and home health aides	107	1.3	4.9
First-line supervisors/managers of correctional officers	37	0.5	11.9
First-line supervisors/managers of police and detectives	84	1.0	10.3
Fire fighters	276	3.4	12.1
Correctional officers and jailers	409	5.1	15.8
Detectives and criminal investigators	66	0.8	19.8
Police and sheriff's patrol officers	618	7.7	10.9
Crossing guards	48	0.6	1.1

continued

TABLE 6.2

Employment of Wage and Salary Workers in State and Local Government, Except Education and Health, by Occupation, *continued*

(thousands)

Occupation	Employment, 2006		Projected change, 2006–2016
	Number	Percent	Percent
Service occupations			
Lifeguards, ski patrol, and other recreational protective service workers	43	0.5	12.2
Building cleaning workers	111	1.4	3.6
Landscaping and groundskeeping workers	91	1.1	4.3
Gaming services workers	32	0.4	21.4
Recreation workers	105	1.3	6.9
Office and administrative support occupations	1,572	19.6	2.0
Bookkeeping, accounting, and auditing clerks	104	1.3	8.5
Court, municipal, and license clerks	108	1.3	8.2
Eligibility interviewers, government programs	80	1.0	0.0
Library assistants, clerical	61	0.8	12.2
Police, fire, and ambulance dispatchers	87	1.1	12.5
Secretaries and administrative assistants	308	3.8	2.2
Office clerks, general	317	4.0	3.1
Construction and extraction occupations	447	5.6	9.9
Construction equipment operators	83	1.0	10.3
Highway maintenance workers	138	1.7	8.8
Installation, maintenance, and repair occupations	302	3.8	10.6
Maintenance and repair workers, general	124	1.5	9.8
Production occupations	143	1.8	10.7
Water and liquid waste treatment plant and system operators	89	1.1	12.1
Transportation and material moving occupations	366	4.6	7.4
Bus drivers, transit and intercity	117	1.5	11.5
Refuse and recyclable material collectors	49	0.6	1.0

Note: Columns may not add to totals due to omission of occupations with small employment.

Source: U.S. Department of Labor, Bureau of Labor Statistics, http://www.bls.gov/oco/cg/print/cgs042.htm.

Chief executives, general and operations managers, and legislators establish government policy and develop laws, rules, and regulations. They are elected or appointed officials who either preside over units of government or make laws. Chief executives include governors, lieutenant governors, mayors, and city managers. General and operations managers include district managers and revenue directors. Legislators include state senators and representatives, county commissioners, and city council members.

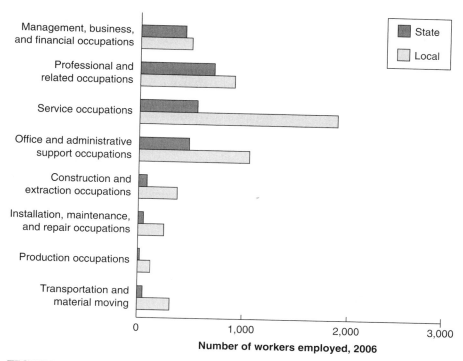

FIGURE 6.2 Local government employs almost four times as many service workers as state government.

Source: U.S. Department of Labor, Bureau of Labor Statistics, http://www.bls.gov/oco/cg/print/cgs042.htm.

Tax examiners, collectors, and revenue agents determine tax liability and collect past-due taxes from individuals and businesses. Urban and regional planners draft plans and recommend programs for the development and use of resources such as land and water. They also propose construction of physical facilities, such as schools and roads, under the authority of cities, counties, and metropolitan areas. Planners devise strategies outlining the best use of community land and identify the places in which residential, commercial, recreational, and other types of development should be located.

Judges arbitrate, advise, and administer justice in a court of law. They oversee legal processes in courts and apply the law to resolve civil disputes and determine guilt in criminal cases. Magistrates resolve criminal cases not involving penitentiary sentences, as well as civil cases involving damages below a sum specified by law.

Social workers counsel and assess the needs of clients, refer them to the appropriate sources for help, and monitor their progress. They interview and investigate applicants and recipients to determine eligibility to receive, or continue receiving, welfare and other types of social assistance. Social and human service assistants' duties vary with specific job titles. These workers include social service technicians, case management aides, social work assistants, residential counselors, alcoholism or drug abuse counseling aides, child abuse workers, community outreach workers, and gerontology aides. Probation officers and correctional treatment specialists assist in rehabilitation of law offenders in custody or on probation or parole.

Court, municipal, and license clerks perform a variety of state and local government administrative tasks. Court clerks prepare dockets of cases to be called, secure information for judges, and contact witnesses, lawyers, and attorneys to obtain information for the court. Municipal clerks draft agendas for town and city councils, record minutes of council meetings, answer official correspondence, keep fiscal records and accounts, and prepare reports on civic needs. License clerks keep records and help the public obtain motor vehicle ownership titles, operator permits, and a variety of other permits and licenses. State and local governments also employ many secretaries and administrative assistants and general office clerks.

Fire fighters control and extinguish fires, assist with emergency medical treatment, and help with the recovery from natural disasters such as earthquakes and tornadoes. Fire inspectors inspect public buildings for conditions that might present a fire hazard. Emergency medical technicians and paramedics assess injuries, administer emergency medical care, and extricate trapped individuals. They transport injured or sick persons to medical facilities.

Police and sheriff's patrol officers and detectives and criminal investigators have duties that range from controlling traffic to preventing and investigating crimes. They maintain order, enforce laws and ordinances, issue traffic summonses, investigate accidents, give evidence in court, serve legal documents for the court system, and apprehend, arrest, and process prisoners. State and local correctional officers guard inmates in jails, prisons, or juvenile detention institutions. Baliffs keep order in courts.

Highway maintenance workers maintain highways, municipal and rural roads, airport runways, and rights-of-way. They patch broken or eroded pavement, repair guard rails and highway markers, plow snow, and mow or clear brush from along roads. Bus drivers pick up and deliver passengers at prearranged stops along their assigned routes. Operators may collect fares, answer questions about schedules and transfer points, and announce stops.

State and Local Government Job Advancement

The education level and experience needed by workers in state and local government vary by occupation. Voters elect most chief executives and legislators, so local support is very important. Taking part in volunteer work and helping to provide community services are valuable ways in which to establish vital community support. Elected chief executives and legislators come from a variety of backgrounds, but must conform to age, residency, and citizenship regulations regarding the positions they seek.

Advancement opportunities for most elected public officials are limited to other offices in the jurisdictions in which they live. For example, a local council member may run for mayor or for a position in state government, and state legislators may decide to run for state governor or for the United States Congress.

A master's degree in public administration is widely recommended, but not required, for city managers. They may gain experience as management analysts or assistants in government departments, working with councils and mayors. After several years, they may be hired to manage a town or a small city and may eventually become manager of a larger city.

Most professional jobs require a college degree. For an entry-level urban or regional planning position, most state and local government agencies require two years of graduate study in urban and regional planning or the equivalent in work experience. To become a judge, particularly a state trial or appellate court judge, one is usually required to be a lawyer. About half of all state judges are appointed; the other half are elected in partisan or nonpartisan elections. Most state and local judges serve fixed terms, ranging from four to six years for limited jurisdiction judges to fourteen years for some appellate court judges.

Most applicants for fire-fighting jobs must have a high school education or its equivalent and pass a civil service examination. In addition, they need to pass a medical examination and tests of strength, physical stamina, coordination, and agility, Experience as a volunteer fire fighter or as a fire fighter in the Armed Forces is helpful, as is completion of community college courses in fire science. Recruits study fire-fighting techniques, fire prevention, local building codes, emergency procedures, and the proper use of rescue equipment. Fire fighters may be promoted depending on written examination results and job performance.

Bus drivers must comply with federal regulations that require drivers who operate vehicles designed to transport sixteen or more passengers to obtain a commercial driver's license from the state in which they live. To qualify for a commercial vehicle driver's license, applicants must pass a written test on rules and regulations and demonstrate that they can operate a commercial vehicle safely. For subway and streetcar operator jobs, applicants with at least a high school education have the best chance.

In some cities, prospective subway operators are required to work as bus drivers for a specified period. Successful applicants generally are in good health, possess good communication skills, and are able to make quick, sound judgments. Because bus drivers and subway operators deal with passengers, they need an even temperament and emotional stability. Driving in heavy, fast-moving, or stop-and-go traffic and dealing with passengers can be stressful.

Police departments in most areas require applicants to be U.S. citizens of good character, at least twenty years old, and able to meet rigorous physical and mental standards. Police departments increasingly encourage applicants to take college courses, and some require a college degree. Many community and junior colleges, as well as colleges and universities, offer programs in law enforcement or criminal justice.

Officers usually attend a local or regional police academy that includes classroom instruction in constitutional law, civil rights, and state and local law. They also receive training in patrol, accident investigation, traffic control, use of firearms, self-defense, first aid, and emergency management. Promotions for police officers are highly influenced by scores on a written civil service examination and subsequent performance evaluations by their superiors.

Wage and Salary Employment in State and Local Governments

Wage and salary employment in state and local governments is projected to increase 8 percent during the 2006–2016 period, slower than the 11 percent growth projected for all sectors of the economy combined. Job growth stems from the rising demand for services at the state and local levels. An increasing population and state and local assumption of responsibility for some services previously provided by the federal government are fueling the growth of these services.

TABLE 6.3

Median Hourly Earnings of the Largest Occupations in State and Local Government, Excluding Education and Hospitals, May 2006

Occupation	State Government	Local Government	All Industries
Business operations specialists, all other	$26.82	$25.73	$26.76
Police and sheriff's patrol officers	25.26	22.69	22.82
Child, family, and school social workers	18.75	20.91	18.02
Fire fighters	17.79	20.00	19.80
Correctional officers and jailers	17.37	16.74	17.19
Executive secretaries and administrative assistants	17.23	18.59	17.90
Highway maintenance workers	15.77	14.99	15.17
Secretaries, except legal, medical, and executive	15.21	14.59	13.20
Maintenance and repair workers, general	14.90	15.85	15.34
Office clerks, general	13.17	12.78	11.40

Source: U.S. Department of Labor, Bureau of Labor Statistics, http://www.bls.gov/oco/cg/print/cgs042.htm.

State and local government job prospects vary by state and region. Overall prospects are favorable. In addition to job openings from employment growth, many opportunities are created by workers who retire from government careers. Many state and local governments are considering cutbacks in retiree pension and benefits programs. Budget cuts may make state and local government jobs attractive to fewer persons. Competition for jobs may be reduced.

Earnings vary by occupation, size of the state or locality, and region of the country. Professionals and managers earn more than other workers. Table 6.3 offers earning comparisons in occupations having the largest employment in state and local government.

Professional and service occupations account for more than half of all jobs in state and local government. Most new jobs stem from steady demand for community and social services, health services, and protective services. For example, increased demand for services for the elderly, the mentally impaired, and children results in steady demand for social workers, registered nurses, and recreation workers. There is strong demand for information technology workers.

Employment in management, business, and financial occupations is projected to grow at about the same rate as overall employment in state and local governments. Employment in office and administrative support occupations is expected to remain close to current levels.

The 2006 median annual salaries of selected executive and managerial occupations in local government, as reported by the International City/County Management Association (ICMA), are shown in Table 6.4. Employer-provided benefits—including health and life insurance plus retirement benefits—are more common among state and local government employees than among workers in the private sector.

TABLE 6.4

Median Annual Salary for Selected Executive and Managerial Occupations in Local Government, 2006

Occupation	Salary
City manager/Chief administrative officer	$92,799
Assistant chief administrative officer	83,155
Engineer	79,648
Chief financial officer	76,101
Fire chief	75,645
Information services director	75,118
Economic development director	73,140
Human resources director	72,527
Public works director	71,360
Human services director	70,958
Chief law enforcement official	69,600
Parks and recreation director	68,284
Health officer	67,275
Purchasing director	63,043
Chief librarian	58,750
Treasurer	54,803
Clerk	45,497
Chief elected official	25,000

Source: U.S. Department of Labor, Bureau of Labor Statistics, http://www.bls.gov/oco/cg/print/cgs042.htm.

Alternatives for Avoiding a Work Stoppage

In those cases where a stalemate is reached and the bargaining process breaks down, alternatives are available for avoiding a work stoppage or strike.

A device sometimes used when labor-management negotiations flounder is *mediation.* The mediator, or in some cases mediators, help carry out negotiations between the disputing parties. They may group both sides around a table and try to find ways to open previously entrenched positions or to point out possibilities for conciliation. When conflicts among the parties push disputes beyond negotiation, the mediator may even put the two sides in separate rooms and run from room to room in a continuing effort to break the deadlock. Some jurisdictions authorize fact-finders to shift to mediation when their recommendations have failed to resolve the differences separating the parties.

Mediation is an art. According to one experienced practitioner, a good mediator should

- Have a good sense of timing, knowing when to advise each side on when to make each move
- Avoid relieving the parties themselves of responsibility to solve the dispute

- Be able to distinguish the power contest between the negotiating parties from internal power struggles (such as union leaders fearful of losing face with their members)
- Avoid passing judgment on the merits of the respective positions[18]

Another alternative to a work stoppage is *fact-finding*. Under this process, an individual or, more frequently, a mutually acceptable panel is set up to review the disputed issues and make recommendations. These recommendations are not binding, but if the fact-finding machinery has been properly constituted, and if its analysis of the facts is accurate, both sides will be under a good deal of pressure to accept its suggestions.

Neither mediation nor fact-finding assures a peaceful settlement to a labor dispute. For that type of guarantee we must turn to a third alternative, *interest arbitration*. This device differs from the other two in one crucial respect: it produces a definite decision that is usually binding on both sides. When binding arbitration has been agreed upon, the arbitrator's word is final and there is no further appeal.

If arbitration is not accepted by either party at the outset, it does not guarantee a peaceful resolution, but it is rarely used without such prior agreement. One typical way of setting up arbitration is for each side to choose a representative and for the two representatives to choose a third member of what then becomes an arbitration panel.

Administrators tend to view third-party proceedings such as fact-finding, mediation, and arbitration with some suspicion. While they recognize that such devices help considerably to avoid strikes, they often feel that they result in decisions injurious from a management perspective. Third parties have nothing at stake except their own future arbitration or mediation business. They show a tendency, it is felt, to split the issue down the middle, with perhaps some leaning toward the labor side. Some administrators question not only the leaning toward labor but also whether most disputes should automatically be split down the middle. They feel many issues do not lend themselves to that type of decision. In any case, management loses control in such proceedings, and decisions are made by those who cannot be fully aware of all their implications and who do not have to live with them.

Unionists have tended to look more favorably on third-party intervention. They have particularly favored arbitration. As a fire fighters' union official once expressed it, without compulsory arbitration in the background, collective bargaining for employees becomes collective begging.[19]

Collective Bargaining for Federal Employees

The Federal Service Labor-Management Relations Statute, Title VII of the Civil Service Reform Act of 1978, allows nonpostal federal employees to bargain collectively through labor organizations of their choice and thereby participate with agency management in the development of personnel policies and practices and other decisions that affect their working lives.[20] The 1970s through 1990s saw the federal labor-management relations program evolve from a simple executive order that provided for consultation between agency management and employee organizations to a formal collective bargaining program established by law.

The program is enforced by an independent administrative agency, the Federal Labor Relations Authority (FLRA), as well as by the federal courts. The latest available data from the Office of Personnel Management (OPM) show that about 1.1 million federal employees, or 60 percent of the total nonpostal federal workforce, were represented by unions. OPM formally acknowledges 79 unions and associations with exclusive recognition in the federal service. Forty affiliated labor organizations are recognized by OPM as bargaining units.[21]

The Lloyd-LaFollette Act of 1912 established the right of federal employees to belong to labor organizations as long as the organizations did not impose a duty on employees to engage in or assist in a strike against the government. But it was not until 1962, when President Kennedy issued Executive Order 10988, that a federal labor-management relations program was officially established.

The order was the result of a presidential task force study that found that 33 percent of federal employees, mostly in the postal service and among blue-collar workers, belonged to employee organizations. Since they lacked guidance, the various agencies of the government had proceeded on widely varying courses in dealing with these organizations. Some, such as the Tennessee Valley Authority and various units of the Department of Interior, had engaged in close to full-scale collective bargaining with the trade unions that represented their employees, but most had done little or nothing.

Among other provisions, Executive Order 10988 recognized the right of federal employees to join, or refrain from joining, employee organizations and established procedures for granting recognition to federal employee organizations. These organizations were given the right to consult or negotiate with agencies on matters that concerned working conditions and personnel policies within the limits of applicable federal laws and regulations.

Certain other matters, including the agency's mission, its budget, its organization and assignment of personnel, and the technology needed to perform its work, were deemed "management's rights" and, therefore, nonnegotiable. The order also allowed individual agencies to establish procedures to deal with grievances, appeals, and negotiation impasses, but it specifically precluded strikes or binding arbitration as means of resolving such disputes. Arbitration hearings by private arbitrators were permitted for employee grievances so long as the arbitrators' decisions were advisory and not binding.

Executive Order 10988 provided for a variety of union recognition policies. The percentage of employees supporting the union in the bargaining unit determined the type of recognition.

- *Exclusive recognition.* A union had to show that it represented at least 10 percent of the employees in the unit. The union then had to be chosen by a majority of the employees of the unit to be their representative.
- *Formal recognition.* A union had to show it represented 10 to 50 percent of the unit employees. If the union could show that 10 to 50 percent of the unit employees belonged to the union, the employer-agency had to consult the union on personnel matters.
- *Informal recognition.* This status was granted if less than 10 percent of the unit employees were members of the union. However, the employer-agency had no obligation to meet, consult, or negotiate with the union.[22]

In 1969, a review of the program by an interagency study committee indicated that the policies of Executive Order 10988 had brought about more democratic management of the workforce and better employee-management cooperation, and that negotiation and consultation had produced improvement in a number of personnel policies and working conditions. The review also found that union representation of employees in exclusive bargaining units had expanded greatly to include 52 percent of the total federal workforce subject to the order.

As a result of the study committee's recommendations, Executive Order 11491 was issued on October 29, 1969. The new order retained the basic principles and objectives underlying Executive Order 10988 and added a number of fundamental changes in the overall labor-management relations structure. A Federal Labor Relations Council (FLRC), composed of the chairman of the Civil Service Commission, the director of the Office of Management and Budget, and the secretary of Labor, was established as a central body to administer the program, make final decisions on policy questions, and adjudicate three types of labor-management disputes:

1. Negotiability appeals
2. Exceptions to arbitration awards
3. Appeals of decisions by the Assistant Secretary of Labor for Labor-Management Relations on unfair labor practice and representation cases

Although the Federal Service Labor Management Relations Statute was modeled after the National Labor Relations Act applied to the private sector, it also carried over many policies and approaches from the executive order program. As a result, federal labor relations bargaining is different from labor-management relations programs in the private sector in several ways:

- *"Bread and butter" issues* that are the focus of private sector bargaining, including wages, fringe benefits, and many others relating to hiring, firing, promoting, and retaining employees, usually cannot be negotiated in federal contracts. Since the first executive order, federal sector bargaining has been limited to the way personnel policies, practices, and procedures are implemented.
- *Traditional bargaining incentives* (i.e., strikes and lockouts) are prohibited.
- *"Agency shop"* or *"fair share" representation fees* are prohibited. Under the federal program, employees are entitled to select a union to represent them, but they cannot be compelled to join or to pay a fee for the representation that the union is required to provide.

Conflicts in State Civil Service and Collective Bargaining Systems

Joel Douglas, professor of public administration at City University of New York and arbitrator of government-employee relations, explores the impacts of the emergence of public sector labor relation systems on the legal structure and the design of state civil service systems. According to Douglas, many jurisdictions have developed "dual personnel systems," with civil service and collective bargaining provisions existing side by side.[23]

University of Maryland Baltimore
Glossary of Labor Relations Terms

Agreement, Collective Bargaining (another term for Memorandum of Understanding/MOU)

A written agreement or contract that is the result of negotiations between an employer and a union. It sets out the conditions of employment (wages, hours, benefits, etc.) and ways to settle disputes arising during the term of the contract. Collective bargaining agreements usually run for a definite period—one, two, or three years.

Arbitration

Where it is available, a method of setting a labor-management dispute by having an impartial third party hold a formal hearing, take testimony, and render a decision. The decision is usually binding upon the parties (i.e., the University, the union, and the employees).

Bargaining Agent

A labor organization which is the exclusive representative of all employees in a bargaining unit, both union and nonunion members.

Bargaining Units

Defined by the Maryland higher education collective bargaining law as three on each UM campus consisting of regular exempt, nonexempt, and sworn police employees.

Checkoff

A provision, which is many times found in the collective bargaining agreement or MOU, that allows union dues, assessments, and initiation fees to be deducted from the pay of union members who decide to use the checkoff. The employer then transfers the payments to the union on a scheduled basis.

Collective Bargaining

A method of mutually determining wages, hours, and terms and conditions of employment through negotiations between representatives of the employer and the union. The results of the bargaining are set forth in a collective bargaining agreement. Collective bargaining determines the conditions of employment for all employees holding jobs in a bargaining unit.

Exclusive Representative

An employee organization that has the right to solely represent the bargaining unit for purposes of collective bargaining.

Fair Share

A fee (usually called an agency fee) paid to the union by members of a bargaining unit who have not joined that union. The fee pays for services and benefits which the union has negotiated for all members of the bargaining unit.

Free Riders

A term used by unions to designate nonmembers within the bargaining unit who obtain, without cost, the benefits of a contract/MOU gained through the efforts of the dues-paying members.

Grievance

A formal complaint usually lodged by an employee or the union alleging a misinterpretation or improper application of one or more terms in a collective bargaining contract/MOU. The method for dealing with grievances is through a grievance procedure negotiated in the union contract/MOU. If a grievance cannot be settled at the supervisory level, it can be appealed to higher levels of management.

Grievance Arbitration

The appeal of grievances to an impartial arbitrator for final and binding determination, sometimes called arbitration of "rights." The arbitrator determines the meaning of the contract/MOU and clarifies and interprets its terms. Arbitration, where it is available, is usually the last step in the grievance procedure.

Grievance Procedure

The steps established in a collective bargaining contract/MOU for the handling of grievances made by or on behalf of employees.

Impasse

A deadlock in negotiations. After bargaining in good faith, the parties have failed to reach an agreement on one or more issues.

Labor Board

Defined by the Maryland higher education collective bargaining law as the State Higher Education Labor Relations Board (SHELRB), an independent state unit. The SHELRB is a five-member panel appointed by the governor after July 1, 2001 and approved by the Senate. The SHELRB is responsible for establishing procedures for and overseeing elections for exclusive representatives, as well as investigating and taking action regarding unfair labor practices.

Labor Organizer

A person usually employed by a union (usually the regional or international union) whose function is to enlist the employees of a particular employer to join the union.

Management's Rights

Certain rights that management maintains as fundamental to the ability to manage and operate the organization. They are not required, negotiable subjects of collective bargaining. These rights are often expressly reserved to management in the management's rights clause of the bargaining agreement. They include the right to hire, promote, suspend, or discharge employees; to direct the work of employees; and to establish operating policies.

Memorandum of Understanding (MOU)/ Labor Contract

The resulting agreement reached by the parties during the negotiations/bargaining process. Also known as a collective bargaining agreement or contract.

Public Employee

A person who is employed by a municipal, county, state, or federal agency or state college or university.

Representation Election

Secret balloting by employees in a bargaining unit for the purpose of selecting a bargaining agent or no representation.

Shop Steward/Steward

A union representative of a group of fellow employees who carries out duties of the union within the workplace. Example: Handling grievances, collecting dues, recruiting new members and monitoring compliance with the contract. The steward usually is either elected by other union members or appointed by higher union officials. The steward usually remains an employee while handling union business. Some release time (with or without pay) may be available to stewards under specific language in many collective bargaining contracts.

Supervisor

An individual (regardless of his/her job description or title) having authority, in the interest of the employer, to hire, transfer, suspend, lay off, recall, promote, discharge, assign, reward or discipline other employees of the employer. A supervisory employee is also one who has responsibility for directing employees, answering their grievances, or recommending disciplinary action, if authority is not merely clerical but requires independent judgment.

Unfair Labor Practice

An act or omission on the part of either the union or management which violates the regulations set forth by the State Higher Education Labor Relations Board.

Source: Abridgment from "Collective Bargaining at UMB: Glossary of Labor Relations Terms" on the University of Maryland, Baltimore, Web site www.umaryland.edu. © 2001 University of Maryland, Baltimore. Reprinted by permission.

Collective bargaining and state civil service merit systems often contradict each other. As of 2000, twenty-nine states had enacted public sector collective bargaining legislation covering state employees.

In the public sector, collective bargaining is multilateral—not bilateral, as in the private sector. Managerial authority is widely shared in the public sector. Multilateral bargaining includes more than two distinct parties; thus, in multilateral bargaining, no clear dichotomy divides union and management. Public sector collective bargaining is highly decentralized. Almost all bargaining is carried out on a single-government-unit basis. Union bargaining agreements exist among 90 unions with 2,218 bargaining units. These agreements cover more than one million federal employees.[24]

Labor relations systems supersede but do not replace existing civil service merit systems. State legislatures often fail to terminate procedures for civil service merit systems, yet they have not successfully integrated labor relations systems with civil service merit systems, resulting in numerous problems. Dual personnel systems are commonplace, but they are not recommended. Collective bargaining and civil service merit systems do not blend well. Civil service merit systems flourish where there is a statutory commitment to merit, subjects have been removed from bargaining and reserved to merit systems, and management rights are designated and are not subject to bargaining.[25]

The structure of civil service and labor relations legislation is consistent, in so far as civil service statutes predate collective bargaining laws in every state. The legislatures' silence enlarges the scope of negotiations and allows issues to be litigated. Confusion exists, however, over primary and concurrent jurisdiction, the scope of bargaining, and election of forum as bilateralism replaces unilateralism in public sector workplace decision making.

Zero-Sum versus One-Ten Power Games?

Traditional labor-management relations are a zero-sum game (one side wins, the other loses). Traditional bargaining focuses on pay and benefits. The end result is to secure more pay to buy a new automobile as increased compensation for a dull, dead-end job. Workers have changed and now demand more of their employment arrangements. "Workers not only want enough pay to enjoy their time off the job, they want satisfaction on the job," according to Robert M. Tobias, president of the National Treasury Employees Union (NTEU) from 1983 to 1999.

IRS employee surveys indicate that employees appreciate challenging work and are most satisfied when their knowledge, skills, and abilities are utilized effectively. Annual reports of the National Partnership Council show that job satisfaction and productivity increase if employees are included in improving work processes and procedures. U.S. Department of Labor studies of state and local governments reveal that including employees in productivity designs results in continuous improvement and employee satisfaction.

A hostile labor-management environment leads to the traditional union focus on processing the grievances of a small number of employees. Employee involvement in creating new work processes, determining organizational strategies, and solving workplace problems abandons a zero-sum game in favor of a game of one-to-ten. Personally secure managers recognize that they do not have all the solutions to workplace problems. Nor do managers have all the knowledge, skills, and abilities to enhance agency productivity and public satisfaction. More personally secure managers thus share authority with adequately trained employees who then exercise discretion and become much more productive.

A one-to-ten game means that if government workers cannot attain a "ten," perhaps they can reach a four, five, or six. For example, teachers could bargain for higher wages, but not be permitted to strike. Or bargaining is permitted, but negotiations on health insurance are not allowed. The situation is not "either-or." Alternatives and flexibility exist. Most government employees do not respond well to an "either-or" (zero-sum) arrangement.

Union leaders and managers are no longer playing a zero-sum game where one side wins and the other goes home empty-handed. Replacing this either-or approach is the one-to-ten game, in which everyone gains something from workplace disagreements. Union leaders are no longer there to protect employees from the vices of management. Manager-union processes now promote improving employee satisfaction; developing up, down, and lateral communications throughout the organizational structure; and focusing on the political and leadership skills required to make significant changes.

Employee protection, therefore, is no longer the only union role. "Unions need to expand their role to include improving employee satisfaction," Tobias stresses. "Doing so will create shared experiences that strengthen the labor community. And a union that focuses on the 95 percent of workers who've never dealt with a formal grievance will increase membership rates and become a vital organization."[26]

Abandonment of the zero-sum adversarial relationship lowers costs. Fewer grievances, arbitrations, unfair labor practices, and lawsuits occur. With the one-to-ten employee enhancement style of management-labor relations, greater human and monetary savings occur. The result is increased productivity and improved employee and consumer-customer-citizen satisfaction.

Radical Individualism and Labor Unions

Public sector labor agreements take place within the cultural context of America's fundamentally egalitarian ideology. Our culture emphasizes individual self-reliance. Citizen status, even personal identity, is derived from individual association with the economy and what one does for a living. Civic membership, as in belonging to a labor union, intersects personal identity with social identity. Social capital may be measured in terms of associational membership and public trust.

Social capital is often said to be on the decline. Expressions of individualism may undermine civic commitment. The decline of political participation follows a very linear trail to the demise of social capital. Welfare-state liberalism, as illustrated by government-funded and -supported public universities, is juxtaposed against neocapitalism. Big business and big government create problems—and often not solutions. More than in comparable countries, Americans think markets are fairer than the mechanisms of local, state, and federal governments.

Corporate formalism, public and private, is accompanied by legalistic notions of the common good. On matters of sex and race, American policy incorporates pharisaic definitions of how governments are to adjudicate "the good life." History shows that labor union membership contributed significantly to the relative affluence and attendant independence of middle-class Americans. (College professors realize the benefits of tenure, a routinized, egalitarian labor guarantee. Many benefit from the sacrifice of the few. Individuals receive benefits and goods even when they do not contribute to the group's efforts.)

Despite renditions of past labor achievements, membership is what facilitates comprehensive labor agreements for government workers. The National Air Traffic Controllers Association (NATCA) succeeded where the defunct Professional Air

Traffic Controllers Organization (PATCO) failed. NATCA, confronting the radical individualism spawned by terrorism, became the first nonpostal employee union to bargain with management over wages. NATCA bargained over money for the 14,300 air traffic controllers it represents and negotiated supervisory staffing levels. The Federal Aviation Administration (FAA), as management, represented the public trust.

NATCA and the FAA—labor and management—met at the critical intersection between personal identity and social indentity. Personal identity focuses on what air traffic controllers do for a living, or their skills, knowledge, and expertise. Social identity promotes the safety of U.S. airline travel. Citizens may disagree as to whether the United States faces a civic identity crisis. September 11 called into question what constitutes civic identity. Airline safety has become not just a social crisis for the greater good, but a personal crisis for anyone who flies airplanes regulated by the FAA. In first class or coach, salaries and benefits of air traffic controllers, articulated by associational membership in the NATCA, a public sector labor union, are of vital concern to all passengers on spaceship earth.[27]

Public Sector Labor Law Impacts

Richard B. Freeman and Casey Ichniowski offer five broad conclusions about the role of labor law in the rise of collective bargaining in the public sector.[28]

1. *The legal environment is critical in determining whether public sector employees bargain collectively with their workers.* The probability that a municipal department is governed by a collective contract is enhanced by favorable state public sector labor laws.
2. *Economic benefits and costs do not readily explain the timing of public sector labor laws.* Public sector labor laws call for legalization of union activities, requiring managers to "meet and confer" with unions, requiring managers to bargain with unions, and mandating arbitration or certain final closure mechanisms to provide a contract.[29] A review of comparative state literature does not explain why certain states enact laws earlier rather than later.[30]
3. *Public sector laws favorable to collective bargaining raise wages in nonunion as well as union departments.* Laws enhance the bargaining power of unions, affect economic outcomes, alter management decision making in both union and nonunion departments. Public sector union members in states favoring collective bargaining receive 6 percent higher salaries, on average, than municipal workers in states with unfavorable laws.[31]
4. *Among states that obligate employers to bargain, wages are no higher with compulsory arbitration than with other dispute resolution mechanisms. Wages are noticeably higher with strike-permitted laws.* Evidence indicates that arbitration laws reduce strike rates. Although compulsory arbitration states do not differ noticeably from duty-to-bargain states, states that permit strikes pay between 2 and 9 percent higher salaries than states prohibiting strikes. In other words, strike-permitted states' laws raise pay; arbitration-permitted states' laws have effectively no impact on pay.[32]

5. *Arbitrators do not favor one side or the other nor respond greatly to the facts of a case when labor and management make "reasonable" proposals; rather, they tend to "split the difference."* Arbitration occurs in a wide range of settings. Most involve a third-party arbitrator or panel of arbitrators hearing and deciding how a dispute is to be resolved. Arbitrators weigh facts but do so differently. Because offers and facts are often unrelated, arbitrators "split the difference" when employers and employees propose alternatives that reflect diverse sets of facts.[33]

The secret to handling all or most of the labor troubles that occur in the public sector is good management. Nearly all sides consider this the sine qua non of good labor relations. Many management people agree that mediocre management probably causes more labor trouble than militant union leadership. Union excesses, say some, spring perhaps most often from managerial misdeeds and mistakes. The real key to achieving peace on the public labor front may lie in developing better policies and better administrators.

Reasons for Union Prominence

The reasons for union prominence in the public sector include (1) changes in the legal environment, (2) changes in public attitudes, and (3) changes in economic conditions. Recent changes in each of these areas will certainly affect the future of public sector unionism, as they have affected its course for the last thirty years.

Changes in the legal environment brought about the striking expansion in public sector union participation between 1960 and 1976. From 1976 through 1986, there was little or no union expansion in the public sector. The proportion of government workers affiliated with unions or unionlike organizations hovered unchanged at around 36 percent.

Changes in public attitudes toward unions paralleled the expansion of public sector unions between 1960 and 1976. By allowing public employees to bargain collectively, legislatures recognized that the sovereignty of state government was not threatened by union activities. The 1976 to 1986 period witnessed a consolidation of public unions. Public attitudes toward public sector unions became less favorable during this period.

Unlike private unions, public sector unions have political power that affects demand for government services, budgets, and outcomes of local elections. Growth in the number of government employees and in budgets results directly from citizen demands for increases in government services.

Changes in economic conditions affect growth in the number of public sector employees, programs, and budgets. When the economy slows, the demand for public services naturally slows as well.

The future of public sector unionism rests on these same three factors. Changes in the legal environment, changes in public attitudes, and changes in economic conditions will shape the future of public sector unionism. Legislation and executive rulings will again be crucial. Union supporters advocate a uniform national law permitting

Student Employees Win Bargaining Rights

Student employees at the University of Washington (UW) now carry union cards. The Washington state legislature granted collective bargaining rights to the approximately 3,700 Academic Student Employees at UW who work, typically, between five and ten years as Teaching, Research, or Staff Assistants. Teaching assistants, readers, graders, and tutors at UW account for approximately 50 percent of UW instructional hours.

"We welcome the passage of this law that extends the many benefits represented by collective bargaining rights to UW's Academic Student Workers," said Kristin Intemann, UW Teaching Assistant in Philosophy. The Public Employment Relations Commission certified the Graduate Student Employee Action Coalition/UAW (GSEAC/UAW). A framework has now been provided for GSEAC/UAW and UW to bargain over wages, benefits, hours, and working conditions.

Collective bargaining for Academic Student Employees is finding a market at universities in California, Massachusetts, and New York.

Source: "GSEAC/UAW Welcomes New Collective Bargaining Law, Files for Union Certification," *UAW News,* March 14, 2002.

government employees to join unions and requiring public sector employees to bargain collectively, but public support for unions has not grown. Women and part-time workers change the composition of the workforce. Demographic trends may again influence the demand for public services, leading to more schools, teachers, and related public services. An increase in the number of schoolteachers will enhance the leverage of government workers. An increase in the number of elderly will increase the demand for government services. The demand for public services may be met through more privatization of government functions, but not all public services are suitable for private sector implementation.[34]

In summary, the argument is made that unions are still needed to protect the worker. Evidence shows that as unions decline, the gap between executive and worker pay is growing. Instead of freeing the worker, automation has made it possible for management to expect even more from employees. Employee participation in management is still controlled by management or administration.[35]

Summary

- Transportation is a catalyst for personal and collective sets of economic improvements.
- A kind of social-work model of unionism replaced the more militant labor versions of petition.
- Unionization is greater in the public sector than in the private sector. The unionization rate in the public sector is about four times that of the private sector.
- Public sector unionism is a product of the Great Society of the 1960s and changed the overall labor movement emphasis from high employment and high wages to redistribution of society's economic resources.
- The decline, transformation, or perhaps reformation of public sector unionism occurs within the context of our changing political culture. Despite being larger than private sector unionism, public unionism is in transition. About 37 percent of government workers engage in collective bargaining. Future government unionization depends upon

organized labor's ability to organize the unorganized.

- Unions (on the positive side) usually prevent strikes or shorten those that do occur. Union leaders much prefer to resolve disputes by negotiation. Public employee unions bring public sector problems before the public.

- Trade unionism, according to its detractors, erodes the concept of government work as a public service. Unions perpetuate some of the worst features of personnel systems. They diffuse responsibility and make accountability more difficult to pinpoint. Unionization greatly increases the political involvement of public employees.

- Within the public sector, local government workers had the highest union membership rate, 41.8 percent. This group includes workers in several heavily unionized occupations, including teachers, police officers, and fire fighters.

- In 2006, wage and salary employment in state and local government, excluding education and hospitals, numbered 8,018,000. Local government units accounted for 69.8 percent of this total.

- The power of public sector labor unions is tenuous. The best organized government employees are teachers. The labor rights of Americans lag behind those of people of other nations.

- In both the public and private sectors, the fundamental role of labor unions is not merely to secure economic benefits, but to take collective action in order to avoid unfair or fraudulent controls by management.

- Major issues in state and local government labor relations focus on the sovereign power of the state and public accountability of government-based unions, perceived pressures of public sector unions on fiscal and budgeting issues, government as the monopoly supplier of certain public goods, and the right of public sector employees to strike.

- When collective bargaining fails, alternatives for avoiding strikes include mediation, fact-finding, and arbitration.

- The increasing financial strain experienced by all levels of government in the 1980s brought on a reaction against growing union influence.

- "Bread-and-butter" issues usually cannot be negotiated in federal government contracts. Strikes, lockouts, and "agency shop" practices are prohibited in the public sector.

- Civil service statutes predate collective bargaining laws in every state. To determine the relationship between the potentially conflicting merit and collective bargaining systems, states have enacted statutes to specify the role of collective bargaining.

- Public sector collective bargaining includes (1) mandatory subjects that must be negotiated, (2) prohibited subjects that may not be bargained, and (3) permissive subjects that may be bargained.

- The District of Columbia and twenty-nine states provide bargaining coverage by statute for all major employee groups. This coverage is realized through a single comprehensive public employee relations policy or separate policies for different functions.

- The decline of labor has accompanied U.S. economic inequality.

- Traditional labor-management relations are a zero-sum game.

- Corporate formalism, public and private, is accompanied by legalistic notions of the common good. History shows that labor union membership contributed significantly to the relative affluence and attendant independence of middle-class Americans.

- The legal environment, economic benefits and costs, favorable collective bargaining laws, compulsory arbitration, strike-permitted laws, and labor-management arbitrators account for many developments in the emergence of collective bargaining in the public sector.

- Explanations for union growth in the public sector include (1) changes in the legal environment, (2) changes in public attitudes, and (3) changes in economic conditions.

- The absolute prerequisite for good labor relations is good management.

Labor Relations
American Dream [1984]
Documentary that follows the story of the dramatic and divisive Hormel strike in Austin, Minnesota, in 1984. Offers lessons for how *not* to "get to yes." Prestige (Miramar). [98 min]

Labor Relations
The Rise of Labor [1969]
A production of Encyclopedia Britannica Educational Corporation. Videocassette release of the 1969 motion picture. Traces history of the American labor movement. Reviews working conditions from the 1800s to the present, effects of early strikes in changing governmental attitudes toward labor, and the organization of AFL-CIO and its impact. [30 min]

Labor History
FAA Air Traffic Control, 1936–1986: Fifty Years of Service [1986]
A history of air traffic control in the United States and the evolution of commercial aviation. [12 min]

Labor History
Organizing America: A History of Trade Unions [2008]
Using interviews, archives, personal accounts, and other sources, this video explores the history of U.S. labor unions in the context of workplace and social issues. Cambridge Educational Films Media Group. [42 min]

Case Study

The FAA, PATCO, and NATCA—and Civil Aviation

The following case study illustrates how economics, job stress, management, government employees, and air safety got caught up in a zero-sum game of partisan, policy, and system politics. The Air Traffic Controllers (ATCs)—exhausted, frustrated, and underpaid, considering their life-and-death responsibilities; positioned with malfunctioning equipment; and burdened by insensitive and ineffective managers—became their own victims.

> They are in violation of the law, and if they do not report for work within forty-eight hours, they have forfeited their jobs and will be terminated.
>
> —*Ronald Reagan, August 3, 1981*
> *PATCO employee ultimatum*

The Federal Aviation Administration (FAA), Professional Air Traffic Controllers Association (PATCO), and National Air Traffic Controllers Association (NATCA) are—or were—regulators and orchestrators of U.S. civil aviation. They fight—or fought—over who controls the federal workplace. Air traffic controllers guide pilots to, around, and from airports throughout the country.

PATCO confronted former President Ronald Reagan and lost. On August 3, 1981, PATCO and almost 13,000 air traffic controllers (ATCs) went on strike after negotiating for months with the federal government.[1] PATCO demanded across-the-board raises of $10,000 for each member, reduction of the work week from 40 to 32 hours, and improved retirement benefits. The media and politicians emphasized PATCO's pay demands. PATCO leaders attempted to focus on hours worked, working conditions, and job pressures.

Two days after the walkout, Reagan fired 11,359 ATCs, about 70 percent of the workforce.[2] Labor law in the United States more often than not supports private property rights. President Reagan had the legal right to fire the PATCO strikers. He declared a lifetime ban on the rehiring of the strikers by the FAA. The turbulent history of FAA-PATCO indicates that both sides took opposing and uncompromising positions. Deep-rooted problems existed.

However, PATCO expected cooperation, if not support, from the Reagan White House regarding the union's call for shorter working hours and higher pay, although PATCO strikers were already the best paid of all AFL-CIO union members. Reagan had sent the union a sympathetic letter when campaigning for the presidency in 1980.

On October 20, 1980, Reagan wrote to PATCO President Robert Poli: "You can rest assured that if I am elected President, I will take whatever steps are necessary to provide our air traffic controllers with the most modern equipment available and to adjust staff levels and work days so that they are commensurate with achieving a maximum degree of public safety."[3] PATCO adherents—along with the Air Line Pilots Association—endorsed Reagan during the 1980 election. Reagan pledged to do whatever was necessary to meet PATCO's needs—and ensure the public's safety. Deregulation—in play since 1978—had worsened already stressful ATC job conditions.

August 3, 1981, was the first day of the strike. The FAA—relying on scabs—was able to keep air traffic at 70 percent of prestrike levels. The FAA's contingency plan functioned smoothly, and the strike's effects were minimized. Approximately 3,000 supervisors, 2,000 nonstriking controllers, and 900 military controllers manned airport towers. The FAA ordered airlines at major airports to reduce scheduled flights. Flights during peak hours were reduced by 50 percent, and nearly 60 percent of small airport towers were shut down indefinitely. Safety was the first priority.

The public—flying or not—sided with the FAA and the federal government. PATCO strikers did not generate much citizen support; for one thing PATCO members earned already above the national salary average. The unionized ATCs did not anticipate public fallout over perceived union disregard for public safety.

Union militants were arrested, jailed, and fined. Some PATCO members jeopardized their home mortgages and economic livelihoods when they decided to strike.

How did the strike affect the U.S. political economy? The airlines employed 340,000 people. Daily commercial flights numbered 14,000. Planes carried 800,000 passengers—60 percent of them business travelers. Air transportation was a $30-billion-per-year business. Air cargo planes moved 10,000 tons daily. Fresh fruit, flower, and fish markets were in jeopardy. Health care priorities depended on access to blood supplies.

The politics of this conflict had a touch of irony. Reagan emerged from the conflict perceived as a strong president, an effective and decisive leader. This view was in direct contrast to the public's view of his predecessor, Jimmy Carter. Reagan pointed out that he was the first president to be a lifetime member of the AFL-CIO. In firing the strikers, Reagan was accused of "brutal overkill." But pilots and machinists crossed PATCO picket lines. Poli was criticized for damaging labor's image, for calling an ill-advised strike.

The 1981 demise of PATCO was not very pretty. "We're not on strike over money. Not 10 or 20 percent of these people would have walked out over money. People are tired of being dumped on, and they want to make it to retirement," said striker Robert Devery.[4] ATC job grievances began during the Carter administration. Reagan decertified the union. He called in military air controllers. He gave the 11,000 strikers an ultimatum: Return to work, or you are fired. Most strikers did not return.

Markets, economic development, and technology highlight the necessity that ATCs enjoy access to a participative model of collective bargaining where work rules, grievance systems, and wage standards can be discussed with higher levels of human civility. An atmosphere of unity and good feeling is essential in this industry. Adaptation to new technologies is omnipresent.

Reagan's PATCO policy—designed to break the strike—began a downward slide to economic conditions that resulted in a less effective labor movement. A weaker labor movement led to a dramatic rise of U.S. income inequality. In 1973, the family income of the richest 5 percent of Americans was 11.3 times the income of the poorest 20 percent. In 1999, the richest made 19.1 times what the poorest earned. Studies indicate that declining unionization caused about one-fifth of this increased inequality.[5]

Twenty years after President Reagan fired the air controllers, NATCA President John Carr stated: "The

PATCO strike was a watershed event in labor history. From those ashes, we have built a relationship with the FAA based on trust, honor, and integrity, and we are doing our best within the limitations of collective bargaining in the federal sector to co-manage the National Airspace System."[6] With twenty years as a job limit for air controllers, retirements could bring a 50 percent job turnover.

George W. Bush, like his father and Reagan, was anything but public-sector-union-friendly. After taking office in 2001, he ordered an end to all labor-management partnerships in the federal government.

The FAA in Civil Aviation History

The Air Commerce Act of May 20, 1926, was the cornerstone of the federal government's regulation of civil aviation. This landmark legislation was passed at the urging of the aviation industry. Industry leaders believed the airplane could not reach its full commercial potential without federal action to improve and maintain safety standards. The Act charged the Secretary of Commerce with fostering air commerce, issuing and enforcing air traffic rules, licensing pilots, certifying aircraft, establishing runways, and operating and maintaining aids to air navigation.

In 1938, the Civil Aeronautics Act transferred federal civil aviation responsibilities from the Commerce Department to a new independent agency, the Civil Aeronautics Authority. In 1940, President Franklin Roosevelt created two agencies—the Civil Aeronautics Administration (CAA) and the Civil Aeronautics Board (CAB). The CAA monitored ATCs, airman and aircraft certification, safety enforcement, and airway development. The CAB monitored safety rule making, accident investigations, and economic regulation of the airlines.

The Federal Aviation Act of 1958 created the Federal Aviation Agency (FAA) as an independent agency. Safety rule making was taken from the CAB and given to the FAA. In 1967, the Department of Transportation (DOT) commenced operations. With a new name, the Federal Aviation Administration (FAA) emerged under the auspices of DOT. The CAB's accident investigation function was transferred to the new National Transportation Safety Board (NTSB). The Airline Deregulation Act of 1978 enhanced the industry's competitive environment.[7]

The FAA is the U.S. government bureaucracy with primary responsibility for the safety of civil aviation. The FAA is headed by an Administrator, who is assisted by a Deputy Administrator. Reporting to the Adminis-

trator are five Associate Administrators who implement the agency's principal functions. The field organization includes nine geographical regions and two major centers. The FAA's major functions include

- Regulating civil aviation to promote safety and fulfill the requirements of national defense
- Encouraging and developing civil aeronautics, including new aviation technology
- Developing and operating a common system of air traffic control and navigation for both civil and military aircraft
- Research and development with respect to the National Airspace System and civil aeronautics
- Developing and implementing programs to control aircraft noise and other environmental effects of civil aviation
- Regulating U.S. commercial space transportation[8]

Nearly 90 percent of the eligible FAA workforce are represented by various unions (see table). Labor organizations representing FAA employees include:

AFGE—American Federation of Government Employees

AFSCME—American Federation of State, County, and Municipal Employees

LIUNA—Laborer's International Union of North America

NAATS—National Association of Air Traffic Specialists

NAGE—National Association of Government Employees

NATCA—National Air Traffic Controllers Association

NFFE—National Federation of Federal Employees

NUDAI—National Union of Drug Abatement Inspectors

PAACE—Professional Association of Aeronautical Center Employees

PASS—Professional Airways Systems Specialists

Union dues are 1.5 percent of step 1 of an employee's federal government grade level. Dues withholding per pay period for 1998 were as follows:[9]

Grade	Dues (per pay period)
FG–9	$19.09
FG–11	23.10
FG–12	27.70
FG–13	32.93
FG–14	38.93

Labor Organizations Representing FAA Employees

Union	Bargaining Units	Labor Agreements	Employees Represented
AFGE	14	5	1,300
AFSCME	5	0	2,200
LIUNA	1	1	150
NAATS	1	1	2,400
NAGE	3	1	400
NATCA (AT)	3	1	15,700
NATCA (AF)	5	1	1,350
NATCA (ABA)	1	0	100
NATCA (AIR)	1	0	530
NATCA (ARC)	1	0	500
NATCA (AFS)	1	0	13
NATCA (AAM)	1	0	42
NATCA (ARP)	1	0	286
NFFE	2	2	1,000
NUDAI	1	0	25
PAACE	3	2	400
PASS (AF/AEA)	1	1	7,500
PASS (AVN)	1	1	250
PASS (AFS)	2	1	3,500
PASS (AIR)	1	0	150
PASS (AOP)	1	0	18
Total	**50**	**17**	**37,814**

Source: FAA Center for Management Development, Palm Coast, FL. "Basic Labor Relations," Overview. Historical Perspective, Stand-Alone Modules (SAMs), 2001; http://www.cmd.faa.gov/LR-SAMs/M-032/Chap-1/032-1-05.htm.

Contract negotiations may begin when:

- The union requests its first meeting with management to discuss a written contract, or submits its contract proposals.
- Management requests a meeting with the exclusive representative to discuss a written contract, or submits its contract proposals.
- Either party notifies the other of its intent to renew, extend, or renegotiate the existing contract—within the time frame specified in the existing collective bargaining agreement.[10]

In 1998, NATCA members negotiated a collective $200 million raise over three years. For the first time, a nonpostal employee union bargained with management over wages. Federal managers, policy makers, and politicians had managed to keep pay off the negotiating table for the forty-year history of modern federal labor relations.

Salaries of controllers in high-traffic centers were increased by as much as $10,000. Reductions in supervisory ranks—decreasing the ratio of managers to front-line personnel from 1-to-7 to 1-to-10—financed the controller salary increases. The NATCA bargained not only over money for the 15,700 air traffic controllers it represented at the time, but also over supervisory staffing levels.[11]

One-to-Ten versus Zero-Sum Labor Decisions

Economics, job stress, and management were the most publicized aspects of the PATCO strike. Except for certain military ATCs, the FAA enjoys a monopoly on hiring and training air traffic controllers. The sensitivity of the culture implies that the economics of air control are a one-to-ten game of labor-management relations—not an absolute zero-sum game, as practiced by President Reagan in 1981.

Aviation employees focus on these factors:

- *New sources of safety data.* Improving air safety depends on collecting and analyzing safety data, developing safer systems, and taking corrective action before accidents occur.
- *Incentives to report safety issues.* Aviation employees are encouraged to report safety problems. Employees who report safety problems are protected. The Justice Department prosecutes potential criminal activities.

- *Reducing accidents and tracking problems.* Accident reduction is a priority. Human performance errors need examination. Pilots and mechanics demand improved training programs. User-friendly technology—in the cockpit and control towers—enhances skills, knowledge, and expertise.[12]

What power government employees enjoy is grounded in politics. Yet the dominant power of the marketplace is obvious. Labor rights in the United States lag behind those in other developed nations. The legal environment is critical. PATCO members violated the law. They decided to strike against the policies of their employer—the FAA. President Reagan acted within the confines of law.

The ATCs—exhausted, frustrated, and underpaid, considering their life-and-death responsibilities; positioned with malfunctioning equipment; and burdened by insensitive and ineffective managers—became their own victims. President Reagan spoke for the community of the collective welfare, national interests, and the greater good.

Questions and Instructions

1. How do issues such as individualism and community impact the FAA, PATCO, NATCA, and civil aviation challenges? Explain.
2. PATCO and NATCA illustrate the dynamics of "New Unionism." How is "New Unionism" different from "Old Unionism"? Explain.
3. Why is the PATCO strike considered the "watershed event" in "New Unionism" labor history? Explain.
4. Why is an atmosphere of unity and good feeling essential in the civil aviation industry? Explain.
5. Nearly 90 percent of eligible FAA workers are represented by unions. Why is this so? Explain.
6. In the public sector, collective bargaining is multilateral—not bilateral, as in the private sector. Using the FAA, PATCO, NATCA, and civil aviation as your illustration, explain why this is so.

7. Union leaders and managers are no longer playing a zero-sum game. How does the zero-sum adversarial relationship lower costs? Using the FAA, PATCO, NATCA, and civil aviation as your illustration, explain why this is so.
8. Social capital may be on the decline. Individualism may undermine civic commitments. Using the FAA, PATCO, NATCA, and civil aviation as your illustration, explain why this is so.
9. The legal environment is critical in determining whether public sector employees bargain collectively with their workers. Using the FAA, PATCO, NATCA, and civil aviation as your illustration, explain why this is so.
10. The ATCs (air traffic controllers) are public sector employees. Aside from obvious safety demands, how are their job assignments crucial to the economy? Explain.

Insights-Issues/The FAA, PATCO, and NATCA—and Civil Aviation

Clearly and briefly describe and illustrate the following concepts or issues. Interpret the word *role* as meaning impacts, applications, importance, effects and/or illustrations of certain facts, concerns, or issues from the case study.

1. Role of individualism and community as impacting the FAA, PATCO, NATCA, and civil aviation.
2. Role of markets, economic development, and technology as impacting the FAA, PATCO, and NATCA—and civil aviation.

3. Role of "New Unionism" and "Old Unionism" as impacting the FAA, PATCO, and NATCA—and civil aviation.

4. Role of federal laws as impacting the FAA, PATCO, and NATCA—and civil aviation.

5. Role of corporate formalism, public and private, and legalistic notions of the common good as impacting the FAA, PATCO, and NATCA—and civil aviation.

Notes

1. Jason Manning, "The Air Traffic Controllers' Strike," 2000, http://wolfstories2.tripod.com/id33.htm.

2. History Channel, "Speeches: Ronald Reagan, Fortieth U.S. President, on the Striking Air-Traffic Controllers," http://www.historychannel.com/speeches/archive/speech_227.htm.

3. Manning, "Air Traffic Controllers' Strike."

4. "When Air Traffic Controllers Took on Ronald Reagan: Lessons of PATCO," *Socialist Worker Online,* August 3, 2001, http://www.socialistworker.org/2001/374/374_10_PATCO.shtml.

5. David Moberg, "The Consequences of the Air Traffic Controllers' Strike, 20 Years Later," *The Progressive Magazine Media Project,* http://www.progressive.org/pmp0701/pmpmj2601.html.

6. "NATCA Marks 20th Anniversary of PATCO Strike," National Air Traffic Controllers Association, AFL-CIO Media Center, August 8, 2001, http://www.natca.org.

7. "A Brief History of the Federal Aviation Administration and Its Predecessor Agencies," http://www.faa.gov/apa/history/briefhistory.htm.

8. "An Overview of the Federal Aviation Administration," http://www.faa.gov/apa/history/ overvue.htm.

9. NATCA: Frequently Asked Questions: "How Much Are Dues?" http://eea.natca.net/faq.htm.

10. "FAA Bargaining Unit Contracts, Collective Bargaining Agreements," http://fedlabor.org/Contracts/.

11. Jonathan Walters, "The Power of Pay," *Government Executive,* January 1, 1999, http://www.govexec.com/news/index.cfm.

12. The White House, Office of the Press Secretary, "New Public-Private Partnerships to Increase Aviation Safety," January 14, 2000, http://clinton4.nara.gov/WH/New/html/20000114 .html.

Sources

FAA Office of Public Affairs, "Historic Labor Agreement for New Partnership," June 15, 1998, http://www.faa.gov/apa/pr/jun/dot11598.html; Owen F. Lipsett, "Should Reagan Fly Off Into The Sunset?" *The Phoenix Online,* February 20, 1998, http://www.sccs.swartmore.edu/org/phoenix/1998/1998-02-20/7.html; Joseph A.

McCartin, "Marking a Tragic Anniversary," *History News Service,* August 3, 2001, http://www2.h-net.msu.edu/~hns/articles/archives/2001/080301a.html; Brian Trumbore, "Educate Yourself: In Honor of Ronald Reagan," http://www.buyandhold.com/bb/en/education/history/2001/ronaldreagan.html.

Notes

1. Stanley Aronowitz, *From the Ashes of the Old: American Labor and America's Future* (New York: Houghton Mifflin Company, 2002).

2. Richard B. Freeman, "Through Pubic Sector Eyes: Employee Attitudes Toward Public Sector Labor Relations in the U.S.," in *Public Sector Employment in a Time of Transition,* edited by Dale Belman, Morley Gunderson, and Douglas Hyatt, pp. 59–84.

3. U.S. Bureau of Labor Statistics, "Table 3: Union Affiliation of Employed Wage and Salary Workers by Occupation and Income 2001, http://stats.bls.gov/news.release/union2.t03.htm; "Union Members Summary: Union Members in 2001," *News,* January 17, 2002, http//stats.bls.gov/news.release/union2.nrO.htm. State union membership rates continue to show a clear geographic pattern. All states in the East North Central, Middle Atlantic, and Pacific regions had union membership rates above the national average of 13.5 percent, while

all states in the East South Central and West South Central regions had below average rates.

4. Steven Greenhouse, "Labor Leader Sounds Do-or-Die Warning," *New York Times,* February 19, 2001. According to a survey tabulated at the Cornell University School of Labor Relations, managers at 70 percent of factories where organizing drives are ongoing threaten to close if workers unionize. Survey data indicate that workers often say threats to discourage them from voting to join labor unions.

5. Greg Tarpinian, "Public Sector Workers and Unions Today," *LABORRESEARCH Online,* May 16, 2001; see http://www.laborresearch .org/dis.shtmlpubsec.txt.

6. Richard B. Freeman, Robert B. Reich, Josh S. Weston, John Sweeney, William J. McDonough, and John Mueller, "Toward a Apartheid Economy?" *Harvard Business Review* 74, no. 5 (September–October 1996): 114–127.

7. Leo Troy, "The Rise and Fall of American Trade Unions: The Labor Movement from FDR to RR," in *Unions in Transition: Entering the Second Century,* ed. Seymour Martin Lipset (San Francisco: ICS Press, Institute for Contemporary Studies, 1986), pp. 75–109. See also Troy, "Is Unionism in Permanent Decline?" *Chicago Tribune,* September 1, 1986, section 1, p. 11.

8. Troy, "Rise and Fall," p. 106.

9. U.S. Department of Labor, Bureau of Labor Statistics, http://www.bls.gov/news.release/ union2.nr0.htm.

10. Rodger Doyle, "U.S. Workers and the Law: Labor Rights of Americans Lag Behind Those of Other Nations," *Scientific American,* August 2001, p. 24.

11. Richard D. Kahlenberg, "Labor Organizing as a Civil Right," *The Century Foundation New Ideas for a New Century,* Idea Brief No. 15, August 2000, www.tcf.org; Richard B. Freeman and Joel Rogers, *What Workers Want* (New York and Ithaca, NY: Russell Sage/Cornell University Press, 1999), p. 1.

12. Dwight Waldo, *The Enterprise of Public Administration: A Summary View* (Novato, CA: Chandler & Sharp, 1980), p. 164.

13. Leo Troy, "Is the U.S. Unique in the Decline of Private Sector Unionism?" *Journal of Labor Research* 11, no. 1 (Spring 1990): 111–114.

14. David Lewin, "Public Employee Unionism in the 1980s: An Analysis of Transformation," in *Unions in Transition: Entering the Second Century,* ed. Seymour Martin Lipset (San Francisco: Institute for Contemporary Studies, 1986), pp. 241–264; see also Chimezie A. B. Osigweh, "Collective Bargaining and Public Sector Union Power," *Public Personnel Management* 14 (Spring 1985): 75–84; Douglas M. McCabe, "Labor Relations, Collective Bargaining, and Performance Appraisal in the Federal Government Under the Civil Service Reform Act of 1978," *Public Personnel Management* 13 (Summer 1984): 133–146; and R. Douglas Collins, "Agency Shop in Public Employment," *Public Personnel Management* 15 (Summer 1986): 171–179.

15. Leo Troy, *The End of Unionism: A Reappraisal* (St. Louis, MO: Center for the Study of American Business, 1994); *The New Unionism in the New Society: Public Sector Unions in the Redistributive State* (Fairfax, VA: George Mason University Press, 1994).

16. Leo Troy, "The End of Unionism: A Reappraisal," *Current,* no. 373 (June 1995): 26–33.

17. Michael Ballot, with contributions from Laurie Lichter-Heath, Thomas Kail, and Ruth Wang, *Labor-Management Relations in a Changing Environment,* 2d ed. (New York: John Wiley & Sons, 1996), pp. 478–482.

18. George Bennet, "Tools to Resolve Labor Disputes in the Public Sector," *Personnel* 50, no. 2 (March–April 1973).

19. *Boston Herald-American,* March 28, 1973.

20. *Federal Labor Relations: A Program in Need of Reform* (Washington, DC: U.S. General Accounting Office, 1991). GAO Publication GAO/GGD–91–101.

21. From http://www.opm.gov/cplmr/html/ unions.asp. For current data on federal labor-management relations, see http://www.opm .gov/lmr/index.asp; also see http://www .federaldaily.com/labor.

22. Ballot, *Labor-Management Relations,* p. 429.

23. Joel M. Douglas, "State Civil Service and Collective Bargaining Systems in Conflict," *Public Administration Review* 52, no. 1 (January/February 1992): 162–172.

24. Stephan Barr, "A Labor-Management Thicket Awaits Bush Administration," *Washington Post,* January 12, 2001, p. B2.

25. Douglas, "State Civil Service."

26. Robert M. Tobias, "Giving Up the Good Fight," *Government Executive,* March 28, 2000, http://www/govexec.com.

27. Robert Bellah et al., "Individualism and the Crisis of Civic Membership," http://www .religion-online.org/cgi-bin/relsearchd.dll/ showarticleitem_id=224; Robert D. Putnam, *Bowling Alone: The Collapse and Revival of American Community* (New York: Touchstone Books, 2000); Jay Walters, "The Power of Pay," *Government Executive,* January 1, 1999, http://www/govexec.com.

28. Richard B. Freeman and Casey Ichniowski, "Introduction: The Public Sector Look of American Unionism," in *When Public Sector Workers Unionize,* ed. Richard B. Freeman

and Casey Ichniowski (Chicago: University of Chicago Press, 1988), pp. 1–15.

29. Richard B. Freeman and Robert G. Valletta, "The Effects of Public Sector Labor Laws on Labor Market Institutions and Outcomes," in *When Public Sector Workers Unionize,* ed. Freeman and Ichniowski (Chicago: University of Chicago Press, 1988), pp. 81–103.

30. Henry S. Farber, "The Evolution of Public Sector Bargaining Laws," in *When Public Sector Workers Unionize,* ed. Freeman and Ichniowski (Chicago: University of Chicago Press, 1988), pp. 129–166.

31. Freeman and Valletta, "Effects of Public Sector Labor Laws."

32. Ibid., pp. 97–99.

33. David E. Bloom, "Arbitrator Behavior in Public Sector Wage Disputes," in *When Public Sector Workers Unionize,* ed. Freeman and Ichniowski (Chicago: University of Chicago Press, 1988), p. 122.

34. Linda N. Edwards, "The Future of Public Sector Unions: Stagnation or Growth?" *AEA Papers and Proceedings* 79, no. 2 (May 1989): 161–165.

35. John Buell, "The Future of Unions," *The Humanist* 57, no. 5 (September–October 1997): 41–42.

Communication and Leadership

Chapter Highlights

Communication and Public Administration

Formal and Informal Communication

The Information Highway

E-Government and Communications

The Other Organization

Upward, Downward, and Lateral Communications

Leadership and Needs of the Situation

Leadership Qualities

Leadership and Charisma

Institutionalizing the American Presidency

The Limits of Leadership

Summary

Student Government Association at Steady State University: Communications

Purposes

The Student Government Association (SGA) at Steady State University (SSU), College Corner, State of Commonwealth, has six major purposes:

- To represent the interest of the student body in student, university, and governmental affairs.
- To provide services that improve the quality of life of SSU students.
- To keep the student body informed of relevant issues.
- To coordinate and regulate student activities and funds in the interests of the student body.
- To maintain an interactive relationship between the student body and the local community.
- To serve as the chief representative body of students at SSU. This mission, as well as our operating procedures, can be found in the SGA constitution, bylaws, and guidelines.

Steady State University (SSU)

Steady State University is a comprehensive, state-funded institution of higher education. Its mission is to provide excellent education. It is located in College Corner, sixty-nine miles from Big Burb, the state capital. Students enrolled at SSU are subsidized by the State of Commonwealth. All SSU graduates are expected to be able to analyze information, think critically, solve problems, communicate effectively, demonstrate competency with computers, and converse in at least one foreign language.

Meetings and Membership

SGA meetings are held every other Tuesday at 6.30 P.M. at 2468 Steady State Alumni Hall, unless otherwise specified. All students are welcome to attend. Any accredited student enrolled at SSU can become a member of the SGA. If you are interested, fill out a membership form at http://www.ssu.edu/sga.

Committees

Within SGA are nine committees, each dedicated to fulfilling a certain part of our mission. These committees are:

- *SSU Campus Improvements.* The purpose of the Campus Improvements Committee is to receive and respond to student concerns and suggestions that focus on physical changes to campus. Past projects include an addition to the Student Center and a twenty-four-hour study area. The committee also works to improve campus safety.
- *Web Administration.* The Web Administration Committee is responsible for maintaining the SGA Web site and providing Web-related assistance to student organizations. Due to the work-intensive nature of the committee, Web Administration members are not required to serve project hours.
- *External Funding.* The External Funding Committee reviews applications for the Club Appropriations Fund, the Nonvarsity Sports Fund, and the Professional Projects Fund. Recommendations for the appropriations of these funds are then presented to the SGA.
- *Intercultural Relations.* Intercultural Relations assists SSU-recognized organizations in promoting intercultural events on campus. The committee helps international and minority groups with programming and publicity for campuswide events, such as campuswide diversity workshops. The committee offers proposals and provides insights to the SGA and the University regarding cultural issues. Specifically, this committee coordinates Diversity Week activities.
- *Issues Committee.* Got a problem? Have you and your friends been discussing things that are missing on campus—services, policies, programs, or people? Are you perturbed by a recent incident on campus? The Issues Committee coordinates investigative panels to examine campus issues brought forward

by members of the SSU student body. This committee recommends likely solutions to the SSU administration.

- *Parent-Alumni Relations.* The Parent-Alumni Relations Committee serves as a liaison to the Parents Association and the Alumni Board and makes recommendations to these two groups on projects that would benefit the student body as a whole. The committee keeps track of SSU SGA alumni and coordinates an SGA reunion reception during Homecoming as well as a student-alumni mentoring program. In addition, this committee seeks new sources of funds for SGA.
- *Student Services and Activities.* The Student Services Committee improves current SSU services and provides new services to help students at SSU. This committee organizes a student-run book sale every semester. This committee also facilitates interorganization activities, organizes four yearly blood drives on campus, and coordinates the SGA Student Leadership Recognition Banquet.
- *Student Activity Fee Board.* The Student Activity Fee Board serves as exchequer for the student body and the independent organization. It provides financial guidance and assistance to the organizations it influences and makes certain all monies are used for their intended purpose. The Student Activity Fee Board provides recommendations and information to the SGA membership free of favoritism or discrimination.
- *University Relations.* The purpose of the University Relations Committee is to act as a direct liaison between students and the University. This committee receives and responds to student complaints that involve University policy and directs those complaints to the proper channels for resolution. Some projects include improvements to the current advising and registration systems.

The SSU Student Council

The SSU Student Council is the legislative body of the Student Government Association. Each council member represents a department, college, institute, or special unit of SSU. Some departments, colleges, institutes, and units have more than one representative. There are sixty-five council members.

The departments, colleges, institutes, and units include accounting, anthropology, applied sciences and technology, architecture, art, biology, business, chemistry, computer science, continuing education, counseling psychology, criminal justice, economics, educational psychology, elementary education, English, finance, geography, geology, gerontology, graduate school, history, humanities, lab school, industry and technology, international programs, journalism, management, marketing, mathematical sciences, military science, modern languages, music, natural resources, nursing, parking services, philosophy, planning, religious studies, physics, physiology and health science, political science, psychology, social work, sociology, special education, speech pathology and audiology, telecommunications, theatre and dance, urban planning, and wellness.

The SSU Student Council meets once each week. Students do not have to be SGA members to come to these sessions. All meetings are open to everyone, and students are welcome to come and participate in the discussions. A special time is reserved every week to hear concerns from any member of the SSU community. This time is called Student Open Forum, and it begins at 7:15 P.M. Students do not have to call anyone or be on the agenda. Just raise your hand, stand up, and say what's on your mind.

Inquiries may be sent by e-mail or snail-mail to:

Student Council President
Steady State University
2468 Steady State Alumni Hall
College Corner, Commonwealth 69069
Phone: (069) 690-6906 or FAX: (069) 690-0696
http://www.ssu.edu/sga

The Lowdown on SSU and SGA

SSU is a formal, government-funded and -regulated organization. It is chartered by the State of Commonwealth and operates according to the laws of Commonwealth and the United States. Communications that occur at SSU do so within the culture of governments and laws. SSU is an opportunity institution.

Formal communications are written. The SGA constitution, bylaws, and guidelines are formal communications. Informal communications are oral. SGA discussions are informal exchanges among council members. (The SGA secretary takes notes on the proposals and conversations, and the notes formalize SGA member comments.) Inflections, gestures, and even body language are part of the informality of SGA debates.

SGA students who come from public administration class think they have experienced a base case of communication overload: too many acronyms, agencies, programs, policies, and problems. SGA members not only decide public policy controversies, they attempt to make common sense of why SSU vice presidents do what they do. SGA members try to find rationality within a university community of ethnic and racial diversity.

The organizational size of the Steady State University contributes to SGA's challenges. SSU has 18,000 graduate and undergraduate students. The larger the government organization, the more likely it is to rely on formal communications. The public character of SSU does not go without notice. Government agencies get their missions from laws, rules, regulations, and money.

SSU did not escape the ravages of the paper revolution. Records are carefully maintained. Every student creates a "paper trail" at SSU with grade sheets. SSU enrollment is the beginning of a process of meeting the requirements of a certain number of courses in a particular academic major. Professors have task specializations. The exponential growth of communications technologies—computers, cell phones, answering machines, photostat machines, and used cars—affords students all kinds of possibilities and some problems.

The small-group dynamic is evident in SGA deliberations. SGA members from the humanities, sciences, and media majors more easily form coalitions to pass legislation than do members from the business and architecture colleges. Primary peer contacts between members take precedence over secondary relationships.

Who makes the rules? SSU SGA students make the rules. A prelaw student usually assumes the task of SGA parliamentarian. Students are primarily interested in keeping tuition fees low and state legislator-taxpayer funding high. Tuition hikes and state subsidies pique the interests of SSU students. SGA leaders have state government funding at the top of their legislative agenda. SSU administrators and professors have little interest in SGA activities.

Lateral communication is prevalent within SGA. All SGA members are students at SSU, and students form a peer group. SGA members furnish emotional and social support to one another as they act on matters that affect the entire student body. Psychological forces cause communication among peers. People in the same boat share the same problems.

Upward communication is not particularly important. In decades past, freshmen paid some attention to the experience and views of seniors. Freshmen today often think they have a better grasp of SSU welfare-state politics than senior SGA leaders. The egalitarian nature of being a SSU student makes downward communication problematic. Everybody is an expert, yet nobody knows a lot about anything. Effective downward communication is rare because SGA leaders often lack skills and knowledge of the issues.

The grapevine flourishes at SSU. The "other" organization within SGA is manned by fraternity members who sit in the back row and poke fun at SGA leaders. SGA formal communication restrains arbitrariness, capriciousness, favoritism, and communication. SGA members tend to obey only those rules in which they believe.

The SSU SGA tries to build rationality from a diversity of issues and student interests. The formal SGA organization cannot exist without its informal counterpart. SSU is a state-funded university. As a unit subject to the laws and budgets of the State of Commonwealth, SGA leaders and members must adhere to all laws—respecting due process, or fairness, in all actions.

Will SGA members make a difference within the SSU, College Corner, or State of Commonwealth communities? Perhaps they will—if they create ideas they can market among other publics, including administrators, professors, alumni, state legislators, and entrepreneurs.

Communication and Public Administration

Communication and public administration, or organizational structure, are crucial factors for achieving the integration and coordination of agency goals, rules, and human resources. Structures, processes, and cultures of government bureaus must be defined and communicated. Organizational structure sways communication direction and substance. Formal communication and the formal authority structure merge. Vertical communication is transmitted between government executives and agency employees. Horizontal communication probes the roles of tasks, work units, and divisions.

Human communication is ongoing, interactive, and dynamic. Communication models find their origins in Greek antiquity. Aristotle recognized the speaker, speech, and audience as communication components. Five hundred years before Christ, the Greek philosopher Heraclitus observed that "a man [or woman] can never step into the same river twice. The man [or woman] is different and so is the river."[1] Change and continuity are interwined in a process of actions that flow through the ages. Communication is a process that flows like a stream through time.

The Politics of Greeting

Male primates have elaborate greeting rituals that include touching one another's genitals. Human males greet one another and interact in a far more casual manner than do women. Women put a great deal of effort into putting others at ease.

Source: Michael Segell, "The Politics of Greeting," *Esquire* 128, no. 1 (July 1997): 84–86.

Communication presents as many problems as any other aspect of administration, if not more. There are, first, the *technical* problems. Communication problems arise not only from information that is too slow, incomplete, or distorted, but also from information that is overabundant. This is the problem of *communication overload*. Occasionally, this communication problem arises by intent. For example, school superintendents sometimes purposely flood their school board members with reports and other documents, which, although completely accurate, are so voluminous it is impossible for the board members to know what is happening. As the board members struggle in vain to keep abreast of the swelling tide of information, the superintendent calmly proceeds to do pretty much whatever he or she wants to do.

Most overload problems, however, arise from sheer force of circumstance, and the circumstances that make for too much communication are increasing all the time. The growing complexity, specialization, and interdependence of today's organizational world are adding to the rising flood of information—a process being aided and abetted by the exponential growth of *communications technology*. An organization may take great care and achieve great success in developing excellent lines and flows of communication, only to sink under the profusion of information that may develop as a result.

Formal and Informal Communication

Communication falls into two basic and easily defined categories, formal and informal. *Formal communication is written communication; informal is oral.* Of course, not all informal communication is verbal. Attitudes and even ideas can be transmitted by means of inflection, gesture, and body language, but although nonverbal communication has a place in organizational life, its role is usually not great and, in any case, it is hard to analyze and define. Consequently, our discussion of informal communication will be directed toward verbal communication. What factors govern the use of one form of communication over the other? Under what conditions does formal communication take precedence over informal, and vice versa?

Usually, two factors foster the use of formal communication. One of these is *organizational size*. As organizations grow, they tend to make increasing use of formal communication and, correspondingly, diminishing use of informal. The other factor is *public character*. Public organizations tend to rely more heavily on formal communication than do private ones.

Formal communication fosters *accountability*. By facilitating accountability, formal communication places natural restraints on arbitrariness, capriciousness, favoritism, and discrimination. By proceeding on formal instructions and keeping records of their transactions, public officials find it much more difficult, although certainly not impossible, to depart from acceptable standards of impartiality and fairness. Of course, the rules and standards may be unfair, but if so, this is at least a matter of public record and can be easily determined. An administrator with integrity will welcome the opportunity to document his or her actions.

Proponents of formal communication argue that it is:

- Official, more binding, and more likely to be obeyed
- Written, more precise, and less likely to be misunderstood
- Inscribed, so that it can be traced at any time and preserved for numerous distributions
- Official, establishing responsibility of the sender and receiver beyond any doubt
- Routinized, saving time and effort otherwise consumed in informal talks, discussions, and even arguments
- More definite, avoiding the embarrassment of the face-to-face contact between persons if the communication is sensitive or painful[2]

The use of the written word tends to encourage its further use, and many governmental and private organizations have found themselves swamped in a *sea of documentation*. Detractors argue that formal communication is:

- Too rigidly defined, limiting information within the department to that sanctioned by the chief executive or supervisor
- Codified by language, obscuring the real meaning of communication, permitting more than one interpretation, or using cautious phraseology and "bureaucratic jargon"
- Substantively superficial, failing to identify the reasons for the message and causing the recipient consternation and frustration
- Costly in terms of secretarial efforts, reproduction costs, and delivery time
- Top-down, reflecting authoritarianism, as the formal arrangement is based on the descent of executive information and not on the ascent of employee concerns
- Impersonal and final, failing to motivate employees
- Elementary and trivial, devaluing the intelligence of recipients
- Divisive, separating personnel into "recipients" and "nonrecipients"[3]

The Information Highway

Technology impacts modes of communication, formal and informal. In an era of faxes, computers, and photocopiers, communication challenges will emerge that are even more complex, demanding, and technical. Cell phones, e-mail, and telephone answering machines contribute to the narrowing of the gulf between formal and informal communication distinctions.

Technology is crucial in the development of the information highway that would link every home to a fiber-optic network over which voice, data, television, and other services would be transmitted. The Internet's architecture is determined by an informal group of U.S.-based software and computer engineers. The Internet's global scope and electronic commerce's growth make its management an international policy issue. Analysts and government believe a hands-off approach is best.[4]

People and organizations, not computers, determine the course of the future. As a form of communication, the Internet can be used by individuals, private corporations, and government agencies for good or bad, but it cannot influence the direction our society chooses to take. The Internet only reflects the society that created it. The development and use of the telegraph and telephone provide a definitive pattern for how the newest form of networked communication, the Internet, will be used in the future.[5]

The lack of accountability and civility has increased as the anonymity in U.S. society has increased, states newspaper columnist Ellen Goodman. She cites the anonymous zones of talk radio and cyberspace among the foxholes for people who want to say anything and everything with impunity.[6]

Despite the downside of the information highway, Internet access has made communication between local government and citizens much easier nationwide. Public records access, personnel postings, permit applications, and legislative updates are available online in many cities and counties.[7]

The technology of the Internet may afford the masses access to much more information and many more options. Internet technology is neither evil nor good. "Thanks to the Internet and satellite TV, the world is being wired together technologically, but not socially, politically, or culturally," concludes *New York Times* columnist Thomas L. Friedman. "We are now seeing and hearing one another faster and better, but with no corresponding improvement in our ability to learn from, or understand, one another. So integration, at this stage, is producing more anger than anything else."[8]

The World Wide Web—the Internet—as Community?

Is the Internet public or private? The World Wide Web is not the domain of any government or group of governments. The Internet functions informally, as a worldwide community of communicators. Is that communication formal or informal? Employ the delete button, and poof—your copy disappears into cyberspace. But if you print your copy, the informality of the Internet becomes formalized by paper and ink.

The Internet was originally formed in 1969 as a military network at the Department of Defense (DOD). The early cyberspace version was called the Advanced Research Projects Agency network (ARPAnet). Nonmilitary users were given access to the network in the 1970s. Universities and companies doing defense-related research came on board first. The WWW began to flourish as most universities and many businesses around the world came online. In 1989, Tim Berners-Lee proposed the World Wide Web project. This endeavor is credited with bringing the Internet to the masses. In 1991, commercial providers began selling Internet connections to individuals, and WWW usage exploded. A new era of computer communications began.

Founded in 1985 as Quantum Computer Services, America Online officially became AOL in 1989. By 1993, AOL had 500,000 members; by 1997, 9 million; by 2001, 21 million. The history of Internet servers encompasses more than merely connections between computers; the purpose is to connect people. In this perspective, AOL is a very large unincorporated world community.

The Internet video business cannot easily be regulated by government administrators. The Internet reaches beyond the sovereignty of states—American and worldwide. Legislators do not dare regulate the likes of YouTube. Approximately three in four U.S. Internet users (nearly 136 million Americans) view online video. Governments suffer from culture lag as they try to keep tabs on Internet communications.

According to a ComScore Video Metrix report, 70 million people viewed more than 2.5 billion videos on YouTube.com in September 2007. YouTube dominates the Internet video business, controlling 27.6 percent of the market. Google sites, led by YouTube, captured the largest video audience with 71.6 million unique viewers, followed by Fox Interactive Media (41.2 million) and Yahoo sites (39.6 million). The average online video viewer consumed sixty-six videos, or more than two per day.

Sources: America Online, http://www.aol.com/nethelp/misc/history.html; Steve Donohue, "YouTube Dominates Internet Video, with 27.3% Share," *Multichannel News*, November 30, 2007.

Employers and E-Mail

Most people are introduced to e-mail and Internet access in the workplace. It's in the workplace that they discover, too often, a lesser-known aspect of this exceptionally fluid and informal form of communication: *It has no guarantee of privacy.* For reasons that have occasioned much armchair psychological speculation, most of those new to e-mail seem to act as if they had a high expectation of privacy—indeed, as if they were talking to intimate friends. E-mailers also frequently blurt out things electronically that would never be said face-to-face.

Source: "Employers and E-mail," Washington Post, April 18, 1998, p. 18A.

The Internet educates people faster than any previous technology the world has known. However, the Internet can just as easily infiltrate the minds of millions with lies, half-truths, and hatreds. "The Internet," says Friedman, "at its ugliest, is just an open sewer: an electronic conduit for untreated, unfiltered information." The Internet and satellite TV may inflame emotions and cultural biases, resulting in less understanding and tolerance. Government programs are built on political consensus. Legislation is enacted for the long term. Compromises are based on education, exchanges, diplomacy, and human interaction.

Advances in the use of information technology (IT) and the Internet continue to change the way that federal agencies communicate, use, and disseminate information, deliver services, and do business. Electronic government (e-government) refers to the use of technology, particularly Web-based Internet applications.

Informal Communication

Oral communication offers a solution to many of the problems encountered in written communication. It does not flood the office worker's desk or clog the files. It can evoke immediate feedback, which, in turn, can lead to a resolution of issues or clarification of misunderstood points. In the process, the one communicating can be assured that his or her information has been received. Speaking and listening permit shading, emphasis, and gesture. Conversation is also significantly more human and often more humane. People are dealing together directly.

Efforts have long been underway to substitute oral for written communication. President Johnson's task force on cutting red tape, for example, urged federal officials to make more extensive use of the telephone and less use of "time-consuming written communications."[9] It is possible that the use of oral communication will grow apace in governmental agencies, although it will most likely never replace formal communication. For reasons noted earlier, the written word and the printed document will probably continue to serve as the mainstay of the communications process in any developed democracy.

Grapevines

Any agency that has an informal organization will also have an informal communications system, often referred to as the "grapevine." Informal organizations are found in almost all organizations; therefore, grapevines are ubiquitous.

The grapevine, or informal communication network in government organizations, can have negative effects such as resentment, embarrassment for upper-level administrators, distorted messages, rumor diffusion, and subversion of administrative decision making. Grapevines develop when employees share common hobbies, lunch schedules, family ties, hometowns, and social relationships. These informal networks operate quickly, often accurately, and with resilience. It is suggested that management should use the network for its own purposes to complement formal networks. Administrators should also be candid about information if possible.[10]

Grapevines can also be terribly efficient. "With the rapidity of a burning powder train," says Keith Davis, a professor of management who has studied grapevines for years, "information flows out of the woodwork, past the manager's door and the janitor's mop closet, through steel walls or construction-glass partitions."[11] What is more, Davis claims, more than three-fourths of this information is accurate.

Even when it is not accurate, says Davis, the grapevine may convey a psychological truth, for many rumors that run rampant through an organization are "symbolic expressions of feelings." If the rumor is that a certain employee is planning to quit, it may reflect the wish on the part of fellow employees that he or she would quit. Or it may reflect the employee's own desire to leave.

Proponents of informal communication argue that it is:

- Less official and less intimidating, enhancing the new flow of ideas and solicits plans without fear of punishment
- Personal, embracing enthusiasm, reflecting the zeal of the participants, and playing down the relevance of dry, bureaucratic logic
- Usually verbal, allowing informal communication, permiting exploration of hidden dimensions of government organization, and facilitating two-way communication
- Revealing of underlying motives and pressures, promoting an atmosphere of free yet discreet discussion, and explaining to employees why the department works the way it does
- Better at refuting rumors and putting an end to office gossip filtering through the formal environment, complete with unanswered questions
- Reflective of a spirit of comraderie that unites workers by the discovery of shared concerns and interests
- Able to sustain a harmonious relationship between officers and their superiors, promoting cooperation based on mutual understanding and concern

Detractors argue that informal communication is:

- Difficult to define or apply in systematic ways
- Inaccurate, spreading half-truths and sometimes resulting in second- and third-hand information being represented as original, factual, and trustworthy
- Indiscriminate, possibly leading to disclosure of classified information
- Emotional, distorting or changing meaning to fit the personal sentiments of the bearer
- Verbal and difficult to trace, making further inquiry problematic
- Of questionable social advantage, as it is only as constructive as participants deem it to be[12]

Formal communication—certainly historic and more traditional—functions as a means of controlling agency activities. Authoritative policies and procedures circulate among personnel. Formal specifications state what is to be done when, where, how, and by whom. Formal communication allows the organization to "track" issues through organization "channels."

Organizations are groupings of social beings, however. A certain amount of informal and personal communication occurs within the ranks. Participants seek the "right" mixture of informal and formal communications. No magic formula exists for arriving at this mixture. A proper blend of formal and informal communications depends upon participants and organization leaders.

The organization's environment and the needs of personnel—along with the maturity and intelligence of leaders—determine the appropriateness of a given mixture of informal and formal communications. Informal communications—in a trustworthy language—may supplement the formal structure. In this fashion, workers are reassured, improve their attitudes, and deepen their commitments to the department.[13]

E-Government and Communications

E-government seeks to improve relationships between the private citizen and public sector services. This mostly informal, sometimes formal, application of government includes every technology from fax machines to wireless Palm Pilots. E-government is not exclusively an Internet-driven activity. Cost-effective and efficient, e-government enhances citizens' access to government information, services, and expertise. Five guiding principles ensure citizen participation in—and satisfaction with—the governing process:

- Building services around citizens' choices
- Making government and its services more accessible
- Promoting inclusive social relations
- Providing information in responsible fashion
- Using human resources effectively and efficiently[14]

E-government, then, is not "just putting government online. It is changing the way agencies interact with citizens, businesses and federal employees as they perform the government's business."[15] The demands for more effective government services increase as the days pass. E-government initiatives keep pace as government leaders and employees search for innovations to meet the demands.

Effective communications are vital to the well-being of American democracy and bureaucracy. Commitments to government online systems lead to:

1. *Connected governments,* or improved communications and information management between federal, state, and local governments—and nongovernmental organizations
2. *Connected communities,* or online integrated services readily available and conveniently accessed twenty-four hours a day, seven days a week, delivered to homes, businesses, and other locations by the Internet and other media
3. *Connected people,* or effective and efficient electronic communication used by elected leaders, government officials, agencies, and the community at large[16]

What do citizens say they want from electronic government services? Peter D. Hart and Robert M. Teeter surveyed 1,003 citizens; 150 government officials in federal, state, and local governments; and 155 institutional customers of government in the business and nonprofit sectors about the potential uses of e-government services, the benefits of e-government, how quickly e-government develops, and what concerns them about the digital divide. Issues of mobility, voting, and recreation were at the top of their lists, which included:

- Driver's license renewal
- Voter registration
- State park information and reservations
- Internet voting
- Access to one-stop shopping (one portal for all government services)
- Birth, death, and marriage certificate retrieval
- State tax filing
- Hunting and fishing licenses
- Accessing medical information from the National Institute of Health[17]

First Amendment advocates claim that e-mails have replaced public meetings and other public information forums. The reasons for these reforms range from expediency to a desire for secrecy. The e-mail technology makes holding public officials accountable more challenging, difficult, and problematic. Discussions and decision making are conducted outside the public view when they should be taking place in public.[18]

Media reporters and freedom of information advocates argue that millions of e-mails coming and going in government circles of partisan, policy, and systems politics entail a "double-edged sword." Texts of e-mails provide access to more information. However, retaining, storing, and maintaining government cyberspace communications in e-mail archives occur within emerging versions of technological political cultures. As Dwight Waldo points out, public and private are not categories of nature. They are categories of history and culture, of law and custom. They are contextual and subject to change and redefinition.[19]

What came about as reforms and communication access evolves into developing human rigidities, technological breakdowns, increased expenses, and new interpretations of bureaucracy and democracy. Government agencies have no obligations to maintain e-mail archives. How long governments should maintain e-mails is not resolved. Issues of electronic transparencies are contextual and subject to change and redefinition. They are matters of public—and private.

The Other Organization

Organizational charts and manuals of procedure rarely provide us with an accurate picture of an organization. What is not official or even readily visible may often be the most important. Even the most formal organizations, which pride themselves on going strictly "by the book," rarely do so. An informal system of authority, which supersedes, at least to some extent, the formal one, may arise. In the army, for example, the lieutenant clearly outranks the sergeant. But when the sergeant has had twenty years of army service and the lieutenant is fresh from a college Reserve Officers Training Program (ROTC), the sergeant, rather than the lieutenant, may end up running the platoon.

Communication also frequently flows through informal channels. The office grapevine is usually faster and more complete than the office memo. Aboard a ship, the real communications center is often not the captain's office, but the kitchen or galley, and navy cooks are usually better sources of news than commanding officers. This is how the term "scuttlebutt" came to have its current meaning. The informal organization may spawn a network of relationships for which the organization chart and the manual of procedure provide few clues.

One of the most extreme examples of how the informal organization can overwhelm the formal organization is the U.S. prison system. Ostensibly, prisons are run by wardens and corrections officers according to prescribed rules and regulations. In practice, this has rarely been the case. Sociologists and criminologists who have studied prisons have found that most prisons have traditionally been run by the prisoners.[20]

In most cases, the informal organization does not loom so large on the administrative scene, and its role should not be overstressed. It usually colors the formal organization but does not radically alter it. No matter how expert and experienced a sergeant may be, and no matter how naive and nervous the lieutenant may be, it is the lieutenant and not the sergeant who bears the final responsibility for the platoon. There is a limit to how much authority the sergeant can acquire and how much the lieutenant can abdicate. Nevertheless, informal elements influence the operation of nearly all organizations, and the administrator must be alert as to what these elements are and what they do.

Two aspects of informal organization merit special attention. One concerns the role of *informal rules;* the other concerns the role of *small groups.*

Whose Rules?

Employees of organizations, like citizens of nations, tend to obey only those rules in which they believe. Workers will accept a rule only if they regard it as legitimate in terms of their values. They will not accept it just because those who issued it had a legal right to do so.

Employees have also become adept at evading rules or bending them to suit their needs and desires, and the more rules the organization tends to set down, the more dexterity its members may show. The informal organization not only achieves frequent and sometimes spectacular success in sabotaging the formal organization's rules, but it also manages to establish and enforce rules of its own. Many of these rules concern work output. Those who exceed the informal quota may be branded as "rate-busters," while those who fail to carry their fair share of the load may earn the title of "slacker" or "chiseler." Seniority is another rule that governs many procedures of many informal organizations. Those with job seniority get the better assignments and more congenial conditions. The most junior members may not only get the less desirable assignments, but may also experience various petty harassments, like being sent to fetch the "left-handed monkey wrench." Sometimes the harassment is not so petty. College fraternities' hazing rituals have resulted in injuries and occasional deaths.

Probably no informal rule is more widespread than the ban on "squealing." This prohibition is instilled in most Americans during their school years and tends to stay with them the rest of their lives. The taboo against "tattling" is so widely and deeply ingrained that even those who would stand to benefit from it tend to dislike it. The "informer" or "spotter," no matter how useful he or she may be, rarely wins esteem in the eyes of management, and though the informer may increase his or her earnings, "squealing" seldom enhances one's chances for promotion.

While the formal organization often encounters difficulty in enforcing its rules, the informal organization usually succeeds in securing support and adherence to its own codes of behavior. Sanctions against offenders can take many forms, not excluding violence.

Many informal rules are benign. While the *golden rule* remains an unattainable goal, it has become a nearly universal governing principle and, as such, governs a good deal of organizational behavior. If people do not naturally love their neighbors as themselves, they do tend to help others who have helped them, or at least try to refrain from injuring them.

The Small Group

The basic unit for the formal organization may be the division, the department, the section, or all three, plus others. The primary basis for the informal organization is usually the small group. Although many informal norms and rules apply organizationwide, many others are promulgated and enforced by small work groups. The small group consists of no set number of individuals. Rather, it designates any group whose members are in continual, face-to-face contact with each other. Such groups often follow the structural lines of the formal organization. The small group in the army infantry is typically the squad. In the university, it is usually the department. Whether it conforms to any formally recognized structure, forces from within customarily dictate a good deal of its behavior.

The importance of the small group springs chiefly from the importance of primary relationships over secondary relationships in human behavior. Those people we work with every day invariably become more important to us than those whom we see infrequently or with whom we conduct relations at a distance. Out of such primary relationships come norms, codes, procedures, and the means for their enforcement. The famed "silent treatment" is most powerfully exercised on those with whom we are in daily contact.

Such are the workings of small groups and informal organizations.

Upward, Downward, and Lateral Communications

Information in government agencies moves in three basic directions:

- Upward from subordinate to superior
- Downward from superior to subordinate
- Horizontally from one organizational unit to another

No matter which way it flows, however, it runs into problems.

Communicating Upward

According to Daniel Katz and Robert I. Kahn, communication up the line may occur in many forms, but such information can be reduced to what the person says:

1. About himself, his performance, and his problems
2. About others and their problems
3. About organizational practices and policies
4. About what needs to be done and how it can be done[21]

The basic problem of upward communication is the nature of the hierarchical administrative structure, because the first role requirement of executives and supervisors is to direct, coordinate, and control the activities of persons below them. Therefore, employees fear that information passed along the hierarchical chain of command may be used for control purposes. The employees are unlikely to pass along information that may affect them adversely. This concern makes the upward route the most difficult.

Communicating Downward

According to Katz and Kahn, there are five varieties of communications down the line, from superior to subordinate:

1. Specific task directives: job instructions
2. Information designed to produce understanding of the task and its relationship to other organizational tasks: job rationale
3. Information about organizational procedures and practices
4. Feedback to the subordinate about his or her performance
5. Information of an ideological character to inculcate a sense of mission: indoctrination of goals[22]

While downward communication is less problematic than upward, communication down the line nevertheless encounters numerous obstacles and impediments. When it is oral, downward communication is subject to almost all the alterations that can creep in when communication moves upward.

When downward communication is written, other difficulties may develop. The message may not be complete, or the recipient may not be willing to accept it. The biggest problem, however, is probably the inability or the refusal of the recipient to absorb the information that seems to be cascading downward. Memorandum senders encounter persistent problems in this respect.

Communicating Laterally

According to Katz and Kahn, communication among peers, in addition to providing task coordination, also furnishes emotional and social support to the individual. The mutual understanding of colleagues is one reason for the power of the peer group. Psychological forces always push people toward communication with peers; people in the same boat share the same problems.

On the other hand, if no problems of task coordination are left to a group of peers, the content of their communication can take forms irrelevant or destructive to the organization's functioning.[23] The communication channels become dysfunctional if line officials in the organizational hierarchy are charged with initiating all communications. The agency softball team or annual picnic, for example, should be informal arrangements for which someone other than the line officials communicates directions.

Staff meetings can be particularly helpful in stimulating lateral communication. Physical arrangements can also play an important role in either helping or hampering lateral communication. Organizational practices designed to resolve other problems may foster lateral communication as well. In-service training, for example, may bring people from various parts of the organization together and result in a good deal of lateral communication. Organizationwide activities, such as bowling teams or hobby clubs, and an organizationally run cafeteria or dining room will also bring employees together and may lead to an interchange of information. Rotation of employees is also useful in improving lateral communication.

Leadership and Needs of the Situation

Anyone who hopes to spell out the qualities of a leader is engaged in a perilous and problematic mission. One helpful observation, however, can be made at the outset. *Leadership is, to a great extent, determined by the needs of the situation.* "It is more fruitful to consider leadership as a relationship between the leader and the situation than as a universal pattern of characteristics possessed by certain people," Douglas McGregor notes.[24] In a similar vein, William J. Reddin, after surveying the research on management style, concludes that "no single style is naturally more effective than others. Effectiveness depends on a style's appropriateness to the situation in which it is used."[25] There is, in short, no ideal leadership style and most probably no ideal leader.

Different types of organizations may demand different types of leaders. Many a successful business executive has failed miserably after attempting to transfer with all his or her administrative prowess to the public sector. Few public sector executives test their leadership skills directing a business firm. If so, they would probably frequently fail. Furthermore, an organization may need different leaders at different stages of its existence.

The relationship of leadership ability to the particular situation that calls the leader into being makes the task of defining and detailing a list of general leadership

Optimism, Conviction, Civility, Humor, and Nostalgia

As president, Ronald Reagan projected optimism, conviction, and nostalgia for a simpler time in America. His memory poignantly beckons Americans once again to recall a political past when presidential leadership seemed simpler and more open than it is today. President Reagan opposed communism and spoke of "the magic of the marketplace," as he unself-consciously put it, that stood for irreducible verities in American government and politics. Conservative scholars ridicule mainstream academics who conclude that Reagan was a mediocre leader. They praise his unwavering devotion to conservatism, his strong leadership, his civility, and his humor.

Sources: New York Times, February 24, 1998, page 20A; see also Stephen Goode, "The Reagan Legacy," *Insight on the News* 13, no. 39 (27 October 1997): 10–14.

qualities elusive and difficult. Certain qualities do, however, seem to characterize most leaders in most situations. Although this list does not constitute a formula, since one could possess all the qualities on the list and still be unable to lead, it does provide a basis from which the student may gain a perspective on one of the most intriguing and enigmatic aspects of the administrative craft.

Leadership Qualities

Probably no quality is more pertinent and pervasive among successful leaders than the quality of *optimism*. To lead successfully, one must believe that his or her leadership will make a difference. No matter how dismal a journey, the leader must be able to see positive results.

That *energy* and *enterprise* must accompany such optimism should be reasonably obvious. This does not mean that every luminary in the ranks of leadership has been a whirlwind of activity, but one cannot hope to meet leadership's obligations without some deliberate and diligent application of one's talents. Leaders often do not seem to be working hard at their jobs, but such appearances can be deceptive. A leader may be relaxed and easygoing, but laziness and indolence will usually lead to failure.

What about *intelligence*? Certainly, it is rare to find a leader who is both dumb and successful, and some have been extraordinarily brilliant. Take Napoleon and William Pitt, those young titans who confronted each other across the English Channel at the beginning of the nineteenth century. Each was at home in a variety of disciplines, including mathematics, languages, and the law. In this country, and during the same period, a president (Thomas Jefferson) had come to power who was accomplished in architecture, science, agriculture, law, political theory, and many other fields of study. Nevertheless, when it comes to correlating intellectual ability with leadership, some qualities seem more crucial than others.

According to Albert C. Yates, good leaders must be virtuous people who can be trusted to make the right choices to restore optimism and spirit to the society. Intelligent leaders without virtue can lead society toward selfishness and cynicism. *Virtue* embodies all that is good and right in human life and is a combination of values such as commitment, integrity, compassion, truth, and competence. A dynamic relationship between leadership and values sustains a good democratic society.[26]

One vital intellectual skill is *verbal ability*. Communication skills usually accompany leadership ability, no matter what the situation. A ditch digger who becomes the foreman of the work gang will probably be able to communicate better than all, or at least most, of the other members of the gang.

Much more complex is the question of *creativity* and *judgment*. The problem is that these two qualities are not always compatible. Good idea people, as Daniel Katz and Robert L. Kahn point out, tend to be enthusiastic and somewhat impulsive and may fail to subject their ideas to searching criticism. They frequently have a hard time translating ideas into action, and when they do, they may fail to follow through because they soon sprout another idea that they want to work on.

Katz and Kahn maintain that leadership puts more of a priority on reasoned judgment than creativity, and if a leader can have only one of these qualities, he or she is better off with the former. One can always make up for lack of creativity by surrounding oneself with people who are creative.[27]

Leadership and Charisma

The relationship between leadership and charisma is important in understanding both. Katz and Kahn argue that charisma originates from people's needs and from dramatic events in association with leadership. Most persons are in no position to evaluate suggestions for organizational change; therefore, charismatic leadership is most appropriate for formulating policies and altering organizational structures. Since followers are often not knowledgeable concerning specific programs for attaining organizational goals, subordinates allow leaders much flexibility for such decisions.

However, as Katz and Kahn emphasize,

> charisma is not the objective assessment by followers of the leader's ability to meet their specific needs. It is a means by which people abdicate responsibility for any consistent, tough-minded evaluation of the outcome of specific policies. They put their trust in their leader, who will somehow take care of things. Charisma requires some psychological distance between leader and follower. Immediate superiors exist in the work-a-day world of constant objective feedback and evaluation. They are very human and very fallible, and immediate subordinates cannot build an aura of magic about them. Day-to-day intimacy destroys illusion. But the leader in the top echelons of an organization is sufficiently distant from the membership to make a simplified and magical image possible.[28]

To put charisma into operation, Katz and Kahn emphasize the use of two particular measures. The degree of emotional arousal among followers and the global character of the leader's power as perceived by followers are crucial for charismatic success. Both adherents and opponents react emotionally to charismatic personalities; the leader's portrait is global and not discriminating. Specific weaknesses are overlooked in the great leader.

Katz delineates three types of interpersonal relations between charismatic personalities and followers:

- One type of charismatic leader may symbolize the followers' *wishful solutions to internal conflicts*. Instead of searching for deeper meanings and motives, followers seek release from their internal conflicts. They project their fears, aggression, and aspirations upon social measures that facilitate symbolic solution. In his or her personality and program, the charismatic leader offers symbolic solution.
- A second type of charismatic leader entails an *aggressor*, or father figure, who possesses overwhelming power; the follower is unable to escape the exercise of such power. In this type of interpersonal relation between leader and followers, there is no new ideology; but the followers identify with the aggressor, or father figure.
- A third type of charismatic leader maintains an *interpersonal relationship void of internal conflict* with followers. In assuming that their charismatic leader may advance their interests, followers magnify the power of their leader.[29]

The concepts of power and leadership enjoy common properties; however, they are not the same. Leaders exercise power. A leadership act involves choosing power instruments. Leadership is the point at which power is activated. Leadership entails attempts on the part of a leader, or influencer, to affect, or influence, the behavior of a follower or followers.

A charismatic leader may fail to fully develop the abilities of subordinates, as they become overly dependent upon the leader. When the leader is absent, the organization tends to flounder, and when he or she departs for good, it may fall to pieces.

Charismatic leadership also may inhibit communication. Subordinates become reluctant to give the leader unpleasant information or advise against policies that may be unwise. Often they lose the ability to discriminate between wise and unwise policies because they have surrendered much of their capacity for independent judgment. This can be crucial, because a charismatic leader may be not only forceful but also foolish.

While charisma is positive in many ways, its main danger in public administration is the possibility that a charismatic leader's personality may negate important advice and challenges from subordinates and citizens.

Max Weber and Charisma Power Centers

Max Weber's three "pure types" of authority are *rational, traditional,* and *charismatic.* In his rational emphasis, Weber believed in the "legality" of patterns of normative rules. He insisted upon the right of those elevated to authority under these rules to issue commands. This focus constituted legal or *rational* authority. In his traditional emphasis, Weber believed in the sanctity of immemorial traditions. He recognized the legitimacy of the status of those exercising authority under such traditions. This focus constituted *traditional* authority. In Weber's charismatic emphasis, the German scholar espoused devotion to the specific and exceptional sanctity, heroism, or exemplary character of an individual person. This focus constituted *charismatic* authority.[30]

In the Bible, the word *charisma* is translated "gifts." In Romans 12, the New English Bible translation, Paul contrasts the "enthusiastic" display of charisma with its institutional dynamics: "The gifts we possess differ as they are allotted to us by God's grace, and must be exercised accordingly: the gift of administration, in administration."[31] Verses 6, 7, and 8 specifically refer to administration and point out how *charisma* in this application could become the focus of ecclesiastical organization and offices.[32]

In 1 Corinthians 12, there is a long passage about "gifts of the spirit." Verse 4 of this chapter refers to such "gifts" as wisdom, knowledge, faith, healing, miracles, prophecy, delineation of true and false spirits, and ecstatic utterances and interpretation of ecstatic utterances.[33] These gifts, or charisma, set apart particular individuals who have and use them.

Weber focused on the function and exercise of power in society. He concluded that there are three major points of influence for examining charismatic leaders and their impacts.

1. *The law and the traditional taboos* of the particular culture or society. These might include laws, rules, regulations, customs, mores, taboos, routines, and certain ascribed standards. These properties are thought to be rational, grounded in prescribed ways of acting and behaving.

Major Concepts in Leadership

A *leader* is a person who has the authority to decide, direct, and represent the objectives and functions of an organization.

A *manager* is a person who has the authority to direct specific organizational resources in order to accomplish objectives.

Authority is the license an organization grants that gives an individual the right to use its powers and resources.

Credibility is the recognition by an organization that one is competent to use its powers.

Source: Robert A. Portnoy, *Leadership: What Every Leader Should Know About People,* 1986. Reprinted by permission of the author.

---

2. *Individual leadership,* largely emotional, which Weber labeled *charisma.* This is also referred to as the *cult of personality.* These personalities might include the president, governor, mayor, coach, pastor, priest, rabbi, or other community leaders. This property is thought to be often irrational, as it goes against the grain of how issues confronting the organization have been handled, dealt with, brokered, and accepted.

3. *The mass of administrators* who carry out the laws and policies of the organization, or government; in short, the bureaucracy, also referred to as the followers. In a governmental office, it's the employees. In U.S. society, it's the citizens. In a religious organization, it's the parishioners. On the state university's athletic teams, it's the players. These properties emphasize a rational response, grounded in prescribed ways of responding to the dictates of leaders, manager, and other authorities.

Charisma, then, is not merely the appearance of a dynamic, excited, motivated, committed, passion-filled person. Charismatic persons persuade followers to change their old ways of responding to the organization's challenges and problems and act in creative, determined, and new ways to accomplish the tasks assigned to the government bureaucracy. In the history of organizations, there are occasions when a great man or woman arrives on the scene or comes from the ranks of the organization.

The immense personal magnetism of the charismatic leader causes followers to rid themselves of their old, dysfunctional ways and become more productive than ever for the new leader and the organization. The charismatic leader dominates decision making regardless of the logic of his or her positions. The followers abandon rational thinking and follow the new leader, perhaps a Pied Piper, into the unknown future of the organization. Charismatic leaders encounter challenges in democratic societies. Their followers are often educated and not easily seduced, for long periods of time, by leaders turned Pied Pipers.[34]

Charismatic Leader Behaviors

Perspectives on charismatic leadership in times of cultural and technological change are pertinent to understanding the dynamics of charisma. What common behaviors do charismatic leaders exhibit?

Robert J. House offers six categories of charismatic leader behaviors:

1. *Role modeling.* The role model espouses a set of values and beliefs in which followers should believe. The model's emotional responses to rewards or punishments elicit similar emotional reactions from followers.
2. *Image building.* In the cult of personality, charismatic leaders portray an image or images to followers. In the institutionalization of charisma, perceptions are as important as realities. Therefore, the creation and maintenance of an image or images are crucial considerations.
3. *Goal articulation.* In organizational leadership, the development of an institutional mission and goals is an ongoing process. The creation and maintenance of an institutional mission and goals require leadership skills whereby the leader merges his personality characteristics with the organization's social structure. The leader provides the organization with a special identity. In pointing out organizational goals, the leader articulates goals that transcend the movement or cause. Such goals are ideological rather than pragmatic. Moral overtones abound.
4. *Exhibiting high expectations and showing confidence.* Charismatic leaders communicate high performance expectations for followers. Such leadership enhances subordinates' self-esteem and affects the goals followers accept for themselves. As the charismatic leader spells out to his followers that they are competent and personally responsible, subordinates perceive themselves as competent. Leaders seek to enhance motivation, performance, and satisfaction in followers.
5. *Effect on followers' goals.* Followers may evaluate their performance according to standards the leader has articulated in terms of specific and high expectations. The leader's expectations allow followers to derive feedback on their personal behaviors.
6. *Emotional arousal.* Adherents and opponents react emotionally to charismatic leaders. The enthusiasm of one group's responses is matched by the mistrust of the other group. The organizational maintenance of emotional arousal is pertinent to the long-term success of the charismatic leader.[35]

House describes four personal characteristics of charismatic leaders. Charismatic leaders exercise *dominance,* personify *self-confidence,* exhibit *influence,* and maintain *strong convictions* in the moral righteousness of their beliefs.[36]

Why does charismatic leadership emerge in the environment of movements for change? What historical circumstances explain such emotional arousals among followers? Weber indicates that charisma and personality blend most readily "in times of psychic, physical, economic, ethical, religious, political distress."[37]

Historical Conditions Favoring Charisma

Erik H. Erikson suggests that large numbers of people become "charisma hungry" under historical conditions in which religion wanes. Charismatic leaders minister well during three kinds of distress:

- One distress condition is *fear.*
- A second, and related, condition is *anxiety.* The condition of people not knowing who they are creates an "identity vacuum" and "anxiety."

- A third historical condition, in Erikson's terms, is *existential dread*. In this type of distress, people experience circumstances in which the rituals of their human existence become dysfunctional. The leader, under such conditions, may offer meaning and provide followers with a greater sense of community, emerging as a charismatic leader. In offering salvation from fear, anxiety, and existential dread, the charismatic leader creates new forms of safety, identity, or rituals.[38]

Crisis, therefore, is important to the emergence of charismatic leadership. Crises foster the emergence of charismatic leaders judged as more effective than the group leaders who emerge in noncrisis situations.[39]

Thus, charismatic movements develop and multiply during times of widespread distress in society. The charismatic leader, by virtue of unusual personal qualities, promises the hope of salvation. Perceived by followers as specifically salvationist or messianic in nature, the charismatic leader offers himself or herself to those persons in distress as peculiarly qualified to lead them from their distressful predicament.

Institutionalizing the American Presidency

The institutionalization of the American presidency and the charismatic leaders who have held the office over the past two centuries point out the historical maturing of one U.S. public sector—government organization. Some charismatic presidents might include Washington, Jefferson, Jackson, Lincoln, Teddy Roosevelt, Franklin Roosevelt, Kennedy, Reagan, and perhaps even Clinton. The test of these charismatic personalities is not whether they had individual dynamism, but whether they influenced the American masses to change their old dysfunctional, perhaps destructive, ways and implement bold changes.

According to Lyn Ragsdale and John J. Thesis III, the presidency becomes institutionalized when it attains high levels of:[40]

- *Autonomy* (the independence of the presidency from other units). The growth of the organization's budget is an indicator of autonomy. The $1.7 trillion budget shapes the stability and value of the U.S. government. As the presidency becomes more institutionalized, administrations offer policy proposals independent of Congress. Since the Great Society of the 1960s, autonomous presidents have acted contrary to the wishes of Congress because of executive access to budgets.
- *Adaptability* (the longevity of units in the presidency). Flexibility permits presidents to create, modify, and eliminate administrative units. Adaptability is the safety valve of an organization's institutionalization. Units may be added to the Executive Office of the President (EOP) by executive order, public law, and presidential reorganization plans.
- *Complexity* (the differentation of subunits and staff in the office). Complexity is an internal aspect of institutionalization. It involves the division of labor and specialization. The unit's differentiation improves its stability and makes it more difficult to dismantle. Complexity also promotes the unit's intricate

internal identity. An indicator of complexity is the organization's total number of units, compartments, divisions, and the like.

- *Coherence* (the ability to manage work volume). Coherence addresses the abilities of the organization to manage its workload. If tasks are erratic or excessive, coherence is low. Workload follows more predicatable patterns as criteria are developed. Clearance procedures for budgets, legislation, and executive orders enhance coherence. The strongest determinants of changing levels of institutionalization are measures of national government activities. Commitments to social security, medical care, unemployment, and education, for example, are illustrated by an ever-expanding social welfare budget. Challenges, problems, and enemies define presidents: Teddy Roosevelt fought the special interests. Franklin Roosevelt fought the Great Depression and World War II. Kennedy adapted to television and confronted the Soviets in Cuba. Reagan, confident yet simplistic in a complex era, cut the federal budget. And Clinton, despite the foibles of his personal life, withstood criticisms of his presidency from a zealous prosecutor and out-of-control media.

Ragsdale and Thesis explore institution and institutionalization. According to these researchers, institutionalization occurs as an organization acquires value and stability as an end itself.

As an organization achieves stability and value, it becomes an institution. Stability denotes that the organization is no longer a mechanistic entity, easily altered or eliminated. Instead, as an organization institutionalizes, it survives various internal

---

The Functions of Institutional Leadership

The relationship between leadership and organizational character is more transparent when examined in the context of the leader's key tasks.

1. *The definition of institutional mission and role.* The setting of goals is a creative task that entails self-assessment and discovery of the true commitments of the organization as determined by effective internal and external demands. The failure to set aims in the light of these commitments is a major source of irresponsibility in leadership.

2. *The institutional embodiment of purpose.* The task of leadership is not only to make policy but to build policy decisions into the organization's social structure. This too is a creative task. It means shaping the "character" of the organization, sensitizing the organization to the complex dynamic of thinking and responding, so that the execution and elaboration of policies, according to their spirit as well as their letter, will be achieved more reliably.

3. *The defense of institutional integrity.* The leadership of any policy fails when it concentrates on sheer survival; institutional survival, properly understood, is a matter of maintaining values and distinctive identity.

4. *The ordering of internal conflict.* Internal interest groups form naturally in large-scale organizations because the total enterprise is, in one sense, a polity composed of a number of suborganizations. The struggle between competing interests always has a high claim on the attention of leadership. This is so because the direction of the enterprise as a whole may be seriously influenced by changes in the internal balance of power.

Source: Phillip Selznick, *Leadership in Administration* (University of California Press, 1984), pp. 61–63.

and environmental challenges and achieves self-maintenance—it exists in the future because it has existed in the past. . . . As an organization institutionalizes, it acquires a distinctive identity, a way of acting, and tasks it acts upon, which are all deemed to be important in and of themselves.[41]

In processes of organizational institutionalization, stability and values merge. The longer the organization exists, the greater the prospects for developing distinguishing structures, capabilities, and liabilities. Personal interests within the organization and the dynamics of the outside environment interact to result in institutionalization.

Themes of instutionalization are illustrated in both public and private organizations. Leaders, or managers, differ. In all organizations, personalities, leaders, and decision-making methods vary. The features of autonomy, adaptability, complexity, and coherence indicate how your college or university has continued through the years and achieved importance despite changes in individual or outside environmental constraints.

The Limits of Leadership

One real, yet often overlooked, or at least underestimated, aspect of leadership is that its diverse literature applies to as many situations as there are government organizations.

"In a bureaucracy that contains people with brains and consciences," wrote Charles Frankel following his tour of duty in Washington, "an unspoken bargain binds the man at the top to his subordinates. If they are to be the instruments of his will, he must, to some extent, be an instrument of theirs."[42] Most writers on administration agree. "A manager is often described as someone who gets things done through other people," notes British organizational theorist Rosemary Stewart. "We tend to forget that this means he is dependent upon them."[43]

In a complex bureaucracy the problem intensifies. Tsar Nicholas II was one of the few truly autocratic rulers of his time. Yet he experienced constant frustration in getting his smallest orders carried out. "I do not rule Russia," the weary monarch once sighed. "Ten thousand clerks do."[44]

American presidents have consistently discovered that their office provides far less power than they expected. Franklin Roosevelt depicted Lincoln as "a sad man because he couldn't get it all at once, and nobody can." Roosevelt's own battles with his bureaucracy are almost legendary. He once wearily described his efforts to balance the special interests of diverse government agencies as akin to boxing a featherbed.

Truman and Eisenhower suffered from the same problem. John F. Kennedy took office with the idea of changing Washington bureaucracy. But he found that when he wanted a simple sign taken down, it did not come down, even after he had given the order for its removal three times.

To many students, the president of the university may appear out of touch with the immediate concerns of the students. College presidents confront the external and internal demands—more conflicting than not—of legislators, trustees, faculty, service staff, and community leaders.

Why Smart People Can Be So Stupid

The behavior of smart people—from presidents to prosecutors to college professors—is sometimes so incredibly stupid as to appear inexplicable. Why do intelligent persons act so dumb—when their lives and livelihoods might be in danger?

Why can smart people be so stupid?

You are in college now. You realize that the attainment of skills, knowledge, and expertise are valuable personal goals. You are learning how to think smart, act smarter than most of your peers, work harder than they, and keep from repeating crucial mistakes in your personal life. Yet no one is immune from doing dumb things.

Bill Clinton engages Monica Lewinsky in sexual hanky-panky in the Oval Office. Richard Nixon covers up the truth about the Watergate break-in. Bobby Knight, a basketball genius, insults friend and foe alike. Teddy Kennedy drinks too much, then drives—and a young woman dies.

According to Robert J. Sternberg, stupidness and smartness are not opposites. Highly intelligent people, says Sternberg, commit singularly idiotic acts. Stupidity is the opposite not of smartness but of wisdom, says Sternberg. In college life, many suffer from an imbalance of foolishness—or in brief, stupidity.

Sternberg emphasizs four main tendencies leading to personal stupidity:

- *The egocentrism fallacy.* We foolishly think we are so incredibly smart. We assume the world should revolve around us and our egocentric personalities.
- *The omniscience fallacy.* As egocentric personalities, we foolishly insist the reason the world revolves around us is because we know much more than others do, or even all we need to know.
- *The omnipotence fallacy.* We believe that the special knowledge we glean in college makes us omnipotent, or all-powerful. We can do whatever we want and get away with stupid actions.
- *The invulnerability fallacy.* We believe we can get away with repeated stupidities because we possess superior intelligence. Therefore, we foolishly feel invulnerable to attack or even perhaps to criticism.

People are not reliable judges of their own stupidity. Smart persons may be unwise. Students would be wise to consider how egocentrism, omniscience, omnipotence, and invulnerability invade their study habits and personal lives.

Sources: Gregory Mott, "Stupidity for Dummies," *Washington Post,* May 7, 2002, p. HE1; Robert J. Sternberg, ed., *Why Smart People Can Be So Stupid* (New Haven, CT.: Yale University Press, 2002).

David Lilienthal, who held such posts as the chairmanships of the Tennessee Valley Authority and the Atomic Energy Commission, once defined leadership as a humanistic art. It requires, he said, "a humanistic outlook on life rather than mere mastery of technique. It is based on the capacity for understanding of individuals and their motivations, their fears, their hopes, what they love and what they hate, the ugly and the good side of human nature. It is an ability to move these individuals, to help them define their wants, to help them discover, step by step, how to achieve them."[45]

The challenge of leadership is thus the challenge of humanism. Its successful exercise lies less and less in giving orders and more and more in developing the innate capacities of human beings. But to this must be joined a sense of mission, bolstered and buttressed by some degree of vision. The story is sometimes told of three stonecutters asked what they were doing. The first replied, "I am making a living." The second, busily at work, answered, "I am doing the best job of stonecutting in the whole country." The third, looking up with a gleam in his eye, said, "I am building a cathedral."[46]

The conclusion is obvious. Only the third person can become an effective manager, or better yet, leader.

Summary

- Administrators and administrative theorists place increasing emphasis on communication.
- Communication problems arise not only from information that is too slow, incomplete, or distorted, but also from information that is too abundant. This is a problem of communication overload.
- Communication falls into two basic categories— formal and informal. Formal communication is written. Informal communication is oral. Formal communication fosters accountability, while informal communication does not produce mounds of paperwork.
- Formal communication restrains arbitrariness, capriciousness, favoritism, and discrimination.
- Organizational size and public character are factors affecting the use of formal communication.
- The informal communications system is often referred to as the "grapevine."
- Organizations are groupings of social beings. A certain amount of informal and personal communication occurs within the ranks. Participants seek the "right" mixture of informal and formal communications.
- The Internet educates people faster than any previous technology that the world has known. The Internet is neither evil nor good.
- Upward communication focuses on the employee, his or her performance, and problems; others and their problems; organizational practices and policies; and what needs to be done and how it can be done.
- Information moves in three basic directions: upward from subordinate to superior, downward from superior to subordinate, and horizontally from one organizational unit to another.
- Downward communication includes job instructions, job rationale, information about organizational procedures and practices, feedback to the subordinate about his or her performance, and indoctrination of goals.
- The growth of specialization and interdependency is making it increasingly vital for information to flow through the organization as well as to move up and down its ranks.
- Informal organization is more important in determining worker cooperation than formal organization. In this "other organization," the output is set by social norms, not individual abilities, and the group greatly influences the behavior of individual workers.
- Employees of organizations, like citizens of nations, tend to obey those rules in which they believe.
- The importance of the small group is based upon the centrality of primary relationships over secondary relationships in human behavior.
- Leadership is, to a great extent, determined by the needs of the situation.
- Leadership qualities include optimism, conviction, humor, civility, energy, enterprise, virtue, intelligence, verbal ability, creativity, and judgment.
- Max Weber's "pure types" of authority are *rational, traditional,* and *charismatic.* Weber believed in the "legality" or rationality of patterns of normative rules and in the sanctity of immemorial traditions. He also espoused devotion to the specific and exceptional sanctity, heroism, or exemplary character of an individual person, or charisma.
- Weber focused on the function and exercise of power in society. He proposed three major points of influence for examining charismatic leaders and their impacts: (1) the law and the traditional taboos of the particular culture or society; (2) individual leadership, largely emotional, which Weber labeled *charisma;* and (3) the bureaucrats, or mass of administrators, who carry out the laws and policies of the organization or government.
- Erik Erikson suggests that large numbers of people become "charisma hungry" under historical conditions in which religion wanes. Particular conditions of distress, namely fear,

anxiety, and existential dread, bring on the dynamics of charismatic leaders.

- Charisma is not the objective assessment of a leader's ability to meet followers' specific needs. It is a means by which people abdicate responsibility for any consistent, tough-minded evaluation of the outcome of specific policies. They trust their leader, who will somehow take care of things.
- The presidency becomes institutionalized when it attains high levels of four features: autonomy, adaptability, complexity, and coherence.

- As an organization achieves stability and value, it becomes an institution. In processes of organizational institutionalization, stability and values merge. The longer the organization exists, the greater the prospects for developing distinguishing structures, capabilities, and liabilities.
- The functions of institutional leadership are (1) definition of the institutional mission and role, (2) institutional embodiment of purpose, (3) the defense of institutional integrity, and (4) the ordering of internal conflict.
- The behavior of smart people is sometimes so incredibly stupid as to appear inexplicable.

VIDEOS AND FILMS

Public Administration in Action

Communication
Communication Breakdown [2007]
Illustrates seven common communication problems that can derail organizations. Includes interactive training scenes, a discussion leader's guide in PDF format, and a Microsoft PowerPoint presentation. Produced by Coastal Training Technologies Corp. [19 min]

Leadership
The Leadership Pill: The Movie [2004]
Illustrates advantages of quality leadership and leading with character. Explores core leadership principles of integrity, partnership, and affirmation. Based on the book *The Leadership Pill*. [23 min]

Leadership
The Leadership-Learning Connection [2002]
Cultivating, recognizing, and applying organizational wisdom. Wise organizations reflect, take the risk to experiment, and take values seriously. Produced by the Center for Performance Assessment. [55 min]

Leadership-Charisma
Patton [1970]
A brilliant and effective military leader who never learned that all great soldiers must be diplomats as well as warriors. Historical moral-ethical emphasis. George C. Scott gives masterful performance as Patton. [171 min]

Case Study

The Supreme Allied Commander

Leadership, to a great extent, is determined by the needs of the situation. Situations create leaders, to be sure, but leaders also create their situations. Such was the case with Dwight D. Eisenhower. The Eisenhower case study describes primarily policy and system politics—or the administrative politics of World War II's ultimate challenges: mayhem, destruction, strengths, weaknesses, deaths, and evil.

> Leaderhip: the art of getting someone else to do something you want done because he wants to do it.
>
> *—Dwight D. Eisenhower*
> *World War II Commander and U.S. President*

Dwight (Ike) David Eisenhower, leader of the posse comitatus to rid the world of Hitler's evils and post–World War II American president, was not charismatic, creative, assertive, or even very politically partisan. According to historian Stephen Ambrose, he exuded the qualities of love, honesty, faithfulness, responsibility, modesty, generosity, duty, and leadership—and a hatred for war.

British Field Marshall Bernard Montgomery was not especially impressed with Ike's soldiering abilities, but recognized "his real strength lies in his human qualities. He has the power of drawing the hearts of men toward him as a magnet attracts the bit of metal. He merely has to smile at you, and you trust him at once."[1]

The *New York Times* polled a group of historians in 1961, asking how they would rank America's presidents. Eisenhower scored a rating of 22. This ranking placed him in the low-average category, rated even below Herbert Hoover. But Eisenhower's contribution to humankind rests not only on his years at 1600 Pennsylvania Avenue.

In some respects, Ike's first fifty years were spent in almost total obscurity. World War II afforded him the chance to move from a lieutenant colonel in 1941 to a five-star general in 1945. He commanded an integrated, multinational alliance of ground, sea, and air forces. As Supreme Allied Commander of the Allied Expeditionary Force, he led the most powerful military force—navy, air force, and army—ever assembled. He was the principal architect of the successful Allied invasion of Europe during World War II—and the subsequent defeat of Hitler and Nazi Germany. Ike's conduct of this command illustrates his administrative leadership skills.

George C. Marshall, Chief of Staff, was the one who chose Eisenhower for this difficult assignment. The difficulties confronting Eisenhower derived not so much from the military as from the political situation. Leadership, to a great extent, is determined by the needs of the situation. All kinds of people, parties, and pressures had to be skillfully managed or led. They included the British armed forces and their various leaders, British public opinion, British political leaders, conflicting French interests, other Allied forces and their governments, exile governments in London, and Ike's own troops, their commanders, his military and political superiors in Washington, and the American press and public opinion.

Ike as an Institutional Leader

Eisenhower frequently evaluated the Allied institutional mission and role. He assessed commitments of the Allied force that by December 1944 numbered 4,500,000. The Americans, British, French, Canadians, and others constituted the Allied social structure, forming the "character" of the Allied organization. These nationalities embodied the purpose of Allied existence. Ike relied on U.S. President Franklin D. Roosevelt (FDR), British Prime Minister Winston Churchill, and Marshall as Allied forces defended the institutional integrity of the Allied operations.

Behind Ike's modest geniality lay a great singleness of purpose. Eisenhower realized that the alliance would falter and flounder unless there was a single overall commander. He made sure that this premise was accepted and acknowledged. He assured Allied forces that all issues would be discussed and decisions arrived at on a basis other than national pride. An integrated command—combining the forces of several nations—is considered Eisenhower's greatest accomplishment.

Eisenhower put first things first. In North Africa, he deferred his integration scheme, important though it was, in order to capture Tunis before the bad weather. Roosevelt urged him to send troops into Rome; the city's liberation would glorify his own reputation and that of the United States. Eisenhower refused. He sought more time to prepare for the invasion of France.

Eisenhower originally wanted to commense an invasion of southern France to accompany the Normandy attack. A shortage of landing craft and related factors forced him to scuttle the idea. British Brigadier General Sixsmith, a biographer, holds the view that this decision "was typical of the man," for "he liked to keep his options open."[2]

As a military strategist, Eisenhower made mistakes. He allowed German military divisions in Sicily to escape. He balked at sending an airborne division to capture Rome. He opened up a gap that permitted Hitler to launch the perilous and costly Battle of the Bulge. It took the Allied forces, despite their complete domination of the air and vast superiority on the ground, nearly a year after they crossed the channel to bring Germany to defeat.

Allied values and identity were uppermost in Eisenhower's thinking. The ordering of internal conflicts challenged Ike almost daily. A great storm over the English Channel forced postponement of the invasion of Europe from June 4 until June 6, 1944. Operation Overlord, as the famous D-Day invasion was named, spoke loudly of values and a distinctive identity. The value was to free Europe from Hitler's slaughterhouse. The identity was to afford as many generals, officers, foot soldiers, and nationalities as possible the opportunity to participate in the overthrow of Nazi Germany.

The Allied landing force included 156,000 men who attacked the Nazis on Normandy's beaches. Some 6,000 ships were joined by thousands of airplanes. Ike was assisted by 16,312 officers and enlisted men. The ordering of internal conflicts underscored the widespread diversity of the mission. The Americans, British, French, Canadians, and others volunteered for the prospect of victory and the chance of injury and death.

Eisenhower's command was crowded with huge military egos—in his theater and among alliance countries. Strong personalities—such as Walter Bedell Smith, Chief of Staff; Omar Bradley; George C. Patton; Montgomery; and Charles de Gaulle, the Free French leader, exerted competing interests and claims on Ike's decision-making options. Despite sharing similar values and a distinctive identity, these military leaders argued over the implementation of military strategies. Ike held deep convictions, which he never ceded or compromised at any point he felt was important.

Behavioral Side of Military Forces

Eisenhower understood the behavioral side of military forces. The challenge of leadership is the challenge of humanism. He realized that the likes of Patton and

Montgomery had strengths, but also displayed weaknesses of person and command. "Morale," Ike once wrote, "is at one and the same time the strongest and the most delicate of growths. It withstands shocks, even disasters, on the battlefield, but can be destroyed utterly by favoritism, neglect, or injustice."[3]

Cries to bring the European war to a speedy end with a minimum of Allied bloodshed required outstanding managerial and human skills. Eisenhower approached this awesome task with modesty and geniality. He shared his thoughts with his subordinates as if they were his equals. He framed his commands as if they were advice.

According to General Sixsmith, he was a superb delegator of authority—yet he was able "to keep his finger on all that was going on. His subordinates were able to see that they were expected to act, they were told what was in Eisenhower's mind, and they knew he would not shrink from responsibility."[4]

Eisenhower issued a directive early in the campaign that newspaper stories criticizing him should not under any circumstances be censored. At the Normandy beach invasion of France, he prepared a statement for use in the event that the invasion failed. In it, Eisenhower accepted full blame for its failure. During the actual campaign across Europe that followed, he discounted persistent attempts in the British press to give all the credit for Allied successes to the British generals.

Eisenhower's managerial skills are illustrated by his tenuous treatment of General George C. Patton. He recognized that Patton was in many ways an excellent combat commander, particularly in tank warfare. He further realized that the Germans had a very high opinion of Patton and feared him as they feared no other Allied combat general. Eisenhower was also painfully aware of Patton's weaknesses, such as his egotism, his officiousness, and his reactionary cast of mind.

When Patton set off an uproar in the United States by slapping American soldiers hospitalized with bad nerves or battle fatigue, Eisenhower refused to relieve him of command. Instead, he ordered Patton to make personal apologies to the slapped men, the medical personnel, and all others concerned. Patton complied, as he was desperate to continue in command. During the savage Nazi combat at the Battle of the Bulge, Patton's troops rescued the besieged U.S. forces. Eisenhower's decision to keep Patton was vindicated.

Eisenhower's toleration of Patton's behavior had limits. After the war ended, Patton insisted on employing ex-Nazis in his occupation zone. Eisenhower moved to replace him. Even at this point, he tried to ease

Patton's humiliation by asking Patton whom he would prefer as his replacement. When Patton named someone who was acceptable to Eisenhower, the American commander appointed him.

Ike's tact and concern were not only evident in giving orders to theater commanders. He also regularly toured the ranks, talking with soldiers, and looking after their well-being. He sharply reproved any base commander who utilized his best facilities for administrative quarters instead of providing them for the rest and relaxation of the fighting troops.

Finally, Eisenhower demonstrated a capacity for communication. As an aide to General MacArthur in the 1930s, Eisenhower drafted most of McArthur's eloquent speeches. As Commander of the Allied forces in World War II, Ike wrote delicate orders that were considered models of tact and understanding. Ike's verbal abilities served him well.

According to Sixsmith, he was by no means a poor strategist, constantly beset as he was by conflicting pressures. In the north, Montgomery insisted that the full Allied thrust be put under his control. He was supported by feverish public opinion in England, not simply because he was their general but also because they feared the German rockets that were being launched from the area that Montgomery was trying to capture.

Farther south, Patton demanded more gasoline, supplies, and troops. American public opinion sought a hero, and Patton could not be completely restrained. Meanwhile, the French were clamoring for the liberation of Paris—a move that would not only detract from the route of advance but could hinder further advances. Supplies and trucks to carry them would have to be siphoned off to maintain the city afterward.

Eisenhower adequately orchestrated the strategist role. He superbly managed his administrative and political roles. At Germany's surrender, General Marshall, effusive in his congratulations to Eisenhower, stated: "You have commanded with outstanding success . . . you have met and successfully disposed of every conceivable difficulty . . . you have triumphed over inconceivable logistical problems and military obstacles . . . you have made history, great history for the good of mankind."[5]

Eisenhower remained in Europe for the duration of World War II. He accepted the unconditional surrender of the German army at Rheims, France, on May 8, 1945.

Maintaining a Mature Objectivity

Eisenhower was committed to maintaining a mature objectivity in his working life. Among his principles were "Remember that belligerence is the hallmark of insecurity" and "Forget yourself and personal fortunes." He was more intelligent than creative, realistic than optimistic—exhibiting good judgment regarding both people and battle scenarios. Whereas Patton and Montgomery might "give into their emotions," Eisenhower—steadfast in the technical expertise of military training—remained decisive but uncharismatic in battle.

As Supreme Commander, Eisenhower was absolutely committed to maintaining harmony among the Allies. He would not tolerate internal bickering or rivalry among commanders. Marshall, FDR, and Churchill supported Eisenhower. Any field commander too far out of line could be relieved of command.

Ike was perceived to be an unassuming but calculated risk-taker. He was a compromiser, yet a stabilizing force. Eisenhower was articulate, charming, confident, tolerant, tactful, and discreet. He ordered internal conflicts quickly and decisively. Eisenhower was a cool property administering a hot item—the most destructive war in the history of the world.

The Eisenhower Case Study describes primarily policy and system politics—or administrative politics. This review tells the story of a leader inside a public institution—the U.S. military. As an administrative leader, Eisenhower implemented the institutional mission and role, embodiment of purpose, institutional integrity, and ordering of internal conflicts.

The war's ultimate challenges—evil, strengths, weaknesses, mayhem, destruction, deaths—were challenges to all humanity. Leaders create their situations, to be sure, but situations also create their leaders. Such was the case with Dwight D. Eisenhower.

Questions and Instructions

1. Can leadership be learned? Explain.
2. The ability to make good decisions is crucial if a leader is to be successful. What does this case study say about President Eisenhower's ability to make decisions?
3. Leaders create their situations, but situations also create their leaders. Which premise seems more applicable to Eisenhower?
4. Why is Eisenhower considered a more effective war administrator than presidential administrator?

5. How did Eisenhower's network of prior associations and preferences contribute to his success as war administrator, yet detract from his record as presidential administrator? Explain.
6. How did the leadership styles of Eisenhower and General Patton differ?
7. What role, if any, did charisma play in Eisenhower's approach to leadership?
8. Why do leaders place more emphasis on reasoned judgment than creativity? In his roles as war and presidential administrators, did Eisenhower exude creativity, exercise good judgment, or both?
9. To lead successfully, a person must believe that his or her leadership will make a difference. In his roles as war and presidential administrators, did Eisenhower make a difference? Explain.

Insights-Issues/The Supreme Allied Commander

Clearly and briefly describe and illustrate the following concepts and issues. Interpret the word *role* as meaning impacts, applications, importance, effects, and/or illustrations of certain facts, concerns, or issues from the case study.

1. Eisenhower's roles as leader and manager. What circumstances afforded Ike opportunities, as Supreme Allied Commander, to emerge as a leader, and when did he act as a manager? Explain.
2. What roles did the political situation play in Eisenhower's leadership as Supreme Allied Commander and as president? Explain.
3. How did Eisenhower define the institutional mission and roles as Supreme Allied Commander? Explain.
4. How did Eisenhower order the internal conflicts as Supreme Allied Commander? Explain.
5. Leadership qualities include optimism, energy, enterprise, intelligence, verbal ability, creativity, and judgment. In what ways did Eisenhower demonstrate some or all of these characteristics? Explain.

Notes

1. The principal source of material for this case study is E. K. G. Sixsmith, *Eisenhower as Military Commander* (New York: Stein & Day, 1973). Another source is Ladislas Fargo, *Patton: Ordeal and Triumph* (New York: Dell Publishing, 1970).
2. Sixsmith, *Eisenhower.*
3. Ibid.
4. Ibid.
5. Ibid.

Sources

Stephen Ambrose, "Character Above All: Dwight D. Eisenhower Essay," http://www.pbs.org/newshour/character/essays/eisenhower.html; "Dwight D. Eisenhower: Biography," *Encyclopedia Americana,* http://www.grolier.com/presidents/ea/bios/34peise.html; "Dwight Eisenhower: 34th President (1953–1961)," http://www.americanpresident.org/kotrain/courses/DE/DE_In_Brief.htm; "Eisenhower, Dwight David (1890–1969)," German Corner Website, German-American Mall; http://www.germanheritage.com/biographies/atol/eisenhower.html; Michael Maccoby, "Making Sense of the Leadership Literature," *Research Technology Management,* 44, no. 5 (September–October 2001): 58–60, http://www.maccoby.com/Articles/LeaderLit.html; John M. Shalikashvili, "The Three Pillars of Leadership," *Defense Issues* 10, no. 42, http://www.defenselink.mil/speeches/1995/s19950412-shali.html.

Notes

1. David K. Berlo, *The Process of Communication: An Introduction to Theory and Practice* (New York: Holt, Rinehart, & Winston, 1960), pp. 23–24; Harold F. Gortner, Julianne Mahler, and Jeanne Bell Nicholson, *Organization Theory: A Public Perspective,* 2d ed. (Fort Worth, TX: Harcourt Brace, 1997), pp. 135–141.
2. See http://www.ualr.edu/dllauferswei/cj3306/formalcomm.html.
3. Ibid.
4. Kenneth Cukier, "Who Runs the Internet?" *World Press Review* 45, no. 5 (May 1998): 39–41.
5. David E. Nye, "Shaping Communication Networks: Telegraph, Telephone, Computer," *Social Research* 64, no. 3 (Fall 1997): 1067–1092.
6. Ellen Goodman, "Anonymity Breeds Incivility," *Boston Globe,* September 5, 1996, p. 17A.
7. Brandi Bowser, "Opening the Window to Online Democracy: www.localgovernment.com," *American City & County* 113, no. 1 (January 1998): 36–38.
8. Thomas L. Friedman, "Global Village Idiocy," *New York Times,* May 12, 2002.
9. *Detroit Free Press,* September 28, 1967.
10. Alan Zaremba, "Working with the Organizational Grapevine," *Personnel Journal* 67, no. 7 (July 1988): 38–41.
11. *Time,* June 18, 1973, p. 67.
12. See http://www.ualr.edu/dllauferswei/cj3306/formalcomm.html.
13. Ibid.
14. UNPAN, "Global Survery of E-Government; What Is E-Government?" See http://upan.org/egovernment2.asp.
15. "Tech Watch: Give Federal Employees Tools to Exploit E-Government," *Federal Times,* December 17, 2001.
16. See http://www.jerseyisc.org/e-government/e-government-introduction.html.
17. Meghan E. Cook, "What Citizens Want from E-Government," Center for Technology in Government, State University of New York, Albany. See http://www.ctg.albany.edu/egov/what_want.html.
18. Henry C. Jackson, "Government's Move to E-mail Eases Access but Worries Some," *Chicagotribune.com,* March 15, 2008.
19. Dwight Waldo, *The Enterprise of Public Administration* (Novato, CA: Chandler & Sharp, 1980), p. 164.
20. Vincent O'Leary and David Duffy, "Managerial Behavior and Correctional Policy," *Public Administration Review* (November–December 1971).
21. Daniel Katz and Robert L. Kahn, *The Social Psychology of Organizations* (New York: John Wiley, 1966), p. 245.
22. Ibid., pp. 245–246.
23. Ibid.
24. Douglas McGregor, *Leadership and Motivation* (Cambridge, MA: MIT Press, 1966), p. 73.
25. William J. Reddin, *Managerial Effectiveness* (New York: McGraw-Hill, 1970), p. 35.
26. "Good Leaders Must First Be Good People," *Black Issues in Higher Education* 13, no. 9 (June 27, 1996): 64.
27. Katz and Kahn, *The Social Psychology of Organizations,* pp. 293–294.
28. Ibid., pp. 545–546.
29. Daniel Katz, "Patterns of Leadership," *Handbook of Political Psychology* (San Francisco: Jossey-Bass, 1973), pp. 216–217.
30. A. M. Henderson and Talcott Parsons, eds., *Max Weber: The Theory of Social and Economic Organization* (New York: Oxford University Press, 1947), p. 328.
31. Rom. 12, New English Bible with Apocrypha.
32. Michael Hill, *A Sociology of Religion* (London: Heinmann Educational Books, 1973), p. 147.
33. 1 Cor. 12:4, New English Bible with Apocrypha.
34. John M. Pfiffner and Frank P. Sherwood, *Administrative Organization* (Englewood Cliffs, NJ: Prentice-Hall, 1960), pp. 55–56.

35. Robert J. House, "A 1976 Theory of Charismatic Leadership," in *Leadership: The Cutting Edge,* eds. James G. Hunt and Lars L. Larson (Carbondale, IL: Southern Illinois University Press, 1977), pp. 193–204.

36. Ibid., p. 204.

37. Reinhard Bendix, *Max Weber: An Intellectual Portrait* (Garden City, NY: Doubleday, 1947), p. 245.

38. Robert C. Tucker, "The Theory of Charismatic Leadership," *Daedalus* 97, no. 3 (Summer 1968): 745.

39. Rajnandini Pillai, "Crisis and the Emergence of Charismatic Leadership in Groups: An Experimental Investigation," *Journal of Applied Social Psychology* 26, no. 6, (March 16, 1996): 543–563.

40. Lyn Ragsdale and John J. Thesis III, "The Institutionalization of the American Presidency, 1924–92," *American Journal of Political Science* 41, no. 4 (October 1997): 1280–1318.

41. Ibid., p. 1282.

42. Charles Frankel, *High on Foggy Bottom* (New York: Harper and Row, 1968), p. 56.

43. Rosemary Stewart, *The Reality of Organizations* (New York: Anchor Books, 1972), p. 48.

44. For an interesting and informative view of some of the tsar's leadership problems, see the earlier chapters of Robert K. Massie, *Nicholas and Alexandra* (New York: Atheneum, 1969).

45. David E. Lilienthal, *Management: A Humanist Art* (New York: Columbia University Press, 1967), pp. 16–17.

46. Peter F. Drucker, *The Practice of Management* (New York: Harper & Row, 1954), p. 122.

C H A P T E R **8**

Taxing, Budgeting, and Spending

Chapter Highlights

Who Gets What Amount of Money?

The Federal Budget Process

Federal Spending

Federal Revenue

Discretionary and Mandatory Spending

Deficit, Surplus, and National Debt

Federal Funds, Trust Funds, and Off-Budget Spending

Phases of the Budget Cycle

The Incrementalism Budgeting Perspective

Roots of the Deficit Problem

Economic Progress, Taxes, and Savings

Federal Spending in the States

State Tax Burdens

Summary

Local Budgets and Ecology

All economic decision making has environmental consequences—just as all environmental decision making has economic consequences. A budget entails outlays of how a community spends citizens' hard-earned dollars for the common good.

Water, air, and land—natural resources—are among the earth's greatest assets. Protecting them means protecting human health, but that protection has costs. Federal and state legislatures set fees for public water supply systems and storm-water permits. The residents of Fountain Inn, State of Commonwealth, found that they had an emerging water crisis after last year's spring floods.

Fountain Inn is located in the scenic rolling hills of the State of Commonwealth, one hour by interstate to Commonwealth's state capital, Big Burb. The town is a progressive, growing community. Despite population increases, Fountain Inn offers the friendliness and closeness of a small town.

In 1970, the town had a population of 3,308, and by 1990, it had jumped to 11,708, a 254 percent increase. The 2000 population was 14,488, increased by 23.74 percent since 1990. Sixty-one percent of the population is under the age of 35, 31 percent under the age of 18, and 24 percent between the ages of 35 and 54.

The town economic base is a combination of small business and heavy industry that moved out of the city center of Big Burb. Many residents commute to Big Burb for their jobs. High-tech industry is beginning to consider Fountain Inn as a location for development opportunities. Stay-at-home moms are utilizing their liberal arts degrees to start entrepreneurial computer-based jobs. Fathers long ago found out that their family responsibilities are more than merely "bringing home the bacon."

Street sweepers and pet-poop patrols could become commonplace in Fountain Inn, located along Commonwealth's primary interstate route, as local communities begin the task of meeting new clean water standards that are applied to storm-water runoff. Elected officials are pressured to raise taxes as they devote more of their cities' budgets to meeting the new water-quality standards required by the federal Environmental Protection Agency (EPA).[1]

Government-imposed regulations constrain or encourage many sorts of activities in order to meet the goals of modern societies. Many existing and emerging town policies have a fundamental flaw: their design and implementation do not adequately consider environmental or ecological impacts.[2]

Towns like Fountain Inn are responsible for local economic and social development, environment and the quality of life, and planning.[3] Specific local government responsibilities include:

- Roads, parks, and cemeteries
- Markets, street traders, and shop licenses
- Local police and fire services
- Street lighting
- Electricity distribution
- Water, sewerage, and rubbish disposal
- Public transport
- Preschool education and primary schools
- Adult education
- Libraries and museums
- Sports stadiums and facilities
- Lowest-level health facilities
- Low-cost housing

Storm-water runoff is excess water that drains off streets, lawns, and parking lots into creeks, rivers, and lakes—many of which are sources of drinking water. The runoff carries with it elements of oil, grease, chemicals, fertilizers, pesticides, fecal material from animals, and other pollutants. Measures for improving the quality of runoff water include sweeping streets to keep excess dirt out of the water, implementing erosion controls at development sites, enforcing animal control ordinances to prevent animal manure from washing down storm drains, and monitoring the use of fertilizer and pesticide applications.

The Commonwealth state Department of Health and Environmental Control (CDHEC) wrote regulations to meet the new storm-water standards. The goal of the new regulations is to control the quality of storm water prior to its release. This ecological ordinance by Fountain Inn means that its city council has no choice but to prepare future budgets to deal with an issue confronting the entire community.

What Commonwealth Citizens Get for Their Tax Money

Commonwealth citizens' taxes pay for several environmental protection programs and services:

- CDHEC emergency responders from the Office of Land Quality deal with about 2,000 oil and hazardous material spills a year.
- The Office of Water Quality upholds standards for 4,500 public water supply systems and more than 2,000 wastewater treatment facilities.

The state's Environmental Permit Programs also:

- Process and issue operating permits to all facilities
- Process and issue permits for new facilities and modifications
- Conduct compliance inspections of all facilities
- Review compliance information generated by all facilities
- Educate the public and facilities on aspects of rule and permit requirements
- Pursue enforcement where warranted
- Provide legal support to permit programs as needed

The implementation of new water runoff standards cannot be financed by state or federal monies; instead, the costs for meeting new runoff standards are met by raising local taxes. "I think there's going to be no other recourse than the necessity to raise taxes," said Tommy Tickedoff, a Fountain Inn councilman.[4]

A budget plan explains how elected government officials would pay for citizen interests and activities. The 2008–2009 proposed city budget sets aside $25,000 to comply with storm-water regulations. But councilman Tickedoff predicts the costs will be substantially higher. Buying a street sweeper may cost the taxpayers between $80,000 and $120,000. The purchase would be funded through the city's general fund on a lease-purchase arrangement over five or six years.

Councilman Tickedoff laments that the new water standard illustrates how the State of Commonwealth dumps unfunded mandates on towns and cities. "There's only so much that local property owners can continue carrying on their backs," he said. "I think the quality of our water is something everyone ought to be concerned about. But some of these regulations seem a little excessive. I don't know how we would be able to have dog-poop police."[5]

Commonwealth state law requires Fountain Inn to implement a Storm-Water Management Plan, which has to incorporate

- Surface drainage and flood protection
- The preservation or rehabilitation of natural systems
- Protection of aquatic habitat and life
- Reduction of storm-water pollutants
- Erosion and sediment controls
- Enhanced aesthetics and recreational opportunities
- Reuse of storm water as a valuable resource
- A comprehensive community education program (awareness raising and action)
- Adequate funding
- Commitment from the Storm-Water Manager[6]

The operation and maintenance of the sanitary sewer system was funded through the Wastewater Revolving Fund. The Fountain Inn city council endorsed the concept of self-sufficiency and agreed to an annual 16.3 percent increase in the fee. The Storm-Water Management Fee supports operating and capital budgets for the Drainage Cost Centers. Revenues are generally consistent, because the fee is based on total impervious area not affected by water. The maintenance program and its components are mandated by the State of Commonwealth Pollution Discharge Elimination System (CPDES) permit.

The Fountain Inn city council established the position of Public Works Manager to operate the Storm-Water Division. He or she will oversee the planning, directing, and implementation of goals, strategies, and programs. Qualifications include a Master's degree in Public Administration and a Bachelor of Science degree in Civil Engineering or a related field.

Local government officials demand more authority—and power—over matters that directly affect them. As local governments gain power and experience, they take over more responsibilities. Next they must consider the matter of costs, raising taxes, and implementing budgets effectively. At this juncture in Fountain Inn politics, the possibility of increasing property taxes merits further notice.

The State of Commonwealth does not permit local governments to incur budget deficits. Raising taxes and cutting spending in order to balance budgets creates a "between a-rock-and-a-hard-place" scenario for Fountain Inn officials—both elected and appointed. Property owners balk at paying higher taxes. Business district entrepreneurs from Fountain Inn's city center offer similar views.

"Public and private are not categories of nature," Dwight Waldo cautioned. "They are categories of history and culture, of law and custom. They are contextual and subject to change and redefinition."[7] Waldo's maxim is causing residents of Fountain Inn to reconsider personal and collective priorities. Government policy of Fountain Inn, as acted upon by its city council, impacts numerous individual and community economic activities.

Civic decisions on the environment have economic consequences. They entail deliberations about the Wastewater Revolving Fund, Storm-Water Management Fees, and services of the Public Works Manager in Fountain Inn's Storm-Water Division. Almost everyone in Fountain Inn agrees economic decisions—by individuals, private businesses, and local government agencies—have consequences for the ecology of their community. The effects are long-term.

Budget making requires compromises as everyone gets taxed, but some residents are assessed more than others. If budgets are instruments of coordination, control, and planning, and if administrative politics is deciding who gets what amount of money, is levying property taxes a matter of "whose ox is being gored" or whose basement is being flooded for the third time this spring?

Notes

1. L. C. Leach III, "Storm Water Rules Could Run Off with City Budgets," *Tribune-Times.* http://tribunetimes.com/stories/2002/04/09/200204092728.htm.
2. "Government Budgets: Green Budget Reform," http://iisdl.iisd.ca/greenbud/default.htm.
3. "The News in Brief . . . Budget Crunch May Harm Environmental Protection," *Financial Times of Indiana,* February 11, 2002.
4. Leach, "Storm Water Rules."
5. Ibid.
6. Peter J. Morison and Geoffrey J. Hunter, "Implementation of Storm-Water Management Plans—It Costs a Lot to Build Bad Products." In Conference proceedings *Thinking Outside the Square—Stormwater Management Strategies in the Hawkesbury–Nepean Catchment,* Stormwater Industry Association: Hawkesbury–Nepean Stormwater Management Workshop. Sydney, Australia, March 6, 2001, pp. 2.1–2.15. http://www.ipwea.au/papers/download/Peter%20Morison.doc.
7. Dwight Waldo, *The Enterprise of Public Administration* (Novato, CA: Chandler & Sharp, 1980), p. 164.

If politics is sometimes defined as the process of deciding who gets what, administrative politics often becomes the process of deciding *who gets what amount of money.* Consequently, whether one department or individual is favored over another or whether one program or policy is supported over another usually translates into a budgetary decision. In this sense, budgets are political documents.

It is not enough, however, to call attention to the political aspects of budgeting to define what budgeting is. Budgets are also instruments of *coordination, control,* and *planning.* They govern nearly all aspects of administration and confer a great deal of power on those who prepare them.

Who Gets What Amount of Money?

Budgeting practices in the United States are the result of American ideology, federalism, and decision-making models. The political environment of budgeting is defined by our democratic ideology, which involves varying concepts of representative government. Democratic ideology is, in turn, defined by the idea of capitalism, a system that assumes that a growth-directed economy supports government's ability to appropriate sufficient funds for public services.

Public sector monies are raised from taxes on *individuals* and *businesses.* It's tough to maintain viable public services if revenues supporting such activities are low or nonexistent. Whether citizen taxpayers are providing education, unemployment compensation, or national defense, they need a growth economy to finance these citizen benefits. From a capitalistic economy we are, therefore, able to afford programs that benefit all citizens. The appropriate mix of capitalism and socialism affects the size and scope of government and budgeting policies.

Deciding which level of government should provide a certain service is a matter of *federalism,* with its ever-changing division of power. The American system of federalism helps determine the scope, size, and nature of national, state, and local budget priorities. If state law conflicts with federal law, state law gives way. If local legislation conflicts with state or federal provisions, local ordinances are overruled.

What Is the Budget?

The federal budget is:

- *A plan for how the government spends your money.* What activities are funded? How much does it spend for defense, national parks, the FBI, Medicare, and meat and fish inspection?
- *A plan for how the government pays for its activities.* How much revenue does it raise through different kinds of taxes—income taxes, excise taxes, and social insurance payroll taxes?
- *A plan for government borrowing or repayment of borrowing.* If revenues are greater than spending, the government runs a surplus. When there is a surplus, the government can reduce the national debt.

- *A plan that affects the nation's economy.* Some types of spending—such as improvements in education and support for science and technology—increase productivity and raise incomes in the future. Taxes, on the other hand, reduce incomes, leaving people with less money to spend.
- *A plan that is affected by the nation's economy.* When the economy is doing well, people earn more and unemployment drops. In this atmosphere, revenues increase and the deficit shrinks.
- *A historical record.* The budget reports on how the government has spent money in the past and how that spending was financed.

Source: Tax Foundation, "How Does Uncle Sam Plan to Spend Your Federal Tax Dollar in FY 2003," http://www.taxfoundation.org/taxdollar.html, 2002.

State boundaries, overlapping jurisdictions, the economic decline of certain states and cities, and suburban growth patterns contribute to the dilemmas of budgeting in a federal system.

The Federal Budget Process

The annual budget process, or appropriations process, involves only one-third of the federal government budget. This one-third, called the discretionary budget, is what Congress debates and sets the levels for on an annual basis. Military and education programs are examples of discretionary spending. For details of this process, see http://www.nationalpriorities.org, on which the next few sections are based.

The other two-thirds of the federal budget consists of mandatory spending, primarily federal entitlement programs such as food stamps and Social Security. Congress sets controls by establishing eligibility rules and other payment guidelines, but the appropriations process is basically automatic. The numbers given in the annual budget are simply estimates based on the eligibility and/or payment rules.

The annual budget process comprises a series of steps visible to the public:

Step 1. The president submits a budget proposal.
Step 2. Congress passes a budget resolution.
Step 3. Congressional subcommittees "mark up" appropriation bills.
Step 4. The House and Senate vote on appropriation bills and reconcile differences.
Step 5. The president signs each appropriation bill, and the budget is enacted.

Within these steps are a number of activities not readily visible to the citizenry. We outline them here in chronological order.

First Monday in February: The president submits a "budget request." The President's Budget is a proposal for the coming fiscal year, which starts on October 1

Federal Budget Process Landmarks

1921:   Bureau of Budget created within Treasury Department

1939:   Bureau of Budget placed in the newly created Executive Office of President. This gives the President greater authority over budget by providing him the responsibility for developing a comprehensive budget to be presented to the Congress.

1970:   Bureau of Budget's functions expanded to oversee management of federal agencies, and renamed as Office of Management and Budget.

1974:   Congressional Budget Act passed. Congress creates Congressional Budget Office to provide an independent source of economic and fiscal analysis. Thus, CBO is on the legislative side, while OMB is on the executive side. CBO and OMB projections and estimates do not necessarily match (this is a good example of the checks and balances). Start of fiscal year moved from July 1 to October 1.

1990:   The Budget Enforcement Act (BEA) passed, which essentially limits discretionary spending, and ensures that new entitlement programs and/or tax cuts do not worsen tax deficit. BEA provisions expired in 2002.

1997:   The Balanced Budget Act passed. According to OMB,

First enacted in 1990 and extended in 1993 and 1997, BEA significantly amended the laws pertaining to the budget process, including the Congressional Budget Act, the Balanced Budget and Emergency Deficit Control Act, and the law pertaining to the President's budget. The BEA constrained legislation enacted through 2002 that would increase spending or decrease receipts.

The BEA divided spending into two types–discretionary spending and direct spending. Discretionary spending is controlled through annual appropriations acts. Direct spending, which is more commonly referred to as mandatory spending, is controlled by permanent laws.

The BEA required budget authority provided in annual appropriations acts for certain specifically identified programs to be treated as mandatory. This is because the authorizing legislation in these cases entitles beneficiaries to receive payment or otherwise obligates the Government to make payment, even though the payments are funded by a subsequent appropriation. Since the authorizing legislation effectively determines the amount of budget authority required, the BEA classified it as mandatory.

The BEA defined categories of discretionary spending and specified dollar limits known as "caps" on the amount of spending in each category. If the amount of budget authority or outlays provided in appropriations acts for a given year exceeded the cap for that category, the BEA required a procedures, called sequestration, for reducing the spending in the category.

The BEA did not cap mandatory spending. Instead, it required that all laws that affected mandatory spending or receipts be enacted on a "pay-as-you-go" (PAYGO) basis. That means that if such a law increased the deficit or reduced a surplus in the budget year or any of the four following years, another law had to be enacted with an offsetting reduction in spending or increase in receipts for each year that was affected. Otherwise, a sequestration would be triggered in the fiscal year in which the deficit would be increased.

and continues through September 30 of the following year. For example, FY2011 begins on October 1, 2010, and ends September 30, 2011.

A lengthy preparation process, largely invisible to the public, determines the shape of the budget. Initially, the president and the cabinet decide on their policy priorities. Based on these priorities, the Office of Management and Budget (OMB) offers guidelines to federal departments and agencies for preparing their strategic plans and budgets. These administrative units then submit their budget requests.

OMB then evaluates these documents and prepares the President's Budget, which is published in six comprehensive volumes:

- Budget of the United States Government
- Analytical Perspectives
- Historical Tables
- Appendix
- Budget Systems and Concepts
- Citizen's Guide to the Federal Budget

February to mid-April: After the president submits the budget, the House and Senate traditionally prepare budget resolutions. A "budget resolution" is a framework for making budget decisions about spending and taxes. It does not set binding spending amounts for particular programs. After the two chambers pass budget resolutions, a joint conference is formed to reconcile differences. Each chamber must approve conference compromises.

Late Spring to Early Fall: The House and Senate subcommittees "mark up" appropriations bills. Based on the budget resolution, the Appropriations Committee of each chamber sets allocations for each of its subcommittees (ten in the House and twelve in the Senate). Each committee takes budget requests and justifications submitted by agencies. Hearings are conducted.

Committee staffs follow up with agencies to obtain answers to questions about agency requests. Having sought comprehensive information, each committee writes a first draft of its appropriation bill. This effort is known as the "chairman's mark." The committee then votes on its bill. After passage, the bill moves back to the Appropriations Committee, which reviews it and sends it to the floor for a vote. Special riders may also be attached. This process of appropriations may include one or more pieces of tax or other legislation affecting federal revenues.

Summer to Early Fall (in practice, through December): The individual appropriation bills are debated and voted on by their respective chambers. After both House and Senate versions of a particular appropriation bill have been passed,

How to Get Involved

Stay informed. A number of nongovernmental organizations provide credible information about the federal budget:

- National Priorities Project
- OMB Watch
- Center on Budget and Policy Priorities
- Women's Action for New Directions
- Center for Community Change
- Coalition on Human Needs

These organizations provide information on their Web sites and have e-mail lists that you can join. These e-mail lists differ in length, frequency, and content.

Contact your legislators. You can e-mail your House representative or visit the Web site of your U.S. senators. "Snail mail" letters tend to be taken more seriously by representatives and their aides than e-mails or telephone calls. Even more effective is visiting your representatives. Make an appointment with them if you are visiting Washington. Representatives and senators also maintain offices in their home districts. These local constituent offices afford opportunities to talk with staff personnel about your concerns. After all, officials are elected to serve you.

Source: http://www.nationalpriorities.org/print/5850.

a conference committee is set up to resolve differences between them. The House and Senate then vote on a conference report for each bill and send it to the president.

October 1: The budget is enacted. The president must sign each appropriation bill after it has passed Congress. When all the bills have been signed, the budget is enacted. However, the process is not normally complete by October 1. In recent years, this budget process has not been finished until December. If the budget is not enacted by October 1, Congress must pass "continuing resolutions" in order for the government to continue its functions. These resolutions simply continue funding for agencies and programs at current levels until the budget for the fiscal year is enacted.

Federal Spending

Federal spending is more than $2 trillion a year and accounts for more than half of all government spending in the United States. The federal government accounts for 20 percent of the U.S. gross domestic product (GDP). But this pattern was not always the case.

In the 1920s, the federal government spent less than $40 billion in today's dollars. This was approximately 3 percent of the GDP. Direct government spending did not have a significant impact on the economy. However, the federal government did allocate land to railroad companies, and to encourage mining, it set low mining fees on public lands.

Federal spending increased significantly during the New Deal and especially during World War II. In 1944, outlays reached an all-time high of 44 percent of GDP. Outside of World War II, the peak in federal spending was in 1983 during the Reagan military buildup.

During the 1990s, federal spending did not keep pace with the expansion of the economy or population growth. Federal spending declined, and by the end of the decade, federal spending was at a low not seen for almost thirty-five years. More recently, federal spending has increased as a result of significant increases in military spending, rising health costs, and a growing number of citizens retiring and collecting Social Security. These historical patterns in federal spending are summarized in Figure 8.1.

In the twenty-first century, federal spending accounts for more than 20 percent of GDP. About one-third of that spending, $818 billion in FY2005, is devoted to Social Security and Medicare—programs aimed at senior citizens, the disabled, and children and spouses of deceased workers (see Figure 8.2).

Spending on the category of "national defense" amounts to 20 percent of total federal spending. This accounting category, however, does not include foreign military financing grants, other military assistance, or military-related expenditures. The high deficits in the 1980s accelerated the accumulation of federal debt. Servicing the debt consumes approximately 7 percent of spending, or about $180 billion. This amount would be much higher—around $270 billion—if it were not offset by interest earned on Social Security trust funds.

The federal government contributes only about 8 percent of total public spending on elementary and secondary education. Education spending, including higher education, consumes less than 3 percent of the federal budget.

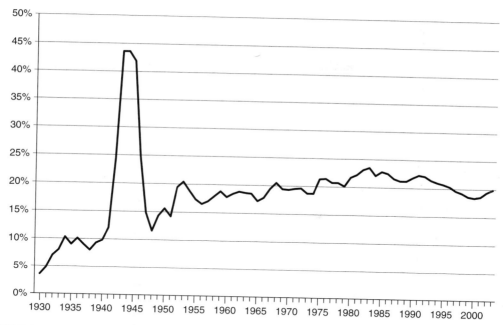

FIGURE 8.1 Federal outlays as a percentage of GDP, 1930–2005

Source: ©2005 National Priorities Project, Inc.

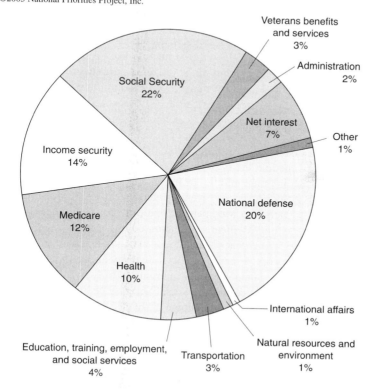

FIGURE 8.2 Total federal outlays, fiscal year 2005

Source: © 2005 National Priorities Project, Inc.

TABLE 8.1	
Total Federal Revenues, Fiscal Year 2005	
Total revenues	$2 trillion
Individual income taxes	$894 billion
Corporate income taxes	$227 billion
Social insurance*	$774 billion
Other	$159 billion

*Includes employment and general retirement, unemployment compensation, and other retirement.

Source: Budget of the U.S. Government, FY2006, Historical Tables.

Federal Revenue

Total federal revenues for fiscal year 2005 amounted to $2 trillion (see Table 8.1). The largest portion, 44 percent, is from individual income taxes. The next largest share is social insurance and retirement receipts, at 38 percent. The remainder consists of corporate income taxes, excise taxes, estate and gift taxes, customs duties, federal reserve deposits, and other receipts.

The U.S. Constitution grants Congress power to "collect taxes, duties, imposts and excises." Early federal government taxation was mostly in the form of excises on goods such as alcohol and tobacco. Although a tax on personal income existed briefly during the Civil War, not until 1913 was the income tax firmly established. At that historical juncture, less than 1 percent of the citizenry paid income taxes.

During World War I, a need for more revenues dominated tax policy making. The top income tax rate rose from 7 percent to 77 percent. Changes occur continuously in the tax code regarding exemptions, deductions, and rates of taxation. During World War II, the number of people subject to the income tax increased tenfold. In the first decade of the twenty-first century, more than 100 million tax returns are filed annually. The federal income tax is progressive, meaning that the rich pay a larger percentage of their income than middle- or low-income taxpayers.

Taxes to finance Social Security were established in 1935. More benefits have been added over time, including Medicare, which provides health care coverage for senior citizens. Taxes to fund Medicare are increased as needs demand. Social Security taxes now stand at 15.3 percent of income, of which half is paid by the employer.

The employee pays 6.2 percent for Social Security and 1.45 percent for Medicare. However, as of 2008, Social Security taxes apply only to the first $102,000 of personal income. This formula causes the Social Security tax to be regressive, in that high-income taxpayers pay a lower percentage of their income than do lower-income taxpayers. About 75 percent of taxpayers actually pay more in payroll taxes (Social Security and Medicare) than they do in individual income taxes.

Corporate income taxes contribute less and less to total tax collections. The burden of taxation has increasingly shifted from corporations to individuals. Over the last half century, corporate taxes have declined from 27 percent of federal revenues to 11 percent (see Figure 8.3). Individual income taxes, meanwhile, have remained relatively stable.

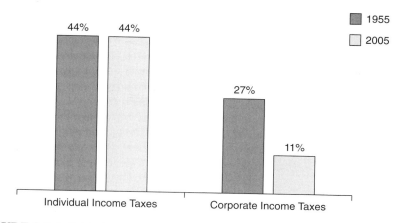

FIGURE 8.3 Individual and corporate income taxes as a share of total federal revenues, 1955 and 2005

Sources: Office of Management and Budget, Budget of the United States Government, Historical Tables, FY2006.

Discretionary and Mandatory Spending

Congress appropriates the federal budget into two types of spending: *discretionary* and *mandatory*. Discretionary spending is subject to the annual appropriations process. Congress directly sets levels of spending on discretionary programs; it may choose to increase or decrease spending on any program in a given year. The discretionary budget is about one-third of total federal spending. Figure 8.4 indicates how discretionary spending was allocated in fiscal year 2005.

About half of the discretionary budget is "national defense." This government-defined category is roughly equivalent to the term, "military." However, it does not include foreign military financing, security assistance, and other programs commonly thought of as military. Discretionary spending also includes education, health, and housing programs.

Mandatory spending consists mostly of entitlement programs, whose funding is determined by eligibility or payment rules. Congress decides to create a program, such as food stamps, and determines who is eligible. It also establishes other criteria for food stamp administration. How much money is appropriated for food stamps each year is then determined by estimates of how many Americans will be eligible and apply for food stamps.

Unlike discretionary spending, Congress does not increase or decrease the food stamp budget each year. It periodically reviews eligibility rules and may alter them in order to include or exclude more recipients. Mandatory spending accounts for two-thirds of the total federal budget. Social Security is by far the largest mandatory federal program. Social Security comprises one-third of mandatory spending and continues to increase as U.S. demographics shift toward an older population. Figure 8.5 shows the breakdown of different types of mandatory spending in fiscal year 2005.

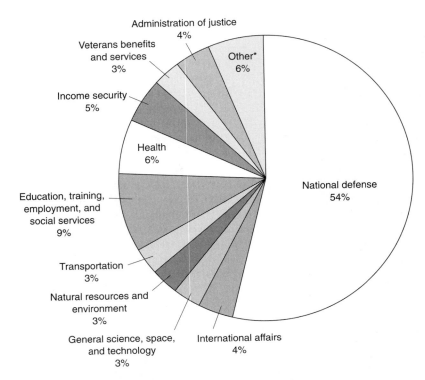

FIGURE 8.4 Federal discretionary budget, fiscal year 2005

*Includes energy, agriculture, commerce and housing credit, community and regional development, general government, and the administration of Medicare and Social Security.

Source: © 2005 National Priorities Project, Inc.

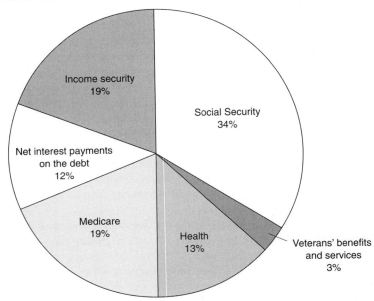

FIGURE 8.5 Federal mandatory spending, fiscal year 2005

Source: © 2005 National Priorities Project, Inc.

Deficit, Surplus, and National Debt

Currently at about $8 trillion, the national debt has assumed political, economic, and even cultural, significance—with both short- and long-range effects. *Debt* is sometimes confused with *deficit*. A deficit occurs when spending exceeds revenues in any given year; a surplus is the opposite—revenues exceed spending. The gross federal debt is the total of all federal net borrowing over the course of years.

The gross federal debt is held by federal entities and by the public. Government trust funds, such as Social Security, are typically required by law to put any surpluses into Treasury securities, which represent shares of debt. Some of the government's debt is actually owned by government trust funds. Intragovernmental holdings include revolving funds, special funds, Federal Financing Bank securities, and other government accounts.

The gross federal debt is also held by the public—individuals, corporations, local, state, and foreign governments, any entity that is not the U.S. federal government. The Federal Reserve System, a federal entity, is an exception. It holds debt that is classified as public. In order to conduct monetary policy, the Fed buys and sells federal securities. If the debt is ever completely eliminated, the Fed may buy securities to conduct policy making.

Figure 8.6 indicates the amount of gross national debt from fiscal year 1940 to its projected level by the end of 2005. Note that the national debt increased noticeably during World War II, grew most rapidly during the 1980s, and as of 2005 hovered at around $8 trillion. It now stands at more than $9 trillion.

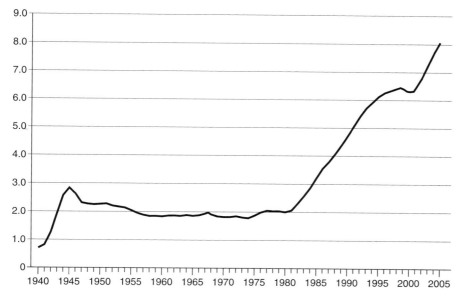

FIGURE 8.6 Gross national debt, 1940–2005 (year end, in trillions of 2005)

*Estimated.

Source: © 2005 National Priorities Project, Inc.

FIGURE 8.7 Gross national debt as a percentage of gross domestic product, 1940–2005 (year end)

*Estimated.

Source: © 2005 National Priorities Project, Inc.

Absolute numbers do not give the whole story, however; the size of the economy also matters. If the economy grows more quickly than the debt, more resources are available to pay back the debt. As a percentage of the economy, the federal debt declined significantly after World War II. Reagan policy making—boosting military spending and promoting tax cuts—resulted in huge federal deficits. In the economic boom of the Clinton years, debt as a percentage of GDP declined (see Figure 8.7).

The huge deficits of the 1980s and budget surpluses of the 1990s are evident in Figure 8.8. In 1998, the federal budget was in surplus for the first time since 1969. The last surplus was in 2001. Beginning in that year, surpluses that in 2000 amounted to $265 billion turned into a $170 billion deficit by 2002. Larger deficits followed in 2003 and 2004. The federal budget is unlikely to yield a surplus again unless significant new tax and/or spending policies are enacted.

Federal Funds, Trust Funds, and Off-Budget Spending

Federal budgeting consists of *federal funds* and *trust funds,* which earmark revenues for particular purposes. Social Security, Medicare, unemployment compensation, federal employment retirement, veterans' retirement, highway construction, and airport development all have their own trust funds. The designation is largely arbitrary, as trust funds and federal funds may finance very similar activities. Trust funds number more than 200; see Figure 8.9 for a breakdown.

Federal fund revenues come from individual, corporate, excise, estate, and gift taxes, special collections, and borrowing. See Figure 8.10 for a breakdown of federal funds budgeting priorities.

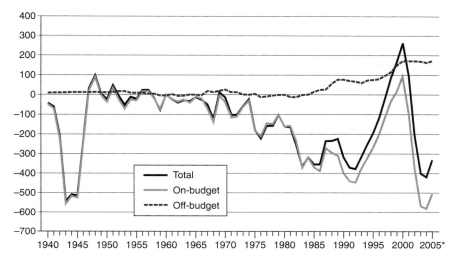

FIGURE 8.8 Federal deficits and surpluses, 1940–2005 (in billions of $2005)

*Estimated.

Source: © 2005 National Priorities Project, Inc.

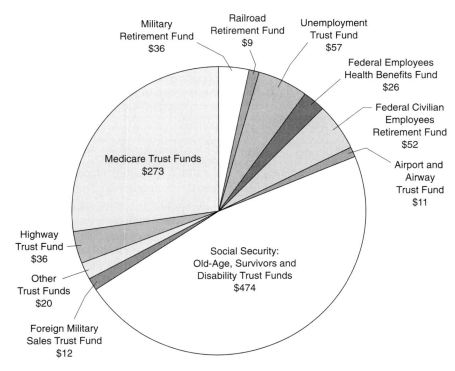

FIGURE 8.9 Federal trust funds, fiscal year 2003 (in billions of dollars)

Source: http://www.nationalpriorities.org/print/5855.

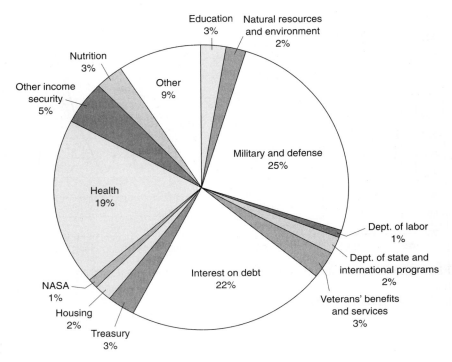

FIGURE 8.10 Federal funds, fiscal year 2002

Sources: Office of Management and Budget, Budget of the U.S. Government, Analytical Perspectives, FY2004.

An *off-budget* program is not considered part of the federal budget and it is not included in the budget totals. As of 2005, off-budget spending totaled $400 billion, compared to an on-budget total of $2 trillion. Social Security trust funds and U.S. Postal Service operations are off-budget tabulations.

A program is typically placed off-budget for political reasons. President Reagan requested that Congress place the strategic petroleum reserve spending off-budget. Instead of raising revenues and/or cutting spending, placement of this program off-budget gave the appearance of a smaller budget deficit. Nonetheless, the federal government still financed this petroleum spending. Placing the savings and loan bailout off-budget permitted the first Bush administration to circumvent congressional balanced budget legislation.

Figure 8.11 indicates the difference between on-budget and off-budget deficits and surpluses. Late 1990s on-budget surpluses were the result of tight fiscal policy and a strong economy. Subsequent on-budget deficits were the result of 2001–2003 tax breaks and higher military spending.

The Social Security trust fund is financed through dedicated payroll taxes. It is positioned off-budget in order to support a decent quality of life for the elderly. Payroll taxes were raised in the late 1980s to anticipate retirement of the baby boomer generation. Government, however, returned to on-budget deficit spending in 2001. The federal government borrows from Social Security surpluses in order to pay for current program demands—rather than taxing and cutting spending now to prepare for future necessities.

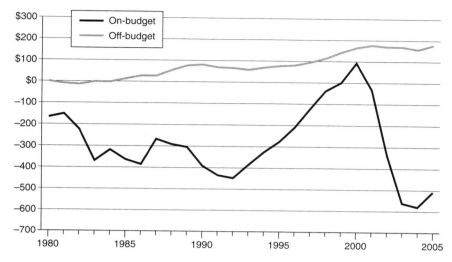

FIGURE 8.11 On-budget and off-budget deficits and surpluses, 1980–2005

Source: © 2005 National Priorities Project, Inc.

Phases of the Budget Cycle

Federal budgeting can be understood in four phases: executive preparation, legislative consideration, implementation and control of the enacted budget, and audit and evaluation. According to Douglas Lee, a "budget, after all, is only an accounting of the financial cost of many political and social decisions.[1] The term *budget* originates from the Middle English word for pouch or purse.[2] Federal budgeting is a continuous and overlapping process, with stages of the budget cycle linked. The findings of audit/evaluation are important data for preparation of future budgets. The federal fiscal year begins in October. Many local governments start their fiscal years in January. Excepting Alabama, Michigan, New York, and Texas, state governments begin their fiscal years in July. The fiscal year in Alabama and Michigan begins in October. New York starts in April, and Texas begins in September. Fiscal years are named after the year in which they end; the federal fiscal year that began on October 1, 2007, was the 2008 fiscal year.

Executive preparation. The president (or governor, mayor, or chief executive on the state and local levels) transmits general directions for department and agency request preparation. The department or agency reviews current operations, program objectives, issues, and future plans as they relate to the upcoming annual budget. Cabinet secretaries and agency heads submit projections for requirements reflecting current operations and future plans. Supporting memoranda and related analytic studies identify major issues, alternatives for resolving issues, and comparisons of costs and effectiveness.

The Office of Management and Budget (OMB) develops economic assumptions, obtains forecasts of international and domestic situations, and prepares fiscal projections. The OMB compiles total outlay estimates for comparison with revenue

Ten Principles of Sound Tax Policy

1. **Transparency is a must.** A good tax system requires informed taxpayers who understand how taxes are assessed, collected and complied with. It should be clear to taxpayers who and what is being taxed, and how tax burdens affect them and the economy.

2. **Be neutral.** The fundamental purpose of taxes is to raise necessary revenue for programs, not micromanage a complex market economy with subsidies and penalties. The tax system's central aim should be to minimize distortions in the economy, and to interfere as little as possible with the decisions of free people in the marketplace.

3. **Maintain a broad base.** Taxes should be broadly based, allowing tax rates to be as low as possible at all points.

4. **Keep it simple.** The tax system should be as simple as possible, and should minimize gratuitous complexity. The cost of tax compliance is a real cost to society, and complex taxes create perverse incentives to shelter and disguise legitimately earned income.

5. **Stability matters.** Tax law should not change continuously, and tax changes should be permanent and not temporary. Instability in the tax system makes long-term planning difficult, and increases uncertainty in the economy.

6. **No retroactivity.** Changes in tax law should not be retroactive. As a matter of fairness, taxpayers should rely with confidence on the law as it exists when contracts are signed and transactions are made.

7. **Keep tax burdens low.** It makes a difference how large a share of national income is taken by government in taxes. The private sector is the source of all wealth, and is what drives increases in the standard of living in a market-based economy. Taxes should consume as small a portion of national income as possible, and should not interfere with economic growth and investment.

8. **Don't inhibit trade.** In our increasingly global marketplace, the U.S. tax system must be competitive with those of other developed countries. Our tax system should not penalize or subsidize imports, exports, U.S. investment abroad or foreign investment in the U.S. Taxes on corporations, individuals, and goods and services should be competitive with other nations.

9. **Ensure an open process.** Tax legislation should be based on careful economic analysis and transparent legislative procedures. Tax legislation should be subject to open hearings with full opportunity to comment on legislation and regulatory proposals.

10. **State and local taxes matter.** The same general principles that apply to federal taxes also apply at the state and local level. Local, state and federal tax systems should be harmonized to the extent possible, including consistent definitions, procedures and rules.

Source: Andrew Chamberlain, Tax Foundation, October 7, 2005, http://www.taxfoundation.org/blog/show/1106.html.

estimates. It develops recommendations for the president on fiscal policy, program issues, and budget levels.

As appropriate, the president discusses budgetary outlook and policies with the director of the OMB and with cabinet secretaries and agency heads. He reviews budget recommendations and decides on department and agency budget estimates, grounding his decisions on overall budget assumptions and policies. He may often revise his budget message. He transmits recommended budget estimates to Congress within fifteen days after Congress convenes.[3]

Legislative consideration. The predominant legislative power in the Western world is the power of the purse.[4] Congress acts on requests for budget authority and does not vote directly on outlays of taxpayer dollars. Instead, Congress grants budget authority to departments and agencies. Budget authority permits the agencies to incur obligations and to spend federal monies. This is accomplished through passage of appropriation bills.

The Congressional Budget Timetable

The Congressional budget process begins nine months prior to the beginning of the budget year, which begins on October 1.

Five days prior to the transmittal of the President's budget to Congress: The Congressional Budget Office (CBO) issues its sequestration preview report for the year beginning October 1 (the budget year).

On or after the first Monday in January, but no later than the first Monday in February: The President's budget is transmitted to Congress.

On or before February 15: The CBO issues its *Budget and Economic Outlook* for the budget year.

February 25: Deadline for Congressional committees to submit their budget estimate to Budget Committees.

April 15: Congress completes action on budget resolution.

June 15: Congress completes action on reconciliation bills.

June 30: House completes action on appropriation bills.

July 15: The OMB (Office of Management and Budget) midsession budget estimate report is due.

August 15: The CBO issues its updated sequestration report.

August 20: The OMB issues its updated sequestration report.

October 1: The new fiscal year begins.

Ten days after the end of the congressional session: The CBO issues its final sequestration report for the year that began on October 1.

Fifteen days after the end of the congressional session: The OMB issues its final sequestration report.

Forty-five days after the end of the congressional session: GAO (General Accounting Office) issues its sequestration compliance report.

Source: http://members.bellatlantic.net/~vze25f7j/budget/timetable.htm.

The budget committees hold hearings as they prepare for the drafting of the first concurrent resolution on the budget. The appropriations committees hold special hearings on the budget overview with the director of the OMB, Secretary of the Treasury, and Chair of the Council of Economic Advisors. Subcommittees of the appropriation committees also hold hearings and review justifications from each department and agency. The House appropriations subcommittees draft appropriation bills and reports. The budget committees receive the views and budget estimates of all committees and draft the first concurrent resolution.

Congress receives the president's budget within fifteen days after Congress convenes. It adopts the first concurrent resolution on the budget by April 15. The House of Representatives debates and passes appropriation bills, with or without amendments. The Senate receives the House-passed versions of appropriation bills and refers them to the Senate Appropriations Committee. The Senate debates and passes appropriation bills with or without amendments. If Senate bills differ from House versions, bills are sent to conference. Conference committees consider items of disagreement between the two houses and make recommendations for resolving differences in conference reports. These reports are submitted to each body for action. Congress adopts the second concurrent resolution of the budget on August 15.

Authorizing legislation is substantive legislation enacted by Congress that sets up or continues the legal operation of a federal program or agency either indefinitely or for a specific period or sanctions a particular type of obligation or expenditure within a program. Authorizing legislation is usually a prerequisite for appropriations. An appropriation act is a statute, under the jurisdiction of the House and Senate Committees on Appropriations, that provides authorization for federal agencies to incur obligations and to make payments out of the treasury for specified purposes. There are thirteen regular appropriation acts enacted annually.

Implementation and control of the enacted budget. Spending of federal taxpayer dollars must proceed in a manner consistent with appropriation laws. Once the appropriation bill is approved, the Treasury Department draws an appropriation warrant, countersigned by the General Accountability Office (GAO) and forwarded to the department or agency. The departments and agencies revise operating budgets in view of approved appropriations and program developments.

The director of the OMB distributes budget authority to each department and agency by time periods, usually every three months, or by activities over the duration of the appropriation. The departments and agencies allot apportioned funds to various programs or activities. The budgetary term for allotments is *apportionment.* Central budget office discretion to curtail allotments is often limited. The term for the president's withholding of federal appropriations is *impounding.* Since 1974, presidents have been able to continue to impound funds. Congress, however, can veto these impoundments.

Audit and evaluation. An audit is an "examination of records, facilities, systems, and other evidence to discover or verify desired information. Internal audits are those performed by professionals employed by the entity being audited; external audits are performed by outside professionals who are independent of the entity."[5] Different forms of audits include:

- Financial audit, or a review of financial records to determine whether the funds were spent legally, if receipts were properly recorded and controlled, and if financial records and statements are complete and reliable.
- Management or operations audit, or a focus on the efficiency of operations, on waste of government resources, and on use and control of resources.
- Program audit, or an examination of the extent to which desired results are being achieved, objectives of the program being met, and whether there might be lower-cost alternatives to reach the desired results.
- Performance audit, a part of sunset legislation, which establishes "a set schedule for legislative review of programs and agencies unless affirmative legislative action is taken to reauthorize them. Thus, the 'sun sets' on agencies and programs,"[6] causing an assessment of the total operations of a department or agency, including compliance, management, and program audits.

To illustrate the focus of each audit, consider a state highway department appropriation to purchase road salt for snow and ice removal. A financial audit considers whether the department purchased the salt, if the salt was actually delivered, if competitive practices were used in selecting a supplier, and if the department spent the correct amount on salt. A management audit considers whether the salt inventory is adequately protected from the environment, if the inventory is adequate or excessive, and if other methods of selecting a supplier would result in lower costs. A program audit considers whether the prevailing level of winter highway clearing is an appropriate use of community resources and if alternatives to deployment of salt would be less costly to the community. Finally, a performance audit examines all operations of the highway department.[7]

The GAO conducts an independent audit of financial records, transactions, and financial management and makes reports to Congress. The departments and agencies review compliance with established policies, procedures, and requirements. They evaluate the accomplishments of program plans and the effectiveness of management and operations. The OMB reviews department and agency operations and evaluates programs and performance. The OMB conducts and guides departments and agencies in organization and management studies and assists the president in improving management and organization of the executive branch.

The Budget and Accounting Act of 1921 set the start of the fiscal year at July 1. It created the Bureau of the Budget (changed in 1970 to the Office of Management and Budget) and the General Accounting Office (changed in 2004 to the General Accountability Office). This legislation authorizes the president's budget message to Congress. The Congressional Budget and Impoundment Control Act of 1974 set the start of the fiscal year at October 1. It created the Congressional Budget Office and House and Senate Budget Committees. It requires the current services budget and congressional budget resolutions.

The Incrementalism Budgeting Perspective

The incrementalism perspective of budgeting states that budgeting is primarily, if not exclusively, a process of political strategy.[8] Budgeting is incremental, says Aaron Wildavsky. "The largest determining factor of the size and content of this year's budget is last year's budget. Most of the budget is a product of previous decisions. . . . The budget may be conceived of as an iceberg with by far the largest part below the surface, outside the control of anyone. Many items in the budget are standard and are simply reenacted every year unless there is a special reason to challenge them."[9]

Incremental budgeting demands little inquiry because the increment, not the base, is considered. Incremental decision making entails routine, requires negotiations and accommodation grounded on mutual respect, is delegated to specialists, and is almost invisible. It is distributive, historical, annual, repetitive, predictable, and automatic. It is rewarding and can create stable coalitions.

Incremental budgeting distributes only the increment, but takes nothing away from anyone; decremental budgeting, meanwhile, redistributes resources from people who absorb cuts in appropriations. Incremental budgeting rewards increments to everyone, as credit for such enhancement is to be shared; decremental budgeting engenders blame for the pain of losing accustomed funding.

The incremental model minimizes the intellectual task of creating a new budget every year, facilitates the political task of adopting a budget, and appears ethical. Such a model, accepting the base as a given, eliminates the necessity for rethinking the entire budget. The political task of building a coalition to support this year's new budget allows a majority of political interests with economic stakes to form and take hold. No one appears hurt; everyone gains a little in incremental budgeting.

Decremental budgeting is chaotic and conflict-laden. It may result in coercion, involve confrontation, and generate mistrust. It is clearly redistributive, breaks precedents, is multiyear, erratic, unpredictable, painful, can foster unstable coalitions, and requires active leadership for overcoming such obstacles.

Decrementalism suggests a centralized political system dominated by top-down budgeting. Incrementalism treats budgeting as a bottom-up process. What's the difference? The budgeting process includes the countervailing forces of centralization and decentralization, autonomy and interdependence, micropolitics and macropolitics. The president and his key advisors dominate the top-down process. A limited number of people are involved in such an approach; the developments are less visible to the public. Top-down strategy confronts the mixture of defense and domestic components of the budget, the budget's size, the impact of the budget on fiscal policies, and the executive's policy initiatives to force cutbacks. As suggested in our discussion of decrementalism, routine is not a common feature of the top-down process.

There have been top-down characteristics of the budgetary process since the passage of the Budget and Accounting Act of 1921. Top-down elements are more difficult to document as the process is less routine, involves fewer people, and receives less publicity, and as such have garnered less attention than the bottom-up developments. Researchers find it difficult to observe, conceptualize, and explain the top-down process. According to budget theorists Barry Bozeman and Jeffrey D. Straussman, such features are often ignored or relegated to historical "disturbances."[10]

Incrementalism reflects the bottom-up budgeting process. The late budget theorist Aaron Wildavsky reported that incrementalism focuses on the significance of adjusting the margins from last year's budgetary base with little, if any, examination of the assumed baseline.

Why the emphasis upon the bottom-up process? First, incrementalism is explainable. Budget variations may be explained by using simple projections. Second, incrementalism gives an adequate account of the bottom-up process. Third, incrementalism is emphasized extensively in the administration and budgeting literature. Finally, incrementalism dominates policy makers' perceptions of how budgeting actually occurs and portrays the actual experience of policy makers themselves.

Top-down and bottom-up processes are operative in every budget cycle. As the demands of the budget cycle change with developments in fiscal policy, presidential leadership, economic growth, foreign conflict, congressional assertiveness, and other factors, the use of the respective processes changes. Although the top-down process of federal budgeting grew more important in the Ford and Carter administrations, the Reagan administration implemented perhaps the most important shift in budget policy, determining that the "controllable" portion of the budget includes entitlements offering social services to the middle class.

The baseline federal outlay projections for entitlements consist of social insurance programs such as Social Security, Medicare, unemployment insurance, and railroad retirement; means-tested programs such as Medicaid, food stamps, assistance payments, supplemental security income, veterans' pensions, guaranteed student loans, and child nutrition; civilian and military employee retirement and disability; and programs offering veterans' benefits, farm price supports, general revenue sharing, and other social services.[11]

The desire to curb the development of middle-class entitlement spending, promote economic changes, and alter public perception of economic issues and economic thinking encouraged Reagan administration policy makers to adopt top-down

Budget Components and Reform Techniques

- **The Capital Budget.** A budget that deals with large expenditures for capital items normally financed by borrowing. Capital projects calls for long-range returns and life spans, are relatively expensive, have physical presence, and involve investments in community facilities. Examples include buildings, roads, and sewage systems.[1]
- **The Operating or Expense Budget.** This is an annual projection of revenues and expenditures for regular and recurring operations of governments that serves as a primary instrument of planning and financial control. Examples of expenditures include wages, salaries, personnel costs, supplies, materials, and travel costs.
- **Performance Budgets.** Performance budgets focus on departmental objectives and accomplishments. They do not emphasize the purchase of resources utilized by the department. This technique accounts for the cost of performing measured accomplishments during the fiscal year. A performance budget includes sections on demand, workload, productivity, and effectiveness.[2]
- **Program Budgets.** In a program budget, the focus is on output. The concept rests not on

what governments purchase, nor on the tasks in which government is involved, but on the outputs of government, as nearly as they can be defined. This technique delineates the goals of a department and categorizes tasks contributing to each goal. The focus is on product, not input. Planning Programming Budgeting Systems, or PPBS, focuses on accountability.[3]

- **Zero-Based Budgets (ZBB).** ZBB requires its practitioners to adopt two basic terms and three procedures for implementation. The ZBB terms are *decision units* and *decision packages*. The ZBB steps are *identification, formation,* and *ranking*.[4]

1. Jonathan Rauch, "A Capital Idea for the Budget," *National Journal* 18, no. 49 (6 December 1986): 2948–2949.
2. John L. Mikesell, *Fiscal Administration,* 135–155.
3. Samuel M. Greenhouse, "The Planning-Programming-Budgeting System: Rationale, Language, and Idea-Relationships," *Public Administration Review* 26, no. 6 (December 1966): 271–277.
4. See Peter A. Pyhrr, "The Zero-Base Approach to Government Budgeting," *Public Administration Review* 37, no. 1 (January–February 1977): 1–8; see also Allen Schick, "The Road from ZBB," *Public Administration Review* 38, no. 2 (March–April 1978): 177–180.

strategies. Bozeman and Straussman state that conventional budgeting wisdom did not keep pace with events. Concluding that budget theory should be reformulated, these theorists argue that the political and economic environments changed and led to a perceived demand for reductions in the rate and level of spending. Such cutback management, they argue, can be achieved only through coordinated fiscal management with top-down strategies. Under such conditions, incrementalism becomes a less satisfactory explanation of federal budgeting.[12]

More federal spending was added to the national debt during Reagan's presidential tenure than was added during all previous administrations combined. Perhaps Reagan's chief contribution to budgetary politics, on the other hand, was calling attention to excessive middle-class entitlements and moving from incremental budgeting to decremental estimates. From domestic to defense spending, the representatives of the American people have yet to find the line items that allow for equal sacrifice in implementing federal budgetary policies.

Budgets are grounded in percentage increments to the historic budget base according to some notion of fairness for continuing the funding of each department and agency. The annual focus is on determining percentage monetary adjustments to existing programs.

Operating departments and agencies are units of government bureaucracies that spend taxpayer monies for the delivery of services. They focus on the clientele they serve. Their purpose is to expand service opportunities.

The office of the chief executive (president, governor, mayor) employs budget specialists to argue on behalf of government departments and agencies and their programs. At the federal level, the budget specialists are located in the OMB. In the states, various titles designate the units of executive office budget specialists. For example, in Mississippi, it's the Budget Office. In Arizona, it's the Finance Division. In Iowa, it's the State Controller's Office. In Kentucky, it's the Office of Policy and Management. In Washington state, it's the Office of Planning and Fiscal Management.

Budget analysts are guided by the priorities of the chief executive. The chief executive must balance the priorities and interests of the population. Departments and agencies have a clientele orientation. Not all programs have equal weight. Those with the strongest support in the legislature will do better in the budgeting process than others.

Elected members of the national, state, and municipal *legislatures* champion the priorities of their constituencies. They advocate programs and projects that benefit the people who elect them.

But legislators often cannot compete with the expertise of chief executives, departments, and agencies. Most state legislators are part-time legislators. The role and institutional history of the national legislatuture are more developed than those at the state, local government, and special district levels.

Executives, department and agency heads, legislators, and numerous clientele use budgetary strategies for maintaining or increasing the monies available to them.[13] These strategies emphasize *cultivating clientele* and *developing confidence.*

Departments and agencies cultivate active clientele for lobbying the legislature and chief executive. Most departments and agencies experience little difficulty in locating clientele. Interest groups find ways to petition government decision making and spend funds. Departments and agencies accessing and servicing large and strategically placed clientele are less likely to have their budgets reduced. They not only concentrate on individual constituencies, but seek to expand their clientele. They proactively secure feedback on their programs and their effectiveness. They want constituents to offer suggestions for improving services.

The development of confidence, or deploying actions of personnel and programs to fit in with the expectations of others playing the power game, is a vital part of group strategies. Budget officials are guardians of the department or agency treasury. Presentations are geared to that end. As guardians, budgeteers espouse the effectiveness of programs and promise efficiency in spending taxpayer dollars. Preparation is important as administrative leaders develop and maintain confidence. Public hearings afford officials opportunities to exude confidence in their department or agency missions and programs. Requests for information must be met promptly and in appropriate detail.

Contingent strategies depend on budget circumstances. In defending its base for budget cuts, officials might suggest that a politically popular program be eliminated. In Indiana, for example, where the political culture nurtures high school basketball programs, budget officials call for reduction of athletic budgets when school districts confront fiscal problems. Officials argue that the community's high school

Budget Terms

Authorizations: Involves the determination of maximum spending levels for each program approved by the legislative branch; the responsibility of standing committees of the U.S. House of Representatives and U.S. Senate.

Appropriations: One of the most crucial aspects of budget making; entails the power to spend or to incur financial obligations; "spending" committees in the U.S. House of Representatives and U.S. Senate exercise major roles in this stage of the budgetary process.

Authorizing Legislation: Legislation enacted by Congress to permit the establishment or continuation of a federal program or agency. Authorizing legislation is normally required before the enactment of budget authority, and such authority is usually provided in separate legislation.

Budget Authority (BA): Authority provided by law to enter into obligations that will result in immediate or future outlays. It may be classified by the period of availability, by the timing of congressional action, or by the manner of determining the amount available.

Budget: The president's request to Congress for new programs, allocation of resources to serve national objectives, embodiment of fiscal policy for programs, and information about the national economy essential for the private sector.

Budget Cycle: Executive formulation and transmittal, legislative authorization and appropriation, budget execution and control, review and audit.

Continuing Resolution: Legislation that provides budget authority for specific ongoing activities when a regular appropriation for those activities has not been enacted by the beginning of the fiscal year. Some continuing resolutions provide interim funding for part of the fiscal year until the regular appropriations bill is enacted. Others provide funding for the full fiscal year.

Fiscal Year: The federal government's yearly accounting period, which begins on October 1 and ends on the following September 30.

Outlays: Government spending. Outlays are payments, normally in the form of checks issued, cash disbursed, and electronic fund transfers, net of refunds, reimbursements, and offsetting collections. Outlays include interest accrued on public issues of the public debt.

Receipts: Government income. All income collected from the public by the federal government in its sovereign capacity, primarily through the exercise of its power to tax.

Sequestration: Reduction of new budget authority or other budgetary resources, as defined in the Balanced Budget and Emergency Deficit Control Act of 1985, as amended.

Administrative Audiences

Thomas J. Anton points out that an administrator must try to appease three audiences:

1. The administrator's own *employees,* who look to the administrator to preserve and, if possible, enhance their working conditions and status. Such considerations can be met by increasing the organization's appropriation.
2. The agency's *clientele group.* The people from this group also desire increased funds for the agency, because they are usually the most direct beneficiaries of the agency's expenditures. These first two pressures for budgeting increases would probably exist under any form of budgeting.
3. Finally, there are the *review officials,* including superiors, budget bureau officials, and legislators. All of these, but particularly the latter, have an interest in being able to cut the budget. In making cuts, they achieve a sense of fulfillment and importance.

Source: Thomas J. Anton, "Roles and Symbols in the Determination of State Expenditures," *Midwest Journal of Political Science* 11, no. 1 (February 1967): 29.

basketball program faces an all-or-nothing choice. Any budgetary reduction would make the program impossible. It might as well be eliminated. In the Hoosier state, high school basketball has a jurisdictional, or statewide, clientele base. Strong clientele may prevent across-the-board reductions. Therefore, Indiana school districts and their elected school boards may decide to cut art, music, or history programs, rather than basketball appropriations.

Departments and agencies prepare their budgets incrementally. The most rational guide for next year's budget is based on the development, implementation, and evaluation of this year's appropriations. Departments and agencies must not strive to be "too successful," for they may "win" their "program war," making next year's budget unnecessary.[14]

Roots of the Deficit Problem

The budget deficit was not of major concern to policy makers from the end of World War II through the mid-1970s. From 1947 until 1974, deficits averaged less than 1 percent of the gross domestic product (GDP). As a result of World War II and the Great Depression, the public debt reached 114 percent of the GDP in 1946. But the budget situation became significantly worse after the mid-1970s. Deficits averaged 2.9 percent of GDP during the last half of the 1970s, 4.0 percent during the 1980s, and during the first three years of the 1990s, 4.4 percent. The public debt increased faster than the economy. The ratio of public debt to GDP more than doubled. In 1992, the federal government had revenues of $1.076 trillion and outlays of $1.475 trillion. The budget deficit equaled 37 percent of revenues.

The deterioration of the country's fiscal circumstances was caused by the interaction of several factors. There were systemic policy mistakes. Unanticipated and unpredictable changes occurred in the fiscal environment. The policy makers had little or no direct control over these changes.

First, an unexpected economic slowdown began in the mid-1970s. The slowdown baffled economists. The rate of economic growth slowed by approximately 1 percent after 1973. From the late 1940s through 1973, real per capita GDP expanded at an average annual rate of 2.5 percent, and real output per hour of labor expanded at an average rate of 2.1 percent. From 1973 through 1995, real per capita GDP expanded at only 1.5 percent a year, and output per hour of labor expanded at only 0.8 percent a year. Federal revenues expand as the economy increases. This economic slowdown had a significant impact on federal budgets.[15]

Second, the domestic entitlements the federal government committed to during the 1962–1972 period contributed significantly to growing deficits. Congress and three presidents enacted laws establishing Medicare, Medicaid, food stamps, guaranteed student loans, Title XX social services, and supplemental security income programs. The slowdown in the economy resulted in a decline in income growth. Increasing numbers of people became eligible for means-tested domestic programs. Unexpected demographic developments made more persons eligible for domestic entitlements: The divorce rate doubled. The fraction of births to unwed mothers more than tripled. The poverty rate declined from 22.4 percent in 1959 to 11.1 percent in 1973. The poverty rate increased an average of more than 14 percent

Fiscal and Monetary Policies

Fiscal policy encompasses federal government policy with respect to taxes, spending, and debt management, and is intended to promote the nation's macroeconomic goals, particularly with respect to employment, gross domestic product, price level stability, and equilibrium in balance of payments. The budget process is a major vehicle for determining and implementing federal fiscal policy.

The other major component of federal macroeconomic policy is monetary policy. Monetary policy entails policies that affect the money supply, interest rates, and credit availability, and is intended to promote maximum sustainable output and employment along with stable prices. Monetary policy is directed primarily by the Board of Governors of the Federal Reserve System and the Federal Open Market Committee. Monetary policy works by influencing the cost and availability of bank reserves.

Source: A Glossary of Terms Used in the Federal Budget Process (Washington, DC: General Accounting Office, March, 1981), pp. 59, 97.

from 1980 through 1995. Health care costs, new entitlement commitments, were unexpectedly expensive. With the enactment of Medicare and Medicaid in 1965, the federal government assumed more responsibility for the provision of health care.

Third, the Reagan administration began the 1980s with large increases in defense spending. The Republican president made an ambitious effort to increase defense capabilities. Defense outlays increased from 4.9 percent of GDP in 1980 to 6.3 percent in 1986. Reagan called for cutbacks on the domestic side of government. Wage increases had elevated many Americans into higher tax brackets. Reagan promoted reductions in tax burdens, an effort that made the deficit problems worse. The nondefense domestic discretionary budget declined from 5.2 percent of GDP in 1980 to 3.8 percent in 1986. However, the Reagan administration could not convince the Democratic Congress to significantly slow the increase in domestic entitlement spending programs.

Finally, the weak cyclical performance of the economy after 1974 contributed to growing deficits. Between fiscal years 1955 and 1974, the economy operated at or above its capacity in twelve of the twenty fiscal years. Between fiscal years 1964 and 1974, the economy operated at or above its capacity in nine of eleven fiscal years. Between fiscal years 1975 and 1996, the economy operated at or above capacity in only four fiscal years. The 1964–1974 period economic indicators were misleading.

The economic practice of sustaining increasing domestic entitlements without corresponding tax increases was sliding into deficit spending. Rising interest rates contributed to economic downturns. The growing size of the structural deficit caused federal expenditures on net interest to rise. Between 1951 and 1977, federal expenditures on net interest amounted to no more than 1.5 percent of GDP. After 1984, they expanded to 3 percent or more. Profound changes occurred in the composition of federal spending and taxes. Entitlements, other mandatory expenditures, and interest payments had lawmakers reconsidering benefit levels and eligibility criteria.[16]

In summary, factors contributing to growing federal deficits over the last thirty years of the twentieth century were:

- The unexpected economic slowdown of the mid-1970s
- Domestic entitlement commitments the federal government enacted between 1962 and 1972

- Reagan administration policies for increasing national defense capabilities and appropriations, decreasing nondefense discretionary budget spending, and reducing tax burdens
- A weak cyclical performance of the economy since 1974

President Clinton did achieve a balanced budget, but George W. Bush reverted to Reagan's legacy of large budget deficits.

According to John Steele Gordon, five trends have increasingly affected government fiscal policies over the last sixty years.

> First, a powerful but fundamentally flawed concept in the discipline of economics has completely changed the way both economists and politicians view the national economy and their responsibilities toward it.
>
> Second, the responsibilities of government in general and the federal government in particular, as viewed by the public, have greatly increased.
>
> Third, a shift in power from the Executive to Congress has balkanized the budget process by sharply limiting the influence of the one politician in Washington whose constituency is national in scope, the President.
>
> Fourth, the decay of party discipline and the seniority system within Congress itself has further balkanized the budget process, dividing it among innumerable committees and subcommittees. This has made logrolling (you vote for my program and I'll vote for yours) the order of the day on Capitol Hill.
>
> Finally, the political-action-committee system of financing congressional elections has given greatly increased influence to spending constituencies (often called special interests, especially when they are funding someone else's campaign) while sharply reducing that of the electorate as a whole, which picks up the tab.[17]

Economic Progress, Taxes, and Savings

Economic progress, central to many of the country's concerns as a society, requires investment, which, over the longer term, depends on savings. The nation's savings consist of the private saving of households and businesses and the savings or lack of savings of all levels of government. In general, government budget deficits represent the opposite of savings; they subtract national savings that could be used for investment. Conversely, government surpluses add to savings.

American hostilities toward taxes are well documented. However, the per capita tax level in the United States is not considered high; the people of the United States are not overtaxed. Taxation as a percentage of national income is lower in the United States than in any other major industrialized country (see Figure 8.12). The opposition to taxes clearly cannot be traced to a heavy tax burden. Citizens rebel against higher taxes because they believe that governments are inefficient—even wasteful—in spending assessed revenues for their various operations.[18]

Since the 1970s, private saving has declined while federal budget deficits have consumed a large share of these increasingly scarce savings. The result has been to decrease the amount of national saving potentially available for investment. The depressing effect of deficits on growth might have been mitigated had they financed higher levels of public investment. However, as a share of gross domestic product (GDP), federal investment spending has declined over the past two decades. Therefore, private saving

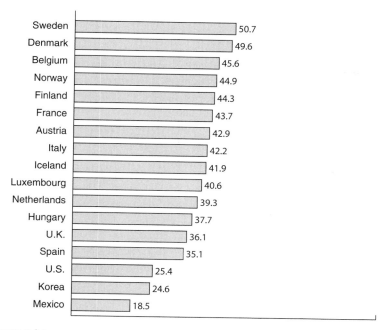

FIGURE 8.12 Total taxes as a percentage of gross domestic product, selected countries, 2003–2004

Source: Organization for Economic Co-operation and Development, "Tax Administration in OECD and Selected Non-OECD Countries: Comparative Information Series (2006)." http://publicagenda.org/issues/factfiles_detail .cfm?issue_type=federal_budget&list=16.

remains low. Federal budget deficits declined significantly from the levels of the 1980s and early 1990s, making available some additional funds for investment.

Total national saving and investment remain significantly below the levels of the 1960s and 1970s. Economists note that these low levels of saving and investment raise concerns for the nation's future productive capacity and future generations' standard of living. The most certain way to increase the resources available for investment is to increase national saving, and the most direct way for the federal government to increase national saving is to achieve and maintain a balanced federal budget. Budget surpluses increase saving and allow the government to reduce the level of federal debt held by the public.

Growing deficits and the resulting lower savings lead to dwindling investment, slower growth, and finally a decline in real gross domestic product. Living standards, in turn, stagnate and fall. Actions on the deficit may be postponed, but they cannot be avoided. By the mid-1990s, robust economic growth and policy action combined to curtail deficit spending for a brief period. Major progress was made on deficit reduction, culminating in the passage of the Balanced Budget Act of 1997.

Policy action accounted for about 25 percent of the late-1990s improvement in the CBO's budget estimates. The remainder of the improvement was due primarily to economic factors.[19] At the close of the century, the decline in the deficit significantly slowed growth in the federal debt held by the public.

The economic benefits of a sustainable budget policy include increased saving and investment levels and faster economic growth, which results in higher living standards. The future implications of current policy decisions are usually not captured in the budget process. The budget is a short-term, cash-based spending plan focusing on the short- to medium-term cash implications of government obligations and fiscal decisions. While the sustainability of the government's fiscal policy is driven primarily by future spending for Social Security and health care commitments, the federal government's commitments and responsibilities extend far beyond these programs.

The main influence of budget policy on long-term economic performance is through the effect of the federal deficit on national savings. Conversely, the rate of economic growth helps determine the overall deficit or surplus through its effect on revenues and spending. Federal deficits reduce national savings, while federal surpluses increase national savings. The level of savings affects investment and, in turn, GDP growth.[20]

Tax policy making combines elements of partisan, policy, and system politics. The citizenry welcomes lower taxes. But do legislators deliver on corresponding government spending cuts? Oftentimes not. Local, state, and federal tax policies determine the range of programs and services government offers.

The purpose of tax policy is to spur economic growth. Expanding economic growth means more revenues for government coffers and more profits and wage increases. Tax policy also includes prospects for balancing budgets, lowering the national debt, and recession spending.

The conventional wisdom is that the Republican Party favors lower taxes and the Democratic Party campaigns for higher taxes. This assertion is partly true, but it is misleading and incomplete. The economy cannot cope with excessively high taxes, but basic government services cannot be provided if taxes are excessively low. The crux of tax policy is to find some happy medium between too few and too many revenues—or between what the state owes the citizenry and what the citizenry owes the government or state.

Democrats favor tax cuts targeting certain segments of the population. Democrats usually do not favor tax cuts for the wealthiest Americans. Republicans promote tax breaks that favor people in all taxing categories. These tax cuts tend to be larger, but require more reductions in government services in order to cover costs.[21]

The 1990s reflected exceptional economic vigor. Output increased nearly 40 percent, investments more than doubled, and consumption grew just over 40 percent. A spending spree reduced personal savings to almost zero. Spending grew faster than the country's earnings. A trade deficit got worse. By the close of 2000, income expenditure excesses climbed to about 4 percent of the United States GDP.

Borrowing and selling assets are ways out of debt for citizens and countries. In the case of nations, creditors and buyers of assets are foreigners. Why be concerned about this development? If the debt is small and remains under control, the creditors are not worried. But if the debt is out of control and the debtor becomes less credible, the creditors may decide not to finance a country's growing debt. This scenario could bring very unpleasant consequences for Americans. Depreciation of the dollar would make imports very expensive and exports very cheap. The trade deficit might be eliminated.[22]

America's persistent and growing trade deficit is rapidly deteriorating. A nation accumulating deeper debts is more and more dependent on its creditors, who are private investors and governments from Europe and Asia. The creditors have no advantage in disrupting their unfettered access to the largest consumer market in the world—producing trade surpluses and greater market shares for their countries. Creditor nations will eventually ask the United States to pay its debts. Creditors want their money. "You can't sustain an empire from a debtor's weakening position—sooner or later, the creditors pull the plug," emphasizes William Greider. Deficits at $400 billion a year will grow the trade debt to alarming levels.[23]

Trade and budget deficits (or balances) appear to be simple, easy to measure and understand, and often raise this commonsense inquiry: "Your family has to keep a balanced budget—why not your government?" However, certain economists argue that the two balances are the least significant and most unreliable indicators of the economy's health and prospects.[24]

A trade deficit (or an import surplus) often reflects strong demands of a booming economy for investment, consumption, and intermediate goods. A trade surplus often reflects weak demands of a depressed, deflationary economy. Internal savings outstrip the availability of domestic opportunities for profitable investment.

In the balanced budget debate, the proportion of any budget that is allocated for public investment in roads and productive infrastructure may go unnoticed. Tax revenues fall and transfer payments rise when the economy is doing poorly. When the economy prospers, as were the circumstances in the mid- to late 1990s, coffers of all governments grow larger.

The budget deficit—or balance—is a certain indicator of what any community, society, or greater good values for that particular year of financial accounting. Budgets are instruments of coordination, control, and planning. They surely can tell us who gets what amount of money. *Washington Post* writer David Broder warns of a "fiscal train wreck that awaits this country unless it mends its ways."[25]

The trade deficit is the broadest measure of foreign trade. It covers not only trade in goods and services; it also follows investment flows between countries. The trade imbalance represents the amount the United States must borrow from foreigners to cover the shortfall between exports and imports.[26]

Foreigners agree to hold dollars in payment for American purchases of cars, televisions, and foreign oil. According to Broder, "almost half the government debt owed to banks or individuals is held by foreign creditors, notably China, Japan, and the OPEC nations, up from 13 percent" in 2003.[27]

The concern is what would occur should foreigners at some point decide they want to hold less in dollar-denominated assets. The widening of the trade deficit causes citizens to question free trade policies, unfair trade competition, and American loss of manufacturing jobs.

Federal Spending in the States

Some states assume much larger federal tax burdens than others. The federal tax burdens on states can be compared with their receipt of federal expenditures. Table 8.2 shows federal spending by state per tax dollar sent to Washington for fiscal year 2005.

Federal spending per dollar of federal taxes is highest in New Mexico ($2.03) followed by Mississippi ($2.02). Alaska, Louisiana, and West Virginia also rank among the five states receiving the most net federal tax dollars. Connecticut, Nevada, and New Jersey rank last among all states in net federal spending received. Although

TABLE 8.2

Federal Spending in Each State Per Dollar of Federal Taxes, Fiscal Year 2005

State	Federal Spending per Dollar of Federal Taxes	Rank
New Mexico	$2.03	1
Mississippi	$2.02	2
Alaska	$1.84	3
Louisiana	$1.78	4
West Virginia	$1.76	5
North Dakota	$1.68	6
Alabama	$1.66	7
South Dakota	$1.53	8
Kentucky	$1.51	9
Virginia	$1.51	10
Montana	$1.47	11
Hawaii	$1.44	12
Maine	$1.41	13
Arkansas	$1.41	14
Oklahoma	$1.36	15
South Carolina	$1.35	16
Missouri	$1.32	17
Maryland	$1.30	18
Tennessee	$1.27	19
Idaho	$1.21	20
Arizona	$1.19	21
Kansas	$1.12	22
Wyoming	$1.11	23
Iowa	$1.10	24
Nebraska	$1.10	25
Vermont	$1.08	26
North Carolina	$1.08	27
Pennsylvania	$1.07	28
Utah	$1.07	29
Indiana	$1.05	30
Ohio	$1.05	31
Georgia	$1.01	32
Rhode Island	$1.00	33
Florida	$0.97	34
Texas	$0.94	35
Oregon	$0.93	36
Michigan	$0.92	37
Washington	$0.88	38
Wisconsin	$0.86	39

continued

TABLE 8.2

Federal Spending in Each State Per Dollar of Federal Taxes, Fiscal Year 2005, *continued*

State	Federal Spending per Dollar of Federal Taxes	Rank
Massachusetts	$0.82	40
Colorado	$0.81	41
New York	$0.79	42
California	$0.78	43
Delaware	$0.77	44
Illinois	$0.75	45
Minnesota	$0.72	46
New Hampshire	$0.71	47
Connecticut	$0.69	48
Nevada	$0.65	49
New Jersey	$0.61	50
District of Columbia	$5.55	na

Source: Tax Foundation.

not a state, the District of Columbia benefited the most—receiving $5.55 in federal outlays for every dollar DC taxpayers sent to the United States Treasury.

Several factors influence this shifting of federal dollars, including the locations of people who receive Social Security, Medicare, and other federal entitlements; the locations of federal employees; federal procurement decisions; and grants to state and local governments.

State Tax Burdens

The 1990s were good times for state and local governments, a period of exceptionally strong growth in most sectors of the economy. The 1990s saw abundant tax revenues in state governments throughout the United States. Income and sales taxes during the 1990s added to the boom for expanding state and local government operations. Income-tax-dependent states witnessed rapid growth in citizens' personal incomes. Strong consumer spending promoted state and local government operations dependent on the sales tax. (Some states rely disproportionately on one or the other.)

During the 1990s, state governments' tax collections grew faster than taxpayers' personal income. As the 1990s came to an end, state tax and fee collections increased by 8 percent. This growth in overall tax collections was substantial when adjusted for inflation. Property, income, and sales taxes all contributed significantly to state and local government budgets.

Various measurements of state tax collections differ substantially. The fiscal year 2005 state tax collections shown in Table 8.3 are based on Bureau of the Census data. The census data record tax collections from various taxes levied at the state level.

TABLE 8.3

Local Government General Revenue* by Source, Fiscal Year 2005

State	From State and Federal Governments	Percentage of General Revenue from Own Taxes					From Non-Tax Charges and Misc.
		Property Taxes	Sales Taxes	Individual Income Taxes	Corporate Income Taxes	Total From Own Taxes	
U.S. Average	38.9%	27.9%	6.2%	1.8%	0.4%	38.8%	22.5%
Alabama	38.5	11.3	12.7	0.8	0.0	28.2	33.3
Alaska	40.4	29.7	7.0	0.0	0.0	38.0	21.6
Arizona	42.7	23.4	10.1	0.0	0.0	36.1	21.2
Arkansas	57.1	8.9	12.4	0.0	0.0	21.8	21.1
California	47.0	17.6	6.3	0.0	0.0	26.5	26.4
Colorado	28.7	26.4	14.1	0.0	0.0	42.8	28.4
Connecticut	33.1	55.9	0.0	0.0	0.0	57.2	9.8
Delaware	49.5 `	21.4	0.4	2.2	0.0	30.3	20.2
D.C.	34.7	14.0	15.7	14.2	2.5	53.0	12.3
Florida	30.7	29.5	6.3	0.0	0.0	38.1	31.1
Georgia	34.1	27.6	10.8	0.0	0.0	40.1	25.8
Hawaii	20.0	43.3	7.8	0.0	0.0	57.7	22.4
Idaho	40.5	27.5	0.5	0.0	0.0	29.8	29.7
Illinois	35.2	38.3	6.9	0.0	0.0	46.7	18.1
Indiana	36.1	33.9	0.4	2.7	0.0	37.6	26.3
Iowa	37.1	31.6	5.0	0.6	0.0	37.8	25.0
Kansas	35.7	31.5	7.2	0.0	0.0	39.3	25.0
Kentucky	43.1	18.7	4.2	8.0	0.0	33.4	23.5
Louisiana	38.0	16.5	21.4	0.0	0.0	39.3	22.8
Maine	31.6	53.0	0.0	0.0	0.0	54.0	14.3
Maryland	31.9	25.1	2.4	17.3	0.0	51.5	16.6
Massachusetts	41.3	43.8	0.6	0.0	0.0	45.5	13.1
Michigan	49.5	27.5	0.6	1.2	0.0	30.0	20.5
Minnesota	48.2	22.1	0.9	0.0	0.0	24.2	27.6
Mississippi	45.5	22.1	0.7	0.0	0.0	23.7	30.9
Missouri	33.5	26.2	13.7	1.7	0.1	44.0	22.6
Montana	43.0	31.3	0.2	0.0	0.0	32.7	24.3
Nebraska	30.6	33.8	5.5	0.0	0.0	44.9	24.5
Nevada	42.3	20.0	6.8	0.0	0.0	31.1	26.6
New Hampshire	33.4	54.0	0.0	0.0	0.0	54.9	11.7
New Jersey	32.6	51.3	0.2	0.0	0.0	52.5	14.9
New Mexico	58.1	13.2	11.0	0.0	0.0	25.7	16.2
New York	36.1	26.7	9.2	5.3	3.3	47.6	16.2
North Carolina	42.5	22.7	6.4	0.0	0.0	30.5	27.1
North Dakota	41.3	31.9	4.2	0.0	0.0	37.1	21.6
Ohio	40.6	26.5	3.6	8.1	0.0	39.4	20.0
Oklahoma	41.0	18.3	14.8	0.0	0.0	34.2	24.8

continued

TABLE 8.3

Local Government General Revenue* by Source, Fiscal Year 2005, *continued*

State	From State and Federal Governments	Percentage of General Revenue from Own Taxes					From Non-Tax Charges and Misc.
		Property Taxes	Sales Taxes	Individual Income Taxes	Corporate Income Taxes	Total From Own Taxes	
Oregon	41.3	26.7	2.1	1.0	0.0	34.6	24.1
Pennsylvania	41.6	28.5	0.9	6.8	0.0	40.0	18.3
Rhode Island	33.9	54.1	0.3	0.0	0.0	55.7	10.5
South Carolina	32.7	28.0	2.6	0.0	0.0	33.7	33.6
South Dakota	33.7	34.7	10.5	0.0	0.0	47.3	19.1
Tennessee	33.5	23.2	10.3	0.0	0.0	35.7	30.8
Texas	29.1	39.8	6.9	0.0	0.0	47.8	23.1
Utah	38.0	25.6	9.8	0.0	0.0	37.4	24.6
Vermont	70.1	16.9	0.5	0.0	0.0	18.0	11.8
Virginia	37.4	31.6	8.1	0.0	0.0	44.3	18.3
Washington	39.8	21.2	9.2	0.0	0.0	34.1	26.1
West Virginia	49.1	23.5	1.4	0.0	0.0	29.2	21.7
Wisconsin	45.3	35.9	1.5	0.0	0.0	38.5	16.1
Wyoming	39.0	22.8	5.7	0.0	0.0	29.9	31.1

*General revenue excludes revenue from utilities, liquor stores, and insurance trusts.

Source: Tax Foundation.

The data are limited to the computation of individual tax burdens by state. Tax incidence analysis best determines tax burdens and which taxpayers ultimately bear the real burden of taxes. Income taxes paid by corporations to one state may not be fully borne by the residents of that state. Some portions of the real tax burdens are borne by residents of other states—as customers, out-of-state employees, or shareholders.

Summary

- The federal budget is a plan for how the government spends your money, how the government pays for its activities, and for government borrowing or repayment of borrowing. It is also something that affects the nation's economy, something that is affected by the nation's economy, and a historical record.
- If politics is sometimes defined as the process of deciding who gets what, administrative politics often becomes the process of deciding *who gets what amount of money.* If budgets are essentially political documents, the politics involved are often veiled.

- It is not enough to call attention to the political aspects of budgeting to define budgeting. Budgets are also instruments of *coordination, control,* and *planning.* They govern nearly all aspects of administration and confer a great deal of power on those who prepare them.
- Public sector budgets are raised from taxes on individuals and businesses. It's tough to maintain effective public services if revenues supporting such activities are low or nonexistent. Whether we are providing national defense or unemployment compensation, we need a *growth economy* to finance government benefits.

- Deciding which level of government should provide a certain service is a matter of federalism, with its ever-changing division of power.
- *Functions of budgeting* include allocating resources to achieve governmental priorities, goals, and policies; raising funds through taxes and loans to finance the budget; stabilizing the economy through fiscal and monetary policies; holding operating agencies accountable for the use of budgeted resources; controlling expenditures; tranferring funds from one level of government to another; achieving planned social and economic development; and improving management in operating departments and agencies.
- During the White House years of George W. Bush, economic and policy changes shifted the federal budget priorities from surpluses to deficits. This shift imposed substantial economic costs upon the citizenry, reducing national savings and resulting in a reduction in Americans' future incomes.
- Bush took office in 2001 with a budget surplus. His own estimates are for a $410 billion deficit in fiscal year 2008 and $407 billion for 2009. Gross federal debt accumulated through all U.S. history totaled 8.9 trillion at the end of fiscal year 2007. That was up sharply from $5.6 trillion at the end of fiscal year 2000.
- The increase in defense spending—from 3.0 percent of GDP in 2001 to 3.9 percent in 2004—largely occurred after the September 11, 2001, terrorist attacks. It included military operations in Afghanistan and Iraq, adding to deficits and then debt. Politically, it helped Bush policy advocates to take the war spending off-budget.
- Tax and spending changes affect incentives to work and save, distribution of disposable income, and the business cycle. President Bush called for making his tax cuts permanent. Revenue loss from the tax cuts resulted in policy changes that enlarged federal deficits. The safety net became more porous.
- Programs that make transfer payments from one age group to another, such as Social Security and Medicare, have profound effects on private savings and the fiscal burdens borne by different generations. The rising deficits come as the United States faces the challenge of fulfilling

Social Security and Medicare promises to retiring baby boomers.
- The annual budget process, or appropriations process, mainly concerns only one-third of the budget. This one-third of the budget, called the discretionary budget, is what Congress debates and sets the levels for on an annual basis. Mandatory spending makes up the other two-thirds of the federal budget.
- Federal spending accounts for more than 20 percent of the Gross Domestic Product (GDP). About one-third of that spending, $818 billion in FY 2005, is devoted to Social Security and Medicare—programs aimed at senior citizens, the disabled, and children and spouses of deceased workers.
- About half of the discretionary budget is "national defense," a government-defined function area that roughly corresponds to the military. Discretionary spending also includes budgeting for education, health, and housing.
- Mandatory spending includes most entitlement programs, which are funded by eligibility rules or payment rules. Social Security is by far the largest mandatory spending program and accounts for one-third of the mandatory budget.
- The gross federal debt has grown to $8 trillion. A significant increase occurred during World War II. The debt increased most rapidly during the 1980s. The gross federal debt is the total of all federal borrowing. A deficit occurs when spending exceeds revenues for one year; a surplus is the opposite, revenues exceed spending. Debt represents the long-term accumulation of deficits.
- Government spending can expand the capacity of the economy. Governments are involved in building transport and communications infrastructures. These investments are necessary for development of a modern economy. Deficit spending may expand the capacity of the economy. Economic growth provides a larger resource, or tax, base to pay back incurred debts.
- The federal budget consists of two major groups of funds: trust funds and federal funds. Trust funds earmark revenues for particular purposes, including Social Security, Medicare, and unemployment compensation. Federal funds constitute all other government funds.

- Transparency, neutrality, broad base, simplicity, stability, no retroactivity, low tax burdens, free trade, openness, and relevance of state and local taxes are ten principles of sound tax policy.
- Main actors in the congressional budgetary process are the Congressional Budget Office (CBO), the House and Senate Committees on the Budget (Budget Committees), and Appropriations Committees in the House and Senate.
- *Stages of the budget cycle* are executive preparation, legislative consideration, implementation and control of the enacted budget, and audit and evaluation.
- Operating departments and agencies, chief executives, and legislatures play roles in the budget process and offer strategies for cultivating clientele and developing confidence in their ideas, priorities, and programs.
- Growing deficits and the resulting lower savings lead to dwindling investments, slower economic growth, and finally decline in real gross domestic product. Living standards, in turn, stagnate and fall.
- Major progress was made on deficit reduction in the 1990s, culminating in the passage of the *Balanced Budget Act of 1997*. Policy action accounted for about 25 percent of the improvement in the Congressional Budget Office's budget estimates. The remainder of the improvement was due primarily to economic factors.
- The roots of federal deficits are grounded in the unexpected economic slowdown in the mid-1970s, the domestic entitlements the federal government committed to during the 1962–1972 period, the Reagan administration's commitment to increased defense spending in the 1980s, and the weak cyclical performance of the American economy after 1974.
- America's persistent and growing trade deficit is rapidly deteriorating.
- *Fiscal policy* entails federal government policies with respect to taxes, spending, and debt management, and is intended to promote the nation's macroeconomic goals, particularly employment, gross domestic product, price level stability, and equilibrium in balance of payments.
- *Monetary policy* entails policies that affect the money supply, interest rates, and credit availability, and is intended to promote

maximum sustainable output and employment along with stable prices.
- Incremental budgeting demands little inquiry because the increment, not the base, is considered.
- Decremental budgeting is chaotic and conflict-laden. It may result in coercion, involve confrontation, and generate mistrust.
- Some states assume much larger federal tax burdens than do others.
- The 1990s were boom times for state and local governments.
- New Mexico draws the most federal dollars per dollar paid in federal taxes ($2.03), followed by Mississippi ($2.02), Alaska ($1.84), Louisiana ($1.78), and West Virginia ($1.76). Federal spending per dollar of federal taxes is the least in New Jersey ($0.61), Nevada ($0.65), Connecticut ($0.69), New Hampshire ($0.71), and Minnesota ($0.72). The District of Columbia draws the most federal spending per dollar of federal taxes, $5.55.
- New York State ranks number one in state and local tax collections per capita, at $5,752 for fiscal year 2005. Indiana, at $3,405, ranks 25. Alabama collected $2,569 for 2005 and ranks 50.
- New Jersey ranks first in state and local property tax collections for fiscal year 2005, at $2,206. Ohio, collecting $1,044, ranks 25. Alabama brings up the rear at $394 for fiscal 2005.
- Most of America's governments divide their budgets into two sections, one for *capital* projects, the other for *expenses.*
- Line-item budgets usually include categories for personnel, equipment, and maintenance, among others.
- Performance budgets, program budgets, and zero-based budgets constitute budgetary reforms.
- The per capita tax level in the United States is not high compared with America's economic competitors. The people of the United States are not overtaxed. Taxation as a percentage of national income is lower in the United States than in any other major industrialized country.
- The American philosophy of taxation is: "Don't tax me. Don't tax thee. Tax the fellow behind the tree."

VIDEOS AND FILMS

Public Administration in Action

Debt

The Public Debt: Breaking the Habit of Deficit Spending [1998]
Explores deficit reduction in domestic spending, defense spending, and raising taxes. Provides context of Reagan administration era. Produced by Domestic Policy Association. [42 min]

Taxes

Taxes in U.S. History [1991]
Whiskey Rebellion, first test of the federal power to tax, 1794; protective tariff issue, 1832; fairness and the income tax, 1909. New York: Joint Council on Economic Education. VHS. [75 min]

Case Study

Budgeting the Department of Homeland Security

The President proposes to create a new Department of Homeland Security, the most significant transformation of the U.S. government in over half-century by largely transforming and realigning the current confusing patchwork of government activities into a single department whose primary mission is to protect our homeland. The creation of a Department of Homeland Security is one more key step in the President's national strategy for homeland security.

—George W. Bush
From the Department of Homeland Security
June 2002

Creating a New and Effective Department of Homeland Security

The President's plan to create a new Department of Homeland Security is indeed ambitious. The following chart illustrates the numerous and disparate organizations involved in Homeland Security and their budget authority by percentage. To achieve an all-encompassing Department that is coordinated in a fiscal and practical sense will require enormous effort and expenditures. (See chart on p. 273.)

To achieve an all-encompassing Department that is effective and fiscally sound requires enormous investment, effort, and coordination. Toward that end, the President's 2009 budget and projected improvements are as follows.

Increases Homeland Security Capabilities

- *Boosts overall spending to secure the homeland.* 10.7 percent growth governmentwide compared to 2008. Within the Department of Homeland Security (DHS), spending will increase by 7.6 percent compared to 2008.

Strengthens Border Security, Interior Enforcement, and Immigration Services

- *Increases Border Patrol agents.* Nearly $500 million for 2,200 new Border Patrol agents, to accomplish the President's goal of more than doubling the size of the Border Patrol—from approximately 9,000 agents to 20,000 agents—since September 11, 2001.
- *Builds SBInet.* Funding to ensure $2 billion over two years to continue to construct the most effective mix of current and next generation

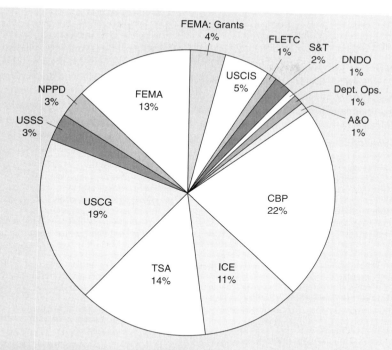

Percent of total budget authority by organization, fiscal year 2009 (Total = $50,502,371,000)

Notes: A&O: Analysis and Operations
CBP: United States Customs and Border Protection
Dept. Ops.: Departmental Management and Operations
DNDO: Domestic Nuclear Detection Office
FLETC: Federal Law Enforcement Training Center
FEMA: Federal Emergency Management Agency
ICE: United States Immigration and Customs Enforcement
NPPD: National Protection and Programs Directorate
S&T: Science and Technology Directorate
TSA: Transportation Security Administration
USCG: United States Coast Guard
USCIS: United States Citizenship and Immigration Services
USSS: United States Secret Service

technology, as well as additional miles of fencing and other infrastructure to protect the border.

- *Supports the Southwest Border Counternarcotics Strategy.* The increased 2009 investments by the Department in personnel and technology will enable DHS and partner agencies to capitalize on an array of intelligence and information sharing programs to much more effectively confront all border threats.
- *Provides additional detention beds.* 1,000 new detention beds, bringing the total number to 33,000 beds, to ensure the continuation of "catch and return."

- *Partners with state and local law enforcement.* Expands the 287(g) program to improve coordination and provide assistance and training in immigration law for state and local law enforcement officials.

Additionally, this Budget supports key reforms in the programs and systems that provide immigration benefits and services, such as:

- *Expands E-Verify, the Employment Eligibility Verification Program.* $100 million to continue expansion and enhancements for the

Internet-based system that helps participating U.S. employers hire and maintain a legal workforce.

- *Reforms existing temporary-worker programs.* Proposes changes to the H-2A, H-2B, and H-1B programs to streamline the process for U.S. employers to hire the labor they need when no Americans are available, while also providing for appropriate labor protections for workers.
- *Improves the background check process for immigration benefit applicants.* Takes steps to eliminate the existing backlog of pending FBI name checks and prevent any new backlog.

Enhances the Security of the Nation's Transportation System

- *Devotes nearly $6 billion to the multilayered, risk-based aviation security system.* (a) $3 billion for over 48,000 Transportation Security Officers and technologies to screen passengers and their baggage for weapons and explosives. (b) $1.2 billion to recapitalize checked baggage screening devices and accelerate deployment of inline systems that will increase baggage throughput up to 300 percent. The Budget proposes temporary security-fee surcharges totaling $426 million that would accelerate the deployment of optimal baggage screening systems and address the need to recapitalize existing equipment deployed immediately after September 11, 2001. (c) $128 million for enhancements at passenger checkpoints to improve the detection of prohibited items, especially weapons and explosives, through the use of additional sensors. (d) Nearly $100 million for air cargo security inspectors, canine teams, and the Certified Shipper Program to achieve 100 percent screening of passenger air cargo in 2010.
- *Enhances security assessments.* Funds security assessments on more than 2.4 million individuals in the nation's transportation system, including commercial HAZMAT drivers, airport and port workers, and international airline flight crews. In addition, TSA will continuously vet 13 million individuals who have already undergone a security assessment. These assessments will be based on terrorism and criminal information from the U.S. intelligence community and FBI databases. And TSA will assume the watch list matching of over two million airline passengers daily with the implementation of Secure Flight.
- *Addresses surface transportation vulnerabilities.* $37 million for surface transportation security, including funding for nearly 100 inspectors to conduct risk-based assessments in the largest mass transit and rail systems.

Reinforces Maritime Safety and Security

- *Recapitalizes assets.* $990 million to fund Integrated Deepwater Systems, a multiyear recapitalization project for the Coast Guard's aircraft and largest seagoing ships that continues to build Maritime Domain Awareness, a major goal outlined in the President's National Strategy for Maritime Security.
- *Supports Transportation Worker Identification Credentials (TWICs).* Issues more than 100,000 TWICs to maritime workers to better safeguard U.S. ports. TWIC is one of the world's most advanced, interoperable biometric credentialing programs and is powered by state-of-the-art technologies.
- *Builds on law enforcement* $17.6 million in new funding to enhance Coast Guard intelligence and investigative capabilities.
- *Supports the Marine Inspection Program.* $20 million in new funding for more marine inspectors to ensure compliance with vessel safety and security standards and to keep pace with the growth in maritime commerce.

Fortifies Cyber Security across the Federal Government

- *Enhances the U.S. Computer Emergency Readiness Team (US-CERT).* $242 million to maintain and expand the capabilities of US-CERT to provide additional network defense measures and increase malware and intrusion analysis capabilities. A more robust US-CERT will increase the cyber security posture of the federal government and help ensure our networks are protected.

Improves BioWatch Capabilities

- *Upgrades the BioWatch Monitoring System.* Increases its investment in Gen 3, the next-generation BioWatch technology, to enable the BioWatch system to become fully automated and reduce detection times to as little as four hours. Completes the full testing and multicity pilots of Gen3 technologies and begins procurement and deployment.

Expands Federal Emergency Management Agency's (FEMA'S) Operational Capacity

- *Expands FEMA capabilities.* $215 million to allow FEMA to implement Phase II of the Vision initiatives, including: completing the conversion of temporary, full-time employees to permanent staff; updating the information technology and logistics systems; meeting requirements of the Post-Katrina Emergency Management Reform Act, such as through the establishment of regional strike teams; and improving emergency communications.
- *Provides grant support.* $2.2 billion in support, primarily in the form of grants, to the Department's state and local partners in homeland security. The Budget continues to emphasize programs that distribute grant awards on the basis of risk, and this year introduces a grant program to help states implement Real ID requirements and provide a more efficient, merit-based allocation of limited resources.

Who Became Part of the Department?

The agencies slated to become part of the Department of Homeland Security are housed in one of four major directorates: Border and Transportation Security, Emergency Preparedness and Response, Science and Technology, and Information Analysis and Infrastructure Protection.

The Border and Transportation Security directorate brings the major border security and transportation operations under one administrative hierarchy, including:

- The U.S. Customs Service (Treasury)
- The Immigration and Naturalization Service (part) (Justice)
- The Federal Protective Service
- The Transportation Security Administration (Transportation)
- Federal Law Enforcement Training Center (Treasury)
- Animal and Plant Health Inspection Service (part) (Agriculture)
- Office for Domestic Preparedness (Justice)

The Emergency Preparedness and Response directorate oversees domestic disaster preparedness training and coordinates government disaster response. It brings together:

- The Federal Emergency Management Agency (FEMA)
- Strategic National Stockpile and the National Disaster Medical System (HHS)
- Nuclear Incident Response Team (Energy)
- Domestic Emergency Support Teams (Justice)
- National Domestic Preparedness Office (FBI)

The Science and Technology directorate seeks to utilize all scientific and technological advantages when securing the homeland. The following assets are part of this effort:

- CBRN Countermeasures Programs (Energy)
- Environmental Measurements Laboratory (Energy)
- National BW Defense Analysis Center (Defense)
- Plum Island Animal Disease Center (Agriculture)

The Information Analysis and Infrastructure Protection directorate analyzes intelligence and information from other agencies (including the CIA, FBI, DIA and NSA) involving threats to homeland security and evaluates vulnerabilities in the nation's infrastructure. It brings together:

- Federal Computer Incident Response Center (GSA)
- National Communications System (Defense)
- National Infrastructure Protection Center (FBI)
- Energy Security and Assurance Program (Energy)

The Secret Service and the Coast Guard are located in the Department of Homeland Security, remaining intact and reporting directly to the Secretary. In addition, the INS adjudications and benefits programs reports directly to the Deputy Secretary as the U.S. Citizenship and Immigration Services.

The effectiveness of the new Department of Homeland Security and how it will affect all aspects of our lives remain to be seen.

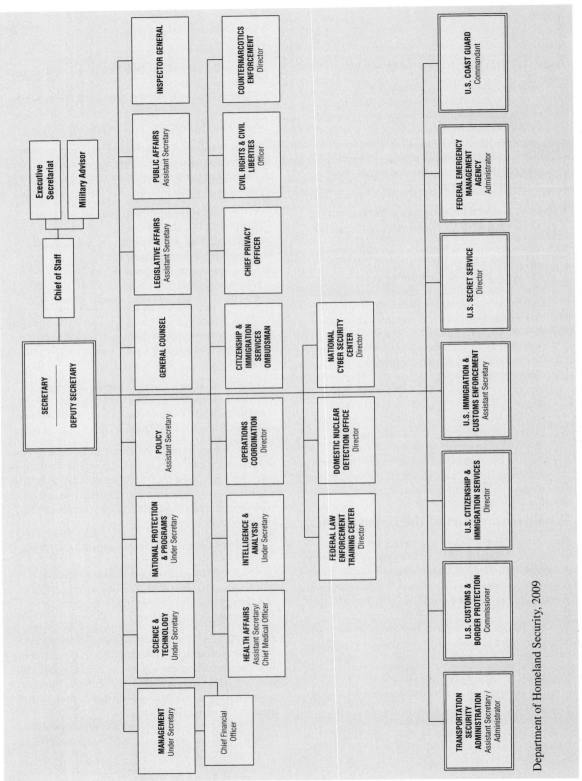

Department of Homeland Security, 2009

Budgeting Priorities at the Department of Homeland Security
(Dollar amounts in millions)

	Actual 2007	Estimate 2008	Estimate 2009
Spending			
Gross Discretionary Budget Authority:			
Departmental Management and Operations	913	840	1,084
Office of the Inspector General	99	109	101
Citizenship and Immigration Services	180	−4	151
U.S. Secret Service	1,277	1,386	1,415
Transportation Security Administration	6,028	6,315	6,423
Federal Law Enforcement Training Center	250	267	274
Immigration and Customs Enforcement	4,446	4,817	5,364
Customs and Border Protection	6,332	7,875	9,494
U.S. Coast Guard	7,079	7,156	7,835
National Protection and Programs Directorate	945	1,016	1,447
Federal Emergency Management Agency	5,875	6,823	5,729
Science and Technology	848	830	869
Domestic Nuclear Detection Office	481	486	564
Total, Gross budget authority	34,753	37,916	40,749
Less fee-funded activities	−2,976	−2,957	−3,139
Total, Discretionary budget authority (net)	31,777	34,959	37,611
Bioshield (non-add)	—	—	2,175
Memorandum:			
Budget authority from enacted supplementals	7,669	5,719	—
Additional funding requirements	—	63	—
Total, Discretionary outlays	39,897	41,071	44,043
Mandatory Outlays:			
Citizenship and immigration Services	1,655	2,390	2,539
Customs and Border Protection	1,035	2,281	1,463
U.S. Coast Guard	1,234	1,395	1,513
Transportation Security Administration	95	424	287
Legislative proposal	—	—	320
All other	−4,730	−5,209	−5,856
Total, Mandatory outlays	−711	1,281	266
Total, Outlays	39,186	42,352	44,309
Credit activity			
Direct Loan Disbursements:			
Disaster Assistance	162	160	160

	Number of Programs	2009 Savings
Major Savings, Discretionary Reductions	1	−1,905

Questions and Instructions

1. Why is a unified homeland security administrative structure preferred over the multidepartmental approach? Explain.
2. In what ways are the challenges of homeland security almost endless? Explain and illustrate.
3. "Terrorism begins and ends with deteriorating human relations." How so? Explain and illustrate.
4. Why do some express concerns about homeland security becoming homeland pork? Explain and illustrate.
5. The Department of Homeland Security takes budgets, skills, knowledge, and expertise from other departments and agencies. Yet the mind-sets of those units are still in play. Why is this so? Explain and illustrate.
6. Why is the material culture of the Department of Homeland Security symbolic? Explain.
7. Do sophisticated technologies really improve our chances of being more secure? Explain.
8. If the costs of creating the Department of Homeland Security are prohibitive, will Americans choose lower budget deficits and less formalized security measures? If so, why? Explain and illustrate.
9. What did Americans do, if anything, to contribute to their status as victims of terror? Explain and illustrate.

Insights-Issues/Budgeting the Department of Homeland Security

Clearly and briefly describe and illustrate the following concepts and issues. Interpret the word *role* as meaning impacts, applications, importance, effects, and/or illustrations of certain facts, concerns, or issues from the case study.

1. Role of increased federal spending (more dollars) in securing the homeland and fighting terrorism.
2. Role of promoting border security, interior enforcement, and immigration services for securing the homeland and fighting terrorism.
3. Role of enhancing the security of the nation's transportation system for securing the homeland and fighting terrorism.
4. Role of expanding FEMA's (Federal Emergency Management Agency) operational capacity for securing the homeland and fighting terrorism.
5. Role of consolidation, reorganization, and positioning of federal agencies into the Department of Homeland Security for securing the homeland and fighting terrorism.

Sources

http://www.whitehouse.gov/omb/budget/fy2009/homeland.html;
http://www.dhs.gov/xabout/history/editorial_0133.shtm.

Notes

1. L. Douglas Lee, "How Congress Handles the Budget," *Wharton Magazine* 4 (Winter 1980): 29.
2. Marshall E. Dimock, Gladys Ogden Dimock, and Douglas M. Fox, *Public Administration* (New York: Holt, Rinehart and Winston, 1983), p. 359.
3. John L. Mikesell, *Fiscal Administration: Analysis and Applications for the Public Sector,* 2nd ed. (Chicago: Dorsey Press, 1986), pp. 75–85.
4. Dimock, Dimock, and Fox, *Public Administration,* p. 367.

5. Peter F. Rousmaniere, *Local Governments Auditing—A Manual for Public Officials* (New York: Council on Muncipal Performance, 1980), p. 83.

6. Advisory Commission on Intergovernmental Relations, "Sunset Legislation and Zero-Based Budgeting," *Information Bulletin* 76, no. 5 (December 1976): 1.

7. Mikesell, *Fiscal Administration,* p. 48.

8. Ibid. pp. 56–60.

9. Aaron Wildavsky, *The Politics of the Budgetary Process* (Boston: Little, Brown and Co., 1984), pp. 63–126.

10. Barry Bozeman and Jeffrey D. Straussman, "Shrinking Budgets and the Shrinkage of Budget Theory," *Public Administration Review* 42, no. 6 (November–December 1982): 509–515. See also Lance T. LeLoup, *Budgetary Politics* (Brunswick, OH: King's Court Communications, 1986), pp. 16–21.

11. Murray L. Weidenbaum, "Budget Dilemma and Its Solution," in *Control of Federal Spending,* ed. C. Lowell Harris (New York: Academy of Political Science, 1985), pp. 47–58.

12. Bozeman and Straussman, "Shrinking Budgets," p. 511.

13. Mikesell, *Fiscal Administration,* pp. 56–60.

14. Ibid.

15. Robert D. Reischauer, "The Budget: Crucible for the Policy Agenda," in *Setting National Priorities: Budget Choices for the Next Century,* ed. Robert D. Reischauer (Washington, DC: Brookings Institution Press, 1997), pp. 4–11.

16. Ibid.

17. John Steele Gordon, "The Federal Debt," *American Heritage* 47, no. 7 (November 1995): 82–92.

18. For more detailed explanations of the comparatively low U.S. tax burden, see Louis Ferleger and Jay R. Mantle, "America's Hostility Toward Taxes," *Challenge* 14, no. 4 (July–August 1991): 54; "No Pain, No Gain: Taxes, Productivity, and Economic Growth," *Challenge* 36, no. 3 (May–June 1993): 11–20; and *A New Mandate: Democratic Choices for a Prosperous Economy* (Columbia, MO: University of Missouri Press, 1994).

19. See *Federal Debt and Interest Costs* (Congressional Budget Office, May 1993), and *Federal Debt: Answers to Frequently Asked Questions* (November 27, 1996).

20. *Budget Issues: Analysis of Long-Term Fiscal Outlook* (Congressional Budget Office, October 1997; GAO/AIMD/OCE-98-19).

21. "Tax & Economic Policy," http://www.onlytheissues.com/politics.cgi?issue=4.

22. Franco Modigliani and Robert M. Solow, "America Is Borrowing Trouble," *New York Times,* April 9, 2001.

23. William Greider, "The End of Empire," *The Nation* 275, no. 9 (September 23, 2002): 13–15.

24. See Charles Wolf, Jr., and Walter Wriston, "Two Deficits That Just Don't Matter," *Hoover Digest,* no. 4 (1997); William A. Niskanen, "The Uneasy Relation Between the Budget and Trade Deficits," *Cato Journal* 8, no. 2 (Fall 1988): 507–532.

25. David S. Broder, "New Task for a Budget Straight-Talker," *Washington Post,* March 16, 2008, p. B7.

26. "Trade Deficit at 2nd Highest Level Ever," *New York Times,* September 8, 2006.

27. Broder, "New Task."

The Productivity Challenge: Working Smarter While Doing More with Less

Chapter Highlights

What Is Excellence?

Efficiency and Effectiveness

Privatization of the Public Sector

Evaluating Government Programs

Citizen-Driven Government Performance

People Crisis and/or Opportunity?

Summary

SETs, Program Evaluation, and College Professors

Student power at Steady State University is known throughout higher education. For example, a nontenured professor was removed as the instructor of an introductory chemistry course when a student petition with signatures from 100 of his 200 students claimed he demonstrated an "inability to teach new information" and a "willful academic demoralization of students."

Three perspectives emerged. Some students said he was a victim of "whiny" students—that he was simply a tough teacher. Many students feared that a low grade in a difficult subject would keep them from admission to graduate school. Others said he ignored student questions—and made tests more difficult than they needed to be.[1]

In a world of "corporate responsibility" and "human error," validity is not easy to access. SETs, or student evaluations of teaching, provide historical trends for rating the production of college professors. The "convergent validity" of student ratings correlates with other measures of teaching effectiveness.[2] Grading practices,

SET ratings, student motivations, and the skills, knowledge, and expertise of professors contribute to program evaluations of higher-education productivity.

How do colleges and universities, especially those that are taxpayer-funded, evaluate teaching effectiveness? Validity, bias, and utility measures are critical. Teaching effectiveness is multidimensional. SETs attempt to measure a composite of delivering instruction, facilitating interactions, and ascertaining student learning. SETs, then, are positively correlated with expected course grades. Pedagogy at SSU focuses on processing as much as content. The SSU administration, after all, pays professor salaries. Student enrollees pay ever-higher tuition fees. The culture for academic disciplines is not well-established at SSU.

Like other state universities, SSU employs SETs for tenure and promotion purposes. Professors initially used SETs for feedback so that they might know student needs. Now the primary purpose is to make personnel decisions—that is, to make decisions for retention, promotion, tenure, and salary increases.

Despite this trend, SSU refuses to confront the problems of defining teaching effectiveness. SSU promotes politically correct or popular standards and perceptions in the classroom. Low student academic preparation is not taken into account. The SSU Teachers' College is known for fostering a grading system where "students pay their fees—and get their Bs."

"Teachers have no duty to teach using a particular style, only to teach successfully," argues Michael Scriven.[3] Elements of success, achievement, excellence, effectiveness, and efficiency are based on teaching and learning cultures. Teaching styles, therefore, constitute but one aspect of a complex evaluative theory of teaching productivity.

Scriven identifies the duties of college professors in the following framework:[4]

1. *Knowledge of subject matter* (curriculum demands)
2. *Instructional competence* (communication, course construction skills)
3. *Assessment competence* (test construction and grading criteria)
4. *Professionalism* (ethics and attitudes)
5. *Nonstandard but contractual duties* (community service)

SETs and program evaluations at Steady State University are *context-dependent:* They take into account constituents' needs, wants, and expectations. Pertinent societal values, customs, and mores are recognized. Relevant laws and statutes, economic dynamics, political forces, media interests, and protocols cannot be ignored by evaluators. The organizational mission, goals, and priorities of Steady State University are driving forces in how professors produce in the classroom. The organizational governance and management of SSU indicate how employees feel and react to policies. SSU's history and current challenges make SETs context-dependent.

The SSU Student Government Association (SGA) contributes to the program evaluation of Steady State professors. The SGA consists of volunteer students, elected by the student body, working for all students at SSU. SGA is composed of legislative, executive, and judicial branches. Getting involved in SGA is simple; students apply for positions and committee memberships, and attend SGA meetings.

The SSU/SGA constitution spells out that SGA:

- Provides a forum for the expression of student views and interests
- Focuses on academic freedoms, academic responsibilities, and student rights
- Seeks to facilitate improvements in student cultural, social, and physical welfare
- Acknowledges that the achievement of skills, knowledge, and expertise is the primary reason for attending SSU
- Promotes the development of more effective instruction standards, classroom facilities, and teaching and learning methods
- Emphasizes student knowledge of history, politics, economics, languages, and cultures
- Recognizes the rights and responsibilities of students in regard to the mission, goals, and priorities of SSU, the community of College Corner, the state of Commonwealth, and humanity[5]

At SSU, taxpayer resources flow to students and student programs. Proactive initiatives are commended and rewarded. Because students learn at different rates, SSU learning is individualized. Students, professors, and administrators recognize that classroom production differs from other kinds of production. Outcomes from SETs are not considered standards. However, SSU professors long ago dismissed SETs as helpful feedback for improving teaching methods.

Market values drive program functions, organization structures, academic standards, and emerging technologies at SSU. Inductive thinking is piecemeal, at best. Senior administrative staff are committed to centralized budgeting methods—or determining who gets what amount of money.

Program evaluation is constant—reflecting the mission, goals, and priorities of SSU. SETs—as

SSU program evaluation techniques—are utilized to promote, penalize, or otherwise discipline professors. Yet SSU administrative leaders insist that professors enjoy academic freedom as they probe the depths of young minds.

Raising agendas and making a difference is what program evaluation—for professors, administrators, and student productivity—is all about at Steady State University. This taxpayer-funded, state-financed university is an "opportunity institution"—a marketplace of student rights, decremental budgeting, fleeting accountability, and routinized program responsibilities.

Notes

1. Robert E. Haskell, "Academic Freedom, Tenure, and Student Evaluation of Faculty: Galloping Polls in the 21st Century," *Education Policy Analysis Archives* 5, no. 6 (February 12, 1997).

2. "Student Ratings of Professors: A Series of Articles in *The American Psychologist,* November 1997," http://www.luc.edu/faculty/eposava/amerpsyc.htm.
3. Michael Scriven, "Duties of the Teacher," *Journal of Personnel Evaluation in Education* 8, no. 2 (1994): 151–184.
4. Ibid.
5. "Buttons Will Go Here!" SGA@OSU, https://you.okstate.edu/sga/.

Sources

Ernest R. House and Kenneth R. Howe, "Deliberative Democratic Evaluation Checklist," October 2000, http://www.wmich.edu/evalctr/checklists/dd_checklist.htm; Benjamin Levin, "Students and Educational Productivity," *Educational Policy Analysis Archives* 1, no. 5 (May 4, 1993), http://epaa.asu.edu/epaa/vln5.html; Daniel L. Stufflebeam, "Evaluation Values and Criteria Checklist," March 2001; Evaluation Checklists Project, www.wmich.edu/evalctr/checklists; "Institutionalizing Evaluation Checklist," July 15, 2002, http://www.wmich.edu/evalctr/checklists/values_criteria.pdf; Phillip N. Venditti, "Defining the Productivity of Community College Administrators," *Leadership Abstracts* 8, no. 4 (April 1995).

What Is Excellence?

Productivity in the public sector refers to excellence in individual and collective performance—especially in times when public employees are expected to do more with less. The employees could be public school teachers, occupational safety inspectors, highway patrol officers, fire fighters, air traffic controllers, maintenance crews removing snow from the streets, or sanitation workers removing waste and technological excess from communities.

Among these areas of worker expertise, there are widely divergent views as to what excellence is. *Excellence,* in its various forms, is based on the cultural context of a particular function. Therefore, measuring excellence and employee productivity in government-funded organizations is a problematic assignment. The public sector usually deals in services, which, because they are intangible and often widely variable, almost always present problems in productivity measurement. Many government experts concede that some public sector functions are not measurable with the mechanisms currently available.

Despite these difficulties, an organization should adapt excellence as its main component. The system should enable an organization to achieve high performance levels from their employees. Outstanding performance not only benefits the organization but also improves the delivery of services to the citizens.[1] Most citizens care about the performance of their public institutions. Parents worry about the quality of their children's schools. City dwellers anxiously scan the latest crime statistics. Drivers pray for better roads, transit riders for dependable buses and subways, air travelers for effective air traffic control.[2]

Posing particular difficulties for analyses are numerous staff operations, such as personnel work and social casework. One has only to think of the complexities involved in trying to measure the productivity of a caseworker in a public welfare office to realize some of the difficulty. Should the caseworker be rated on how many cases he or she clears from the welfare rolls, or on how many people he or she adds? Using either standard can produce distortions.

Efficiency and Effectiveness

Related to these problems is the central task of distinguishing between efficiency and effectiveness. Efficiency means *doing things well,* while effectiveness means *doing the right things well. Efficiency,* essentially, is the input of labor, capital, and other resources into an effort matched against the output of product, regardless of the mechanism selected to gauge output. *Effectiveness,* meanwhile, calls for a preestablished standard of comparison; a focus upon a certain quality of production; an ability to mobilize, organize, and direct resources for specified purposes, taken within a certain cultural context.

Government Performance Perceptions

Mark Abramson explains citizen dissatisfaction with government performance with four points of emphasis:

Democracy is "messy." Democratic governments are designed to promote equity and fairness. Pluralism is central to the way American society is organized. The inherent nature of our government admits to inefficiency and ineffectiveness. Citizens expect only satisfactory—not optimum—performance from government units. Democracy is not cost-effective.

Government takes a "bum rap." The media, politicians, academics, and government oversight agencies accentuate what's wrong with government bureaucracies. U.S. public bureaucracies are not actually the stereotyped discriminators and bunglers they are made out to be. They are not homogeneous, antipoor, and antiminority. Markets are not perfect. Public and private are not categories of nature. They are categories of history and culture, of law and custom. They are contextual and subject to change and redefinition. Societies do not fail because governments are ineffective.

Government must "shape up." Disincentives must be overcome. Government support systems should encourage and reward public administrators rather than penalize them for taking risks. No public philosophy exists for judging the effectiveness of government programs. Partisan consensus for maintaining the government welfare state prevents some government agencies from being downsized. Innovations threaten the status quo.

The country must "shape up." Productivity problems are not unique to government operations. The performance of the nation as a whole, not only the public sector, is important for a national common purpose. Federal deficits are traced to a society grounded in short-term consumer decision making with little, if any, long-term commitments to values that promote savings and investments for the future.

Terror attacks on the World Trade Center and Pentagon disrupted government consensus for government policy making—what citizens owe the state (society) and what the state owes its citizens. Political dissensions prevent the nation (government) from "shaping up." The citizenry is divided on many issues. Partisan politics takes priority over policy and system politics. Policy fragmentation is a catalyst for enhanced economic disparities.

Sources: Mark A. Abramson, "The Public Manager and Excellence," *The Bureaucrat* 14, no. 3 (Fall 1985): 9–13; see also Charles T. Goodsell, *The Case for Bureaucracy: A Public Administration Polemic* (Chatham, NJ: Chatham House Publishers, 1983), pp. 55–60.

Government, Morality, and Family

The government has a role to play in restoring morality to public life, argues William R. Marty. Marty says that government should not reflect the views held by religious fanatics or libertarian lunatics, but strive to guarantee that government institutions that support moral growth remain strong. This government role involves support for the traditional family struc-ture, guarantees some degree of moral education in the schools, and gives parents flexible choices in the education of their children.

Source: William R. Marty, "Government, Morality, and the Family," *Journal of Interdisciplinary Studies* 7, nos. 1–2 (Annual 1995): 1–25.

As one commentator noted, a man might be efficient in driving nails into a table. Effectiveness enters the picture when we question whether he should be driving nails into a table at all. Questions regarding quality make the public productivity measurer's task still more of a hazard and a hassle. A fiddler isn't necessarily producing more by fiddling faster. Nor can a pianist be hailed as especially productive for playing Chopin's Minute Waltz in fifty seconds. On a more mundane and realistic level, a narcotics squad that made a lot of arrest quotas for their narcotic divisions had to change them when they realized that such productivity measures were not producing "quality" arrests—in other words, arrests of major dealers.[3]

Privatization of the Public Sector

Privatization means that a service previously produced by a government agency is now produced by a nongovernmental organization. The government may sell to private buyers, or a private concern may sell to government. *Contracting out,* as it is often called, is thought to be more efficient because:

- It harnesses competitive forces and brings the pressure of the marketplace to bear on inefficient workers.
- It permits better management, free of most of the distractions characteristic of overtly political organizations.
- It places the costs and benefits of managerial decisions more directly on the decision maker, whose own rewards are directly at stake.[4]

As government at all levels has come under attack, the conclusion that the private sector performs and produces more effectively has received considerable credibility. If privatization is the answer in general, however, no one seems to agree on the particulars, such as what products will be produced privately or what provisions for private entrepreneurship will follow.

Conflicting definitions of privatization center around provision, or providing, and production, or producing.[5] Executives, legislators, and judges make and interpret policies that provide services. Government functions as buyer and seller. A good example of services that are privatized to varying degrees are security services. One can lay out a four-part scheme of possible overlap of sectors, government and nongovernment, providing and producing security services. Of the four possibilities, there are two admixtures of responsibility and two possibilities where one sector or the other takes full responsibility for the provision and production of security.

- *Case 1.* Government does both. The legislature writes the law and provides the money; the Department of Corrections runs the prison. Neither function is private.
- *Case 2.* Production is private. The City of Bloomington decides to provide security when the high school hockey teams play at the city arena. The city contracts with Pinkertons for the guards.
- *Case 3.* Provision is private. Government sells to private buyers. The North Stars hockey team wants security at Metropolitan Sports Center, and it contracts with the Bloomington city police.
- *Case 4.* Both activities are private. A department store decides that it wants uniformed security and employs (or contracts privately for) its own guards. Government performs neither activity.[6]

The policy decision in Case 1, the pure-case public sector, shows government as a public bureau producing the service. Case 2 entails the controversial system of a government contracting out. Case 3 illustrates government selling services to a private buyer. Case 4 portrays a pure case of a private agency selling to a private buyer. Of the two words, *provision* is the more complicated to explain. The word *providing* can be confusing. For example, society (or government) provides medical care to the elderly; however, medical doctors are the providers. To provide in this context means to make policy, to decide, to buy, to regulate, to franchise, to finance, to subsidize.

A publicly provided service is described in this manner:

1. The decision whether to have the service (and the decisions about who shall have it and how much of it) is a political decision.
2. Government arranges for the recipients not to have to pay directly for the service themselves.
3. Government selects the producer that will serve them.

A privately provided service is described in this way:

1. Individuals and nongovernmental organizations make their own decisions whether or not to have the service.
2. If they choose to have it, they pay for it in full out of their own resources, whatever these may be.
3. They select the producer themselves.[7]

There are mixed cases of public and private provisions as well. Government may provide a service and allow citizens to decide whether to use it. The financing of such provisions may be divided between public and private sectors as users finance part and the government pays part of the costs. Some citizens (the wealthy) may pay the full cost of provisions, while government picks up the complete tab for others (the poor). Government may finance the complete cost but permit the user to choose the vendor. The provision of schools is financed, publicly, via taxes.

Nontax devices, such as regulations and franchising, are used as well. Government regulations require restaurant owners to clean the premises themselves at their own expense; in franchising provision of water, gas, or electricity, government allows a monopoly to develop, which, in turn, permits an average price, overcharging some customers while subsidizing others. In privatizing the provision of services, government withdraws or reduces its role as buyer, regulator, standard setter, or decision maker.

Now let us examine the concept of *production* as it applies to activities of government. Government officials decide to produce the services they determine should be provided. In other words, government operates, delivers, runs, performs, sells, and administers services. As emphasized, service production is less complicated than service provision. Production may be divided into line services and support or staff services; production may be divided into labor-intensive functions, equipment and facilities; production may focus on the substance of the work or on the management or administration of work. For example, a municipality may divide refuse collection among several garbage collection companies, or the management of worker pension funds among several financial institutions.

In privatizing public sector production, the question of competition is an important one. If the shift is merely from a public sector provider to a single private sector one, a monopoly supplier still exists. The deregulation of railroads, aviation, trucking, banking, health care, and telecommunications has taken place in the private sphere to encourage competition. Despite such efforts, questions concerning competitiveness remain.

The neat distinctions between government's primary policy decision providing a service and the secondary decision producing a service are not, in reality, easily discerned. The Federal Aviation Administration administers air safety for public and private good. The Department of Defense contracts with private providers for base support and maintenance. Pinkerton and Wells Fargo, private security firms, have a long history of public service. Public day-care centers allow young mothers economic opportunities in the private sphere.

Privatization of some government services, notably Social Security and the Postal Service, has been considered to decrease costs and increase efficiency. Proponents think that the competition created by contracting out will improve federal government programs. So far, many state and local governments are experimenting with privatization, but the federal government resists. Unions oppose the practice because they fear the adverse effects on employee salaries and benefits.[8]

The George W. Bush administration did not need approval of Congress to place nearly half the federal civilian workforce, approximately 850,000 government jobs, in the private contractor competitive marketplace. The Bush privatization plan is a major expansion of trends taking place in government at all levels for the past two decades. According to OMB, 60 percent of the privatized jobs make their way to small businesses and companies owned by women and minorities.

Bush's goal is to "create a market-based government unafraid of competition, innovation and choice." Savings from privatization plans are targeted to be 20 to 30 percent. However, after taking over government jobs, contractors may perform poorly or encounter legal or financial trouble. Bobby L. Harnage, Sr., president of the American Federation of Government Employees, a government union representing

Public versus Private Postal Productivity

Perhaps the most maligned public agency is the U.S. Postal Service (USPS). The cost of a first-class stamp has risen in the past and will certainly rise steadily in the future. Statutes prohibit private firms from competition with the U.S. Postal Service for first-class service. It is possible that private entrepreneurs could find cheaper, more effective ways to deliver a huge volume of first-class mail, but the U.S. Postal Service is more than a national post office. USPS is a conduit, a catalyst for undergirding capitalism by facilitating consumer advertising through the mail, for bolstering the free press, disseminating information through newspapers and magazines, and for promoting commerce in general.

By comparison, United Parcel Service (UPS) delivers twice the number of parcels as the U.S. Postal Service, with lower rates, faster deliveries, and an 80 percent lower damage rate, and still makes a profit. But will UPS deliver your favorite fashion catalog, news magazine, or church bulletin for mere pennies? The U.S. Postal Service subsidizes at a reasonable cost many and varied cultural, economic, and even political activities in the United States.

600,000 federal workers, protested that Bush had "declared all-out war on federal employees." Harnage insisted that federal employees almost always offer more expertise and experience than outside contractors.[9]

Contract compliance programs help companies comply with numerous laws governing contracts and subcontracts with the federal government, avoid criminal prosecution, and reduce violation fines. Contract compliance programs include:

- Codes of ethics to be adhered to by private sector employees
- Strategies for effective delegation of responsibilities
- Procedures for reporting violations, corrective measures for noncompliance, and constant evaluation of the compliance program
- A records management system for keeping records for the contract duration as specified by law.[10]

Privatization is an effective way of providing necessary services usually provided by the government while overcoming the problem of shrinking federal, state, and local government budgets and ailing infrastructure. The government plays the role of prudent purchaser and manager of services offered by private sector contractors. Privatization aims at creating a market-driven partnership for the betterment of taxpayers, although it faces resistance from citizens who fear elimination of services.[11] Privatizing government functions, then, is seen as a way of increasing efficiency and producing significant savings.

Empirical evidence usually shows private enterprises to be more efficient than public enterprises. Public sector productivity is lower than private sector productivity, labor costs are higher in the public sector than in the private sphere, and public utilities are less cost-effective than private utilities.[12] On the other hand, no one promised that democratic government was cost-effective, at least when measuring efficiency. *Fairness* is a more accurate standard for ascertaining the effectiveness of government services.

Employee Motivation Indicators and Peformance Guidelines

Gordon Maner, Carl Vinson Institute of Government, suggests certain indicators of lack of employee motivation:

- *Little interest in achieving established goals.* Poorly motivated employees do not envision work unit goals as important. They will not work to reach goals. They may reject supervisor efforts to motivate them for personal or other reasons.
- *Unsatisfactory output and quality.* Poorly motivated employees are not careful workers. They often will not complete tasks adequately.
- *Absenteeism or tardiness.* Poorly motivated employees tend to arrive late or be absent from work. Absenteeism is considered a crucial indicator for detecting employee dissatisfaction.
- *Time killing/clock-watching activities.* Poorly motivated employees show signs of boredom with assigned tasks and responsibilities. However, they make no efforts to change employment.
- *Frequent request for help in solving minor problems.* Poorly motivated employees lack initiative in completing challenging tasks.
- *No desire to improve job knowledge.* Poorly motivated employees need attitude adjustments:

"Why should I learn more?—I will still be doing the same old job." Improvements could lead to different opportunities for promotion, transfer, or the expansion of current tasks.

Maner recommends guidelines for correcting and improving employee performance. He emphasizes that constructive confrontation is a basic duty of any supervisor. The challenge, notes Maner, is to get employees to accept corrections without resentment. The guidelines are:

- *Know the attitudes and personality traits* of the employee you confront. Watch for indicators of frustration.
- *Be sure your own attitude is one of genuine helpfulness.* Exercising one's authority for authority's sake is not productive. The employee should not be confronted in anger; allow yourself to calm down. Think rationally before approaching an employee regarding improvement in his or her performance.
- *Get all the facts first.* Looking the role and doing the job are two separate things. Job performance may not reflect employee appearance, credentials, or communication skills.

Source: Software Techniques, 13105 Booker T. Washington Highway, Hardy, VA 24101. See http://www.softwaretech.com/hrad/articles/.

Evaluating Government Programs

Taxing, budgeting, and government spending priorities place program evaluation *at the center, not at the periphery,* of policy making in the public sector. To improve the effectiveness of program evaluation, such priorities need to assume their rightful place at the center of the policy-making and budget-making processes. Program evaluation needs consideration alongside financial and political lines. When Planning Programming Budgeting Systems (PPBS) began to diminish in the federal bureaucracy, many found a replacement in another analytical device—program evaluation. Some state and municipal governments have warmly welcomed this technique and have set up offices to evaluate their program performance.

According to Ralph C. Chandler and Jack C. Plano, program evaluation is

an assessment of the effectiveness of a program through the application of a research design aimed at obtaining valid and verifiable information on the structure, processes, outputs, and impacts of the program. Program evaluation is an effort to help decision makers determine whether to maintain, modify, or discontinue a specified program. Program evaluation is concerned with whether program activities have been successful in resolving the public problem identified, and the extent to which other factors may have contributed to the problem's resolution."[13]

There are three phases in program evaluation:

1. Selection and identification of goals and objectives of the program
2. Execution of the evaluation according to scientific guidelines
3. Feedback on results and recommendations

The overall goals of program evaluation, or PE as it is sometimes called, can be simply stated. PE increases our understanding of government activities, leads to governmental improvements, and produces financial savings. The tools it uses seem familiar—for the most part, they greatly resemble the types of analytical devices developed for PPBS, zero-based budgets (ZBB), and management by objectives (MBO).

Legislative backing and buttressing have played a major role in the flourishing of program evaluation at all government levels.

The productivity challenge in the public sector is hampered by structural and environmental barriers; therefore, the need for evaluation of productivity is always present. In the private sphere, technology becomes an intervening factor between monetary rewards and corporate failures. However, productivity indices in the public sector are grounded in politics, with merit principles sometimes receiving less emphasis. As citizens, elected officials, and administrators consider the effectiveness of the bottom-line delivery of public services, there will be enhanced interest in pro-active, rather than reactive, program evaluations and employee performance evaluations.

Citizens and policy makers seek evidence regarding program results from taxpayer-supported programs. Program evaluation efforts may identify problems and demonstrate results. Findings may impact state policies. In California, program evaluation of welfare reforms, smoking prevention efforts, and state prison drug treatment programs resulted in definitive policy impacts.

The California legislature recognizes that high-priority program evaluation projects need adequate planning, time, and resources. Guidelines, in the form of questions, are posted as the legislature drafts legislative language calling for the evaluation of state-sponsored programs. Policy makers utilize guidelines with pertinent questions for the strategic investment of limited evaluation resources.

The guideline inquiries are:

1. Is evaluation of this program an important investment of state resources?
2. What questions does the legislature need to have answered about this program?
3. What will it take to answer the legislature's questions—and can adequate resources be provided?
4. What will it take to ensure credible evaluation findings?
5. Who should be involved in this evaluation—from inception to results?
6. When should evaluation findings be expected from this program?
7. What is the role of state agencies in this evaluation?
8. What information needs to be available for statewide evaluation?

Problems with program evaluation results may arise. Policy makers, legislative staff, and state government evaluation specialists reveal that evaluation reports sometimes do not focus on key policy questions. Legislators seek analytical reports when reviews merely describe clients and activities. Certain key stakeholders may be omitted. Findings may be misunderstood and not utilized. The request for program evaluation may come too soon in the life of the government program. Earmarked funding may prove inadequate for the rigorous work demanded. If the evaluator is not independent of the program, evaluation findings may lack credibility. Local government programs may not be required to collect standardized data.[14]

The United States Department of Education shifted in 2002 to a new approach to program evaluation—the Performance-Based Data Management Initiative. This centralized, consolidated, electronic system replaces the department's myriad data collections. The reform dramatically reduces reporting burdens on elementary and secondary schools. The focus is to gather much better data about program effectiveness.[15]

The Centers for Disease Control (CDC) Office on Smoking and Health (OSH) assists state tobacco control program managers and staff in the planning, design, implementation, and use of comprehensive evaluations of tobacco control efforts. Tobacco use is the leading preventable cause of death and disease in the United States—contributing to more than 430,000 deaths annually.

Tobacco control programs are designed to reduce disease, disability, and death related to tobacco use. To determine the effectiveness of prevention and control programs, evaluators document and measure program implementation and effects.

Program evaluation examines implementation protocols and operations, effectiveness, and accountability. CDC goals call for preventing the initiation of tobacco use among young people, promoting quitting among young people and adults, eliminating nonsmokers' exposure to environmental tobacco smoke (ETS), and identifying and eliminating disparities related to tobacco use and its effects among different population groups.

Measuring Government Operations

Harry P. Hatry and Diana R. Dunn offer ways of measuring the effectiveness of a government-operated recreation facility.

Accessibility. The number of people who reside within so many miles or so many minutes of the facility, proximity to public transportation, and other data on convenience of location determine its accessibility.

Usage. Likewise, the number of persons using the facility, how often they use it, and for how long are indicators of unit productivity. How often do citizens come to the facility, what services do they use, and how long do they stay?

Safety. What is the rate of injury at the facility? What about crime? Is the facility dangerous? The lack of recreation outlets may be linked to increased crime.

Attractiveness. Does the facility contribute to the neighborhood's physical design? Does it upgrade the neighborhood? What are its impacts on property values? How is commerce affected?

Overall satisfaction. This focus combines accessibility, use, safety, attractiveness, and culture impacts. How does the facility affect egalitarian values, mores, and citizen behavior? Is recreation afforded all citizens, or merely segments of the state and community?

Are community and state recreation opportunities excellent, good, fair, or poor?

Source: Harry P. Hatry and Diana R. Dunn, *Measuring the Effectiveness of Local Government Services: Recreation* (Washington, DC: Urban Institute, 1971).

Accountability includes assessing and documenting the effectiveness of programs, measuring program outcomes, documenting implementation and cost effectiveness, and increasing the impact of programs. Strategies stress community mobilization, policy and regulatory action, and the strategic use of media. Program evaluation examines the effectiveness of these strategies for meeting program goals.[16]

Performance-Based Management

Transportation services—more than other government-produced programs—are likely to be routinized into performance measurement within a strategic planning framework. The Pennsylvania Department of Transportation (PENNDOT) creates a new agency agenda every four years. PENNDOT is committed to managing change.

A scorecard of measures clearly link performance metrics with agency goals and objectives. PENNDOT defines effective scorecard measures as those that make a difference to customers and stakeholders, drive behavior throughout the organization, and can be utilized for evaluation and decision making. PENNDOT, a public sector agency with 12,000 employees, commenced a four-year improvement program designed to combine measurable targets of organization performance with rigorous strategic planning practices. Findings focused on effectively setting directions, achieving market-based results, and sustaining cultural changes.

The tasks of PENNDOT's strategic management system transcend partisan politics with an emphasis on policy and system transportation politics. The tasks are divided into four phases: determine the approach, develop the agenda, align market-based plans, and manage with measures.

Phase 1: Determine the approach (1998). Proposed agency goals and objectives are reviewed according to leadership direction, client expectations, client service capabilities, priority tasks and strategies, and plans and performance targets. Continuous feedback and performance measurement promote objectives and measures that assess performance from both process and product perspectives—taking into account internal and external factors.

Phase 2: Develop the agenda (1999). PENNDOT gathers data from clients, stakeholders, partners, and employees. Despite this empirical emphasis, replacing opinions with facts remains a challenge. Extensive surveys and interviews supplement existing data—suggesting value-added strategies. Strengths, weaknesses, opportunities, and threats (SWOT) are probed from reviewing internal and external data. Goals and objectives are not divorced from performance measurement targets. According to David Margolis, "front-end feedback data" identify "meaningful back-end performance measures."[17]

Phase 3: Align market-based plans (2000). Agency agenda offers perspectives for initiating the alignment phase. Decision makers adopt thirteen high-level goals and twenty-one strategic objectives from eight strategic focus areas. A scorecard of measures helps determine whether agency goals and objectives are supported. Indicators suggest measures for short- and long-term targets. SWOT and agency agenda commence the process, and PENNDOT units develop objectives and scorecards. Workshops permit employees—and managers—to consider top-down directives in the context of bottom-up priorities. Market plans and budget outlines focus on strategies and performance targets. A higher degree of program alignment is confirmed.

Motivation and Empowerment

The promotions are gone. A raise is out of the question. Budget cuts prevent managers from providing public sector employees any material incentives. How do managers motivate or empower government employees? People view themselves as outstanding rather than ordinary. If managers encourage employees, they must empower them, too.

Three secrets of empowerment are:

- Managers must share information with employees. Employees want to be partners in the operation. They want to know about the budget.
- Managers must project a vision. A clear vision often means a clear purpose. Employees want to

understand what managers are trying to accomplish. Being empowered is knowing what to do.

- Managers, part of the supervisor hierarchy, will be replaced by teams. Empowered teams may say "no" to the status quo. Teams may create a vision and determine goals, and they are less expensive to the taxpayer.

Empowerment, says Ken Blanchard, begins with vision—meaning purpose, values, image, and goals. People would rather be outstanding than ordinary. Employees must be partners with management, not adversaries.

Source: Ken Blanchard, "Motivation Q&A with Ken Blanchard," http://www.smartbiz.com/sbs/arts/pos6.htm.

Phase 4: Manage with measures (2001). Workshops give employees opportunities to create dashboard measures for supplementing market-based scorecards. Leading indicators and interim outcome measures are added. Dashboards monitor progress toward scorecard metrics and fundamental core market-based targets. Dashboards permit tactical and resource decisions at monthly reviews. Decision makers emphasize proactive problem solving—not reactive thinking. Continuous improvement is a constant theme.

Lessons learned from PENNDOT's strategic planning and performance measurement improvement efforts include:

- Senior PENNDOT leaders were engaged throughout the process.
- Widespread participation took place throughout PENNDOT with ongoing feedback.
- An "adapt, don't adopt" philosophy developed as a mechanism for evaluating the best practices and policies.

Before performance-based management at PENNDOT, decisions occurred within the partisan and ideological parameters of Pennsylvania state government. PENNDOT's focus on strategic planning and performance measurement favors policy and systemwide decision making as evolving, policy-neutral tools. Partisan politics is secondary; policy and system politics are primary. Agency missions, meaningful data, and market results dominate performance-based management at the Pennsylvania Department of Transportation (PENNDOT).

Citizen-Driven Government Performance

Over the last decade, a market has developed for citizen-driven, results-oriented government performance. The emphasis is on assessing and improving how local governments serve their communities. Involvement of community stakeholders in assessing performance is a priority; citizen-driven influence is paramount. Elected leaders and government services respond to community needs and priorities—as stakeholders get involved, participate, and contribute.

How do citizens think impartial experts rate agency performance? What grades do these experts give your city bureaucracies—A, B, C, D, or worse? Is performance improving or deteriorating? How city services should be measured draws little political consensus. However, democratic institutions—cities, towns, counties, states, and even the country—function effectively only with satisfactory levels of trust in government and the long-term health of legally formalized communities.[18]

Improvements in the performance of governments—all 87,525 in the United States—is a widespread expectation for democratic capitalism. The principal idea of the Government Performance and Results Act of 1993 is that federal agencies will produce strategic policy-making plans for revitalizing government units.

The Pew Charitable Trust, in a private sector project called "Grading Governments," generously funded researchers at the Maxwell School of Citizenship and Public Affairs at Syracuse University to study forty federal agencies, all fifty state governments, and forty major units of local government. At the federal level, financial management, human resource management, deployment of information technology, executive leadership capacity, and managing for results—or measuring unit performance—are management categories studied by the Syracuse researchers.

No universally accepted term exists for measuring an organization's performance. Productivity, work measurement, and effectiveness describe similar challenges dictated by the concept of "performance measurement." According to Paul D. Epstein, performance measurement is government's mechanism for providing a quality product at a reasonable cost. Based on the Civil Service Reform Act of 1978, performance measurement, as defined by the GAO in 1980, includes measures of productivity, effectiveness, quality, and timeliness. Different performance measures supplement each other—and should not be perceived as divergent or contradictory.

Grading the American States

With states emerging from the worst financial crisis in fifty years, the Government Performance Project (GPP) spent 2004 and the beginning of 2005 assessing the quality of management performance. They found that all states faced similar economic challenges, but their reactions differed widely. Some states developed truly innovative responses, while others drifted behind. Their different managerial responses have significant implications for their citizens, both now and in the years to come.

The report of the GPP's research team, made up of academics and journalists, grades states on how well they manage their money, people, infrastructure, and information—the foundation necessary to successfully provide services to citizens. The goal of the project is to give states information they can use to improve management and achieve their goals. The project's overall findings are summarized in Table 9.1.

In the Money category, states showed considerable ingenuity in dealing with the fiscal crisis of the past few years. Many of them made a renewed commitment to get back to the basics—to improve long-term planning, replenish rainy day funds, and revisit revenue estimating techniques. In this category, Delaware takes one of three top grades for its strong financial performance with good structural balance, innovative purchasing and contracting systems, and a strong commitment to assessing the fiscal impact of policy decisions.

In managing People, a wave of retirements looms on the horizon. In more than half the states, one in five state government employees will be retiring in the next

TABLE 9.1

Government Performance Project: Grading the States 2005

	Overall	Money	People	Infrastructure	Information
Alabama	C–	C	C+	D	C
Alaska	C+	C	C+	C+	C
Arizona	B	B	B	B–	B–
Arkansas	C+	B–	C	C+	C+
California	C–	D	C–	C	C
Colorado	C+	C–	C+	C+	C+
Connecticut	C+	C	B	C+	C–
Delaware	B+	A	B–	B+	B
Florida	B–	C+	B–	B+	B
Georgia	B	B–	A	C+	B–
Hawaii	C	C	B	C–	D
Idaho	B–	B+	B	C+	C+
Illinois	C+	B	C	C+	C+
Indiana	C+	C	C	B–	C
Iowa	B	B+	B	B	B
Kansas	B	B+	B–	B–	B–
Kentucky	B+	B+	B	B+	B
Louisiana	B	B+	B	C+	A–
Maine	B–	B–	B–	B	C+
Maryland	B	B	B–	A–	C+
Massachusetts	C+	C+	C+	C–	C+
Michigan	B+	B	B	B+	B+
Minnesota	B+	A–	B+	B	B+
Mississippi	C+	B–	C+	C+	C+
Missouri	B	B	B–	B–	A–
Montana	C+	C+	C+	B–	C
Nebraska	B	B+	B–	B+	C+
Nevada	B–	C+	C+	B+	B–
New Hampshire	C	C	C+	C+	C–
New Jersey	B–	C+	B	B–	C
New Mexico	C+	B	C+	D+	B
New York	B–	C+	B–	B+	C+
North Carolina	C+	B–	C+	C+	C+
North Dakota	B–	B–	B–	B–	C
Ohio	B	B+	B–	A–	C+
Oklahoma	C+	B–	B–	C–	C
Oregon	C+	D	B–	B	B
Pennsylvania	B	B+	B–	B+	B
Rhode Island	C+	C+	D+	B–	C+
South Carolina	B	B+	A–	C+	B
South Dakota	B–	B+	B–	B	D

continued

TABLE 9.1

Government Performance Project Grading the States 2005, *continued*

	Overall	Money	People	Infrastructure	Information
Tennessee	C+	B–	C–	B–	C+
Texas	B	B	B	B–	B
Utah	A–	A	B+	A	A–
Vermont	B	B+	B	B–	B–
Virginia	A–	A	A–	A	A–
Washington	B+	A–	B+	B	A–
West Virginia	C+	B–	C	C	C+
Wisconsin	B–	B–	B	C	B–
Wyoming	C	B	D+	C	C

Source: The Pew Center on the States, Government Performance Project, http://www.gpponline.org/States.aspx.

five years. A reasonable number of states are paying close attention to workforce planning, but others, limited by budget cutbacks or simple lack of interest, have not made planning a priority. Georgia, the only state receiving a grade of "A," has integrated workforce planning with the state's strategic planning process. Carrying planning one step further, the state creates employee performance plans that outline the skills each employee needs to move up the career ladder.

With regard to Infrastructure, new accounting regulations require states to estimate the value of their inventory, which forces them to acknowledge how much they defer in maintenance costs. The budget crisis has led more states to push more maintenance off into the future. The best of the pack in 2005 for Infrastructure is Utah. The state requires future maintenance costs to be included in the state operating budget for all new construction. With a statewide capital plan that looks out five years (and longer for transportation projects), the state has its infrastructure systems firmly under control.

And finally, in the category called Information, more and more states are developing and using performance information, and the technology to support this process is improving. States know more than ever about how programs are performing. Executive-branch agencies tend to make the most use of the information; state legislatures the least. Louisiana is a high performer in this category. Agencies report on their performance quarterly through a database available to the public. The legislature analyzes performance measures and uses them to make funding decisions. In addition, the state has a strong performance auditing record.

Performance Measurement in Local Governments

Performance management contributes to better decision making, performance appraisal, accountability, service delivery, public participation, and civic discourse.[19] Performance measurements, as shown in Table 9.2, include input, outputs or workload, outcome or effectiveness, cost-effectiveness, and productivity indicators. Explanatory information probes indicators for service efforts and accomplishments.

TABLE 9.2

Types of Performance Measurement Indicators: An Example

Municipal Function	Input Measures	Output/ Workload Measures	Efficiency Measures	Effectiveness Measures	Productivity Measures	Explanatory Information
Sanitation	The amount of labor-hours of the Sanitation Department, the budget of the Sanitation Department; number of vehicles	Tons of refuse collected; miles of road cleaned; number of customers served	Employee-hours per ton of refuse collected; dollars spent for one mile of snow removal	Percentage of clean streets (e.g., measured by periodical visual inspection; citizen surveys)	Cost per mile of a clean street (i.e., total cost of all road cleaning divided by the total miles of clean streets)	Composition of solid waste; climatic conditions; terrain; crew size of vehicles; type of vehicles

Source: From "Citizen-Driven Government Performance," www.newark.rutgers.edu. Reprinted by permission of Professor Marc Holzer.

Designing and implementing a performance measurement system requires a thorough understanding of what the program is attempting to accomplish and who the clientele are, as well as a knowledge of the public services currently provided by the government unit. Steps in the process include the following.

Step 1: Identification of a program. Government activities are identified by distinct programs. Street resurfacing, patching, seal coating, and repairing are part of street maintenance. Animal control, the clerk's office, code enforcement, corrections, courts, fire prevention, fire suppression, housing code enforcement, landfill operations, library, parks maintenance, police patrol, recreation services, senior services, waste collection, street cleaning, utility billing, wastewater collection, and water distribution are popular local government programs. These programs are included in the city's operating budget.

Step 2: Statement of purpose. Preparation of a well-articulated statement of purpose for a program reflects a clearly understood mission. Programs are not self-serving. They provide services to the citizens of a certain government jurisdiction.

Step 3: Identification of program inputs, outputs, efficiency, and productivity indicators. Operating budget, number of labor-hours, and full-time-equivalent employees are delineated. Outputs reflect workload measures—or the quantity of service delivered to users. Unit of output spells out the quantity of each service. Efficiency and productivity measures address how the service is provided, and efficiency measures focus on costs (dollars and/or employee hours).

Step 4: Setting targets for accomplishment. Service effectiveness and quality measures are established. How do government officials determine if objectives are met? Goals, quantities, dates, and targets are closely adhered to. The goals of a program are set according to a specified period of time. Quantities include percentages for recognizing achievements; dates focus on a time frame. Targets include input and output factors.

Step 5: Monitoring. Continuous monitoring of targets is a given. Monitoring is a way of keeping tabs on program operations. Monitoring gauges whether the target has been reached or not. Is everything going as a planned? Are there seasonal or cyclical patterns to clientele satisfaction? Data gathering should be reasonable—and not overwhelm the unit's fiscal and human capacities. Monitoring varies according to the service and the target.

Step 6: Performance reporting. Indicators are summarized. Results are compared to set targets. Reports include comparisons with previous time frames, similar jurisdictions, technically developed standards or norms, geographic areas of clientele within the same jurisdiction, and public sector/private sector costs and results. Performance reporting includes the program name, unit jurisdiction, purpose statement, workloads/outputs, inputs, productivity and/or efficiency ratios, and synopses of explanatory information.

Success: Measures of Careers Well-Lived?

What is success? By what yardstick does one measure it? What are the means (career, job, lifestyle) by which success (productivity, achievement) is measured?

"Defining one's own success," says Linda Gast, "means ascribing to a personal set of values and beliefs. It means that we must know what our values are and commit ourselves to living and accomplishing in accordance with those values. . . . When we choose to define our success by our own values, our decisions have a firmer foundation."

An employee's acceptance of or change in jobs based on the degree to which those jobs embrace, express, or fit his or her personal values puts compensation packages, job responsibilities, and advancement options in perspective.

How do we want our successes—and achievements—to be judged? By whose standards are our efforts to be evaluated? Are we judged by our own values, or the values of others? How do we live out our values in our everyday lives?

"Success," writes Bill Galston, former deputy assistant to President Clinton, "is intimately connected with integrity. By integrity I mean not honest and honorable deeds, but, more broadly, living in accordance with one's deepest convictions about what gives life purpose and meaning." Personal convictions of integrity vary widely from person to person. Integrity is often met at the junction of personal honesty and professional productivity.

"Integrity may seem straightforward," suggests Galston, "but the appearance is deceptive. . . . there is no guarantee that our understanding of life's meaning and purpose will correspond to our natural talents." We may produce at a high level of performance in a field we consider of secondary importance. Or we may perform in mediocre fashion in a field that we think is fundamental. A measure of dissatisfaction—and even unhappiness—often results.

Does success bring happiness? Not necessarily, says Galston. Integrity is not always sufficient for happiness. The mismatch between our convictions (values) and talents (personal skills) affects how we perceive factors both internal and external to us.

"Success," concludes Galston, "is the skillful exercise of integrity in those choices and acts that are within our power. . . . there is no guarantee that each person's beliefs about what really matters will fit together into a harmonious whole." Or to reverse the predicament, as Galston states, "*Failure* means a high level of moral discomfort with the choices that have defined one's life."

Definitions of success—and achievement— emphasize the personal and ethical measures of careers well-lived.

Source: Linda Gast and William A. Galston, "Viewpoint: Success: What Is Your Yardstick?" *University of Maryland Magazine,* Spring 2000, pp. 6–7.

Step 7: Analysis and action. Well-developed performance measurement systems permit clientele to recognize weaknesses, strengths, threats, and opportunities. Relevant actions may be taken. Unit growth capabilities may be diagnosed.[20]

People Crisis and/or Opportunity?

People are the federal government's most valuable asset. Studies of private and public sector organizations show that high-performing organizations value and invest in their employees—their human capital—and align their "people policies" to support organizational performance goals. In the federal government, however, strategic human capital management is a pervasive challenge.[21]

The GAO includes human capital on its high-risk list. Critical skill shortages in federal departments and agencies cause difficulties in the implementation of the programs and agendas of the president and Congress.[22] Several reforms are in process.

First, an emphasis on workforce planning and restructuring requires federal agencies to flatten their organizational hierarchy and improve their work processes. To optimize the services provided to citizens, federal employees must understand the link between their daily work and the results their government employer seeks to achieve.

Second, administrative reforms must recast job descriptions. Job responsibilities need restructuring to make work more interesting and promote greater employee teamwork. The very way in which agencies design work for their employees needs rethinking. Narrow job descriptions are not attractive to employees who are likely to strive to make contributions in the public arena.

Third, performance management measures are ineffective. The Government Performance and Results Act (GPRA) requires agencies to be performance-driven. But agencies must restructure their performance appraisal systems to measure individual performance against target outcomes.

Finally, recruitment for hard-to-fill positions needs reevaluation.

Agencies evaluated in this study include the Federal Aviation Administration, the Office of Personnel Management, the Veterans Benefits Administration, the Internal Revenue Service, and the Federal Emergency Management Agency. By studying the efforts of these five agencies, the GAO found that directly involving employees in performance planning and important agency decisions empowered the workforce. The provision of regular training to employees, proactive communication with unions on personnel changes, and serious efforts to make human resources a visibly high priority resulted in positive employee impacts.

For the initiatives GAO reviewed, agencies had to overcome organizational and cultural barriers—including lack of trust, resistance to change, lack of buy-in from front-line employees and managers, and workload demands. The agencies developed open communication with employees and reevaluated their systems for reassigning and hiring personnel.[23]

According to the GAO, granting employees decision-making authority not only improved morale, but also streamlined government processes. Once managers and employees perceived the benefits of improved communication and new personnel practices, they adapted to agency changes.

Motivation techniques can be applied in an attempt to improve government employee productivity. However, the bottom line of technique effectiveness entails the mix of partisan, policy, and systems politics. Government productivity gets its energy from continuing expansion of democratic capitalism. Each public sector unit finds its raison d'etre in the political economy of its geographic jurisdiction.

Personnel and motivation are better than ever. Most government employees join the public sector workforce because they like what they do. If partisans cannot agree on what bottom-line policy principles should exist, the public administrative sector systems may become dysfunctional—at least in part. Public sector productivity remains uniquely political.

Summary

- Program evaluations are context-dependent.
- Market values drive program functions, organization structures, standards, and emerging technologies.
- Most citizens care about the *performance* of their public institutions.
- Productivity in the public sector refers to excellence in individual and collective performance. There are widely divergent views as to what excellence is because excellence is based on the cultural context of a particular function.
- *Efficiency* means doing things well; *effectiveness* means doing the right things well.
- Efficiency is essentially the input or contribution of labor, capital, and other resources into an effort measured against the output produced, regardless of the mechanism selected to gauge output.
- Effectiveness calls for a preestablished standard of comparison; a focus on a certain quality of production; and an ability to mobilize, organize, and direct resources for specified purposes, all taken within a certain cultural context.
- The reasons for citizen complaints with government performance are: Democracy is messy. Government takes a bum rap. Government must shape up. The country must shape up.
- Democratic governments are designed to promote equity and fairness. Pluralism is central to the way American society is organized.
- Government has a role to play in restoring morality to public life.
- Privatization of public responsibilities center around *provision,* or providing, and *production,* or producing, of goods and services. *Privatization,* often called contracting out, means that a service previously produced by a government agency is now produced by a nongovernmental organization.
- Program evaluation increases our understanding of government activities, leads to governmental improvements, and produces financial savings.
- Accessibility, use, safety, attractiveness, and overall satisfaction constitute preset ways of measuring the effectiveness of public services.
- The purposes of program evaluation are to bring rigorous analytical perspective to influence agency budget requests, assess agency effectiveness for meeting program objectives established by elected leaders, and develop program performance measures for agency implementation.
- Transportation services—more than other government produced programs—are likely to be routinized into performance measurement within a strategic planning network.
- Empowering employees begins with vision— meaning purpose, values, image, and goals.
- Performance measurement includes indicators of productivity, effectiveness, quality, and timeliness.
- Information provided by performance measurement includes inputs, outputs, outcomes, and efficiency.
- The purpose for doing performance measurement focuses on setting goals and objectives, planning,

- allocating resources, monitoring and evaluating results, and modifying program plans to enhance performance.
- According to Government Performance Project indicators, Delaware captures top grades for performance in the area of money management, with good structural balance, innovative purchasing and contracting systems, and a strong commitment to assessing the fiscal impact of policy decisions.
- Georgia scored the top grade for integrated workforce planning, creating employee performance plans that outline the skills each employee needs to move up the career ladder.
- Utah scores at the top in infrastructure, requiring that future maintenance costs be included in the state operating budget for all new construction; the statewide capital plan projects five years and longer for transportation projects.

- Louisiana scores well in the development and use of performance information, with agencies reporting on their performance quarterly through a database available to the public.
- Performance measurement in local governments contributes to better decision making, performance appraisal, accountability, service delivery, participation, and civic discourse.
- Personal convictions of integrity vary widely from person to person.
- The mismatch between our convictions, or values, and talents, or personal skills, affects how we perceive factors both internal and external to us.
- Failure implies a high level of moral discomfort with the choices that define a person's life.
- People are government's most valuable asset.
- Most government employees join the public sector workforce because they like what they do.

VIDEOS AND FILMS

Public Administration in Action

Performance
Performance Issues [2007]
Probes causes for low productivity. Features vignettes illustrating common workplace problems facing supervisors. Produced by Coastal Training Technologies Corp.

Productivity
Project Management for Improved Productivity [2002]
Based on the book *Project Management*. Covers basic principles and tools, including timelines and schedules. [28 min]

Fairness
The Fairness Factor [1999]
Evaluation and Discipline: How to Manage Performance and Discipline to Maximize Productivity and Minimize Legal Liability. Specifies steps to be taken when conducting performance reviews or disciplinary sessions. [20 min]

Innovation
Challenges of Innovation [2003]
Discusses how unprecedented technological progress during the twentieth century brought new, complex challenges to the delivery of education. Addresses use of technology as a learning tool in current environment of high-stakes testing and accountability—and standards-based teaching. [60 min]

Case Study

"Going Postal" Injures Performance, Kills Motivation

The United States Postal Service (USPS)—a government corporation—is a conduit for freedom and capitalism. "Going postal" became part of the American vocabulary of workplace violence. USPS had an employee crisis. Services and the economy were endangered. In the case study that follows, grievance reforms emerged as a by-product of workplace violence.

> Workplace violence isn't a remote risk. And the hurt can cut deeply into the bottom line.
>
> *—John P. Mello, Jr.*
> *Woonsocket, Rhode Island*

Thomas McIlvane had been fired from his job at the United States Postal Service (USPS), Royal Oak Post Office, Royal Oak, Michigan, for alleged time-card fraud. Less than one week after his dismissal was upheld by an arbitrator, McIlvane went on a killing spree that wounded five and murdered four USPS employees. Then McIlvane turned the gun on himself.[1]

The post office killer had previously been dishonorably discharged from the U.S. Marines. (Allegedly, he had run a car over with a tank.) The rifle he used at Royal Oak was illegal. His dishonorable discharge prohibited McIlvane from owning firearms. No background check was required.

Patrick Sherrill, a full-time substitute letter carrier and ex-Marine sharpshooter, murdered fourteen USPS employees in Edmond, Oklahoma. He, too, committed suicide. The morning before the murders, Sherrill met with Richard Esser, who later was among the dead, and Bill Bland to discuss his work performance. Police sources said that Bland threatened to terminate Sherrill; the USPS claimed they made no efforts to terminate the murderer.[2]

Was Sherrill's killing rampage—the third worst mass murder in American history—an act of revenge? The details were not clear. Coworkers viewed Sherrill as often angry and frequently depressed. But no real evidence came forth that his work performance had ever been seriously questioned. However, it was said that Sherrill preferred keeping his own company to the usual workplace socialization. At best enigmatic, he was not well understood by those who knew him. His workplace mayhem was seemingly without purpose.

The USPS has gotten a "bad rap" for public sector workplace violence, as is illustrated by the deaths in Royal Oak and Edmond. "Going postal" has become part of the American vocabulary of violence. The USPS had an employee crisis. Incidents of murder and mayhem were isolated. Could anything come out of events that were so evil? Performance and motivation at the USPS, a conduit to American capitalism, were in serious jeopardy.[3]

Employers are increasingly aware that employee motivation and unit productivity are linked. Partisan, policy, and system politics support the government's public services improvement agenda. New technologies impact the ways we live and work. High-performing employers excel at instilling employee motivation. Workforce strategies link motivation, individual performance, and unit performance.

USPS, a public sector corporation, was forced to resolve citizen concerns regarding employee tensions, safety, and security in its workplaces. "Going postal" not only threatened USPS employees, it endangered services, and therefore, the economy. Like air traffic control and the interstate highway system, the USPS functions to promote personal exchanges and economic developments—namely, freedom and capitalism.

USPS as Conduit for Freedom and Capitalism

Each week the USPS delivers billions of pieces of mail—including letters, bills, advertisements, and packages. It employs about 860,000 persons. Qualification is based on an examination. The number of qualified applicants continues to encourage keen competition as applicant numbers are expected to exceed the number of job openings.

The nationwide private mailing industry generates $155 billion yearly, excluding postage, and employs 6.2 million people. USPS employees carry more mail to more people over a larger geographic area than postal employees in any other country. Three of the postal service's six product lines—correspondence and transactions, business advertising, and expedited delivery—would qualify as Fortune 500 companies.[4]

USPS serves 7 million customers daily through 38,000 retail outlets. Mail is collected from more than 312,000 street mail collection boxes. Every two weeks,

USPS pays out $1.6 billion in employee salaries and benefits. The average carrier delivers about 2,500 pieces of mail a day to 500 addresses. Many postage stamps raise awareness of social issues.[5]

Postal clerks, typically classified by job duties, perform a variety of functions. They may work as window or counter clerks; sell stamps, money orders, postal stationary, envelopes, and boxes; weigh packages to determine postage; and check packages for satisfactory mailing conditions. Distribution clerks sort local mail for delivery to individual customers. Mail processors operate optical character readers (OCRs) and barcode sorters for scanning, coding, and sorting mail. Carriers cover routes by foot and/or vehicle.

Working conditions vary. Window clerks usally work in clean, well-ventilated, and well-lit buildings. They rarely work at night. They may, however, deal with upset customers, stand for long periods, and be held accountable for the assigned stock of stamps and funds. Despite the use of automated equipment, postal clerks may have to do physically demanding work. Most carriers begin work in the morning. Overtime hours are frequently required during peak delivery times. Employment of postal service workers is expected to decline slightly through 2010.[6]

Approximately 40,000 postal workers are hired each year. Retirements, transfers, departures, and deaths open the way for new hires. USPS advertises internally. The Office of Personnel Management (OPM) has no jurisdiction. In 1971, the politicized Post Office Department became the United States Postal Service—an independent, public corporation.

The Postal Pay Act determines pay scales, which are not part of the General Pay Schedule. The Postal Service pays extra compensation, overtime, and night shift differentials. Special pay scales are used for rural letter carriers. A cost-of-living adjustment (COLA) accrues to the employee salary base at the rate of 1 cent per hour for each .4-point increase in the Consumer Price Index. Benefits include vacation and sick leave, health and life insurance, and retirement considerations.

Classification requirements must be met for carrier, clerk, machine distribution clerk, flat-sorting machine opeator, mail handler, mail processor, and automated mark-up clerk positions. You must be eighteen or older to apply. Applicants do not have to be U.S. citizens. Physical requirements are determined by the job. Carriers must be able to lift a 70-pound mail sack. All applicants must be able to efficiently perform their assigned duties. USPS maintains a comprehensive program to ensure a drug-free workplace. Employees are scheduled for drug screening tests. Veterans receive a five- or ten-point hiring preference.[7]

Postal Service Violence in a Larger Context

Death, we might argue, is a very personal matter. At some juncture, every living thing—plant, animal, human, even government bureaucracy—is going to die. The workplace violence in Royal Oak and Edmond remains a personal matter for those postal workers who met untimely deaths and for their families and loved ones. But violence in postal offices occurs in a comparative context of nationwide employment.

The mass murders affected the employment, training, performance, motivation, and psyches of USPS employees and their citizen clients. In 1998, postal officials asked Joseph A. Califano, Jr., chairman of the United States Postal Service Commission on a Safe and Secure Workplace and president of the National Center on Addiction and Substance Abuse (CASA) at Columbia University, to investigate.

The Commission's staff included sixty professionals—including sixteen with doctorates and fifteen with master's in business, communications, computer engineering, criminology, economics, education, government, history, journalism, linguistics, medicine, psychiatry, psychology, public health, public policy, social work, sociology, and statistics—one medical doctor, and three attorneys. CASA conducted demonstration programs at thirty-eight sites in twenty-five cities in sixteen states.

CASA prepared a 249-page report. The commission examined twenty-nine incidents of workplace homicide involving postal workers as either victims or perpetrators from 1986 to 1999. According to the two-year report, postal workers are no more likely to commit or be victims of violence, and only a third as likely as those in the general national workforce, to be homicide victims (0.26 vs. 0.77 per 100,000 workers each year between 1992 and 1998).

Fifteen postal employee perpetrators killed thirty-four postal employees. Nineteen nonpostal workers killed fourteen postal employees. Fourteen out of fifteen postal perpetrators had troubled histories of violence, mental illness, substance abuse, and/or criminal convictions. Male veterans were no more likely than other male postal employees to commit homicides. Guns were used in all the homicides committed by postal employee perpetrators and by 90 percent of the homicides committed by nonpostal perpetrators. Motives included robbery, problems in intimate relationships, and employment termination.

"'Going postal' is a myth, a bad rap," concluded Califano, "causing unnecessary apprehension and fear among 900,000 postal workers. This report should shatter the myth that postal workers are more violent than other workers and discourage the pejorative use of that expression."[8]

The dynamics of "going postal" did affect the USPS employment environment. The commission survey found postal employees to be less angry, aggressive, hostile, depressed, and stressed than those in the national workforce and better suited to cope. However, USPS management and workers expressed more negative attitudes about work.

Postal workers project that they are

- Nearly six times more likely than those in the national workforce to be victims of violence by coworkers (17 versus 3 percent). In reality, the probability is almost identical (4 percent versus 3 percent).
- Less confident in management's fairness and honesty (37 percent versus 60 percent).
- Less likely to agree that their employer—USPS— takes action to protect them (52 percent versus 70 percent).[9]

USPS Grievance Reforms as a By-Product of Violence

In the early 1990s, USPS encountered an employee crisis. The shootings received media attention, but these incidents were isolated. In some respects, the internal battles of USPS local units mirrored the depressing, deadly chaos that USPS's government—and very corporate—image portrayed to the country. Charges of racial discrimination, sexual harassment, and similar management abuses and informal complaints resulted in 30,000 grievance filings per year.

Some complaints escalated into costly litigation. In 1994, as part of a settlement of a class-action lawsuit, lawyers at USPS created REDRESS™ to settle disputes using neutral outside mediators. The program was tested in certain cities before going national in 1997.

The results proved spectacular. The first twenty-two months of full operation of REDRESS saw 17,645 informal disputes mediated. Eighty percent of those were resolved. Formal complaints, which peaked at 14,000 in 1997, declined by 30 percent. Prior to REDRESS, USPS employee-management disputes lasted for years. The REDRESS program offered disgruntled workers mediation.

Attempts to short-circuit controversies can prompt justice. An employee who filed an informal complaint would agree to employ REDRESS. A meeting would be set up, and a mediator would hear both sides of the dispute. In most instances, the mediator would propose a solution within a day. REDRESS made mediation available at any stage of the grievance process—not just the beginning.

REDRESS emerged as a very productive tool for USPS. Corporate America took notice. High-profile racial discrimination and sexual harassment class-action lawsuits against industry giants like Texaco and Coca-Cola point out that government agencies are not the only jurisdictions in which professional conflicts and controversies occur.[10]

Cynthia J. Hallberlin, former chief legal council at USPS, placed issues of employment productivity and motivation at USPS in perspective: "You're never going to get rid of conflict," Hallberlin said, "you just want to handle it better."[11]

Questions and Instructions

1. For whom, if anyone, are USPS production services efficient, effective, and/or excellent? Explain and illustrate.
2. How do USPS dynamics afford commentary on adages such as "democracy is messy," "government takes a bum rap," "government must shape up," and "the country must shape up"? Illustrate.
3. What are the limitations for further privatization of postal service tasks and functions? Explain.
4. How is the USPS a conduit for freedom and capitalism? Explain and illustrate.
5. Did any good come out of the evils of the Royal Oak and Edmond mass murders? What insights were gleaned about conflicts and fairness? Explain.
6. How do effective USPS job classifications promote a more effective postal workforce? Explain.

7. People work for one of three basic reasons: money, people, and job. Place in rank order the reasons why USPS employees are likely to toil as postal workers. Explain your rankings.
8. Was the report of the United States Postal Service Commission on a Safe and Secure Workplace a product of inductive thinking, deductive thinking, or a combination of the two? Why?
9. Assuming issues of labor, management, technology, volume, and nationwide consumer demand for personal economy will continue, can the USPS be "reinvented" to promote both egalitarian access and efficiency?

Insights-Issues/"Going Postal" Injures Performance, Kills Motivation

Clearly and briefly describe and illustrate the following concepts and issues. Interpret the word *role* as meaning impacts, applications, importance, effects, and/or illustrations of certain facts, concerns, or issues from the case study.

1. Role of USPS production services as efficient, effective, and/or excellent—for whom?
2. Role of USPS as a conduit for freedom and capitalism.
3. Role of mass murders in raising the agenda for evaluating morale factors in 38,000 labor-intensive USPS units.
4. Role of USPS Commission on a Safe and Secure Workplace as an inductive or deductive (or combination) contributor to solutions.
5. Roles of money, people, and jobs as reasons why employees work.

Notes

1. Violence Policy Center, "Where'd They Get Their Guns? An Analysis of the Firearms Used in High-Profile Shootings, 1963 to 2001," November 14, 1991, http://www.vpc.org/studies/wgun911114.htm.
2. "A Public Awakening—The Edmond Post Office Massacre," http://www.svn.net/mikekell/v5.html.
3. National Center on Addiction and Substance Abuse at Columbia University, *Postal Commission Releases Groundbreaking Report on Workplace Violence,* August 31, 2000, http://www.casacolumbia.org/newsletter1457/newsletter_show.htm?doc_id=34000.
4. Stephen Barr, "Struggling Postal Service Makes Case for Transformation," *Washington Post,* May 14, 2002, p. B2.
5. United States Postal Service, "Postal Facts," http://www.usps. com/history/pfact00.htm.
6. Jonathan W. Kelinson, *1998–99 Occupational Outlook Handbook,* Bureau of Labor Statistics, "Postal Clerks and Mail Carriers," http://www.umsl.edu/services/govdocs/ooh9899/135.htm.
7. Dennis V. Damp, *Post Office Jobs: How to Get a Job with the U.S. Postal Service,* 2nd ed. (La Crosse, WI: Brookhaven Press, 2000), http://federaljobs.net/uspscont.htm.
8. "'Going Postal' Is a Myth, Report Says," *CNEWSFeatures,* August 31, 2000, http://www.fan590.com/CNEWSFeatures0008/31_postal.html.
9. National Center on Addiction and Substance Abuse at Columbia University, *Postal Commission.*
10. Mickey Meese, "Companies Adopting Postal Service Process," *New York Times,* September 6, 2000, http://www.spea.indiana.edu/icri/nytsepa.htm.
11. Ibid.

Sources

American Management Association, "Motivating for Results: Bringing Out the Best in People," http://www.amanet.org/seminars/cmd2/2275.htm; Kathy Bunch, "When Employees Turn Deadly at Work," February 26, 2001, http://my.webmd.com/printing/article/1685.51170; Bureau of Labor Statistics, Occupational Outlook Handbook, 2002–03 edition, http://stats.bls.gov/oco/ocos141.htm; "Case Studies: Research & Ideas," http://www.theworkfoundation.com/casestudies/casestudy05.jsp; Debbie DeVoe and Loretta W. Prencipe, "Mastering Motivation," *InforWorld,* November 16, 2001, http://staging.infoworld.com/articles/pe/xml/01/11/19/011119pemotivate.xml?Template=/storypa; Colin Johnson, "Federal Employees—'Give Us a Chance to Do Our Jobs,'" http://www.brook.edu/dybdocroot/comm/news/1030publicservice.htm; John P. Mello, Jr., "Hell in Your Hallways," http://www.cfo.com/printarticle/0, 5317, 1477!,00.html; "Productivity Bonus Program," http://www.tipc.state.tx.us/overview/pbp/pbp.htm.

Notes

1. G. Chris Hartung, "Institutionalized Excellence: Not Just More Pop Government Jargon?" *Public Management* 78, no. 7 (July 1996): 25–29.
2. David Osborne, "Grading Governments, *Washington Post,* April 13, 1997, p. A8.
3. *New York Times,* April 20, 1971.
4. E. S. Savas, *Privatizing the Public Sector* (Chatham, NJ: Chatham House, 1982), p. 89.
5. Ted Kolderie, "The Two Different Concepts of Privatization," *Public Administration Review* 46, no. 4 (July–August 1986): 285–291.
6. Kolderie, "Two Different Concepts," p. 285.
7. Ibid., p. 286.
8. Richard L. Worsnop, "Privatizing Government Services: Can For-Profit Businesses Do a Better Job?" *CO Researcher* 6, no. 30 (August 9, 1996): 699–717.
9. Richard W. Stevenson, "Government Plan May Make Private Up to 850,000 Jobs," *New York Times,* November 15, 2002, http://www.nytimes.com/2002/11/15/politics/15PRIV.html?pagewanted=print=top.
10. Richard D. Lieberman, "The 'Criminalization' of Government Procurement," *Civil Engineering* 63, no. 3 (March 1993): 68–70.
11. Charles R. Rendall, "Privatization: A Cure for Our Ailing Infrastructure?" *Civil Engineering* 66, no. 12 (December 1996): 6.
12. Steve H. Hanke, "Privatization: Theory, Evidence, and Implementation," *Proceedings of the Academy of Political Science* 35, no. 4 (1985): 101–113.
13. Ralph C. Chandler and Jack C. Plano, *The Public Administration Dictionary* (New York: John Wiley & Sons, 1982), p. 91.
14. David A. Dowell, "Guidelines for Legislative Language for State Program Evaluation," Long Beach, CA: California State University, 1998, http://www.csulb.edu/~ddowell/guidelines.htm.
15. David Thomas, "Department of Education Announces New Approach to Program Evaluation," http://www.ed.gov/PressReleases/04-2002/04052002a.html.
16. Centers for Disease Control and Prevention, "Introduction to Program Evaluation for Comprehensive Tobacco Control Programs," February 6, 2002, http://www.cdc.gov/tobacco/evaluation_manual/executive_summary.html.
17. David Margolis, "Performance-Based Management in PENNDOT," *PA Times* 25, no. 6 (July 2002): 3.
18. "Editor's Notebook," *Government Executive Magazine,* January 1, 1997; http://www.govexec.com/news/index/cfm.
19. David Osborne and Peter Plasrik, "Grading Governments," http://www.psgrp.com/resources/Publications/op4-13.html.
20. The National Center for Public Productivity, "A Brief Guide for Performance Measurement in Local Government," http://newark.rutgers/~ncpp/Manual.htm.
21. Gail C. Christopher and Robert J. O'Neill, Jr., "The Federal Government's People Crisis," *Federal Times,* December 2000.
22. General Accounting Office, *Human Capital: Practices That Empowered and Involved Employees,* GAO-01-1070, September 14, 2000.
23. Kellie Lunney, "Managers Should Involve Employees in Decision Making," *Government Executive Magazine,* October 10, 2001, http://www.govexec.com.

Administrative Law and Government Regulations

Chapter Highlights

The Impact of Administrative Growth on Democratic Ideals and Administrative Law

Traditional and Contemporary Cornerstones of American Administrative Law

What Is Administrative Law?

Administrative Law Judges and Federal Regulations

Internal and External Administrative Controls

The Whistle-Blower as Tell-All

Law and Control: How Much Is Enough?

Government Regulation

Market Failure and Regulations

Is the United States a Regulatory State?

Economic, Social, and Subsidiary Regulations

Administrative Rules and Rule Making

The Administrative Procedure Act

What Is the Public Interest?

Sunset Limited Jettisoned into Regulatory History

Amtrak's eastbound Sunset Limited, a passenger train headed for Mobile, Alabama, during the early hours of September 22, 1993, was about to meet its final destiny and the subsequent deaths of 47 of the more than 220 people aboard. The accident not only cost lives but resulted in almost $20 million in equipment damage—plus an unknown amount of civil liability.

The Amtrak train, speeding at 72 miles per hour, derailed off the CSX railway bridge built in 1909, as three locomotives and the first four passengers cars were jettisoned into the Big Bayou Canot, a shallow waterway not suitable for commercial barge navigation.

The south Alabama fog settled across the landscape that fateful morning. Willie Odom was working the midnight-to-6 A.M. shift as pilot of the Mauvilla towboat. Captain Odom was navigating his towboat—pushing six 1,500-ton barges aligned side by side in three rows. Each barge was 195 feet long and 35 feet wide. The barge flotilla moved at three to four knots, or less than five miles per hour. The weight of the towboat accumulated about 9,000 tons of deadly force.[1]

Odom became disoriented by the dense fog. The captain thought his towboat and barges were moving along the Mobile River. The six heavily laden barges pushed coal, cement, and wood chips from Mobile to Birmingham and Tuscaloosa. The railroad bridge stood about seven feet above the water. Barges could not pass under the structure. The CSX freight railway owned the bridge. A CSX official phoned the United States Coast Guard to report the derailment.

Odom was lost in the fog, but he did not know it until he "heard this noise—whoosh!—and I seen this fire."[2] Odom's barges had nudged out the alignment of the center portion of the three-section railroad bridge. A single railroad track was suddenly out of line—by 28 inches. A heavy girder was directly in the path of the speeding locomotives. A tremendous impact ensued. Lives would be lost—and many more lives would be changed forever.

The railroad safety system had been in use for a century. The circuit track system automatically turns signals red if a bridge collapses. If a rail is broken, the small electrical current passing through it is turned off, and the "fail-safe" signals turn red. The barge collision shifted the CSX track, but it did not break it. Towboats were not intended to float under this trestle.

Accident Aftershocks Effect Regulations

The aftershocks of this horrible accident continue to affect government regulations monitoring inland operators of towing vessels.

The masters, pilots, tankermen, and deckhands laboring in the country's towboat industry had toiled in obscurity—excepting an occasional oil spill or drowning. "The industry as a whole was invisible," noted Captain John Sutton, a towboat pilot from Hahnville, Louisiana, and past president of the American Inland Mariners Association. The phrase *human error* was taking on new meaning. Odom's wrong turn made headlines and history. The towboat industry would change.[3]

The Coast Guard (USCG) had failed to establish higher standards for the licensing of inland operators of towing vessels. The new rule making affects 13,024 mariners employed by 1,252 towing companies, on 5,400 registered towing vessels.[4] The preamble to the new rule states: "This rule will place its primary economic burden on the mariner, not on the mariners' employer."[5]

The Coast Guard, as government regulator, sought inputs on new regulations from towboat owners, employees, and clients. The USCG received 787 comment letters in its original Notice of Proposed Rule Making (NPRM) and conducted extensive public hearings before issuing its regulations. The USCG encouraged the public to participate in towboat rule making by submitting comments and related materials.[6]

The USCG, in its discussions of comments and regulatory changes, promulgated standards for the apprentice mate (steersman), assistance towing, grandfathering of licenses, horsepower, proficiency demonstrations, refresher courses and training, examiners and exam centers, responsibility of the master, safety, costs, and whistle-blowers.

The National Transportation Safety Board (NTSB) investigates accidents, identifies human errors and facilitating factors, and recommends changes, corrections, and strategies to government and industry officials who effect changes and enhance safety measures. The NTSB found that Odom, the towboat operator, had no experience in operating barges in fog. Though he had radar on his tug, the captain had no formal training in the use and interpretation of radar technologies. The towboat company was of no assistance to Odom. The tow was not equipped—nor was it required to be equipped—with a compass or charts to assist in correcting human errors. Neither the company nor the USCG required formal radar training.

The NTSB assessed blame on Odom's inexperience with radar, the company's failure to provide Odom with proper radar training, and the USCG's reluctance to establish more strict licensing standards for towboats and captains. Would radar skills have prevented this disaster? Marsh and mud, consistent with the bayou's geography, are very poor reflectors. As long as expectations for tugboat equipment and pilot skills are low, the public may never find out. (The USCG reviewed 12,000 towboat accidents between 1982 and 1991. It determined that only 18 percent were caused by equipment or structural failure. The Coast Guard attributed 62 percent of towboat accidents to human error.)

Interest groups, including the American Waterways Operators Association, the American

Inland Mariners Association, and the National Association of Maritime Educators (NAME), became involved in the rule-making debate and provided input to the USCG regulators. NAME insisted that

- The USCG did not possess sufficient first-hand experience working in the commercial towing industry.
- The Coast Guard had not adequately monitored licensing of towing vessels in the past.
- The USCG was overly dependent on information provided by representatives of large towing companies.
- The mariners working in the towing industry are—for the most part—not represented by labor unions.
- The new rules promulgated by the USCG regulate the mariner while refusing to adequately or effectively regulate the towing vessel.[7]

Change in Industry Culture?

The media coverage of the Amtrak disaster and USCG investigations has brought to the inland mariner-towboat industry what some call a "change in culture." Operators are attending radar classes, having their skills evaluated and licenses restricted, and asking why the death rate in the industry is eight times the national average. Prior to September 22, 1993, few persons outside the industry cared about its trial-by-fire methods or tendency to lose deck-hands. The emphasis on merit and skills was irritating to the older masters and pilots. They relied more on intuition than formal training.

"Individual human errors do not occur in a vacuum," stated Jim Hall, then chairman of the National Transportation Safety Board (NTSB). "They take place within a cultural, social, and organizational context. That is, there are underlying causes and conditions that shape, facilitate, or even nurture the behavior and actions of an accident-causing individual. These causes and conditions arise from government, industry, or individual company policies, procedures, and programs that either do not exist or do not properly address the issues at hand."[8]

If a CSX freight train had jettisoned off a century-old railway trestle that September morning, who would have noticed? The deaths would have been minimized. The relationships between the towboat industry, government, and citizens would not have been altered. Regulations would not be an issue. But that scenario is not reality—and it is not regulatory history.

Notes

1. Don Phillips, "Towboat Captain May Have Hit Railroad Bridge in Fog," *Washington Post,* September 24, 1993, p. 2.
2. Jim Morris, "New Rules Pushing Towboat Industry: Aftershocks Still Being Felt in Wake of Deadly 1993 Accident," *Houston Chronicle,* December 15, 1996, p. 1, http://www.chron.com/ content/chronicle/page1/96/12/15/barges.html.
3. Ibid.
4. Richard A. Block, "Interim Rule for Licensing Towing Vessel Officers," *N.A.M.E. Newsletter,* no. 86 (December 1999), http://www.metbooks.com/name/name86.html.
5. Gulf Coast Mariners Association, "Rule Making and Regulations: Towing Vessel Licensing," http://gulfcoastmariners. org/gulf/rulemaking_license.htm.
6. Block, "Interim Rule."
7. Gulf Coast Mariners Association, "Rule Making."
8. Jim Hall, Remarks before the International Marine Transit Association, Vancouver, Canada, September 23, 1996, http://www.ntsb.gov/speeches/former/hall/jh960923.htm.

Source

U.S. Department of Transportation, Coast Guard, "Licensing and Manning for Officers of Towing Vessels," *The Federal Register,* Vol. 64, No. 223, pp. 63213–63235, http://frwebgate .access.gpo.gov/cgi-bin/getdoc.cgi?

Defining Administrative Law

Administrative law is an amorphous body of law. . . . Administrative law is created or affected by the activities of government agencies. The term *administrative law* is akin to many other conceptual terms and is hard to define.

—*Joseph J. Simeone*

Administrative law controls a system: a system which, in the simplest terms, has only one goal: to deliver government services to its citizens.

—*Charles Koch, Jr.*

1. That branch of law concerned with the procedures by which administrative agencies make rules and adjudicate cases; the conditions under which these actions can be reviewed by courts. 2. The legislation that creates administrative agencies. 3. The rules and regulations promulgated by administrative agencies. 4. The law governing judicial review of administrative actions.

—*Jay M. Shafritz*

Broadly speaking, administrative law deals with (1) the ways in which power is transferred from legislative bodies to administrative agencies; (2) how administrative agencies use power; and (3) how the actions taken by administrative agencies are reviewed by the courts. More specifically, administrative law is concerned with the legal developments which have so dramatically increased the powers and scope of the administrative branch.

—*Kenneth F. Warren*

Sources: Joseph J. Simeone, "The Function, Flexibility, and Future of United States Judges of the Executive Branch," *Administrative Law Review* 44, no. 1 (Winter 1992): 159–161; Charles Koch Jr., *Administrative Law and Practice* (New York: West Publishing Co., 1985); Jay M. Shafritz, *The Dorsey Dictionary of American Government and Politics* (Chicago: The Dorsey Press, 1988); Kenneth F. Warren, *Administrative Law in the Political System,* 3d ed. (Upper Saddle River, N.J.: Prentice Hall, 1997), p. 23.

The Impact of Administrative Growth on Democratic Ideals and Administrative Law

The United States, a country espousing democratic capitalism, exists in the era of the *administrative state.*

The administrative presidency, with corresponding implications for state governors, county executives, and municipal mayors, finds philosophical origins in George Washington's first cabinet. Thomas Jefferson, the original "outsider" advocating states' rights and decentralization of power, called for the pluralist model of presidential leadership. Alexander Hamilton—called our first accountant of the nation's purse—called for a strong chief administrator with direct, accountable lines of program authority.

Jefferson represented values of equality of uniform participation, or democratic ideals, while Hamilton called for efficient administration, articulated in hierarchy and bureaucracy. How has the emergence of the modern administrative state redefined the basic democratic principles of our 1787 U.S. Constitution? Tenets of administrative law are grounded in constitutionalism, shared governmental powers, popular government, individualism, and political equality.[1]

Constitutionalism. A constitutional governmental system regards the people, not the government, as sovereign. The rule of law emphasizes supremacy of the law and the notion of limited government. A constitutional government is politically legitimate if it rests securely on popular consent.

Many Americans believe that the growth of administrative expertise challenges the primacy of democratic constitutionalism. According to this argument, administrative discretion permits public administrators to "govern" the United States, and governmental regulations are threats to democratic constitutionalism. The undemocratic character of administrative experts compromises constitutional democracy. The new cadre of governmental experts forms an administrative elite that evolves into a democratically irresponsible oligarchy.

Shared Powers. The division of powers among the chief executive, administrative, legislative, and judicial branches and among different levels of government permits each political entity a limited check over the powers of other authorities in the governmental system. Decision-making powers in this system are not monopolized by a single governmental branch. Presidents, legislators, and judges tend to delegate more of their prescribed powers to government bureaucrats as the weight of increasing governmental regulation increases.

The expansion of administrative policy-making powers is enhanced as other branches of government become increasingly bogged down with peripheral concerns. Public administrators, for example, absorb more power as constitutionally elected politicians agonize over the role of government in the resolution of moral dilemmas. Many citizens perceive the public administration system as a closed political system that circumvents the open decision-making structure authored by the constitutional framers. Political bureaucracy emerges with a less than well-defined philosophy of the public interest.

Popular Government. Democratic government implies that the ultimate determination of public policy resides with the people. Stressing majority will, individual rights, and liberty, popular government is the opposite of absolutism. The shift of power from political institutions to administrative agencies raises questions about the democratic functioning of popular government.[2]

If public policy making is "farmed out" to government bureaucrats, how "popular" can government be? The administrative state, grounded in structures, functions, and rationality, may not be suited to the flexibility required to meet the public's demands. A system based on knowledge, skills, and expertise conflicts with a system based on partisan politics and spoils. All government officials, elected and appointed, are servants of the people and should be held accountable for their performance in the public's interest. It can be difficult to ensure that a nonelected official can be that accountable.

Individualism. Freedom, personal well-being, and capabilities of individuals may conflict with the regulation of society by public bureaucracies. According to some, bureaucracy stymies the will of citizens, expressing the powers of the system and not the individual.

The tug of war between societal rights and individual rights challenges the political consensus of democratic governments. Regulatory agencies prescribe rules that may destroy the freedom of individuals, with new structures of apolitical power over individuals emerging in their place.

In balancing societal and individual rights, government regulators are called upon to implement guidelines of federal, state, and local laws in a "fair" manner. Issues of administrative law ultimately involve questions of due process of law. The

---

Why Administrative Law Matters

1. The growth of government by public administrators is the most important political innovation in modern times.
2. In the present day, the effects of administrative government influence us literally every moment of our lives.
3. Bureaucratic government has provided no utopian cure for the shortcomings of free enterprise.

4. Administrative law seeks to reduce the tendencies toward arbitrariness and unfairness in bureaucratic government.
5. Administrative law, a relatively new and open-ended field of law, has not yet succeeded in playing its assigned role effectively.

Source: Lief H. Carter, *Administrative Law and Politics: Cases and Comments* (Boston: Little, Brown, 1983), p. 4.

---

question is, due process or fair treatment for whom? Liberty is sacrificed and our way of life is altered when an administrative agency or a court makes a decision that benefits a larger group at the expense of the individual. The rights of the individual—bolstered by the Fourth Amendment to the U.S. Constitution, which monitors unreasonable searches and seizures, and the Fifth Amendment, which guards against self-incrimination—can be undermined by the exercise of excessive regulatory control.

Political Equality. Grounded in democratic philosophies of equality under the law and equal opportunity for all persons, government is to treat and represent all persons equally. Laws forbid arbitrary treatment of citizens by government officials, but in practice U.S. administrative agencies do not afford complete equality to all persons or groups. The reality of U.S. political bureaucracy is that preferential treatment is given to special interests.

Sexual and racial discrimination are well known and publicized aspects of our society. Since the Great Society of the 1960s, citizen groups have been organized to represent the interests of women and minorities. Affirmative action programs call for special compensatory measures from government to rectify past discriminatory practices by society. In theory, at least, the rule-of-law principle demands that government bureaucrats treat all individuals equally. Public bureaucracy, as prescribed by Max Weber's "ideal type," rests upon knowledge, skills, and expertise, and not upon equality or political influence.

Constitutionalism, shared powers, popular government, individualism, and political equality are the political philosophies upon which administrative laws find implementation in modern American society. The individual needs the assurance of protection in law from the potential misuse of regulatory power. The conflicts between individual citizens and their governments and the resolution of these conflicts by the law allow understanding of how these philosophies are played out in American life.

Prospects for federal government growth after September 11, 2001, are juxtaposed for comparison and contrast to the four periods of previous bureaucratic growth as categorized and described by James Q. Wilson, later supplemented by Kenneth F. Warren (Table 10.1).

TABLE 10.1

James Q. Wilson's Four Periods of Bureaucratic Growth

Period	Focus	Key Acts Passed
1887–1890	Control monopolies and rates	Interstate Commerce Act Sherman Act
1906–1915	Regulate product quality	Pure Food and Drug Act Meat Inspection Act Federal Trade Commission Clayton Act
1930–1940	Extend regulation to cover various socioeconomic areas, especially new technologies	Food, Drug, and Cosmetic Act Public Utility Holding Company Act National Labor Relations Act Securities and Exchange Act Natural Gas Act
1960–1979	Expand regulation to make America a cleaner, healthier, safer, and fairer place to live and work	Economic Opportunity Act Civil Rights Acts of 1960, 1964, and 1968 National Environmental Policy Act Clean Air Act Occupational Safety and Health Act
1978–1993	Deregulation movement as a reaction to bureaucratic overexpansion	Paperwork Reduction Act Air Deregulation Act Radio and TV deregulation Banking deregulation

Sources: James Q. Wilson, "The Rise of the Bureaucratic State," *Policy Making,* ed. Francis E. Rourke, 4th ed. (Boston: Little, Brown, 1986), pp. 125–148; and Kenneth F. Warren, *Administrative Law in the Political System,* 3d ed. (Upper Saddle River, N.J.: Prentice-Hall, 1997), p. 45.

Traditional and Contemporary Cornerstones of American Administrative Law

The traditional cornerstones of administrative law are the independent regulatory agency, a uniform administrative procedure law (Administrative Procedure Act, 1946, as amended), substantial evidence judicial review, and notice and comment ruling.[3]

The *independent regulatory agency,* as a descriptive concept, is a misnomer. All agencies are, in unique ways, dependent directly upon the executive and legislative branches of government and indirectly upon the judicial branch. The independent agencies, as they are called, emerged from the American constitutional provision of separation of powers.

There are three types of regulation. The best known is old-style economic regulation. The second type, the new social regulation, is a product of the 1970s. A third type of regulation is subsidiary regulation.[4] Economic regulation emerged from the social and economic challenges of the 1930s. From the devastating consequences of the Depression, the New Deal created the Federal Deposit Insurance Corporation (FDIC), Tennessee Valley Authority (TVA), Federal Communications Commission (FCC), Securities and Exchange Commission (SEC), National Labor Relations Board (NLRB), and Civil Aeronautics Board (CAB). These regulatory bodies were established from 1933 through 1938.

After World War II, other agencies were created to monitor and confront emerging national problems. The Atomic Energy Commission (AEC), Selective Service System (SSS), National Aeronautics and Space Administration (NASA), Federal Maritime Commission (FMC), Equal Employment Opportunity Commission (EEOC), Environmental Protection Agency (EPA), Occupational Safety and Health Administration (OSHA), and Consumer Product Safety Commission (CPSC) were created to administer and regulate, respectively, programs concerning atomic energy, military conscription, space exploration, shipping, employment discrimination, environmental protection, occupational safety, and consumer product safety. In addition, there is a need to regulate the activities of agencies implementing Social Security, medical care, welfare, food stamps, veterans' benefits, and internal revenue programs.

The development and enactment of a *uniform administrative procedure law* is the second traditional cornerstone of administrative law. The Administrative Procedure Act, enacted in 1946, brings a degree of standardization to administrative practices and procedures and public access to those procedures. Before the enactment of APA, administrative practice and procedure questions were decided on a constitutional basis. The APA brought order from chaos. Unless they can find a justifiable exception, agencies must follow the fundamental outlines of APA's broad and general statute. Such legislation was an advance of immeasurable proportions in administrative law and the protection of citizen rights.

Judicial review is the third traditional cornerstone of administrative law. Substantial evidence review is a dominant feature of administrative practice and procedure. The courts may rule on the merits of agency action if things go askew. Derived from statutory and nonstatutory sources, judicial review permits judges to scrutinize allegedly illegal administrative actions. Judicial review, as a basic right, rests on the congressional grant of general jurisdiction under Article 3 of the U.S. Constitution.

The *rule-making procedure* (notice and comment ruling) constitutes the fourth and final traditional cornerstone of administrative law. Rule making guides the subsequent application of policy, and, it is argued, clear rules promote fairness. Rule making is also a forceful, efficient, yet democratic way for agencies to implement their mandates. Prior to the advent of rule making, agencies resorted to policy interpretation on a case-by-case, ad hoc basis. Rule making is a more rational means of policy making than adjudication, because adjudication is reactive and potentially disjointed. Rule making is more comprehensive, facilitating planning and coordination.

Contemporary pressing demands call attention to new cornerstones of administrative law. These are public participation in the administrative process, administrative process in informal and discretionary governmental activity, and the evolving definition of the mission of administrative agencies and development of effective oversight of their activities.[5]

The courts have held that *public participation* is pertinent to sound and equitable decision making in administrative processes. Until the mid-1960s, the prevailing perspective was that the agency was representative of the public interest. The courts insisted upon citizen rights to participate in the administrative process; Congress and the agencies soon recognized the validity of public participation as well.

The *administrative process in formal and discretionary governmental activity* is a second contemporary cornerstone. The development of procedural law to cover persons in public institutions, aliens, and the governance of educational institutions emphasizes the broadening development for protecting the rights of citizens in previously neglected areas. Aspects of administration once thought purely discretionary are subject to regulation as well.

A third, and final, contemporary cornerstone of administrative law is the *continuing definition of the mission of administrative agencies and development of effective oversight of their activities.* Each new administration advocates regulatory reform, but each administration fails to redefine the mission with sweeping regulatory reform. Congress may strengthen its oversight functions by demanding better analyses of the potential effects of proposed legislation, stronger program evaluation requirements in legislation, greater oversight of program design and development of regulations, and more use of program evaluation information. The final cornerstone, then, is the continuing development and fulfillment of mission and likewise improvement in oversight.

What Is Administrative Law?

There is no commonly agreed upon subject matter of administrative law. There are, however, certain parameters wherein the application of administrative law is appropriate.

Bernard Schwartz argues that administrative law does not relate to public administration in the same manner that commercial law relates to commerce and land law relates to land. Rather, the definition of administrative law centers around powers and remedies to answer the following questions: (1) What powers may be vested in administrative agencies? (2) What are the limits of those powers? (3) What are the ways in which agencies are kept within these limits?[6]

All law may be generally categorized as either procedural or substantive. For example, the Environmental Protection Agency establishes New Source Performance Standards that prohibit emissions from industrial, stoker-fired boilers in excess of 0.10 pound of fly ash per million BTU of heat input. The Administrative Procedure Act specifies that such a rule be published in the *Federal Register* so that interested persons may comment before the ruling becomes final. The requirement for publishing the rule in the *Federal Register* is procedural; the rule for limiting emissions from stoker-fired boilers is substantive.[7]

Administrative law originates primarily from interpretations of legal statements that describe procedures agencies follow. Such judicial interpretations emanate primarily but not exclusively from due process clauses as detailed in constitutions, from applicable administrative procedure statutes, and sometimes from clauses within statutes establishing an agency and also prescribing a procedure to follow.

Administrative law is not regulatory law. The differences between regulatory and administrative law will be discussed later in the chapter. Numerous government agencies and departments, cooperating with legislatures, create regulatory laws that affect even the most trivial of activities. Several of the more recognizable regulatory agencies are the Federal Communications Commission (FCC), which regulates broadcasting and interstate telephone rates; the Occupational Safety and Health Administration (OSHA), which regulates the safety of the workplace; and the Food and Drug Administration (FDA), which tests drugs for marketing and monitors the contents of the food we eat. The laws, consent decrees, rules, and regulations made and enforced by these agencies are not administrative law. Instead, "regulatory law governs the citizenry; administrative law governs the government. We might say that administrative law governs the bureaucracy as other constitutional provisions govern the judicial, legislative, and presidential powers in government."[8] Administrative law applies legal principles originating from statutes, common law, constitutions, and regulatory laws to the government agencies affected.

In attempting to set up standards for administrative due process, the courts, basing their findings on the federal government's Administrative Procedure Act and similar state acts and on their new interpretations of the Constitution, have worked out a fairly strict set of rules that administrators must follow. These rules have developed to meet four basic due process requirements:

1. Adequate notice
2. Disclosure of reasons
3. The right to a hearing
4. The right to further appeal

Administrative Law Judges and Federal Regulations

The Administrative Procedure Act of 1946 ruled out any evidence that would be "irrelevant, immaterial or unduly repetitious," but did not go so far as to outlaw hearsay evidence as such. In 1971, the Supreme Court held that uncorroborated hearsay evidence can constitute "substantial evidence," sufficient to support an administrative ruling.[9] This did not mean that all such evidence was to be indiscriminately accepted. It would have to be relevant and reliable and support the point for which it was being used. Material "without a basis in evidence having rationality and probative force" would not meet the Court's standard.

Such a ruling does not close the door on the issue but only opens it wider. Hotly contested disputes can erupt at any time on whether a particular piece of hearsay evidence meets the criteria for relevance and probative value. Many, meanwhile, still question whether any hearsay evidence should be allowed to influence administrative action. The consequences of administrative decision making can frequently exceed those of a court trial, therefore it is only right and proper, so the argument goes, that those who would have to bear these consequences should benefit from the safeguards enjoyed by those subject to a court trial. Others contend, however, that there is nothing inherently evil about hearsay evidence. Such evidence is admissible in even criminal trials in most countries in the world, including most democratic countries. To bar it from the hearing room, they contend, would only hinder administrative tribunals from making informed and judicious decisions.

The dilemma of hearsay evidence is not the only controversy confronting administrative law judges. The prospect that the administrative law judges prosecute and adjudicate cases brought before him or her is a very serious concern. When an agency discharges or demotes an employee or deprives an individual or a group of some benefit or right, the agency first brings the charges and then, during the hearing, sits in judgment on these charges. In effect, it seems to be sitting in judgment on itself. To many lawyers, this is inherently unfair and contrary to both the spirit and intent of due process. They claim the affected party should possess the right to have the charges decided by a completely external body.

While most administrative agencies adjudicate their own charges and complaints, they usually use special employees to do so. These officials are customarily called hearing examiners in most local and some state bureaucracies, but in a few states as well as at the federal level they bear the more prestigious title of administrative law judges. Formerly referred to as "Washington's hybrids," "the hidden judiciary," "trial examiner," or a "hearing officer," they adjudicate cases for federal agencies.[10]

The administrative law judge exercises his or her prerogatives when a corporation or a private citizen disputes the decision of a federal department or agency. For example, if your grandfather is denied a disability pension from the Social Security Administration or if a state university is charged with unfair labor practices by the faculty union, the administrative law judge decides the case. Until 1978, the 1,100 administrative law judges were called "hearing officers." They, according to the United States Supreme Court, are "functionally comparable" to federal court judges. The Office of Personnel Management certifies the administrative law judge and maintains a central registry from which agencies select judges. Administrative law judges (ALJs) then interpret federal regulations enforced by a particular department or agency to which they are assigned.

Although federal ALJs are employees of the agency whose cases they adjudicate, their qualifications and civil service status have given them virtual immunity from normal agency pressures. They frequently counteract and contradict the policies of their agencies. When the Social Security Administration attempted to use the Reagan administration's stricter guidelines to pare nearly a quarter million people from the rolls of its recipients, it found itself on a collision course with its ALJs. The ALJs, using the more liberal standards of the Supreme Court, reinstated approximately three-fifths of those who appealed their loss of benefits. Their actions infuriated the heads of Social Security, who overruled many of the reinstatements. This, in turn, riled the ALJs, who felt they had acted as they should, as independent judicial officers and not as "mere bureaucrats."

Judicial review of agency action provides controls over administrative behavior. For the person who is harmed by a particular agency decision, judicial review operates to provide relief. Over a period of years, judicial review has evolved into a complex system of statutory, constitutional, and judicial doctrines. These doctrines define the proper boundaries of the oversight system. The trend of judicial decisions and the APA is to make judicial review more widely and easily available.[11]

Despite the independence and integrity that ALJs have usually shown, some observers continue to express doubts as to whether an agency employee should preside over a case in which the agency itself is a party of interest. Suggestions have been made to divorce ALJs completely from any particular agency, setting up, in effect, a new administrative unit in the federal bureaucracy that would assign them to different agencies as cases arose. This would give them more independence, but would reduce their expertise in the matters under dispute, for they would no longer be specialized in the work of one agency.

Critical examination of the formal agency adjudicative process and the role of the ALJ reveals two trends. First, there is growing dissatisfaction with formal trial procedures for resolving licensing, merger, and related economic regulation policy issues. Second, the number of benefits and enforcement cases has increased dramatically. Enforcement is another growth area. ALJs discipline license holders, revoke licenses, issue cease-and-desist orders, and impose civil money penalties.

ALJs deal with license and route certification of transportation by air, rail, motor vehicle, or ship; regulate radio and television broadcasting; establish rates for gas, electrical, communication, and transportation services; monitor compliance with federal standards relating to interstate trade, labor-management relations, advertising, communications, consumer products, food and drugs, corporate mergers, and antitrust; regulate health and safety in mining, transportation, and industry; regulate trading in securities, commodities, and futures; and adjudicate claims relating to Social Security benefits, workers' compensation, international trade, and mining. The brief history of ALJs reflects tension between the need for fact-finder independence and the need for policy and management control.

Internal and External Administrative Controls

In the fifty-first of their famous *Federalist Papers,* James Madison and Alexander Hamilton pointed out,

> If men were angels, no government would be necessary. If angels were to govern men, neither external nor internal controls on government would be necessary. In framing a government which is to be administered by men over men, the great difficulty lies in this: you must first enable the government to control the governed; and in the next place oblige it to control itself. A dependence on the people is, no doubt, the primary control of the government; but experience has taught mankind the necessity of auxiliary precaution.[12]

As the writers of *The Federalist Papers* perceptively noted, there are two aspects of administrative control, internal and external.

Internal control is the control that agencies exercise over their own constituent elements, be they subunits or individuals. Staff units and their personnel frequently perform a controlling function even when they have no authority or mandate to do so. This is what frequently makes them suspect to line employees. Staff services provide internal control, even when they are not expressly designed to do so. Many staff services are, however, expressly designed with a control function in mind.

Internal control mechanisms include the *personnel department.* If it enjoys appropriate authority, the personnel department influences how line departments and line officials confront personnel problems. The *budget office* of any agency or any government obviously exercises a high degree of control, for it may decide who gets what amount of money for what purpose. Another staff department that exercises financial control is the *purchasing office*. Perhaps the most important financial control unit is the *auditing branch*. *Field inspections* support internal controls.

External control over administration is exercised primarily by the *legislative branch of government*. Legislatures *control expenditures* and *confirm appointments*. The best-known power legislative bodies exercise over administrative ones is the *power to investigate and expose*. The authority of the "independent" prosecutor in the Watergate and Monica Lewinsky controversies originated with legislative prerogatives to investigate the professional—and personal—activities of the president. The General Accountability Office is the investigative arm of Congress and is charged with examining all matters relating to the receipt and disbursement of public funds.

The Whistle-Blower as Tell-All

A form of government employee control at times controversial, yet often effective, is that of *whistle-blower*. The term *whistle-blower* was originated by Ralph Nader to categorize those public employees who, in effect, blow the whistle on acts by their own agencies when they deem such acts to be improper.[13] Some of the more famous whistle-blowers during the early 1970s were Gordon Rule, the Navy's director of procurement, who challenged extravagant cost overruns and claims for extra compensation by Navy suppliers; A. Ernest Fitzgerald, the Pentagon cost analyst who called attention to similar cost overruns in conjunction with the Air Force's C-5A transport jet; Frank Serpico, the New York City police officer whose reports on corruption in his department touched off a wide-ranging investigation that culminated in numerous indictments and shake-ups in the city's constabulary; and Linda Tripp, a secretary in the Clinton White House, who secretly recorded telephone conversations with Monica Lewinsky, the intern with whom President Clinton had "inappropriate intimate contact."

Many factors account for the growing prominence of whistle-blowers as agents of administrative control. One of them is the development of *administrative law* and the safeguards it extends to public employees. When the Nixon administration attempted to discharge Fitzgerald, for example, by eliminating his job, he fought back through the courts and won.[14] A midwestern high school teacher fired after he sent a letter to a local newspaper criticizing his school board won similar reinstatement. In general, the courts have become increasingly protective of whistle-blowing employees.

A second factor that has encouraged whistle-blowing has been the development of the *news media*. In this connection, the press has long played an active and aggressive role in controlling administrative actions. "I fear three newspapers more than I fear three thousand bayonets," Napoleon once remarked, while an English contemporary, philosopher Jeremy Bentham, observed that "Without publicity, all checks are inefficient; in comparison to publicity, all checks are of small account."[15]

The development of broadcast journalism, particularly television news, and the growth of public awareness and interest in government have made the news media a form of control that rivals, if it does not exceed, that exerted by legislative bodies.

Ethics: Public Administration's Challenge of the Twenty-First Century

Honesty, fairness, and productivity are characteristics of American patriotism and must be practiced consistently by every government employee. Even from the point of view of effectiveness, it is smart for public administrators to be moral in carrying out government functions. The credibility of government is at stake. Laws, rules, and regulations of government should be grounded in ethics, integrity, and organization commitments.

Government employee performance and policy leadership should reflect emphasis on the following themes:

- Make ethics a part of employee orientation and training programs.
- Include ethics in the performance evaluations and regular feedback provided to employees.

- Publicize ethical dilemmas and the organization's perception of them.
- Review management practices in different parts of the organization to help identify existing or potential ethics problems.
- Develop a code of ethics.
- The actions of top government officials must be consistent with their expectations for employee conduct. Leadership by example is an effective tool to establish an ethical perspective among members of the federal, state, or local government organization.

Source: Stephan J. Bonczek, "Ethics: Challenge of the 1990s: A Local Government Perspective," *Public Management* 72, no. 8 (July 1990): 17–19.

This is particularly true in the United States, which does not have a government-owned television and radio network and has a long muckraking tradition. The media are not only important for what they do on their own but for the help they provide other forms of control. The media have encouraged and strengthened whistle-blowing by providing considerable publicity to the whistle-blowers. The press also has stimulated legislative control by providing headlines and coverage for legislative exposés. Furthermore, many newspapers and radio and TV stations act as ombudspersons, soliciting citizen complaints against the bureaucracy and then checking them out.

A third instrument of control over an administrative agency is its *clientele.* For reasons that will be more fully discussed later in the chapter, administrators, particularly in the United States, need considerable cooperation from their clientele, and the clientele often seize upon this to exercise some countervailing influence over administrators. Sometimes this takes dramatic and violent forms, such as the client takeovers of welfare offices, the student rebellions of the 1960s, and the prison riots of the early 1970s. More often, however, clients exercise control by refusing to comply with policies they do not like.

Finally, a form of control that often receives little attention but that plays an important role in constraining many administrative agencies is the control exercised by *competing agencies.* Agencies are frequently locked in combat over jurisdiction, funding, and so on. In their continual jousting for power and position, agencies tend to control each other. James Madison saw this as one of the most effective forms of control. In a well-known passage in *The Federalist* he noted, "Ambition must be made to counteract ambition . . . the constant aim is to divide and arrange the several offices in such a manner that each may be a check on the other—that the private interest of every individual may be a sentinel over the public rights."[16]

Law and Control: How Much Is Enough?

Democratic government rests on such principles as accountability and responsibility. We have seen that the realization of these principles requires a comprehensive system of administrative control. The public has a right to demand and administrators have a need to accept a widespread network of restraints and restrictions on administrative activity. *Democratic government is controlled government.*

Carried too far, however, administrative control can render government ineffectual and even inert, leaving the way clear for less savory and less responsible forces to operate. As we saw in our examination of administrative law, the judicialization of the administrative process has proved a bonanza to various business interests that use the safeguards imposed on administrative agents to perpetuate or prolong questionable activities. Too much control also breeds a climate of conflict and distrust that can result in dysfunctional behavior.

Government Regulation

Government regulations affect all Americans—through the food and beverages we consume, the medications our doctors prescribe, the way we invest our savings, how we develop private property, and the procedures by which we operate profit-making businesses. The direct costs of regulation are typically imposed on businesses and governments. These costs, however, are passed along to consumers.

Critics of regulation point out that federal agencies have not developed systems for making rational, well-informed decisions on ways to allocate human resources efficiently—to maximize health, safety, and environmental protection. Would citizens rather have local health boards not inspect restaurants, the Food and Drug Administration not regulate prescription drugs, the zoning commission not

Regulatory Agencies

Office of Information and Regulatory Affairs	Fish and Wildlife Service
Office of Management and Budget	Food and Drug Administration
Animal and Plant Health Inspection Service	Food Safety and Inspection Service
Antitrust Division	International Trade Commission
Bureau of Alcohol, Tobacco and Firearms	Mine Safety and Health Administration
Commodity Futures Trading Commission	National Highway Traffic Safety Administration
Comptroller of the Currency	National Labor Relations Board
Consumer Product Safety Commission	Nuclear Regulatory Commission
Federal Aviation Administration	Occupational Safety and Health Administration
Federal Communications Commission	Office of Thrift Supervision
Federal Election Commission	Securities and Exchange Commission
Federal Energy Regulatory Commission	Small Business Administration
Federal Maritime Commission	Surface Transportation Board
Federal Motor Carrier Safety Administration	
Federal Railroad Administration	*Source:* http://www.regulation.org.
Federal Trade Commission	*Note:* See the Appendix for Web sites of many regulatory agencies.

check the use of private property, the Securities and Exchange Commission not monitor financial investments, and government safety experts not probe the quality of our automobiles? As imperfect as they are, government regulations are here to stay.

No better illustration exists of what citizens owe the country, and what the country owes them. The conflicts between public and private are never ending. Regulations typically do not require substantial burdens of taxation or government spending, but they act as hidden taxes. The indirect costs are passed along to consumers, employees, and employers. Regulatory impacts are more difficult to measure. From this perspective, regulations are politically convenient ways to implement public policies. This appeals especially in times of fiscal budget constraint.[17]

Market Failure and Regulations

Regulations take force because the market or markets fail or otherwise do not work effectively. U.S. regulations commenced with the establishment of the Interstate Commerce Commission in 1887. Information is a scarce commodity. Decision makers cannot collect all relevant information; they act in a state of partial ignorance and uncertainty. They use the best source of information available: what has just happened. Government oversight and information occur in this perspective. Public choice may be defined as "the economic study of nonmarket decision making, or simply as the application of economics to political science."[18] Public choice assumes that rational individuals pursue their own interests.

Market failure. The normal operations of the marketplace fail to protect the public from actual or potential abuses of power by business firms, leading to calls for regulation.

Transportation regulation. The Interstate Commerce Act of 1887 established the Interstate Commerce Commisson (ICC). Federal supervision focused on interstate commerce, while states supervised intrastate commerce.

Governmental oversight and information. A regulatory agency focuses its attention on a particular industry or on a narrow area of human behavior. The agency develops an "expertise" in its area of regulation. However, governmental oversight addresses the boundaries of the expertise function, asking if the function of regulation is the economic well-being of an industry.

Public choice. In the 1980s, elected officials acted not to further the overall social good, but to bolster chances of their reelection to public office. This meant that government decision makers might capitulate to interest group pressures rather than acting for the good of the entire community.

Is the United States a Regulatory State?

In 1789, Congress granted the president the prerogative to select an administrator to "estimate the duties payable on imports." Since then, Congress continues to delegate rule-making power to administrative agencies. The full scope of regulatory power, in addition to the power to formulate rules, includes the authority for interpreting laws and regulations, enforcing rules and regulations, trying cases concerning violations of those rules, holding hearings investigating and adjudicating such circumstances,

Introduction to Laws and Regulations

Laws and regulations are a major tool in protecting the environment. Congress passes laws that govern the United States. To put those laws into effect, Congress authorizes certain government agencies, including the Environmental Protection Agency (EPA), to create and enforce regulations. The following is a basic description of how laws and regulations come to be, what they are, and where to find them, with an emphasis on environmental laws and regulations.

1. **Creating a Law**

   Step 1: A member of Congress proposes a bill. A bill is a document that, if approved, will become a law.

   Step 2: If both houses of Congress approve a bill, it goes to the president, who has the option to either approve it or veto it. If approved, the new law is called an Act, and the text of the Act is known as a public statute. Some of the better-known laws related to the environment are the Clean Air Act, the Clean Water Act, and the Safe Drinking Water Act.

   Step 3: Once an Act is passed, the House of Representatives standardizes the text of the law and publishes it in the *United States Code.* The U.S. Code is the official record of federal laws.

2. **Putting the Law to Work**

   Now that the law is official, how is it put into practice? Laws often do not include all the details. The *U.S. Code* would not tell you, for example, what the speed limit is in front of your house. To make the laws work on a day-to-day level, Congress authorizes certain government agencies, including the EPA, to create regulations. Regulations set specific rules about what is legal and what isn't. For example, a regulation issued by EPA to implement the Clean Air Act might state what levels of a pollutant—such as sulfur dioxide—are considered safe. It would tell industries how much sulfur dioxide they can legally emit into the air and what the penalty will be if they emit too much. Once the regulation is in effect, EPA then works to help Americans comply with and enforce the law.

3. **Creating a Regulation**

   First, an authorized agency, such as the EPA, decides that a regulation may be needed. The agency researches it and, if necessary, proposes a regulation. The proposal is listed in the *Federal Register* so that members of the public can consider it and send their comments to the agency. The agency considers the comments, revises the regulation accordingly, and issues a final rule. At each stage in the process, the agency publishes a notice in the *Federal Register.* These notices include the original proposal, requests for public comment, notices about public meetings where the proposal will be discussed, and the text of the final regulation.

and imposing sanctions on violators. In a single agency, administrative regulatory power combines legislative, executive, and judicial powers.[19]

Administrative power expands as the power and responsibilities of government in our society expand. An industrialized, urbanized, interdependent society requires a more active role for government. The protection of individual rights, mediation of disputes, provision of benefits, and stabilization of the economy reflect accepted activities of modern U.S. government.

Federal departments and agencies such as the FDA, EPA, OSHA, and at least fifty others are called *regulatory agencies.* They are empowered to create and enforce rules—regulations—that carry the full force of law. According to the Office of the Federal Register, in 1970 the Code of Federal Regulations (CFR) contained 54,834 pages; in 1998 it contained 134,723 pages, filling 201 volumes and 19 feet of shelf space. The General Accounting Office (GAO) reported that between 1996 and 1999, a total of 15,286 new federal regulations went into effect, of which 222 were classified as "major" rules.[20]

(The *Federal Register* includes other types of notices, too.)

- *Federal Register* notices related to the environment are available on the EPA's Web site (www.epa.gov).
- A complete record of *Federal Register* notices issued by the entire federal government is available from the Government Printing Office (www.gpo.gov).

4. **Carrying Out the Law**

Among the environmental laws enacted by Congress through which EPA carries out its efforts are the following:

1938 Federal Food, Drug, and Cosmetic Act
1947 Federal Insecticide, Fungicide, and Rodenticide Act
1948 Federal Water Pollution Control Act (also known as the Clean Water Act)
1955 Clean Air Act
1965 Shoreline Erosion Protection Act
1965 Solid Waste Disposal Act
1970 National Environmental Policy Act
1970 Pollution Prevention Packaging Act
1970 Resource Recovery Act
1971 Lead-Based Paint Poisoning Prevention Act
1972 Marine Protection, Research, and Sanctuaries Act
1972 Ocean Dumping Act
1973 Endangered Species Act

1974 Safe Drinking Water Act
1974 Shoreline Erosion Control Demonstration Act
1975 Hazardous Materials Transportation Act
1976 Resource Conservation and Recovery Act
1976 Toxic Substances Control Act
1977 Surface Mining Control and Reclamation Act
1978 Uranium Mill-Tailings Radiation Control Act
1980 Asbestos School Hazard Detection and Control Act
1980 Comprehensive Environmental Response, Compensation, and Liability Act
1982 Nuclear Waste Policy Act
1984 Asbestos School Hazard Abatement Act
1986 Asbestos Hazard Emergency Response Act
1986 Emergency Planning and Community Right to Know Act
1988 Indoor Radon Abatement Act
1988 Lead Contamination Control Act
1988 Medical Waste Tracking Act
1988 Ocean Dumping Ban Act
1988 Shore Protection Act
1990 National Environmental Education Act

Source: Environmental Protection Agency, www.epa.gov. See Carol Browner, "Creating a Healthier Environment: How EPA Works for You," *EPA Journal* 21, no. 1 (Winter 1995): 33–49.

Administrative regulatory powers are vested in state and local government agencies as well. State regulatory powers and responsibilities include licensing of physicians, barbers, lawyers, architects, cosmeticians, liquor dealers, and funeral directors. States regulate commerce within their boundaries and supervise the governance of all public educational institutions. Local government agencies enforce building codes and fire, health, and safety regulations and standards. Agencies of state or local governments may also be charged with implementation of national programs via functional federalism.

The process of regulation is not widely understood. Regulation is the way in which a national priority or concern is translated into a specific rule. Regulation does not commence when a government department or agency issues a ruling. Regulation has it origins in Congress, when the national legislature passes a law establishing a regulatory agency, providing a mandate to issue rules governing a particular activity. The writing of a particular statute is usually the most important action of an extended rule-making process. The regulatory department or agency cannot cure basic defects in the enabling legislation.

First, Congress perceives a "market failure," or private sector inability to achieve a social goal. Departments or agencies promulgate regulations in response to laws passed by Congress to correct that market failure. Regulatory proceedings are not mere matters of procedure and conformance. Regulations originate from demands for clean air, safe drinking water, safe workplaces, reliable financial markets, improved medicines, and competitive industries. The regulatory process, however, is fundamentally bureaucratic—with all the powers and defects of government institutions—and at best is a blunt and imperfect mechanism for attempting to create a better society.[21]

As argued earlier in the chapter, the United States is a *regulatory state*. The vast majority of direct contacts for most citizens are likely to be with federal, state, or local administrative agencies. We are a society in which nearly every activity, whether of organizations or individuals, is included in the scope of administrative regulation and control. Overhead operations, independent regulatory commissions, cabinet departments, independent agencies, government corporations, the Executive Office of the President (EOP), and assorted other federal agencies of more and lesser consequence issue administrative regulations daily in the *Federal Register* and annually in the *Code of Federal Regulations.*

Overhead units carry out functions for the entire federal government. The General Accountability Office (GAO), Government Printing Office (GPO), Congressional Budget Office (CBO), Office of Management and Budget (OMB), General Services Administration (GSA), and Office of Personnel Management (OPM) issue regulations and administer support functions for most of the federal bureaucracy.

Since the creation of the Interstate Commerce Commission more than one hundred years ago, *independent regulatory commissions* have been prominent in the government regulation of business. Such commissions are multiheaded, bipartisan in composition, organizationally separated from other departments and agencies, and not directly in the president's chain of command. They provide nonpartisan flexibility, continuity, and expertise in the regulatory process; assign commissioners with terms longer than the president's; protect commissioners from presidential dismissal; and allow lengthy tenure for maximizing commissioner expertise and independence. These characteristics and aspirations may not be realized in each commission on every day of every year; however, these commissions possess widespread responsibilities for regulating specific industries and for protecting consumers and workers.

Examples of prominent, independent regulatory commissions are the Federal Communications Commission (FCC), Surface Transportation Board, Nuclear Regulatory Commission (NRC), Postal Rate Commission, Securities and Exchange Commission (SEC), Federal Maritime Commission (FMC), Federal Reserve System (FED), Consumer Product Safety Commission (CPSC), and Equal Employment Opportunity Commission (EEOC).

Cabinet departments enjoy regulatory power of a scope, type, and impact similar to that of independent regulatory commissions. Major distinctions between the two types of agencies include administrative form and operations within executive departments or agencies. Cabinet agencies are led by a single administrator; cabinet secretaries are directly responsible to the president for programming. For example, the Food and Drug Administration (FDA), within the Department of Health and Human Services (HHS), is responsible for ensuring the purity and safety of food, drugs, and cosmetics; the Internal Revenue Service (IRS), within the Treasury Department, implements tax laws; and the Occupational Safety and Health Administration (OSHA), within the Department of Labor, attempts to ensure that places of work are free from hazards affecting the health and safety of workers.

Independent agencies, such as the Federal Emergency Management Agency (FEMA), the National Foundation for the Arts and Humanities, and the Small Business Administration (SBA), share characteristics in common with independent regulatory commissions and cabinet departments. Independent agencies are accountable to the president for direction and control; they have a single administrative leader, and they are not positioned within a cabinet department.

Government corporations, such as Amtrak, a passenger railroad; the Federal Deposit Insurance Corporation (FDIC), an insurance company; the Tennessee Valley Authority (TVA), an electric power generating facility; and the U.S. Postal Service, issue regulations as well. Such public corporations are multiheaded (with a board of directors); however, the president may dismiss corporation board members.

Distrust and dislike of the chief executive may encourage the establishment of independent regulatory commissions. A powerful clientele group, such as the environmental lobby, may call for the promotion and protection of a particular concern or interest within a single-headed independent agency. An agency within a department may seek refuge there from hostile or corrupt influences.

The total administrative regulatory process includes ten procedures, or steps. Most regulatory activities do not touch all ten bases, either because the rule is obeyed without discussion or controversy or the agency does not actively enforce the regulation. The procedures or steps of the administrative regulatory process are summarized in Table 10.2.

TABLE 10.2

Steps of the Administrative Regulatory Process

Step 1:	Authorizing legislation
Step 2:	Agency interpretation-enforcement (rule making)
Step 3:	Complaint
Step 4:	Investigation
Step 5:	Informal proceedings
Step 6:	Prosecution
Step 7:	Formal hearing (adjudication)
Step 8:	Agency review
Step 9:	Judicial review
Step 10:	Agency enforcement

Source: Florence Heffron with Neil McFeeley, from *The Administrative Regulatory Process,* 1983. Reprinted by permission of Pearson Education, Inc.

Economic, Social, and Subsidiary Regulations

Social regulatory programs deal with health, safety, and environmental issues. Social regulatory agencies are limited to a specific policy area, but they have power to regulate across all industries. Social regulatory agencies include the Environmental Protection Agency (EPA), Drug Enforcement Administration (DEA), Food and Drug Administration (FDA), Occupational Safety and Health Administration (OSHA), National Transportation Safety Board (NTSB), and National Labor Relations Board (NLRB). The social regulatory functions are divided into (1) consumer safety and health, (2) transportation, (3) job safety and other working conditions, (4) environment, and (5) energy.

Economic regulatory agencies focus on specific industries. Economic controls include the use of price ceilings and service parameters. The Federal Communications Commission (FCC), Federal Deposit Insurance Corporation (FDIC), and Federal Trade Commission (FTC) are economic regulatory agencies. Economic regulatory tasks are divided into (1) finance and banking, (2) industry-specific regulation, and (3) general business.[22]

The costs of compliance with federal requirements have shifted over the decades. Thomas Hopkins identifies three groups of federal regulation compliance requirements:

- *Environmental and risk reduction regulations* attempt to lessen pollution and other societal risks. These include air emission and water pollution, solid waste disposal regulation, handling and labeling of hazardous materials, noise regulations, superfund compliance, and nuclear power safety.
- *Price and entry control regulations* restrict rates on business entry and include government controls on labor markets and on product prices and availability.
- *Paperwork regulations* entail tax compliance procedures. Taxpayers spend time complying with the intricacies of the tax code.[23]

Public sector expenditures are a small proportion of the total cost of regulation by society. Regulatory behaviors fall into three categories: economic, social, and subsidiary regulations.

Economic Regulations

What we will call *Regulation I,* or *economic regulation,* focuses on market aspects of industrial behavior, including rates, quality, and quantity of service, and competitive practices within a specific industry or segment of the economy. Categories of economic regulation include finance and banking, industry-specific regulation, and general business regulation.

Economic regulation is usually industry-specific and focuses on market structure and firm conduct, regulating the entry, exit, merger, and rates within markets.[24] For example, the ICC regulates railroads and trucking, and the FCC regulates communications. The ICC and FCC each concentrate on a specific industry, and each agency has no other responsibilities. Regulation I also concerns enforcement of congressionally mandated antitrust policies. The Justice Department and FTC regulate the frequency of mergers and combinations within particular industries. The goal of antitrust policies is maintaining and restoring competition within the market system. Competition and economic efficiency are objectives of Regulation I.

One of the most criticized forms of economic regulation is the effort of the FTC to demand that businesses tell consumers the truth, the whole truth, and nothing but the truth. The disclosure of full and accurate information by business, however, should prove compatible with desired outcomes of sellers and buyers in the market system.

Social Regulations

Regulation II, or *social regulation,* controls the nature and types of goods and services and production processes. Social regulations involve consumer safety and health, job safety and working conditions, environment, and energy.

Social regulation usually cuts across industries, regulating issues such as employment opportunity, environmental protection, and occupational safety.[25] Social regulation seeks control or elimination of socially harmful impacts occurring as by-products of the production process and protection of consumers and the public from unsafe or unhealthy products. If conservatives find Regulation I unpopular, they believe Regulation II an anathema. Regulation II focuses on the subtle regulation of clean air, occupational safety, poison prevention, boat safety, lead-based paint elimination, product safety, political campaigns, pesticide control, water pollution, noise control, flood disaster, energy, commodity futures trading, hazardous materials transportation, and similar potential abuses.

Regulation II covers more industries and directly affects more consumers than Regulation I. For example, OSHA's regulations govern the activities of every employer whose business affects commerce. In other words, government is involved with detailed, sometimes minute, facets of the production process.

Two concerns are raised by Regulation II. First, the apparatus of the presidency concentrates significant power and influence regulating health, safety, and environmental activities. Second, the accretion of new regulatory powers and controls could undermine citizens' faith in government, a negative reaction to the overstrengthening of government and regulatory excesses of the mid-1970s.

Social regulation may be costly because certain regulatory decisions are grounded in grossly inadequate information. Even if information is forthcoming, regulatory decisions may reflect the most extreme and unrealistic assumptions about the problem's potential social interference. There could be strong resistance to alternative and innovative problem solutions. Figures 10.1 and 10.2 summarize the increases in administrative costs and staffing related to federal regulation over the past several decades.

Subsidiary Regulations

Regulation III, or *subsidiary regulation,* entails all regulatory activities accompanying Social Security, Medicare, Medicaid, Aid to Families with Dependent Children (AFDC), food stamps, veterans' benefits programs, Internal Revenue Service regulatory concerns, and categorical grant program regulations. Clientele of subsidiary regulations include individuals and state and local governments.

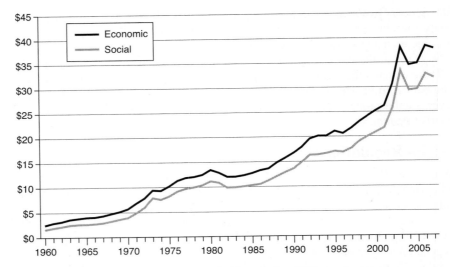

FIGURE 10.1   Administrative costs of federal regulation (billions of constant 2000 dollars)

Source: Susan Dudley and Melinda Warren, *Moderating Regulatory Growth: An Analysis of the U.S. Budget for Fiscal Years 2006 and 2007* (St. Louis, MO: Weidenbaum Center, Washington University, May 2006), 2007 Annual Report, Regulators' Budget Report 28, http://wc.wustl.edu, p. 7.

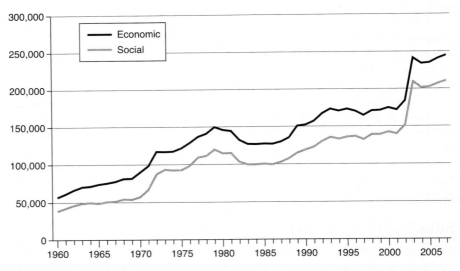

FIGURE 10.2   Staffing of federal regulatory agencies (full-time equivalent personnel)

Source: Susan Dudley and Melinda Warren, *Moderating Regulatory Growth : An Analysis of the U.S. Budget for Fiscal Years 2006 and 2007* (St. Louis, MO: Weidenbaum Center, Washington University, May 2006), 2007 Annual Report, Regulators' Budget Report 28, http://wc.wustl.edu, p. 8.

Federal Trade Commission

The Federal Trade Commission (FTC) enforces a variety of federal antitrust and consumer protection laws. The Commission has enforcement and administrative responsibilities under forty-six laws in three categories: (1) statutes relating to both competition and consumer protection, (2) statutes relating principally to the competition mission, and (3) statutes relating principally to the consumer protection mission.

The FTC seeks to ensure that the nation's markets function competively—that they are vigorous, efficient, and free of undue restrictions. The Commission also works to enhance the smooth operation of the marketplace by eliminating acts or practices that are unfair or deceptive. The FTC's efforts are directed toward stopping actions that threaten consumer opportunities to exercise informed choice. When requested, the Commission undertakes an economic analysis to support its law enforcement efforts and to contribute to the policy deliberations of Congress, the executive branch, other independent agencies, and state and local governments.

In 1914, Congress passed the Federal Trade Commission Act (FTCA)—Public Law Number 203—thereby creating the FTC. The protection of business and competition was its original intent; no direct responsibility to protect consumers was included. The FTC found that the interests of business and consumers were not mutually exclusive. Rogue businesses could steal clients from a competitor by deceiving consumers. The FTC is the primary federal agency responsible for preventing citizens from being deceived, or otherwise injured, by advertising and other marketing practices.

The phrase *unfair methods of competition* is not defined in the FTCA. The vagueness is permitted to allow the FTC to adapt to the ever-changing marketplace. The courts support this leverage. The FTC addresses vertical and horizontal restraints. Vertical restraints entail agreements between companies and suppliers that might harm competition. Horizontal restraints occur when direct competitors enter into a competition-limiting agreement. The FTC may intervene when the intent of the parties is to reduce competition—as in mergers and buyouts.

The FTC files a complaint when it has reason to believe that the law has been or is being violated, and it appears to the Commission that a proceeding is in the public interest. The complaint is not a finding or ruling that the defendants violated the law. Cases are decided by the courts.

The FTC works for the consumer to prevent fraudulent, deceptive, and unfair business practices in the marketplace—providing information to help consumers spot, stop, and avoid them. The FTC enters Internet, telemarketing, identify theft, and other fraud-related complaints into Consumer Sentinel, a secure online database available to civil and criminal law enforcement agencies throughout the United States.

Copies of complaints and Stipulated Final Judgments and Orders are available from the FTC's Web site, http:/www.ftc.gov, and also from the FTC's Consumer Response Center, Room 130, 600 Pennsylvania Avenue NW, Washington, DC 20580. Citizens may file a complaint or get free information on 150 consumer topics by calling 1-877-FTC-HELP (1-877-382-4357) toll-free, or they may use the complaint form at http://www.ftc.gov.

Sources: Jef Richards, "The Federal Trade Commission," http://www.museum.tv/archives/etv/F/htmlF/federaltrade/federaltrade.htm; Federal Trade Commission, http://www.ftc.gov/ftc/mission.htm.

The general public has mixed feelings toward Regulation III. Americans would like to believe that there is no such thing as a free lunch. Freeloaders, welfare cheats, and food stamp chiselers invoke citizen suspicion, mistrust, and hostility. Most Americans do, however, consider Social Security, unemployment compensation, and veterans' benefits as legitimate.

Unless there are clear and specific regulations for such benefit programs, the opportunities for cheating are almost limitless, making the costs and benefits of Regulation III difficult to quantify. Programs range from deciding eligibility for benefit programs to providing equal sports opportunities for women in college and equal educational opportunities for the handicapped. Costs are largely intangible; the market value is not readily apparent.

Economic, social, and subsidiary regulations are diverse, contradictory, and value laden. The growth of administrative regulatory power changes responsibilities and relationships among branches and levels of government. Regulations control or restrict one's choices and/or behavior and are blamed for all sorts of societal ills, including inflation, recession, and the demise of the family, individual initiative, and the federal system. Despite criticisms, the societal conditions demanding counterbalance to the vast power that private corporations and industry exercise over the lives, health, safety, and happiness of Americans are still evident. In addition, nationwide polls indicate that the American public supports, generally, the concept of regulations.[26]

Administrative Rules and Rule Making

Rule making and adjudication are not the same process. Rule making, in general, focuses on the future and is broad in scope. Adjudication is particular, focusing on an instance in the present or the past. Prior to the adjudication of a person's rights, the individual is entitled to a hearing under the due process clause of the Fifth Amendment for federal agencies and the Fourteenth Amendment for state agencies. The development of administrative rules follows the commercial development of the American West, tragedies of transportation accidents, development of the federal government as collector of revenues, government as benefit provider, and the populist rebuttal to the exploitation of the farmer by the rail trust.[27]

Regulatory law and administrative law, as stated earlier, work in tandem, but are not the same thing. *Congress does not like controversy.* Congress is a provincial political institution. In other words, members of Congress do not enjoy conflict-laden issues where they are likely to have constituents split over the solutions. Each member of Congress comes from a narrow, provincial political base. Each member of Congress looks out for his or her district's narrow economic interests and not those of the entire nation. Partly because Congress is composed of politicians representing 535 political jurisdictions, they pass laws that do not speak clearly. It is not difficult, therefore, to explain the presence of vague, ambiguous, and general laws that allow wide human discretion.

Administrative agencies serve to interpret the vagueness, ambiguity, and generality of these laws. For example, the FCC, by rule, restricts the number of commercial broadcasting stations a private corporation may operate. The IRS, by rule, determines which groups in society must pay or are exempted from paying taxes. The FCC creates communications law; the IRS makes tax law. Independent regulatory commissions, cabinet agencies, independent agencies, public corporations, and the EOP have similar functions.

The Administrative Procedure Act

The Administrative Procedure Act, although not a comprehensive code of administrative procedure, provides a general framework of fundamental importance. The APA, in the minds of some authorities, serves as the "Magna Carta of administrative law." Regulatory law regulates citizen behaviors; administrative law oversees the administrative discretion of bureaucrats.

Types of Agency Rules

There are four types of rules formulated and enforced by agencies:

- Legislative or substantive rules—presuming they are authorized by statute, do not exceed or contradict the statute, and are applied according to correct procedure—have the force and effect of law.
- Interpretative rules advise clientele on what the agency interprets a statute or regulation to mean. Interpretative rules examine the construction of a law that an agency administers.

- Procedural rules regulate an agency's internal practices. All agencies establish rules governing their own procedures.
- General policy statements are philosophical commentary and are not accountable to the rule-making provisions of the APA. Procedural, interpretative, and general policy statements are published in the *Federal Register.*

Source: Stanley A. Reigel and P. John Owen, *Administrative Law: The Law of Government Agencies* (Ann Arbor, MI.: Ann Arbor Science, The Butterworth Group, 1982), pp. 39–59.

Judges interpret legal statements and prescribe the procedures that agencies and their employees follow. Judicial interpretation originates from constitutions; the primary, but not exclusive, origin for interpretation comes from due process clauses. Judges also interpret administrative procedure statutes, if applicable; some clauses within a statute require agencies to follow certain procedures, including conducting a full hearing. Administrative law, meanwhile, applies legal principles originating from statutes, common law, constitutions, and regulatory law.[28] Public administrators, as implementors of regulatory law, implement rules. The terms *rule* and *regulation* are nearly synonymous. Unless rules are successfully undermined in a lawsuit as unconstitutional, rules have the force of law. What is a rule? The APA defines a rule as

> the whole or a part of an agency statement of general or particular applicability and future effect designed to implement, interpret, or prescribe law or policy or describing the organization, procedure, or practice requirements of an agency and includes the approval or prescription of the future of rates, wages, corporate or financial structures or reorganizations thereof; prices, facilities, appliances, services, or allowances thereof; or of valuations, costs, or practices bearing on any of the foregoing.[29]

The first of the two types of rule making delineated by the APA is informal or "notice and comment" rule making. The characteristics of this procedure are advance notice and public participation. Notice of proposed rule making gives the time, place, and nature of the rule-making proceeding, refers to the authority, or statute, under which the rule is proposed, and includes the terms or substance of the proposed rule or a description of the subjects and issues therein.

The second type of rule making, "on the record" formal rule making, occurs when a "trial-type" hearing precedes rules. The hearing is an adversarial process entailing production of evidence, testimony by witnesses, cross-examination, and representation by counsel. The more formal requirements apply when a statute determines that rules must be cited "on the record after opportunity for an agency hearing."

The *Federal Register* and the *Code of Federal Regulations* publish notices of proposed rule making. The Federal Register Act of 1935 established a system of federal rules publication. The Act designated the *Federal Register* as the official publication of federal rules, regulations, orders, and other documents of "general applicability and legal effect." On March 14, 1936, the *Federal Register* began publishing every day, Monday through Friday. In 1936, the *Register* published 2,620 pages of rules, orders, and other actions; in 1980, the *Register* totaled more than 87,000 pages.[30]

After each year, the issues of the *Register* are bound and indexed. The regulations published in the *Federal Register* for the preceding year are codified with regulations previously issued and still in effect. The *Code of Federal Regulations,* a collection of paperback books grouped together by agency, is divided into fifty titles, with each title more or less representing a particular agency or a broad subject area.

The *Federal Register* turned seventy years of age on March 14, 2006. The first issue was 16 pages; the seventieth anniversary edition came in at 256 pages. The first year, 1936, recorded 2,620 pages. The inaugural edition included rules for the new Social Security system. It published trade practices for buttons on clothes and ivory.[31]

In 2004, the total page count was 75,675 (see Figure 10.3). The seventieth anniversary issue included final and proposed rules from the Department of Agriculture outlawing the spread of pine shoot beetles in six states. The *Register* that day published a Department of Commerce regulation imposing a temporary ban on pollock fishing in the Gulf of Alaska.

Bruce James, head of the U.S. Government Printing Office, stated that Congress passed legislation in 1935 authorizing the *Federal Register*'s existence after

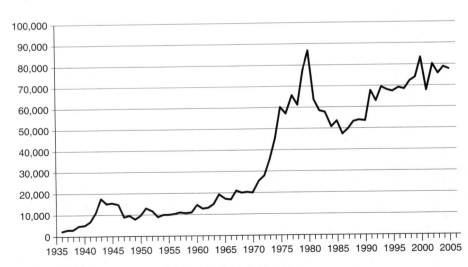

FIGURE 10.3 Growth in number of *Federal Register* pages.

Source: Susan Dudley and Melinda Warren, *Moderating Regulatory Growth: An Analysis of the U.S. Budget for Fiscal Years 2006 and 2007* (St. Louis, MO: Weidenbaum Center, Washington University, May 2006), 2007 Annual Report, Regulators' Budget Report 28, http://wc.wustl.edu, p. 9.

The *Federal Register* and The *Code of Federal Regulations*

- The *Federal Register,* published daily, Monday through Friday, provides a uniform system for making available to the public regulations and legal notices issued by federal departments and agencies. These include presidential proclamations and Executive Orders and federal agency documents having general applicability and legal effect, documents required to be published by act of Congress, and other federal agency documents of public interest.
- The *Code of Federal Regulations* is a codification of the general and permanent rules published in the *Federal Register* by the executive departments and agencies of the federal government. The *Code* is divided into fifty titles which represent broad areas subject to federal regulation. Each title is subdivided into chapters which usually bear the name of the issuing agency. Each chapter is further subdivided into parts covering specific regulatory areas.
- The *Federal Register* and the *Code of Federal Regulations* must be used together to determine the latest version of any given rule. Each volume of the *Code* contains amendments published in the *Federal Register* since the last revision of that volume of the *Code.* Source citations for the regulations are referred to by volume number and page number of the *Federal Register* and date of publication.

acknowledging that "no real place [existed] to capture the work of what the agencies were doing." The *Register* was sent gratis to 1,300 public and research libraries. The 1936 mail subscription was $10 annually. Today the *Register*'s fee is $929 annually.

The *Register* came to the Internet in the 1990s. The masses were brought into the government's rule-making processes. The free online service caused the number of paid subscribers to decrease from 35,000 to fewer than 2,000. The Internet service posts more than 100 million documents annually—at no cost. Federal departments and agencies post proposed rules and regulations for publication in the *Register.* Time for public comment is offered. Final rules that carry the force of law are published.

The 6,653-page antitrust settlement between the Justice Department and Microsoft Corporation, published on May 3, 2002, was the largest single document ever to appear in the *Federal Register.* The *Federal Register* is published every federal workday. It includes presidential proclamations, executive orders, and legal notices.

The Stages of Rule Making

Stage 1: Origin of rule making activity
Stage 2: Origin of individual rule making
Stage 3: Authorization to proceed with rule making
Stage 4: Planning the rule making
Stage 5: Developing the draft rule
Stage 6: Internal review of the draft rule
Stage 7: External review of the draft rule
Stage 8: Revision and publication of a draft rule
Stage 9: Public participation
Stage 10: Action on the draft rule
Stage 11: Post-rule-making activities

Administrative Responsibility

Administrative responsibility incorporates accountability, competence, fairness, and responsiveness.

- *Accountability* is answerability—answering, in particular, to someone or something outside the organization. Accountability also refers to direction and control, so that if things go wrong, someone is held liable.
- *Competence* implies expertise, prudence, and care for consequences rather than negligence. Recognizable objective standards guide the formulation and implementation of public policy.

- *Fairness* combines the individual concern for due process with the notion of justice and is designed to protect the individual from arbitrary and capricious decisions.
- *Responsiveness* acknowledges an organization's yielding to citizen demands for policy change and entails the initiation of proposed solutions for problems.

Source: Paul N. Tramontozzi with Kenneth W. Chilton, *U.S. Regulatory Agencies Under Reagan, 1980–1988* (St. Louis, MO: Center for the Study of Business, 1987), pp. 11–14.

What Is the Public Interest?

In casting about for answers to the question of responsibility, we are at the outset likely to come across the phrase "the public interest." Many see the entire solution to the question neatly encapsulated in this phrase, as though an administrator need only resolve to serve the public interest, and his or her problems concerning responsibility will vanish.

This solution, like so many other easy solutions to difficult problems, raises more questions than it answers. The most basic is this: *What is the public interest?* Walter Lippman once claimed that "The public interest may be what men would choose if they saw clearly, thought rationally, and acted disinterestedly and benevolently."[32] This leaves us with the task of defining "clear" vision and "rational" thought, concepts that, in practice, seem susceptible to varying interpretations. Even deciding what course of action is "benevolent" and "disinterested" may produce more controversy than it settles. "It may be somewhat difficult for some readers to accept the conclusion that there is no public interest theory worthy of the name," concluded political scientist Glendon Shubert.[33]

Another maxim that often presents itself is "following one's conscience." This, too, fails to furnish a usable guideline. The enforcers of the Inquisition who burned thousands of heretics at the stake felt they were following the most lofty appeals to conscience. The same can be said for many other appalling actions that people have perpetrated on others. As Carl Friedrich noted, "Autocratic and arbitrary abuse of power has characterized the officialdom of a government service bound only by the dictates of conscience."[34]

While Friedrich rules out the use of conscience as a means of ensuring responsibility, he does have some positive ideas to offer in its place. "We have a right to call such a policy irresponsible if it can be shown that it was adopted without proper regard to the existing sum of human knowledge concerning the technical issues involved; we have also a right to call it irresponsible if it can be shown that it was

Types of Accountability

There are four types of accountability:

- *Bureaucratic accountability* entails an organized and legitimate superior/subordinate relationship with close supervision or a surrogate system of standard operating procedures or clearly stated rules and regulations.
- *Legal accountability,* similar to bureaucratic accountability, is grounded upon relationships between a controlling party outside the agency, typically lawmakers, and members of the organization. Bureaucratic accountability portrays a hierarchical relationship, grounded upon the ability of supervisors to reward or punish subordinates, while legal accountability presents a relationship of two relatively autonomous parties, involving a formal or implied trustee agreement between the public agency and its legal monitor.

- *Professional accountability* relies upon skilled and expert employees for providing appropriate solutions. Deference to expertise within the agency is the key to professional accountability.
- *Political accountability* asks: Whom does the public administrator represent? The general public, elected officials, agency heads, agency clientele, special interest groups, and future generations constitute potential constituencies. The key relationship is between the public administrator and his or her constituents.

Source: Barbara S. Romzek and Melvin J. Dubnick, "Accountability in the Public Sector: Lessons from the Challenger Tragedy," *Public Administration Review* 47, no. 3 (May/June 1987): 227–238.

adopted without proper regard for existing preference in the community and more particularly its prevailing majority."[35]

In keeping with this admonition, Friedrich sees the solution to the question of administrative responsibility as lying in two areas: *professionalism* and *participation.* Professionals usually have been conditioned to uphold certain standards, and they usually subscribe to a code of ethics that governs the practice of their profession. As Friedrich sees it, professionalism constitutes something of an "inner check" on administrative irresponsibility. Participation, meanwhile, means that administrators must consult more interests and listen to more points of view. Allowing divergent parties to share in decision making should make that process less arbitrary and subjective and more responsive and responsible.

To Friedrich's twin safeguards of professionalism and participation can be added a third protective device: *publicity.* Directing the public spotlight onto administrative decision making should make such decision making more responsible. Secrecy has rarely led to improved administrative decisions or better administrative behavior.

Professionalism, participation, and publicity do not in themselves guarantee responsible administration. Professionals can act irresponsibly, and shared decision making can produce irresponsible decisions. Publicity can, on occasion, distort an administrator's perspective, because what is immediate "good press" is not always most beneficial to the public. These caveats notwithstanding, these three "Ps"—professionalism, participation, and publicity—provide a basis for better public management. As they become more a part of bureaucratic behavior, such behavior may move closer toward meeting the desires and demands of the American people.

Summary

- The principles of *administrative law* are grounded in constitutionalism, shared powers, popular government, individualism, and political equality.
- Independent regulatory agencies, uniform administrative procedure law, judicial review, and rule making are traditional cornerstones of administrative law. Public participation in the administrative process, the administrative process in formal and informal governmental activity, and the evolving definition of the mission of administrative agencies and development of oversight of their activities are contemporary cornerstones of U.S. administrative law.
- Honesty, fairness, and productivity are characteristics of American patriotism and must be practiced by every government employee. Even from the standpoint of effectiveness, it is smart for public administrators to be moral in carrying out government functions. The credibility of government is at stake. Laws, rules, and government regulations should be grounded in ethics, integrity, and organizational commitments.
- The United States has entered the era of the *administrative state.*
- Administrative law and regulatory law act in tandem, but they are not the same. Agencies and departments, cooperating with legislatures, create regulatory law. *Regulatory law* governs the private activities of citizens; *administrative law* governs the regulators, applying principles originating from statutes, common law, constitutions, and regulatory laws. The provisions of adequate notice, disclosure of reasons, the right to a hearing, and right to further appeal entail a set of rules that administrators must follow to meet due process requirements.
- After a century of intense litigation and adjudication, the field of administrative law is still alive with issues. Hearsay evidence and the double role of judge and prosecutor are key controversies of administrative law, affecting public administrators and clientele.
- The major aspects of the *administrative process* include delegation of power, judicial review, the investigatory power, the rule-making process, the right to be heard, adjudicatory policy making, informal activity and the exercise of discretion, remedies against improper administrative acts, and opening up the government.
- Administrative agencies adjudicate individual claims or cases. The procedures are diverse. Administrative hearings focus on disputed questions of fact.
- An administrative hearing has no jury. The administrative law judge, or hearing examiner, is likely to be concerned about overall policies. The particular merits of one party's case have less consequence.
- Agencies accomplish most work with informal procedures. They exercise discretion granted to them by statute.
- Judicial review of agency action provides controls over administrative behavior. For the person who is harmed by a particular agency decision, judicial review operates to provide relief.
- The question of administrative control has two distinct aspects—*internal* and *external* controls.
- Democratic government rests on principles such as *accountability* and *responsibility;* the realization of such principles requires a comprehensive system of administrative control. The public has a right to demand, and administrators have a need to accept, a widespread network of restraints and restrictions on administrative activity. Democratic government is *controlled* government.
- Regulations take force because the market or markets fail or otherwise do not work effectively. U.S. regulatory activities began with the establishment of the Interstate Commerce Commission in 1887. Decision

makers cannot collect all relevant information, so they use the best source of information available: what has just happened. Government oversight and information reflect this perspective.

- The full scope of *regulatory power*—in addition to the power to formulate rules—includes the authority for interpreting laws and regulations, enforcing rules and regulations, trying cases concerning violations of those rules, holding hearings for investigating and adjudicating such circumstances, and imposing sanctions on violators. Administrative regulatory power combines legislative, executive, and judicial powers.

- The United States is a *regulatory state* where nearly all activities of organizations and individuals are part of administrative regulations and controls. There are three types of regulatory behaviors: *economic, social,* and *subsidiary.*

- *Economic regulation* is the more traditional, industry-specific form of regulation. These regulators employ economic controls such as price ceilings and service parameters. These departments and agencies regulate a broad base of activities in particular industries. Examples of economic regulatory agencies are the Federal Communications Commission (FCC), the Federal Deposit Insurance Corporation (FDIC), and the Federal Trade Commission (FTC).

- *Social regulation* focuses on achieving cleaner air, equal employment opportunity, safer work environments, and consumer safety. Social regulatory departments and agencies are limited to a specific issue, but their prerogatives include regulatory powers that penetrate and spread through industry boundaries. Illustrations are the Environmental Protection Agency (EPA), the Drug Enforcement Agency (DEA), and National Labor Relations Board (NLRB).

- *Subsidiary regulation* includes regulatory activities related to Social Security, Medicare, Medicaid, food stamps, veterans' benefits, and other entitlement programs.

- The *Federal Register* provides a uniform system for making available to the public regulations and legal notices issued by federal departments and agencies. The *Register* includes presidential proclamations and Executive Orders and federal agency documents having general applicability and legal effect.

- The *Code of Federal Regulations* is a codification of the general and permanent rules published in the *Federal Register* by the executive departments and agencies of the federal government. The *Federal Register* and The *Code of Federal Regulations* are used in tandem to determine the latest version of any rule or regulation.

- Administrative power expands as the power and responsibilities of government expand. An industrialized, urbanized, interdependent society requires a more active role for government.

- Rule making and adjudication are not the same. *Rule making* is general and focuses on the future. *Adjudication* is particular, focusing on the present or the past. Administrative agencies interpret vagueness, ambiguity, and generality of laws; public administrators, as implementors of regulatory law, interpret rules. The terms *rules* and *regulations* are synonymous. There are four types of agency rules: legislative, or substantive, rules; interpretative rules; procedural rules; and general policy statements.

- *Administrative responsibility* entails the ideas of *accountability, competence, fairness,* and *responsiveness.* Executive control, pluralism, professionalism, and representative bureaucracy are especially important for achieving administrative responsibility. There are four types of accountability: bureaucratic, legal, professional, and political.

- *Professionalism, participation,* and *publicity* contribute significantly to administrative responsibility and provide a sound basis for better public management.

VIDEOS AND FILMS

Public Administration in Action

History

The Regulators: Our Invisible Government [1983]

Examines how federal regulators implement and enforce the laws enacted by Congress. Probes Environmental Protection Agency's guidelines to regulate pollution. A Reagan administration era perspective. [49 min]

Regulation

The Nature of Money [2000]

Presents a brief overview of the history of money and explains how the Federal Reserve creates and measures the money supply. Discusses the structure and functions of the Federal Reserve. Distributed by Insight Media. [30 min]

Regulation

Monetary Policy [2000]

Explains the basic principles of macroeconomics and discusses dual problems of unemployment and inflation—and their effects on the economy and individual well-being. Distributed by Insight Media. [30 min]

Regulation

Transportation—The Sunset Limited: Death on the Bayou [1998]

A Discovery Channel production. Market failures occur in water and passenger rail transportation modes. Six barges crash into century-old railroad bridge. Safety regulations fail. NTSB investigates as 47 people die in the carnage. [52 min]

Ethics

Winning, Greed, and Self-Interest [1994]

A production of Public Affairs Television. Princeton, NJ: Films for the Humanities and Sciences. Series title: The Moyers Collection. Discusses lack of ethical standards in our society and the philosophy of winning, greed, and self-interest. [30 min]

Ethics

All the President's Men [1976]

Role of the press and *Washington Post* reporters Bob Woodward and Carl Bernstein in the Watergate scandal. The accuracy of this film approaches that of a documentary. This movie is the way most Americans remember the Watergate crisis. [135 min]

Ethics

Quiz Show [1994]

Reveals moral weaknesses in the American social fabric, exposing a willingness to compromise intellectual integrity and public trust for the sake of celebrity and material gain. Produced and directed by Robert Redford. [133 min]

Case Study

Whistle-Blowing at the FBI

Administrative laws outline the prospects and limits of whistle-blowers. The FBI and CIA reflect developments of policy and system politics, but impact partisan politics. Whistle-blowers emerge as agents of administrative control. Breaking through the FBI culture to fight terrorism makes the job of FBI whistle-blower ever more challenging. The case study that follows illustrates that point.

If she sees something she believes is wrong, she is not going to sweep it under the carpet.

—*A former coworker of FBI Agent Coleen Rowley,*
May 25, 2002

As whistle-blower, FBI Agent Coleen Rowley insisted that the public interest was more important than that of her employer. She blew the whistle on the nation's premier law enforcement agency. She ignited a storm of criticism of the bureau's management practices.

The FBI, she said, discouraged innovation. Investigators felt overcome with paperwork. Agents who sought to cut through many layers of risk-adverse superiors in Washington were punished. Rowley operated from a field office. Seven to nine levels of officials at headquarters often second-guess the decisions of agents in the field.[1] Rowley has been praised for her courage in criticizing senior FBI officials over the September 11 massacre.

Rowley, General Counsel with the FBI's Minneapolis field office, wrote to Director Robert Mueller on May 21, 2002: "I have deep concerns that a delicate and subtle shading/skewing of facts by you and others at the highest levels of FBI management has occurred and is occurring. I feel certain facts have been omitted, downplayed, glossed over and/or mischaracterized in an effort to avoid or minimize personal and/or institutional embarrassment on the part of the FBI and/or perhaps even for improper political reasons."[2]

What Is a Whistle-Blower?

A whistle-blower is a person who takes a concern about fraud or mistreatment outside of the organization in which the abuse or suspected abuse is occurring and with which the whistle-blower is affiliated. Not all whistle-blowing is adversarial to the affected organization. That the organization cannot correct its own problems, nevertheless, is an embarrassment.

Rowley emerged as "an American hero," wrote John Carlson, newspaper columnist for *The Des Moines Register.* The mother of four, Rowley exuded the values of integrity, honesty, courage, and patriotism. As a kid, the bespectacled Rowley was "gutsy," observed Carlson. As a forty-seven-year-old whistle-blower, armed with a law degree, she carried out a "full-bore butt-kicking of her (FBI) bosses."[3] Rowley was the Iowa kid who knew—in the fifth grade—that she wanted to be an FBI agent. Well-schooled to be a whistle-blower, Rowley was said to be straightforward, intelligent, thoughtful, outspoken, but not out of control. FBI coworkers back home described the career official as a model agent.

FBI headquarters officials refused permission for Minneapolis agents to obtain warrants to search suspected terrorist Zacarias Moussaoui's computer and other properties. Rowley reported that her superiors at headquarters prevented field agents from pursuing their suspicions of Moussaoui, the so-called twentieth highjacker, and part of a larger conspiracy involving flight training and airplanes. After September 11, they found that Moussaoui had ties to several hijackers. The Minneapolis FBI agent was determined to bring the truth to power—focusing on the FBI's "willful refusal to investigate and a deliberate suppression of information."[4]

Rowley hand-delivered her thirteen-page memo to FBI Director Mueller and the staff of the U.S. Senate Intelligence Committee. Democrat Diane Feinstein of California and Republican Richard Shelby of Alabama, ranking members on the committee, also received copies. Whistle-blower Rowley provided specifics of persons within the FBI hierarchy who blocked the investigation of Zacarias Moussaoui—charged as a co-conspirator in the September 11, 2001, suicide hijackings that killed more than three thousand persons.

The FBI claims that Moussaoui, a thirty-four-year-old French-Morrocan, Islamic fundamentalist, paid $8,000 cash for training to fly a Boeing 747 at a Minneapolis-area flight school. However, Moussaoui was only interested in steering a jumbo jet in flight—not in learning how to take off or land. French intelligence sources reported that Osama bin Laden's Al Qaeda organization had recruited Moussaoui.[5]

According to Rowley, Minneapolis FBI agents became so frustrated by inaction at FBI headquarters that they went directly to the CIA for assistance in establishing a case against Moussaoui. They did this without the knowledge of their FBI superiors. Officials at FBI headquarters reprimanded them for breach of Bureau protocol. Rowley, knowing the consequences of speaking truth to power, sought federal whistle-blower protection. FBI Director Mueller asserted that Rowley faced no retaliation or intimidation for writing her letter or talking to the Committee. Rowley's right to criticize the structure, culture, and mission of the FBI is protected by amendments of the Whistle-blower Protection Act (WPA).

Bill Miller and Dan Eggen, reporters for the *Washington Post,* wrote that Rowley's FBI whistle-blower statement was "a scathing indictment of FBI culture and its impact on the way FBI headquarters handled the case of Zacarias Moussaoui."[6] Daniel Franklin, writing in the *American Prospect,* stated: "As in most bureaucracies, the bureau was more concerned with upholding the chain of command than with increasing its effectiveness."[7]

To his credit, Mueller welcomed Rowley's criticisms of FBI policies and personnel. The FBI's insular culture was called into question.[8]

In July 2001, Kenneth Williams wrote a memo from the FBI's Phoenix office to two task forces at FBI headquarters, including the Radical Fundamentalist Unit task force and the Osama bin Laden task force. The memo addressed the frequency of Middle Eastern men enrolled in flying lessons. On August 15, 2001, Moussaoui came to the attention of FBI agents in Minneapolis. The agents received information about Moussaoui's flight training. The FBI, working with the U.S. Immigration and Naturalization Service, detained Moussaoui on visa violations.[9]

On December 11, 2001, a federal grand jury in Alexandria, Virginia, indicted Moussaoui on six counts of conspiracy—accusing him of plotting with bin Laden and members of Al Qaeda to murder thousands of people at the World Trade Center and the Pentagon. Bin Laden and the nineteen dead hijackers were named as unindicted co-conspirators.[10]

Terrorism and the FBI Culture

Mueller used the opportunity provided by Rowley not to be defensive about the FBI and its culture lag over the events of September 11. The director led the greatest reorganization of the FBI in its history. He appeared to be employing Rowley's thirteen-page memo as his reorganizing principle. Mueller directed that the FBI be decentralized. More control was given to agents in the field. The first priority of the FBI would be the prevention of terrorism.

The FBI suffered a terrorism "rethink." The whistle-blower counterterrorism initiative produced a plan whereby 3,718 agents and other law enforcement officials focus on counterterrorism—up from 2,178. A shift of 480 FBI agents were reassigned from fighting drugs, white-collar crime, and violent crime.[11]

Rowley charged that the FBI operates in "a climate of fear which has chilled aggressive . . . law enforcement action."[12] In a police agency where hierarchy and "do it my way or hit the highway" are readily acceptable modes of operation, protecting whistle-blowers' "freedom to warn" tolerates drawbacks. Increasing and centralizing the power of FBI headquarters could reinforce the paralyzing culture of fear. The vulnerabilities of terror might be exacerbated by promoting excessive government secrecy.

The reorganization chart does not address the cultural problems facing the FBI. When Rowley hand-delivered her memo to Mueller, she circumvented eight different layers of leadership. FBI headquarters personnel chastised her for not following bureau protocol. They made direct contact with the CIA's Counterterrorism Center.

The FBI must change not only what it does, but how it thinks, how it perceives itself, and the people and agencies with whom it works. Not everyone agrees on what the "cultural problems" of the Bureau are. "If the Bureau's recent history proves anything," Franklin writes, "it's that it can't fix a problem that its own agents don't perceive."[13]

The FBI is America's national police force. Its jurisdictions are controlled by law. The personnel department, budget office, auditing branch, and field inspections are internal FBI controls. The fallout from September 11 brought the FBI, as a bureaucracy, challenges of great magnitude. New funding included a $1.5 billion budget increase. The investigative latitude for agents was made more liberal. Agents could open preliminary investigations and maintain them for a year without approval from headquarters.

FBI mistakes reflect an inability to digest an overabundance of resources—not a lack of them. Between 1997 and 2002, the Bureau increased its payroll by 1,000 employees. Virtually all new hires were positioned at headquarters. Almost none were stationed in field offices. Rowley bypassed eight layers of administrative leaders to get her message to Mueller.

Police bureaus are quasimilitary operations. Obeying the chain of command is priority. Administrative law—by promoting whistle-blowers—seeks to reduce arbitrariness and unfairness in government. Rowley, from her perspective, tried to change internal FBI practices.

External controls are found in the legislative branch of government. Legislators control expenditures and confirm appointments. They have the power to investigate and expose. Congress and its committees write laws for agents to obey and implement. Through the General Accountability Office (GAO), representatives seek audits of departments, agencies, and bureaus. Rowley carried her message to the very top of her government bureaucracy—the FBI. But she also contacted prominent members of the U.S. Senate Judiciary Committee.

Administrative laws outline the prospects and limits of whistle-blowers. The FBI reflects policy and system politics—but impacts partisan politics. The consensus of partisan politics is that the activities of the FBI and CIA should enhance, even promote, electoral politics or democracy. The most effective way to fight terrorism is through popular—and elected—governments. Administration of the FBI and CIA depends on shared powers—among democratic institutions and with citizens.

The FBI and CIA are competing agencies. The FBI focuses on internal terrorism. The CIA pursues terror on an international scale. In the culture of the Cold War, these distinctions may have been easier to define. In post–September 11 politics, FBI-CIA activities are often blurred. Clientele responding to the agenda raised by this whistle-blower included the media, FBI employees, the security establishment, Congress, the executive, and the American people.

Government employees must be able to speak truth to power. This employee's predicament reminds citizens of government bureaucracy's need to protect a whistle-blower's "freedom to warn." Civil liberties may be in the balance. A culture of fear and excessive government secrecy promote "risk-adverse careerism" at security agencies.[14]

Mrs. Rowley is a portrait in American individualism. She made a difference.

Questions and Instructions

1. The FBI and the intelligence community are cited for not being prepared for major terrorist attacks. How do the developments and facts from this case study enable the FBI, as a public organization, to be better prepared in the future? Explain and illustrate.

2. Coleen Rowley charged that the FBI operated in "a climate of fear" which "chilled" agressive law enforcement. Explain.

3. How does increasing and centralizing the power of institutions (like the FBI) reinforce the paralyzing culture of fear which, in turn, exacerbates the vulnerabilities to terror? Explain and illustrate.

4. How are the Bureau's "cultural problems" of serious consequence to FBI operations? Explain and illustrate.

5. Why did Coleen Rowley seek whistle-blower status at the FBI? In what ways did Rowley breach Bureau protocols? Explain and illustrate.

6. FBI Director Robert Mueller welcomed criticism from Coleen Rowley—asserting that she would face no retaliation or intimidation for writing her memo or talking to the joint Senate-House Intelligence Committee. Why were these decisions in the best interests of the country and the FBI? Explain and illustrate.

7. Prior to September 11, 2001, why were security agencies—including the FBI—preoccupied "above all" with questions of administrative procedure? Explain and illustrate.

8. What actions, if any, did Coleen Rowley take to merit being called "an American hero"? What values did she espouse in this case study? Explain and illustrate.

9. New investigatory powers provided to FBI agents allow them to visit Internet sites, libraries, churches, and political organizations as they seek to find and prosecute terrorists. Do these FBI prerogatives infringe on citizens' civil rights and liberties? Explain and illustrate.

10. How are internal and external administrative controls manifest in this case study? Explain and illustrate.

Insights-Issues/Whistle-Blowing at the FBI

Clearly and briefly describe and illustrate the following concepts and issues. Interpret the word *role* as meaning impacts, applications, importance, effects, and/or illustrations of certain facts, concerns, or issues from the case study.

1. Role of whistle-blower Coleen Rowley (individualism) in efforts to refocus (culture) and reorganize (administrative structure) the FBI.

2. Role of the Bureau's "cultural problems" in refocus (priorities) and reorganization (administrative procedures and structures).
3. Role of partisan, policy, and systems politics in the terror debate.
4. Role of the expansion of FBI powers, the culture of fear, and the guarantee of political freedoms.
5. Role of internal and external administrative controls in—and of—the FBI.

Notes

1. David Johnston and Neil A. Lewis, "Traces of Terror: The Congressional Hearings; Whistle-Blower Recounts Inside the FBI," *New York Times,* June 7, 2002, p. 1A; Dan Eggen, "FBI Whistle-Blower Assails Bloated Bureaucracy," *Washington Post,* June 7, 2002, p. A2.
2. "Coleen Rowley's Memo to FBI Director Robert Mueller," *Time,* http://www.time.com/time/nation/printout/0,8816,249997,00.html.
3. John Carlson, "As an Iowa Kid, FBI Memo Writer Was Sharp, Gutsy, Neighbor Recalls," *Des Moines Register,* May 29, 2002, http://desmoinesregister.com/news/stories/c5917686/18308626.html.
4. Patrick Martin, "New Evidence that U.S. Government Suppressed September 11 Warnings," *Sierra Times,* May 27, 2002, http://www.sierratimes.com/cgi-bin/warroom/printpage/cgi?forum=15&topic=25.
5. Ibid.
6. Bill Miller and Dan Eggen, "FBI Culture Blamed for Missteps on Moussaoui," *Washington Post,* May 25, 2002, p. A1, http://www.washingtonpost.com/ac2/wp-dyn/ A7214-2002May24?language=printer.

7. Daniel Franklin, "Dollars Don't Do It: Throwing Money at the FBI Only Deepens the Problem," *American Prospect* 13, no. 13, http:// www.prospect.org/print-friendly/print/V13/13/franklin-d.html.
8. Richard S. Dunham, "Of Zipped Lips and Blown Tips," BusinessWeek Online, May 29, 2002, http://www.businessweek.com/print/bwdaily/dnflash/may2002/nf20020529_9307.htm.
9. Franklin, "Dollars Don't Do It."
10. Jerry Seper, "Moussaoui's Notes Say He Is a Terrorist," *Washington Times,* July 3, 2002, http://asp.washtimes.com/printarticle.asp?action=print@ArticleID=20020703-70254835.
11. "FBI Has a Terrorism Rethink," *News12.com,* May 30, 2002, http://www.news24.com/News24/World/Americas/0,1113,2-10-33_1192314,00.html.
12. Martin Edwin Andersen, "Rowley's Risk," *Washington Times,* May 30, 2002, http://www.washtimes.com/op-ed/20020530-1343644.htm.
13. Franklin, "Dollars Don't Do It."
14. Andersen, "Rowley's Risk."

Sources

David Corn, "The Loyal Opposition: Playing The 9/11 Blame Game," http://www.tompaine.com/feature.cfm/ID/5714/view/print; Edward Helmore, "Agent Blasts FBI Over September 11, 'Cover-Up,' " *Guardian Unlimited,* http://www.guardian.co.uk/september11/story/0,11209,722428,00.html; "Leadership the Issue, Not Expanded Powers, in FBI Misadventures," *Gainesville Times,* June 1, 2002, http://www.gainesvilletimes.com/news/stories/20020601/opinion/426174.html; David Risen and David Johnston, "Traces of Terror: The Intelligence Reports; Agent Complaints Lead FBI Director to Ask for Inquiry," *New York Times,* May 24, 2002, p. 1A; Laura Rosen, "Seeking a Higher Intelligence: Will Congress Push for Real Reform in the CIA and FBI?" *American Prospect,* 13, no. 12, http://www.prospect.org/print-friendly/print/V13/12/rosen-1.html; Jerry Seper, "Moussaoui's Notes Say He Is a Terrorist," *Washington Times,* http://asp.washtimes.com/printarticle.asp?action-print&ArticleID-20020703-70254835; "Sharp Note from a Whistle-Blower," *Los Angeles Times,* May 28, 2002, http://www.smh.com.au/articles/2002/05/28/1022243318693.html.

Notes

1. Jerre S. Williams, "Cornerstone of American Administrative Law," *Administrative Law Review* 28 (1976): v–xii.
2. Florence Heffron and Neil McFeeley, *The Administrative Regulatory Process* (New York: Longman, 1883), pp. 347–371.
3. Williams, "Cornerstone," pp. v–xii.
4. Kenneth F. Warren, *Administrative Law in the American System* (St. Paul, MN: West, 1982), pp. 111–122.
5. Dwight Waldo, *The Enterprise of Public Administration: A Summary View* (Novato, CA: Chandler & Sharp, 1980). See especially Chapter 6, "Bureaucracy and Democracy: Reconciling the Irreconcilable," pp. 81–98.
6. Bernard Schwartz, *Administrative Law* (Boston: Little, Brown, 1976), p. 2.
7. Stanley A. Reigel and P. John Owen, *Administrative Law: The Law of Government Agencies* (Ann Arbor, MI: Ann Arbor Science, The Butterworth Group, 1982), pp. 4–5.
8. Lief H. Carter, *Administrative Law and Politics: Cases and Comments* (Boston: Little, Brown, 1983), p. 60.
9. *Richardson v. Perales,* 402 US 389 (1971).
10. "The 'Hidden Judiciary' and What It Does," *U.S. News & World Report,* November 1, 1982.
11. "Administrative Law and Procedure—Continued," *West Legal Directory,* July 4, 2002, http://www.wld.com/conbus/weal/wadmin2.htm.
12. Alexander Hamilton, John Jay, and James Madison, *The Federalist Papers* (New York: Modern Library, n.d.), p. 337.
13. Ralph Nader, Peter Petkas, and Kate Blackwell, eds., *Whistle-Blowing* (New York: Bantam Books, 1972).
14. Ibid., pp. 39–55.
15. Quoted in George E. Berkley, *The Democratic Policeman* (Boston: Beacon Press, 1969), pp. 159–160.
16. Hamilton, Jay, and Madison, *The Federalist Papers*, p. 337.
17. "Why Regulation Matters," The Regulation Home Page, regulation.org, http://www.regulation.org/whyregs.html.
18. Daniel J. Gifford, *Administrative Law: Cases and Materials* (Cincinnati: Anderson, 1992), pp. 1–9.
19. Florence Heffron with Neil McFeeley, *The Administrative Regulatory Process* (New York: Longmans, 1983), pp. 1–23.
20. Robert Longley, About.com: US Government Info; see http://usgovinfo.about.com/library/weekly/blfedregs.htm?
21. Murray Weidenbaum, *A New Approach to Regulatory Reform* (St. Louis, MO: Center for the Study of American Business, 1998), pp. 2–3. See also Thomas D. Hopkins, *Regulatory Costs in Profile* (St. Louis, MO: Center for the Study of American Business, 1996).
22. Susan Dudley and Melinda Warren, "Regulatory Response: An Analysis of the Shifting Priorities of the U.S. Budget for Fiscal Years 2002 and 2003," Mercatus Center, Arlington, VA, and the Murray Weidenbaum Center on the Economy, Government, and Public Policy, St. Louis, MO, 2002, www.mercatus.org & www.wc.wust.edu.
23. Hopkins, *Regulatory Costs,* pp. 3–12; Weidenbaum, *A New Approach*, pp. 2–8.
24. Douglas R. Wholey and Susan M. Sanchez, "The Effects of Regulatory Tools on Organizational Populations," *Academy of Management Review* 16, no. 4 (October 1991): 743–767.
25. Wholey and Sanchez, "The Effects of Regulatory Tools," pp. 743–767.
26. Heffron with McFeeley, *The Administrative Regulatory Process,* pp. 347–371.
27. James T. O'Reilly, *Administrative Rule Making: Structuring, Opposing, and Defending Federal Agency Regulations* (New York: McGraw-Hill), pp. 4–6.
28. Lief H. Carter, *Administrative Law and Politics: Cases and Comments* (Boston: Little, Brown, 1983), pp. 14–39.

29. Administrative Procedure Act, P.L. 404, 60 Stat. 237(1946), 5 U.S.C.A. 551.

30. William F. West, *Administrative Rule-Making: Politics and Processes* (Westport, CT: Greenwood Press, 1985), p. 17.

31. Darlene Superville, "*Federal Register* Celebrates 70th Birthday," *Boston Globe*, March 14, 2006.

32. Walter Lippman, *The Public Philosophy* (Boston: Little, Brown, 1955), p. 42.

33. Glendon A. Shubert, Jr., *The Public Interest* (New York: Free Press, 1952), p. 223.

34. Carl Friedrich, "Public Policy and the Nature of Administrative Responsibility" in *The Politics of the Federal Bureaucracy,* ed. Alan A. Altshuler (New York: Dodd, Mead, 1968), p. 417.

35. Ibid.

Web Sites

Students will find these government and other Web links useful for studying for academic assignments, conducting research, and seeking internships and post-college jobs.

American Political Science Association
http://www.apsanet.org

American Society for Public Administration
http://www.aspanet.org

Animal and Plant Health Inspection Service
http://www.aphis.usda.gov/

Budgeting, Spending, Taxing
http://www.concordcoalition.org

Bureau of Alcohol, Tobacco, and Firearms
http://www.atf.treas.gov/

Chicago Tribune
http://www.chicagotribune.com

Chronicle of Higher Education
http://www.chronicle.com

Commodity Futures Trading Commission
http://www.cftc.gov/

Consumer Product Safety Commission
http://www.cpsc.gov/

Current Population Survey (union statistics database)
http://www.unionstats.com

Federal Communications Commission
http://www.fcc.gov/

Federal Aviation Administration/Regulations
http://www.faa.gov/

Federal Election Commission
http://www.fec.gov/

Federal Energy Regulatory Commission
http://www.ferc.gov/

Federal Government Employment
http://www.jobsfed.com/

Federal Maritime Commission
http://www.fmc.gov/

Federal Motor Carrier Safety Administration
http://www.fmcsa.dot.gov/

Federal Railroad Administration
http://www.fra.dot.gov/

Federal Register/Regulations
http://www.archives.gov/federal-register/

Federal Trade Commission
http://www.ftc.gov/

Federation of State PIRGs [Public Interest Research Group]
http://www.uspirg.org

Fish and Wildlife Service
http://www.fws.gov/

Food Safety and Inspection Service
http://www.fsis.usda.gov/

Food and Drug Administration
http://www.fda.gov/

Government Printing Office access CFR
http://www.gpoaccess.gov/INDEX.HTML

International City Management Association
http://icma.org

International Trade Commission
http://www.usitc.gov/

Journal of Homeland Security and Emergency Management
http://www.bepress.com/jhsem/policies.html

Labor Research Association
http://www.workinglife.org/wiki/resources

Los Angeles Times
http://www.latimes.com

Mine Safety and Health Administration
http://www.msha.gov/

National Constitution Center
http://www.constitutioncenter.org

National Highway Traffic Safety Administration
http://www.nhtsa.dot.gov/

National Labor Relations Board
http://www.nlrb.gov/

National Priorities
http://www.nationalpriorities.org

New York Review of Books
http://www.nybooks.com

New York Times
http://www.nytimes.com

New York Transit Museum
http://www.nytransitmuseum.com

Nuclear Regulatory Commission
http://www.nrc.gov/

Occupational Safety and Health Administration
http://www.osha.gov/

Office of Management and Budget
http://www.whitehouse.gov/omb/

Office of Information—Regulatory Affairs
http://www.whitehouse.gov/OMB/inforeg/

Presidential Studies Quarterly
www.polisci.tamu.edu/journals/presquarterly/

Public Performance-Rutgers University
http://www.ncpp.us/

RAND Corporation for Statistical Analysis
http://www.rand.org/

Small Business Administration
http://www.sba.gov/

Securities and Exchange Commission
http://www.sec.gov/

State Government Performance
http://www.pewcenteronthestates.org/gpp_report_card.aspx

Surface Transportation Board
http://www.stb.dot.gov/

U.S. Bureau of Labor Statistics
http://www.bls.gov/

U.S. Census Bureau
http://www.census.gov/

U.S. Department of Education
http://www.ed.gov/index.jhtml

U.S. Department of Health & Human Services
http://www.hhs.gov/

U.S. Department of Housing and Urban Development
http://www.hud.gov/

U.S. Department of Labor
http://www.dol.gov/

U.S. Federal Labor Relations Authority
http://www.flra.gov/

U.S. Government's Official Web Portal
http://www.usa.gov/

U.S. Merit Systems Protection Board
http://www.mspb.gov/sites/mspb/default.aspx/

U.S. Office of Personnel Management
http://www.opm.gov/

U.S. Supreme Court
http://supremecourtus.gov/

USA Jobs
http://www.usajobs.gov/

USA Today
http://www.usatoday.com

Washington Post
http://www.washingtonpost.com

The White House
http://www.whitehouse.gov/

Credits

Chapter 1
Page 6: Source: Michael M. Harmon and Richard T. Mayer, *Organization Theory for Public Administration* (Boston: Little, Brown, 1986). See "Defining Organization," pp. 17–21. **Page 8:** Source: Glen J. Godwin and William T. Markham, "First Encounters of the Bureaucratic Kind: Early Freshman Experiences with a Campus Bureaucracy," *Journal of Higher Education* 67, no. 6 (November–December, 1996): 660–692. **Page 20:** Source: Robert T. Golembiewski, Frank Gibson, and Geoffrey Y. Cornog, *Public Administration: Readings in Institutions, Processes, Behavior, Policy* (Chicago: Rand McNally, 1976), pp. 1–10. **Page 22:** *American Heritage College Dictionary,* 4th Edition. Copyright © 2007 by Houghton Mifflin Harcourt Publishing Company. Adapted and reproduced by permission from *The American Heritage College Dictionary,* 4th Edition.

Chapter 2
Page 37: Source: Lane Kenworthy, "Equality and Efficiency: The Illusory Trade-off," *European Journal of Political Research,* Vol. 27, No. 2, 1995, pp. 225–254. **Page 51:** Table 2.3, Reprinted by permission of Center for Responsive Politics. **Page 52:** Table 2.4, Reprinted by permission of Center for Responsive Politics. **Page 53:** Table 2.5, Reprinted by permission of Center for Responsive Politics. **Page 53:** Table 2.6, Reprinted by permission of Center for Responsive Politics.

Chapter 3
Page 64: Source: http://www.fas.org/irp/congress/2001_hr/071801_kelly. **Page 69:** Table 3.1, Source: U.S. Office of Personnel Management. **Page 71:** Source: "The Controversy over Local Government Structure," http://www.ppic.org/publications/PPIC112. **Page 74:** Figure 3.1, Source: http://www.doe.gov/organization/orgchart.htm. **Page 79:** Source: Bradley R. Schiller, "All Welfare Is Local," *The New York Times,* January 28, 1997, p. A21. **Page 84:** Figure 3.2, Source: J. Steven Ott. From *The Organizational Culture Perspective,* 1989. Reprinted with permission of the author. **Page 86:** Source: Alan Brinkley, "The Culture of Corruption," *Los Angeles Times,* November 2, 1997, p. M1.

Chapter 4
Page 96: Source: Richard D. Lamm, "The Elusive Concept of Community," *Kettering Review,* 28–36. **Page 100:** Source: Daniel Bell, "The Protestant Ethic," *World Policy Journal* 13, No. 3 (Fall 1996): 35–38. **Page 101:** Source: Michael M. Harmon and Richard T. Mayer, *Organization Theory for Public Administration* (Boston: Little, Brown, 1986). See Chapter 3, "The Normative Context of Public Administration," pp. 34–53. **Page 103:** Source: Carl F. Horowitz, "The Shaming Sham," *The American Prospect,* No. 31 (March–April 1997): pp. 70–76. **Page 109:** Source: Michael M. Harmon and Richard T. Mayer, *Organization Theory for Public Administration* (Boston: Little, Brown, 1986), p. 158. **Page 113:** Source: Roger Harrison. Reprinted by permission of *Harvard Business Review.* From "Understanding Your Organization's Character," by Roger Harrison, *Harvard Business Review,* May/June 1972. Copyright © 1972 by Harvard Business School Publishing Corporation; all rights reserved.

Chapter 5
Page 121: Source: C. J. Chivers, "For Black Officers, Diversity Has Its Limits," *New York Times,* April 2, 2001. **Page 126:** Source: Katy Saldarini, "2000 Plum Book Lists Sought-After Jobs in Next Administration," *Government Executive,* November 10, 2000. **Page 127:** Table 5.1, Source: www.bls.gov. **Page 128:** Table 5.2, Source: www.bls.gov. **Page 132:** Table 5.3, Source: U.S. Office of Personnel Management. **Page 133:** Table 5.4,

Source: U.S. Office of Personnel Management.
Page 135: Source: Stephen Barr, "Website Encourages
Young People to Think About Working for Uncle
Sam," *The Washington Post,* July 13, 2001, p. B02.
"Government Jobs for Students: New Website Helps
Find Summer and Temporary Jobs," http://www
.usgovinfo.about.com/library/weekly. **Page 140:**
Table 5.6, Source: Congressional Budget Office,
Characteristics and Pay of Federal Civilian Employees
(Washington, DC: CBO, March, 2007). **Page 141:**
Source: Merit Systems Protection Board, "New MSPB
Report Finds That Federal Entry-Level New Hires May
Not Be What Most People Expect," February 8, 2008.
Page 142: Source: Congressional Budget Office,
Characteristics and Pay of Federal Civilian Employees
(Washington, DC: CBO, March, 2007). **Page 143:**
Source: Congressional Budget Office, *Characteristics
and Pay of Federal Civilian Employees* (Washington,
DC: CBO, March, 2007). **Page 148:** Source: "The
Origins of Affirmative Action" by Marquita Sykes, as
appeared on the Web site, www.now.org, 4/2/02.
Reprinted by permission of the National Organization
for Women, Inc. **Page 149:** Source: U.S. General
Accounting Office, "Enhanced Agency Efforts Needed
to Improve Diversity as the Senior Corps Turn Over,"
October 15, 2003. GAO-04-123T. **Page 152:** Source:
Joseph R. Grima, "Administrative and Civil Service
Reform," The World Bank Group, http:www1
.worldbank.org/publicsector/civilservice/individual.htm.
Page 153: Source: "Assistant Professor Faculty
Position" ad from the University of Texas at Arlington,
School of Social Work Web site, www.uta.edu/ssw/ad.
Reprinted by permission of the University of Texas at
Arlington, School of Social Work.

Chapter 6
Page 164: Source: Richard C. Kearney, *Labor Relations
in the Public Sector,* 4th Edition (New York: Taylor and
Francis, 2009). Reprinted by permission. **Page 170:**
Source: Robert Samuelson, "Work Ethic vs. Fun Ethic,"
The Washington Post, September 3, 2001 p. A21.
Page 171: Figure 6.1, Source: http://www.bls.gov/opub/
ted/2007/feb/wk1/art05.htm. **Page 173:** Source: Michael
Ballot, with contributions from Laurie Lichter-Heath,
Thomas Kail, and Ruth Wang, *Labor-Management
Relations in a Changing Environment,* 2nd ed. (New
York: John Wiley & Sons, pp. 474–478, 1996).
Page 175: Table 6.1, Source: www.bls.gov/oco/cg/print/
cgs042.htm. **Page 177:** Table 6.2, Source: www.bls.gov/
oco/cg/print/cgs042.htm. **Page 179:** Figure 6.2, Source:
http://www.bls.gov/oco/cg/print/cgs042.htm. **Page 182:**

Table 6.3, Source: www.bls.gov/oco/cg/print/cgs042
.htm. **Page 183:** Table 6.4, Source: www.bls.gov/oco/cg/
print/cgs042.htm. **Page 187:** Source: Abridgment from
"Collective Bargaining at UMB: Glossary of Labor
Relations Terms" on the University of Maryland,
Baltimore, Web site, www.umarlynad.edu. © 2001
University of Maryland, Baltimore. Reprinted by
permission. **Page 193:** Source: UAW News, "GSEAC/
UAW Welcomes New Collective Bargaining Law, Files
for Union Certification," March 14, 2002. **Page 198:**
Table, Source: FAA Center for Management
Development, Pal Coast, FL. "Basic Labor Relations,"
Overview, Historical Perspective, Stand-Alone Modules
(SAMs), 2001; http://www.cmd.faa.gov/LR-SAMs/
M-032/Chap-1.

Chapter 7
Page 207: Source: Michael Segell, "The Politics of
Greeting," *Esquire* 128, No. 1 (July 1997): 84–86.
Page 209: Sources: America Online, Steve Donohue,
"YouTube Dominates Internet Video, with 27.3%
Share," *Multichannel News,* November 30. 2007.
Page 210: Source: "Employers and E-mail," *The
Washington Post,* April 18, 1998, p. 18A. **Page 217:**
Sources: *The New York Times,* February 24, 1998, p. 20A;
see also Stephen Goode, "The Reagan Legacy,"
Insight on the News 13, No. 39 (27 October 1997):
10–14. **Page 221:** Source: Robert A. Portnoy,
*Leadership: What Every Leader Should Know About
People,* 1986. Reprinted by permission of the author.
Page 224: Source: Phillip Selznick, *Leadership in
Administration* (University of California Press, 1984),
pp. 61–63. **Page 226:** Sources: Gregory Mott, "Stupidity
for Dummies," *The Washington Post,* May 7, 2002,
p. HE01; Robert J. Sternberg, ed., *Why Smart People Can
Be So Stupid* (New Haven, CT: Yale University Press,
2002).

Chapter 8
Page 239: Source: Tax Foundation, "How Does Uncle
Sam Plan to Spend Your Federal Tax Dollar in FY
2003," http://www.taxfoundation.org/taxdollar.html,
2002. **Page 241:** Source: http://www.nationalpriorities
.org/print/5850. **Page 243:** Figure 8.1, Courtesy of
National Priorities Project. **Page 243:** Figure 8.2,
Courtesy of National Priorities Project. **Page 244:**
Table 8.1, Source: Budget of the U.S. Government,
FY2006, historical tables. **Page 245:** Figure 8.3,
Courtesy of National Priorities Project. **Page 246:**
Figure 8.4, Courtesy of National Priorities Project.
Page 246: Figure 8.5, Courtesy of National Priorities

Project. **Page 247:** Figure 8.6, Courtesy of National Priorities Project. **Page 248:** Figure 8.7, Courtesy of National Priorities Project. **Page 249:** Figure 8.8, Courtesy of National Priorities Project. **Page 249:** Figure 8.9, Courtesy of National Priorities Project. **Page 250:** Figure 8.10, Courtesy of National Priorities Project. **Page 251:** Figure 8.11, Courtesy of National Priorities Project. **Page 252:** Source: Andrew Chamberlain, Tax Foundation, October 7, 2005, http://www.taxfoundation .org/blog/show/1106.html. **Page 253:** Source: http:// members.bellatlantic.net. **Page 259:** Source: Thomas J. Anton, "Roles and Symbols in the Determination of State Expenditures," *Midwest Journal of Political Science* 11, No. 1 (February 1967): 29. **Page 261:** Source: *A Glossary of Terms Used in the Federal Budget Process* (Washington, DC: General Accounting Office, March 1981), pp. 59, 97. **Page 263:** Figure 8.12, Source: Organization for Economic Co-operation and Development, "Tax Administration in OECD and Selected Non-OECD Countries: Comparative Information Series (2006)," http://publicagenda.org/ issues/factfiles. **Page 267:** Table 8.2, Source: Tax Foundation. **Page 268:** Table 8.3, Source: Tax Foundation.

Chapter 9

Page 283: Sources: Mark A. Abramson, "The Public Manager and Excellence," *The Bureaucrat* 4, No. 3 (Fall 1985): 9–13; see also Charles T. Goodsell, *The Case for Bureaucracy: A Public Administration Polemic* (Chatham, NJ: Chatham House Publishers, 1983), pp. 55–60. **Page 284:** Source: William R. Marty, "Government, Morality, and the Family," *Journal of Interdisciplinary Studies* 7, No. 1–2 (Annual 1995): 1–25. **Page 288:** Source: Software Techniques, 13105 Booker T. Washington Highway, Hardy, VA 24010. See www.softwaretech.com. **Page 290:** Source: Harry P. Hatry and Diana R. Dunn, *Measuring the Effectiveness of Local Government Services: Recreation* (Washington, DC: Urban Institute, 1971). **Page 292:** Source: Ken Blanchard, "Motivation Q&A with Ken Blanchard," www.smartibz.com. **Page 294:** Table 9.1, Source: The Pew Center on the States, Government Performance Project, http://www.gpponline.org/States.aspx. **Page 296:** Table 9.2, Source: From "Citizen-Driven Government Performance" on Web site www.newark .rutgers.edu. Reprinted by permission of Professor Marc Holzer. **Page 297:** Source: Linda Gast and William A. Galston, "Viewpoint: Success: What Is Your Yardstick?" *University of Maryland Magazine,* Spring 2000, pp. 6–7.

Chapter 10

Page 306: Source: U.S. Department of Transportation, Coast Guard, "Licensing and Manning for Officers of Towing Vessels," *The Federal Register,* Vol. 64, No. 223, pp. 63213–63235. **Page 311:** Source: Lief H. Carter, *Administrative Law and Politics: Cases and Comments* (Boston: Little, Brown, 1983), p. 4. **Page 312:** Table 10.1, Sources: James Q. Wilson, "The Rise of the Bureaucratic State," *Policy Making,* ed. Francis E. Rourke, 4th ed. (Boston: Little, Brown, 1986), pp. 125–148; and Kenneth F. Warren, *Administrative Law in the Political System,* 3rd ed. (Upper Saddle River, NJ: Prentice-Hall, 1997), p. 45. **Page 319:** Source: Stephen J. Bonczek, "Ethics: Challenge of the 1990s—A Local Government Perspective," *Public Management* 72, No. 8 (July 1990): 17–19. **Page 325:** Table 10.2, Source: Florence Heffron with Neil McFeeley, from *The Administrative Regulatory Process,* 1983. Reprinted by permission of Pearson Education, Inc. **Page 328:** Figure 10.1, Source: Susan Dudley and Melinda Warren, "Moderating Regulatory Growth: An Analysis of the U.S. Budget for Fiscal Years 2006 and 2007," Murray Weidenbaum Center on the Economy, Government, and Public Policy at Washington University and Mercatus Center at George Mason University, May 2006. **Page 328:** Figure 10.2, Source: Susan Dudley and Melinda Warren, "Moderating Regulatory Growth: An Analysis of the U.S. Budget for Fiscal Years 2006 and 2007," Murray Weidenbaum Center on the Economy, Government, and Public Policy at Washington University and Mercatus Center at George Mason University, May 2006. **Page 329:** Sources: Jef Richards, "The Federal Trade Commission," www.museum.tv. **Page 331:** Source: Stanley A. Reigel and P. John Owen, *Administrative Law: The Law of Government Agencies* (Ann Arbor, MI: Ann Arbor Science, The Butterworth Group, 1982), pp. 39–59. **Page 332:** Figure 10.3, Source: Susan Dudley and Melinda Warren, "Moderating Regulatory Growth: An Analysis of the U.S. Budget for Fiscal Years 2006 and 2007," Murray Weidenbaum Center on the Economy, Government, and Public Policy at Washington University and Mercatus Center at George Mason University, May 2006. **Page 334:** Source: Paul N. Tramontozzi with Kenneth W. Chilton, *U.S. Regulatory Agencies Under Reagan, 1980–1988* (St. Louis, MO: Center for the Study of Business, 1987), pp. 11–14. **Page 335:** Source: Barbara S. Romzek and Melvin J. Dubnick, "Accountability in the Public Sector: Lessons from the Challenger Tragedy," *Public Administration Review* 47, No. 3 (May/June 1987): 227–238.

Index